## TO THE READER

§ Scientology® is a religious philosophy containing pastoral counseling procedures intended to assist an individual to attain spiritual freedom. The mission of the Church of Scientology is a simple one—to help the individual attain full awareness of himself as an immortal being, and of his relationship to the Supreme Being. The attainment of the benefits and goals of Scientology requires each individual's dedicated participation as only through his own efforts can he himself, as a spiritual being, achieve these.

§ This is part of the religious literature and works of the Founder of Scientology, L. Ron Hubbard. It is presented to the reader as part of the record of his personal research into life, and should be construed only as a written report of such research and not as a statement of claims made by the church or the author.

§ Scientology and its sub-study, Dianetics, as practiced by the church, address only the "thetan" (spirit). Although the church, as are all churches, is free to engage in spiritual healing, it does not, as its primary goal is increased *spiritual awareness* for all. For this reason, the church does not wish to accept individuals who desire treatment of physical illness or insanity but refers these to qualified specialists of other organizations who deal in these matters.

§ The Hubbard Electrometer is a religious artifact used in the church confessional. It, in itself, does nothing, and is used by ministers only, to assist parishioners in locating areas of spiritual distress or travail.

§ We hope the reading of this book is only the first stage of a personal voyage of discovery into the new and vital world religion of Scientology.

This book belongs to: _____

Date _____

THE BOARD OF DIRECTORS
CHURCHES OF SCIENTOLOGY

# YOU CAN ALWAYS WRITE TO RON

All mail addressed to me shall be received by me. I am always willing to help. By my own creed, a being is only as valuable as he can serve others.

Any message addressed to me and sent to the address of the nearest Scientology Church listed in the back of this book, will be forwarded to me directly.

# DIANETICS AND SCIENTOLOGY
# TECHNICAL DICTIONARY

by

# L. Ron Hubbard

Publications Organization

Los Angeles

Published by
Church of Scientology of California
Publications Organization United States
4833 Fountain Ave., East Annex
Los Angeles, California 90029


*The Church of Scientology of
California is a non-profit organization.*


*Scientology is an applied religious philosophy.
Dianetics® and Scientology® are registered names.*

First printing 1975
Second printing, November 1975
Third printing 1978
Fourth printing 1979
Fifth printing 1979

*The E-meter is not intended or effective for
the diagnosis, treatment or prevention of any
disease.*

*A Dianetics Publication.
Dianetics is the trademark of L. Ron Hubbard
in respect of his published works.*

ISBN 0-88404-037-2

Printed in the U.S.A. by Kingsport Press, Inc.

Typeset by Freedmen's Organization, Los Angeles, California

# Contents

# Guide to the Dictionary

This is the long awaited and much heralded *Dianetics and Scientology Technical Dictionary*. It contains and defines almost all of the words and abbreviations used in connection with auditing technology and with the training of auditors to date in Dianetics and Scientology. Many words have several definitions taken from various periods of the development of Dianetics and Scientology.

A large amount of L. Ron Hubbard's books, tape lectures, articles and technical bulletins etc. were researched for many years by a team of researchers. The period from 1950 to 1975 was heavily consulted for the terms and their definitions.

The student can readily see the progressive development through time of the vocabulary of Dianetics and Scientology by its Source and Founder, L. Ron Hubbard as well as the changes that have come about through his continued research. More important however, is the fact that *all* of the materials of the subjects remain valid and in force today.

In compiling this dictionary the researchers and editors have chosen to omit the conventional use of the ellipsis (. . .) which would indicate an intentional omission of words in the definition. This is so that each definition imparts a complete uninterrupted thought to the reader and allows him to form a concept of the word without distraction or the inclusion of data not contributory to the *definition*.

The references at the end of each definition allow the reader to consult the Source of the definition if further information is desired.

In addition to giving an understanding of the vocabulary of the subjects and clearing up misunderstood words and abbreviations in connection with Dianetics and Scientology, there is a further major use for this dictionary; The student requiring information about any area of Dianetics or Scientology need only look up the words connected with that area and he will be provided with references to appropriate material for further study of that area.

As the Tone Scale is referred to in many definitions a full Tone Scale appears at the end of the dictionary before the reference summary.

**The Editors**

# Note

While this dictionary has attempted to include all Dianetic and Scientology technical words and philosophic terms, there is a chance you might find some words not included.

If you discover any missing words, please write them to:

Dictionary Staff
LRH Personal Secretary
Saint Hill Manor
East Grinstead
Sussex, England

**The Editors**

# Introduction

In the early sixties the research which I did on study and study materials brought to view the necessity of an accurate and modernized dictionary of Dianetics and Scientology.

Despite the pressing need of this so many other research projects existed that I did not have an opportunity to personally engage upon this work of definitions. All of the grades and OT levels remained to be researched in full and therefore I relegated any dictionary compilations to staff action.

Almost all the words used in Dianetics and Scientology are defined in the early bulletins in which they first appeared. However, a complete dictionary is a vital necessity and use of it can mean the difference between understanding and not understanding; being able to be an auditor and not being one.

Philosophy has always had the liability of gathering to itself a great many new words and labels. The reason for this is that the philosopher finds phenomena in the physical universe or in the mind or humanities which have not hitherto been observed or properly identified. Each one of these tends to require a new word for its description. In actual fact this cycle of new observations requiring new labels is probably the growth of language itself. Language is obviously the product of unsung observers who then popularized a word to describe what had been observed.

The system which has been followed in Dianetics and Scientology in labelling phenomena or observed things was originally to make verbs into nouns or vice versa. The practice of developing new nomenclature was actually held to a minimum. However, it was found that many old words in the field of philosophy, when used, conveyed to people an entirely new idea. The exactness of Dianetics and Scientology required a more precise approach. This approach was achieved by special naming with an eye to minimal confusion with already supposed or known phenomena. The Dianetics and Scientology vocabulary is nevertheless not large.

It is interesting that many Dianetics and Scientology terms have moved sideways into society and are in common use today.

In the search which brought about Dianetics and Scientology many new phenomena were encountered which resulted, for the first time, in a workable, predictable science of the humanities. The introduction of a few words of new meaning to make this possible seems to be a small price to pay.

It is the hallmark of the Dianeticist and Scientologist that he uses these words even in his common conversation with ease and facility.

The student who is not completely conversant with these exact words as contained in this dictionary will find himself drowsing over his bulletins and utterly appalled when he tries to obtain results which are not forthcoming due to his lack of understanding of some small word.

The liability of misunderstood words is not a monopoly of Dianetics and Scientology. In broader university subjects you will find that not only the vocabulary of the subject, but the subject itself is often completely and totally misunderstood, leaving the student ARC broken, upset and even riotous.

Whereas the subject of misunderstood words or understood words is, in itself, a broad one, it does not comprise, in itself, the entire technology of study.

I hope this dictionary will be of use. Not only in clarifying some of the phenomena of existence, but also speeding greatly your study of Dianetics and Scientology and the results you will be able to attain thereby.

# DIANETICS AND SCIENTOLOGY
# TECHNICAL DICTIONARY

# A

**A**, affinity. (5904C08)

**AA**, attempted abortion. (*DMSMH*, p. 245)

**A=A=A, 1. anything equals anything equals anything.** This is the way the reactive mind thinks, irrationally identifying thoughts, people, objects, experiences, statements, etc., with one another where little or no similarity actually exists. (*Scn AD*) **2.** we have a broad dissertation on this in *Dianetics: The Modern Science of Mental Health* as it affects insane behavior. Everything is everything else. Mr. X looks at a horse knows it's a house knows it's a school teacher. So when he sees a horse he is respectful. (HCO PL 26 Apr 70R) **3.** this is the behavior of the reactive mind. Everything is identified with everything on a certain subject. (PDC 20)

**ABCD, 1.** these are the steps designation of the second run through of R3R as given in the commands for R3R. Usually the auditor simply writes **ABCD** on his worksheet which shows he has given the command required and designated under **A**, under **B**, under **C**, under **D**, as and when he gives them to the preclear. (LRH Def. Notes) **2.** after the first time through an incident in Dn and when pc has recounted it, the auditor tells pc, **A.** "Move to the beginning of the incident." **B.** "Tell me when you are there." **C.** When pc has said he is, "Scan through to the end of the incident." **D.** "Tell me what happened." (BTB 6 May 69R II)

1

**ABERRATE,** to make something diverge from a straight line. The word comes basically from optics. (*Dn 55!*, p. 65) —*adj.* **Aberrated,** departed from rationality, deranged. (*EOS*, p. 14)

**ABERRATED BEHAVIOR,** destructive effort toward pro-survival data or entities on any dynamic or effort toward the survival of contra-survival data or entities for any dynamic. (*Scn 0-8*, p. 86) See ABERRATION.

**ABERRATED PERSONALITY,** the **personality** resultant from superimposition, on the genetic **personality**, of personal characteristics and tendencies brought about by all environmental factors, pro-survival and **aberrational.** (*SOS* Gloss)

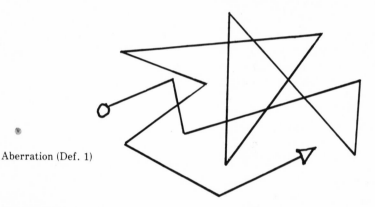

Aberration (Def. 1)

**ABERRATION, 1.** a departure from rational thought or behavior. From the Latin, *aberrare,* to wander from; Latin, *ab,* away, *errare,* to wander. It means basically to err, to make mistakes, or more specifically to have fixed ideas which are not true. The word is also used in its scientific sense. It means departure from a straight line. If a line should go from A to B, then if it is "**aberrated**" it would go from A to some other point, to some other point, to some other point, to some other point, to some other point and finally arrive at B. Taken in its scientific sense, it would also mean the lack of straightness or to see crookedly as, in example, a man sees a horse but thinks he sees an elephant. **Aberrated** conduct would be wrong conduct, or conduct not supported by reason. When a person has engrams, these tend to deflect what would be his normal ability to perceive truth and bring about an **aberrated** view of situations which then would cause an **aberrated** reaction to them. **Aberration** is opposed to sanity, which would be its opposite. (LRH Def. Notes) **2.** an **aberrated** person wanders from his self-determined course. He no longer goes where he wants to go now, but goes where he has wanted to go in the past. His course is, therefore, not rational, and he seems to go wherever the environment pushes him. He has as many **aberrations** as he has hidden contra-survival decisions in his past. (*Abil 114A*) **3.** mental derangement, any irrational condition. (*DMSMH*, p. 102) **4.** the **aberree's** reactions to and difficulties with his current environment. (*DTOT*, p. 127) **5.** the manifestation of an engram, and is serious only when it influences the competence of the individual in his environment. (*Scn Jour 28-G*) **6.** the degree of residual plus or minus randomity accumulated by compelling, inhibiting or unwarranted assisting of efforts on the part of other organisms or the physical (material) universe. (*Scn 0-8*, p. 86)

**ABERRATIVE VALENCE,** people from whom one felt that one could not withhold anything were the most **aberrative valences** on the case. We thus have a new definition for **aberrative valences,** namely the "cannot withhold from" **valence.** (PAB 128)

**ABERREE, 1.** a neologism meaning an **aberrated** person. (*DMSMH*, p. 22) **2.** a person not released or cleared. (*DMSMH*, p. 286) **3.** anybody who has one or more engrams. (*EOS*, p. 90) **4.** was sometimes used in the early days of Dn to designate an **aberrated** person. (LRH Def. Notes)

**ABILITY,** to observe, to make decisions, to act. (SH Spec 131, 6204C03)

**ABILITY GAIN,** the pc's recognition that pc can now do things he could not do before. (HCOB 28 Feb 59)

**ABILITY RELEASE,** expanded Grade IV release. (CG&AC 75) See GRADE IV RELEASE.

**ABILITY TO THINK,** the capability of the mind to perceive, pose and resolve specific and general problems. (*DASF*, p. 90)

# ABRIDGED STYLE AUDITING

**ABRIDGED STYLE AUDITING,** (Level III style), by **abridged** is meant "abbreviated," shorn of extras. Any not actually needful auditing command is deleted. In this **style** we have shifted from pure rote to a sensible use or omission as needful. We still use repetitive commands expertly, but we don't use rote that is unnecessary to the situation. (HCOB 6 Nov 64)

**ABSOLUTE OVERT ACT,** an **absolute overt act** would be something destructive on all eight dynamics. (5901C04)

**ABSOLUTE RIGHTNESS,** the immortality of the individual himself, his children, his group, mankind and the universe and all energy—the infinity of complete survival. (*DASF*, p. 80)

**ABSOLUTE WRONGNESS,** the extinction of the universe and all energy and the source of energy—the infinity of complete death. (*DASF*, p. 80)

**ABSOLUTE ZERO, 1.** something that does not have mass, doesn't have wave-length, doesn't have location and does not have time. (UPC 11) **2. absolute zero** would be a no-motion, a no-temperature condition. (SH Spec 96, 6112C21)

**AC, Ability Congress.** (HCOB 29 Sept 66)

**ACAD, Academy.** (BPL 5 Nov 72R)

**ACADEMY,** in Scn the **academy** is that department of the technical division in which courses and training are delivered; Department 11, Division 4. (BTB 12 Apr 72R) *Abbr.* Acad.

**ACC, Advanced Clinical Course.** (PAB 71)

**ACCELERATION PROCESS,** this was an experimental rundown run in 1970-1971. It consisted of running down prior ARC breaks preceding engrams; it was superseded by L-10 and Expanded Dianetics. Mentioned in HCOB 21 Dec 69, *Solo Auditing and R6EW*. (LRH Def. Notes)

**ACCEPTABLE EFFECT,** one which is real. The person is certain that an **effect** of some kind or other has occurred. (5707C25)

**ACCEPTANCE LEVEL, 1.** the degree of a person's actual willingness to **accept** people or things, monitored and determined by his consideration of the state or condition that those people or things must be in for him to be able to do so. (*PXL Gloss*) **2.** what he really could have. (XDN No. 4, 7204C07)

**ACCEPTANCE LEVEL PROCESSING,** that **process** which discovers the lowest **level** of **acceptance** of the individual and discovers there the prevailing hunger and feeds that hunger by means of mock-ups until it is satiated. The **process** is not a separate process itself, but is actually a version of Expanded Gita. (PAB 15)

**ACCESSIBILITY, 1.** the willingness of the preclear to **accept** auditing and the ability of the auditor and the preclear to work as a team to increase the position of the preclear on the tone scale. (*SOS*, Bk. 2, p. 187) **2.** the **accessibility** of an individual has to do with his own ability to communicate with his environment and to communicate with his own past. (5011C22) **3.** generally, the desire of the individual to attain new and higher levels of survival and the betterment of mind and body. (*SOS*, Bk. 2, p. 185)

**ACCIDENT-PRONE,** a case where the reactive mind commands **accidents.** He is a serious menace in any society for his **accidents** are reactively intentional and they include the destruction of other people who are innocent. (*DMSMH*, p. 153)

**ACC TRs,** TRs which have been used on the **1st South African ACC** and are a version of the E-meter drills. (HCOB 30 Apr 60)

**ACK, acknowledgement.** (HCOB 23 Aug 65)

**ACK'ED, acknowledged.** (*BCR*, p. 23)

**ACKNOWLEDGEMENT,** something said or done to inform another that his statement or action has been noted, understood and received. "Very good," "Okay," and other such phrases are intended to inform another who has spoken or acted that his statement or action has been accepted. An **acknowledgement** also tends to confirm that the statement has been made or the action has been done and so brings about a condition not only of communication but of reality between two or more people. Applause at a theater is an **acknowledgement** of the actor or act plus approval. **Acknowledgement** itself does not necessarily imply an approval or disapproval or any other thing beyond the knowledge that an action or statement has been observed and is received. In signaling with the morse code the receiver of a message transmits an R to the sender as a signal that the message has been received, which is to say **acknowledged.** There is such a thing as **over-acknowledgement** and there is such a thing as **under-acknowledgement.** A correct and exact **acknowledgement** communicates to someone who has spoken that what he has said has been heard. An **acknowledgement** tends to terminate or end the cycle of a communication, and when expertly used can sometimes stop a continued statement or continued action. An **acknowledgement** is also part of the communication formula and is one of its steps. The Scientologist, sometimes, in using Scientologese abbreviates this to **"Ack"**; he **"acked"** the person. (LRH Def. Notes)

**ACT,** a stage of processing. Applies solely to the particular process in use at a certain case level. (*AP&A* Gloss)

Action (Def. 4)

**ACTION, 1.** a motion through space having a certain speed. (SH Spec 42, 6410C13) **2. action**=motion or movement=an act=a consideration that motion has occurred. (*FOT*, p. 19) **3.** doingness directed towards havingness. (*Scn 8-8008*, p. 26) **4. action** consists of energy outputs and inputs. **Action** is energy interchanges on a gross mest level. (5203CM05A)

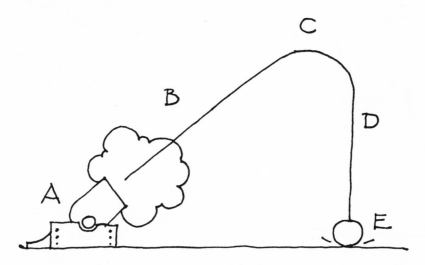

Action Cycle

**ACTION CYCLE,** the creation, growth, conservation, decay and death or destruction of energy and matter in a space. **Action cycles** produce time; an **action cycle** goes from 40.0 to 0.0 on the tone scale. (*Scn 0-8*, p. 25)

**ACTION DEFINITION,** see DEFINITIONS, TYPES OF.

**ACTION PHRASES, 1.** words or **phrases** in engrams or locks (or at 0.1 in present time) which cause the individual to perform involuntary **actions** on the time track. **Action phrases** are effective in the low tone ranges and not effective in the high ranges. As a case progresses up the scale, they lose their power. Types of **action phrases** are bouncer, down bouncer, grouper, denyer, holder, misdirector, scrambler, and the valence shifters corresponding to these. (*SOS* Gloss) **2.** those which seem to order the preclear in various directions. The **action phrases** are bouncers such as, "Get up," "Get out"; holders such as "Stay

7

here," "Don't move"; misdirectors such as "Don't know whether I'm coming or going," or "Everything is backwards"; down-bouncers such as "Get under," or "Go back"; groupers such as "Everything happens at once," "Pull yourself together"; call-backs such as "Come back," "Please come"; and one other, the denyer, which states that the engram does not exist, such as "There isn't anything here," "I can't see anything." There is also the valence shifter which shifts the individual from his own identity to the identity of another; the valence-bouncer, which prohibits an individual from going into some particular valence; the valence denyer, which may even deny that the person's own valence exists; and the valence-grouper, which makes all va-lences into one valence. These are all the types of **action phrases**. (*SOS*, pp. 181-182)

**ACTUAL**, that which is really true; that which exists despite all apparencies; that which underlies the way things seem to be; the way things really are. (*FOT*, p. 20)

**ACTUAL CYCLE OF ACTION**, CREATE, create-create-create, create-counter-create, no creation, nothingness. CREATE= make, manufacture, construct, postulate, bring into beingness= CREATE. Create-create-create=create again continuously one moment after the next=SURVIVAL. Create-counter-create=to create something against a creation=to create one thing and then create something else against it=DESTROY. No creation =an absence of any creation=no creative activity. An **ACTUAL cycle of action** then consists of various activities, but each and every one of them is creative. The **cycle of action** contains an APPARENCY of SURVIVAL, but this is actually only a continuous creation. (*FOT*, pp. 20-21)

**ACTUAL GOAL**, the dominating significance of the thetan's own causation which binds together the masses accumulated by the reliable items of an actual GPM. (HCOB 13 Apr 64, *Scn VI Part One Glossary of Terms*)

**ACTUAL GPM**, the composite black mass of all the pairs of reliable items and their associated locks, dominated and bound together by the significance of an actual goal and having a definite location as a mass on the time track. (HCOB 13 Apr 64, *Scn VI Part One Glossary of Terms*)

**ACTUALITY**, (Scientology Axiom 27), an **actuality** can exist for one individually, but when it is agreed with by others it can then be said to be a reality. (*PXL*, p. 175) **2.** one's attitude towards his own universe. (*Scn 8-8008*, p. 28)

**ACUTE**, immediate, right now. It doesn't mean exaggerated. Medically it means simply right now, and rather temporary. (SH Spec 31, 6401C28)

**ACUTE INSANITY**, one which flares into existence for a few moments or a few days and then subsides, leaving a relatively normal person. (*DASF*, p. 77)

**AD or A.D., after Dianetics** (1950) e.g. 1965=**AD** 15. (HCOB 23 Aug 65)

**ADAPTIVE POSTULATE**, a pre-Dianetic error that an individual was healthy so long as he was adjusted to his environment. Nothing could be less workable than this **"adaptive" postulate.** Man succeeds because he adjusts his environment to him, not by adjusting himself to the environment. (*SA*, p. 112)

**AD COURSES**, see ADVANCED COURSES.

**ADDITIVE**, a thing which has been **added.** This usually has a bad meaning in that an **additive** is said to be something needless or harmful which has been done in **addition** to standard procedure. **Additive** normally means a departure from standard procedure. For example, an auditor puts different or **additional** words into a standard process or command. It means a twist on standard procedure. In common English, it might mean a substance put into a compound to improve its qualities or suppress undesirable qualities. In Dn and Scn it definitely means to **add** something to the technology procedure resulting in undesirable results. (LRH Def. Notes)

**ADMIN, administration** or **administrator.** (HCOB 23 Aug 65)

**ADMINISTRATION (ADMIN)**, a contraction or shortening of the word **administration, admin** is used as a noun to denote the actions involved in **administering** an organization. The clerical and executive decisions, actions and duties necessary to the running of an organization, such as originating and answering mail, typing, filing, dispatching, applying policy and all those actions, large and small which make up an organization. **Admin**

is also used to denote the action or fact of keeping auditor's reports, summary reports, worksheets and other records related to an auditing session. "He kept good **admin**," meaning that his summary report, auditor's report and worksheets were neat, exactly on pattern, in proper sequence and easily understood as well as complete. "His **admin** was bad"; from the scribble and disorderly keeping of records of the session while it was in progress one could not make out what had happened in the session. You will also see the word **admin** in connection with the three musts of a well-run organization. It is said that its ethics, tech and **admin** must be "in," which mean they must be properly done, orderly and effective. The word derives from **minister**, which means to serve. **Administer** means to manage, govern, to apply or direct the application of laws, or discipline, to conduct or execute religious offices, dispense rights. It comes from the Latin, *administrare*, to manage, carry out, accomplish, to attend, wait, serve. In modern English, when they use **administration** they mean management or running a government or the group that is in charge of the organization or the state. (LRH Def. Notes)

**ADMIN TRs,** the purpose of these **TRs** is to train the student to get compliance with and complete a cycle of action on **administrative** actions and orders, in spite of the randomities, confusions, justifications, excuses, traps and insanities of the third and sixth dynamics, and to confront such comfortably while doing so. (BTB 7 Feb 71)

**ADMIRATION, 1.** is the very substance of a communication line, and it is that thing which is considered desirable in the game of the three universes. (*COHA*, p. 203) **2.** a particle which unites and resolves, like the universal solvent, all types of energy, particularly force. (PAB 8)

**ADVANCED CLINICAL COURSE, 1.** basically a theory and research course which gives a much further insight into the phenomena of the mind and the rationale of research and investigation. (PAB 71) **2.** L. Ron Hubbard's special **courses** personally taught by him, scheduled by him, and sponsored for him by an HCO office. (HCO PL 24 Feb 60) *Abbr.* ACC.

**ADVANCED COURSES, 1.** Solo Audit Course, Clearing Course or OT courses. (HCO PL 12 Aug 71 II) **2.** above VA processes, one enters the field of **advanced courses,** specifically dealing with materials of which one has to solo audit in order to attain the stable gains of the grade. (HCO PL 28 Mar 70) *Abbr.* Ad Crses.

**ADVANCED ORGANIZATION, 1.** the **advanced** courses were at first separate in the Office of LRH at Saint Hill and then became the **Advanced Orgs (AOs)** under the Sea Org. (HCOB 8 Oct 71 II) **2.** that **organization** which runs the **advanced** courses. Its products are Clears and OTs. (FO 508)

**ADVANCE PROGRAM, 1.** the major actions to be undertaken to get the case back on the class chart from wherever he had erroneously gotten to on it. The **advance program** consists of writing down in sequence every needful step and process missed on the class chart by the case which is now to be done. It gets the preclear or pre-OT up to where he should be. (HCOB 14 Jun 70) **2.** this is what was called a "return program" in the *C/S Series.* The name was changed from "return" to **"advance"** as more appropriate. (HCOB 25 Jun 70 II)

**A.E.S.P., attitudes, emotions, sensations, pains.** (BTB 8 Jan 71R)

**AESTHETIC MIND,** many more **mind** levels apparently exist above the analytical level. There is, for instance, clear evidence that there is an **aesthetic mind** level, which is probably immediately above the analytical mind level. The **aesthetic mind** would be that **mind** which, by an interplay of the dynamics, deals with the nebulous field of art and creation. It is a strange thing that the shut-down of the analytical mind and the aberration of the reactive mind may still leave in fairly good working order the **aesthetic mind.** (*SOS,* Bk. 2, p. 234)

**AESTHETIC PRODUCT, 1.** Dn Axiom 169: any **aesthetic product** is a symbolic facsimile or combination of facsimiles of theta or physical universes in varied randomities and volumes of randomities with the interplay of tones. (*AP&A*, p. 99) **2.** Dn Axiom 170: an **aesthetic product** is an interpretation of the universes by an individual or group mind. (*AP&A*, p. 99)

**AESTHETICS,** the study of ideal form and beauty—it is the philosophy of art, which itself is the quality of communication. (*B&C*, p. 15)

# AFFINITY

**AFFINITY, 1.** the feeling of love or liking for something or someone. **Affinity** is a phenomena of space in that it expresses the willingness to occupy the same place as the thing which is

Affinity (Def. 1)

loved or liked. The reverse of it would be antipathy, "dislike" or rejection which would be the unwillingness to occupy the same space as or the unwillingness to approach something or someone. It came from the French, *affinite*, **affinity**, kindred, alliance, nearness and also from the Latin, *affinis*, meaning near, bordering upon. (LRH Def. Notes) **2.** the ability to occupy the space of, or be like or similar to, or to express a willingness to be something. (SH Spec 83, 6612C06) **3.** the relative distance and similarity of the two ends of a communication line. (*Dn 55!*, p. 35) **4.** emotional response; the feeling of affection or the lack of it, of emotion or misemotion connected with life. (HCOB 21 Jun 71 I) **5.** the attraction which exists between two human beings or between a human being and another life organism or between a human being and mest or theta or the Supreme Being. It has a rough parallel in the physical universe in magnetic and gravitic attraction. The **affinity** or lack of **affinity** between an organism and the environment or between the theta and mest of an organism and within the theta (including entheta) of the organism brings about what we have referred to as emotions. (*SOS* Gloss) **6.** in its truest definition which is coincidence of location and beingness, that is the ultimate in **affinity**. (9ACC-10, 5412CM20)

**AFFINITY SCALE, 1.** a **scale** which refers to the individual's relation with other people. The **affinity scale** may refer, at any particular time, to just one or to a small number of people. But as **affinity** is suppressed repeatedly, the individual will begin to take on an habitual tone level, on the **affinity scale,** an habitual reaction to almost all people. (*NOTL*, p. 102) **2.** the **affinity scale** includes most of the common emotions, apathy, grief, fear, anger, hostility, boredom, relief, contentment, enthusiasm, exhilaration, inspiration. (*SOS* Gloss)

**AFTER THE FACT ITEMS,** [in New Era Dn] **1.** an **"after the fact"** running **item** is one which clearly has an earlier thing before it, yet, by its very wording, prohibits reaching the earlier thing. (HCOB 20 Jul 78) **2.** the item is after the fact of having been run over. (HCOB 20 Jul 78)

**AGAINST SCIENTOLOGY,** attention off **Scientology** and protesting **Scientology** behavior. (HCOB 19 Aug 63)

**AGAINST SESSION,** attention off own case and talking at the auditor in protest of auditor, PT auditing environment or Scn. (HCOB 19 Aug 63) See also OUT OF SESSION.

**AGE FLASH,** the auditor says, "When I snap my fingers an **age** will occur to you. Give me the first number that comes into your mind." He then snaps his fingers, and the preclear gives him the first number which comes into his head. (*SOS*, Bk. 2, p. 51)

**AGONY,** is the deep emotion of boredom. Boredom, in essence, is the warning signal that **agony** is on its way. (5312CM20)

**AGREEMENT, 1.** a mutual knowingness, a mutual postulatingness towards certain end products. (SH Spec 71, 6110C25) **2.** two or more people making the same postulates stick. (SH Spec 62, 6110C04) **3.** ability to co-act with or mimic or be mimicked by. (5303M24) **4.** a specialized consideration, it is shared in common, and this we call an **agreement.** (5702C26)

**AHMC, Anatomy** of the **Human Mind Course.** (CG&AC 75)

**AICL, Advanced Indoctrination Course Lectures.** (HCOB 29 Sept 66)

**ALCOHOL,** is meant whiskey, beer, wine, vodka, rum, gin, etc.— in other words, any fermented or distilled liquor or drink of any kind or fumes of such with some percentage of **alcohol** content. (HCOB 15 Jun 71R III)

**ALL THE WAY SOUTH,** *Slang.* that state of mind at the extreme bottom where the fellow must have total effect on self and could not possibly make any effect of any kind on anybody else. It's below death. (5707C25)

**ALLY, 1.** this is a noun which means an individual who cooperates with, supports and helps another for a common object; a supporter, a friend. In Dn and Scn, it basically means someone who protects a person who is in a weak state and becomes a very strong influence over the person. The weaker person, such as a child, even partakes the characteristics of the **ally** so that one may find that a person who has, for instance, a bad leg, has it because a protector or **ally** in his youth had a bad leg. The word is from French and Latin and means to bind together. (LRH Def. Notes) **2.** by **ally** in Scn, we mean a person from whom sympathy came when the preclear was ill or injured. If the **ally** came to the preclear's defense or his words and/or actions were aligned with the individual's survival, the reactive mind gives that **ally** the status of always being right—especially if this **ally** was obtained during a highly painful engram. (HCOB 20 Mar 70)

**ALLY COMPUTATION,** little more than a mere idiot calculation that anyone who is a friend can be kept a friend only by approximating the conditions wherein the friendship was realized. It is a **computation** on the basis that one can only be safe in the vicinity of certain people and that one can only be in the vicinity of certain people by being sick or crazy or poor and generally disabled. (*DMSMH*, p. 243)

**ALTER-IS, 1.** a composite word meaning the action of **altering** or changing the reality of something. Is-ness means the way it is. When someone sees it differently he is doing an **alter-is**; in other words, is **altering** the way it **is**. This is taken from the *Axioms*. (LRH Def. Notes) **2.** to introduce a change and therefore time and persistence in an as-is-ness to obtain persistency. An introduction of an **alter-is** is therefore the addition of a lie to the real which causes it to persist and not to blow or as-is. (HCOB 11 May 65)

**ALTER-IS-NESS, 1.** the consideration which introduces change, and therefore time and persistence into an as-is-ness to obtain persistency. (*PXL*, p. 154) **2.** the effort to preserve something by **altering** its characteristics. (*PXL*, p. 53)

**ALTER-IST,** the control case, the person obsessively controlling things, *and* himself, is an **alter-ist**. He's got to change, change. Well, he's lost too much. Now he's got to change everything but he's not satisfied with anything. (*PXL*, p. 54)

**ALTERNATE, 1.** occurring by turns; succeeding each other; one and then the other. (HCOB 10 May 65) **2.** in auditing, **alternate** means two questions run one after the other, consecutively, one command positive followed by one negative. (HCOB 4 Dec 59)

**ALTERNATE CONFRONT,** (PROCESS), "What can you **confront?**" "What would you rather **not confront?**" (HCOB 16 Jun 60)

**ALTITUDE, 1.** a prestige which the auditor has in the eyes of the preclear. A somewhat artificial position of the auditor which gives the preclear greater confidence and therefore greater ability to run than he would otherwise have. (*SOS* Gloss) **2.** a difference of level of prestige—one in a higher **altitude** carries conviction to one on a lower **altitude** merely because of **altitude.** (*DMSMH*, p. 343)

**AMNESIA,** a guy who is so spooked that he doesn't dare remember ten seconds ago. He has had some experience earlier than which he is not going to remember, including the experience, so he's only willing to remember some moment after that experience. (SH Spec 72, 6607C28)

**ANALYTICAL,** capable of resolving, such as problems, situations. The word **analytical** is from the Greek *análysis* meaning resolve, undo, loosen, which is to say take something to pieces to see what it is made of. This is one of those examples of the shortcomings of the English language since no dictionary gives the word **analytical** any connection with thinking, reasoning, perceiving, which in essence is what it would have to mean, even in English. (LRH Def. Notes)

**ANALYTICAL ATTENUATION,** see ANATEN.

**ANALYTICAL MIND, 1.** the conscious aware **mind** which thinks, observes data, remembers it, and resolves problems. It would be essentially the conscious **mind** as opposed to the unconscious mind. In Dn and Scn the **analytical mind** is the one which is alert and aware and the reactive mind simply reacts without **analysis.** (LRH Def. Notes) **2.** that **mind** which combines perceptions of the immediate environment, of the past (via pictures) and estimations of the future into conclusions which are based upon the realities of situations. The **analytical mind** combines the potential knowingness of the thetan with the conditions of his surroundings and brings him to independent conclusions. This **mind** could be said to consist of visual pictures either of the past or the physical universe, monitored by, and presided over, by the knowingness of a thetan. The keynote of the **analytical mind** is awareness, one knows what one is concluding and knows what he is doing. (*FOT*, pp. 57-58) **3.** there is considerable dissertation in *Dianetics: The Modern Science of Mental Health* concerning the "awareness of awareness unit." When this subject was first under investigation it was established that all was not a machine. Somewhere, in tracing back the various lines, it was necessary to strike a cause point, either simply to assume that there was a cause point or to discover one. Two words were used in connection with this causative agent. One of them was "**analytical mind,** and the other, much more properly, the "awareness of awareness unit." The awareness of awareness unit, as its name implies, is aware of being aware, or aware of being alive. When one was looking at or discussing the **analytical mind,** one was aware of something else: that the awareness of awareness unit became connected in some fashion with computers, or analyzers, in order to handle and control the remainder of the physical being. The term "**analytical mind**" then meant the awareness of awareness unit plus some evaluative circuit or circuits, or machinery, to make the handling of the body possible. (*Dn 55!*, p. 11) **4.** that part of the being which perceives, when the individual is awake or in normal sleep (for sleep is not unconsciousness, and anything the individual has perceived while he was asleep is recorded in the standard memory banks and is relatively easy for the auditor to recover). (*SOS*, Bk. 2, p. 230) **5.** we say the **analytical mind** is kind of a misnomer because most people think it's some kind of a computing machine, and it's not. It's just the pc. It was a mistake made in early Dianetics in research. There was something there doing a lot of thinking and computing and so I called it the **analytical mind,** to differentiate this, because at the time we didn't know anything much about thetans. We mean the thetan. (SH Spec 23, 6106C29)

**ANALYTICAL THOUGHT, 1. thought** which directly observes and **analyzes** what it observes in terms of observations which are immediately present. (*COHA*, p. 196) **2.** rational **thought** as modified by education and viewpoint. (*DMSMH*, p. 79)

**ANALYZER,** the **analytical** mind. (*DMSMH*, p. 44)

**ANATEN, 1.** an abbreviation of **analytical attenuation** meaning diminution or weakening of the **analytical** awareness of an individual for a brief or extensive period of time. If sufficiently great, it can result in unconsciousness. (It stems from the restimulation of an engram which contains pain and unconsciousness.) (*Scn AD*) **2.** simply a drop in ARC to an extreme. (PAB 70) **3.** unconscious. (SH Spec 229, 6301C10) **4.** dope-off. (*Abil 52*)

**ANATOMY OF THE HUMAN MIND COURSE,** a basic Scn **course** which teaches observation and understanding of the fundamentals of the **human mind**. It includes demonstrations of the parts of the **human mind**. There are no prerequisites for this **course**. (CG&AC 75) *Abbr.* AHMC.

**ANCHOR POINTS, 1.** assigned or agreed-upon **points** of boundary, which are conceived to be motionless by the individual. (PDC 13) **2. points** which are **anchored** in a space different to the physical universe space around a body. (*FOT*, p. 63) **3.** those places which we called in *Advanced Procedures and Axioms* the sub-brains of the body; control centers, epicenters. (5410C10D) **4.** the **points** which mark an area of space are called **anchor points**, and these, with the viewpoint, alone are responsible for space. (*Scn Jour*, Iss 14-G) **5.** space is the viewpoint of dimension. The position of the viewpoint can change, the position of the dimension points can change. A dimension point is any point in a space or at the boundaries of space. As a specialized case those **points** which demark the outermost boundaries of the space or its corners are called in Scientology **anchor points**. An **anchor point** is a specialized kind of dimension point. (*Scn 8-8008*, p. 16) **6.** any kind of a **point**, any kind of a particle, any kind of electron, or anything which anybody believes is an actual **point**. There is nothing more real than a real **anchor point**. (2ACC-1A 5311CM17)

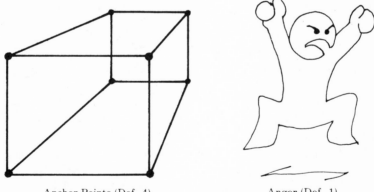

Anchor Points (Def. 4)                    Anger (Def. 1)

**ANGER, 1.** true **anger** is a hate hold. At exactly 1.5 on the tone scale we have a total ridge. It's hate. When we move a little above or a little below 1.5 we get a dispersal. (5904C08) **2. anger** is simply the process of trying to hold everything still. (5203CM09A)

**ANSWER HUNGER,** an unfinished cycle of communication generates what might be called **"answer hunger."** An individual who is waiting for a signal that his communication has been received is prone to accept any inflow. When an individual has, for a very long period of time, consistently waited for **answers** which did not arrive, any sort of **answer** from anywhere will be pulled in to him, by him, as an effort to remedy his scarcity of **answers**. Thus he will throw engramic phrases in the bank into action and operation against himself. (*Dn 55!*, p. 65)

Antagonism

**ANTAGONISM,** at the level of tone 2.0, affinity is expressed as **antagonism,** a feeling of annoyance and irritation caused by the advances of other people toward the individual. (*SOS*, p. 56)

**ANTI Q AND A TR, 1.** *commands:* basically "Put that (object) on my knee." Student is to get the coach to place the object that he has in his hand on the knee of the student. *Purpose:* (a) to train student in getting a pc to carry out a command using formal communication NOT tone 40. (b) to enable the student to maintain his TRs while giving commands. (c) to train the student to not get upset with a pc under formal auditing. (HCOB 20 Nov 73 I) **2.** to get this disease (**Q&A**) out of an HGC requires that auditors go through an **anti Q and A** handling. (HCOB 20 Nov 73 II)

**ANTISOCIAL PERSONALITY, 1.** there are certain characteristics and mental attitudes which cause about 20 per cent of a race to oppose violently any betterment activity or group. Such people are known to have **antisocial** tendencies. (*ISE*, p. 9) **2.** we're calling it a suppressive because it's more explicit. (SH Spec 78, 6608C25) See also SUPPRESSIVE PERSON.

**ANXIETY,** constant irresolute computation. Constant computation on a certain point or a certain problem. That is what worry is and that is what **anxiety** is. (T-80-2A 5205C20)

**AO, Advanced Org.** (HCOB 8 Oct 71 II)

**AP, aberrated personality.** (*DMSMH*, p. 124)

**APA, American Personality Analysis,** the **personality** test. (BTB 3 Nov 72R) See OCA.

**APATHY, 1.** complete withdrawal from person or people. There is in **apathy** no real attempt to contact one's self and no attempt to contact others. Here we have a null point of dissonance which is on the threshold of death. (*SOS*, p. 57) **2.** a very docile and obedient, if sick, state of not-beingness. (*HFP*, p. 56) **3.** no effort, all counter-effort. (*AP&A*, p. 33) **4. apathy** actually is a motionless enturbulence. It's an enturbulence cancelling itself out to the degree that it appears to be motionless. (5206CM25A) **5. apathy,** near death, imitates death. If a person is almost all wrong, he approximates death. He says, "What's the use? All is lost." (*NOTL*, p. 20)

Apathy (Def. 2, 5)

**APPARENCY, 1.** noun, something that seems to be, that **appears** to be a certain way; something **appears** to be but is different from the way it looks. It is from the Latin, *apparere*, to **appear**. In Dianetics and Scientology it is used to mean something that looks one way but is, in actual fact, something else. "Gives an **apparency** of health" whereas it's actually sick. (LRH Def. Notes) **2.** what **appears** to be as distinct from what actually is. (*FOT*, p. 19)

**APPARENT CYCLE OF ACTION**, create, then survive, then destroy; or creation, survival, destruction. (*FOT*, p. 18)

**APPETITE OVER TIN CUP**, *Slang.* a pioneer Western U.S. term used by riverboat men on the Missouri; it means thrown away violently, like "head over heels," "bowled over." (LRH Def. Notes)

**APPLIED PHILOSOPHY**, one which has to do with doing and action. One which **applies** to living—not just a theory, but one where the theory can be used to help you get on better in life. (BTB 4 Mar 65R)

**APPRENTICE SCIENTOLOGIST**, one who knows how to know, how to study, what life is about. (*BCR*, p. 14)

**ARBITRARY, 1.** something which is introduced into the situation without regard to the data of the situation. (SH Spec 83, 6612C06) **2.** an order or command introduced into the group in an effort to lay aside certain harm which may befall the group or in an effort to get through a period, fancied or real, of foreshortened time. (*NOTL*, p. 136) **3.** an order or command which was issued without explanation, and demanded instantaneous action on the part of other members of the group. (*NOTL*, p. 131)

**ARC, Anti-Radiation Congress.** (HCOB 29 Sept 66)

**ARC, 1.** a word from the initial letters of **Affinity, Reality, Communication** which together equate to Understanding. It is pronounced by stating its letters, **A-R-C.** To Scientologists it has come to mean good feeling, love or friendliness, such as "He was in **ARC** with his friend." One does not, however, fall out of **ARC,** he has an **ARC** break. (LRH Def. Notes) **2. ARC**=Understanding and Time. **A**=Space and the willingness to occupy the same space of. **R**=Mass or agreement. **C**=Energy or Recognition. (HCOB 27 Sept 68 II) **3. affinity** is a type of energy and can be produced at will. **Reality** is agreement; too much agreement under duress brings about the banishment of one's entire consciousness. **Communication,** however, is far more important than **affinity** or **reality,** for it is the operation, the action by which one experiences emotion and by which one agrees.

(PAB 1) **4.** the triagonal manifestation of theta, each aspect affecting the other two. (*SOS* Gloss)

**ARC BREAK, 1.** a sudden drop or cutting of one's affinity, reality, or communication with someone or something. Upsets with people or things come about because of a lessening or sundering of affinity, reality, or communication or understanding. It's called an **ARC break** instead of an upset, because, if one discovers which of the three points of understanding have been cut, one can bring about a rapid recovery in the person's state of mind. It is pronounced by its letters **A-R-C break**. When an **ARC break** is permitted to continue over too long a period of time and remains in restimulation, a person goes into a "sad effect" which is to say they become sad and mournful, usually without knowing what is causing it. This condition is handled by finding the earliest **ARC break** on the chain, finding whether it was a **break** in affinity, reality, communication, or understanding and indicating it to the person, always, of course, in session. (LRH Def. Notes) **2.** an incomplete cycle of some kind or another. It's a lowering of Affinity, Reality and Communication, so we call it an **ARC break**. It's a sudden down curve. It's a highly technical term. It means exactly what it says but its incept and so forth is an incompete cycle of action. (SH Spec 65, 6507C27) *Abbr.* ARCX.

**ARC BREAK ASSESSMENT, 1.** reading an **ARC break** list appropriate to the activity to the pc on a meter and doing nothing but locating and then indicating the charges found by telling the pc what registered on the needle. (HCOB 7 Sept 64 II) **2.** it isn't auditing because it doesn't use the auditing comm cycle. You don't ack what the pc says, you don't ask the pc what it is. You don't comm. You **assess** the list between you and the meter, same as no pc there. Then you find what reads and you tell the pc. And that's all. (HCOB 7 Sept 64 II)

**ARC BREAK LONG DURATION,** spotted by a person who has led a sad or subdued or rather suppressed sort of life and is probably around .8 on down on the tone scale. (LRH Def. Notes)

**ARC BREAK NEEDLE, 1.** a "floating needle" occurring above 3.0 or below 2.0 on a calibrated Mark V E-meter with the pc on two cans. An **ARC break needle** can occur between 2.0 and 3.0 where bad indicators are apparent. (HCOB 21 Oct 68) **2.** An F/N with bad indicators is an **ARC break needle.** These include propitiation. It is quite usual that a pc has just mentioned grief when the **ARC break needle** turns on, or some gloomy idea. A real F/N means the pc is out the top; an **ARC break needle** means he's out the bottom. He ceases to mock up, through grief. (HCOB 5 Oct 68) **3.** may be dirty, stuck or sticky, but may also give the appearance of floating. The pc will be upset and out of comm at the same time. (HCOB 21 Sept 66)

**ARC BREAK STRAIGHTWIRE,** "Recall an **ARC break.**" "When?" (HCOB 3 Feb 59)

**ARC BROKEN PCs,** they gloom and misemote. They criticize and snarl. Sometimes they scream. They blow, they refuse auditing. If an auditor's **pc** isn't bright and happy, there's an **ARC break** there with life or the bank or the session. (HCOB 29 Mar 65)

**ARC ENGRAM,** see SECONDARY ENGRAM. (*NOTL*, p. 35)

**ARC LOCKS, 1.** a type of **lock** which results when **affinity, communication,** or **reality** is forced upon the individual by the environment when he does not want it, when it is not rationally necessary, or when one or more of these is inhibited or denied to the individual by others in the environment. (*SOS*, p. 113) **2.** "permanent" encystments of entheta resulting from the enturbulation of theta by enforcements or inhibitions of **affinity, reality** or **communication** and the trapping of this enturbulated theta by the physical pain of some engram or chain of engrams whose perceptics are approximated in the present-time enturbulation. **Locks** are analytical experiences. (*SOS* Gloss)

**ARC SECONDARIES, ARC** locks of such magnitude that they must be run as engrams in processing. Or, since locks are often run as engrams, **ARC** locks of great magnitude. (*SOS* Gloss)

**ARC STRAIGHTWIRE,** see STRAIGHTWIRE.

**ARC STRAIGHTWIRE RELEASE, recall release.** Freedom from deterioration; has hope; knows he/she won't get any worse. (*Scn 0-8*, p. 137)

**ARC TRIANGLE, 1.** it is called a **triangle** because it has three related points: **affinity, reality** and the most important, **communication.** Without **affinity** there is no **reality** or **communication.** Without **reality** or some agreement, **affinity** and **communication** are absent. Without **communication,** there can be no **affinity** or **reality.** It is only necessary to improve one corner of this very valuable **triangle** in Scn in order to improve the remaining two corners. The easiest corner to improve is **communication:** improving one's ability to **communicate** raises at the same time his **affinity** for others and life, as well as expands the scope of his agreements. (*Scn AD*) **2.** this **triangle** is a symbol of the fact that **affinity, reality,** and **communication** act together as a whole entity and that one of them cannot be considered unless the other two are also taken into account. (*NOTL*, p. 20)

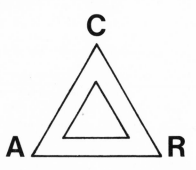

ARC Triangle

**ARCU, Affinity, Reality, Communication, Understanding.** (HCOB 6 Aug 68)

**ARF,** see AUDITOR REPORT FORM.

**ART,** the quality of communication. It therefore follows the laws of communication. Too much originality throws the audience into unfamiliarity and therefore disagreement, as communication contains duplication and "originality" is the foe of duplication. Technique should not rise above the level of workability for the purpose of communication. Perfection cannot be attained at the expense of communication. (HCOB 30 Aug 65)

**ASHO, American Saint Hill Organization** (BPL 5 Nov 72RA)

**AS-IS,** to view anything exactly as it is without any distortions or lies, at which moment it will vanish and cease to exist. (*Scn AD*)

**AS-IS-NESS, 1.** the condition of immediate creation without persistence, and is the condition of existence which exists at the moment of creation and the moment of destruction and is different from other considerations in that it does not contain survival. (*PXL*, p. 154) **2. as-is-ness** would be the condition created again in the same time, in the same space, with the same energy and the same mass, the same motion and the same time continuum. (*PXL*, p. 68) **3.** something that is just postulated or just being duplicated—no alteration taking place. **As-is-ness** contains no life continuum, no time continuum. (*PXL*, p. 91)

**ASMC, Anatomy** of the **Spirit** of **Man Congress.** (HCOB 29 Sept 66)

**ASSERTED,** another name for suggested, used mainly in check out of a goal to be sure, and occasionally in routine nulling when pc is declaring "it is my goal." (HCOB 1 Aug 62)

**ASSESS IN DIANETICS,** means choose, from a list or statements which item or thing has the longest read or the pc's interest. The longest read will also have the pc's interest oddly enough. (HCOB 23 Apr 69)

**ASSESSING BY ELIMINATION, 1.** doing it twice because of a possible instant read fault. **Assessing by elimination** is done on double (2 item) reads. But a hot auditor does it on best largest instant read. (BTB 11 Apr 74) **2.** after the first **assessment** the auditor continues to **assess** the reading items on the list **by elimination** down to ONE item. Sometimes some items will read three or four times, but the action is the same. The auditor **assesses** the reading items **by elimination** down to one item. (BTB 20 Aug 70R) [N.B. This action is revised by HCOB 14 Mar 1971R, *F/N Everything* and HCOB 20 Apr 72 Iss. II, *C/S Series 78 Product, Purpose and Why and WC Error Correction.*]

**ASSESSING, METHODS OF, 1.** the auditor starts at the top and takes up each read until he gets one to F/N. In this case the auditor does not do "Itsa earlier itsa." He just cleans each read.

(HCOB 28 May 70, *Correction Lists, Use Of*) **2.** the auditor starts from the top and on each read cleans it and does itsa earlier itsa to F/N or to a clean no-read and goes on. (HCOB 28 May 70, *Correction Lists, Use Of*) [N.B. the actions described in 1 and 2 above are revised according to HCOB 14 Mar 1971R, *F/N Everything.*] **3.** method 3—you take a prepared list and you read it to the pc, and you read the next one to the pc, and the first one that reads you then take it down earlier similar, earlier similar, earlier similar, earlier similar, until it F/Ns. (7106C12) **4.** the whole list is rapidly **assessed** over and over until one item stays in and that is given to the pc. (HCOB 28 May 70, *Correction Lists, Use Of*) [N.B. this action in 4 above is revised according to HCOB 14 Mar 1971R, *F/N Everything.*] **5.** method 5—all the way through and then you sort out the reads accordingly, and get them into a sequence that will F/N. (7106C12) **6.** method 6—the L-10 method of **assessing** a prepared list. You look at the pc and ask him directly every question on the list. (7106C12)

**ASSESSMENT,** an inventory and evaluation of a preclear, his body and his case to establish processing level and procedure. (HCOB 3 Jul 59, *General Information* )

**ASSESSMENT, 1.** is an action done from a prepared list. There is no other word that goes with that. **Assessment** does not go with anything else but that. That is all that **assessment** means. It is associated with a prepared list. Only a prepared list. (Class VIII No. 11) **2. assessment** isn't auditing, it is simply trying to locate something to audit. You say the word right to the pc's bank. (Class VIII No. 11) **3. assessment** is done by the auditor between the pc's bank and the meter. There is no need in **assessing** to look at the pc. Just note which item has the longest fall or BD. The auditor looks at the meter while doing an **assessment.** (HCOB 21 May 69) **4.** the whole action of obtaining a significant item from a pc. (HCOB 5 Dec 62) **5.** any method of discovering a level on the pre-hav scale for a given pc. (HCOB 7 Nov 62 III)

**ASSESSMENT BY INSTANT READ,** E-meter drill 24. Purpose: to train the student auditor to **assess** a list accurately and rapidly by **instant read.** (*EMD*, p. 47)

# ASSESSMENT BY TONE ARM

**ASSESSMENT BY TONE ARM,** E-meter drill 23. Purpose: to train the student auditor to **assess** a list accurately by selecting that item which, upon brief discussion, produces the most movement of the **tone arm.** (*EMD*, p. 46)

**ASSESSMENT FOR LONGEST READ,** calling off the items the pc has given and marking down the **reads** that occur on the meter. The pc is not required to comment during this action and it is better if he does not. (HCOB 29 Apr 69)

**ASSESSMENT TRs,** used to get a list to read. **Assessment** questions are delivered with impingement, the auditor accenting or "barking" the last word and syllable. An **assessment** is done crisply and businesslike with real punch (not shouting) so each line is *to* the pc. This is not to say that an **assessment** is done tone 40 or with antagonism. It's friendly but businesslike and impinges. (BTB 13 Mar 75)

**ASSESS ON PRE-HAV,** to **assess** the whole **pre-hav** scale. (HCOB 13 Jul 61)

**ASSIST, 1.** an action undertaken by a minister to **assist** the spirit to confront physical difficulties which can then be cared for with medical methodology by a medical doctor as needful. (*Abil MA, 241*) **2.** anything which is done to alleviate a present time discomfort. (*Abil 73*) **3.** simple, easily done processes that can be applied to anyone to help them recover more rapidly from accidents, mild illness or upsets. (*Scn AD*) **4.** the processing given to a recently injured person in order to relieve the stress of live energy which is holding the injury in suspension. (*Scn 8-8008*, p. 38) See also CONTACT ASSIST, TOUCH ASSIST, AUDITING ASSIST.

**ASSIST ENGRAM,** in the case of the manic, the fanatic or the zealot an engram has entirely blocked at least one of the purpose lines deriving from a dynamic. The engram may be called an **assist engram.** Its own surcharge (not the dynamic force) leads the individual to believe that he has a high purpose which will permit him to escape pain. This "purpose" is a false purpose not ordinarily sympathetic with the organism, having a hectic quality derived from the pain which is part of it, even though that pain is not wittingly experienced. This **assist engram** is using the native ability of the organism to accomplish its false "purpose" and brings about a furious and destructive effort on the part of the individual who, without this **assist engram** could have better accomplished the same goal. The worst feature of the **assist engram** is that the effort it commands is **engramic** dramatization of a particular sort, and if the **engram** itself is restimulated the individual becomes subject to the physical pain and fear which the entire experience contained. Therefore, the false purpose itself is subject to sporadic "sag." (*DTOT*, p. 77)

**ASSOCIATIVE DEFINITION,** see DEFINITIONS, TYPES OF.

**ASSOCIATIVE RESTIMULATORS, 1.** those things connected with the **restimulator.** (*DMSMH*, p. 354) **2.** a perceptic in the environment which is confused with an actual **restimulator.** (*DTOT* Gloss)

**ASSUMPTION, 1.** the name given to the act of a theta being taking over a mest body. This is occasionally found to be part of the record of the GE strong enough to be audited. It is the sensation of being taken over thoroughly, sometimes contains the shock of contact. The **assumption** takes place in most cases just prior to birth for every GE generation. (*HOM*, p. 37) **2. assumption** point: where the thetan has taken over the body. (PAB 8)

**ASTRAL BODIES,** somebody's delusion. **Astral bodies** are usually mock-ups which the mystic then tries to believe real. He sees the **astral body** as something else and then seeks to inhabit it in the most common practices of "**astral** walking." Anyone who confuses **astral bodies** with thetans is apt to have difficulty with theta clearing for the two things are not the same order of similarity. (*Scn 8-8008* Gloss)

**ATE, Auditors' Training Evening.** (HCOB 29 Sept 66)

**ATTENTION, 1.** when interest becomes fixed, we have **attention.** (*COHA*, p. 99) **2.** a motion which must remain at an optimum effort. **Attention** is aberrated by becoming unfixed and sweeping at random or becoming too fixed without sweeping. (*Scn 0-8*, p. 75)

**ATTENTION UNIT, 1.** a theta energy quantity of awareness existing in the mind in varying quantity from person to person. (HCOB 11 May 65) **2.** actually energy flows of small wavelengths and definite frequency. These are measurable on specifically designed oscilloscopes and meters. No special particle is involved. (*Scn 8-80*, p. 45)

**ATTENTION VALENCE, 1.** the **valence** one has assumed because it got **attention** from another **valence**. (PAB 95) **2.** one has become the **valence** B because one wants **attention** from C. Example—one becomes mother because mother received **attention** from father while self did not. (*FOT*, p. 95)

**AUD, auditor.** (HCOB 23 Aug 65)

**AUD C, Auditors' Congress.** (HCOB 29 Sept 66)

**AUDIO IMAGERY,** when a person can recall things he has heard by simply hearing them again. (*Exp Jour Winter-Spring 1950*)

**AUDIO-SEMANTIC,** part of the standard banks, a special part of sound files; the recording of words heard. (*DMSMH*, p. 46)

**AUDIT FOREVER CASE,** the grind case, the **audit forever case** is an afraid to find out case. (HCOB 15 Mar 62)

**AUDITING, 1.** the application of Scn processes and procedures to someone by a trained **auditor**. (BTB 30 Sept 71 IV) **2.** the action of asking a preclear a question (which he can understand and answer), getting an answer to that question and acknowledging him for that answer. **Auditing** gets rid of unwanted barriers that inhibit, stop or blunt a person's natural abilities as well as gradiently increasing the abilities a person has so that he becomes more able and his survival, happiness and intelligence increase enormously. (BTB 30 Sept 71 IV) **3.** Scn processing is called **auditing** by which the **auditor** (practitioner) listens, computes, and commands. (*FOT*, p. 88) **4.** to get a result on a pc. (SH Spec 71, 6607C26) **5.** an activity of an **auditor** taking over the control of and shepherding the attention of a pc so as to bring about a higher level of confront ability. (SH Spec 48, 6108C31) **6.** directing the pc's attention on his own case and directing his ability to talk to the **auditor**. (SH Spec 49, 6109C05) **7.** the reversing of other-determined flows by gradient scales, putting the pc at cause again. (HCOB 7 May 59) **8.** a communicating process or a communication process with the end goal of raising the ability of another person so that he can handle his bank, body, others, and environment in general. (5707C17)

**AUDITING ASSIST,** the **Auditing Assist** is done by a trained **auditor** using an E-meter. It consists of "running out" the physically painful experience the person has just undergone, accident, illness, operation or emotional shock. This erases the "psychic trauma" and speeds recovery to a remarkable degree. (HCOB 2 Apr 69)

**AUDITING BY LIST, 1.** a technique using prepared **lists** of questions. These isolate the trouble the pc is having with **auditing.** Such **lists** also cover and handle anything that could happen to a student or staff member. (LRH ED 257 Int) **2.** the earlier genus of this process was sec checking on the Joburg. Any **list** can be used. The questions asked are generalized and without time limiters; i.e. Has a withhold been missed? Have you been given a wrong goal? etc. If the line when asked has an instant read, say "That reads" then "What do you consider this could be?" or "What considerations do you have about this?" Let the pc answer all he wants to. This is continued until the line goes clean. If the line does not read say "That's clean" and move on to the next line of the **list.** This process gets charge off the case. (HCOB 23 Apr 64) [This process was later revised as follows.] **3.** we now F/N everything, we do not tell the pc what the meter is doing. This changes **auditing by lists** in both respects. We do not say to the pc, "That's clean" or "That reads." Use any authorized published **list.** Green Form for general review, L1C for ARC breaks, L4B for listed items, list errors. You are looking for an instant read that occurs at the end of the exact syllable of the question. If the question reads look expectantly at the pc. You can repeat the question by just saying it again if pc doesn't begin to talk. (HCOB 3 Jul 71) [The above is a brief summary only. The full exact procedure can be found in the referenced HCOBs.]

**AUDITING COMMAND, 1.** a certain, exact **command** which the preclear can follow and perform. (*FOT*, p. 88) **2.** an **auditing**

# AUDITING COMMAND CYCLE

**command,** when executed, has had performed exactly what it said and nothing else. An **auditing command** has no understoods about it. There is no pre-arrangement about an **auditing command** except maybe knowing the language. (SH Spec 25, 6107C05)

**AUDITING COMMAND CYCLE,** auditor asks, pc replies and knows he has answered, auditor acknowledges. Pc knows auditor has acknowledged. That is a full **auditing command cycle.** (HCOB 12 Nov 59)

**AUDITING COMM CYCLE,** this is the **auditing comm cycle** that is *always* in use: 1) is the pc ready to receive the command? (appearance, presence), 2) auditor gives command/question to pc (cause, distance, effect), 3) pc looks to bank for answer (itsa maker line), 4) pc receives answer from bank, 5) pc gives answer to auditor (cause, distance, effect), 6) auditor acknowledges pc, 7) auditor sees that pc received ack (attention), 8) new **cycle** beginning with (1). (HCOB 30 Apr 71)

**AUDITING CYCLE, 1.** the basic of **auditing** is an **auditing cycle** of command which operates as an attention director. Call it a restimulator if you want, but it's an attention director, eliciting a response from the pc to as-is that area and who knows he has done so when he receives from the practitioner an acknowledgment that it has occurred. That is the **auditing cycle.** (SH Spec 189, 6209C18) **2.** there are basically two communication **cycles** between the auditor and the pc that make up the **auditing cycle.** They are cause, distance, effect with the auditor at cause and the pc at effect, and cause, distance, effect, with the pc at cause and the auditor at effect. These are completely distinct one from the other. (HCOB 23 May 71R IV)

**AUDITING GOOFS,** minor unintentional omissions or mistakes in the application of Scn procedures to a person by a trained Scientologist. (*ISE*, p. 37)

**AUDITING OUT SESSIONS,** now and then it is necessary to **audit out** an **auditing session** or all **auditing.** One does this by R3RA, running the incident narrative to erasure and only going earlier similar if it starts to grind very badly or, if all **auditing,** handling it **session** by **session** as a chain. (HCOB 22 Jun 78R)

**AUDITING PROCEDURE,** the general model of how one goes about addressing a preclear. (*FOT,* p. 96)

**AUDITING SESSION, 1.** a precise period of time during which the **auditor** listens to the preclear's ideas about himself. (*Abil*

*155*) **2.** a period in which an **auditor** and preclear are in a quiet place where they will not be disturbed. The **auditor** gives the preclear certain and exact commands which the preclear can follow. (*FOT*, p. 88)

**AUDITING SUPERVISOR,** on the Saint Hill Special Briefing Course and in academies, **supervision** of the **auditing** section is done by the **auditing supervisor,** and auditing instructor or instructors. The **auditing supervisor** (or in some cases the course supervisor as at Saint Hill) assigns all sessions and teams. (HCO PL 21 Oct 62)

**AUDITOR, 1.** one who listens and computes; a Scn practitioner. (HCOB 26 May 59) **2.** one who has been trained in the technology of Scn. An **auditor** applies standard technology to preclears. (*Aud 38 UK*) **3.** a person who through church training becomes skilled in the successful application of Dn and Scn to his family, friends and the public to achieve the ability gained as stated on the Gradation Chart for his class of training. (FBDL 18, 2 Dec 70) **4.** Scn processing is done on the principle of making an individual look at his own existence, and improve his ability to confront what he is and where he is. An **auditor** is the person trained in the technology and whose job it is to ask the person to look, and get him to do so. The word **auditor** is used because it means one who listens, and a Scn **auditor** does listen. (*Scn 0-8*, p. 14) **5.** the word **auditor** is used, not "operator" or "therapist," because **auditing** is a cooperative effort between the **auditor** and the patient, and the law of affinity is at work. (*DMSMH*, p. 175) *Abbr.* Aud.

**AUDITOR CLEARANCE, 1.** rudiment: "Is it all right if I audit you?" (HCOB 21 Mar 61) **2.** beginning rudiment: "Are you willing to talk to me about your difficulties?" (HCOB 21 Dec 61)

Auditor

# AUDITOR COMM LAG

**AUDITOR COMM LAG,** lack of speed in giving commands. (HCOB 9 Aug 69)

**AUDITOR C/S,** a sheet on which the **auditor** writes the C/S instructions for the next session. (BTB 3 Nov 72R)

**AUDITOR EXPERTISE DRILLS, drills** to improve the quality of auditing by familiarizing auditors with the exact procedure of each auditing action through the use of **drills.** These **drills** are numbered as **Expertise Drill-1 (ED-1), Expertise Drill-2 (ED-2),** etc. (BTB 20 Jul 74)

**AUDITOR PRESENCE, 1.** the impingement on a pc; familiarity, certainty that something is going to happen, not scared of confronting; ability to make an impact. (6102C14). **2.** the **auditor** is as real and has as much **presence** to the pc as the rudiments stay in and has as little **presence** as the rudiments go out. (SH Spec 78, 6111C09)

**AUDITOR REPORT FORM, 1.** an **auditor's report form** is made out at the end of each session. It gives an outline of what actions were taken during the session. (BTB 6 Nov 72R VI) **2.** they give the details of the beginning of the session, condition of pc, what's intended, the wording of the process, total TA action. (HCOB 24 Jul 64) *Abbr.* ARF.

**AUDITOR RUDIMENT, 1.** O/Ws off on **Auditor** or **Auditors** or **PCs** until OK to be audited. (HCOB 8 Jan 60) **2. Auditor** Clearance is the most important of the **rudiments** because if the **Auditor** is not cleared negative results will be obtained on the profile of the preclear. To handle charge on the **Auditor,** TR 5N should be run if charge does not blow on a little two-way comm. Overt-Withhold on the **Auditor** is far too accusative and invalidates the PC. (HCOB 25 Jan 61) **3. Auditor** Clearance, "Is it all right if I Audit you?" if not, clear objection, or use TR5N or "Who should I be to Audit you?" or "Who am I?" depending on nature of the difficulty. (HCOB 21 Mar 61) [Note this HCOB was later revised by the next referenced HCOB] **4. Auditor** Clearance, "Are you willing to talk to me about your difficulties?" (HCOB 21 Dec 61)

**AUDITOR RUNDOWN,** this is an intensive which fully handles any case reasons why an **auditor** might have difficulty and enables him to move forward without any losses or failures from past efforts to help people stopping him. (LRH ED 301 INT)

**AUDITOR'S CODE, 1.** a list of the things one must or must not do to preserve the theta-ness of theta and to inhibit the enturbulation of theta by the **auditor.** (*SOS,* Bk. 2, p. 12) **2.** a collection of rules (do's and don'ts) that an **auditor** follows while **auditing** someone, which ensures that the preclear will get the greatest possible gain out of the processing that he is having. (*Scn AD*) **3.** the governing set of rules for the general activity of auditing. (*FOT*, p. 88) **4.** the **Auditor's Code** was evolved from years of observing processing. It is the technical **code** of Scientology. It contains the important errors which harm cases. It could be called the moral **code** of Scn. (*COHA*, p. 3)

**AUDITOR'S HANDBOOK,** the manual current at the time of the Phoenix Lectures which contained the *Axioms* and the Route One and Route Two processes of Intensive Procedure. It forms the basis of and is wholly included in *The Creation of Human Ability*. (*PXL* Gloss)

**AUDITOR TRAINEE PROGRESS BOARD,** a vertical **auditor trainee progress board** is kept by the intern supervisor. This has a space under each of the headings, left to right. Boxes along the top, left to right, serve to indicate the exact action the **trainee** is doing. The **trainee's** name is on a tab that is pinned to the space. The name tab is merely dated each time it is moved to the right. Thus the intern super can chase up any faltering student. (HCOB 7 Jan 72)

**AUTOGENETIC,** there are two kinds of illness: the first could be called **autogenetic,** which means that it originated within the organism and was self-generated, and exogenetic, which means that the origin of the illness was exterior. Psychosomatic illness would be **autogenetic,** generated by the body itself. (*DMSMH*, p. 92)

**AUTOMATIC BANK,** when a pc gets picture after picture after picture all out of control. This occurs when one isn't following an assessed somatic or complaint or has chosen the wrong one which the pc is not ready to confront or by overwhelming the pc with rough TRs or going very nonstandard. (HCOB 23 Apr 69)

**AUTOMATICITY, 1.** a sudden very rapid machine-gun fire outflow of answers given by the preclear. (HCOB 10 May 65) **2.** non-self-determined action which ought to be determined by the individual. The individual ought to be determining an action and he is not determining it. That's a pretty broad consideration. It's something not under the control of the individual. But if we said, something not under the control of the individual, as a total, unqualified definition of **automaticity,** we would have this, then: that car that just went down the street would be an **automaticity** to you. You didn't have control of it. So this is not a precision definition. The precision definition has "which ought to be under the control of the individual." (*Abil 36*) **3.** anything that goes on running outside the control of the individual. (*Abil SW*) **4.** something set up **automatically** to run without further attention from yourself. (2ACC-6A 5311CM20) **5.** there are three kinds of **automaticities**, those which create things, and those which make things persist, and those which destroy things. (2ACC-19A 5312CM09)

**AUTOMATIC MOCK-UP,** a picture of something which didn't really happen. (PAB 99)

**AUX. P.H.,** **auxiliary pre-hav** scale. (HCOB 3 Dec 61)

**AVU, 1. Authority** and **Verifications Unit.** (HCO PL 15 Aug 73) also known as **2. Authorizations** and **Verifications Unit.** (HCO PL 28 Jul 73RA)

**AWARENESS, 1.** the ability to perceive the existence of. (HCOB 4 Jan 73) **2. awareness** itself is perception. (2ACC-8B 5311CM24)

**AWARENESS LEVEL,** see AWARENESS SCALE.

**AWARENESS OF AWARENESS UNIT, 1.** an actuality of no mass, no wave-length, no position in space or relation in time, but with the quality of creating or destroying mass or energy, locating itself or creating space, and of re-relating time. (*Dn 55!*, p. 29) **2.** the individual himself. (5410CM20) **3.** the thetan is the **awareness of awareness unit.** (5410C10D)

**AWARENESS SCALE,** there are fifty-two levels of **awareness** from Unexistence up to the state of Clear. By "level of **awareness**" is meant that of which a being is **aware.** A being who is at a level on this **scale** is **aware** only of that level and the others below it. (HCO PL 5 May 65)

**AXIOMS, 1.** the **Axioms** are agreed-upon considerations. They are the central considerations which have been agreed upon. They are considerations. A self-evident truth is the dictionary definition of an **axiom.** No definition could be further from the truth. In the first place, a truth cannot be self-evident because it is a static. So, therefore, there is no self-evidency in any truth. There is not a self-evident truth, never has been, never will be. However, there are self-evident agreements and that is what an **axiom** is. (5501C21) **2.** statements of natural laws on the order of those of the physical sciences. (*DMSMH*, p. 6)

# B

**BACHELOR OF SCIENTOLOGY**, the standard **B Scn**/HCS course is in actuality the 20th ACC. The tapes to be used are the 20th ACC tapes. The texts are *Scientology Clear Procedure Issue One* and *ACC Clear Procedure* as published in booklet form. The **B Scn**/HCS course is five weeks in length. If comm course and upper indoc have not been covered by the student, the course becomes seven weeks in length. (HCOB 26 Dec 58) *Abbr.* B. Scn.

**BACK TO BATTERY**, *Slang.* an artillery term. A gun, after it fires, is said to go **out of battery**, which is to say, it recoils. Then after it's fired it's supposed to go **back to battery**, which is sitting the way you see them in photographs. They use the term in slang to indicate somebody who is now fixed up. So this guy will be all right for something or, what he has had will now be over. I could give you a purer definition, and say it is a completed case for that level, but the C/S doesn't normally think like that. (7204C07 SO II)

**BAD CONTROL**, a fallacy actually, control is either well done or not done. If a person is controlling something he is controlling it. If he is **controlling** it poorly, he is not **controlling** it. A machine which is being run well is controlled. A machine which is not

35

being run well is not being **controlled.** Therefore we see that **bad control** is actually a **not-control.** People who tell you that **control** is **bad** are trying to tell you that automobile accidents and industrial accidents are good. (*POW*, p. 40)

**BAD INDICATORS,** the condition isn't getting any better, not getting a lessening of the condition. Because we're not getting a lessening of the condition we therefore have losses. (SH Spec 3, 6401C09) See also INDICATORS.

Bad Indicators

**BAD MEMORY, 1.** accumulated occlusion of it all, but it's nevertheless nonconfront. (SH Spec 72, 6607C28) **2.** interposed blocks between control center and facsimiles. (*HFP* Gloss) See also AMNESIA.

**BAD NEEDLE,** a rock slam or a dirty **needle** or a stuck **needle** or a stage four **needle.** (HCO PL 30 Aug 70)

**BANK, 1.** the mental image picture collection of the pc. It comes from computer technology where all data is in a "**bank.**" (HCOB 30 Apr 69) **2.** a colloquial name for the reactive mind. This is what the procedures of Scn are devoted to disposing of, for it is only a burden to an individual and he is much better off without it. (*Scn AD*) **3.** merely a combination of energy and significance and this comprises a mass that sits there in its own made up space, and it's plotted against the pc's experiential track known as time. (SH Spec 65, 6507C27) See also REACTIVE MIND.

**BANK-AGREEMENT,** the common denominator of a group is the reactive **bank.** Thetans without **banks** have different responses. They only have their **banks** in common. They agree then only on **bank** principles. The **bank-agreement** has been what has made the earth a hell. (HCO PL 7 Feb 65)

**BANK BEEFING UP,** the sensation of increasing solidity of masses in the mind. (HCOB 19 Jan 67)

**BANK MONITOR,** the *file clerk* is the **bank monitor.** "He" **monitors** for both the reactive engram **bank** and the standard **banks.** (*DMSMH*, p. 198) See FILE CLERK.

**BANKY,** *Slang.* a term which means that a person is being influenced by his **bank** and is displaying bad temper, irritability, lack of cooperation and the signs of dramatization. He is being irrational. (*Scn AD*)

**BARK,** assessments are done to impinge and get a meter to read. The auditor **barks** the last word and the last syllable so it does impinge. You don't drop your voice or downcurve your voice tone at the end of the line as that will cost you reads. You punch the last sylable to make it read and *to* the pc. The accent is at the end of the sentence routinely, not on the earliest part. (BTB 13 Mar 75)

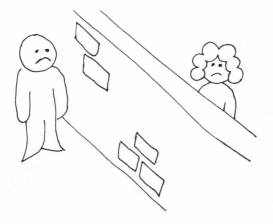

Barrier (Def. 2)

matter

**BARRIER, 1.** something which an individual cannot communicate beyond. (*Dn 55!*, p. 126) **2.** space, energy, matter and time—each is only a **barrier** to knowingness. A **barrier** is a **barrier** only in that it impedes knowingness. (*COHA*, p. 151) **3.** from Scientology Axiom 28: Barriers consist of Space, Interpositions (such as walls and screens of fast-moving particles) and Time. (*COHA*, p. 18)

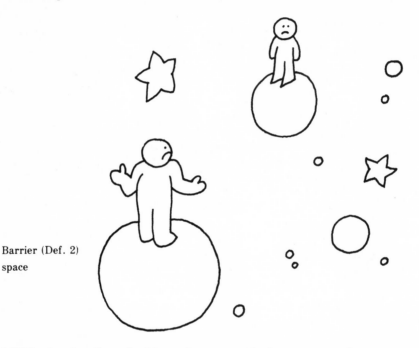

Barrier (Def. 2)
space

**BASIC, 1.** the first incident (engram, lock, overt act) on any chain. (HCOB 15 May 63) **2.** the first experience recorded in mental image pictures of that type of pain, sensation, discomfort, etc. Every chain has its **basic.** It is a peculiarity and a fact that when one gets down to the **basic** on a chain, (a) it erases and (b) the whole chain vanishes for good. **Basic** is simply earliest. (HCOB 23 Apr 69)

**BASIC AREA, 1.** the time track from the first recording on the sperm or ovum track to the first missed menstrual period of the mother. (*SOS* Gloss) **2.** early prenatal. (*DMSMH*, p. 224)

**BASIC AUDITING, 1.** the fundamental and most important elements of **auditing**—the skill of handling and keeping the preclear in session, proper use of the **auditing** communication cycle, the repetitive use of the **auditing** communication cycle to flatten a process, the correct application of the technology of Scn, and the ability to use and read an E-meter correctly. (*Scn AD*) **2.** the handling of the pc as a being, the **auditing** cycle, the meter. (HCOB 26 Nov 63)

**BASIC-BASIC, 1.** this belongs in Scn, not Dn. It means the most **basic basic** of all **basics** and results in clearing. It is found on the Clearing Course. (HCOB 23 Apr 69) **2.** the first engram on the whole time track.(HCOB 15 May 63) **3.** any similar circumstance repetitive through a person's whole track has a first time it occurred and that first time that it occurred we call **basic-basic.** (SH Spec 69, 6110C19)

**BASIC CYCLE OF ACTION,** create, resist effects (survive) and destroy; create an object, have it resist effects (survive) and then destroy it; create a situation, continue it and change it, and destroy or end it. (*COHA*, p. 249)

**BASIC ENGRAM,** the earliest **engram** on an **engram** chain. (*DTOT*, p. 112) See also BASIC.

**BASIC GOAL,** that **goal** native to the personality for a lifetime. It is second only in importance to survival itself. It is incident to the individuation of the person. A child of two knows its **basic goal.** It is compounded from genetic generations of experience. It can be found and reduced in some long past heavy effort facsimile such as death. It is neither advisable nor inadvisable to tamper with it. Much experience aligns on it. Desensitized, it would be supplanted by another **basic goal.** (*AP&A*, p. 42)

**BASIC INDIVIDUAL, 1.** the **basic individual** is not a buried unknown or a different person, but an intensity of all that is best and most able in the person. The **basic individual** equals the same person minus his pain and dramatizations. (*DTOT*, pp. 36-37) **2. basic individual** and Clear are nearly synonymous since they denote the unaberrated self in complete integration and in a state of highest possible rationality. A Clear is one who has become the **basic individual** through auditing. (*DTOT*, p. 34) See also CLEAR.

**BASIC LIE,** the **basic lie** is that a consideration which was made was not made or that it was different. (*PXL*, p. 181)

**BASIC OVERT ACT,** making somebody else want mest. (HCOB 17 Mar 60)

**BASIC PERSONALITY, 1.** a person's own identity. (*FOT*, p. 31) **2.** the **basic personality**, the file clerk, the core of "I" which wants to be in command of the organism, the most fundamental desires of the **personality**, may be considered synonymous for our purposes. (*DMSMH*, p. 394) **3.** the individual himself. (*DMSMH*, p. 394) *Abbr.* B.P. (BP).

**BASIC PRINCIPLE OF EXISTENCE,** the **basic principle of existence** is survival and that is only true for the body. A spirit cannot help but survive whether in heaven or in hell or on earth or in a theta trap. (*Abil Mi 5*)

**BASIC PROGRAM,** the **program** laid out in the Classification and Gradation Chart. (HCOB 12 Jun 70)

**BASIC PURPOSE,** it is a clinical fact that **basic purpose** is apparently known to the individual before he is two years of age: talent and inherent personality and **basic purpose** go together as a package. They seem to be part of the genetic pattern. (*DMSMH*, p. 238)

**BASICS OF SCIENTOLOGY,** axioms, scales, codes, fundamental theory about the thetan and the mind. (HCOB 3 May 62)

**BASIC TRUTH,** a static has no mass, meaning, mobility, no wave-length, no time, no location in space, no space. This has the technical name of **"basic truth."** (*PXL*, p. 180)

**BA STEPS, bring about steps**—R6 material. (HCOB 23 Aug 65)

**B.D., before Dianetics.** (*DMSMH*, p. 266)

**BD, blowdown.** (SH Spec 309, 6309C19)

**B.E., before earth.** (5203CM10)

**BEAUTY, beauty** is a wave-length closely resembling theta or a harmony approximating theta. (*Scn 8-80*, p. 26)

**BE, DO, HAVE,** see CONDITIONS OF EXISTENCE.

**BEEP METER,** a machine developed by Volney Mathison for chiropractors from a model furnished him by a chiropractor. Wherever a person has a painful spot on his body, if you put the electrode on it, the machine goes **"beep,"** but right alongside of the painful spot, it doesn't **beep.** (ESTO 6, 7203C03 SO III)

**BEFORE EARTH,** a theta line incident. There is a **before earth** and a before mest universe in all banks. The incidents are not dissimilar. The only thing remarkable about these **before** incidents is that they are a very definite degradation and condemnation of the preclear. (*HOM*, p. 66) *Abbr.* B.E.

**BEGINNING RUDIMENTS, 1. rudiments** at the **beginning** of session involve: (1) getting pc comfortable in environment; (2) getting pc willing to talk to auditor about pc's own case; (3) getting off withholds; (4) checking for and handling PTPs. The above are the **beginning rudiments.** (HCOB 14 Dec 61) **2.** are normally devoted to getting the atmosphere and the environment out of the road, so you can audit the pc. (SH Spec 45, 6108C24)

**BEHAVIOR PATTERNS,** conflicts in the commands contained in engrams and conflicts between the basic drive and the engramic contents combine into **behavior patterns.** (*DTOT*, p. 55)

**BEING, 1.** a viewpoint; he is as much a **being** as he is able to assume viewpoints. (*Scn 8-8008*, p. 17) **2.** an energy production source. (*Scn 8-80*, p. 33) See also THETAN.

**BEINGNESS, 1.** the result of having assumed an identity. (LRH Def. Notes) **2.** in terms of human experience, **beingness** is space. Space is a viewpoint of dimension. The points which mark an area of space are called anchor points, and these, with the viewpoint, alone are responsible for space. The creation of anchor points, then, is the creation of space, which is, in itself, the creation of **beingness.** The essential in any object is the space which it occupies. Thus, the ability to be an object first depends upon the ability to be the space which it occupies. (*Scn Jour 14-G*) **3.** essentially, an identification of self with an object. (*COHA*, p. 76)

Beingness (Def. 1)
see definition on
previous page

**BEINGNESS OF MAN,** essentially the **beingness** of theta itself acting in the mest and other universes in the accomplishment of the goals of theta and under the determination of a specific individual and particular personality for each being. (*Scn 8-8008*, p. 11)

**BEINGNESS PROCESSING,** is an alter-isness **process.** When a case is extremely inverted it is necessary to get the case up to a level where it can identify itself with *something.* **Beingness** is essentially identification of self with an object. In running **beingness processing** it will be discovered that the imagination of the preclear revives to a marked extent. **Beingness processing** recovers the various valences which the thetan is trying to avoid. The matter of valences is also a matter of packages of abilities, and where an individual is unable to be something which has certain definite abilities, he also cannot achieve those abilities, and this, in itself, is the heart of disability. (*COHA*, pp. 76-79)

**BEING OTHER BODIES, 1.** out of valence; being another identity than his own. He's in one **body** and he's **being another body.** (5904C08) **2.** that's shame. There is an emotion of shame connected with **being other bodies.** One is ashamed to be oneself, he is somebody else. (5904C08)

**BELOW THE CENTER LINE,** the American APA has a **center line** which is zero, above which we get plus and **below** which we get minus. An OCA is essentially the same thing, except the OCA has a better center graph. There are two conditions here **below the center line:** any negative, and "in the white." (7203C30SO)

**BENEFIT,** defined as that which would enhance survival. (*Scn 8-8008*, p. 6)

**B.E.R., bad exam report.** (BTB 5 Nov 72R III) See also RED TAG.

**BETRAYAL, 1.** a **betrayal** is help turned to destruction. The dichotomy of destroy is destroy-help. When help fails destruction occurs, or so goes the most basic consideration behind living. (HCOB 6 Feb 58) **2.** the knock-in of anchor points. One's anchor points are pulled out and then they are suddenly knocked in. That operation, when done exteriorly by somebody else is **betrayal.** (Spr Lect 17 5304CM08)

**BETTER,** negative gain. Things disappear that have been annoying or unwanted. (HCOB 28 Feb 59)

**BETTERMENT,** to us, is a lessening of a bad condition. (SH Spec 3, 6401C09)

**BETTERMENT LAG,** how many hours you have to process a preclear before he can become cause. (5410CM06)

**BETWEEN-LIVES AREA, 1.** the experiences of a thetan during the time **between** the loss of a body and the assumption of another. (*PXL*, p. 105) **2.** at death the theta being leaves the body and goes to the **between-lives area.** Here he "reports in," is given a strong forgetter implant and is then shot down to a body just before it is born. At least that is the way the old Invader in the earth area was operating. (*HOM*, p. 68)

**BETWEEN SESSIONS,** we don't mean overnight. We mean solely, strictly, completely and utterly if they get out of the auditor's sight at any time during a break. (SH Spec 7, 6106C05)

**BIG MIDDLE RUDIMENTS,** the **big mid ruds** can be used in the following places: At the start of any session. Examples: "Since the last time I audited you . . ." "Since the last time you were audited . . ." "Since you decided to be audited . . ." In or at the end of any session. Examples: "In this session . . ." On a list. Examples: "On this list . . ." "On (say list question) . . ." On a goal or item. Example: "On (say goal or item) . . ." Here is the correct wording and order of use for **big mid ruds**. ". . . has anything been suppressed?" ". . . is there anything you have been careful of?" ". . . is there anything you have failed to reveal?" ". . . has anything been invalidated?" ". . . has anything been suggested?" ". . . has any mistake been made?" ". . . is there anything you have been anxious about?" ". . . has anything been protested?" ". . . has anything been decided?" (HCOB 8 Mar 63) *Abbr.* B.M.R.

**BIG THETA BOP,** one-third of the dial back and forth or one-half of the dial back and forth, something like that. That's a **bop** on the loss of and still trying to hold onto the home universe. (PDC 15)

**BIG TIGER,** the same drill as the **tiger** drill except that it additionally uses nearly found out, protest, anxious about and careful of. One shifts to **big tiger** when making sure of the last item in on the list or a goal that fires strongly. (HCOB 29 Nov 62) See also TIGER DRILL.

**BIRTH, 1. birth** is one of the most remarkable engrams in terms of contagion. Here the mother and child both receive the same engram which differs only in the location of pain and the depths of "unconsciousness." Whatever the doctors, nurses and other people associated with the delivery say to the mother during labor and **birth** and immediately afterwards before the child is taken away is recorded in the reactive bank, making an identical engram in both mother and child. (*DMSMH*, p. 136) **2. birth** is ordinarily a severely painful unconscious experience. It is ordinarily an engram of some magnitude. Anyone who has been **born** then possesses at least one engram. (*DTOT*, p. 52)

**BIs, bad indicators.** (BTB 6 Nov 72RA IV)

**BLAB,** *Slang.* there may once in a while be a person who reads nicely at their clear reading with no action and you're very suspicious the guy isn't Clear. This could be a complete **"blab"**

no responsibility case—a mockery of Clear. (HCOB 26 May 60, *Security Checks*)

**BLACK AND WHITE, 1.** the name of a string of incidents where the theta body was implanted with electronic waves. (5208 CM07C) **2.** the two extreme manifestations of perception on the part of the preclear. Seeing **whiteness** or color the thetan is able to discern or differentiate between objects, actions and spatial dimensions. Energy can also manifest itself as **blackness**. (*Scn 8-8008*, p. 50) **3.** a rapid process which eliminates the need for running single incidents, locks, or secondaries, and is effective only in occluded cases. Wide-open cases cannot see **black** or **white**, but see color. These black areas, which are curtains over occluded facsimiles along the time track, erase, or become white, when attention is centered on them, and turning the field white by concentrating on the aesthetic band is the only concern of the auditor or preclear. Heavy somatics may be expected during **"black and white"** processing, but these can be avoided by keeping the field white. (*Scn 8-80* Gloss)

**BLACK DIANETICS, 1.** hypnotism. (5109C17A) **2.** There are those who, to control, resort to narcotics, suggestion, gossip, slander— the thousands of overt and covert ways that can be classified as **Black Dianetics**. (*Scn Jour* Iss 3G)

**BLACK FIELD,** just some part of a mental image picture where the preclear is looking at **blackness**. It is part of some lock, secondary or engram. In Scn it can occur (rarely) when the pc is exterior, looking at something **black**. It responds to R3R. (HCOB 23 Apr 69)

**BLACK FIELD CASE,** a **case** that could not run engrams because he could not see them. (HCOB 14 Jan 60)

**BLACK FIVE, 1.** a heavily occluded case characterized by mental pictures consisting of masses of **blackness**. This is a **"step V"** in early procedures such as Standard Operating Procedure 8. (*PXL*, p. 141) **2.** a level of nonperception, whether the person is seeing **blackness** or invisibility. (SH Spec 271, 6305C20) **3.** a no-responsibility case. (*COHA*, p. 161)

# BLACKNESS

**BLACKNESS, 1.** usually the protective coating between the preclear and the pictures. (*Abil SW*, p. 15) **2.** both of these conditions regarding blackness exist. The machine that makes **blackness** and having a **black** picture in restimulation; there is also simply the **blackness** of looking around inside a head. (*Abil SW*, p. 15) **3.** the **blackness** on the case is indicative of a scarcity of viewpoints, a necessity for safeguarding and protective "screens," a defensive and propitiative attitude towards existence, too much loss of allies and good, too much loss of space and finally and most importantly, loss of those who have evaluated for the preclear. The sudden departure of the person who has evaluated for the preclear results in loss of that viewpoint which the preclear unwittingly had assumed. (PAB 8) **4.** either the pc's unwillingness to face things or his basic bank. It cures if you do Dianetics by gradients. (HCOB 3 Apr 66)

**BLACKNESS OF CASES,** the **blackness of cases** is an accumulation of the **case's** own or another's lies. (*PXL*, p. 183)

Black Panther (Def. 2)

attack

flee

avoid

neglect

succumb

**BLACK PANTHER MECHANISM, 1.** in Dn considerable slang has been developed by patients and Dianeticists and they call the **"Black Panther Mechanism"** a neglect of the problem. One supposes this stems from the ridiculousness of biting **black panthers.** (*DMSMH*, p. 147) **2.** there are five ways in which a human being reacts toward a source of danger. Let us suppose that a particularly black-tempered **black panther** is sitting on the stairs and that a man named Gus is sitting in the living room. Gus wants to go to bed. But there is the **black panther.** The problem is to get upstairs. There are five things that Gus can do: (1) he can go *attack* the **black panther;** (2) he can run out of the house and *flee* the **black panther;** (3) he can use the back stairs and *avoid* the **black panther;** (4) he can *neglect* the **black panther;** and (5) he can *succumb* to the **black panther.** These are the five **mechanisms.** All actions can be seen to fall within these courses. And all actions are visible in life. (*DMSMH*, pp. 147-148)

**BLAME, 1.** it's simply punishing other bodies. (5904C08) **2.** when one individual assigns cause to another entity, he delivers power to that entity. This assignment may be called **blame,** the arbitrary election of cause. (*DAB*, Vol. II, p. 233) **3. blame** is the negation of your responsibility. You can **blame** self, that's the last stage, or you can **blame** somebody else. That's an effort not to be responsible. (5112CM28B)

**BLANKET,** to settle down over a mest body (one or more mest bodies). (5206CM26B)

**BLANKETING,** this incident consists of throwing oneself as a thetan over another thetan or over a mest body. **Blanketing** is done to obtain an emotional impact or even to kill. It is strongest in sexual incidents where the thetan throws two mest bodies together in the sexual act in order to experience their emotions. (*HOM*, p. 62)

**BLINDNESS,** extreme unawareness. (PAB 117)

**BLIND REPAIR,** when no FES is done, or when the pc has lost his folder, one is doing a **blind repair.** The progress program and advance program may have holes in them. (HCOB 6 Oct 70)

**BLINKLESS TR 0,** there is no such thing. Sitting with any attention on the body just isn't confront—you aren't doing the drill right. If your body blinks then OK, but if you are making it blink by having attention on the eyes then your **TR 0** is out. (HCOB 8 Dec 74)

**BLOCKING OUT,** identifying incidents on the time track by dating, moving the time track to that date, asking the pc what is there, finding the duration, moving the pc through it to the end, asking the pc what happened, checking for earlier beginning, moving the pc through the incident again. (SH Spec 272, 6306C11)

**BLOW,** *n.* **1.** the sudden dissipation of mass in the mind with an accompanying feeling of relief. (*Scn AD*) **2.** a definite manifestation and the pc must say "something **blew"** or "it disappeared" or "it's gone" or "it vanished," not "I feel lighter." (HCOB 24 Sept 71) **3.** the phenomena of obsessive efforts to individuate. (HCOB 12 Jan 61) **4.** departures, sudden and relatively unexplained, from sessions, posts, jobs, locations and areas. (HCOB 31 Dec 59) —*v. Slang.* **1.** unauthorized departure from an area, usually caused by misunderstood data or overts. (HCOB 19 Jun 71 III) **2.** leave, get out, rush away, cease to be where one should really be or just cease to be audited. (*BCR*, p. 23)

**BLOWDOWN, 1.** a tone arm motion to the left made to keep the needle on the dial. (HCOB 29 Apr 69) **2.** a period of relief and cognition to a pc while it is occurring and for a moment after it stops. When the auditor has to move the tone arm from right to left to keep the needle on the dial and the movement is .1 divisions or more, then a **blowdown** is occurring. (HCOB 3 Aug 65) **3.** a movement of the needle from left to right as you face a meter with a hang-up at the right. That's got to be included in training. It's whether or not the needle stays over to the right that makes the **blowdown,** not what you do with the tone arm. (SH Spec 21, 6406C04) **4.** the meter reaction of having found the correct by-passed charge. (HCOB 19 Aug 63) *Abbr.* BD.

**BLOWING BY INSPECTION,** an auditor may occasionally encounter a pc who erases chains before he can even tell about them. Along about Step 3 of R3RA, the TA **blows** down, the needle F/Ns, the pc says, "It's gone," and VGI's come in. This is called **blowing by inspection** and occurs once in a while with a fast running pc on a light chain. (HCOB 26 Jun 78 II)

**BLOW-OFFS,** see BLOW.

**BLOW-UP,** in the low tone arm case, means a sudden approach of the tone arm from a non-optimum (below 2.0) reading toward the optimum read. (HCOB 1 Sept 60)

**BLUE SHEET,** Return Programs (now called Advance Programs) are on bright **blue sheets.** (HCOB 25 Jun 70)

**B.M.R., big mid ruds.** (SH Spec 320, 6310C31)

**BOARD POLICY LETTERS,** color flash—green ink on cream paper. These are the issues of the Boards of Directors of the

Churches of Scientology and are separate and distinct from those HCO Policy Letters written by LRH. Only LRH issues may be printed green on white for policy and only LRH issues may have the prefix HCO. These **Board** issues are valid as **Policy.** The purpose of this distinction is to keep LRH's comm lines pure and to clearly distinguish between Source material and other issues and so that any conflict and/or confusion on Source can easily be resolved. (BPL 14 Jan 74R I) *Abbr.* BPL.

**BOARD TECHNICAL BULLETIN,** color flash—red ink on cream paper. These are the issues of the Boards of Directors of the Churches of Scientology and are separate and distinct from those HCO Bulletins written by LRH. Only LRH issues may be printed red on white for Technical Bulletins and only LRH issues may have the prefix HCO. These **Board** issues are valid as **tech.** The purpose of this distinction is to keep LRH's comm lines pure and to clearly distinguish between Source material and other issues and so that any conflict and/or confusion on Source can easily be resolved. (BPL 14 Jan 74R I) *Abbr.* BTB.

**BODHI, 1.** one who has attained intellectual and ethical perfection by human means. This probably would be a Dn Release. (*PXL*, p. 18) **2. Bodhi** means enlightenment or, alternately, one who has attained intellectual and ethical perfection by human means. (*HOA*, Intro)

**BODY, 1.** a carbon-oxygen engine which runs at 98.6°F. The theta being is the engineer running this engine in a *Homo sapiens*. (*HOM*, p. 42) **2.** a solid appendage which makes the person recognizable. (PAB 125) **3.** an identifying form or non-identifiable form to facilitate the control of, the communication of and with, and the havingness for the thetan in his existence in the mest universe. (HCOB 3 Jul 59) **4.** the thetan's communication center. (*CFC*, p. 9) **5.** a carbon-oxygen engine which runs on low combustion fuel, generally derived from other life forms. The **body** is directly monitored by the genetic entity in activities such as respiration, heartbeat and endocrine secretions; but these activities may be modified by the thetan. (*Scn 8-8008*, p. 8) **6.** a physical object. It is not the being himself. As a **body** has mass it tends to remain motionless unless moved and tends to keep going in a certain direction unless steered. (HCOB 10 May 72)

**BODY IN PAWN,** an incident of protecting **bodies.** Societies have gone totally batty on the track with this and we call it **bodies in pawn.** (5904C08)

**BODY MOTION,** any **motion** of the **body** which causes the tone arm to move falsely up or down. **Body motion** is never recorded in a session. (*EMD*, p. 25)

**BODY-PLUS-THETAN SCALE,** from 0.0 to 4.0 on the tone scale, and the position on this **scale** is established by the social environment and education of the composite being and is a stimulus-response **scale.** (*Scn 8-8008*, p. 76)

**BODY REACTIONS,** one of the ten main needle actions of an E-meter. The deep breathing of a preclear, a sigh, a yawn, a sneeze, a stomach growl can any one of them make a needle react. They're not important once you know what they are. (*EME*, pp. 18-19)

**BODY VALENCE,** human identity. (HCOB 14 Jul 56)

**BOGGED STUDENT,** he is groggy or puzzled or frowning or even emotionally upset by his misunderstood words. When not caught and handled he will go to sleep or just stare into space. (HCO PL 26 Jun 72)

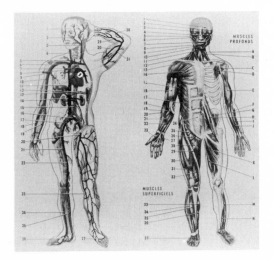

Body (Def. 5)

**BOIL-OFF,** *v.* to become groggy and seem to go to sleep. (*HFP*, p. 100) —*n.* **1.** usually a flow running too long in one direction. (7204C07 SO III) **2.** a manifestation of unconsciousness, is very mild, and simply means that some period of the person's life wherein he was unconscious has been slightly restimulated. (*Scn Jour ISS. 14-G*) **3.** a state of unconsciousness produced by a confusion of effort impinging upon one area. It is a slow motion unconsciousness. (PDC 29) **4.** a condition of somnolence which is sometimes indistinguishable from sleep. (*SOS*, Bk. 2, p. 133) **5. boil-off** was originally and sedately named "comatic reduction," but such erudition has been outvoted by the fact that it has never been used. (*DMSMH*, p. 303) **6.** it actually is a flow which is run too long in one direction. That's what **boil-off**, anaten, etc. is. (SH Spec 229, 6301C10)

**BONUS PACKAGE,** occasionally you get a **bonus package** off one list. In addition to the item you are looking for, sometimes two R/Sing items will show up on the same list opposing each other and blow. They oppose each other, not what you're listing. (HCOB 23 Nov 62) *Abbr.* BP.

**BOOK AND BOTTLE,** Opening Procedure by Duplication. Its goal is the separating of time, moment from moment. This is done by getting a preclear to duplicate the same action over and over again with two dissimilar objects. In England this process is called **"Book and Bottle,"** probably because these two familiar objects are the most used in doing Opening Procedure by Duplication. (*Dn 55!*, p. 114)

**BOOK AUDITOR, 1.** someone who has successfully applied Scn from a **book** to help someone else and who has received a **Hubbard Book Auditor** certificate for doing so. (*Scn AD*) **2.** someone who has studied **books** on Scn and listens to other people to make them better. (*Abil 155*)

**BOOK ONE CLEAR,** Mest Clear. (*Abil 87*) See also MEST CLEAR.

**BOOK ONE OF DIANETICS,** *Dianetics: The Modern Science of Mental Health.* (HCO PL 25 Jan 57)

**BOOK ONE OF SCIENTOLOGY,** *Scientology: The Fundamentals of Thought.* (HCO PL 25 Jan 57)

**BOREDOM, 1. boredom** is not just not doing anything. **Boredom** is an eddying back and forth which on its lower harmonic becomes pain and on a lower harmonic becomes agony. (2ACC-28B, 5312CM20) **2. boredom** is not a state of inaction. It is a state of idle action, vacillating action where penalties are yet in existence, and where they are grave, but a state in which one has decided he can't really do anything about them. It's just a high-toned apathy. (PDC 59)

Boredom (Def. 2)

**BORROWED FACSIMILES, facsimiles** that aren't yours. That is to say they are **borrowed** from people or they're photographed or they're taken right straight out of other theta beings, just outright stolen; we call it **borrowing.** (5207CM24B)

**BOTTOM TERMINAL,** the **terminal** farthest from present time. (SH Spec 306, 6309C11)

**BOUNCER, 1.** an engram which contains the species of phrase, "can't stay here," "Get out!" and other phrases which will not permit the preclear to remain in its vicinity but returns him to present time. (*DTOT*, p. 129) **2.** the preclear may be in an engram and yet be **bounced** into present time. This creates a situation in which the preclear seems to be in present time but is actually under considerable tension being held in an engram. (*SOS*, p. 106)

**BP, bonus package.** (HCOB 23 Nov 62)

**B.P., basic personality.** The attention units called **basic personality.** (*DMSMH*, p. 124)

**BPC, by-passed charge.** (HCOB 23 Aug 65)

**BPI,** designation on HCO Policy Letters and HCO Bulletins indicates dissemination and restriction as follows: **Broad Public Issue.** Give to HCOs of all types, all staff of central organizations, field Auditors, put in magazines, do what you like with it. (HCO PL 22 May 59)

**BPL, Board Policy Letter.** (BPL 14 Jan 74R I)

**BRACKET, 1.** the standard **bracket** is a five-way **bracket.** The general form of this is as follows: you . . . terminal; terminal . . . you; terminal . . . another; another . . . terminal; terminal . . . terminal. (HCOB 30 Apr 61) **2.** the word **bracket** is taken from the artillery, meaning to enclose with a salvo of fire. A **bracket** is run as follows: first one gets the concept as happening to the preclear. Then one gets the concept of the preclear making it happen (or thinking or saying it) to another. Then one gets the concept as being directed by another at others. (*Scn 8-80*, p. 40) **3.** with these three things: the thetan trying to put up mock-ups of his own which persist; trying to divert the mock-ups of others; and trying to observe what others are doing to others; we have what we call a **bracket** in Scn. (PAB 11) **4.** the individual does it himself, somebody else does it, others do it, or the individual does it to somebody else, or somebody does it to him or others do it to others. (PDC 31)

**BRAIN, 1.** another part of the nervous system which receives and sends impulses to the body parts. (*SPB*) **2.** a neuro-shock absorber. It has very little to do with thinking. (SH Spec 75, 6608C16) **3.** a very mechanical rattletrap sort of a switchboard that's been thrown together by you in order to translate thought into action and to coordinate energy. (5203CM03B)

**BREAK-ENGRAM, 1.** a late **engram** which crosses chains of **engrams** would be a "cross engram." If such an **engram** resulted in a loss of sanity it would be called a "**break-engram.**" (*DMSMH*, p. 144) **2.** the secondary **engram** after the receipt of which the individual experienced a lowering of general tone to

2.5 or below and became therefore unable to cope with his environment. (*DTOT* Gloss)

**BREAKING A CASE,** *Slang.* meaning that one **breaks** the hold of the preclear on a nonsurvival facsimile, never breaking the preclear or his spirit, but **breaking** what is breaking the preclear. (*HFP* Gloss)

**BRIDGE, THE, 1.** the route to Clear, **the bridge,** which we call the *Classification, Gradation and Awareness Chart.* (*Aud 107 ASHO*) **2.** a term originating in early Dn days to symbolize travel from unknowingness to revelation. (*Aud 72 ASHO*)

**BROKEN,** *Slang.* used in the wise of **"breaking** a case," meaning that one **breaks** the hold of the preclear on a nonsurvival facsimile. Used in greater or lesser magnitude such as **"breaking** a circuit"** or **"breaking** into a chain"** or **"breaking** a computation."** Never breaking the preclear or his spirit, but **breaking** what's breaking the preclear. (*HFP* Gloss)

**BROKEN DRAMATIZATION,** where the individual has been prevented from carrying out the commands of the engram which is restimulated by present time environmental perceptics. (*SOS,* Bk. 2, p. 118)

**BROKEN DRAMATIZATION LOCKS, locks** in which the chief factor is that the individual has been prevented from completing the dramatization of a restimulated engram. These are most abundant at the 1.5 level. (*SOS* Gloss)

**B.S., Beginning Scientologist.** (HCOB 23 Aug 65)

**B. Scn., Bachelor** of **Scientology.** (HCOB 23 Aug 65)

**B.T., before time.** (5203CM10A)

**BTB, Board Technical Bulletin.** (BPL 14 Jan 74R I)

**BUBBLE GUM INCIDENT, 1.** an incident on the track where you are hit with motion and finally develop an obsession about motion. (I wish you to carefully note these very technical terms like **bubble gum.**) (5206CM23A) **2.** the first incident on the track that has any words in it and is usually the last incident on the track of any magnitude that has any words in it for millions of years afterward. It sits there all by itself. It's a verbal implant, a thought implant. (5206CM25B)

**BUDDHA,** simply one who has attained bodhi. There have been many **buddhas** and there are expected to be many more. (PAB 32)

Buddha

**BUGGED,** the word **bugged** is slang for snarled up or halted. (HCO PL 29 Feb 72 II)

**BULL-BAITING,** in coaching certain drills, the coach attempts to find certain actions, words, phrases, mannerisms or subjects that cause the student doing the drill to become distracted from the drill by reacting to the coach. As a **bullfighter** attempts to attract the **bull's** attention and control the **bull,** so does the coach attempt to attract and control the student's attention, however the coach flunks the student whenever he succeeds in distracting the student from the drill and then repeats the action until it no longer has any effect on the student. Taken from a Spanish and English sport of **"baiting"** which means "to set dogs upon a chained **bull,"** but mainly "to attack or torment especially with persistent insult, criticism or ridicule." Also "to tease." (LRH Def. Notes)

**BUREAU 5,** (Continental Liaison Office) **Bureau 5** covers the standard functions done in Scientology Church Tech and Qual Divisions. (SO ED 96 Int)

**BUTTERED ALL OVER THE UNIVERSE, 1.** a preclear who does not know where he is. The preclear has used remote viewpoints, and has left remote viewpoints located all over everywhere to such a degree that the preclear thinks he is anyplace rather than where he is. (*Dn 55!*, pp. 145-146) **2.** in his effort to control, a thetan spreads himself further and further from the universe, and in his failures to control, withdraws from things he has attempted to control but leaves himself connected with them in terms of 'dead energy.' Thus we get the manifestation **'buttered all over the universe.'** (*COHA*, p. 123) **3.** *Colloquial;* a thetan unknowingly in contact with a large part of a universe. (*COHA*, p. 74) **4.** the lower harmonic of exteriorization, which is: "I don't want to be there and I've backed out in spite of myself." (5411C29) **5.** the super reach case. He isn't withdrawing, he's reaching, compulsively and he can't stop himself. (2ACC-29A, 5312CM20)

**BUTTON(S), 1.** items, words, phrases, subjects or areas that cause response or reaction in an individual by the words or actions of other people, and which cause him discomfort, embarrassment, or upset, or make him laugh uncontrollably. (*Scn AD*) **2.** things in particular that each human being finds aberrative and has in common. (*HFP*, p. 127) **3.** restimulators, words, voice tones, music, whatever they are—things which are filed in the reactive mind bank as parts of engrams. (*DMSMH*, p. 74) **4.** (suppress **button**, invalidate **button**, etc.), it is called a **button** because when you push it (say it) you can get a meter reaction. (HCOB 29 Jan 70)

**BUTTON CHART,** chart of attitudes toward life. This might be called a **"button chart"** for it contains the major difficulties people have. (*HFP*, p. 38)

**BY-PASS CIRCUITS,** see DEMON CIRCUITS.

**BY-PASSED CHARGE, 1.** mental energy or mass that has been restimulated in some way in an individual, and that is either partially or wholly unknown to that individual and so is capable of affecting him adversely. (*Scn AD*) **2.** when one gets a lock, a lower earlier incident restimulates, that is **BPC.** It isn't the auditor **by-passing** it. One handled later charge that restimmed earlier **charge**. That is **BPC** (tech of '62), and that is all that the term means. "Earlier **charge** restimmed and not seen" would be another name for it. (HCOB 10 Jun 72 I) **3.** reactive **charge** that has been **by-passed** (restimulated but overlooked by both pc and auditor). (*BCR*, p. 21) *Abbr.* BPC.

**BY-PASSED CHARGE ASSESSMENT, 1.** auditing by list to help the preclear find **by-passed charge.** The moment the correct **by-passed charge** is found the preclear feels much better. (*Scn AD*) **2.** a **BPC assessment** is actual auditing (Level III). Here one cleans each smallest read of a question (but not cleaning cleans), before going onto the next question, handling originations by the pc and acknowledging. One never does this with an ARC broken pc. With an ARC break one just ploughs on looking for a big read and indicates it to pc. (*BCR*, p. 41) **3.** a **by-passed charge assessment** is auditing because you clean every read of the needle on the list being assessed. The pc is acked, the pc is permitted to itsa and give his opinions. But you never do a **by-passed charge assessment** on an ARC broken pc. These two different activities (**by-passed charge assessment** and ARC break assessment) unfortunately have the word **assessment** in common and they use the same lists, therefore some students confuse them. (HCOB 7 Sept 64 II)

**BY-PASSED ITEM,** when a list has been made and includes a reliable item and that reliable item was not used to find an **item** in opposition to it, the **item** which was not so found is called a **by-passed item.** (HCOB 17 Nov 62)

# C

**CALIBRATION,** finding and marking the correct positions on the tone arm dial so that TA 2 and TA 3 positions are known precisely by the auditor at start of session. (*EMD*, p. 16A)

**CALL-BACK,** a type of action phrase which would, in present time, cause the preclear to move back to another position in space, and when contained in an engram would pull the preclear down from present time into the engram. (*SOS*, p. 105)

**CAL-MAG FORMULA,** working on this in 1973, for other uses than drug reactions, I found the means of getting **calcium** into solution in the body along with **magnesium** so that the results of both could be achieved. (HCOB 5 Nov 74)

**CANCELLER, 1.** in Dn processing we used to use what was called a "**canceller**." At the beginning of the session, the preclear was told that anything which had been said to him would be **cancelled** when the word **cancelled** was uttered at the end of the session. This **canceller** is no longer employed, not because it was not useful but because lock scanning provides the means of scanning off all the auditing. This is a far more effective and positive mechanism than the **canceller**. (*SOS*, Bk. 2, pp. 228-229) **2.** a contract with the patient that whatever the auditor says will not become literally interpreted by the patient or used by him in any way. It prevents accidental positive suggestion. (*DMSMH*, p. 200)

**CANNED LIST,** *Slang.* a pre-prepared and issued list. (7204C07 SO I)

**CANS,** electrodes for the E-meter. Steel soup or vegetable cans, unpainted, tops cleanly removed, label and glue washed off, tin plated or not, have been standard for many years. It is with these that calibration has been done. (HCOB 14 Jul 70)

Cans

**CAN'T HAVE, 1.** it means just that—a depriving of substance or action or things. (HCO PL 12 May 72) **2.** denial of something to someone else. (BTB 22 Oct 72) **3.** a moment of pain or unconsciousness is a moment of **can't have.** If, at a certain moment, an individual **couldn't have** the environment, **couldn't have** the circumstances he was undergoing then it is a certainty that he'll pile up an engram right at that spot in time. (*Abil 34*)

**CAS, Church** of **American Science.** (PAB 74)

**CASE,** the whole sum of past by-passed charge. (HCOB 19 Aug 63)

**CASE ANALYSIS, 1.** the determination of where pc's attention (at current state of case) is fixed on the track and restoring pc's determinism over those places. (HCOB 28 Feb 59) **2.** the steps for **case analysis** are (1) discover what the pc is sitting in, (2) get the lies off, (3) locate and indicate the charge. (HCOB 14 Dec 63)

**CASE CRACKING SECTION,** a **section** in the Dept. of Review in the Qualifications Division of a Scientology Church. This **section** audits cases (students or HGC pcs or other pcs in difficulty such as field auditor rejects) to a result. (HCO PL 24 Apr 65)

**CASE V, 1.** the definition of a **case V** is no mock-ups, only blackness. (*Scn 8-8008*, p. 120) [For a complete list of the eight levels of case of SOP 8-C, see STATES OF CASE SCALE.]

**CASE GAIN, 1.** the improvements and resurgences a person experiences from auditing. (*Scn AD*) **2.** any case betterment according to the pc. (*Abil 155*)

**CASE HISTORIES,** reports on patients, individual records. (PAB 82)

**CASE LEVEL,** see STATE OF CASE SCALE.

**CASE PROGRESS SHEET,** a **sheet** which details the levels of processing and training the pc has achieved while moving up the grade chart. It also lists incidental rundowns and setup actions the pc has had. The **sheet** gives at a glance the pc's **progress** to OT. (BTB 3 Nov 72R)

**CASE, STATES OF,** see STATE OF CASE SCALE.

**CASE SUPERVISOR, 1.** that person in a Scientology Church who gives instructions regarding, and **supervises** the auditing of preclears. The abbreviation **C/S** can refer to the **Case Supervisor** or to the written instructions of a **case supervisor** depending on context. (BTB 12 Apr 72R) **2.** the **C/S** is the **case supervisor.** He has to be an accomplished and properly certified auditor and a person trained additionally to **supervise cases.** The **C/S** is the auditor's "handler." He tells the auditor what to do, corrects his tech, keeps the lines straight and keeps the auditor calm and willing and winning. The **C/S** is the pc's case director. His actions are done *for the pc.* (*Dn Today*, Bk. 3, p. 545) *Abbr.* C/S. See also C/S.

**CATATONIA, 1.** a psychiatric name for withdrawn totally. (HCOB 24 Nov 65) **2. catatonia** means the person is lying still in apathy unmovingly and not reaching anything. (SH Spec 303, 6309C05)

**CAUSATION,** imposing time and space upon objects, people, self, events and individuals. (*Scn 8-80*, p. 44)

**CAUSE, 1. cause** could be defined as emanation. It could be defined also, for purposes of communication, as source-point.

(*FOT*, p. 77) **2.** a potential source of flow. (*COHA*, p. 258) **3.** is simply the point of emanation of the communication. **Cause** in our dictionary here means only "source point." (*Dn 55!*, p. 70)

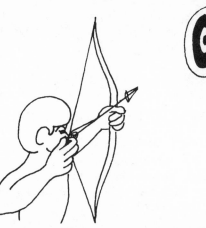

Cause (Def. 2)

**"CAVE IN,"** (noun) **"CAVED IN"** (adjective), mental and/or physical collapse to the extent that the individual cannot function causatively. The individual is quite effect. A U.S. Western term which symbolized mental or physical collapse as like being at the bottom of a mine shaft or in a tunnel when the supports collapsed and left the person under tons of debris. (LRH Def. Notes)

**CC, Clearing Course.** (HCO PL 6 Sept 72 II)

**CCHs, 1.** a highly workable set of processes starting with **control**, going to **communication** and leading to **havingness** in that order. The **CCHs** are auditing specifically aimed at and using all the parts of the two way comm formula. (BTB 12 Sept 63) **2.** several associated processes which bring a person into better **control** of his body and surroundings, put him into better **communication** with his surroundings and other people, and increase his ability to **have** things for himself. They bring him into the present, away from his past problems. (*Scn AD*) **3.** actually, **control**, **communication** and **havingness**. When you apply **control**, you obtain **communication** which gives the preclear **havingness**. And it is a method of entrance on cases which is rather infallible. (SH Spec 9, 6106C07)

**CCH-0,** the sum of **CCH-0** is find the auditor, find the auditing room, find the pc, knock out any existing PT problem, establish goals, clear help, get agreement on session length and get up to the first real auditing command. **CCH-0** isn't necessarily run in that order and this isn't necessarily all of **CCH-0**, but if any of these are seriously scamped, the session will somewhere get into trouble. (*SCP*, p. 8)

**CCH OB,** clear help in brackets with a meter, running meter toward a freer needle. (PAB 138)

**CDEI, curiosity, desire, enforcement, inhibition.** (BTB 1 Dec 71RB II)

**CDEINR, curious, desired, enforced, inhibited, no, refused.** (BTB 1 Dec 71RB II)

**CELL, 1.** the virus and **cell** are matter and energy animated and motivated in space and time by theta. (*Scn 0-8*, p. 75) **2.** a unit of life which is seeking to survive and only to survive. (*DMSMH*, p. 50)

**CEN-0,** designation on HCO Policy Letters and HCO Bulletins indicates dissemination and restriction as follows: to go to all staff of **Central Organizations only** plus HCO Area Sec, HCO Cont, HCO WW. (HCO PL 22 May 59)

**CEN-O-CON,** designation on HCO Policy Letters and HCO Bulletins indicates dissemination and restriction as follows: to go to Association Secretaries or **Organization Secretaries** of **Central Organizations only,** not to staff; also to HCO Area Sec, HCO **Cont,** HCO WW. (HCO PL 22 May 59) **2.** modifies HCO PL 22 May 59, HCO Policy Letters which are marked **CenOCon** may be issued to all staff including HASI Personnel. (HCO PL 25 Jun 59)

**CENT, central.** (BPL 5 Nov 72RA)

**CENTRAL ORG (ORGANIZATION),** Church of Scientology (Class IV). (HCO PL 6 Feb 66)

**CERT,** see CERTIFICATE.

**CERTAINTY, 1.** the degree of willingness to accept the awareness of an is-ness. (SH Spec 84, 6612C13) **2.** knowledge itself is **certainty**; knowledge is not data. Knowingness is **certainty**. Sanity is **certainty**, providing only that that **certainty** does not fall beyond the conviction of another when he views it. To obtain a **certainty** one must be able to observe. (*COHA*, p. 187) **3.** knowingness—knowing one knows—a state of beingness. (PAB

29) **4.** measurement of the effort and locations and distances necessary to make two points coincide at a certain instant in time. And that is really a low level **certainty**. That is **certainty** in terms of motion. (5311CM17A) **5.** clarity of observation. (*COHA*, p. 190)

**CERTAINTY PROCESSING,** the **processing** of **certainties.** The anatomy of maybe consists of uncertainties and is resolved by the **processing** of **certainties.** (*Scn 8-8008*, p. 126)

**CERTIFICATE,** an award given by the Hubbard Communications Office to designate study and practice performed and skill attained. It is not a degree as it signalizes competence whereas degrees ordinarily symbolize merely time spent in theoretical study and impart no index of skill. (Aud 2 UK) *Abbr.* Cert.

Certificate

**CERTIFICATION COURSE,** you teach the student the theory in the **certification course** and the drills and key processes for the grade in the classification course. (HCOB 22 Sept 65)

**CERTIFICATION EXAM,** this is a written test taken from the HCOBs, tapes, policy letters of the theory material the student studies. (FO 1685)

**CHAIN, 1.** a series of recordings of similar experiences. A **chain** has engrams, secondaries and locks. (HCOB 23 Apr 69) **2.** incidents of similar nature strung out in time. (SH Spec 70, 6607C21) **3.** a series of incidents of similar nature or similar subject matter. (HCOB 1 Mar 62)

**CHAIN OF INCIDENTS, 1.** when one speaks of a **chain of incidents,** one means usually a **chain** of locks or a **chain** of engrams or a **chain** of secondaries which have similar content. (*SOS*, Bk. 2, p. 194) **2.** a whole adventure or activity related by the same subject, general location or people, understood to take place in a long time period, weeks, months, years or even billions or trillions of years. (HCOB 15 May 63) See also CHAIN.

**CHANGE, 1.** a shift of location in space. (SH Spec 4, 6105C26) **2.** essentially the redirection of energy. When **change** is too rapid or too slow both beingness and havingness suffer. (*Scn 8-8008*, p. 103)

**CHANGE OF CHARACTERISTIC, 1.** one of the ten main needle actions of an E-meter. A **change of characteristic** occurs when we hit on something in the preclear's bank. It occurs only when and each time we ask that exact question. As the question or item alone changes the needle pattern, we must assume that that is it and we use it. It is not much used but must be known. (*EME*, pp. 15-16) **2.** the meter on a certain question has its needle shift into a different action than it was in. It resumes its old action when you no longer ask the question. (SH Spec 1, 6105C07)

Chain

# CHANGE OF SPACE PROCESSING

**CHANGE OF SPACE PROCESSING,** the object of **change of space processing** is to get all areas into present time. Originally it could be conceived that only the place where the preclear is is in present time, that all other places are in past time to the degree that they are far from the preclear. **Change of space processing** is done in this fashion: "Be at the place where you entered the mest universe," "Be at the center of this room," "Be at the place where you entered the mest universe," "Center of this room," "Entrance point," "Room" and so forth until the entrance point is in present time. The preclear should be made to run **change of space** on any area until that area is in present time. (*COHA*, p. 38)

**CHANGE OF VIEWPOINT,** the primary requisite of the **viewpoint** is that it has position relative to points. A **change of viewpoint** necessitates a **change** of positions rather than a **change** of idea. The **change** of position is primary; the **change** of idea is secondary. (PAB 8)

**CHANGE PROCESSES,** 1. resistance to **change** prevents the pc from having, and as the ideas of **change** are sorted out the pc has increased havingness. (HCOB 27 Apr 61) 2. if a pc is bad off on **change** (which includes about eighty per cent of the pcs you get), he cannot run another auditing command cleanly as he never really runs the command but runs something else. Therefore the only thing that can be run is a **change process** and it must be run until motion is removed from the tone arm. There are many, many versions of **change.** To get the best result, adapt a **process** to the pc. (HCOB 27 Apr 61)

**CHAOS,** 1. all points in motion—no points fixed. (5410CM07) 2. there's nothing traveling in one direction and there's nothing in alignment. (PDC 59)

**CHAOS MERCHANT,** the slave master, the fellow who's trying to hold everybody down, the fellow who's trying to keep everybody shook up one way or the other and so he can't ever get up again, the fellow who makes his money and his daily bread out of how terrible everything is. (SH Spec 328, 6312C10) See also MERCHANTS OF CHAOS.

**CHARGE, 1.** harmful energy or force accumulated and stored within the reactive mind, resulting from the conflicts and unpleasant experiences that a person has had. Auditing discharges this **charge** so that it is no longer there to affect the individual. (*Scn AD*) **2.** the electrical impulse on the case that activates the meter. (HCOB 27 May 70) **3.** stored energy or stored recreatable potentials of energy. (HCOB 8 Jun 63) **4.** the stored quantities of energy in the time track. It is the sole thing that is being relieved or removed by the auditor from the time track. (HCOB 13 Apr 64, *Scn VI Part One Tone Arm Action*) **5.** emotional **charge** or energy. (*NSOL*, p. 29) **6.** the accumulation of entheta in locks and secondaries which **charges** up the engrams and gives them their force to aberrate. (*SOS* Gloss) **7.** by **charge** is meant anger, fear, grief, or apathy contained as misemotion in the case. (*SOS*, p. 108) See also CHRONIC CHARGE.

**CHARGE UP, charge** that is restimulated but not released causes the case to **"charge up"** in that **charge** already on the time track is triggered but is not yet viewed by the pc. (HCOB 8 Jun 63)

**CHARGED UP,** the key-in and additional locks begin to give the engram more and more entheta, and it becomes more and more powerful in its effect upon the individual. It has to be, in short, **charged up** in order to affect the individual. (*SOS*, Bk. 2, p. 137)

**CHART OF ATTITUDES, 1.** a **chart** on which are plotted with the numerical values of the emotional tone scale the gradient **attitudes** that fall between the highest and lowest states of consideration about life. Example: top-CAUSE; bottom-FULL EFFECT. (*PXL* Gloss) **2.** a **chart of attitudes** toward life. This might be called a "button chart" for it contains the major difficulties people have. It is also a self-evaluation chart. You can find a level on it where you agree and that is your level of reaction toward life. (*HFP*, p. 38)

**CHC, Clean Hands Congress.** (HCOB 29 Sept 66)

**CHECKLIST,** a **list** of actions or inspections to ready an activity or machinery or object for use or estimate the needful repairs or corrections. This is erroneously sometimes called a "checksheet" but that word is reserved for study steps. (HCOB 19 Jun 71 III)

# CHECKOUT

**CHECKOUT,** the action of verifying a student's knowledge of an item given on a checksheet. (HCOB 19 Jun 71 III)

**CHECKSHEET,** a list of materials, often divided into sections, that give the theory and practical steps which, when completed, give one a study completion. The items are selected to add up to the required knowledge of the subject. They are arranged in the sequence necessary to a gradient of increasing knowledge on the subject. After each item there is a place for the initial of the student or the person checking the student out. When the **checksheet** is fully initialed, it is complete, meaning the student may now take an exam and be granted the award for completion. Some **checksheets** are required to be gone through twice before completion is granted. (HCOB 19 Jun 71 III) *Abbr.* c/sheet or ch. sheet or √sht.

**CHECKSHEET MATERIAL,** the policy letters, bulletins, tapes, mimeo issues, any reference book or any books mentioned on the **checksheet.** (HCO PL 16 Mar 71)

**CHEMICAL RELEASE,** drugs (or alcohol) give an enforced moment or period of **release.** It is surrounded in mass. They are deadly because they give the sensation of **release** while actually pulling in mass. (HCOB 23 Sept 68)

**CHEW AROUND,** tendency on the part of preclears to change the direction or position of the energy masses which they are handling, and when this is the case there is a certain loss of havingness by reason of heat and friction. (PAB 52)

**CHEW ENERGY,** *Slang.* just "**chewing** the **energy** around" doesn't make it persist, but, with all this **chewing** he isn't as-ising anything. All he is doing is moving mass "A" to position "B." Anybody who is doing this gets no cognition out of it at all. He is waiting for that piece of **energy** to tell him something, and this tells you a great deal about the preclear who couldn't run an engram. He was waiting for the MEST to say something. (PAB 56)

**CHKSHT,** checksheet. (BPL 5 Nov 72RA)

**CHRONIC CHARGE,** charge is an impulse to withdraw from that which can't be withdrawn from or to approach that which can't be approached, and this, like a two pole battery, generates current.

This constantly generated current is **chronic charge**. (HCOB 8 June 63)

**CHRONIC ENGRAM,** an **engram** which has been more or less continuously restimulated so that it has become an apparent portion of the individual. (*DTOT,* p. 45)

**CHRONIC HIGH TA,** one which is found high two sessions running (consecutive). **"High"** means around 4.0 or above. But 3.8 can also be called **"high"** if it occurs at session beginning too often. (HCOB 13 Feb 70) See also HIGH TA.

**CHRONIC INSANITY, 1.** an acute **insanity** with the time factor lengthily extended. (*DASF*) **2.** one which, having appeared, does not subside but holds the individual in an abnormal state. (*DASF*)

**CHRONIC SOMATIC, 1.** a stuck moment on a time track, which is the stable datum of a prior confusion. (SH Spec 61, 6110C03) **2.** an obvious demonstration of a help-failure cycle where the individual has used an effort to help and has failed and has gotten a **somatic** back. (5112CM30A) **3.** psychosomatic illness, as it is called in the field of medicine, is named in Dn a **chronic somatic,** since it is not an illness, and cannot be diagnosed as such but is only some former pain which is in restimulation. (*SOS,* p. xv) **4.** a psychosomatic illness, since it is discovered that psychosomatic illness is only the restimulated **somatic** of some engram and goes away when the engram is contacted and reduced or erased. (*SOS,* p. 26) **5.** simply an area of randomity, a theta facsimile of past pain, effort, counter-effort, that has swamped the individual. It throws him all out of whack. As far as atoms and molecules are concerned, he suffers pain. (5109CM24B)

**CHUG,** a needle reaction in which the needle in falling appears to encounter, penetrate and surge beyond a "skin." (HCOB 13 Apr 64, *Scn VI Part One Glossary of Terms*)

**CIRCUIT, 1.** a part of an individual's bank that behaves as though it were someone or something separate from him and that either talks to him or goes into action of its own accord, and may even, if severe enough, take control of him while it operates.

A tune that keeps going around in someone's head is an example of a **circuit**. (*NOTL* Gloss) **2.** just an identity that is so dominant that it balls up a whole section of the whole track. It takes a large section of the whole track and bundles it all up in a black ball and it's full of pictures. (SH Spec 105, 6201C25) **3.** a **circuit** has no livingness in it. It is simply a motivated mass. (SH Spec 21, 6106C27) **4.** matter, energy, space and time at a mental level, enclosing thought. (6009C13) **5.** a mechanism which becomes an identity in itself, with its own "I" which takes a piece of the analyzer, walls it off with the charge, and thereafter dictates to the preclear. In olden times, these were called demons. (*SOS*, Bk. 2, p. 202) **6.** divisions of your own mind that seem to make up other personalities and these other personalities affect you and argue with you and so forth. (5203CM05D)

**CIRCUIT CASES,** the auditor will encounter many cases which resolve very rapidly. These account for fully 50% of the people who come to him, but he will also encounter many people whose cases are resistive and he will encounter a small handful who wouldn't let anything happen if the auditor used a shotgun on them. These are classified as **"circuit cases."** (PAB 19)

**CIRCUITRY, 1.** consists of "you" phrases. They are the phrases addressed from an exterior "I" to "you." "I have to tell you" is still a "you" addressing the "I." These phrases are received from persons who seek to nullify the independence of judgment of others. (*NOTL*, p. 49) **2. circuitry** is an escape from knowing. It is knowingness in a substitute for lack of knowing. When a thetan escapes from knowing, he sets up a **circuit**. (SH Spec 68, 6110C18)

**CLASS, 1.** refers to the level of **classification** of an auditor. (BTB 12 Apr 72) **2.** a technical certificate in Scn goes by **classes** on the gradation chart. (HCO PL 13 Mar 66) *Abbr.* Cl.

**CLASS 0,** see HRS.

**CLASS I,** see HTS.

**CLASS II,** see HCA.

**CLASS III,** see HPA.

**CLASS IV,** see HAA.

**CLASS V,** see HVA.

**CLASS VI,** see HSS.

**CLASS VII,** see HGA.

**CLASS VIII,** see HSTS.

**CLASS VIII C/S-6,** list useful in running out past bad auditing. (HCOB 28 Mar 74)

**CLASS VIII DRUG RUNDOWN,** one of the steps in a complete **drug rundown.** It consists of listing and rehabbing all drugs, 3-way recalls, secondaries, and engrams of taking and giving **drugs.** (HCOB 31 Aug 74)

**CLASS IX,** Hubbard Advanced Technical Specialist. The **Class IX** Course is taught at Saint Hill organizations and contains data concerning advanced procedures and developments since Class VIII. (CG&AC 75)

**CLASS X,** an advanced Scn course available only on Flag. It teaches L-10 OT, an upper level rundown whose basic tech comes from research into increasing OT powers. (CG&AC 75)

**CLASS XI,** an advanced Scn Course, available to Sea Org auditors only and is taught on Flag. It teaches L-11, the New Life Rundown and L-11X, the New Life Expansion Rundown. (CG&AC 75)

**CLASS XII,** an advanced Scn course available to Sea Org auditors only and is taught on Flag. It teaches L-12, the Flag OT executive Rundown. (CG&AC 75)

**CLASS CHART,** see CLASSIFICATION GRADATION AND AWARENESS CHART.

**CLASSIFICATION, 1. classification** means that we require certain actions to have been done or conditions to have been attained before an individual is **classified** on that level and we let him go on. (*Aud 107 ASHO*) **2.** an award earned by an auditor that entitles him to audit certain levels of processes, and that shows that he has attained the ability and skill to do so by actual test. (*Scn AD*)

# CLASSIFICATION COURSE

**CLASSIFICATION COURSE,** the practical drills and student auditing portion of an auditor training **course.** After completion of the **classification course** the auditor is **classified** to that level and may audit pcs professionally on the processes of that level. (*PRD* Gloss)

**CLASSIFICATION EXAM,** this is a practical **exam.** The test consists of a checkout of TR-4, any of the meter drills of the level, and the auditing of a doll on the process or processes of that level with full TRs and admin. (FO 1685)

**CLASSIFICATION GRADATION AND AWARENESS CHART,** the route to Clear, the Bridge. On the right side of the **chart** there are various steps called the states of release. The left-hand side of the **chart** describes the very important steps of training on which one gains the knowledge and abilities necessary to deliver the grades of release to another. It is a guide for the individual from the point where he first becomes dimly aware of a Scientologist or Scn and shows him how and where he should move up in order to make it. Scn contains the entire map for getting the individual through all the various points on this **gradation scale** and for getting him across the Bridge to a higher state of existence. (*Aud 107 ASHO*)

Clay Demo

**CLAY DEMO,** abbreviation for **clay demonstration.** A Scn study technique whereby the student **demonstrates** definitions, principles, etc. in **clay** to obtain greater understanding by translating significance into actual mass. (BTB 12 Apr 72R)

**CLAY TABLE,** a **clay table** is any platform at which a student, standing or sitting, can work comfortably. The surface must be smooth. A **table** built of rough timber will serve but the top surface where the work is done should be oil cloth or linoleum. Otherwise the **clay** sticks to it and it cannot be cleaned and will soon lead to an inability to see clearly what is being done because it is stained with **clay** leavings. (HCOB 10 Dec 70 I)

**CLAY TABLE CLEARING, 1.** a process of **clearing** words and symbols. (HCOB 9 Sept 64) **2.** as one Scn remedy for increased IQ and destimulation, **clay table clearing** is audited by an auditor in a session. The entire effort by the auditor in a session of **clay table clearing** is to help the pc regain confidence in being able to achieve things by removing the misunderstandings which have prevented that achievement. (HCOB 18 Aug 64)

**CLAY TABLE HEALING,** gets the pc to name the condition *the pc* requires to be handled and gets the pc to represent this in **clay.** The whole process is flat when the condition has vanished. **Clay table healing** is a very precise series of actions. (HCOB 9 Sept 64) [The above is a very brief summary only. The full series of steps can be found in the referenced HCOB.] *Abbr.* CTH.

**CLAY TABLE IQ PROCESSING, 1.** trace back (with no meter) what *word* or term the pc failed to grasp in the subject chosen. Get the pc to make up the mass represented by the word in **clay** and any related masses. Get them all labeled and explained. **I.Q.** (**intelligence quotient** or the relative brightness of the individual) can be rocketed out of sight with HGC use of a **clay table.** (HCOB 17 Aug 64) **2.** the original issue of "**Clay Table Clearing**" was called "**Clay Table I.Q. Processing.**" (HCOB 27 Sept 64)

**CLAY TABLE PROCESSING, 1.** the **clay table** presents us with a new series of **processes.** The preclear is made to make in **clay** and labels whatever he ,or she is currently worried about or hasn't understood in life. The essence of **clay table processing** is to get the pc to work it out. In auditing the pc tells the auditor. This is still true in **clay table processing.** (HCOB 17 Aug 64) **2.** the pc handles the mass. The auditor does not suggest subjects or colors or forms. The auditor just finds out what should be made and tells the pc to do it in **clay** and labels. And keeps calling for related objects to be done in **clay**. (HCOB 17 Aug 64)

**CLAY TABLE TRACK ANALYSIS,** a training activity for Class VI. (HCOB 18 Aug 64)

**CLAY TABLE TRAINING,** the student is given a word or auditing action or situation to demonstrate. He then does this in **clay**. (HCOB 11 Oct 67)

**CLEAN HANDS,** in order for an auditor who is regarded as a security risk to be considered to have **clean hands**, it is necessary for him to receive a **Clean Hands** Clearance Check from HCO. If on completion there are questions which are alive or if there are any missed or partial withholds the person must go back to the HGC to have them **cleaned** up before he is considered to have **clean hands**. If no questions are alive and there are no missed or partial withholds, then the person will be awarded a **Clean Hands** seal on his certificate and will be considered to be in good standing with HCO. (HCO PL 27 Feb 62)

**CLEANING A CLEAN, 1.** attempting to **clean** up or deal with something that has already been **cleaned** up or dealt with or that wasn't troublesome to the person in the first place. (*Scn AD*) **2.** there is nothing there yet the auditor tries to get it and the pc ARC breaks. This is **cleaning a clean** with an E-meter. (HCO PL 16 Apr 65) **3.** this is the same as asking a pc for something that isn't there and develops a "withhold of nothing." (HCOB 13 Apr 64, *Scn VI Part One Tone Arm Action*)

**CLEAN NEEDLE, 1.** a **needle** that acts when the auditor speaks and does nothing the rest of the time. (*EMD*, p. 42) **2.** it is a total uniform speed. There is not the faintest tick in it. There is not the faintest speed-up. There is nothing. It is just like molasses pouring out of the barrel—and there it is, and that's a **clean needle**. (SH Spec 224, 6212C13) **3.** one which flows, producing no pattern or erratic motions of the smallest kind with the auditor sitting looking at it and doing nothing. A **clean needle** is not just something that doesn't react to a particular question. It's a lovely slow flow, usually a rise, most beautifully expressed on a Mark V at 64 sensitivity. (HCOB 30 Dec 62)

**CLEAR,** *n.* **1.** a thetan who can be at cause knowingly and at will over mental matter, energy, space and time as regards the first dynamic (survival for self). The state of **Clear** is above the release grades (all of which are requisite to **clearing**) and is attained by completion of the **Clearing Course** at an Advanced Organization. (*Scn AD*) [In 1978 the Founder released HCOB 24 September 1978, Issue III, *Dianetic Clear* which states "The state of Clear can be achieved on Dianetics."] **2.** a **Clear**, in an absolute sense, would be someone who could confront anything and everything in the past, present and future. (*Abil Mi 256*) **3.** a **Clear** is not an all-knowing being. A **Clear** is somebody who has lost the mass, energy, space and time connected with the thing called mind. (SH Spec 80, 6609C08) **4.** a picture is completely unnecessary for any kind of a recall at all which is probably about the only change there has been from the definition of a Book One **Clear.** (SH Spec 59, 6504C27) **5.** a **Clear** has no vicious reactive mind and operates at total mental capacity just like the first book (*DMSMH*) said. In fact every early definition of **Clear** is found to be correct. (HCOB 2 Apr 65) **6.** the name of a button on an adding machine. When you push it, all the hidden answers in the machine **clear** and the machine can be used for a proper computation. So long as the button is not pressed the machine adds all old answers to all new efforts to compute and wrong answers result. Really, that's all a **Clear** is. **Clears** are beings who have been **cleared** of wrong answers or useless answers which keep them from living or thinking. (*Aud 4 UK*) **7.** a **Clear** has risen from the analogy between the mind and the computing machine. Before a computer can be used to solve a problem, it must be **cleared** of old problems, of old data and conclusions. Otherwise, it will add all the old conclusions into the new one and produce an invalid answer. Processing **clears** more and more of these problems from the computer. The completely **cleared** individual would have all his self-determinism in present time and would be completely self-determined. (*Abil 114A*) **8.** a thetan **cleared** of enforced and unwanted behavior patterns and discomforts. (HCOB 8 May 63) **9.** simply an awareness of awareness unit which knows it's an awareness of awareness unit, can create energy at will, and can handle and control, erase or re-create an analytical mind or reactive mind. (*Dn 55!*, pp. 17-18) **10.** a person who can have or not have at will anything in the universe. (5412CM06) **11.**

an unaberrated person. He is rational in that he forms the best possible solutions he can on the data he has and from his viewpoint. He obtains the maximum pleasure for the organism, present and future, as well as for the subjects along the other dynamics. The **Clear** has no engrams which can be restimulated to throw out the correctness of computation by entering hidden and false data in it. (*DMSMH*, p. 111) **12.** one who has become the basic individual through auditing. (*DTOT*, p. 33) —*v.* **1. to clear:** to release all the physical pain and painful emotion from the life of an individual. (*DMSMH*, p. 170)

**CLEARED CANNIBAL,** the individual without engrams seeks survival along all of the dynamics in accordance with his breadth of understanding. This does not mean that a Zulu who has been **cleared** of all his engrams would not continue to eat missionaries if he were a **cannibal** by education; but it does mean that he would be as rational as possible about eating missionaries; further, it would be easier to re-educate him about eating missionaries if he were a **Clear.** (*SOS*, p. 110)

**CLEARED THETA CLEAR, 1.** a person who is able to create his own universe; or, living in the mest universe is able to create illusions perceivable by others at will, to handle mest universe objects without mechanical means and to have and feel no need of bodies or even the mest universe to keep himself and his friends interested in existence. (*Scn 8-8008*, p. 114) **2.** next level above **theta clear** (which is **cleared** of need to have a body). All of a person's engrams have been turned into conceptual experience. He is **clear** all the way along the track. He can really deliver the horsepower. (5206CM26A) **3.** one who has full recall of everything and full ability as a thetan. (*Scn 8-80*, p. 59)

**CLEARED WORD,** a word which has been **cleared** to the point of full conceptual understanding. (HCOB 23 Mar 78R)

**CLEARING, 1.** a gradient process of finding places where attention is fixed and restoring the ability of the pc to place and remove attention under his own determinism. (HCOB 28 Feb 59) **2.** what is **clearing** but regaining awareness that one is himself, and regaining confidence. (HCOB 1 Feb 58)

**CLEARING COMMANDS, 1.** when running a process newly or whenever the preclear is confused about the meaning of the **commands, clear** the **commands** with the preclear, using the dictionary if necessary. The auditor reads the **commands** one at a time to the pc and asks the pc "What does this **command** mean to you?" (HCOB 14 Nov 65) **2. clear** the **commands** (or questions or list items) by first **clearing** in turn each word in backwards sequence of the words in the **command**. (e.g. if **command** is "Do fish swim?" **clear** "swim" then "fish" then "do.") This prevents the pc starting to run the process by himself while you are still **clearing** the words. (BTB 2 May 72R)

**CLEAR MOCKERY,** a condition in which the thetan thinks of himself as dead. If you just ask him, "How could you help me?" although he is sitting here at 3 on the dial, there is no action on the needle. The needle is stiff. He is all machine motivated. You'll find in his normal course of endeavor he has all kinds of bad luck. He doesn't quite groove in but basically this: he doesn't believe anything can be done. No help, no doingness. (SH Spec 1, 6105C07)

**CLEAR OT,** our definition of an **operating thetan** is that of a **Clear Operating Thetan.** This is a proofed-up being who no longer has a bank, and who has experience. This is a completely stable state—a being who won't hit the banana peel. (SH Spec 82, 6611C29)

**CLEAR READ,** when a preclear is **Clear** he may occasionally get some tone arm motion due to purely body electronics but in the main **reads** at male or female on the tone arm (3 or 2) according to his or her sex. (*EME*, p. 11)

**CLEAR THINKING,** a **Clear** does not have any "mental voices." He does not **think** vocally. He **thinks** without articulation of his thoughts and his thoughts are not in voice terms. He thinks at such speed that the word stream of consciousness would be left at the post. (*DMSMH*, p. 87)

**CLOSED TERMINALS,** when one begins to identify, one has "**closed terminals**" too **closely**, and believes one **terminal** is another **terminal**. (PAB 63) See also SNAPPING TERMINALS.

**CLOSURE MECHANISM** (of problems), problems **close** in on one as an actual mental mass when one invents solutions for them. The solution is *not* the problem so does not as-is or erase. When one invents problems or conceives of problems as simply problems, the mental mass moves *away* from him in space. This can be demonstrated to a pc (who can see mental mass) by having him invent some solutions. A mental mass will move in on him. But when he invents problems the mental mass moves away. See HCOB 11 June 57, page 6. In considerable use in 1955 in London. (LRH Def. Notes)

**COACH,** to train intensively by instruction, demonstration and practice. In training drills, one twin is made the **coach** and the other the student. The **coach** in his **coaching** actions, **coaches** the student to achieve the purpose of the drill. He **coaches** with reality and intention following exactly the materials pertaining to the drill to get the student through it. When this is achieved the roles are then reversed—the student becoming the **coach** and the **coach** becoming the student. (HCOB 19 Jun 71 III)

**CO-AUDIT,** *n.* a team of any two people who are helping each other reach a better life with Scn processing. (*Abil 155*)

**CO-AUDITING,** is an abbreviation for **cooperative auditing.** It means a team of any two people who are helping each other reach a better life with Scn processing. (*Aud 90 UK*)

**CO-AUDITING TEAM,** where two people **audit** each other alternately. There is also the three-way **team,** in which three people **co-audit.** This has the advantage of keeping altitude for each auditor, since in the triangle, none is being processed by anyone he is **auditing.** (*SOS,* Bk. 2, pp. 266-267)

**CO-AUDITOR,** one who **audits** another **co-auditor** under supervision and after training at a given level. (*Aud 2 UK*)

**CODE,** collection of rules (do's and don'ts). (BTB 30 Sept 71 IV)

**CODE OF A SCIENTOLOGIST,** the **Code of a Scientologist** was evolved to safeguard **Scientologists** in general, and is subscribed to by leading **Scientologists.** (*COHA,* p. 7)

**CODE OF HONOR, 1.** the ethical **code** of Scn; the **code** one uses, not because he has to, but because he can afford such a luxury. (*COHA* Gloss) **2.** the **Code of Honor** clearly states conditions of acceptable comradeship amongst those fighting on one side against something which they conceive should be remedied. Anyone practicing the **Code of Honor** would maintain a good opinion of his fellows, a much more important thing, than having one's fellows maintain a good opinion of one. (PAB 40)

**COFFEE GRINDER,** an alternate name for Facsimile One. (*HOM*, p. 64) See FACSIMILE ONE.

**COF,** designation on HCO Policy Letters and HCO Bulletins indicates dissemination and restriction as follows: HCO **City Offices** and all their field Auditors, HCO Franchises, central organizations, HCO Area, continental and HCO WW. (HCO PL 22 May 59)

**COFFEE SHOP AUDITING, 1.** out of session auditing of someone. (HCOB 20 Apr 72 II) **2.** meterless fool-around, often by students, stirring up cases. (HCOB 8 Mar 71)

**COFFIN CASE,** a preclear who lies in the position of a dead man, with arms folded. This is a grief engram having to do with the death of some loved one, and with the preclear in the valence of the loved one. (*SOS*, p. 112) See also CORPSE CASE.

**COG, cognition.** (HCOB 23 Aug 65)

**COGNITING,** as-ising aberration with a realization about life. (HCOB 26 Apr 71 I)

**COGNITION, 1.** as-ising aberration with a realization about life. (HCOB 26 Apr 71 I) **2.** a pc origination indicating he has "Come to realize." It's a "What do you know, I . . ." statement. (HCOB 14 May 69 II) **3.** something a pc suddenly understands or feels. "Well, what do you know about that?" (HCOB 25 Feb 60) *Abbr.* Cog.

**COGNITION SURGE,** a release of electrical charge. It goes along with the person having a **cognition.** (SH Spec 9, 6106C07)

**COLD,** an extreme stillness. (SH Spec 56, 6109C20)

**COLOR-VISIO AND TONE-AUDIO,** when a person can imagine in terms of **color** motion pictures with **sound.** (*Exp Jour, Winter-Spring 50*)

**COMANOME, 1.** once upon a time, engrams were called **coma-nomes.** (5009CM23B) **2.** a period of unconsciousness which contained physical pain and apparent antagonism to the survival of the individual. (*Exp Jour, Winter-Spring 1950*) See ENGRAM.

**COMATIC REDUCTION,** boil-off was originally and sedately named **comatic reduction** but such erudition has been outvoted by

the fact that it has never been used. (*DMSMH*, p. 303) See
BOIL-OFF.

**COMBINATION VALENCE,** one which has all the characteristics
of the terminal and oppterm. (SH Spec 105, 6201C25)

**COMBINED TERMINAL,** an item or identity the pc has both
been and opposed produces therefore both pain and sensation
when it is "late on the track," which is to say, after the fact of
many terminals and opposition terminals. The **combination
terminal** is the closure between terminal and opposition terminal
lines which possesses attributes of both and the clarity of
neither. It signifies a period toward the end of a game. It is
found most commonly when the pc's case is only shallowly
entered. They exist on all cases but are fewer than terminals
and opposition terminals. *Symbol.* COTERM. (HCOB 8 Nov 62)

**COME ALIVE,** on a second or third assessment items which were
at first null or reading poorly will be found to **come alive** and
read well. The pc by being audited has had an increase of ability
to confront. The result is that items beyond his reach previously
(and did not read well) are now available and can be run easily.
(HCOB 29 Apr 69)

**COMM, communication.** (HCOB 23 Aug 65)

**COMMAND PHRASES,** statements that group, bounce or deny.
(HCOB 15 May 63) See ACTION PHRASES.

**COMMAND POSTS, 1.** control centers. (5110CM11B) **2.** epicenters which stand along the nerve channels of the body and
are like switchboards. (*HOM*, p. 25)

**COMMAND SOMATIC,** a **somatic** brought from a different part of
the time track by some **command** phrase, such as "My arm
hurts." The preclear may have this **somatic** while running a
prenatal engram although he was only three days conceived in
the incident. **Command somatics** occur where the preclear is out
of valence. (*SOS* Gloss)

**COMM COURSE,** because the H.A.S. Course is a **course** about
**communication** it is often called the **Comm Course.** (HCO PL 15
Apr 71R) See H.A.S. COURSE.

**COMM CYCLE, communication cycle.** (HCOB 23 Aug 65)

**COMMENT,** a statement or remark aimed only at the student or the room. (HCOB 16 Aug 71 II)

**COMM LAG, communication lag.** (*Abil SW*)

**COMM LINE,** see COMMUNICATION LINE.

Communication (Def. 9)

**COMMUNICATION, 1.** the consideration and action of impelling an impulse or particle from source point across a distance to receipt point with the intention of bringing into being at the receipt point a duplication and understanding of that which emanated from the source point. (HCOB 5 Apr 73) **2.** the first and most basic definition of any part of **communication** is that **communication** or any part thereof is a consideration. As duplication is a consideration, **communication** is possible to the degree that the preclear can freely make considerations. (*COHA*, pp. 170-171) **3.** the operation, the action, by which one experiences emotion and by which one agrees. **Communication** is not only the modus operandi, it is the heart of life and is by thousands of per cent the senior in importance to affinity and reality. (PAB 1) **4.** any ritual by which effects can be produced and perceived. Thus a letter, a bullet, the output of theta "flitter" are all, to us, **communication.** (PAB 4) **5.** the ability to translate sympathy or some component of sympathy from one terminal to another terminal. (Spr Lect 5, 5303CM25) **6.** an interchange of energy from one beingness to another; in the thetan and in *Homo sapiens* **communication** is known as perception. (*Scn 8-8008*, p. 21) **7.** the handling of particles, of motion. (PAB 1) **8.** the interchange of perception through the material universe between organisms or the perception of the material universe by sense channels. (*Scn 0-8*, p. 83) **9.** the interchange of ideas across space. (*Scn 0-8*, p. 36) **10.** the use of those sense channels with which the individual contacts the physical universe. (*DAB*, Vol. II, p. 218)

**COMMUNICATION BRIDGE, 1.** it simply closes off the process you were running, maintains ARC, and opens up the new process on which you are about to embark. (PAB 151) **2.** before a question is asked, the preclear should have the question discussed with him and the wording agreed upon as though he were making a contract with the auditor. This is the first part of a **communication bridge.** It precedes all questions but when one is changing from one process to another the **bridge** becomes a **bridge** indeed. (PAB 88) **3.** the reason we use a **communication bridge** is so a pc will not be startled by change, for if we change too rapidly in a session, we stick the preclear in the session every time. We give him some warning; and that is what a **communication bridge** is for. (PAB 151)

**COMMUNICATION CHANGE,** by **communication change** we also mean perception **change.** (PAB 1)

**COMMUNICATION COURSE, 1.** because the H.A.S. Course is a **course** about **communication**, it is often called the **Comm Course** (**comm** being for **communication**). (HCO PL 15 Apr 71R) **2.** a basic Scn **course** consisting mainly of the TRs; also called the H.A.S. (Hubbard Apprentice Scientologist Course). (*PRD* Gloss) See H.A.S. COURSE.

**COMMUNICATION CYCLE, 1.** a **cycle** of **communication** and two-way communication are actually two different things. A **cycle** of **communication** is not a two-way communication in its entirety. In a **cycle** of **communication** we have Joe as the originator of a **communication** addressed to Bill. We find Bill receiving it and then Bill originating an answer or acknowledgement back to Joe and thus ends the **cycle.** (*Dn 55!*, p. 82) **2.** consists of just cause, distance, effect with intention, attention, duplication and understanding. (HCOB 23 May 1971R IV) *Abbr.* comm cycle.

**COMMUNICATION FORMULA, 1. communication** is the interchange of ideas or objects between two people or terminals. The

**Formula** of **Communication** and its precise definition is: Cause, Distance, Effect with Intention and Attention and a duplication at Effect of what emanates from Cause. (*PXL* Gloss) **2.** the **formula** of **communication** is: Cause, Distance, Effect with Intention, Attention and Duplication with Understanding. (HCOB 5 Apr 73)

**COMMUNICATION LAG,** the length of time intervening between the asking of the question by the auditor and the reply to that specific question by the preclear. The question must be precise; the reply must be precisely to that question. It does not matter what intervenes in the time between the asking of the question and the receipt of the answer. The preclear may outflow, jabber, discuss, pause, hedge, disperse, dither or be silent; no matter what he does or how he does it, between the asking of the question and the giving of the answer, the *time* is the **communication lag.** The near answer, a guessing answer, an undecided answer, are alike imprecise answers, and are not adequate responses to the question. On receipt of such questionable answers, the auditor must ask the question again. That he asks the question again does not reduce the **communication lag;** he is still operating from the moment he asked the question the first time. And if he has to ask the question 20 or 30 times more in the next hour in order to get a precise and adequate answer from the preclear, the length of time of the **lag** would be from the asking of the first question to the final receipt of the answer. Near answers to the question are inadequate, and are, themselves, simply part of the **communication lag.** (PAB 43)

**COMMUNICATION LAG INDEX, 1.** the length of time it takes to get a logical answer. (Spr Lect 3, 5303CM24) **2.** the most important method of telling whether or not a person is sick or well. A person who answers quickly (and rationally) is in much better condition than a person who answers after a long consideration. (PAB 2)

**COMMUNICATION LINE, 1.** the route along which a **communication** travels from one person to another. (*Scn AD*) **2.** any sequence through which a message of any character may go. (*SOS*, p. 94)

# COMMUNICATION PROCESS

**COMMUNICATION PROCESS,** any **process** which places the preclear at cause and uses **communication** as the principal command phrase. (HCOB 7 Aug 59)

**COMMUNICATION SCALE,** refers to the individual's ability to **communicate** with other people (in relation to his position on the tone scale). (*NOTL*, p. 103)

**COMMUNICATIONS RELEASE,** expanded Grade 0 release. (CG&AC 75) See GRADE 0 RELEASE.

**COMPARABLE MAGNITUDE, 1.** similar importance. (PAB 126) **2.** a datum can only be evaluated by comparison with another datum of **comparable magnitude.** This means the basic unit must therefore, be two. (*SOS* Gloss) *Abbr.* Comp Mag.

**COMPARTMENTING THE QUESTION, 1.** reading it word by word and phrase by phrase to see if any one word or any one phrase falls rather than the question as a whole. (HCOB 28 Sept 61) **2.** using the prior reads occurring at the exact end of the minor thoughts to dig up different data not related to the whole thought. (HCOB 25 May 62)

**COMPLETE,** the reverse of quickie. To make whole, entire or perfect; end after satisfying all demands or requirements. (HCOB 19 Apr 72)

**COMPLETE CASE,** a **case** is not **complete** unless the lowest incomplete grade chart action is **complete** and then each **completed** in turn on up. (HCOB 26 Aug 70)

**COMPLETE LIST, 1.** a **list** which has only one reading item on **list.** (HCOB 1 Aug 68) **2.** any **list listed** for assessment that does not produce a dirty needle while nulling or tiger drilling. (HCOB 12 Nov 62)

**COMPLETION, 1.** a **completion** is the **completing** of a specific course or an auditing grade meaning it has been started, worked through and has successfully ended with an award in Qual. (HCOB 19 Jun 71 III) **2.** a finished level or rundown. (HCO PL 29 Aug 71)

**COMP MAG, comparable magnitude.** (BTB 20 Aug 71R II)

**COMPOSITE ILLNESS,** an **illness composed** of many somatics. (HCOB 19 Jul 69)

**COMPULSION, 1.** an engramic command that the organism must do something. (*DTOT*, p. 58) **2.** things pc feels **compelled** to do. (BTB 24 Apr 69)

**COMPULSIVE COMMUNICATION,** an outflow which is not pertinent to the surrounding terminals and situation. In other words, **compulsive communication** is an outflow which is not in reality with the existing reality. (*Dn 55!*, p. 93)

**COMPULSIVE EXTERIORIZATION,** a manifestation which we call in Scn "doing a bunk," in other words, running away. (*Dn 55!*, p. 136)

**COMPUTATION,** technically, that aberrated evaluation and postulate that one must be consistently in a certain state in order to succeed. The **computation** thus may mean that one must entertain in order to be alive or that one must be dignified in order to succeed or that one must own much in order to live. A **computation** is simply stated. It is always aberrated. A **computation** is as insidious as it pretends to align with survival. All **computations** are nonsurvival. **Computations** are held in place wholly to invalidate others. (*AP&A*, p. 41)

**COMPUTATIONAL ALTITUDE,** signifying that the individual has an outstanding ability to think, to **compute** upon data. Albert Einstein had **computational altitude.** (*SOS* Gloss)

**COMPUTING PSYCHOTIC, 1.** a **psychotic** who from his reactivity figure-figures. He's inconstant in his conduct, he's **compu-tive.** He figures it all out, he's got explanations. His **psychosis** is derived because these are crazy explanations. He's obsessively solving a problem that does not exist. (SH Spec 83, 6612C06) **2.** the **computing psychotic** passes quite commonly for a normal. Here the individual is taking dictation solely from a facsimile of some past moment of pain and is acting upon the advice of that "circuit" and is calling it thought. The **psychotic** personality is distinguished by its irrationality and its perversion of values. The distinguishing characteristic of the **computing psychotic** is his utter inability to change his mind. (*AP&A*, p. 38)

**CONCENTRATION,** duration of a mock-up in present time. (Spr Lect 4, 5303M24)

**CONCEPT, 1.** a high wave thought, above perception or reason or single incidents. (*Scn 8-80*, p. 29) **2.** that which is retained after something has been perceived. (*DMSMH*, p. 46)

**CONCEPT RUNNING,** the preclear "gets the idea" of knowing or not being and holds it, the while looking at his time track. The **concept runs** out, or the somatic it brings on **runs** out, and the **concept** itself is **run.** It is not addressed at individual incidents but at hundreds. (*Scn 8-80*, p. 29)

**CONCLUSION,** the theta facsimiles of a group of combined data. (*Scn 0-8*, p. 78)

**CONDITION, 1.** anything called for as a requirement before the performance, completion or effectiveness of something else; provision; stipulation. Anything essential to the existence or occurrence of something else; external circumstances or factors. Manner or state of being. Proper or healthy state. (HCOB 11 May 65) **2.** a circumstance regarding a mass or terminal. (PAB 126)

**CONDITIONS BY DYNAMICS,** an ethics type action. Have the person study the **conditions** formulas. Clear up the words related to his **dynamics** one to eight, and what they are. Now ask him what is his **condition** on the **first dynamic.** Have him study the formulas. Don't buy any glib PR. When he's completely sure of what his **condition** really is on the **first dynamic** he will cognite. Similarly go on up each one of the **dynamics** until you have a **condition** for each one. Continue to work this way. Somewhere along the line he will start to change markedly. (HCO PL 4 Apr 72) [The above is a brief summary only. The full procedure will be found in the referenced HCO PL.]

**CONDITIONS (ETHICS),** in Scn the term also means the **ethics conditions** (confusion,* treason, enemy, doubt, liability, non-existence, danger, emergency, normal, affluence, power change, power). The state or **condition** of any person, group or activity can be plotted on this scale of **conditions** which shows the degree of success or survival of that person, group or activity at any time. Data on the application of these **conditions** is contained in the **ethics** policies and tapes of Scn. (BTB 12 Apr 72R) [*The ethics condition of confusion came later than the date of this

BTB and is added here by the editor in order that all the current ethics conditions are included.]

**CONDITION OF BEING,** see CONDITIONS OF EXISTENCE.

be

do

have

Conditions of Existence

**CONDITIONS OF EXISTENCE,** there are three **conditions of existence.** These three **conditions** comprise life. They are BE, DO and HAVE. The **condition** of being is defined as the assumption (choosing) of a category of identity. An example of beingness could be one's own name. Another example would be one's profession. The second **condition of existence** is doing. By doing, we mean action, function, accomplishment, the attainment of goals, the fulfilling of purpose, or any change of position in space. The third **condition** is havingness. By havingness we mean owning, possessing, being capable of commanding, positioning, taking charge of objects, energies or spaces. These three **conditions** are given in an order of seniority (importance) where life is concerned. (*FOT,* pp. 26-27)

**CONDUCT SURVIVAL PATTERN,** the **conduct survival pattern** is built upon the equation of the optimum solution. It is the basic equation of all rational behavior and is the equation on which a Clear functions. It is inherent in man. In other words, the best solution to any problem is that which will bring the greatest good to the greatest number of beings. (*DMSMH*, p. 34)

**CONF, conference.** (HCOB 29 Sept 66)

**CONFESSION,** a limited effort to relieve a person of the pressure of his overt acts. (HCOB 21 Jan 60, *Justification*)

**CONFESSIONAL, 1.** sec checking done in session not for security purposes is called a **confessional.** (HCOB 14 Oct 72) **2.** in an effort to get around what was thought to be a public relations scene, the name "security checking" was changed to "Integrity Processing." This was also a PR error because the actual truth of the matter is it originated as **"confessional"** and should have simply been changed back to "handling of **confessions.**" This administrative demand of name alteration threw the original issues on "sec checking" into disuse. Additionally "Integrity Processing" did not include all the tech of sec checking. There should be no further confusion in this matter. "Sec checking," "Integrity Processing" and **"confessionals"** are all the exact same procedure and any materials on these subjects is interchangeable under these titles. (HCOB 24 Jan 77)

**CONFESSIONAL AID (E-METER),** the **confessional aid** assists the minister in locating and relieving the spiritual travail of individual parishioners in the Scn confessional. The **confessional aid** does not diagnose or treat human ailments of body or mind, nor does it affect the structure or any function of the body; its use is directed as an article of faith of the Church of Scientology, and was never intended for use outside of the Scientology ministry. (HCO PL 9 Jul 69) See also E-METER.

**CONFRONT,** *n.* **1.** an action of being able to face. (HCOB 4 Jan 73) **2.** the ability to be there comfortably and perceive. (HCOB 2 Jun 71 I) **3. confront** itself is a result and an end product. It itself isn't a doingness, it's an ability. (SH Spec 21, 6106C27) —*v.* to face without flinching or avoiding. (HCOB 4 Jan 73)

**CONFRONTING, 1.** the ability to be there comfortably and perceive. (HCOB 2 Jun 71R-1) **2.** the ability to front up to. (SH Spec 84, 6612C13)

Confront

**CONFRONT PROCESS, 1.** the **confront process** for a pc from the *Thirty-Six Presessions*. The **confront process** gets the preclear to present time from areas on the track where his attention was fixed by an earlier process. (*EME*, p. 20) **2.** it should move pc on the track, going further into the past and easier and easier into present time. Pc's pictures should improve on a **confront process.** (HCOB 23 Sept 60)

**CONFUSION, 1.** a **confusion** can be defined as any set of factors or circumstances which do not seem to have any immediate solution. More broadly, a **confusion** in this universe is random motion. (*POW*, p. 21) **2.** plus randomity. It means motion unexpected above the tolerance level of the person viewing it. (*Abil 36*) **3.** a number of force vectors traveling in a number of different directions. (UPC 11) **4.** a **confusion** consists of two things, time and space; change of particles in, predicted or unpredicted, and if they are unpredicted changes in space you will have a **confusion.** (SH Spec 58, 6109C26)

Confusion (Def. 1)

# CONNECTEDNESS

**CONNECTEDNESS,** the basic process on association of theta with mest. All forms and kinds of association, including being caught in traps, prone to become identifications as in Dn. **Connectedness** puts the thetan at cause in making the mest (or people when run outside) connect with him. (*SCP*, p. 28)

**CONSCIOUS,** when the individual is "unconscious" in full or in part, the reactive mind is cut in full or in part. When he is fully **conscious**, his analytical mind is fully in command of the organism. (*DMSMH*, p. 59)

**CONSCIOUSNESS, 1.** awareness of now. (*DTOT*, p. 24) **2. consciousness** is awareness. Awareness itself is perception. (2ACC-8B, 5311CM24)

Conservatism

**CONSERVATISM,** at 3.0 on the tone scale we have the person who is democratic, but who is somewhat more **conservative** than the liberal at 3.5 in his attitudes and more given to social regulations, being more in need of them. (*SOS*, p. 124)

**CONSIDER,** think, believe, suppose, postulate. (PAB 82)

**CONSIDERATION, 1.** a thought, a postulate about something. (BTB 1 Dec 71R IV) **2.** a **consideration** is a continuing postulate. (5702C26) **3.** the highest capability of life, taking rank over the mechanics of space, energy and time. (*COHA* Gloss)

**CONSULTANT,** an instructor who is on duty sporadically or from time to time but not routinely in any one place. (HCOB 23 Apr 59)

**CONT, continue** (-d) (-ing), **continental.** (BPL 5 Nov 72RA)

**CONTACT ASSIST,** the patient is taken to the area where the injury occurred and makes the injured member gently **contact** it several times. A sudden pain will fly off and the injury if minor, lessens or vanishes. This is a physical communication factor. The body member seems to have withdrawn from that exact spot in the physical universe. The restoration of awareness is often necessary before healing can occur. The prolongation of a chronic injury occurs in the absence of physical communication with the affected area or with the location of the spot of injury in the physical universe. (HCOB 2 Apr 69)

**CONTAGION OF ABERRATION, 1.** entheta, in proximity to theta, makes entheta out of it. From this we have the **contagion of aberration.** (*SOS*, Bk. 2, p. 24) **2.** people under stress, if aberrated, dramatize engrams. Such dramatization may involve the injury of another person and render him more or less "unconscious." The "unconscious" person then receives as an engram the dramatization. (*DMSMH*, p. 134)

**CONTAGION OF ERROR,** on a course where the students audit each other a **contagion of error** can occur. For example, student A does a bad assessment on student B. Student B is then likely to give a bad assessment to his next pc and you soon have a whole rash of bad assessments. A similar phenomenon occurs when students are permitted to get the answers to their queries from other students. (HCOB 20 May 69)

**CONTINUING OVERT ACT, continually** committing **overts** before, during and after processing. The person who is not getting case gains is committing **continuing overts.** (HCOB 29 Sept 65 II)

**CONTINUING OVERT CASE,** who commits **overts** even when being audited and between sessions. (HCOB 1 Jun 65)

**CONTINUOUS MISSED WITHHOLD,** a **continuous missed with-hold** occurs when a person feels some way and anyone who sees him **misses** it. Example: a doctor feels very unconfident of his skill. Every patient who sees him **misses** the fact that he is not confident. This reacts as a **missed withhold**. It is of course based upon some bad incident that destroyed his confidence (usually of an engramic intensity). (HCOB 15 Dec 73)

**CONTINUOUS OVERT,** this is not quite the same as *The Continuing Overt Act*, HCOB 29 Sept 65. In that type the person is repeating overt acts against something usually named. In the **continuous overt** a person who believes he is harmful to others may also believe that many of his common ordinary actions are harmful. He may feel he is committing a **continuous overt** on others. Example: a clothing model believes she is committing a fraud on older women by displaying clothing to them in which they will look poorly. In her estimation this is a **continuous overt** act. (HCOB 15 Dec 73)

**CONTINUOUS OVERTS CASE,** here's one that commits antisocial acts daily during auditing. He's psychotic, he'll never get better, case always hangs up. We can even solve that case. (HCOB 4 Apr 65)

**CONTRA-SURVIVAL ENGRAM, 1.** any kind of **engram** which lies across the dynamics and has no alignment with purpose. (*DMSMH*, p. 262) **2.** a **contra-survival engram** contains physical pain, painful emotions, all other perceptions and menace to the organism. It contains apparent or actual antagonism to the individual. (*DMSMH*, p. 62)

**CONTROL, 1.** you are stating a greater truth when you say that **control** is predictable change than if you say **control** is start, change and stop because start and stop are, of course, necessary to change. You might say the thinking or philosophic definition would be *predictable change*. (5703C10) **2.** when we say **control**, we simply mean willingness to start, stop and change. (*Dn 55!*, p. 100) **3.** positive postulating, which is intention, and the execution thereof. (*Scn 0-8*, p. 36)

**CONTROL CASE, 1.** the **case** where **control** is obsessive or other-determined, or where the individual is **controlling** things out of compulsion or fear. (*Dn 55!*, p. 100) **2.** the person who feels he must be cold blooded in order to be rational is what is called in Dianetics a **"control case,"** and on examination will be found to be very far from as rational as he might be. People who cannot experience emotion because of their aberrations are ordinarily sick people. (*SA*, p. 94)

**CONTROL CENTER, 1.** the **control center** of the organism can be defined as the contact point between theta and the physical universe and is that **center** which is aware of being aware and which has charge of and responsibility for the organism along all its dynamics. (*Scn 0-8*, p. 84) **2.** every mind may be considered to have a **control center.** This could be called the "awareness of awareness unit" of the mind, or it could be called simply "I". The **control center** is cause. It directs, through emotional relay systems, the actions of the body and the environment. It is not a physical thing. (*HFP*, p. 30)

**CONTROL CIRCUIT,** the **control circuit** may conduct itself as an interior entity which takes the preclear out of the auditor's hands. When preclears are very hard to handle, take the bit in their teeth and try to run their own cases despite anything the auditor may do, they are running on **control circuits,** recorded commands which make the preclear misbehave under auditing. (*SOS*, Bk. 2, p. 204)

**CONTROL-CONCEPT PROCESSING,** you just get the **concept** of "you can't **control** it" and the **concept** that "you can **control** it." (5209CM04B)

**CONTROL PROCESSES, processes** which place the pc's body and actions under the auditor's **control** to invite **control** of them by the pc. (HCOB 29 Oct 57)

**CONTROL TRANSFER,** a specialized kind of **transfer** wherein the thetan having devoted himself to a mest body now begins to **control** the environment and other people for his body much as he **controls** the body. (*HOM*, p. 78)

**CONTROL TRIO,** a three-stage process on a heavy spotting **control.** It runs in this fashion. "Get the idea that you can have that (object)." And when this is relatively flat, "Get the idea of making that (object) remain where it is" (or continue where it is) and "Get the idea of making that (object) disappear." This is actually a very fine process and undercuts (runs on a lower case than) **trio** itself. (*SCP*, p. 22)

**CONVERSATION,** the process of alternating outflowing and inflowing communication. (*Dn 55!*, p. 63)

**COO,** designation on HCO Policy Letters and HCO Bulletins indicates dissemination and restriction as follows: HCO **City Offices only,** not to be shown or given to HCO franchise holders or field Auditors; also goes to central organizations, HCO Area, HCO Cont, HCO WW. (HCO PL 22 May 59)

**COPY,** *n.* **1.** a duplicate, distinguished from a perfect duplicate, in that it does not necessarily occupy the same space, same time, nor use the same energies as the original. (*COHA* Gloss) **2.** the word "duplicate" is used, rather sloppily, to indicate a **copy.** However, a **copy** is not a complete duplicate; a **copy** is a facsimile. (*COHA*, p. 82) **3.** something that a thetan on his own volition simply made of an object in the physical universe with full knowingness. (*PXL*, p. 65) —*v.* to make another one just like it. (*COHA*, p. 34)

**CORPSE CASE,** a pc who would lie upon the couch with his arms crossed neatly all ready for a lily and would always audit in this fashion. The preclear is so fixed in a death that he is trying to make everything unreal, and the only real thing, to him, would be the unreality of death. (PAB 50) See also COFFIN CASE.

**CORRECTION LIST, 1.** a **list** of prepared questions on a mimeod sheet which is used by the auditor for the repair of a particular situation, action, or rundown. (BTB 7 Nov 72 I) **2.** the various **lists** designed to find by-passed charge and repair a faulty auditing action or life situation. (HCOB 28 May 70)

**COTERM, combined terminal.** (HCOB 8 Nov 62)

**COUNTER-CREATE,** see CREATE-COUNTER-CREATE.

**COUNTER-EFFORT, 1.** the **effort** which **counters** one's survival. (5203CM06A) **2.** any **effort** the environment can exert against you. (5203CM04B) **3.** what we're talking about when we talk about a **counter-effort** is the force of impact of an engram. The force of impact which gives the pc an engram is a **counter-effort.** (5206CM25A)

**COUNTER-EMOTION,** any **emotion** that is **countering** an existing **emotion.** (SH Spec 84, 6612C13)

**COUNTER-THOUGHT,** you think one thing somebody else thinks another. Their **thought** is **counter** to your **thought.** (*HFP*, p. 115)

**COURAGE,** the theta force necessary to overcome the obstacles in surviving. (*SOS*, p. 139)

**COURSE ADMINISTRATOR,** the **course** staff member in charge of the course materials and records. (HCOB 19 Jun 71 III)

**COURSE CHECKSHEET,** see CHECKSHEET.

**COURSE MATERIALS,** in Scn and Dn **course materials** are defined as those books, tapes, magazines, HCO Bulletins, HCO Policy Letters and other authorized technical issues listed on the checksheets of courses designed for use by the Church's public. (BTB 24 Nov 71 II)

**COURSE SUP, course supervisor.** (HCOB 23 Aug 65)

**COURSE SUPERVISOR, 1.** the instructor in charge of a **course** and its students. (HCOB 19 Jun 71 III) **2.** basically, someone who in addition to his other duties can refer the person to the exact bulletin to get his information and never tells him another thing. (6905C29) *Abbr.* Crse Sup.

**COURSE SUPERVISOR CORRECTION LIST,** a **correction list** designed to help locate the individual reasons a **supervisor** has for not fully applying the study tech in **supervision.** (HCOB 27 Mar 72R II)

**COVERT AUDITING,** some students **covertly audit.** In "talking" to someone they also seek to **audit** that person "without the person knowing anything about it." This of course is nonsense since auditing results are best achieved in a session and a session depends upon a self-determined agreement to be audited. (HCOB 17 Oct 64 III)

**COVERT HOSTILITY,** around 1.1 on the tone scale we reach the level of **covert hostility.** Here the hatred of the individual has been socially and individually censured to a point where it has been suppressed, and the individual no longer dares demonstrate hate as such. He yet possesses sufficient energy to express some feeling on the matter, and so what hatred he feels comes forth **covertly.** All manner of subterfuges may be resorted to. The person may claim to love others and to have the good of others as his foremost interest; yet, at the same moment, he works, unconsciously or otherwise, to injure or destroy the lives and reputations of people and also to destroy property. (*SOS*, p. 56)

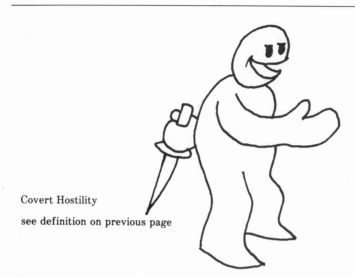

Covert Hostility

see definition on previous page

**CR, cramming.** (HCOB 16 Jun 71 III) [Replaced now by BTB 16 Jun 71RA III.]

**CRAMMING, 1.** a section in the Qualifications Division where a student is given high pressure instruction at his own cost after being found slow in study or when failing his exams. (HCOB 19 Jun 71 III) **2.** the **cramming** section teaches students what they have missed. This includes trained auditors who wish to be brought up-to-date on current technical developments. (HCO PL 13 May 69)

**CRAMMING ORDER, 1.** a **cramming order** is written to handle a specific situation. If that is not handled, the situation will worsen or change, thus the original **cramming order** will not sufficiently handle if it is stale dated. (BTB 21 Jan 73R) **2.** there is a certain technology on how to write up a **cramming order:** (1) isolate the exact outnesses in the folder; (2) order those HCOBs or PLs crammed; (3) now look in a slightly wider circle around the data flunked and get which basic is involved (i.e. Auditor Code, TRs, metering, handling the session, handling the pc as a being, etc.) and get that **crammed,** too. (BTB 12 Dec 71R)

**CREAK,** a stiffness, and out-of-plumbness, an unchanging situation, a no-energy flow. (HCOB 13 Apr 64, *Scn VI Part One Glossary of Terms*)

**CREATE**, make, manufacture, construct, postulate, bring into beingness. (*FOT*, p. 20)

**CREATE-COUNTER-CREATE**, to **create** something against a **creation**, to **create** one thing and then **create** something else against it. (*FOT*, pp. 20-21)

**CREATE-CREATE-CREATE**, **create** again continuously one moment after the next=SURVIVAL. (*FOT*, p. 20)

**CREATIVE IMAGINATION, imagination,** whereby in the field of aesthetics the urges and impulses of the various dynamics are interwoven into new scenes and ideas. (*SOS*, Bk. 2, p. 101)

**CREATIVE PROCESSING, 1.** the exercise by which the pc is actually putting up the physical universe. (SH Spec 52, 6502C23) **2. creative processing** consists of having the preclear make, with his own **creative** energies, a mock-up. (*COHA* Gloss)

**CRIMINAL, 1.** one who is unable to think of the other fellow, unable to determine his own actions, unable to follow orders, unable to make things grow, unable to determine the difference between good and evil, unable to think at all on the future. Anybody has some of these; the **criminal** has ALL of them. (*NSOL*, p.78) **2.** one who thinks help cannot be on any dynamic or uses help on anyone to injure and destroy. (HCOB 28 May 60) **3. criminals** are people who are frantically attempting to create an effect long after they know they cannot. They cannot then create decent effects, only violent effects. Neither can they work. (*FOT*, pp. 31-32)

**CRISS-CROSS**, see 3DXX.

**CRITICAL THOUGHT, 1.** a symptom of an overt act having been committed. (SH Spec 37, 6409C01) **2.** a **critical** pc=a withhold from the auditor. (HCOB 23 Aug 71)

**CRITICISM, 1.** most **criticism** is justification of having done an overt. There are rightnesses and wrongnesses in conduct and society and life at large, but random, carping 1.1 **criticism** when not borne out in fact is only an effort to reduce the size of the target of the overt. (HCOB 21 Jan 60, *Justification*) **2.** a

**criticism** is a hope that they can damage, and that's what a **criticism** is, with an inability to do so. (SH Spec 119, 6202C22)

**CR0000-1,** a drill to train the student to raise his awareness of the condition of the pc called "Set up for a perfect session" drill. (HCOB 16 Jun 71 III) An auditor must be able to see when a pc has not eaten or slept, or what his tone level is, or is the pc auditable. [This HCOB is cancelled and replaced by BTB 16 Jun 71RA III and the drill renamed "Ideal Session Start."]

**CR0000-2,** a drill to train an auditor to increase session pace when auditing a fast pc. Its name is *Rapid TR-2*. This is basically a correction drill for auditors who tend to lose session control by slow acknowledgements inviting endless itsa. (BTB 16 Jun 71R II)

**CR0000-3,** an E-meter drill to train an auditor to confront an E-meter. If a student has difficulty doing the preceding E-meter drills, this drill is done. It is a gradient step towards greater session control. The student confronts the E-meter and does nothing else for two hours. (BTB 16 Jun 71R II)

**CR0000-4,** a drill to train an auditor to be able to *see* the pc, the pc's hands on the cans, the meter plus any reads, and the worksheets without having to *look* at any one of them. The auditor is trained to widen his/her vision until the auditor can see the meter, the pc, the pc's hands on the cans, and the worksheets effortlessly. (BTB 16 Jun 71R II)

**CR0000-5,** E-meter trim check drill. A drill to train an auditor to be able to do a trim check effortlessly in a session without distracting the pc in any way. (BTB 16 Jun 71R II)

**CROSS ENGRAM,** an **engram** which embraces more than one engram chain. The receipt of the **cross engram,** containing as it does the convergence of two or more engram chains, is often accompanied by a "nervous breakdown" or the sudden insanity of an individual. A **cross engram** may occur in a severe accident, in prolonged or severe illness under antagonistic circumstances, or a nitrous oxide operation. (*DTOT*, p. 115)

**CROSSOVER, 1.** the area in the center of a GPM is the **crossover.** This means the RI's which cause the pc to become an opponent of his own goal. (HCOB 4 Apr 63) **2. crossover** means where the individual ceases to be for the goal, and starts to be against the goal. (SH Spec 329, 6312C12)

**CRS, course.** (BPL 5 Nov 72RA)

**C/S,** a **case supervisor** direction of what to audit on a pc. (HCOB 23 Aug 71)

**C/S, 1. case supervisor.** (HCOB 23 Aug 71) **2. commodore's staff.** (BPL 5 Nov 72 RA)

**CSC, Clearing Success Congress.** (HCOB 29 Sept 66)

**C/S 53,** the basic list to get TA up or down into normal range. Assessed M-5, reading items handled then reassessed etc. to F/Ning assessment. Done well with good basic auditing this action should not need to be frequently repeated on a case. TA going high or low in later auditing after **C/S 53** already fully handled is normally handled with the correction list for that action (e.g. L4BR when TA high after listing or WCCL on word clearing, etc.). EP is **C/S 53** F/Ning on assessment with TA in normal range. (BTB 11 Aug 72RA) [This list has been revised a number of times and its current number is C/S 53RK.]

**CS-5, Commodores Staff 5** Qualifications. (BPL 5 Nov 72RA)

**CS-4, Commodores Staff 4** Training and Services. (BPL 5 Nov 72RA)

**C/SHEET,** also **ch. sheet** or √ **sht.** Abbreviation for **checksheet.** (BTB 12 Apr 72R)

**C/SING IN THE CHAIR,** the auditor may not **C/S in the auditing chair** while auditing the pc. If he has no case supervisor he writes the C/S before session and adheres to it in session. To do something else and not follow the C/S is called **C/Sing in the chair** and is very poor form as it leads to Q & A. (HCOB 23 Aug 71)

**CS-1, 1.** a general **C/S** which covers the basics of getting a pc sessionable. The product is an educated pc who can run Scn or Dn easily and get case gain. (BTB 8 Jan 71R) **2.** purpose: to give pcs new to Dn or Scn and to give previously audited pcs as needed, the necessary data and R-factor on basics and auditing procedure so that he understands and is able and willing to be audited successfully. (BTB 8 Jan 71R)

**C/S-6,** see CLASS VIII C/S-6.

**CT, clay table.** (HCOB 6 Nov 64)

**CTH, clay table healing.** (HCOB 27 Apr 65)

**CULTURE,** the pattern (if any) of life in the society. All factors of the society, social educational, economic, etc., whether creative or destructive. The **culture** might be said to be the theta body of the society. (*SOS* Gloss)

**CURVE,** throw a **curve** means to give an unexpected contrary datum. Also to shift reality. **Curve** itself is also the ordinary dictionary meaning. (LRH Def. Notes)

**CUTATIVE,** an invented word to mean the impulse to shorten or leave out or the thing left out. (HCO PL 26 Sept 70 III)

**CUT COGNITION,** you taking too soon an F/N (F/N indicated at the first twitch) you **cut** the **cognition** and leave by-passed charge (a withheld cognition). (HCOB 14 Mar 71R)

**CYCLE, 1.** in Scn, a **cycle** just means from the beginning to the conclusion of an intentional action. (*Aud 39*) **2.** a span of time with a beginning and an end=a section of the totality of time with a beginning and an end=in beginningless and endless time one can set out periods which do have a beginning and an end insofar as action is concerned. (*FOT*, p. 19)

**CYCLE OF ACTION, 1.** the sequence that an **action** goes through, wherein the **action** is started, is continued for as long as is required and then is completed as planned. (*Scn AD*) **2.** the creation, growth, conservation, decay and death or destruction of energy and matter in a space. **Cycles of action** produce time. (*PXL*, p. 8) See also ACTUAL CYCLE OF ACTION.

**CYCLE OF AN ORGANISM,** the **cycle of an organism,** a group of organisms or a species is inception, growth, re-creation, decay and death. (*HFP*, p. 172)

**CYCLE OF AN OVERT,** it goes like this. (1) a being doesn't get the meaning of a word or symbol. (2) this causes the being to misunderstand the area of the symbol or word (who used it, whatever it applied to). (3) this causes the being to feel different from or antagonized toward the user or whatever of the symbol and so makes it all right to commit an overt. (4) having committed the **overt,** the being now feels he has to have a motivator and so feels caved in. This is the stuff of which Hades is made. This is the trap. This is why people get sick. This is stupidity and lack of ability. (HCOB 8 Sept 64)

**CYCLE OF A UNIVERSE,** could be said to be the cycle of creation, growth, conservation, decay and destruction. This is the **cycle** of an entire **universe** or any part of that **universe**. It is also the cycle of life forms. (*Scn 8-8008*, p. 97)

**CYCLE OF MIS-DEFINITION,** (1) a person didn't grasp a word, then (2) didn't understand a principle or theory, then (3) became different from it, commits and committed overts against it, then (4) restrained himself or was restrained from committing these overts, then (5) being on a withhold (inflow) pulled in a motivator. Not every word somebody didn't grasp was followed by a principle or theory. An overt was not committed every time this happened. Not every overt committed was restrained. So no motivator was pulled in. Every nattery or nonprogressing student or pc is hung in the above 1,2,3,4,5 cycle. And *every* such student or pc has a **misdefined** word at the bottom of that pile. (HCOB 21 Feb 66)

**CYCLE OF MOTION,** go from a no change to a change to a no change. (SH Spec 14, 6106C14)

**CYCLE OF RANDOMITY,** the **cycle of randomity** is from static, through optimum, through randomity sufficiently repetitious or similar to constitute another static. (*HFP*, p. 174)

**CYCLE OF SURVIVAL,** conception, growth, attainment, decay, death, conception, growth, attainment, decay, death, over and over again. (*HFP*, p. 20)

**CYCLE OF THE ROCK,** a person (1) failed to communicate himself; (2) started using something to communicate with; (3) put the last item on automatic and it created for him; (4) it failed. **The rock,** itself, when first located will be a solution to many earlier **cycles** as described above. And so, a **rock** is peeled off **cycle** by **cycle** as above. (HCOB 29 Jul 58)

**CYCLIC PROCESS,** a repetitive **process** which causes the preclear to **cycle** on the time track as in recall type processes. (HCOB 29 Sept 65, *Cyclical and Non-Cyclical Processes*)

# CYCLIC PSYCHOTIC

**CYCLIC PSYCHOTIC,** a **psychotic** who becomes completely enturbulated during certain periods of the day, or of the week, or of the month. This type is generally running on a time factor contained in the engram. The incident may have occurred on the twenty-fifth of the month and continued to the thirtieth of every month. Or the incident may have occurred at ten o'clock at night so the **psychotic** is only insane at ten o'clock every night. (*SOS*, Bk. 2, p. 190)

# D

**DA, Dn Auditor.** (*Scn Jour Iss. 31-G*)

**DAC, Dianetic Auditor Course.** (BTB 12 Apr 72R) [The course teaching Dianetics prior to the Hubbard Standard Dianetics Course (HSDC).]

**DANGEROUS AUDITOR, 1.** an **auditor** who consistently does things that are upsetting to a pc's case. (HCOB 12 Feb 66) **2.** the **auditor** who gets off safe withholds is **dangerous** and the auditor who gets off unsafe withholds is safe. An **auditor** who will not pull dangerous withholds from the pc is a **dangerous auditor.** (SH Spec 113, 6202C20) **3.** the **auditor** who is afraid to find out, afraid to be startled, afraid to discover something, afraid of what they will discover. This phobia prevents the "**auditor**" from flattening anything. This makes missed withholds a certainty. (HCOB 3 Mar 62)

**DANGEROUS ENVIRONMENT,** see SCIENTOLOGY ZERO.

**DATA,** consists of the postulates or assignment of value of thetans; that's **data,** that's all **data** is. (15ACC-12, 5610C30)

**DATA ALTITUDE,** signifying that the individual has a fund of knowledge gathered from books and records, or sometimes from experience, with which others are not familiar. The college professor has a **data altitude.** (*SOS* Gloss)

**DATE FLASH,** the auditor says to the preclear, "When I snap my fingers, a **date** will **flash.** Give me the first response which comes into your mind," (snap!). The preclear then gives the first **date** which comes into his mind. (*SOS,* Bk. 2, p. 51)

**DATE/LOCATE, 1.** a process to **date** and **locate** a flat point in a process that appears overrun. (HCOB 24 Sept 71) *Abbr.* D/L. **2.** the essence of the drill is to bring a pc to PT by erasing the **date** by spotting and the **location** by spotting, as the pc is out of PT fixed by both **date** and **location.** (HCOB 24 Sept 74R) *Abbr.* D/L.

**DATUM, 1.** a piece of knowledge, something known. Plural, **data.** (BTB 4 Mar 65) **2.** anything of which one could become aware, whether the thing existed or whether he created it. (*Scn 8-8008,* p. 6) **3.** an invented, not a true, knowingness. (*COHA,* p. 151) **4.** anything which proceeds from a postulate. (PDC 14) **5.** a theta facsimile of physical action. (*Scn 0-8,* p. 78) **6.** a facsimile of states of being, states of not being, actions or inactions, conclusions, or suppositions in the physical or any other universe. (*Scn 0-8,* p. 67)

**DB, degraded being.** (*Abil 272*)

**DCG,** see DIANETIC COUNSELING GROUP.

**DD, Doctor** of **Divinity.** (HCOB 23 Aug 65)

**DEAD BODY,** physical universe matter, energy, space and time *minus* life energy. (*SA,* p. 27)

**DEAD HORSE,** *Slang.* **1.** a list which even with good auditing, failed for any other reason to produce a reliable item. (HCOB 5 Dec 62) **2.** if no slam occurs anywhere on a listing list with the mid ruds in for the session, that's a **dead horse.** (SH Spec 219, 6211C27) **3.** an item listed from a non-reading question will give you a **dead horse** (no item). (HCOB 1 Aug 68)

**DEAD-IN-'IS-'EAD CASE,** *Slang.* a **case** totally associating all thought with mass. Thus he reads peculiarly on the meter. As he is audited he frees his thinkingness so that he can think without mass connotations. (HCOB 17 Mar 60)

**DEAD LIST,** null list. (HCOB 29 Jan 70)

**DEADLY QUARTET,** these processes are **four** in number. They are designed as classes of processes to handle these **four** points:

(1) help factor, (2) control factor, (3) pc communication factor, (4) interest factor. Unless these **four** points are present in a session, it is improbable, in a great number of cases that any real, lasting gain will be made. (HCOB 21 Apr 60)

**DEAD THETAN, 1.** doesn't put out any current. Doesn't react on a meter. Only the body reacts so it looks like a clear read (false read). An ARC break of long duration reads the same way. (LRH Def. Notes) **2.** a false clear read. (HCOB 17 Oct 69) **3.** clear read without tone arm motion and tight needle. That's your lowest case range, save one. There is one below that. (SH Spec 300, 6308C28). **4.** he's so "dead in his head" he thinks he's elsewhere while he's there. (SH Spec 1, 6105C07) **5.** he thinks of himself as **dead** and he is totally incapable of influencing the E-meter. (SH Spec 1, 6105C07)

**DEAFNESS,** the individual simply shutting out sounds. Some **deafness** is occasioned by entirely mechanical trouble with the recording mechanism but most **deafness,** particularly when partial, is psychosomatic or caused by mental aberration. (*SA,* p. 85)

**DEAR ALICE,** see TR-1.

Death (Def. 1)

**DEATH, 1.** a state of beingness rather than an action. It means a fellow's no longer inhabiting a body. (SH Spec 15X, 6106C15) **2.** a separation occurs between the thetan and the body. However, he takes old facsimiles, energy phenomena and bric-a-brac that he feels he cannot do without, with him and attaches it to the next body he picks up. (PAB 130) **3.** cessation of creation. An individual becomes sufficiently morose on the idea of creation that he can actually bring about the condition of inability to create. (*FOT*, p. 67) **4. death** equals life minus thought equals mest. (*NOTL*, p. 14) **5. death** is abandonment by theta of a life organism or race or species where these can no longer serve theta in its goals of infinite survival. (*Scn 0-8*, p. 75) **6.** life's operation of disposing of an outmoded and unwanted organism so that new organisms can be born and can flourish. (*SA*, p. 30) **7.** a limited concept of the **death** of the physical part of the organism. Life and the personality go on. The physical part of the organism ceases to function. And that is **death.** (*SA*, p. 30) **8.** a name assigned to what is apparently the mechanism by which theta recovers itself and the bulk of its volume from the mest, so as to be able to accomplish a more harmonious conquest of the mest in a next generation. (*SOS*, Bk. 2, p. 249)

**DEATH FACSIMILE BOP,** a little hunt, a little nervous twitch of the needle. (5410CM21)

**DEATH TALKER,** at 1.5 on the tone scale is the **death talker** who is going to save something from destruction by creating great havoc. This person will not listen to a creative and constructive plan unless he can see ways and means of using it to destroy. Warmongers and dictators are markedly in this band. (*SOS*, p. 145)

**DEATH WISH,** succumb postulates. (HCO PL 27 Apr 69)

**DEATH ZONE,** below 2.0 on the tone scale is the **death zone,** and here as the tone lowers increasingly, more danger exists that all the remaining theta will suddenly at one fell swoop become entheta. (*SOS*, Bk. 2, p. 13)

**DEBUG,** to get the snarls or stops out of something. (HCO PL 29 Feb 72 II)

**DE-CERTIFICATION,** cancellation of an auditor's **certificates. Certificates** "pulled" is a measure taken by HCO when these conditions exist: (a) the auditor has consistently refused supervised processing; (b) the auditor has committed antisocial acts liable for prosecution under criminal law, or (c) continues to associate with a **de-certified** auditor and balks efforts of HCO to bring the person into an HGC for auditing. (HCOB 22 May 60)

**DECLARE,** an action done in Qual after a pc has completed a cycle of action or attained a state. The pc or pre-OT who knows he made it must be sent to Exams and Certs and Awards to attest. A **declare** completes his cycle of action and is a vital part of the action. (HCOB 19 Jun 71 II)

**DECLARE?,** "Preclear has reached a grade or release. Please look at preclear and pass on to Certs and Awards." (HCOB 23 Aug 65)

**DED, 1.** an incident the preclear does to another dynamic and for which he has no motivator—i.e. he punishes or hurts or wrecks something the like of which has never hurt him. Now he must justify the incident. He will use things which didn't happen to him. He claims that the object of his injury really **DEserveD** it, hence the word **DED,** which is a sarcasm. (*HOM,* p. 75) **2.** an overt act without having a justification for it in the first place. The motivator is on the wrong side of the overt act and that motivator on the wrong side of an overt act is called a **DED.** It's a **deserved** action. (5206CM24C)

**DED-DEDEX, 1.** the overt-motivator sequence went backwards. You hit Joe, then he hits you. Although it went this way you had it figured out that he must have hit you first. So you invented something that he did to you to motivate your hitting him. (SH Spec 83, 6612C06) **2.** overt-motivator sequence; when somebody has committed an overt, he has to claim the existence of motivators—the **Ded-Dedex** version of Dn. (HCOB 7 Sept 64 II) **3.** where the preclear all out of his own imagination has done something to somebody else and then it has been done to him. (PAB 18)

**DEDEX, 1.** an incident which happens to a preclear after he has a **DED.** It is always on the same chain or subject, is always after the **DED.** It means the **DED EXposed.** It is covered guilt. (*HOM,* p. 75) **2.** deserved action explained would be one interpretation of **DEDEX.** The deserved action. This is why the action was deserved. This is why he blew Joe Blink's head off, because twenty years later a fellow by the name of Cuffbah tapped him on the temple. (PDC 29) **3.** motivator. (*Scn 8-80,* p. 32)

**DEEP PROCESSING,** deep processing addresses basic cause and locates and reduces moments of physical pain and sorrow. (*SA*, p. 61)

**DEFINITION PROCESSES,** the first thing to know about **definition processes** is that they are separate and distinct and stand by themselves as **processes.** Remedy A and Remedy B. The purpose of **definitions processing** is fast clearing of "held down fives" (jammed thinking because of a misunderstood or misapplied datums) preventing someone getting on with auditing or Scn. (HCOB 21 Feb 66)

**DEFINITIONS, TYPES OF,** (a) **differentiative defintion**—one which compares unlikeness to existing states of being or not being. (b) **descriptive definition**—one which classifies by characteristics, by describing existing states of being. (c) **associative definition**—one which declares likeness to existing states of being or not being. (d) **action definition**—one which delineates cause and potential change of state of being by cause of existence, inexistence, action, inaction, purpose or lack of purpose. (*AP&A*, pp. 65-66)

**DEGRADATION, 1.** the lower harmonic of apathy. (SH Spec 70, 6110C24) **2.** an inability to handle force. (PDC 48) **3.** being big and getting small and not at your own request. (PDC 34)

**DEGRADED BEING, degraded beings** find *any* instruction painful as they have been painfully indoctrinated with violent measures in the past. They therefore alter-is any order or don't comply. A **degraded being** is not a suppressive as he can have case gain. But he is so PTS that he works for suppressives only. He is sort of a super-continual PTS beyond the reach really of a simple S & D and handled only at Sect 3 OT Course. **Degraded beings**, taking a cue from SP associates, instinctively resent, hate and seek to obstruct any person in charge of anything or any Big Being. (HCOB 22 Mar 67)

**DEI SCALE, Desire-Enforcement-Inhibit Scale.** (PAB 50)

**DELUSION, 1.** a belief in something which is contrary to fact or reality resulting from deception, misconception or misassignment. (HCOB 11 May 65) **2.** what one person thinks is, but others don't necessarily. (SH Spec 72, 6607C28) **3.** the postulation by the imagination of occurrences in areas of plus or minus randomity. (*Scn 0-8*, p. 90) **4. delusion** is imagination out of control. (*Scn Jour, Iss. 14-G*)

**DEMO,** abbreviation for **demonstration.** Usually refers to either a clay **demo** or to a **demonstration** done with a "**demo** kit." (BTB 12 Apr 72R)

Demo Kit

**DEMO KIT, demonstration kit.** Consists of various small objects such as corks, caps, paper clips, pen tops, batteries—whatever will do. These are kept in a box or container. Each student should have one. The pieces are used while studying to represent the things in the material one is demonstrating. It helps hold concepts and ideas in place. A **demo kit** adds mass, reality and doingness to the significance and so helps the student to study. (HCOB 19 Jun 71 III)

**DEMON,** *Slang.* a by-pass circuit in the mind, called **demon** because it was long so interpreted. Probably an electronic mechanism. (*DMSMH* Gloss) **2.** a bona-fide **demon** is one who gives thoughts voice or echoes the spoken word interiorly or who gives all sorts of complicated advice like a real, live voice exteriorly. (*DMSMH*, p. 88) **3.** Dn use of the word is descriptive slang. (*EOS*, p. 16)

**DEMON CIRCUIT, 1.** that mental mechanism set up by an engram command which, becoming restimulated and super-charged with secondary engrams, takes over a portion of the analyzer and acts as an individual being. Any command containing "you" and seeking to dominate or nullify the individual's judgment is potentially a **demon circuit.** It doesn't become a real live **demon circuit** until it becomes keyed-in and picks up secondary engrams and locks. (*NOTL*, p. 80) **2.** a heavily charged portion of the analytical mind which has been captured by the reactive mind and does its bidding, walled off by charge into a separate entity. (*SOS*, p. 67) **3,** any **circuit** that vocalizes your thoughts for you. That's not natural. It's an installed mechanism from engrams and it slows up thought. (*DASF*)

**DENYER, 1.** a phrase which obscures a part of track by implying it is not there or elsewhere or should not be viewed. (HCOB 15 May 63) **2.** any phrase that you could think of in any language that would **deny** a person knowledge of something would be classified as a **denyer.** (SH Spec 81, 6111C16) **3.** a species of command which, literally translated, means that the engram doesn't exist. "I'm not here," "This is getting nowhere," "I must not talk about it," "I can't remember," etc. (*DMSMH*, p. 213) **4.** a command which makes the pc feel there is no incident present. (*DMSMH*, p. 213)

**DEPARTMENT OF PERSONAL ENHANCEMENT, the Department of Personal Enhancement** Division V, Qualifications is held responsible for these things. (1) That no misunderstood words exist amongst staff, Auditors or in the Church public. (2) That all training and auditing programs of staff, students, Auditors, internes or public are in correct sequence without skipped gradient and *done.* (3) That all staff cases are progressing satisfactorily with good OCA (APA) gains and that *no* no-case-gain cases are on staff. (HCO PL 16 Feb 72)

**DEPARTMENT OF SPECIAL CASES, the** HCO PL which makes Dept 10 a **Department of Special Cases** is cancelled. Dept 10 must remain as the Department of Tech Services. Drug Cases (for whom the **Department of Special Cases** was primarily established) are audited in the HGC or Co-Audit on the HSDC Course. (HCO PL 26 Aug 72—*Cancellation issue* of HCO PL 2 Feb 72 II)

**DEPLETION OF HAVINGNESS, the** truth of something, even when arrived at by the route of subjection and force, will as-is the something and cause its vanishment, and thus it is no longer had. This is called by auditors the **depletion of havingness.** (5601C31)

**DEPOSIT, a deposit** is a confused solid ridge area in the body. (5206CM24B)

**DEPT, department.** (BPL 5 Nov 72RA)

**DEPT 10s, see** DEPARTMENT OF SPECIAL CASES.

**DERAILER,** a type of phrase in an engram which throws the preclear "off the track" and makes him lose touch with his time track. This is a very serious phrase since it can make a schizophrenic and something of this sort is always to be found in schizophrenia. Some of its phrases throw him into other valences which have no proper track, some merely remove time, some throw him bodily out of time. "I don't have any time" is a **derailer.** "I'm beside myself" means that he is now two people, one beside the other. "I'll have to pretend I am somebody else" is a key phrase to identity confusion, and many more. (*DMSMH*, p. 335)

**DESCRIPTION PROCESSING, processing** which uses as-isness in present time to remedy the restimulations beheld by the thetan. The total command content of **description processing** is the phrase *"How does . . . seem to you now?"* This is used over, and over, and over by the auditor. In the blank he puts any difficulty the preclear is having. (*COHA*, p. 85)

**DESCRIPTIVE DEFINITION,** see DEFINITIONS, TYPES OF.

**DESTIMULATE, 1.** settle out. (HCOB 16 Aug 70) **2.** to take away the restimulation. **Destimulate** does not mean the erasure of the original incident, it means simply the knock out of the point of restimulation. (SH Spec 84, 6612C13)

**DESTIMULATED,** simply knocking out the key-ins of the original charge, you didn't knock out the original incidents, you just knocked out the moments when the original incident was keyed in. (SH Spec 300, 6308C28)

**DESTIMULATION, 1.** the action of deleting the moments of restimulation of the reactive mind or some portion of it, so that it moves away from the preclear and he is no longer connected to it. (*Scn AD*) **2.** to pull the pc out of the charge not try to erase the charge. To knock out the key-ins that keep the charge pinned to the individual. (SH Spec 9, 6403C10)

**DESTROY,** create-counter-create=to create something against a creation=to create one thing and then create something else against it=**destroy.** (*FOT*, p. 20)

**DESTRUCTION,** the apparent cycle of action contains **destruction,** but the actual cycle of action tells us what **destruction** is. **Destruction,** in terms of action, is a creation of something against a creation of something else. There is another type of **destruction** and this is no more creation. If one stops making something completely and ceases to be a party to its manufacture, it no longer exists for one. (*FOT*, pp. 21-22)

**DETACHED, 1.** chronically out of valence to the point of no case gain. (HCOB 10 Sept 68) **2.** the person that you run into that takes no responsibility for anything in life and that sort of thing. He isn't where he is looking from, see? He's **detached.** We use that word advisedly. You see, he's **detached** from existence, he hasn't got anything to do with it. Existence is up here and he's sitting back, "has nothing to do with me." (SH Spec 48, 6411C04)

**DETECTING METER,** a **meter** which **detects** flows and ridges around your preclear. (PDC 29)

**DFT,** see DIANETIC FLOW TABLE.

**DHARMA,** the name of a legendary Hindu sage whose many progenies were the personification of virtue and religious rites. **Dharma** is a mythological figure and we have the word **Dharma** almost interchangeable with the word Dhyana. But whatever you use there you are using a word which means knowingness. That's what that word means. (7ACC-25, 5407C19)

**DHYANA, 1.** the word **Dhyana** is almost interchangeable with the word Dharma. But whatever you use, you are using a word which means knowingness. **Dhyana**—that's knowingness. It means knowingness. It means lookingness. (7ACC-25, 5407C19) **2. Dhyana** could be literally translated as Indian for Scn, if you want to say it backwards. (7ACC-25, 5407C19)

**DIANAZENE,** a formula combined with vitamins and other minerals to make the intake of nicotinic acid more effective. **Dianazene** runs out radiation—or what appears to be radiation. It also proofs a person up against radiation in some degree. It also turns on and runs out incipient cancer. (*AAR,* pp. 123-124)

**DIANETIC ASSESSMENT LIST,** a **list** of somatic items given by a pc and written down by the auditor with the reads marked that occur on the meter. (BTB 7 Nov 72 IV)

**DIANETIC ASSIST, 1.** the auditor may take an individual who has been injured and run the injury as an engram even though it contains extensive unconsciousness. The last engram on the case has had relatively little chance to become charged up by locks and secondaries, and so is available for auditing regardless of the pre-existing engrams on the case. (*SOS,* Bk. 2, p. 157) **2.** running out the physically painful experience the person has just undergone, accidents, illness, operation or emotional shock. This erases the "psychic trauma" and speeds recovery to a remarkable degree. (HCOB 2 Apr 69)

**DIANETIC AUDITING, 1.** the application of **Dn** procedures to an individual to help him become well and happy. (*DPB*, p. 11) **2.** the tracing of experience. (SH Spec 70, 6607C21) **3. Dianetic auditing** includes as its basic principle, the exhaustion of all the painfully unconscious moments of a subject's life. By eradicating pain from the life of an individual, the auditor returns the individual to complete rationality and sanity. (*DTOT*, p. 68)

**DIANETIC AUDITOR, 1.** a person capable of resolving mental and physical problems by his ability to find and run engrams and secondaries. (HCOB 6 Apr 69) **2.** a **Dianetic auditor** would use **Dn** to handle the lack of well-being of the pc. (HCOB 6 Apr 69 II) **3.** one who has had case gain on **Dn**, and has been able to administer **Dn** so as to give case gains with it and that is what a **Dianetic auditor** is. It is not somebody who has been through the checksheets a large number of times or somebody who knows the Director of Certs and Awards. (6905C29)

**DIANETIC CASE COMPLETION, 1.** all somatic chains that were in restimulation have been traced to basic and blown. The pc is now happy and healthy. Other engrams and chains can exist back on the track but as they are not in restimulation they have no effect on the person. (*Dn Today*, p. 63) **2.** a healthy, happy, high IQ human being; freedom from those things which make a person susceptible to, or "hold in place" physical illness. (*Scn 0-8*, p. 137)

**DIANETIC CLEAR, 1.** the state of **Clear** can be achieved on Dn. It is not however attained by feeding people cognitions; **Clears** are made through auditing. The state of **Dn Clear** means the pc has erased his Dn case or mental image pictures. The discovery that a **Dn Clear** must not be run on engrams, R3RA or any version of R3R, results in an expansion of the Non-Interference Zone. (HCOB 25 Jun 70RA II) **2.** the state of **Clear** can be achieved on Dianetics. The state of **Dianetic Clear** means the pc has erased his Dianetic case or mental image pictures; he has attained the ability to be at cause over mental matter, energy, space and time on the first dynamic. (HCOB 24 Sept 78 III)

**DIANETIC CLEAR REHAB,** the state of **Dn Clear** is checked and rehabilitated which is a very fast action in most cases. It has to be verified because if the person didn't make it he has to go onto the Clearing Course and if he did really make **Dn Clear**, to do the Clearing Course would be disastrous because, of course, he's already **Clear**. (LRH ED 301 INT)

**DIANETIC COUNSELING GROUP,** the **Dn Counseling Group** consists of in full action, Hubbard **Dn Counselors,** the administrative few people, even if only part time, to handle the admin of the unit, and a Hubbard Dn Graduate in order to teach Hubbard **Dn Counselors** out in the field, and a Scn auditor to hold down review. (6905C29) *Abbr.* DCG.

**DIANETIC FLOW TABLE,** a chronological list of **Dn** items run, from earliest to latest, with the **flows** that have been run. (HCOB 3 Nov 72R)

**DIANETIC INFORMATION GROUP,** a **group** formed to provide **information** on the results of **Dn** and its applications. The membership is open to doctors, dental surgeons, pharmacists and qualified nurses. (*STCR*, p. 104) *Abbr.* D.I.G.

**DIANETICIST,** a skilled user of **Dianetic** therapy. (*DTOT* Gloss)

**DIANETIC LIST,** in Scn lists there's only one item. On **Dn lists** there can be a dozen, for a **Dn list** isn't really a list. It isn't trying to isolate the mental troubles of the pc. A **Dn list** is simply the pc's physical aches and pains. (HCOB 21 May 69)

**DIANETIC PRECLEAR,** one who is being processed toward the objective of a well and happy human being. (HCOB 6 Apr 69)

**DIANETIC RELEASE, 1.** the **release** has reached a point where he no longer has psychosomatic illnesses, where he has good stability and where he can enjoy life. If one simply took all the secondary engrams off a case, one would have a **Dianetic Release.** (*SOS*, p. 19) **2.** a preclear in whom the majority of emotional stress has been deleted from the reactive mind. Has had many large gains from **Dn,** is not yet a **Dn** Case Completion. (*DTOT* Gloss)

**DIANETIC REVERIE,** see REVERIE.

**DIANETICS, 1.** *DIA* (Greek) through, *NOUS* (Greek) soul deals with a system of mental image pictures in relation to psychic (spiritual) trauma. The mental image pictures are believed on the basis of personal revelation to be comprising mental activity created and formed by the spirit, and not by the body or brain. (BPL 24 Sept 73 V) **2. Dn** addresses the body. Thus **Dn** is used to knock out and erase illnesses, unwanted sensations, misemotion, somatics, pain, etc. **Dn** came before Scn. It disposed of body illness and the difficulties a thetan was having with his body. (HCOB 22 Apr 69) **3.** a technology that runs and erases locks, secondaries and engrams and their chains. (HCOB 17 Apr 69) **4. Dn** could be called a study of man. **Dn** and Scn, up to the point of stable exteriorization, operate in exactly the same field with exactly the same tools. It is only after man is sufficiently exteriorized to become a spirit that we depart from **Dn;** for here, considering man as a spirit, we must enter the field of religion. (PAB 42) **5.** a precision science. It stems from the study and codification of survival. (*COHA*, p. 148) **6.** a system of coordinated axioms which resolve problems concerning human behavior and psychosomatic illnesses. (5110CM08B) **7. Dn** is *not* psychiatry. It is *not* psycho-analysis. It is *not* psychology. It is *not* personal relations. It is *not* hypnotism. It is a science of mind. (*DMSMH*, p. 168) **8.** the route from aberrated or aberrated and ill human to capable human. (HCOB 3 Apr 66) *Abbr.* Dn.

**DIANETIC SPECIALIST,** HGDS. (HCOB 20 Apr 72)

**DIANOMETRY, 1.** that branch of **Dn** which measures thought capacity, computational ability and the rationality of the human mind. By its axioms and tests can be established the intelligence, the persistency, the ability, the aberrations and existing or potential insanity of an individual. (*DASF*) **2.** "Thought measurement," derived from the Greek for thought, and, unscholarly enough, the Latin for mensuration. (*DASF*)

**DICHOTOMY, 1.** can-can't is the plus and minus aspect of all thought and in Scn is called by a specialized word, **dichotomy.** (*FOT*, p. 100) **2.** a pair of opposites, such as black-white, good-evil, love-hate. (*COHA* Gloss) **3.** opposites; two things which when interplayed, cause action. (5209CM04B)

**DIFFERENTIATION, 1.** the ability to locate things in time and space. (5209CM04B) **2.** simply the distance between the particles. (PDC 28)

**DIFFERENTIATIVE DEFINITION,** see DEFINITIONS, TYPES OF.

**D.I.G., Dianetic Information Group.** (*STCR*, p. 104)

**DILETTANTISM,** is supposed to mean good at many things, but actually I would rather extend its meaning a little bit to saying unprofessional at everything. (SH Spec 33, 6408C04)

**DIMENSION,** the distance from the point of view to the anchor point that is in space. (Spr Lect 14, 5304CM07)

**DIMENSION POINT,** any **point** in a space or at the boundaries of space. As a specialized case, those **points** which demark the outermost boundaries of the space or its corners are called in Scn anchor **points.** (*Scn 8-8008,* p. 16)

**DINKY DICTIONARIES, (dinky:** small, insignificant); in learning the meaning of words small **dictionaries** are very often a greater liability than they are a help. The meanings they give are often circular. Like "CAT: an animal." "ANIMAL: a cat." They do not give enough meaning to escape the circle. The meanings given are often inadequate to get a real concept of the word. The words are too few and even common words are often missing. (HCOB 19 Jun 72)

**DIP,** a falling needle. (*EME,* p. 14) See FALL.

**DIR, director.** (BPL 5 Nov 72RA)

**DIR CERTS AND AWARDS, Director** of **Certificates and Awards.** (HCOB 23 Aug 65)

**DIRECTION-REVERSAL,** confuses left and right. (PAB 12)

**DIRECTIVE LISTING,** that Routine 3 activity which **directs** the pc's attention while **listing** to the form of the inevitable reliable item, providing it can be predicted. (HCOB 8 Apr 63)

**DIRECT STYLE AUDITING,** (Level IV style), by **direct** we mean straight, concentrated, intense, applied in a **direct** manner. By **direct**, we don't mean frank or choppy. On the contrary, we put the pc's attention on his bank and anything we do is calculated only to make that attention more **direct.** (HCOB 6 Nov 64)

**DIRECT VALENCE,** a **valence** by which the pc has transferred identity with someone who has **directly** confronted him. (PAB 95)

**DIR EXAMS, Director** of **Examinations.** (HCOB 23 Aug 65)

**DIR REV, Director** of **Review.** (HCOB 23 Aug 65)

**DIR TECH SERVICES, Director of Technical Services.** (HCOB 23 Aug 65)

**DIRTY NEEDLE,** the following is the only valid definition of a **dirty needle**: an erratic agitation of the needle which is ragged, jerky, ticking, not sweeping, and tends to be persistent. It is not limited in size. A **dirty needle** is caused by one of three things: (1) The auditor's TRs are bad. (2) The auditor is breaking the Auditor's Code. (3) The pc has withholds he does not wish known. The definitions of a **dirty needle** as "a small rock slam" and "a smaller edition of a rock slam" in HCOB 13 August AD 12, "Rock Slams and **Dirty Needles**," are cancelled. The definition of a **dirty needle** as "a minute rock slam" in HCOB 1 August AD 12, "Routine 3GA, Goals, Nulling by Mid Ruds," is cancelled. All definitions which limit the size of a **dirty needle** to "one quarter an inch" or "less than one quarter of an inch" are cancelled. A **dirty needle** is not to be confused with an R/S. They are distinctly different reads. You never mistake an R/S if you have ever seen one. A **dirty needle** is far less frantic. The difference between a rock slam and a **dirty needle** is in the *character of the read*, not the size. Persistent use of "fish and fumble" can sometimes turn a **dirty needle** into a rock slam. However until it does it is simply a **dirty needle**. Auditors, C/Ses, supervisors must must must know the difference between these two types of reads cold. (HCOB 3 Sept 78) *Abbr.* D.N.

**DIRTY READ,** *symbol* **D.R.**—a more or less instant response of the needle which is agitated by a major thought; it is an instant tiny (less than a quarter of an inch) agitation of the needle and is in fact a very small cousin of a rock slam but is not a rock slam. It does not persist. (HCOB 8 Nov 62)

**DIRTY 30,** Opening Procedure by Duplication has been doing things to cases hitherto untouched by extensive and intricate auditing. Because this process is very arduous to run on people below boredom on the tone scale and because it has very often been used on people on whom it should not be used, it was early called **"Dirty 30."** Actually **"Dirty 30"** is **Procedure 30** which encompassed what is now R2-17 and two other steps. (PAB 48)

**DISABILITY RUNDOWN,** handles anything the pc considers a **disability**; mental, physical or otherwise. It handles everything from being too short to not being able to speak Arabic or not wanting to go to parties. It takes each **disability** and handles it with R3RA. (HCOB 22 Jun 78R)

**DISAGREEMENT REMEDY**, a procedure for handling **disagreements** which is done by a Class III or above auditor. (BTB 22 Mar 72R)

**DISASSOCIATION**, mis-identification. (17ACC-4, 5702C28)

**DISCHARGED, 1.** an incident which is **discharged** is no longer capable of restimulation. It is not now an inert incident, it is a gone incident. The batteries in it have been short-circuited. That's the end of it. (SH Spec 300, 6308C28) **2.** where you get a condition of restimulation which is then let off, that is not **discharged**, it is destimulated. **Discharged** means that the incident is now incapable of being restimulated. (SH Spec 300, 6308C28)

**DISCHARGING**, erasing. (SH Spec 300, 6308C28)

**DISHONESTY**, one would not be **dishonest** unless he wished to seek advantage for himself or his group at the expense of some other self or group. That's **dishonesty**. It is seeking an illegitimate advantage and it's illegitimate just because it violates somebody's survival too much. (5108CM13B)

**DISINTEGRATING ROCKET READ**, a **read** that starts out like a mad thing, and turns into a fall. (SH Spec 274, 6306C13)

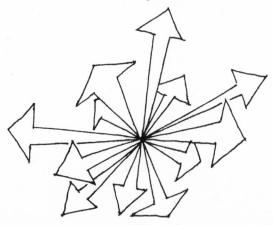

Dispersal
explosion

**DISPERSAL**, a series of outflows from a common point. A **dispersal** is, primarily a number of flows extending from a common center. The best example of a **dispersal** is an explosion. There is such a thing as an **in-dispersal**. This would be where the flows are all traveling toward a common center. One might call this an implosion. Outflow and inflow from a common center are classified under the word **dispersal.** (*Scn 8-8008*, p. 17)

**DISPERSED,** hiding oneself, being vague, not there most of the time. (*FOT*, p. 29)

**DISPERSION,** theta turning into entheta and the inhibition of the flow of free theta. (*SOS*, p. 114)

**DISSEMINATING SCN,** getting the materials of **Dn** and **Scn disseminated** widely and by efficient presentation. (BPL 15 Mar 60)

**DISTRACTION,** a **distraction** is something that is not relevant to the pc's case and is ineffective. (SH Spec 78, 6111C09)

**DIVISION OF TA,** one **division of TA** is from 1 to 2 or similarly from 2 to 3. It doesn't matter which way it moves. (SH Spec 1, 6105C07)

**DIZZINESS,** a feeling of disorientation and includes a spinniness, as well as an out-of-balance feeling. (HCOB 19 Jan 67)

**D/L, date/locate.** (HCOB 29 Oct 71R)

**Dn, Dianetics.** (HCOB 23 Aug 65)

**D.N., dirty needle.** (HCOB 17 May 69)

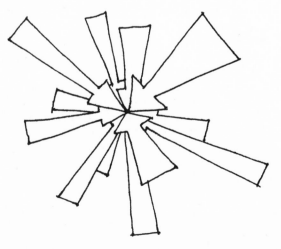

Dispersal
implosion

**DO A BUNK, 1.** an English slang term which meant "run away or desert." (7204C07 SO III) **2.** the body goes collapse; the heart is still beating, the lungs are still breathing, because the G.E. runs those, but the thetan—he's **done a bunk.** (PDC 9) **3.** that's what we say colloquially, means on his way over the hills and far away and he's just now passing Galaxy 18. (PDC 46) **4.** the person shoots out of his head and he's on his way. He hit the dispersal just adjacent to a ridge. (PDC 23)

**DOCTOR OF DIVINITY,** religion is basically a philosophic teaching designed to better the civilization into which it is taught. Backed fully by the precedent of all the ages concerning teachings, a Scientologist has a better right to call himself a priest, a minister, a missionary, a **doctor of divinity**, a faith healer or a preacher than any other man who bears the insignia of religion of the western world. I do not see any inconsistency of any kind in the issuance to those well-schooled and well-skilled in Scn the degree of **Doctor of Divinity** as a passport into those areas where they are needed. (PAB 32)

**DOCTOR OF SCIENTOLOGY, 1.** the **Doctor of Scn** degree is senior to HGA. It is an honor award and may be made by nomination or selection for those who are consistently producing excellent results in their own field. (PAB 6) **2. Doctor of Scn** abroad [away from the USA] was equivalent to HGA in 1956. (HCOTB 12 Sept 56)

**DOCTRINE OF THE STABLE DATUM,** a confusing motion can be understood by conceiving one thing to be motionless. Until one selects one **datum**, one factor, one particular in a confusion of particles, the confusion continues. The one thing selected and used becomes the **stable datum** for the remainder. A **stable datum** does not have to be the correct one. It is simply the one that keeps things from being in a confusion and on which others are aligned. (*POW*, pp. 23-24)

**D OF ESTIMATIONS, Director of Estimations.** In 1965, head of the **Department of Estimations,** now called Tech Services which is in charge of getting pcs to session, having auditing rooms and materials available for auditors, keeping up pcs' status and scheduling boards, and taking care of and safeguarding pc folders and records. (*PRD* Gloss)

**D OF P, Director of Processing.** (HCOB 23 Aug 65)

**D OF T, Director of Training.** (HCOB 23 Aug 65)

**DOG CASE,** *Slang.* **1.** a **case** nobody can make anything out of. (HCOB 5 Mar 71 II) **2.** the pc is not running well. Such a **case** is the result of a flub always. (HCOB 19 Mar 71, *C/S Series 30*)

**DOG PC,** an auditor who cannot audit, whose TRs are out, whose metering is bad and who never keeps the code always says his **pcs** are "**dogs.**" (HCOB 15 Jun 72)

**DOING,** the action of creating an effect. An effect in creation is action. (*FOT*, p. 31)

**DOING A BUNK,** see DO A BUNK.

**DOINGNESS,** what one ought to be **doing** in order to get creation or do creation. (SH Spec 19, 6106C23)

**DOING THE FOLDER,** refers to the technical supervision of case reports. (*ISE*, p. 45)

**DO-IT-YOURSELF PROCESSING,** the HAS co-audit which seeks to improve cases and further interest people in Scn so that they will take individual HGC processing and individual training. (HCO PL 14 Feb 61)

**DOMINATION,** forcing the other person to do exactly what is desired with the mechanism of recrimination and denial of friendship or support unless instant compliance takes place. It seeks by anger and outright criticism, accusations, and other mechanisms to pound another individual into submission by making him less. (*SA*, p. 167)

**DOMINATION BY NULLIFICATION,** this is covert and quite often the person upon whom it is exerted remains unsuspecting beyond the fact that he knows he is very unhappy. This is the coward's method of **domination.** The person using it feels that he is less than the individual upon whom he is using it and has not the honesty or fortitude to admit the fact to himself. He then begins to pull the other individual "down to size," using small carping criticisms. The one who is seeking to **dominate** strikes heavily at the point of pride and capability of his target and yet, if at any moment the target challenges the **nullifier,** the person using the mechanism claims he is doing so solely out of assistance and friendship or disavows completely that it has been done. (*SA*, p. 167)

**DOPE-OFF, 1.** the phenomenon of a person getting tired, sleepy, foggy (as though **doped** ). One of the phenomena of going past a misunderstood word. (BTB 12 Apr 72) **2.** a state of lessened awareness, still above unconsciousness, and manifested principally by communication lag. **Dope-off** is also caused by impaired havingness. (*COHA* Gloss)

**DOUBLE ACKNOWLEDGMENT, 1. double acknowledgment** is not, repeat not, the giving of more than one good or thank you. **Double acknowledgment** only occurs when the auditor assumes the cycle has ended but the preclear then draws the auditor's attention to the fact that it didn't end and the auditor has to **acknowledge** again in order to end that cycle. (BTB 29 Jun 62) **2.** this occurs when the pc answers up, the auditor then **acknowledges,** and the pc then finishes his answer, leaving the auditor with another **acknowledgment** to do. (HCOB 12 Nov 59)

**DOUBLE ASSESS,** (Expanded Dianetics term from tape 7203C30, "Expanded Dianetics") the act of taking various parts or terminals of the pc's environment as mentioned in worksheets or health form such as "home," "job," "Ohio," etc., making it into a list, **assessing** it for best read (**assessment number one** ) and then taking that item (such as "home") and listing out the pains, sensations, emotions and attitudes connected with it (**assessment number 2**) and running it with Dianetics, or otherwise using the result in processing. (LRH Def. Notes)

**DOUBLE QUESTION,** a type of Q and A. The auditor asks a question. The pc answers. The auditor asks a question about the answer. (HCOB 24 May 62)

**DOUBLE TERMINALING, 1.** the process known as **double terminaling** is an assist. One **double terminals** as follows: he has the preclear mock up something or someone facing its duplicate, then he gets another such pair beside, in any position, the first pair. It will be noted that the mock-ups discharge one against the other like electrical poles. A **double terminal** may also consist of an unmatched pair such as a mock-up of a husband facing a wife and, parallel to this, the husband facing the wife again. Or a person facing an inanimate object, then, beside that pair, the same person as another mock-up facing the same object as another mock-up. It will be observed that when TWO pairs are used, there are, even so, only TWO COMMUNICATION LINES. The lines are more important than the **terminals**; one wants two communication lines, parallel to each other. This, of course, requires four **terminals**. (PAB 1) **2. double terminaling** simply puts up two pairs of matched **terminals**. The pairs may each be of two different things but each pair contains one thing the same as the other pair; in other words, husband and wife is one pair and husband and wife is the other pair. These, parallel, give the two **terminal** effect necessary for a discharge. (*COHA*, p. 213) **3.** there are a number of processes which could include **double terminals**. One **terminal** made to face another **terminal** in terms of mock-up can be discharged one against the other in such a way as to relieve aberration connected with things similar to the **terminal** thus mocked up. One takes two pairs of such **terminals** and standing them in relationship to each other, discovers that he has now four **terminals** but these four **terminals** furnish only two lines. These two lines will discharge one against the other. (*Scn 8-8008*, p. 32)

**DOUBLE TERMINALS,** you mock up four of the same person or two of one person, two of another person, in such a way as to give you four **terminals** with an identical line. (Spr Lect 13, 5304CM07)

**DOUBLE TICK,** dirty needle. (HCOB 25 May 62)

**DOUBT, doubting** expresses the inability to find out. (SH Spec 39, 6108C15)

**DOWN-BOUNCER,** this type of phrase is one which tells the person to "get down" or "get back" and keeps the preclear below the actual incident in which he is held. (*SOS*, p. 106)

**DOWN SCALE,** on the tone scale to go **down scale** one must decrease his power to observe. (*COHA*, p. 200)

**DOWN THE TRACK,** not in present time. (HCOB 16 Jul 69)

**D.R., dirty read.** (HCOB 23 Aug 65)

**DRAMATIZATION, 1.** to repeat in action what has happened to one in experience. That's a basic definition of it, but much more important, it's a replay now of something that happened then. It's being replayed out of its time and period. (SH Spec 72, 6607C28) **2.** the duplication of an engramic content, entire or in part, by an aberree in his present time environment. Aberrated conduct is entirely **dramatization.** The degree of **dramatization** is in direct ratio to the degree of restimulation of the engrams causing it. (*DTOT*, p. 74) **3.** complete **dramatization** is complete identity. It is the engram in full force in present time with the aberree taking one or more parts of the *dramatis personae* present in the engram. (*DTOT*, p. 75) **4.** thinking or acting in a manner that is dictated by masses or significances contained in the reactive mind. When **dramatizing,** the individual is like an actor playing his dictated part and going through a whole series of irrational actions. (*PXL* Gloss)

**DRAMATIZE,** to go through the cycle of action demanded by an engram. (*SOS*, Bk. 2, p. 29)

**DRAMATIZING PSYCHOTIC,** the **dramatizing psychotic** is not always looked upon as insane. Whether or not he is classified as insane depends upon whether or not he is of obvious menace to other *Homo sapiens.* He is fixed in one facsimile which he plays over and over to the environment around him. He is controlled by his environment to the extent that anything in his environment turns on his **dramatization.** He is disastrous to have around. Inaccessible persons passing for normals are sometimes **dramatizing psychotics** who **dramatize** infrequently—perhaps only once or twice a day. The **dramatizing psychotic** lives mainly in the illusion of his own facsimile with its surroundings, not actual surroundings. He is definitely not in present time at any time. (*AP&A*, p. 38)

**DREAM, 1.** a pretended knowingness about location. (SH Spec 50, 6109C06) **2.** the imaginative reconstruction of areas of randomity or the re-symbolization of the efforts of theta. (*Scn 0-8*, p. 90) **3.** a **dream** in its normal function is that powerful and original mechanism called the imagination compositing or creating new pictures. (*DTOT*, p. 89) **4.** a frantic effort to orient, just to locate himself so that he can feel secure, that's what a **dream** is and a **dream** of course is pretended knowingness because he is at none of these places. (SH Spec 39, 6108C15) **5. dreams** follow a sudden loss. It's an effort to orient oneself and get something back. (HCOB 29 Mar 65)

**DRIFT DOWN,** not actual tone arm action. The pc is just **drifting** toward the read of an item. In this the tone arm does not go up or down, back and forth. It just **drifts** slowly and evenly down and stays there. (HCOB 11 Apr 62)

**DRIFT UP,** occurs during prepchecking or listing. The constantly rising needle gradually raises the tone arm up to a high read which finally just stays there. This **drift up** is not actually tone arm motion. It is just the pc's refusal to confront. (HCOB 11 Apr 62)

**DRILLS,** exercises, processes. (PAB 82)

**DRIVE,** the dynamic thrust through time toward the attainment of the goal. (*DTOT*, p. 29)

**DROP,** a falling needle. (*EME*, p. 14) See FALL.

**DRUG CASES, cases** who seek in processing the delusions or madness which exhilarated them on **drugs.** (HCOB 25 Nov 71 II)

**DRUG REHAB,** see CHEMICAL RELEASE. See REHABBING DRUGS.

**DRUG RUNDOWN,** the **drug rundown** consists of: (1) TRs 0-4, 6-9 *FLAT.* (2) Full C/S 1, where not done, to fully educate the pc. (3) Objectives—full battery to full EPs per basic books and early HCOBs on them. (4) Class VIII **Drug** Handling—list and rehab all **drugs,** 3-way recalls, secondaries and engrams of taking and giving **drugs.** (5) AESP's on each reading **drug** listed separately and handled with R3R, each **drug** to full F/N assessment of **drug** list. (6) "No interest" **drug** items—all reading ones run where they exist. (7) Prior assessment—AESP's listed separately and run R3R, prior to first **drug** or alcohol taken. (HCOB 31 Aug 74)

# DRUG RUNDOWN REPAIR LIST

**DRUG RUNDOWN REPAIR LIST,** will handle bypassed charge caused by endless **Drug RDs.** (HCOB 19 Sept 78 I)

**DRUGS, 1.** by **drugs** (to mention a few) are meant tranquilizers, opium, cocaine, mariguana, peyote, amphetamine and the psychiatrists' gift to Man, LSD which is the worst. Any medical **drugs** are included. **Drugs** are **drugs.** There are thousands of trade names and slang terms for these **drugs.** Alcohol is included as a **drug** and receives the same treatment in auditing. (HCOB 15 Jul 71 III) **2. drugs** essentially are poisons. The degree they are taken determines the effect. A small amount gives a stimulant. A greater amount acts as a sedative. A larger amount acts as a poison and can kill one dead. This is true of any **drug.** (HCOB 28 Aug 68 II)

Drugs (Def. 1)

**DRY RUN,** a no-auditing situation. You're **running** an electrical circuit with no current. (SH Spec 295, 6308C15)

**D. SCN, Doctor** of **Scientology,** honorary award for the application of **Scn** processes, principles, books or literature. (HCOB 23 Aug 65) See DOCTOR OF SCIENTOLOGY.

**D. SCN. ABROAD,** see DOCTOR OF SCIENTOLOGY.

**DTS, Director** of **Tech Services.** (HCOB 23 Aug 65)

**DUB-IN, 1.** any unknowingly created mental picture that appears to have been a record of the physical universe but is in fact only an altered copy of the time track. (HCOB 15 May 63) **2.** the phrase out of the motion picture industry of putting a sound track on top of something that isn't there. (SH Spec 78, 6608C25) **3.** a recording which is being manufactured by a recording. (5811C07) **4.** imaginary recall—there is no pain **dub-in.** (*DASF*)

**DUB-IN CASE,** this guy is manufacturing incidents and saying they're real. (5206CM24F)

**DUNNAGE,** *Slang.* **1.** the stuff you put around the cargo to keep it straight in a ship. (*PXL*, p. 244) **2.** extra and relatively meaningless talk. (PAB 38) **3.** irrelevant remarks aimed solely to stay in communication with the preclear. (*COHA*, p. 88)

**DUPLICATION, 1.** cause, distance, effect, with the same thing at effect as is at cause. (5411CM01) **2.** the flow of creation. **Duplication** is the process by which a thing persists. (2ACC-13A, 5311CM30)

**DUPLICATIVE QUESTION (TR-3),** a drill to teach a student to **duplicate** without variation an auditing question. Each time newly, in its own unit of time, not as a blur with other questions, and to acknowledge it. (HCOB 16 Aug 71 II)

**DWINDLING ROCK SLAM,** one which diminishes item by item, written thing by written thing. It's less and less and less and less, and finally a dirty needle. Then there isn't even a dirty needle and it's gone. (SH Spec 194, 6209C25)

**DWINDLING SANITY,** a **dwindling** ability to assign time and space. (*Scn 8-80*, p. 44)

**DWINDLING SPIRAL, 1.** one commits overt acts unwittingly. He seeks to justify them by finding fault or displacing blame. This leads him into further overts against the same terminals which leads to a degradation of himself and sometimes those terminals. (HCOB 21 Jan 60, *Justification*) **2.** as life progresses, more and more theta becomes fixed as entheta in locks and secondary engrams, and less and less theta is available to the organism for purposes of reason. This is called the **dwindling spiral.** It is so called because the more entheta there is on the case, the more theta will be turned into entheta at each new restimulation. It is a three-dimensional vicious circle which carries the individual down the tone scale. (*SOS*, Bk. 2, p. 26)

**DYNAMIC, 1.** any one of the eight subdivisions of the **dynamic** principle of existence—SURVIVE. (*PXL*, p. 49) **2. dynamic** is the ability to translate solutions into action. (*HFP*, p. 171) **3.** the tenacity to life and vigor and persistence in survival. (*DMSMH*, p. 38)

**DYNAMIC ASSESSMENT,** you run on the E-meter a **dynamic assessment** and pick up any **dynamic** that gives a change of needle pattern or take any **dynamic** which makes needle drop no matter how slight. Having located the **dynamic** we now ask the pc for any terminal he or she thinks would represent that **dynamic.** (HCOB 4 Feb 60)

**DYNAMIC ASSESSMENT BY ROCK SLAM,** listing and assessing to find the **rock slam** on the pc. (SH Spec 204, 6210C30)

**DYNAMIC DEFINITION,** action **definition.** (5110CM08B) See DEFINITIONS, TYPES OF.

**DYNAMICS,** there could be said to be eight urges (drives, impulses) in life. These we call **dynamics.** These are motives or motivations. We call them the eight **dynamics.** The **first dynamic** —is the urge toward existence as one's self. Here we have individuality expressed fully. This can be called the **self dynamic.** The **second dynamic**—is the urge toward existence as a sexual or bisexual activity. This **dynamic** actually has two divisions. **Second dynamic** (a) is the sexual act itself and the **second dynamic** (b) is the family unit, including the rearing of children. This can be called the **sex dynamic.** The **third dynamic**—is the urge toward existence in groups of individuals. Any group or part of an entire class could be considered to be a part of the **third dynamic.** The school, the society, the town, the nation are each part of the **third dynamic,** and each one is a **third dynamic.** This can be called the **group dynamic.** The **fourth dynamic**—is the urge toward existence as mankind. Whereas the white race would be considered a **third dynamic,** all the races would be considered the **fourth dynamic.** This can be called the **mankind dynamic.** The **fifth dynamic**—is the urge toward existence of the animal kingdom. This includes all living things whether vegetable or animal. The fish in the sea, the beasts of the field or of the forest, grass, trees, flowers, or anything directly and intimately motivated by life. This could be called the **animal dynamic**. The **sixth dynamic**—is the urge toward existence as the physical universe. The physical universe is composed of matter, energy, space and time. In Scn we take the first letter of each of these words and coin a word, mest. This can be called the **universe dynamic**. The **seventh dynamic**—is the urge toward existence as or of spirits. Anything spiritual, with or without identity, would come under the heading of the **seventh dynamic**. This can be called the **spiritual dynamic**. The **eighth dynamic**—is the urge toward existence as infinity. This is also identified as the Supreme Being. It is carefully observed here that the science of Scn does not intrude into the **dynamic** of the Supreme Being. This is called the **eighth dynamic** because the symbol of infinity ∞ stood upright makes the numeral "8." This can be called the **infinity** or **God dynamic**. (*FOT*, pp. 36-38)

Dynamics

first dynamic
self dynamic

second dynamic (Def. b)
sex dynamic

# DYNAMICS

third dynamic
group dynamic

fourth dynamic
mankind dynamic

fifth dynamic
animal dynamic

sixth dynamic
universe dynamic

seventh dynamic
(ancient Greek symbol
for spirit)
spiritual dynamic

eighth dynamic
(symbol for infinity)
infinity or God dynamic

131

# DYNAMIC STRAIGHTWIRE

**DYNAMIC STRAIGHTWIRE,** do a survey, one time on the pc, not every session, to discover any errors in his **dynamics.** On pcs not familiar with Scn terms use the following words: self, sex, family, children, groups, mankind, the animal kingdom, birds, beasts, fish, vegetables, trees, growing things, matter, energy, space, time, spirits, souls, gods, God. Assess with this question only, "Tell me something that would represent (each of the above, one after the other)." When one changes the pattern of the needle action or when it is definitely balmy, write it down. When list is completed take these items written down and run: "Think of something you have done to (selected terminal you wrote down)." "Think of something you have withheld from (selected terminal, same one)." Run these terminals one each, one after the other, until pc seems flat. (HCOB 16 Feb 59)

# E

**EARLIER SIMILAR, 1.** whenever an auditor gets a read on an item from rudiments or a prepared list it must be carried to an F/N. If you know bank structure you know it is necessary to find an **earlier** item if something does not release. What has been found as a read on a prepared list *would* F/N if it were the basic lock. So if it doesn't F/N, then there is an **earlier** (or an **earlier** or an **earlier**) lock which is preventing it from F/Ning. Example: auditor asks for an **earlier similar** ARC Break. (HCOB 14 Mar 71R) *Abbr.* E/S.

**E/B, earlier beginning.** (7203C30)

**ECHO INVALIDATION,** pc names an item and auditor says, "That isn't it." This is not just bad form but a very vicious practice that leads to a games condition. The **invalidation** of each item makes the pc very dizzy and very desperate. (HCOB 13 Apr 64, *Scn VI Tone Arm Action*)

**ECHO METERING,** the pc says, "You missed a suppress. It's . . ." and the auditor reconsults the meter asking for a suppress. That leaves the pc's offering an undischarged charge. Never ask the **meter** after a pc volunteers a button. Example: You've declared suppress clean, pc gives you another suppress. Take it and don't ask suppress again. That's **echo metering.** If a pc puts his own ruds in, don't at once jump to the **meter** to put his ruds in. That makes all his offerings missed charge. (HCOB 13 Apr 64, *Scn VI Part One Tone Arm Action*)

**ED-1, -2,** etc., **Expertise Drill.** (BTB 20 Jul 74) See AUDITOR EXPERTISE DRILLS.

**EDUCATION, 1.** the conveyance of ideas, patterns and creations from one person to another for knowing retention and conscious use by the second person. (HCOB 27 Apr 71) **2.** basically, fixing data, unfixing data and changing existing data, either by making it more fixed or less fixed. (BTB 14 Sept 69 I) **3.** learning, knowing or accomplishing the knowingness of a certain subject, and would be in the direction of accomplishing certain actions professionally. One expects an **educated** person to be able to accomplish certain things in the subject he is **educated** in. He should be able to accomplish the actions and results that are taught in the subject. (*Abil 190*) **4.** the activity of relaying an idea or an action from one being to another, in such a way as not to stultify or inhibit the use thereof and that's about all it is. You could add to it that it permits, then, the other fellow to think on this subject and develop. (SH Spec 33, 6408C04) **5.** the process by which the individual is given the accumulated data of a long span of culture. It can, no less validly than personal experience, solve many of his problems. (*SOS*, Bk. 2, p. 9)

**EDUCATIONAL DIANETICS,** contains the body of organized knowledge necessary to train minds to their optimum efficiency and to an optimum of skill and knowledge in the various branches of the works of man. (*DMSMH*, p. 152)

**EFFECT, 1.** receipt point and what is received at the receipt point. (PAB 30) **2.** a potential receipt of flow. (*COHA*, p. 258)

**EFFECT GOALS,** ambition to be an effect rather than a cause. (*COHA*, p. 200)

**EFFECT SCALE,** a **scale** which tells you how much cause the individual dare be by measuring how much **effect** he's willing to suffer. At the top of the **scale** the individual can give or receive any **effect,** and at the bottom of the **scale** he can receive no **effects** but he still feels he must give a total **effect.** (5904C08)

**EFFORT, 1.** the physical force manifestation of motion. A sharp **effort** against an individual produces pain. A strenuous **effort** produces discomfort. **Effort** can be recalled and re-experienced by the preclear. No preclear below 2.5 should be called upon to use **effort** as such as he is incapable of handling it and will stick in it. The essential part of a painful facsimile is its **effort**, not its perceptions. (*HFP* Gloss) **2.** directed force. (*Scn 0-8*, p. 75) **3.** making two things coincide at one point or stop coinciding at a point or change coincidence at a point. (2ACC-31B, 5312CM22) **4.** condensed feeling. (2ACC-21A, 5312CM11)

**EFFORT-POINT**, that area from which a person exerted **effort**, and that area into which that person received **effort**. (*PXL*, pp. 257-258)

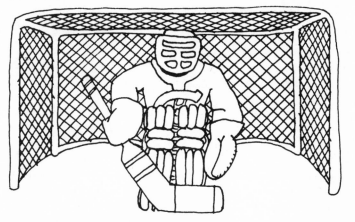

Effect

**EFFORT PROCESSING, 1.** the bank can be considered to have three layers. **Effort**-Emotion-Thought. **Effort** buries emotion. Emotion buries thought. A physical aberration or physical disability is held in place by a **counter-effort**. **Effort processing** removes the **effort** which uncovers the pc's own *emotion* and removes the *emotion* which uncovers and blows the pc's thoughts and postulates about the disability as these are the aberrative source of it. (BTB 1 Dec 71R IV) **2.** processing which lifts up for emphasis the fact that only one's self-determinism is important, and that the **efforts** and the **counter-efforts** against it are the aberrative factor. Rediscovering times for the preclear when he gave up his self-determinism, and erasing the **efforts** involved in these postulates and incidents is giving back that individual's happiness and assisting him to move again in a survival direction. (*DAB*, Vol. II, p. 105)

**8-C, 1. control (Routine 8-Control).** (HCOB 20 Aug 71 II) **2.** essentially and intimately the operation of making the physical body contact the environment. (5410CM08) **3.** name of a process. Also used to mean **good control.** (HCOB 23 Aug 65)

**8D, Standard Operating Procedure 8D,** 1954. Primarily for heavy cases the goal of this **procedure** was "to bring the preclear to tolerate any viewpoint." (*PXL*, p. 205)

**8-80,** see TECHNIQUE 8-80.

**8-8008,** see SCIENTOLOGY 8-8008.

**EIGHT,** the symbol of **infinity** ∞ stood upright makes the numeral "8." (PAB 83)

**EIGHTH DYNAMIC,** see DYNAMICS.

**8 LEVELS OF CASES,** see STATE OF CASE SCALE.

**8RB,** word clearing series **8RB,** the standard C/S for word clearing Method 1 in session. (HCOB 30 Jun 71R II)

**EJECTOR,** species of command. These are colloquially called "bouncers." They include such things as "Get out!" "Don't ever come back," "I've got to stay away," etc. etc., including any combination of words which *literally* mean **ejection.** (*DMSMH*, p. 213)

**ÉLAN VITAL,** theta, life force, life energy, divine energy, the energy peculiar to life. (*SOS*, Bk. 2, p. 21)

**ELECTRICAL,** is the bridge between sensation and pain and is difficult to classify as either pain or sensation when it exists alone. (HCOB 8 Nov 62) [This definition of electrical is a specialized definition of the word in terms of how it applies in the field of perceptics. Only the technical usage of the word as it is used in Dn and Scn is defined here.]

**ELECTRICITY,** a flow manifestation of force. (5312CM17)

**ELECTRONICS,** lower and cruder manifestations of the same order of actuality as thought. (*Scn 8-8008* Gloss)

**ELECTROPSYCHOMETER,** it's an electrical means of measuring the spirit. It's exactly what its name says, **electropsychometer.** It's called for short, **E-meter.** (Class VIII, No. 7) See also E-METER.

**EMERGENCY AUDITOR,** this person is the person called upon by the group auditor to assist a preclear in the group who has hit a sudden "grief charge" or who is consistently "boiling-off." (*GAH*, p. iii)

**EM, E-meter.** Where **EM** is followed directly by a number (e.g. **EM** 16) it refers to the **E-meter** drill of that number. (BTB 12 Apr 72R)

E-meter

**E-METER, 1.** the **Hubbard Electrometer** is a religious artifact used in the Church confessional. It, in itself, does nothing, and is used by ministers only, to assist parishioners in locating areas of spiritual distress or travail. (BPL 24 Sept 73R II) **2. Hubbard Electrometer.** An electronic instrument for measuring mental state and change of state in individuals, as an aid to precision and speed in auditing. The **E-meter** is not intended or effective for the diagnosis, treatment or prevention of any disease. (*Scn AD*) **3.** used to verify the preclear's gain and register when each separate auditing action is ended. (HCOB 5 Apr 69R) **4.** means an **"electro-psychometer,"** an instrument which measures emotional reaction by tiny electrical impulses generated by thought. (HCOB 6 Sept 71) **5.** the **meter** tells you what the preclear's mind is doing when the preclear is made to think of something. The **meter** registers before the preclear becomes conscious of the datum. It is therefore a pre-conscious **meter**. It passes a tiny current through the preclear's body. This current is influenced by the mental masses, pictures, circuits and machinery. When the unclear pc thinks of something, these mental items shift and this registers on the **meter**. (*EME*, p. 8)

**E-METER CALIBRATION,** see CALIBRATION.

**E-METER CHECK,** see METER CHECK.

**EMOTION, 1.** a response by wave-length affecting an individual or another which produces a sensation and a state of mind. (SH

Spec 83, 6612C06) **2. emotion** is three things—engramic response to situations, endocrine metering of the body to meet situations on an analytical level and the inhibition or the furtherance of life force. (*Scn 0-8*, p. 66) **3.** a manifestation, a condition of beingness which is the connector between thought and effort. The tone scale is a direct index of **emotion.** (5203CM05B) **4.** the intention to exert effort bridges into the body by **emotion.** In other words, the physical-mental bridge is **emotion. Emotion** is motion. (5203CM04B) **5. emotion** could be called the energy manifestation of affinity. As used in Dn, **emotion** could be called the index of the state of being. In the English language, **"emotional"** is often considered synonymous with "irrational." This would seem to assume that if one is **emotional** one cannot be reasonable. No more unreasonable assumption could possibly be made. (*SOS*, p. 48) **6.** this word is redefined in Dn and is given an opposite for comparison, "misemotion." Previously the word **emotion** was never satisfactorily defined. Now it is defined as an organism manifestation of position on the tone scale which is rationally appropriate to the present time environment and which truly represents the present time position on the tone scale. Rational affect. (*SOS* Gloss)

**EMOTIONAL CHARGE, emotional charge** may be contained in any engram: the **emotion** communicates, in the same tone level, from the personnel around the "unconscious" person into his reactive mind. Anger goes into an engram as anger, apathy as apathy, shame as shame. Whatever people have felt emotionally around "an unconscious" person should be found in the engram which resulted from the incident. (*DMSMH*, p. 251)

**EMOTIONAL CURVE, 1.** the drop from any position above 2.0 to a position below 2.0 on the realization of failure or inadequacy. It is easily recovered by preclears. (*AP&A*, p. 24) **2.** the drop or rise from one level of **emotion** to another. (*HFP*, p. 120)

**EMOTIONAL SCALE,** refers to the subjective feelings of the individual, in relation to his position on the tone scale. (*NOTL*, p. 102)

**EMOTIONAL TONE SCALE,** see TONE SCALE.

**EMOTION-POINT,** that point from which a person **emotes**, and at which he **emoted**. (*PXL*, p. 257)

**EMPIRICAL FACT,** one that is established by observation, not established by theory or reason. (SH Spec 61, 6110C03)

**END OF CYCLE,** a finite stop. (5311CM24)

**END OF CYCLE PROCESSING,** in **end of cycle processing** you merely keep mocking up a finished, completed task, a goal, and so on up to a point where you've obtained that goal. (5312CM21)

**END OF ENDLESS DRUG RUNDOWN,** the steps of the **Drug RD** have been rearranged to prevent this **endless** running and allow the **rundown** to be taken to a flat point of freedom from the harmful effects of this lifetime **drugs** and an F/Ning **drug** list. (HCOB 19 Sept 78 I)

**END OF ENDLESS INTERIORIZATION REPAIR RUNDOWN,** is the superbly workable new process just developed to handle any needed **Int repairs.** It resolves any **Int** troubles that might persist even after a pc has had an **Int Rundown** done totally standardly. It does not replace the **Int Rundown**; rather, it complements it, when necessary, as it runs **Int** by Recalls. We audit out the **Int** engrams on the **Int Rundown.** Then if **repair** is needed, the **End of Endless Int Repair RD** can be used to clean it up smoothly with Recalls. It is the answer to overrepair of **Int** on any pc. Additionally, it can be used for handling **Int repair** on Clears, OTs and Dn Clears. (HCOB 4 Jan 71R)

**END PHENOMENA, 1.** "those indicators in the pc and meter which show that a chain or process is **ended.**" It shows in Dianetics that basic on that chain and flow has been erased, and in Scientology that the pc has been released on that process being run. A new flow or a new process can be embarked upon, of course, when the **end phenomena** of the previous process is attained. The 0 to IV Scientology **end phenomena** are: (A) floating needle, (B) cognition, (C) very good indicators, (D) release. (HCOB 20 Feb 70) **2.** the auditor does not call F/Ns when running Dianetics until the *full* **EP** of the chain is reached. (1) When it appears that you have reached the basic incident of the chain and that it is erasing, after each pass through the auditor asks, "Has it erased?" (2) The meter will have been F/Ning for some time. (3) When the pc has stated that it has erased the auditor should also expect a cognition volunteered by the pc. (4) The auditor should expect to see very good indicators (VGIs). (5) If no postulate made during the time of the incident has come off and been volunteered by the pc the auditor should ask, "Did you make a postulate at the time of that incident?" Note that the postulate may have come off in the form of a cognition and on the other hand may not have even though a cognition was given. Only when these latter steps have occurred can one consider that the **EP** of a Dianetic incident or chain has been obtained. (HCOB 7 July 78) *Abbr*. EP.

**END RUDIMENTS, rudiments** to make the pc feel ok by session **end.** They are to clean up additional residual charge left by reason of the session and they are to put the pc in a frame of mind to **end** the session. (SH Spec 121, 6203C01)

**END WORD, 1.** the common denominator to the whole of a GPM. (SH Spec 50, 6412C22) **2.** the final **word** of a goal. (HCOB 17 Aug 64)

**ENERGY, 1. energy** would simply mean a potential of motion or power. It would be a force or flow or the potential force or flow from something to something; or the ability to accomplish work; or the ability to make motion or movement. It's potential or actual motion or force. (SH Spec 84, 6612C13) **2. energy** derives from imposition of space between terminals and a reduction and expansion of that space. (*COHA*, p. 256) **3.** there are three kinds of **energy**. There's a flow, and then there's a dispersal, and then there's a ridge. (PDC 18) **4.** a mass of particles which is a mass of motion. (5203CM04B) **5.** postulated particles in space. (*PXL*, p. 150) **6. energy** is subdivisible into a large motion, such as a flow, a dispersal, or a ridge, and a small motion which is itself commonly called a "particle" in nuclear physics. Agitation within agitation is the basic formation of particles of **energy**, such as electrons, protons and others. (*Scn 8-80*, p. 43)

Energy (Def. 1)

**ENFORCED AFFINITY,** the demand on the individual that he experience or admit **affinity** when he has not felt it. People lower toned than the preclear commonly command his **affinity**; and when **affinity** is given but not felt locks are formed which are quite enturbulative should engrams underlie such an enforcement. (*SOS*, Bk. 2, p. 72)

**ENFORCED COMMUNICATION,** the demand on the individual that he experience or admit **communication** when he has not felt it. **Enforced communication** is productive of all manner of aberration and physiological changes in the individual. When the individual is **forced** to listen to something he would not ordinarily listen to if left to his own self-determinism, his hearing to that degree is impaired. When he has been **forced** to touch something which he would not ordinarily touch, his tactile is thus impaired. When he has been **forced** to talk when his self-determinism says he should remain silent, his speech **communication** is impaired. (*SOS*, Bk. 2, pp. 72-73)

**ENFORCED HAVE,** making someone accept what they didn't want. (HCOB 3 Jun 72R)

**ENFORCED OVERT HAVE, forcing** upon another a substance, action or thing not wanted or refused by the other. (HCO PL 12 May 72)

**ENFORCED REALITY,** the demand on the individual that he experience or admit **reality** when he has not felt it. Any time a person is made to agree by **force** or threat or deprivation, to another's **reality** and yet does not feel that **reality** himself, an aberrative condition exists. (*SOS*, Bk. 2, pp. 72-73)

**ENGRAM, 1.** a mental image picture which is a recording of a time of physical pain and unconsciousness. It must by definition have impact or injury as part of its content. (HCOB 23 Apr 69) **2.** a specialized kind of facsimile. This differs from other mental pictures because it contains, as part of its content, unconsciousness and physical pain. (*Dn 55!*, p. 12) **3.** a complete recording, down to the last accurate detail, of every perception present in a moment of partial or full unconsciousness. (*Scn 0-8*, p. 11) **4.** a theta facsimile of atoms and molecules in misalignment. (*Scn 0-8*, p. 81) **5.** a unit of force which is held in because one has chosen force itself for his randomity. (5312CM13) **6.** the word **engram** is an old one borrowed from biology. It means simply, "a lasting memory trace on a cell." It may be engraved on more than the cell, but up against Dn processing, it is not very lasting. (*SOS*, p. 10) **7.** physical pain, enmest and entheta held at a specific point on the time track. (*SOS*, Bk. 2, p. 25) **8.** a severe physical pain causes considerable analytical attenuation, shutting off the analyzer thoroughly for a period of time. This, technically, is an **engram**, although any incident, painful or not, contained in the reactive mind, and occluded by anaten can be considered an **engram**. (*SOS*, p. 80) **9.** a recording which has the sole purpose of steering the individual through supposed but usually nonexistent dangers. (*SOS*, p. 10) **10.** a severe area of plus or minus randomity of sufficient volume to cause unconsciousness. (*Scn 0-8*, p. 81) **11.** a moment when the analytical mind is shut down by physical pain, drugs or other means, and the reactive bank is open to the receipt of a recording. (*DMSMH*, p. 153) **12.** simply moments of physical pain strong enough to throw part or all the analytical machinery out of circuit; they are antagonism to the survival of the organism or pretended sympathy to the organism's survival. That is the entire definition. Great or little unconsciousness, physical pain, perceptic content, and contra-survival or pro-survival data. (*DMSMH*, p. 68) **13.** not a sentient recording containing meanings. It is merely a series of impressions such as a needle might make on wax. These impressions are meaningless to the body until the engram keys-in, at which time aberrations and psychosomatics occur. (*DMSMH*, p. 131) **14.** a bundle of data which includes not only perceptics and speech present but also metering for emotion and state of physical being. (*DMSMH*, p. 245) **15.** an apparent surcharge in the mental circuit with certain definite finite content. That charge is not reached or examined by the analytical mind but that charge is capable of acting as an independent command. (*DTOT*, p. 43)

**ENGRAM BANK,** a colloquial name for the reactive mind. It is that portion of a person's mind which works on a stimulus response basis. (*PXL* Gloss)

**ENGRAM CHAIN,** a basic **engram** and a series of similar incidents. (*DTOT*, p. 112) See CHAIN.

**ENGRAM COMMAND,** any phrase contained in an **engram**. (*DMSMH* Gloss)

**ENGRAMIC THOUGHT, 1. thought** that demands immediate action without examination by the analytical mind. (*Scn Jour*

28-G) **2.** irrational identity **thought** by which the mind is made to conceive identities where only vague similarities may exist. **Engramic thinking** can be stated by A equals A equals A equals A equals A. (*DTOT*, p. 64)

Engram (Def. 1, 2)

**ENMEST, 1.** another word meaning **enturbulated mest.** (*SOS*, p. 5) **2.** below 2.0 on the tone scale **mest** is considered to be confused and **enturbulated** and is referred to as **enmest.** Mest, in a life form, is an orderly array above 2.0 on the tone scale. (*SOS*, p. 41) **3. enmest** could be considered mest with a somehow reversed polarity. It is fighting to get free from theta. The entrapped **enmest** seeks to fight away from anything which even closely resembles **entheta** and so attacks all theta. (*DAB*, Vol. II, p. 136) **4.** mest which has been **enturbulated** by entheta or crushed too hard into theta and rendered less usable. (*SOS* Gloss)

**ENTHETA, 1.** means **enturbulated theta** (thought or life); especially refers to communications, which, based on lies and confusions, are slanderous, choppy or destructive in an attempt to overwhelm or suppress a person or group. (*Scn AD*) **2.** theta which has been confused and chaotically mixed with the material universe and which will lie in this confusion until death or some other process disenturbulates it. Theta, below 2.0 on the tone scale, we call **entheta.** (*SOS*, p. 41) **3.** anger, sarcasm, despair, slyly destructive suggestions. (*HTLTAE*, p. 88)

**ENTITIES,** ridges on which facsimiles are planted. Each one of those things can be a thinking **entity.** It thinks it's alive. It can think it's a being, as long as energy is fed to it. (PDC 36)

**ENTRAPMENT,** the opposite of freedom. A person who is not free is **entrapped.** He may be **trapped** by an idea; he may be **trapped** by matter; he may be **trapped** by energy or space or time; or he may be **trapped** by all of them. The more thoroughly a person is **trapped,** the less free he is. He cannot move, he cannot change, he cannot communicate, he cannot feel affinity and reality. Death itself could be said to be man's ultimate in **entrapment;** for when a man is totally **entrapped,** he is dead. (*Abil 254*)

**ENTURBULATE,** cause to be **turbulent** or agitated and disturbed. (*Scn AD*) [The mechanics of enturbulation can be found in *SOS* Chapter One.]

**ENVIRONMENT, 1.** the physical universe, security, it's right there, it's solid. This is the space of the room, the floor, the ceiling, the walls, the objects there, and if we happen to be looking *through* these things, then it's the walls in the next room, and up through the roof, the air about the house and down through, it's the earth underneath the house. (*PXL*, pp. 218-219) **2.** the surroundings of the preclear from moment to moment in particular or in general, including people, pets, mechanical objects, weather, culture, clothing or the Supreme Being. Anything he perceives or believes he perceives. The objective **environment** is the **environment** everyone agrees is there. The subjective **environment** is the **environment** the individual himself believes is there. They may not agree. (*HFP* Gloss)

**ENVIRONMENTAL ABERRATION,** the result of **aberrated** persons and situations in the individual's present-time **environment.** This is normally temporary, but cumulative **environmental** entheta has a chronic effect in the case. (*SOS*, Bk. 2, p. 103)

**EO, Ethics Officer.** (HCO PL 7 Mar 72R)

**EP, end phenomena.** (HCOB 20 Feb 70)

**EPICENTER,** the **epicenters** would be such parts of the body as the "funny bones" or any "judo-sensitive" spots: the sides of the neck, the inside of the wrist, the places the doctors tap to find out if there is a reflex. Those things are sub-brains picked up on the evolutionary line probably. They have a monitoring effect on the body and the individual. (PAB 2)

**EPICENTER THEORY,** the **theory** of **epicenters** merely states that there is an evolution of command posts and that those command posts remain structurally visible in the organism. They can be found in the organism and they still behave as lower echelon command posts, control centers in other words. (5110CM11B) See also EPICENTER.

**EPISTEMOLOGY,** a philosophical term meaning "the study of knowledge." (*Abil Ma 270*)

**E. PURP, (Ev Purp) evil purpose.** (HCOB 28 Mar 74)

**ERASE,** to recount an engram until it has vanished entirely. There is a distinct difference between a reduction and an **erasure.** If the engram is early, if it has no material earlier which will suspend it, that engram will **erase.** (*DMSMH*, p. 287)

**ERASED,** the words "vanished" or **"erased,"** when applied to an engram which has been treated mean that the engram has disappeared from the engram bank. It cannot be found afterwards except by search of the standard memory. (*DMSMH*, p. 207)

**ERASING AUDITING,** treating the session as an incident and **erasing** it as a lock. (SH Spec 70, 6607C21)

**ERASURE, 1.** the act of **erasing,** rubbing out, locks, secondaries or engrams. (HCOB 23 Apr 69) **2.** apparent removal of the engram from the files of the engram bank and refiling in the standard bank as memory. (*DMSMH*, p. 286) **3. erasure**, in essence, is a knowingness process rather than an energy rub-out process. It teaches somebody that he can duplicate the experience and is still alive. (5312CM16)

**E/S, earlier similar.** (HCOB 14 Mar 71R)

**ESPINOL,** this society belongs nominally to the **Espinol United Stars.** This is sun twelve and it is one little tiny pinpoint. Their whole title is **"Espinol United Stars,** moons, planets and asteroids this part of the Universe is ours—this quarter of the Universe is ours"—it translates better. (SH Spec 281, 6307C09) [Note on SH Spec 297, 6308C21 LRH refers to this as the **Espinol Confederacy** a civilization, duration of which was probably on the order of a few hundred thousand years and which engaged in implanting.]

**ESTO, Establishment Officer.** An **ESTO** is a third dynamic auditor who deaberrates a group by cleanly organizing it so it can produce. (FSO 529)

**ETH?,** "This preclear may be an **ethics** case, roller coaster or no case gain." (HCOB 23 Aug 65)

**ETHICAL CODE,** an **ethical code** is not enforceable, is not to be enforced, but is a luxury of conduct. A person conducts himself according to an **ethical code** because he wants to or because he feels he is proud enough or decent enough, or civilized enough to so conduct himself. An **ethical code**, of course, is a **code** of certain restrictions indulged in to better the manner of conduct of life. (PAB 40)

**ETHICAL CONDUCT, conduct** out of one's own sense of justice and honesty. When you enforce a moral code upon people you depart considerably from anything like **ethics.** People obey a moral code because they are afraid. People are **ethical** only when they are strong. (*Dn 55!*, p. 25)

**ETHICS, 1.** the term is used to denote **ethics** as a subject, or the use of **ethics,** or that section of a Scientology Church which handles **ethics** matters. (BTB 12 Apr 72R) **2. ethics** actually consist, as we can define them now in Dn, of rationality toward the highest level of survival for the individual, the future race, the group, and mankind, and the other dynamics taken collectively. **Ethics** are reason. The highest **ethic** level would be long-term survival concepts with minimal destruction, along any of the dynamics. (*SOS*, p. 128) **3. ethics** has to do with a code of agreement amongst people that they will conduct themselves in a fashion which will obtain to the optimum solution of their problems. (5008C30) **4.** the rules or standards governing the conduct of the members of a profession. (HCO PL 3 May 72) **5. ethics** is a personal thing. By definition, the word means "the study of the general nature of morals and the specific moral choices to be made by the individual in his relationship with others." (*AHD*) When one is **ethical** or "has his **ethics** in" it is by his own determination and is done by himself. (HCOB 15 Nov 72 II) **6.** that which is enforced by oneself, his belief in his own honor, and good reason, and optimum solution along the eight dynamics. (PDC 37)

**ETHICS BAIT,** a person in continual heavy **ethics** or who is **out ethics.** (HCO PL 4 Apr 72)

**ETHICS CASES,** SPs and PTSes. (HCOB 3 Apr 66)

**ETHICS REPAIR LIST,** this is a bright new tool I have developed which will clean up the individual's past **ethics** or justice track, and which will clear any 3rd and 4th dynamic engrams on **ethics** and justice—something which has never been done before in this universe or any other. It is a brand new idea. (HCOB 5 Nov 78 I)

**EUPHORIA,** gleeful happiness about something. (SH Spec 59, 6504C27)

**EVALUATION, 1.** telling the pc what to think about his case. (HCOB 4 Aug 60) **2. evaluation** for a person could be defined as the action of shaking his stable data without giving him further stable data with which he can agree or in which he can believe. (PAB 93) **3.** the reactive mind's conception of viewpoint. (*COHA*, p. 208) **4.** the shifting of viewpoints or the effort to do so. (PAB 8)

**EVALUATION OF DATA,** a **datum** is as understood as it can be related to other **data.** (*SOS* Gloss)

**EVIL, 1.** that which inhibits or brings plus or minus randomity into the organism, which is contrary to the survival motives of the organism. (*Scn 0-8*, p. 92) **2.** may be classified as those things which tend to limit the dynamic thrust of the individual, his family, his group, his race, or life in general in the dynamic drive, also limited by the observation, the observer and his ability to observe. (*DTOT*, pp. 20-21) **3. evil** is the opposite of good, and is anything which is destructive more than it is constructive along any of the various dynamics. A thing which does more destruction than construction is **evil** from the viewpoint of the individual, the future, group, species, life, or mest that it destroys. (*SOS*, Bk. 2, p. 34)

**EVIL PURPOSE,** destructive intentions. (7203C30SO) *Abbr.* Ev purp.

**EVOLUTION,** there are four **evolutionary** tracks, evidently. Organism **evolution,** through natural selection, accident and (evidence suggests) outright planning. Mest **evolution,** brought about through the agency of life organisms. Theta **evolution,** a postulated process of learning in theta as a whole or as entities. And present time ladder-of-support **evolution,** in which less complicated organisms support more complicated organisms. (*SOS* Gloss)

**EXAGGERATERS,** engramic commands which give the aspect of too much pain and too much emotion. (*DMSMH*, p. 347)

**EXAMINER,** that person in a Scientology Church assigned to the duties of noting pc's statements, TA position and indicators after session, or when pc wishes to volunteer information. (HCO PL 4 Dec 71 V)

**EXAM REPORT,** a **report** made out by the Qual Examiner when the pc goes to **Exams** after session or goes on his own volition. It contains the meter details, pc's indicators and the pc's statement. (BTB 3 Nov 72R)

**EXCALIBUR, 1. "Excalibur"** was an unpublished book written in the very late 1930's. Only fragments of it remain. (HCOB 17 Mar 69) **2.** an unpublished work most of which has been released in HCOBs, PLs and books. (HCO PL 26 Apr 70)

**EXCHANGE BY DYNAMICS,** a person who doesn't produce becomes mentally or physically ill. For his **exchange** factor is out. The remedy is rather simple. First one has to know all about **exchange** as covered in the product clearing policy letters. Then he has to specially clear this up with people who do not produce. Clear up the definitions of **dynamics** then have the person draw up a big chart and say what he gives the **first dynamic** and what it gives him. And so on up the **dynamics.** Now, have him consider "his own **second dynamic.**" What does his **second dynamic** give his **first dynamic.** What does his **second dynamic** give the **second dynamic** and what does it give him. And so on until you have a network of these **exchange** arrows, each both ways. Somewhere along the way he will have quite a cognition. That, if it's a big one is the end phenomena of it. And don't be surprised if you see a person now and then change his physical face shape. (HCO PL 4 Apr 72) [The above is a brief summary of the action. Full data can be found in the referenced HCO PL.]

**EXCHANGED VALENCE, 1.** one has directly superimposed the identity of another on his own. Example, daughter becomes own mother to some degree. (*FOT*, p. 95) **2.** a direct assumption of another **valence.** (HCOB 14 Jul 56)

**EX DN, Expanded Dianetics.** (BTB 20 Aug 71R II)

**EXECUTIVE OR BUSINESSMAN'S INTENSIVE,** this enables an **executive** or **businessman** to face situations of stress with calmness and frees him from past **business** stresses. (LRH ED 301 INT)

**EXHIBITIONISTIC,** displaying himself too thoroughly, being too much there at all times. (*FOT*, p. 29)

**EXISTENCE, 1.** an **existing** state or fact of being; life; living; continuance of being; and occurrence; specific manifestation. (HCOB 11 May 65) **2.** apparency, reality, livingness. (*FOT*, p. 26)

**EXOGENETIC,** there are two kinds of illness: the first could be called *autogenetic*, which means that it originated within the organism and was self-generated, and **exogenetic**, which means that the origin of the illness was exterior. The Pasteur germ theory would be the theory of **exogenetic**—exteriorly generated —illness. (*DMSMH*, p. 92)

**EXPANDED DIANETICS,** that branch of **Dn** which uses **Dn** in special ways for specific purposes. It is not HSDC Dn. Its position on the grade chart would be just above Class IV. Its proper number is Class IVA. It uses **Dn** to change an Oxford Capacity Analysis (or an American Personality Analysis) and is run directly against these analysis graphs and the *Science of Survival* "Hubbard Chart of Human Evaluation." **Expanded Dianetics** is not the same as Standard Dn as it requires special training and advanced skills. The main difference between these two branches is that Standard Dn is very general in application. **Expanded Dn** is very specifically adjusted to the pc. Some pcs, particularly heavy drug cases, or who have been given injurious psychiatric treatment or who are physically disabled or who are chronically ill or who have had trouble running engrams (to name a few) require a specially adapted technology. (HCOB 15 Apr 72) *Abbr.* Ex Dn, XDn.

**EXPANDED DIANETIC SPECIALIST,** an **HGDS** (**Hubbard Graduate Dianetic Specialist**). (HCOB 15 Apr 72R)

**EXPANDED GITA,** an extension of **Give** and **Take** processing. **Expanded Gita** remedies contra-survival abundance and scarcity. (*COHA*, p. 227)

**EXPANDED LOWER GRADES,** pcs won't like being told they "have to have their **lower grades** rerun." Actually that's not a factual statement anyway. The **lower grades** harmonic into the OT levels. They can be run again with full 1950-1960 to 1970 processes as given on the SH courses all through the 1960's. These are now regrouped and sorted out and are called **Expanded Lower Grades.** (HCOB 25 Jun 70 II)

**EXPERIENCE, 1.** the doingness of a beingness. (SH Spec 107, 6201C31), **2. experience** has normally to do with action. Let's orient that just a tiny bit better and say **experience** is a test or perception of existence. (PDC 5)

**EXPLOSION,** an outflow of energy usually violent but not necessarily so, from a more or less common source point. (*Scn 8-8008*, p. 49)

**EXT, 1.** extended. (Class VIII No. 11) **2. exterior.** (HCOB 5 Apr 71)

**EXTENDED HEARING, 1.** too high an alertness to sounds. This accompanies, quite ordinarily, a general fear of the environment or the people in it. (*SA*, p. 85) **2.** able to **hear** much more acutely. (*DMSMH*, p. 94)

**EXTENSION COURSE,** consists of a textbook and a series of lessons done on a glued-top tablet, one sheet per lesson, eight questions or exercises per lesson. The **extension course** should give the taker a passing knowledge of Dn and Scn terminology, phenomena and parts. (HCOB 16 Dec 58)

**EXTERIOR,** the fellow would just move out, away from the body and be aware of himself as independent of a body but still able to control and handle the body. (Spec Lect 7006C21)

**EXTERIORILY DETERMINED,** compelled to do or repressed from doing without his own rational consent. (*DMSMH*, p. 229)

**EXTERIORIZATION, 1.** the state of the thetan, the individual himself, being outside his body. When this is done, the person achieves a certainty that he is himself and not his body. (*PXL* Gloss) **2.** the phenomenon of being in a position or space dependent upon only one's consideration, able to view from that space the body and the room as it is. That is **exteriorization.** One can view the body or control the body from a distance. (5702C28)

**EXTERIORIZATION RUNDOWN,** a remedy designed to permit the pc to be further audited after he has gone **exterior.** The **Ext Rundown** is not meant to be sold or passed off as a method of **exteriorizing** a pc. (HCOB 2 Dec 70, C/S Series No. 23, *Exteriorization Summary*) [NOTE: the above HCOB has since been revised to HCOB 17 Dec 71R, C/S Series 23RA, *Interiorization Summary*. All references to Exteriorization Rundown in the former HCOB have been changed to Interiorization Rundown in the latter HCOB. This is also known as Interiorization Rundown, Int Rundown, Int-Ext Rundown, Ext-Int Rundown.] *Abbr.* Ext RD or Int RD.

**EXTRAORDINARY SOLUTIONS, extraordinary solutions** are only required when the basics of auditing are violated, and that is an **extraordinary solution,** definition of—that activity which somebody thinks he ought to do because all the basics of auditing have been flubbed. (SH Spec 60, 6109C28)

**EXTRAPOLATING,** getting some more and some more and some more application of the same datum. Theoretical adding up of data. (5211C10)

**EXT RD, Exteriorization Rundown.** (HCOB 12 Apr 71, C/S Series 35, *Exteriorization Errors*) [NOTE: The above HCOB has since been revised to HCOB 16 Dec 71RA, Revised 19 Sept 74, C/S Series 35RA *Interiorization Errors*. All references to Ext RD in the former HCOB have been changed to Int RD in the latter HCOB.]

**EXTROVERSION, 1. extroversion** means nothing more than being able to look outward. An **extroverted** personality is one who is capable of looking around the environment. A person who is capable of looking at the world around him and seeing it quite real and quite bright is, of course, in a state of **extroversion.** (HCOB 23 Jan 74RA) **2.** the preclear ceasing to put his attention on his mind, but putting his attention on the environment. We see this happen often in the Opening Procedure of 8-C where the preclear has the room suddenly become bright to him. He has **extroverted** his attention. He has come free from one of these communication tangles out of the past and has suddenly looked at the environment. (*Dn 55!*, p. 94)

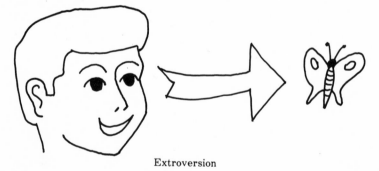

Extroversion

**EXTROVERT,** *n.* one whose available energy is being applied to the world and people around him rather than being applied to the past, or even to any great degree, the present. He does a lot of future planning, a lot of action. Every effort is into the future. (5112CM29B)

# F

**F, fall.** (HCOB 29 Apr 69)

**F, female;** the E-meter basically registers the **female** body at 2.0 on the tone arm. When a preclear is Clear he may occasionally get some tone arm motion due to purely body electronics but in the main reads at male or **female** on the tone arm (3 or 2) according to his or her sex. (*EME*, pp. 8 and 11)

**FABRICATOR,** see LIE FACTORY.

**FAC, Foundation Auditor's Course.** (HCOB 29 Sept 66)

**FAC ONE,** see FACSIMILE ONE.

**FACSIMILE, 1.** any mental picture, that is unknowingly created and part of the time track is a **facsimile**, whether an engram, secondary, lock or pleasure moment. (HCOB 15 May 63) **2.** a theta recording. All physical perceptions, all effort, emotion and thought which a person experiences are recorded continuously, and these recordings are called **"facsimiles."** They are not dependent upon an organism for their continued existence. Any **facsimile** which has been recorded is there to be recalled—when the individual has risen high enough on the tone scale, when he has regained enough of his self-determinism. (*Abil 114A*) **3.** an energy picture made by a thetan or the body's machinery of the physical universe environment. It is like a photograph. It is made of mental energy. It means copy of the physical universe. (PAB 99) **4.** the pictures contained in the reactive mind. (*Dn 55!*, p. 12) **5.** a full **facsimile** is a sort of three-dimensional color picture with sound and smell and all other perceptions plus the conclusions or speculations of the individual. (*HFP*, p. 27) **6.** a simple word meaning a picture of a thing, a copy of a thing, not the thing itself. (*HFP*, p. 25) **7.** a **facsimile** is an energy picture which can be reviewed again. A **facsimile** contains more than fifty easily identified perceptions. It also contains emotion and thought. (*Scn 8-8008*, p. 37) **8.** means the physical universe impression on thought and it means that section of thought which has a physical universe impression on it and it has a time tag on it. (5203CM03B)

**FACSIMILE BANK,** mental image pictures; the contents of the reactive mind; colloquially, **"bank."** (*PXL*, p. 52)

**FACSIMILE ONE, 1.** the basic on the service **facsimile** chain. (HCL 15, 5203CM10) **2.** it is called **facsimile one** because it is the first proven-up whole track incident which, when audited out of a long series of people, was found to alleviate such things as asthma, sinus troubles, chronic chills and a host of other ills. (*HOM*, p. 64) **3.** the one basic engram on top of which all this life engrams are mere locks. (*HYLBTL?* Gloss) *Abbr.* Fac One.

**FACTORS,** the **Factors** are the summation of the considerations and examinations of the human spirit and the material universe completed between A.D. 1923 and 1953. (*COHA*, p. 183)

**FACTUAL HAVINGNESS,** purpose: to remedy **havingness** objectively. To bring about the preclear's ability to **have** or **not have,** his present time environment and to permit him to alter his considerations of what he **has,** what he would continue and what he would permit to vanish. (HCOB 3 Jul 59)

**FADE-AWAY QUESTIONS, questions** to which, because of the characteristics of the mind, there is no possible answer. One of these is "Give me an unknown time." As soon as the preclear starts to answer such a **question,** he of course has as-ised a certain amount of unknownness and will know the time. The answer to a **fade-away question** is measurable, however, it could be said arbitrarily to be answered when the preclear has as-ised enough unknownness to give a known time. There are relatively few of these questions. (PAB 43)

**FAILED CASE, 1.** a **case** in which thought can always be over-powered by mest. The pc's inability to make his thinkingness prevail against mest has failed too often and cannot change. Only mest changes, therefore. This is usually the below zero on the APA pc. (HCOB 9 Sept 57) **2.** medically ill or injured cases. (HCOB 12 Mar 69)

**"FAILED" SESSIONS FORMULA,** when you have an auditor giving a **failed session,** you ASK THE PC WHAT THE AUDITOR DID. Then you get a hold of the auditor and get it corrected. You send the pc to review. (LRH ED 18 INT)

**FAILURE, 1.** at 0.0 on the tone scale, we have **failure.** It's an emotion. It's just a little bit below apathy. It's a realization that one has **failed.** (5904C08) **2.** a cycle of action which one thinks he has completed which suddenly is demonstrated not to have been completed. (2ACC-31B, 5312CM22) **3.** the inability to handle that which has been started after that course of action is entered. (PDC 5)

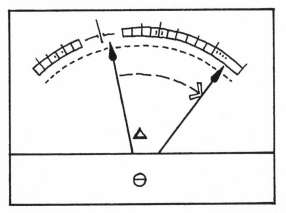

Fall

**FALL, 1.** small **fall** (a quarter to half an inch), **fall** (about 1 to 2 inches), long **fall** (2 to 3 inches), long **fall** blowdown (long **fall** followed by a "blowdown" or TA motion downward). All **falls** are to the right. The E-Meter measures the awareness depth of the pc. On things which do not read on assessment you would find his reality poor. Things that read well on assessment will be found to be things on which a pc has a high reality and a high interest level. (HCOB 29 Apr 69) **2.** a **fall** follows at once at the end of the last word of the question asked. (LRH Def Notes) **3.** a movement of the needle to your right as you face the meter. It can take place anywhere on the dial. It can be a short movement or a long movement even necessitating adjustment of the tone arm. The movement can be either fast or slow. (*BIEM*, p. 41) **4.** also called a drop, a dip, and a register. It denotes that a disagreement with life on which the preclear has greater or lesser reality has met the question asked. (*EME*, p. 14)

**FALL ON HIS HEAD,** *Slang.* this refers to the fact of a person failing in one area or another. A pc **"falls on his head"** when he has been improperly audited or attests to grades or actions he has not really attained and then is continued on higher actions or levels of auditing. An administrator **falls on his head** by failing to handle situations and apply correct policy to an area he is responsible for thereby causing the area and himself to fail. A U.S. Western term meaning a person who has erred and **fallen** from grace such as a horseman who is bucked off a horse. (LRH Def. Notes)

**FALSE,** contrary to fact or truth; without grounds; incorrect. Without meaning or sincerity; deceiving. Not keeping faith. Treacherous. Resembling and being identified as a similar or related entity. (HCO PL 3 May 72)

**FALSE CLEAR,** a preclear whose circuits have been charged to the point where the auditor cannot find an engram and so assumes that he has a Clear, when he does not. (*SOS*, Bk. 2, p. 272)

**FALSE CLEAR READ,** see DEAD THETAN.

**FALSE FOUR,** the laughter and gaiety which the preclear exhibits when he has thoroughly exhausted an incident of charge. There is nothing really **"false"** about **false four,** except that it is often of very short duration. (*SOS* Gloss)

**FALSE MOTIVATOR,** when a person commits an overt or overt of omission with **no motivator,** he tends to believe or pretends that he has received a **motivator** which does not in fact exist. This is a **false motivator.** (HCOB 1 Nov 68 II)

**FALSE OVERTS,** the person has been hit hard for no reason. So they dream up reasons they were hit. (HCOB 1 Nov 68 II)

**FALSE PIANOLA CASE,** a **case** with dub-in circuitry. It is very highly supercharged control circuitry. This person will run on the track, go into this, or go into that, and can go on for years and years. Evidently has very good recall. Has visio and sonic. The only trouble is "I" isn't even there. Sixty per cent of the material he gives you is strictly dub-in. (*NOTL*, p. 67)

**FALSE READ, 1.** if a rud gets any comment, natter or protest or bewilderment, put in **false** and clean it. "Has anyone said you had a . . . when you didn't have one?" is the answer to protested ruds. (HCOB 15 Aug 69) **2.** thinking something read which really didn't. Protest can then give you a **read.** Clean up questions with "protest," "suppress," "invalidate" buttons where pc says there's nothing there. (BTB 6 Jun 68R)

**FALSE SOLUTIONS,** the pretended knowingness that you see on the case. (SH Spec 43, 6108C22)

**FALSE TA,** two conditions in hands or feet can produce an incorrect **TA** position. The dry condition produces a **false high TA.** The overly wet condition produces a **false low TA.** The TA depends on normally moist hands. This does not mean the meter works on "sweat." It does mean the meter works only when there is correct electrical contact. (HCOB 23 Nov 73)

**FALSE TA CHECKLIST,** normally done early in auditing, especially if TA high or low. Prevents unnecessary repair due to wrong cans or grip. Is usually only done once. Do not suddenly interject this action into the middle of a session nor change from cans to footplates mid session due to TA going high. (BTB 11 Aug 72RA) ·

**FALSE III,** an OT who gaily went up the grades without doing them. You don't have to know more about it than that. (HCOB 24 May 69)

**FALSE VALENCE,** a personality which never existed. (PAB 95)

**FAST FLOW,** the student attests his theory or practical class when he believes he has covered the materials and can do it. There is no examination. (LRH ED 2 INT)

**FAST FLOW STUDENT,** the **fast flow student** passes courses by an attestation at Certs and Awards that he (a) enrolled properly on the course, (b) has paid for the course (or signed a no-charge invoice for 2½ or 5 year contracted staff), (c) has studied and understands all the materials on the checksheet, (d) has *done the drills* called for by the checksheet, (e) can produce the result required in the course materials. Twin checkouts are suspended. Examinations are not required. (HCO PL 31 Aug 74 II)

**FAT FOLDER,** a lengthily audited case. (HCOB 6 Oct 70)

**F.C., file clerk.** (*Hubbard Chart of Human Evaluation*)

**FC, Freedom Congress.** (HCOB 29 Sept 66)

**FC, Founding Church** of Scientology. (HCOB 23 Aug 65)

**FCCI, Flag Case Completion Intensive.** (BTB 22 Oct 72)

**F.D., Fellow** of **Dianetics.** (*Scn Jour, Iss. 31-G*)

**FDN, Foundation.** (BPL 5 Nov 72RA)

**FEAR, 1.** a condition of alertness for counter-efforts that threaten survival. (HCL 7, 5203CM06A) **2.** a fast uncontrolled flow. (PDC 8) **3.** the emotion of **fear** and the dispersal of energy are one and the same thing because the dispersal of energy makes one feel like he wants to run away. (5208CM07C)

Fear

**FEAR MERCHANTS,** see MERCHANTS OF FEAR.

**FEELING SHUT-OFF, 1.** a case which manifests no emotion or cannot feel pain when emotion and pain should be present in some incident is suffering from a **"feeling" shut-off.** (*DMSMH,*

p. 319) **2.** this most likely will be found in the prenatal area. The word "feeling" means both pain and emotion: thus, the phrase "I can't feel anything," may be an anesthetic for both. (*DMSMH*, pp. 319-320) **3.** a **"feeling" shut-off** can deny all somatics so that the patient does not feel them. If the patient seems insensible to trouble on the track, be sure that he has a **feeling shut-off.** (*DMSMH*, p. 326)

**FELLOW OF SCIENTOLOGY,** this is an honorary award for signal contributions to Scn technology beyond the scope of a new process. The work must be complete and approved. Usually reserved for a Class IV or V auditor. (HCO PL 12 Aug 63, *Certs and Awards* )

**FES, folder error summary.** (BTB 3 Nov 72R)

**FFD, full flow Dn.** (HCOB 4 Apr 71-IR)

**FFT, full flow table.** (HCOB 4 Apr 71-IR) See DIANETIC FLOW TABLE.

**FIELD, 1.** anything interposing between pc (thetan) and something he wishes to see, whether mest or mock-up. **Fields** are black, grey, purple, any substance, or invisible. In any **field** a pc was effect in an incident where he was being kept from going away. As all **fields** are incidents, and as a pc is the one who mocks up these incidents, all **fields** can be cleared by attaining knowing cause. (HCOB 1 Feb 58)

**FIELD AUDITOR, 1.** anyone who is active in the **field,** professionally, is classified as **"field auditor."** (HCOB 26 Oct 56) **2.** a **field auditor** professionally processes preclears up to his classification but not power processes or above. He can run study courses. (HCO PL 21 Oct 66 II)

**FIFTEEN,** *n.* a designation to denote a finished case, solely for case recording to designate a case advanced to current completion. This was a number system for preclears. A case is noted on record by the act number to which it has been advanced. (*HFP* Gloss)

**FIFTH DYNAMIC,** see DYNAMICS.

**FIFTH INVADER FORCE,** a thetan from the **fifth invader force** believes himself to be a very strange insect-like creature with unthinkably horrible hands. He believes himself to be occupying such a body, but is in actuality simply a unit capable of producing space, time, energy and matter. (*Scn 8-8008*, p. 132)

**FIFTH STAGE RELEASE,** see STAGES OF RELEASE.

**FIGURE-FIGURE CASE,** *Slang*. **1.** somebody who will not ever admit to having done something to anybody. The person cannot face any terminal subjectively for fear of having ruined it or for fear of ruining it. (HCOB 3 Sept 59) **2.** a person who is firmly convinced he is a body and is therefore being a body always has to have a reason for or a significance. Hence we get **figure-figure-figure.** Given a fact there must always be a reason for the fact. (PAB 24)

**FILE CLERK, 1.** Dn auditors' slang for the mechanism of the mind which acts as a data monitor. Auditors could get instant or "flash" answers direct from the **file clerk** to aid in contacting incidents. (*PXL*, pp. 207-208) **2.** the **file clerk** is the bank monitor. "He" monitors for both the reactive engram bank and the standard banks. When he is asked for a datum by the auditor or "I," he will hand out a datum to the auditor via "I." If we had a big computing machine of the most modern design, it would have a "memory bank" of punched cards or some such thing and it would have to have a selector and feeder device to thrust out the data the machine wants. The brain has one of these—it could not operate without it. This is the bank monitor—the **file clerk.** (*DMSMH*, p. 198) **3.** a response mechanism which is instantaneous. One could postulate that the **file clerk** is a group of attention units with ready access to the reactive mind and to the standard memory banks, and which in common mental operation forwards data through to "I" as memory. (*SOS*, Bk. 2, p. 162)

**FIRE, 1.** *v.* rocket read. (HCOB 30 Mar 63) **2.** the auditor *must* be very sure of his rocket read. The correct RI will **fire** once when the pc says it. (HCOB 13 May 63)

**FIREFIGHT,** the action of a quarrel between an auditor and a pc is called a **firefight.** (HCOB 21 Apr 71RB)

**FIRST DYNAMIC,** see DYNAMICS.

**FIRST GOAL CLEAR,** one GPM run gives a **first goal clear.** (HCOB 9 Jul 63)

**FIRST GPM, 1.** the latest **GPM** on the track. (SH Spec 251, 6303C21) **2.** meaning the **first** one contacted by the auditor, always, not the earliest one on the track. (HCOB 30 Mar 63)

**FIRST OVERT,** would be the **first overt** on a chain of overts. (SH Spec 84, 6612C13)

**FIRST PHENOMENON,** when a student misses understanding a word, the section right after that word is a blank in his memory. You can always trace back to the word just before the blank, get it understood and find miraculously that the former blank area is not now blank in the bulletin. The above is pure magic. (HCO PL 24 Sept 64)

**FIRST POSTULATE,** not know. (PAB 66)

**FIRST (1ST) STAGE RELEASED OT,** if a being is a 1st, 2nd, or 3rd stage release and has also become exterior to his body in the process, we simply add "OT" to the state of release. This is all that is meant when a person is called a **First Stage Released OT.** The person has not only come out of his bank but also out of his body. (HCOB 12 Jul 65) See also STAGES OF RELEASE.

**FIRST VALENCE,** the preclear's "own valence," which is his own concept of himself. (PAB 95)

**FISH AND FUMBLE,** cleaning a dirty needle. (HCOB 14 Jun 62)

**FISHING A COGNITION,** this is general ARC, answering the preclear's origin process. When the preclear experiences a somatic, when he sighs, when he gives a reaction to a tone 40 process, the auditor repeats the process two or three more times (random number) and then pausing the process asks the preclear, "How are you doing now?" or "What is going on?" and finds out what happened to the preclear just as though the auditor has not noticed that the preclear had a reaction. The auditor does not point out the reaction but merely wants a discussion in general. During this discussion he brings the preclear up to at least a **cognition** that the preclear has had a somatic or a reaction and then merely continues the process without further bridge. This is done randomly. It is not always done every time the preclear experiences a reaction. (HCOB 11 Jun 57 Reissued 12 May 72)

**5000 OHMS,** the exact value for tone arm position 2 on the E-meter. **Ohms** is the term used for the unit used in measuring electrical resistance on a line. (*EMD*, p. 16A)

**FIXATED PERSON RUNDOWN,** this enables a **person** to overcome the condition of having his attention **fixated** on one **person.** (LRH ED 301 INT)

**FIXED ATTENTION UNITS, attention units** which are caught somewhere down the time track in one incident or another in the form of entheta. (HCOB 11 May 65)

**FIXED IDEA,** is something accepted without personal inspection or agreement. (HCO PL 19 May 70)

**FIXED THETA,** entheta. (*SOS*, Bk. 2, p. 10)

**FLAG,** the Church of Scn of California operates a marine mission aboard a chartered vessel. This marine mission is commonly referred to as **Flag.** It is operated under the aegis (protection, support) of the Church of Scientology of California (BPL 9 Mar 74)

Flag

**FLASH ANSWER, 1.** the first **flash** response, the first impression a person receives in **answer** to a question. (*SOS*, Bk. 2, p. 51) **2.** instantaneous reply, the first thing that **flashes** into the preclear's mind at the snap of the auditor's fingers. (*SOS*, p. 104)

**FLAT,** meaning that the incident when **"flat"** has been discharged of all bad consequences to the preclear. (*HYLBTL?* Gloss)

**FLAT BALL BEARING,** *Slang.* **1.** a defective product; a nonoperational person or thing. (*PRD* Gloss) **2.** cases that don't roll on the assembly line of the HGC. Qual is wholly in the **flat ball bearing** business. The HGC and Academy are wholly in the assembly line business, dealing in fairly round ball bearings. (HCOB 6 Aug 65)

**FLAT BY TA,** the test of **"flat"** is the **TA** moving only one-quarter to one-eighth of a division up or down in twenty minutes of auditing; not cumulative movement such as "the TA moves 1/16th twice so that's 1/8th of a division—" This is wrong. If it moves from 2.25 to 2.50 to 2.25 two or three times in twenty minutes, this is called **flat** and has moved only one-quarter of a **TA** division. This is right. (HCOB 23 May 61)

**FLAT COMM LAG, 1.** the point at which the auditing question or command is no longer producing change of **communication lag.** (*PXL*, p. 45) **2.** a **comm lag** is **flat** when it is consistent. A person may have an habitual **lag** of ten seconds. He may say everything after a ten-second pause. (*Abil SW*)

**FLAT METER,** a cadmium cell **meter** discharges very suddenly when it does go **flat.** In mid session the **meter** can run out of battery. If the needle doesn't snap to the right hard or if it doesn't quite get there on test, then that **meter** will go **flat** in mid session and give false TA and no reads or TA on hot subjects. (HCOB 24 Oct 71)

**FLAT POINT (CCHs),** three cycles with no change in comm lag, no physically observed change, and the pc doing it. (BTB 12 Sept 63R)

**FLAT PROCESS, 1.** a **process** is continued as long as it produces change and no longer, at which time the **process** is **flat.** (*PXL*,

p. 45) **2.** a **process** is **flat** when 1) there is the same lag from the moment the command is given until the time the preclear answers the command at least three times in a row, 2) a cognition occurs, 3) the tone arm action is flat, 4) a major cognition occurs, 5) an ability regained. (SH Spec 290, 6307C25) **3.** a question is **flat** when the communication lag has been similar for three successive questions. Now, that's a **flat** question. The comm lag might be five seconds, five seconds, and five seconds. We would still say with some justice that the *question* lag was **flat**. However, the process lag would not be **flat** until the actual normal exchange lag was present. The question would no longer influence the communication factors of the preclear when the process was **flat**. (*Abil SW*)

**FLAT QUESTION,** see FLAT PROCESS.

**FLATTEN A PROCESS, 1.** to continue a process as long as it produces change and no longer. (*Scn AD*) **2. flattening** something means to do it until it no longer produces a reaction. (HCOB 2 Jun 71 I) See also END PHENOMENA.

**FLIP-FLOPPING,** a process by which the preclear's excess motion was taken off. We would say, "Mock up a man and make him **flip-flop**," and then make him insist that the body **flip-flop** even further and even more wildly until he himself knew that he was making the body **flip-flop.** We would do this with a woman's body and would eventually take the motion off the case that was inhibiting the preclear from controlling the body. This is actually a motionectomy. (*SCP*, p. 15)

**FLOATER,** an engram which has not been restimulated in the individual during the lifetime succeeding it. A **floater** has not accumulated locks since it has not been restimulated. (*DTOT*, p. 45)

**FLOATING NEEDLE, a floating needle** is a rhythmic sweep of the dial at a slow, even pace of the **needle.** That's what an **F/N** is. No other definition is correct. (HCOB 21 July 78) *Abbr.* F/N.

**FLOATING TA,** the pc is so released the needle can't be gotten onto the dial. The needle is swinging wider than the meter dial both ways from center and appears to lay first on one side and then the other. The TA can't be moved fast enough to keep the extreme floating needle on the dial. (HCOB 24 Oct 71)

**FLOW, 1.** an impulse or direction of energy particles or thought or masses between terminals. (HCOB 3 Feb 69) **2.** the progress of particles or impulses or waves from point A to point B. **Flow** has the connotation of being somewhat directional. (SH Spec 84, 6612C13) **3.** a progress of energy between two points. The points may have masses. The points are fixed and the fixedness of the points and their opposition produce the phenomena of **flows.** (HCOB 1 Feb 62) **4.** a change of position of particles in space. (PDC 30) **5.** any line of **flow,** whether contracting or lengthening, is called a **flow.** A common manifestation is seen in an electric light wire. (*Scn 8-80,* p. 43)

**F-1, flow one,** something happening to self. (HCOB 4 Apr 71-1R)

**F-2, flow two,** doing something to another. (HCOB 4 Apr 71-1R)

**F-3, flow three,** others doing things to others. (HCOB 4 Apr 71-1R)

**F-0, flow zero,** self doing something to self. (HCOB 4 Apr 71-1R)

**FLUB,** *Slang. n.* **1.** an error. (HCOB 21 Aug 70) —*v.* **2.** to blunder or make a mess of. (BTB 3 Jul 73 I)

**FLUBBED COMMANDS, commands** used incorrectly. (HCOB 9 Aug 69)

**FLUB CATCH, 1.** to notice, intercept and handle after the fact of the motion or action, a blunder or mistake being made. (BTB 3 Jul 73 I) **2. flub**=to blunder or make a mess of. **Catch**=to intercept the motion or action of. It is a term coined and used to cover that exact action. **Flub catch**=to notice, intercept and handle *after the fact* of the motion or action, a blunder or mistake being made. (BTB 3 Jul 73 I)

**FLUB CATCH SYSTEM, 1.** on Flag, an FES is carefully done so as to detect areas of out tech in the world. This is called the **"Flub Catch System."** Auditors and C/Ses so detected are sent to cramming in their areas to smooth out their tech, knowledge, or TRs, all to improve delivery of tech. (HCOB 6 Oct 70) **2. flub catch** means that **system** which detects, orders and gets corrected out tech. In other words, it catches the **flub.** (FO 2442R)

**FLUNK,** *v.* **1.** to make a mistake. Fail to apply the materials learned. Opposite of pass. (HCOB 19 Jun 71 III) —*n.* **1.** in the grading of sessions, a **flunk** is given when (1) the F/N did not get to examiner and didn't occur at session end, (2) major errors or flubs occurred like no EP, multiple somatic, unflown ruds, etc. (3) the C/S was not followed or completed, (4) Auditors' Rights listed errors occurred, (5) no F/N and BIs at examiner. (HCOB 21 Aug 70) **2.** in TRs, if the student falters, comm lags, fumbles a command or fails to get an execution on coach, coach says **"flunk"** and they start at beginning of command cycle in which error occurred. (HCOB 11 June 57)

**FLYING NEEDLE, 1.** an F/N that is a real F/N and so forth, takes off, it **flies.** You can see it disconnect from the bank and start to function. So it's just a colloquialism; **fly a needle,** float a **needle, F/N,** that's all. (Class VIII No. 2) **2.** an earlier definition—a constant rise, constant rapid rise. (SH Spec 181, 6208C07)

**F/N, floating needle** or **free needle.** (HCOB 2 Aug 65)

**F/NING AUDITOR,** an **auditor** who is auditing well could be said to be **F/Ning** the whole time. (HCOB 5 Oct 71)

**F/NING LIST,** meaning the whole **list** (all items and any added ones) **F/N** throughout the assessment of the *full* **list** with no reads or slows in the **F/N** as all the items are called. (BTB 27 Jul 71 II)

**F/NING STUDENTS, 1. students** who study well are said to be **F/Ning students.** (HCOB 5 Oct 71) **2.** one who is tearing along successfully in his studies. (BTB 7 Feb 72RA II)

**FOLDER, 1.** a **folded** sheet of cardboard which encloses all the session reports and other items. The **folder** is foolscap size, light card, usually blue or green in color. (BTB 3 Nov 72R) **2.** a compilation of data—the records kept by an auditor. (*Abil 218*)

Folder

**FOLDER ERROR SUMMARY**, a **summary** of auditing **errors** in a **folder** and on a pc's case not corrected at the time the **summary** is done. (BTB 3 Nov 72R) *Abbr.* FES.

**FOLDER SUMMARY,** the **folder summary** is kept up every session by the auditor and is stapled to the left inside front cover of the **folder** as a running **summary** for C/S use. The **folder summary** is made up of all actions in consecutive date order and showing *what* was run plus the result at end of process, session time, admin time and exam result—F/N, VGIs or BER. (BTB 5 Nov 72R III) *Abbr.* F/S.

**FOOTPLATES,** metal **footplates** connected to the meter and the pc barefooted in session to handle false TA. (HCOB 24 Oct 71)

# FORCE

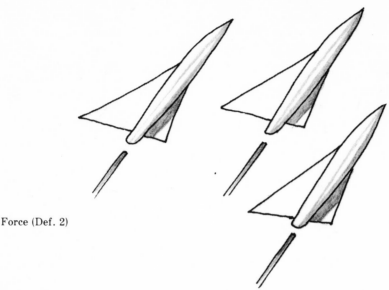

Force (Def. 2)

**FORCE, 1.** random effort. (*Scn 0-8*, p. 75) **2.** energy with some direction. (PDC 56) **3. force** of course is made up of time, matter, energy, flows, particles, masses, solids, liquids, gasses, space and locations. (HCOB 16 Jun 70)

**FORCE FIELD,** actually nothing more or less than wave emanation like you get out of the headlight of a car. You change the wave-length of the headlight of a car and speed it up enough and hit somebody with it, it'll knock him down. That's an electronic **field.** That's a **force** screen. (5206CM28A)

**FORCE SCREEN,** see FORCE FIELD. (5206CM28A)

**FORGET, 1. forget** is a harmonic of not know. (SH Spec 14, 6106C14) **2.** an occlusion of observation. (SH Spec 58, 6109C26)

**FORGETFULNESS, 1.** rapidity of change of state, unpredicted. (HCOB 17 Mar 60) **2.** an individual starts to **forget** when he's lost too much. He just dramatizes loss, too bad to remember. (HCAP-8, 5411C29)

**FORGETTER, 1.** a **forgetter** mechanism is "Put it out of my mind," "If I remembered it I would go mad," "Can't remember," and just plain "I don't know," as well as the master of the family of phrases, "Forget it!" All bar information from the analyzer. A whole case, freshly opened, may keep answering everything with one of these denyers. A **forgetter,** used by an ally, all by itself and with practically no pain or emotion present will submerge data which, in recall, would not be aberrative but which, so buried—by a **forgetter**—makes things said just before it aberrative and literal. (*DMSMH*, p. 270) **2.** any engram command which makes the individual believe he can't remember. (*NOTL* Gloss)

**FORGETTING,** the process of not knowing the past. (*FOT*, p. 85)

**FORMAL AUDITING, 1.** control by ARC. ARC **formal auditing** is not chatty or yap-yap, but it is itself. It has warmth, humanity, understanding and interest in it. (HCOB 2 Apr 58) **2.** auditing done by use of model session and exact TRs. (LRH Def. Notes)

**FORMULA,** a method of getting a case started. The numbers are in order of development, not case level. (HCOB 1 Dec 60)

**FORMULA H,** the effort to reach and withdraw, to grasp, and let go of oneself, of others for themselves, of oneself, for others and others for oneself and others for others: For force, perception and admiration when run resolve the tenacity of engrams. **Formula H** is called **Formula H** because the **H** stands for **hope.** (PAB 9)

**FORMULA 19, F19** (a process name). (BTB 20 Aug 71 II)

**FOUNDING SCIENTOLOGIST,** if you were with Scn before 1964 you were an old-timer, a **Founding Scientologist.** (HCO PL 5 Feb 64)

**40** (as in GF+40), the addition no. **40** items are the original seven resistive cases. (HCOB 10 Jun 71 I)

**4.0,** a **4.0** on the tone scale is, by definition, one who has had all entheta in his current life converted to theta. (*SOS*, Bk. 2, p. 120)

**FOUR FLOWS,** see QUAD FLOWS.

**IV RUNDOWN,** originally developed to catch cases that had somehow gotten up to OT III and were falling on their heads. It is a collection of actions. [See the referenced HCOB for full explanation and use of this rundown.] (HCOB 30 Jun 70R)

**FOURTH DYNAMIC,** see DYNAMICS.

**FOURTH DYNAMIC ENGRAM, 1.** the basic aberration of the planet. (LRH Def. Notes) **2.** the humanitarian objective is to make a safe environment in which the **fourth dynamic engram** can be audited out. By **engram** we mean the mental block that prevents peace and tolerance. By **fourth dynamic** we mean that impulse to survive as mankind instead of just individuals. (Ron's Jour 68)

**FOURTH FLOW, flow 0.** (HCOB 7 Mar 71)

**FOURTH POSTULATE,** remember. (PAB 66)

**FOURTH STAGE RELEASE,** to obtain **Fourth Stage Release** one has to take the lock end words off the R6 bank. (HCOB 5 Aug 65)

**FOUR UNIVERSES,** the four are: thetan or spirit, mind or brain, body or male body or female body, and physical universe or earth or continent or town or house or dwelling. (HCOB 29 Sept 59)

**FRAGILE TA, 1. TA** susceptible to being stuck high or stuck low or stuck dead thetan. (SH Spec 302A, 6309C03) **2.** just one wrong date or duration in R3R or just one wrong RI in R3N and tone arm action ceases, the **TA** going way up or down and staying there. (HCOB 28 Jul 63)

**FRANCHISE,** now termed mission; a group granted the privilege of delivering elementary Scn and Dn services. Does not have church status or rights. (BTB 12 Apr 72R)

**FRANCHISE HOLDER,** a professional auditor with a classification to Level III or over who practices Scientology full or part time for remuneration, who conducts processing and training privately or to groups, whose understanding and experience of Dn and Scn is sufficiently broad for him to be publicized to others as a stable terminal, who has signed a franchise agreement, who receives bulletins, policy letters, advice, advertising, technical information, services and administrative data and who in return for same maintains regularly a weekly report and a weekly tithe to the church. (HCO PL 2 Jan 65)

**FREEDOM, 1.** ability to create and position energy or matter in time and space. (*Scn 8-8008* Gloss) **2.** the absence of barriers. (*Dn 55!*, p. 55) **3.** lots of space, and ability to use it. (PDC 35) **4.** the component parts of **freedom,** as we first gaze upon it, are then: affinity, reality, and communicaton, which summate into understanding. Once understanding is attained **freedom** is obtained. (*Abil Mi 258*)

**FREEDOM RELEASE,** expanded Grade III release. (CG&AC) See GRADE IV RELEASE.

**FREE NEEDLE,** floating needle, **free needle** are the same thing. (HCOB 2 Aug 65)

**FREE NEEDLE-ITIS,** *Slang.* the auditor who is so unsure of what a **floating needle** is and whose TRs and basics are out, calls **floating needles** all over the place on the pc, when the **needle** is in fact not **floating** is said to have **free needle-itis.** *Itis* means, properly, an inflammatory disease. It is used to indicate "obsession with" or a mental obsession. In this case, it would mean an auditor who is obsessed with calling **free needles** (**floating needles**) on the E-meter when they don't exist. (LRH Def. Notes)

**FREE THETA,** attention units **free** enough to be directed of your own volition. (*Scn Jour 18-G*)

**FREE THETAN,** was somebody who was **free** of a body. He wasn't **free** of organizational commitments or ethics but he was **free** of a body, he didn't require any body. (SH Spec 268, 6305C23)

**FREE TRACK,** that part of the **time track** that is **free** of pain and misadventure is simply called the **free track,** in that the pc doesn't freeze up on it. (HCOB 15 May 63)

**FREEZE,** stand completely still. (LRH Def. Notes)

# FREEZES

**FREEZES,** in CCHs **freezes** may be introduced at end of cycle, this being after the "Thank you" and before the next command, maintaining a solid comm line, to ascertain information from the coach or to bridge from the process. (HCOB 5 Jul 63)

**F/S, folder summary.** (BTB 23 Sept 71)

**F. SCN, Fellow** of **Scientology. F. Scn** is not an auditing degree. It is an honorary award extended by the HASI for spectacular contribution to the science itself. The **F. Scn** award carries with it the specific addition to the science for which the rating was awarded. An **F. Scn** is not necessarily a skilled or degreed auditor. (*Scn Jour, Iss 31-G*)

**FULL FLOW DIANETICS,** all former **Dianetic** items ever run are listed and what **flows** have been run on them and to what end phenomena. Such a list is then handled from the earliest forward by A) completing the bogged **flow** and B) completing the missing **flow** if it reads. (HCOB 7 Mar 71)

**FULL RESPONSIBILITY,** the willingness to mock or unmock barriers at will. (2ACC-4B, 5311CM18)

**FUTURE,** on the time track, that area later than present time. Perception of the **future** is postulated as a possibility. The creation of **future** realities through imagination is a recognized function. (*SOS* Gloss)

# G

**GAEs, gross auditing errors.** (HCOB 21 Sept 65)

**GAINS,** see ABILITY GAIN, INTELLIGENCE GAIN and CASE GAIN.

**GALACTIC CONFEDERACY,** the former political unit of which the solar system was a part. (LRH Def. Notes)

**GAME, 1.** any state of beingness wherein exist awareness, problems, havingness and freedom (separateness) each in some degree. (PAB 73) **2.** a contest of person against person, or team against team. (PAB 84) **3.** all **games** are continuing by definition, since an unstarted **game** isn't a **game** and a finished **game** isn't a **game.** (PAB 101) **4.** a **game** consists of freedoms, barriers, and purposes. (*POW,* p. 60)

**GAME CONDITIONS, game conditions** are: attention, identity, effect on opponents, no-effect on self, can't have on opponents and goals and their areas, have on tools of play, own goals and field, purpose, problems of play, self-determinism, opponents, the possibility of loss, the possibility of winning, communication, non-arrival. (*FOT,* pp. 93-94)

# GAMES CONDITION

Game (Def. 2)

**GAMES CONDITION, 1.** when you say **games condition** you mean that somebody's power of choice has been subjugated against his will into a fixated activity from which he must not take his attention. (SH Spec 32, 6107C20) **2.** the word **games condition** is a derogatory actually. There is a technical thing goes along. When you say **games condition** you mean a package, and the package has to do with this: It means a *fixated* attention, an inability to escape coupled with an inability to attack, to the *exclusion* of other **games**. There is nothing wrong with having games. There is a lot wrong with being in a **games condition** because it is unknown, it is an aberrated activity, it is reactive, and one is performing it way outside of his power of choice and without his consent or will. (SH Spec 32, 6107C20) **3.** have for self and can't have for others; now that is a true **games condition.** (SH Spec 32, 6107C20) *Abbr.* G.C.

**GAMES CONDITION PROCESS,** when you say **games condition process** you mean that it is an interchangeable negative bracket. In other words, it's interchanged between Person A and Person B, or Person B and Person C, and Person C and Person D. It is basically a denial of interchange. (SH Spec 32, 6107C20)

174

**GARBAGE,** *Slang.* **1.** the term **garbage** isn't used much more but it meant dub-in. (5009CM23B) **2. garbage** was technically called delusion in the philosophic work of Dn but the term is too harsh and critical, for who has not some misconception of a past incident? (*DMSMH*, p. 191)

**G.C., games condition.** (HCOB 20 Aug 56)

**GE, genetic entity.** (PDC 43)

**GENERALITY, 1.** a **general** or nonspecific statement which is applicable to all and used in Scn to connotate a statement made in an effort to either hide cause or to overwhelm another person with the all-inclusive. (HCOB 11 May 65) **2.** any unspecifity or unspecific statement or indication tends toward a **generality.** It is the substitute of a plural for a singular. (SH Spec 84, 6612C13) **3.** multiple subject, not specific, such as "dogs" or "the public." (*BCR*, p. A-4)

**GENERAL O/W (OVERT-WITHHOLD),** "What have you done?" "What have you withheld?" (HCOB 3 Jul 62)

**GENERAL TRs,** are for use in regular auditing. They are natural, relaxed, while fully controlling the session and the pc. (BTB 13 Mar 75)

**GENETIC,** by line of protoplasm and by facsimiles and by mest forms the individual has arrived in the present age from a past beginning. **Genetic** applies to the protoplasm line of father and mother to child, grown child to new child and so forth. (*HFP* Gloss)

**GENETIC BEING,** see GENETIC ENTITY.

**GENETIC BLUEPRINT, 1.** the facsimiles of the evolutionary line. (*HFP*, p. 28) **2.** the plans of construction of a new body in the orthodox manner of conception, birth, and growth. (*HFP*, p. 76)

**GENETIC ENTITY, 1.** that beingness not dissimilar to the thetan which has carried forward and developed the body from its earliest moments along the evolutionary line on earth and which, through experience, necessity and natural selection, has

175

employed the counter-efforts of the environment to fashion an organism of the type best fitted for survival, limited only by the abilities of the **genetic entity.** The goal of the **genetic entity** is survival on a much grosser plane of materiality. (*Scn 8-8008*, p. 8) **2.** formerly referred to as the somatic mind. It has no real personality, it is not the "I" of the body. This is the "mind" of an animal, a dog or a cat or a cow. (*HOM*, pp. 13-14) **3.** that **entity** which is carrying along through time, that is making the body through the time stream, through the action of sex and so forth. (5410C10D) *Abbr.* GE.

**GENETIC INSANITY, genetic insanity** is limited to the case of actually missing parts. A very small percentage of insanity falls into such a category and its manifestation is mental dullness or failure to coordinate and beyond these has no aberrative quality whatever. (*DMSMH*, p. 134)

**GENETIC LINE, 1.** the **genetic line** consists of the total of incidents which have occurred during the evolution of the mest body itself. The composite of these facsimiles has the semblance of a being. This being would be called the **genetic entity** or the **GE.** The **GE** is not an actual individual but a composite, of individualities assumed in the single lives along the evolutionary track. (*HOM*, p. 23) **2.** protoplasm line. Its cycle is preconception, conception, birth, procreation, preconception and so on. That unending string of protoplasm goes through earth time. (HCL 15, 5203CM10A) **3.** a series of mocked up automaticities which produce according to a certain blueprint from the earliest times of life on this planet through until now. (PAB 130)

**GENETIC PERSONALITY,** personal characteristics and tendencies derived from the three inheritance sources (mest, organic line, theta). This might be said to be basic **personality,** or the core of basic **personality.** (*SOS* Gloss)

**GEN NON-REMIMEO,** [designation on HCO Policy Letters and HCO Bulletins indicates dissemination and restriction as follows:] All Saint Hill Staff, eight duplicated copies only are sent to each organization. (HCO PL 25 Jan 66)

**GEOGRAPHICAL ANTIPATHIES,** pain and unconsciousness have taken place at some point on the globe, some city, some ocean, some altitude, some depth. Afterwards, he avoids such a point. (PAB 9)

**GF, green form.** (HCOB 6 Mar 71 I)

**GF40RB,** expanded **green form forty revised.** See GF40XRR.

**GF40XRR, (green form forty expanded, revised, revised),** a correction list used to handle resistive cases (TA in normal range but not responding well to auditing). Assess M3 with all reading items taken to F/N per instructions, then handled in depth with L&N and R3R processes. Normally done only once if done properly. EP is all reading items handled, pc no longer resistive and making good progress in auditing. Note that a pc can be made to appear resistive by poor basic auditing and failure to use the right correction list when needed. (BTB 11 Aug 72R) **2.** this correction list was further revised in December 1974 and renumbered as **Expanded GF40RB** (HCOB 30 Jun 71R)

**GF MS, goals finder model session.** (HCO PL 8 Dec 62)

**GIs, good indicators.** (HCOB 9 May 69 II)

**GITA, give** and **take** processing. Expanded **Gita** was developed from phenomena discovered after I developed creative processing. It was originally plain **GIve** and **TAke** processing, hence the **Gita.** (PAB 16)

**GLEE,** a kind of insanity. **Glee** is a special kind of embarrassed giggling. You'll know it when you see it. When you see **glee** on some fellow on a post, realize it's because he doesn't understand what he's doing. He's ignorant about something and above that is confusion and above the confusion is **glee.** (HCOB 20 Sept 68)

**GLEE OF INSANITY, 1.** a specialized case of irresponsibility. A thetan who cannot be killed and yet can be punished has only one answer to those punishing him and that is to demonstrate to them that he is no longer capable of force or action and is no longer responsible. He therefore states that he is **insane** and demonstrates that he cannot possibly harm them as he lacks any further rationality. This is the root and basis of **insanity.** (*Scn 8-8008*, p. 55) **2.** also called the **"glee of irresponsibility."** Manifestation which takes the form of an actual wave emanation resulting basically from the individual dramatizing the condition of "must reach—can't reach, must withdraw—can't withdraw." (*PXL* Gloss)

177

**GLIBIDITY,** *Slang.* a condition in which a person gives very **glib** answers. (SH Spec 41, 6409C29)

**GLIB STUDENT,** one who can confront the words and ideas. He cannot confront the physical universe or people around him and so cannot apply. He does not *see* mest or people. The reason for this is that he is below nonexistence on one or more dynamics and so cannot align with the others. (HCOB 26 Apr 72)

**GLUM AREA,** that **area** which when the pc is supposedly "itsaing" about it, makes him **glum** and the TA rise, indicating that a service facsimile is doing the confronting on that **area** and not the pc. (HCOB 16 Oct 63)

**GMTH, CCH-1** is known as **"Give me that hand."** (PAB 133)

**GOAL, 1.** the prime postulate. It is the prime intention. It is a basic purpose for any cycle of lives the pc has lived. (SH Spec 160, 6206C12) **2.** a solution to the problems which have been given the person usually by terminals. (SH Spec 5, 6106C01) **3.** the significance which surrounds the terminal. (SH Spec 5, 6106C01) **4.** a whole track long-term matter. (HCO PL 6 Dec 70)

**GOAL OF DIANETICS,** a world without insanity, without criminals and without war—this is the **goal of Dn.** (*SOS,* p. v)

**GOAL OF LIFE,** the **goal of life** can be considered to be infinite survival. Man, as a life form, can be demonstrated to obey in all his actions and purposes the one command: "SURVIVE!" (*DMSMH,* p. 19)

**GOAL OF PROCESSING,** to bring an individual into such thorough communication with the physical universe that he can regain the power and ability of his own postulates. (*COHA,* p. xi)

**GOAL SERIES,** the actual **goals** in their sequence and pattern that repeats over and over forward through time. (HCOB 13 Apr 64, *Scn VI Part One Glossary of Terms*)

**GOALS FINDER, 1.** a person in an organization who has no other post or activity of any kind. He is simply **Goals Finder** and keeps more or less regular auditing hours. The **Goals Finder finds**

goals of staff members when they are ready. (HCO PL 10 Sept 62) **2.** the title **Goals Finder** is changed herewith to "A Clearing Consultant." (HCO PL 11 Apr 63) [The above are quoted from HCO PLs of the referenced date, however, the post of Goals Finder does not exist as such in today's Church of Scientology.]

**GOALS FINDER MODEL SESSION,** where the pc has been well prepchecked and is well under auditor control, a **goal finder** in an **R-3GA session** may omit rudiments in **model session,** using only **goals** for **session,** and havingness, **goals** and gains at end and general O/W mid ruds and random ruds where needed in the **session.** (HCOB 15 Oct 62)

**GOALS LIST,** a full **list** of **goals** including childhood **goals,** withheld **goals,** antisocial **goals,** and (by meter reaction on question) "Any **goal** you have not told me about." Auditor gets every possible **goal** until the meter is null on the question of **goals** the pc might have. (HCOB 6 Apr 61)

**GOALS PLOT,** the pattern of the pc's actual **goals.** (HCOB 13 Apr 64, *Scn VI Part One Glossary of Terms*)

**GOALS PROBLEM MASS, 1.** the **goal** has been balked for eons by opposing forces. The **goal** pointed one way, the opposing forces point exactly opposite and against it. If you took two fire hoses and pointed them at each other, their streams would not reach each other's nozzles, but would splatter against one another in midair. If this splatter were to hang there, it would be a ball of messed up water. Call hose A the force the pc has used to execute his **goal.** Call hose B the force other dynamics have used to oppose that **goal.** Where these two forces have perpetually met, a mental mass is created. This is the picture of any **problem**—force opposing force with resultant **mass.** Where the pc's **goal** meets constant opposition, you have in the reactive mind the resultant **mass** caused by the two forces— **Goal**=force of getting it done, Opposition=force opposing it getting done. This is the **goal problem mass.** (HCOB 20 Nov 61) **2.** is fundamentally founded on a **goal.** They're a conglomeration of identities which are counter-opposed, and these identities are hung up on the postulate-counter-postulate of a **problem.** (SH Spec 243, 6302C26) **3.** constituted of items, beingnesses, that the person has been and has fought. (SH Spec 137, 6204C24) **4.** the **problem** created by two or more opposing ideas which being opposed, balanced, and unresolved, make a **mass**. It's a mental energy **mass**. (SH Spec 83, 6612C06) **5.** items (valences) in opposition to one another. Any pair of these items, in opposition to each other, constitute a specific **problem**. (HCOB 23 Nov 62)

**GOALS TERMINAL,** something that epitomizes both the **goal** and the resistive modifier. (SH Spec 76, 6111C07)

**GOES THROUGH 7,** around the whole TA dial and back up. (HCOB 20 Aug 63)

**GO IN,** to **go in;** the act of the verb interioriz*ing.* (HCOB 4 Jan 71 II)

**GOING UP THE POLE,** *Slang.* that's when somebody doesn't even begin to handle energy, but he just suddenly somehow or other latches onto about 40.0 and goes out the top and still holds onto the mest body on the bottom and he's done the incredible thing of making a circle out of all this. He's joined 0.0 up against 40.0 and to listen to the guy and to talk to the guy you couldn't really tell whether he's ecstatically alive or fatally dead. (PDC 27)

**GOOD AUDITOR,** one who knows Scn and its techniques and who **audits** with all basics in. (*Aud 1 UK*)

**GOOD AUTOMATICITY,** that which raised the self-determinism of others and let them more and more on a rising scale, think, act and provide for themselves. (PDC 21)

**GOOD CASE CONDITION,** attained the level of **case** for which the church is classified and now in training during staff study time for admin or tech certification. (HCO PL 21 Oct 73R)

**GOOD CONDUCT,** to do only those things which others can experience. (HCOB 1 Mar 59)

**GOOD/EVIL,** for the purpose of Dn and Scn **good** and **evil** must be defined. Those things which may be classified as **good** by an individual are only those things which aid himself, his family, his group, his race, mankind or life in its dynamic obedience to the command, modified by the observations of the individual, his family, his group, his race, or life. As **evil,** may be classified those things which tend to limit the dynamic thrust of the individual, his family, his group, his race, or life in general in the dynamic drive, also limited by the observation, the observer and his ability to observe. **Good** may be defined as constructive. **Evil** may be defined as destructive—definitions modified by viewpoint. (*DTOT*, p. 21)

**GOOD INDICATORS, 1.** what you are treating is getting better, by which we mean, less present; betterness to us is less present, his bad ankle is getting better. We mean the badness of the ankle is less present so that's a **good indicator.** How much less present, is the degree of the **goodness** of the **indicator.** (SH Spec 3, 6401C09) **2.** those **indicators** of a person (or group) indicating that the person is doing well, e.g. fast progress, high production statistics, person happy, winning, cogniting, are said to be **good indicators.** (BTB 12 Apr 72R) *Abbr.* GIs.

Good Indicators (Def. 2)

**GOOD PHYSICAL CONDITION,** not suffering from **physical** illness, not PTS, not currently **physically** damaged by accident. (HCO PL 21 Oct 73R)

**GOVERNOR,** mentioned in a lecture in the autumn of 1951. The speed of a preclear is the speed of his production of energy. The most important step in establishing a preclear's self-determinism, the goal of the auditor, is the rehabilitation of the preclear's ability to produce energy. (*Scn 8-80*, p. 33)

**G PLUS M, goal plus modifier.** (SH Spec 90, 6112C07)

**GPM, goals problem mass.** (HCOB 23 Aug 65)

**GRAD, Graduate.** (BPL 5 Nov 72RA)

**GRADATION,** it means there are **grades,** as to a road, or steps which are a **gradual grade** up. (*Aud 107 ASHO*)

**GRADATION CHART,** see CLASSIFICATION GRADATION AND AWARENESS CHART.

**GRADE, 1.** the word used to describe the attainment of level achieved by a preclear. **Grade** is the personal points of progress on the bridge. A preclear is **Grade 0, I, II, III, IV, V, VA** or **VI** depending on the technology successfully applied. (*Aud 72 UK*) **2.** a series of processes culminating in an exact ability attained, examined and attested to by the pc. (HCOB 23 Aug 71) **3. grade** and level are the same but when one has a **grade** one is a pc and when one has a level one is studying its data. (HCOB 2 Apr 65)

**GRADE 0, Communications Release.** Ability to communicate freely with anyone on any subject. (CG&AC75)

**GRADE I, Problems Release.** Ability to recognize the source of problems and make them vanish. (CG&AC75)

**GRADE II, Relief Release.** Relief from hostilities and the sufferings of life. (CG&AC75)

**GRADE III, Freedom Release.** Freedom from the upsets of the past and ability to face the future. (CG&AC75)

**GRADE IV, Ability Release.** Moving out of fixed conditions and gaining abilities to do new things. (CG&AC75)

**GRADE IV, NEW. Grade IV** has been improved enormously by including and refining formerly Class VI materials. The engram running part cannot be run on Clears but the listing processes can. It is guaranteed to make the preclear fully and completely right. (LRH ED 301 INT)

**GRADE V, Power Release.** Ability to handle power. (CG&AC75)

**GRADE VA, Power Plus Release.** Recovery of knowledge. (CG&AC75)

**GRADE VI, Whole Track Release.** Return of powers to act on own determinism. (CG&AC75)

**GRADE VII, Clear.** Ability to be at cause over mental matter, energy, space, and time on the first dynamic (survival for self). (CG&AC75)

**GRADIENT, 1.** a **gradual** approach to something, taken step by step, level by level, each step or level being, of itself, easily surmountable—so that, finally, quite complicated and difficult activities or high states of being can be achieved with relative ease. This principle is applied to both Scn processing and training. (*Scn AD*) **2.** a steepening or an increasing from the slight to the heavy. (HCOB 3 Apr 66) **3.** the essence of a **gradient** is just being able to do a little bit more and a little bit more and a little bit more until you finally make the grade. (*Scn 0-8*, p. 15)

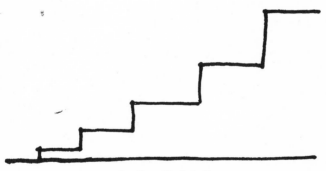

Gradient (Def. 1, 2)

**GRADIENT SCALE, 1.** the term can apply to anything, and means a **scale** of condition **graduated** from zero to infinity. Absolutes are considered to be unobtainable. (*Scn 8-8008*, p. 104) **2.** the tool of infinity-valued logic. It is a tenet of Dn and Scn that absolutes are unattainable. Terms like good and bad, alive and dead, right and wrong are used only in conjunction with **gradient scales.** On the scale of right and wrong, everything above zero or center would be more and more right, approaching an infinite rightness, and everything below zero or center would be more and more wrong, approaching an infinite wrongness. The **gradient scale** is a way of thinking about the universe which approximates the actual conditions of the universe more closely than any other existing logical method. (*SOS* Gloss)

**GRADIENTS OF CASES,** the degree to which the person is overwhelmed by the bank. (SH Spec 46, 6108C29)

**GRAND TOUR, 1.** the process R1-9 in *The Creation of Human Ability.* (*PXL* Gloss) **2. Grand Tour** is the Route 1 or exteriorized version of Spotting Spots. The auditor asks the preclear to be in a spot of a certain description, such as his home town, asks him to be in the auditing room, asks him to be in his home town, asks him to be in the auditing room. (PAB 51) **3.** a very simple process. What you do is run change of space with enough interesting locales in it, to show the pc that he can choose around a great deal of universe and look at a great many things. (5410CM10C) **4.** a process used on an exteriorized thetan to free him from the craving for mass and to bring into present time a greater portion of the mest universe. (*COHA* Gloss)

**GRANT BEINGNESS,** the ability to assume or **grant** (give, allow) **beingness** is probably the highest of human virtues. It is even more important to be able to permit (allow) other people to **have beingness** than to be able oneself to assume it. (*FOT,* p. 27)

**GREASING THE TRACK,** merely by running the preclear through various parts of his life, up and down the **track,** the auditor may relieve enough anaten and misemotion from the case to permit somatics to occur. This was once upon a time known as **"greasing the track."** However one should not run a preclear into a somatic unless one intends to reduce it or to discover the basic on the chain and reduce that. (*SOS,* p. 84)

**GREASY ON THE TRACK,** *Slang.* attention of the pc hard to control. (SH Spec 302A, 6309C03)

**GREEN FORM, 1.** used for general case cleanup particularly on an out-rud type pc or when ruds won't fly. It is not used to handle high or low TA. Assessed M5 to provide data for the C/S then each read handled in accordance with C/S Series 44R. EP is each read handled to its EP. May be reassessed after handling all reading items if heavily charged on first assessment. Can also be done M3 to a good win and F/N VGIs. (BTB 11 Aug 72RA) **2.** in HGC the **Green Form** is done on the order of the case supervisor to detect reasons for case trouble; prepared list. (HCO PL 7 Apr 70RA) *Abbr.* GF.

**GREEN FORM 40 EXPANDED,** this detects and handles any reason why a case might be resistive to processing, thus handling any tendency towards slow gain and making it possible for such cases to make faster gains in future processing. (LRH ED 301 INT)

**GREEN SHEET**, an Expanded Dianetics program is written on a **green sheet.** (BTB 6 Nov 72R II)

**GR ENG INT, group engram intensive.** (HCOB 5 May 70)

**GRIEF, 1.** a ridge and is occasioned by loss. (*Scn 8-8008*, p. 21) **2.** 0.5 on the tone scale. (*SOS*, p. 57) **3. Grief** takes place where one recognizes his loss and failure as in the death of somebody he loved and tried to help. (*HFP*, p. 85)

Grief

**GRIEF CHARGE**, an outburst of tears that may continue for a considerable time, in a session, after which the preclear feels greatly relieved. This is occasioned by the discharge of **grief** or painful emotion from a secondary. (*Scn AD*)

**GRINDING, 1.** charge is held in place by the basic on a chain. When only later than basic incidents are run charge can be restimulated and then bottled up again with a very small amount blown. This is known as **"grinding out"** an incident. An engram is getting run, but as it is not basic on a chain, no adequate amount of charge is being relieved. (HCOB 8 Jun 63) **2.** going over and over and over and over a lock, secondary or engram without obtaining an actual erasure. The Dn auditor who puts the pc through an incident four or five times without erasure or appreciable reduction is encountering **"grinding."** (HCOB 1 May 69) **3.** a level below ARC breaking. A pc who just sits there and **grinds** is very often not up to getting ARC broken. (SH Spec 66, 6110C12)

**GROOVE IN THE QUESTION,** there are a variety of ways to do this, e.g., ask what the **question** means. What period or time the **question** covers. What activities would be included. Where the pc has been that might be something to do with the **question**. If any other people are likely to be involved. In other words you are steering the pc's attention to various parts of his bank and getting him to have a preliminary look. When this has been done, using very good TR 1, you give him the **question** again. (BTB 18 Dec 72)

**GROSS AUDITING ERRORS,** the five **gross auditing errors** are: (1) can't handle and read an E-meter; (2) doesn't know and can't apply technical data; (3) can't get and keep a pc in session; (4) can't complete an auditing cycle; (5) can't complete a repetitive auditing cycle (including repeating a command long enough to flatten a process). (HCOB 21 Sept 65) *Abbr.* GAEs.

**GROUP ANALYTICAL MIND,** the true **analytical mind** of the **group** is the composite of the **analytical minds** of the members of the **group** as guided by the rationale and ethics which initially founded the **group** or which it has developed into a culture. (*NOTL*, p. 137)

**GROUP AUDITOR, 1.** one who stands in front of, sits in front of, or relays by loudspeaker system to a **group** (and a **group** consists of two or more people), **auditing,** so as to improve their condition of beingness as thetans. (*PXL*, p. 284) **2.** a **group auditor** is one who administers techniques, usually already codified, to **groups** of children or adults. (*GAH*, p. i)

**GROUP AUDITOR'S HANDBOOK,** this was a 1954 compilation of **group auditing** sessions resulting from the Advanced Clinical Courses of that year. (*PXL*, p. 288)

**GROUP BANK,** see GROUP ENGRAM.

**GROUPED,** meaning everything in the same place. (21ACC-5, 5901C30)

**GROUP ENGRAM, 1.** each time instantaneous action is demanded of the **group** by compressed time situations, and commands are given by the selected individual or individuals to cope with those moments of emergency, it can be observed that an **engram** has been implanted in the **group**. The instantaneous orders and commands are indicators of an **engram**. The **engram** actually was received during a moment of shock when the ideals, ethics, rationale and general thought and energy of the **group** collided forcefully with mest. (*NOTL*, p. 132) **2.** a **group** is composed of individuals. If they have a **group engram,** it only has force because of basics on that subject in their banks. Thus, if they are cleaned up on the general subject, the general **group engram** should blow off and disappear. (HCOB 27 Feb 70)

**GROUP ENGRAM INTENSIVE,** this is a process run to help a Scientology Church. A **group** is composed of individuals. If they have a **group engram** it only has force because of basics on that subject in their banks. Thus, if they are cleaned up on the general subject, the general **group engram** should blow off and disappear. This is done on every member of the **group.** Listing, nulling and TRs must be flawless. (HCOB 27 Feb 70)

**GROUPER, 1.** species of command which, literally translated, means that all incidents are in one place on the time track: "I'm jammed up," "Everything happens at once," "Everything comes in on me at once," "I'll get even with you," etc. (*DMSMH*, p. 213) **2.** anything which pulls the time track into a bunch at one or more points. When the **grouper** is gone the time track is perceived to be straight. (HCOB 15 May 63) **3.** is a number of incidents becoming located apparently in one time instant. (SH Spec 56, 6109C20) **4.** action phrase which would tend to bunch all incidents in one place, creates the illusion that the time track is collapsed and that all incidents are at the same point in time. Example: "Pull yourself together," "It all happens at once." (*SOS*, p. 103)

**GROUP PROCESSING,** techniques, usually already codified, administered to **groups** of children or adults. The **group** (preclears) is usually assembled and seated in a quiet room where they will not be disturbed by sudden noises or entrances. The group auditor then takes his position in the front of the **group** and talks to them briefly about what he is going to do and what he expects them to do. The auditor then begins with his first command. (*GAH*, p. i)

**GROUP REACTIVE MIND,** could be considered to lie in the actions of those individuals set up for emergency status during compressed time emergencies, which is to say, the **reactive mind** is composed of the composite engrams of the **group** itself. (*NOTL*, p. 136)

**GROUP THETA,** the **theta** of a **group** would be its ideas, ideals, rationale and ethic. This is an actual force. The culture is an accumulated soul which flows over and through a number of individuals and persists after the death of those individuals via other individuals or even other **groups.** (*DAB*, Vol. II, p. 136)

**GROUP THINK,** the common denominator of the **group** is the reactive bank. Thetans without banks have different responses. They only have their banks in common. They agree then only on bank principles. Person to person the bank is identical. So constructive ideas are *individual* and seldom get broad agreement in a human **group.** (HCO PL 7 Feb 65)

**GUARD OF THE LEFT,** you've got *suppress,* you've got *careful of,* and you've got *fail to reveal.* These buttons: suppress, careful of and fail to reveal produce sensation. When the goal doesn't fire it's in the **left-hand column.** (SH Spec 195, 6209C27)

**GUARD OF THE RIGHT,** *invalidate, suggest* and *mistake.* These buttons produce pain. The goal fires falsely on the buttons on the **right.** (SH Spec 195, 6209C27)

**GUIDING SECONDARY STYLE, 1.** steer plus itsa. You **guide** the guy into talking about something and get a tone arm blowdown and then you make him talk about it. You get the tone arm action out of it, and then while he's talking about it he mentions several new things that give him tone arm action so you note those things down and you come back afterwards and talk about those things. (SH Spec 47, 6411C17) **2.** differs from proper guiding style and is done by: (1) steering the pc toward revealing something or something revealed; (2) handling it with itsa. (HCOB 21 Feb 66)

**GUIDING STYLE AUDITING (LEVEL TWO STYLE),** the essentials of **Guiding Style Auditing** consist of two-way comm that steers the pc into revealing a difficulty followed by a repetitive process to handle what has been revealed. (HCOB 6 Nov 64)

**GUILT COMPLEX,** before you felt sympathy, you offended in some way. You did something. Then you were sorry for it. The offense may have taken place years or only minutes before your sympathy came about. This is the emotional curve of sympathy. It goes from antagonism or anger down to sympathy. This used to be called a **"guilt complex."** (*HFP*, pp. 125-126)

**GUK BOMB,** I have found that 600 milligrams of Vitamin E (minimum) assists Scn processing very markedly. It works by itself but is best taken with an old time **"Guk Bomb."** The formula of the **bomb** is variable but is basically 100 mg. of Vitamin B1, 15 gr. of calcium and 500 mg. of Vitamin C. (HCOB 27 Dec 65)

# H

**HAA, 1. Hubbard Advanced Auditor:** a Class IV auditor. This level teaches about service facsimiles and ability. Processes taught include certainty processing and overt justification processes. (CG&AC 75) **2.** an alternate name for **HAA** in 1956 was B Scn or Bachelor of Scn abroad. (HCOTB 12 Sept 56) [The term HAA is today used as in def. 1 above.]

**HABIT, 1.** that stimulus-response reaction dictated by the reactive mind from the content of engrams and put into effect by the somatic mind. It can be changed only by those things which change engrams. (*DMSMH*, p. 39) **2.** simply something one cannot stop. Here we have an example of no control whatever. (*POW*, p. 46)

**HABIT RELEASE,** Grade IV Release. (HCOB 22 Sept 65) [The current name for Grade IV Release is Ability Release.] See GRADE IV.

**HALF-ACKNOWLEDGEMENT, 1.** a continue, an encouragement. (SH Spec 53, 6503C02) **2.** sometimes a pc gets scared or lonesome and you have to give him an uh-huh to encourage him. (SH Spec 70, 6607C21)

# HALLUCINATIONS

**HALLUCINATIONS, 1.** imagined realities with which nobody else agrees. (*HFP*, p. 41) **2.** we call a mental image picture an "**hallucination**" or more properly an automaticity (something uncontrolled) when it is created by another and seen by self. (*FOT*, p. 57) **3.** things seen that aren't there. (7203C30SO) **4.** a person imagining and not knowing he was imagining would be a person who was **hallucinating.** (5203CM04B)

**HALLUCINATORY CAUSE,** the thetan considers that he is actually being more **cause** (going down the sub-zero scale). This is the exact reverse of the reality of the situation. He is becoming more and more effect. (BTB 6 Feb 60)

**HANDLE,** finish off, complete, end cycle on. Service and **handling** are the same thing. When you give service, you **handle.** Part of **handling** cases is **handle** N-O-W! One way or another, one gets the pc **handled.** (HCOB 15 Jan 70 II)

**HANDLING AN ORIGINATION, handling an origination** merely tells the person, "All right, I heard it, you're there." You might say it is a form of acknowledgement but it's not. It is the communication formula in reverse; but the auditor is still in control if he **handles** the **origin.** (PAB 151) See TR-4.

**HANG-FIRE,** delayed firing. After the trigger is pulled a gun sometimes doesn't go off. This is called a "**hang-fire**" or delayed fire if it then goes off late. (LRH Def. Notes)

**HANG-UP,** stuck (on time track). (*HFP*, p. 101)

**HAPPINESS,** is not itself an emotion. It is a word which states a condition, and the anatomy of that condition is interest. **Happiness,** you could say, is the overcoming of not unknowable obstacles toward a known goal. (8ACC-4, 5410CM06)

**HARD WAY TRs,** demand for a start, two hours of no twitch, no blink, no eye redness, no unconscious, no wiggle TR Zero. Really real TRs beginning with Zero. Like the bulletin. (LRH ED 143 INT)

**HAS,** abbreviation for **1. Hubbard Apprentice Scientologist.** (HCOB 23 Aug 65) **2. Hubbard Association of Scientologists.** (PAB 75) **3. HCO Area Secretary.** (HCOB 20 Nov 71)

**HAS CO-AUDIT,** using precise processes developed for this section only, the **HAS Co-audit** (do-it-yourself processing) seeks to improve cases and further interest people in Scn so that they will take individual HGC processing and individual training. (HCO PL 14 Feb 61)

**HAS COURSE,** a **course** in elementary communication and control. Consists of training drills on communication and to put the student at cause over the environment. There are no prerequisites. The graduate is awarded the certificate of **Hubbard Apprentice Scientologist.** (CG&AC 75)

**HASI, Hubbard Association** of **Scientologists, International.** (PAB 74)

**HAS SPECIALIST RUNDOWN,** the **HAS** and establishment officers are peculiarly subject to efforts to unstabilize them. The **HAS Specialist Rundown** consists of processes which increase the ability to hold a position. (HCOB 20 Nov 71)

**HASUK, Hubbard Association** of **Scientologists** of the **United Kingdom.** (PAB 75)

**HAT, 1.** slang for the title and work of a post in a Scientology Church. Taken from the fact that in many professions such as railroading the type of **hat** worn is the badge of the job. (HCO PL 1 Jul 65 III) **2.** term used to describe the write ups, checksheets and packs that outline the purposes, know-how and duties of a post. It exists in folders and packs and is trained in on the person on the post. (HCO PL 22 Sept 70)

**HATE, 1.** a total ridge. (5904C08) **2.** around 1.5 on the tone scale affinity has almost reversed itself. Its dissonance has become **hate,** which can be violent and is so expressed. Here, actually, we have a factor of entheta repelling theta. (*SOS*, p. 56)

**HATS, Hubbard Advanced Technical Specialist.** A Class IX auditor. This level teaches advanced procedures and developments since Class VIII. It is available at Saint Hill organizations. (CG&AC 75)

**HAV, havingness.** (BTB 20 Aug 71 II)

**HAVING,** to be able to touch or permeate or to direct the disposition of. (PAB 83)

**HAVINGNESS, 1.** that which permits the experience of mass and pressure. (*A&L*, p. 8) **2.** the feeling that one owns or possesses. (SH Spec 84, 6612C13) **3.** can be simply defined as ARC with the environment. (SH Spec 294, 6308C14) **4.** that activity which is run when needed and when it will not violently deflect the pc's attention. (SH Spec 85, 6111C28) **5.** the result of creation. (SH Spec 19, 6106C23) **6.** the ability to duplicate that which one perceives, or create a duplication of what one perceives, or to be willing to create a duplication of it. But it's duplication. (1SHACC-10, 6009C14) **7.** ability to communicate with an is-ness. The ability to conceive an is-ness and communicate with it. (17ACC-4, 5702C28) **8. havingness** is the concept of being able to reach or not being prevented from reaching. (SH Spec 126, 6203C29) **9.** the need to **have** terminals and things to play for and on. (*Dn 55!*, p. 137) *Abbr.* Hav.

**HBA, Hubbard Book Auditor.** (HCOB 23 Aug 65) See BOOK AUDITOR.

**HC, Hubbard Consultant.** (HCOB 19 Jun 71 III)

**HCA, 1. Hubbard Certified Auditor.** A Class II auditor. This level teaches about overt acts and withholds. Among the processes taught are responsibility processes and integrity processes. (CG&AC 75) **2.** an early course taught in Scientology Churches only. The certificate of **HCA** (or HPA, the British equivalent) was awarded by examination only. (HCOTB 12 Sept 56) [The current usage of HCA is as in def. 1 above.]

**HCA/HPA,** [At one time HCA and HPA were equivalent certificates, HCA being the American designation and HPA, the British. Data on this appears in HCOTB 12 Sept 56 and HCO PL 1 Oct 58. The current usages of each of these designations are listed separately under each.]

**HCA LECT, Hubbard Certified Auditors Course Lectures.** (HCOB 29 Sept 66)

**HCAP, Hubbard Certified Auditor Course, Phoenix.** (HCOB 29 Sept 66)

**HCI, Hubbard College** of **Improvement.** (FSO 65) [The name of the Academy on Flag.]

**HCL, Hubbard College Lectures.** (HCOB 29 Sept 66)

**HC LIST, 1.** the arbitrary name of the Data Series Correction List. (FO 3179) **2.** it's called an **HC List** because there was one time going to be something called a **Hubbard Consultant** and we've still got the **list**. It's an out-point/plus-point list and it's simply assessed and handled. (ESTO 4, 7203C02 SO II)

**HCO, Hubbard Communications Office.** (BPL 5 Nov 72RA)

**HCOB, Hubbard Communications Office Bulletin.** (HCOB 4 Sept 71 III)

**HCO PL, Hubbard Communications Office Policy Letter.** (HCO PL 24 Sept 70R)

**HCS, Hubbard Clearing Scientologist**—formerly Level IV certificate. (HCOB 23 Aug 65)

**HDA, Hubbard Dianetic Auditor.** (HCOB 23 Aug 65) [An HDA is a graduate of the Dianetic Auditor's Course, forerunner to the HSDC. A graduate of the HSDC is known as an HDC, which is the current certificate awarded to a Dn auditor.]

**HDC, Hubbard Dianetic Counselor.** A graduate of the HSDC. (CG& AC 75) See HUBBARD STANDARD DIANETICS COURSE.

**HDG, Hubbard Dianetic Graduate.** One who is trained to teach the Dianetic Course after graduating from the HSDC. (BTB 12 Apr 72R)

**HDRF, Hubbard Dianetic Research Foundation,** Elizabeth, New Jersey, U.S.A. The first organization, founded by others in 1950, May. Closed 1951 as I had no control of it and the directors mismanaged it. (LRH Def. Notes)

**HEALTH FORM, 1.** a **form** done by an auditor. It is metered. The end product of this **form** is entirely to pick out what to audit. (HCOB 19 May 69) **2.** as one needs a guide to know what to audit on a case, the **Dn health form** is an essential auditing action. You take up and audit each symptom or complaint one after the other. You audit the most available symptom first. Sooner or later the pc will have a well, healthy body, **health**, stability, and a sense of well-being. (HCOB 19 May 69, *Health Form, Use Of*)

**H, E & R, human emotion and reaction.** (HCOB 3 Dec 73)

**HEAT,** the physical sensation associated with the release of energy in the form of **heat** which is attendent to actual GPMs, their RIs and associated locks. (HCOB 13 Apr 64, *Scn VI Part One Glossary of Terms*)

**HEAVILY CHARGED CASE**, by which is meant a **case** with a very **heavy** burden of secondaries. (*SOS*, p. 82)

**HEAVY FACSIMILE**, a **heavy facsimile** is an experience, complete with all perceptions, emotions, thoughts and efforts, occupying a precise place in space and a moment in time. It can be an operation, an injury, a term of **heavy** physical exertion, or even a death. It is composed of the preclear's own effort and the effort of the environment (counter-effort). (*AP&A*, p. 28)

**HELATROBUS**, an interplanetary nation. A little pip squeak government, didn't amount to very much. (SH Spec 268, 6305C23)

**HELATROBUS IMPLANTS, 1.** call them the heaven **implants**, they are the **implants implanted** by **Helatrobus.** (SH Spec 268, 6305C23) **2.** are actually a long chain of engrams, each of which has basics. (SH Spec 272, 6306C11) **3. implants** which begin with the electronic clouds over planets, and the dichotomy, plus and minus, and so forth and sweep on through in a certain series. (SH Spec 266, 6305C21)

**HELD-DOWN FIVES**, jammed thinking because of a misunderstood or misapplied datums. (HCOB 12 Nov 64) See also HELD-DOWN SEVEN.

**HELD-DOWN SEVEN**, *Slang.* **1.** an enforced wrong datum. (*EOS*, p. 52) **2.** jammed thinking because of a misunderstood or misapplied datum. (HCOB 12 Nov 64) [This term stems from an analogy made by LRH comparing the reactive mind to a computer or adding machine in which the number seven (or five) had been shorted out so that it was always added in in every computation. Of course it could not compute correctly or get correct answers from data as long as this condition existed.] (*EOS*, p. 51)

**HELLO AND OKAY**, a very basic process which resolves chronic somatics, eye difficulties, any specific item is to have the affected part or bad area of energy say **"Hello"** and **"Okay"** and "All right" until it is in good condition. (*Dn 55!*, p. 143) ["Hello" and "Okay" process commands can be found in HCOB 22 Mar 58, *Clearing Reality.*]

**HELP, help** is the key button which admits auditing. **Help** is the make-break point between sanity and insanity. That a person cannot accept **help** along some minor line does not mean that he is insane, but it certainly means he has some neurotic traits. (HCOB 5 May 60)

**HELP FACTOR,** the willingness to assist. This also has to do with cause—what can the individual cause? An organization which cannot **help** anybody will have a tendency to fail. (ESTO No. 8, 7203C06SO)

**HELP PROCESSING,** there are probably thousands of ways help could be run. But the one general **process** on **help** that would rank high would be "What have you **helped?**" "What have you **not helped?**" alternated. This is the best way I know of to run the sense of what **help** one has given plus what **help** one has withheld. This lets the pc as-is his failures to **help** as well as his denials of **help.** (HCOB 12 May 60)

**HEV, Human Evaluation Course.** (HCOB 29 Sept 66)

**HGA, 1. Hubbard Graduate Auditor.** Class VII auditor. Only available to Sea Org or five year contracted Church staff. This level teaches the power processes and review auditing. It is not a prerequisite to Class VIII, however. It is delivered in Church of Scientology Saint Hill organizations. (CG&AC 75) **2.** in 1956, an **HGA** was also to be known as D. Scn or Doctor of Scientology abroad. (HCOTB 12 Sept 56) See DOCTOR OF SCIENTOLOGY. **3.** an honor award and may be made by nomination or selection; either way it is for those who are consistently producing excellent results in their own fields and to form a grade by which these recruits can be recognized. (PAB 6) [Current usage of the term HGA is as in def. 1 above.]

**HGC, Hubbard Guidance Center.** (HCOB 23 Aug 65)

**HGC ADMIN, Hubbard Guidance Center Administrator.** (HCOB 23 Aug 65)

**HGDS, Hubbard Graduate Dianetic Specialist.** An Expanded Dianetics auditor. (CG&AC 75) See also EXPANDED DIA-NETICS.

**HIDDEN DATA LINE,** some students have believed there was a **"hidden data line"** of tech in Scn, a **line** on which Scn tech was given out by me but not made known to students. This started me looking, for there is no such **line.** The *whole* of technology is released in HCO Bulletins and HCO Policy Letters and tapes I do and release. I don't tell people anything in some private way, not even instructors. The *apparency* is somebody's pretense to know from me more than is on the tapes and in books and mimeos, or, brutally, somebody's alter-is of materials. This *looks* like a **"hidden data line."** It surely isn't. (HCO PL 16 Apr 65)

**HIDDEN STANDARD, 1.** a **hidden standard** is a problem a person thinks must be resolved before auditing can be seen to have worked. It's a **standard** by which to judge Scn or auditing or the auditor. This **hidden standard** is always an old problem of long duration. It is a postulate-counter-postulate situation. The source of the counter-postulate was suppressive to the pc. (HCOB 8 Nov 65) **2.** is not just a physical or mental difficulty but one by which the pc measures his case gains. A case measurement thing used secretly by the pc. (BTB 18 Sept 72) *Abbr.* HS.

**HIGH CRIME CHECKOUTS, 1.** starrated **checkouts** on all processes and their immediate technology and on relevant policy letters on HGC interns or staff auditors in the Tech Division or staff auditors or interns in the Qual Division for the levels and actions they will use before permitting them to audit church pcs and on supervisors in Tech and Qual who instruct or examine. (HCO PL 8 Mar 66) **2. high crime checkouts** are done by auditors to their highest class. Any new procedure must be drilled on a doll in addition to the **high crime checkout** before the OK to audit chit is issued. (BTB 5 Sept 72RA) [High crime checkouts are so named because it is an ethics offense in the nature of a high crime for failing to insist upon this policy or preventing this policy from going into effect or minimizing the checkouts or lists.]

**HIGH CRIMES,** suppressive acts. (*ISE,* p. 48)

**HIGH SCHOOL INDOCTRINATION,** an extremely precise activity which consists of teaching an auditor not to let a preclear stop him. (HCOB 4 Oct 56)

**HI HI INDOC,** tone 40 8-C. (PAB 113)

**HIGH TA, 1.** 3.5 or up at session start. (HCOB 3 Jan 70) **2.** a **high TA** in Scn is always an overrun. In Dn it means an engram too late on the chain to erase is in restimulation. (HCOB 28 Apr 69) **3. high TA** means the person can still stop things and is trying to do so. However, all one has to do is restimulate and leave unflat an engram chain to have a **high TA. High TA** is reflecting the force contained in the chain. (HCOB 16 Jun 70)

**HIGH-TONE INDIVIDUAL,** thinks wholly into the future. He is extroverted toward his environment. He clearly observes the environment with full perception unclouded by undistinguished fears about the environment. He thinks very little about himself but operates automatically in his own interests. He enjoys existence. His calculations (postulations and evaluations) are swift and accurate. He is very self-confident. He *knows* he knows and does not even bother to assert that he knows. He controls his environment. (*AP&A*, p. 37)

**HI-LO TA, high low TA.** (HCOB 1 Jan 72RA)

**HI-LO TA ASSESSMENT FOR CONFESSIONALS.** See HI-LO TA ASSESSMENT FOR INTEGRITY PROCESSING.

**HI-LO TA ASSESSMENT FOR INTEGRITY PROCESSING,** this list is used to get a TA in normal range before proceeding into an **Integrity Processing** session. It is used after any possible false TA has been checked for and handled, if TA is still below 2.0 or at 3.5 or above. (BTB 6 Dec 72R)

**HIPS, Hubbard Integrity Processing Specialist.** (HCO PL 24 Dec 72)

**HIT,** punished, hurt, etc. (HCOB 1 Nov 68)

**HO-HUM,** minus randomity. (*Abil 36*)

**HOLDER, 1.** any engram command which makes an individual remain in an engram knowingly or unknowingly. (*DMSMH* Gloss) **2.** a species of command. These include such things as "stay here," "sit right there and think about it," "come back and sit down," "I can't go," "I mustn't leave," etc. (*DMSMH*, p. 213)

**HOLLOW SPOT,** a segment of the body which has such a hard impact in the center that all attention units in a mock-up will flow out from the center. It's an outflow from a central point but the point is a counter-effort. (5206CM24B)

**HOME UNIVERSE,** the **universe** a thetan made for himself. (SH Spec 83, 6612C06)

**HOMO NOVIS, 1. Homo** man, **novis** new. (*BCR*, p. 12) **2.** a theta-animated mest body possesed of new and desirable attributes; a mest clear, a good, sane rational mest being about a skycraper higher than *Homo sapiens.* (*HOM*, p. 40) **3.** the Second Stage Release is definitely **Homo novis.** The person ceases to respond like *Homo sapiens* and has fantastic capability to learn and act. (HCOB 28 Jun 65)

**HOMO SAPIENS, 1.** a mest body, whether it belongs to the race of man or the race of ants is yet but an animated vegetable. Given a theta being to guide it, it becomes part of a composite such as **Homo sapiens.** By itself, the body would live, walk around, react, sleep, kill, and direct an existence no better than that of a field mouse, or a zombie. Put a theta being over it and it becomes possessed of ethics and morals and direction and goals and the ability to reason; it becomes this strange thing called **Homo sapiens.** (*HOM*, p. 42)

**HONEST COMPLETION,** means a student who has studied all the materials of the course using full study tech. Has done the demonstrations and drills, and can effectively apply the materials of the course. (HCO PL 16 May 73R)

**HOPE,** the desire that sometime in the future one will cease to have something which he no longer wants but can't seem to get rid of or that one will acquire something he wants. (2ACC-31A, 5312CM22)

**HOPE FACTOR, 1.** validating those good indicators which are present [in the pc]. (SH Spec 3, 6401C09) **2.** something can be done about it. (SH Spec 297, 6308C21)

**HOT QUESTION,** question with reaction on it. (SH Spec 63, 6110C05)

**HOT SPUR LINE,** where there is a senior review C/S there is a **hot spur line** from the C/S to the senior C/S and back to the C/S. This is not necessarily an instant line. It can be a 12-hour lag line. New tech in use, fantastic completions and "dog cases" nobody can make anything out of go on this senior C/S **hot spur line.** (HCOB 5 Mar 71)

**HPA, Hubbard Professional Auditor.** A Class III auditor. This level deals with ARC and ARC breaks. Listing and nulling and two-way comm are taught at this level, as well as change processes and ARC Break SW. (CG&AC 75)

**HPC LECT, Hubbard Professional Course Lecture.** (HCOB 29 Sept 66)

**HPCS, Hubbard Professional Course Supervisor.** (HCO PL 27 Oct 70)

**HPCSC, Hubbard Professional Course Supervisor's Course.** (HCO PL 27 Oct 70 II)

**HQS, Hubbard Qualified Scientologist.** A basic Scn course which teaches about co-auditing and how to handle other people, with group auditing. It consists of, in part, TRs 0 to 4 and 6 to 9, plus students actually co-audit on CCHs, Op Pro by Dup and *Self Analysis* lists. There is no prerequisite for this course. (CG&AC 75)

**HRS, Hubbard Recognized Scientologist.** A Class 0 auditor. This level teaches about communication. Processes taught are Level 0 processes and ARC SW processes. (CG&AC 75)

**HS, hidden standard.** (HCOB 10 Jun 72 V)

**HSCSC, Hubbard Senior Course Supervisor Course.** The **HSCSC** covers the total expertise of the technology of supervising. (FBDL 328)

**HSDC, Hubbard Standard Dianetics Course.** (BTB 12 Apr 72R)

**HSS, Hubbard Senior Scientologist.** A Class VI auditor. An **HSS** is a graduate of the Saint Hill Special Briefing Course. This course consists of the full practical application of Scn grades, repair, setups, assists and special cases tech up to Class VI. (CG&AC 75)

**HSST, Hubbard Specialist** of **Standard Tech,** Class VIII Case Supervisor. (CG&AC 75)

**HSTS, Hubbard Standard Technical Specialist.** A Class VIII auditor. The Class VIII Course teaches exact handling of all cases up to 100 per cent result, as well as Class VIII procedures, all case setup actions, all processes and corrective actions, as well as *flubless* Class VIII auditing. (CG&AC 75)

**HTS, Hubbard Trained Scientologist.** A Class I auditor. This level teaches about problems. The processes taught include objective processes and Level I processes, such as help and control processes. (CG&AC 75)

**HUBBARD COMMUNICATIONS OFFICE,** purpose: to be the office of LRH. To handle and expedite the **communication** lines of LRH. To prepare or handle the preparation of manuscripts and other to-be-published material of Scn. To keep, use and care for LRH's **office** equipment. To assist the Churches of Scientology and their people. To set a good example of efficiency to the Churches. (HCO PL 12 Oct 62)

**HUBBARD COMMUNICATIONS OFFICE BULLETIN, HCOBs** written by LRH only. These are the technical issue line. They are valid from first issue unless specifically cancelled. All data for auditing and courses is contained in **HCOBs.** They are distributed as indicated, usually to technical staff. They are red ink on white paper, consecutive by date. (HCO PL 24 Sept 70R)

**HUBBARD COMMUNICATIONS OFFICE POLICY LETTER, HCO PLs** written by LRH only. This is a permanently valid issue of all Third Dynamic, organization and administrative technology. These, regardless of date or age, form the know-how in running a Scientology Church, organization, group or company. The bulk of hat material is made up from **HCO PLs.** They are printed in green ink on white paper and are distributed to all staff or as indicated or as made up in packs. (HCO PL 24 Sept 70R)

**HUBBARD CONSULTANT,** A **Hubbard Consultant** is skilled in testing, two-way comm, consultation, programming and interpersonal relations. This is the certificate especially awarded to persons trained to handle personnel, students and staff. These technologies and special training were developed to apply Scn auditing skills to the field of administration especially. An **HC** is requisite for course supervisors and student consultants. (HCOB 19 Jun 71 III) *Abbr.* HC.

**HUBBARD ELECTROMETER,** is called an **E-meter** for short. Technically it is a specially developed Wheatstone bridge well known to electrically minded people as a device to measure the amount of resistance to a flow of electricity. (*BIEM,* p. 1) See E-METER.

**HUBBARD GUIDANCE CENTER,** that department of the technical division of a Scientology Church which delivers auditing. Department 12, Division 4. (BTB 12 Apr 72R) *Abbr.* HGC.

**HUBBARD NEW ERA DIANETICS AUDITOR** (provisional), has successfully completed the **New Era Dn** Course and has the skill and knowledge to make a truly well and happy human being. (WIS, p. 32) *Abbr.* HNEDA.

**HUBBARD NEW ERA DIANETICS AUDITOR** (validated), has successfully completed the **New Era Dn** Course and Internship and is a flubless **New Era Dn Auditor.** (WIS, p. 34) *Abbr.* HNEDA.

**HUBBARD NEW ERA DIANETICS GRADUATE** (provisional), has successfully completed the **New Era Dn Graduate** (C/S) Course and has the ability to case supervise **New Era Dn**. (WIS, p. 34) *Abbr.* HNEDG.

**HUBBARD NEW ERA DIANETICS GRADUATE** (validated), has successfully completed the **New Era Dn Graduate** (C/S) Course and Internship and is a flubless **New Era Dn** Case Supervisor. (WIS, p. 34) *Abbr.* HNEDG.

**HUBBARD STANDARD DIANETICS COURSE,** teaches about the human mind, mental image pictures, the time track, locks, secondaries and engrams. The processes taught are Standard Dn auditing and Dn assists. (CG&AC 75) *Abbr.* HSDC.

**HUMAN ENGINEERING,** it's adapting the machinery to fit the person. It's adapting machinery and spatial arrangements and desks and chairs and things like that. The adjustment of the machinery and spatial arrangements to the people who are operating it is important. (ESTO No. 12, 7203C06 SO II)

**HUMAN EVALUATION,** a diagnosis of behavior. (5108CM13A)

**HUMANITARIAN OBJECTIVE,** the **humanitarian objective** is to make a safe environment in which the fourth dynamic engram can be audited out. By engram we mean the mental block that prevents peace and tolerance; by fourth dynamic we mean that impulse to survive as mankind instead of just individuals. Obviously we must do this. (Ron's Jour 68)

**HUMAN MIND,** see MIND.

**HUMOR, humor** is rejection. The ability to reject. The ability to throw something away. That is **humor.** (8ACC-27, 5411CM05)

**HURDY-GURDY SYSTEM,** a "hurdy-gurdy" was a musical instrument played by turning a crank so that a wheel striking strings in turn caused music. The **"hurdy-gurdy" system** was so called because the auditor went round and round the points of the ARC triangle (A-R-C) plus enforced and dominate, inhibit and nullify on persons the pc had known, session after session to restore his memory. Mentioned on page 65, Book 2, *Science of Survival* and described in full later in that same chapter on pages 77-83. (LRH Def. Notes)

**HVA, 1. Hubbard Validated Auditor.** A Class V auditor. This level is taught at Church of Scientology Saint Hill organizations and contains materials about the chronological development of Scn with full theory and application. (CG&AC 75) **2.** Class V reviews all the classes and retrains where necessary and awards permanent classification for all the lower certificates as well as Class V. (*Aud 8 UK*)

**HYPER-SONIC,** if a person hears voices which have not existed and yet supposes that these voices really spoke, we have "over-imagination." In Dn imaginary sound recall would be **hyper-sonic, (hyper**=over). (*DMSMH*, p. 188)

**HYPER-VISIO,** if a person sees scenes which have not existed and yet supposes these scenes were real, we have "over imagination." In Dn imaginary sight recall would be **hyper-visio, (hyper**=over). (*DMSMH*, p. 188)

**HYPNOTISM, 1.** an address to the reactive mind. It reduces self-determinism by interposing the commands of another below the analytical level of an individual's mind; it enturbulates a case markedly, and materially aberrates human beings by keying in engrams which would otherwise lie dormant. (*SOS,* Bk. 2, p. 220) **2.** a continuing inflow without an opportunity on the part of the subject to outflow. (*Dn 55!*, p. 63) **3.** the process of restimulating states of apathy by the introduction of additional engramic content which would thereafter be as compulsive as the other data in the incident. (5109CM17B) **4.** amnesia trance for the purpose of planting suggestions. (*Exp Jour Winter-Spring 1950*)

**HYPO-HEARING,** a condition in which a person has something he is afraid to **hear.** He plays the radio very loudly, makes people repeat continually and misses pieces of the conversation. Men and women are "hysterically" deaf without any conscious knowledge of it. Their **"hearing** just isn't so good." In Dn, this is being called **hypo-hearing, (hypo**=under). (*DMSMH*, p. 189)

**HYPO-SIGHT,** the person who is always losing something when it lies in fair view before him, who misses signposts, theater bills and people who are in plain sight is "hysterically" blind to some degree. He is afraid he will see something. In Dn this is being called, since the word "hysterical" is a very inadequate and overly dramatic one, **hypo-sight, (hypo**=under). (*DMSMH*, p. 189)

**HYSTERIA,** the phenomenon of being out of control. (*AAR*, p. 91)

# I

**"I", 1.** the will, the determining force of the organism, the awareness. (*DMSMH*, p. 87) **2.** the awareness of awareness unit. (*NOTL*, p. 69) **3.** the thetan, the center of awareness, that part of the total organism that is fundamentally cause. (*COHA* Gloss)

**IATROGENIC,** means illness generated by doctors. An operation during which the doctor's knife slipped, and accidentally harmed the patient might cause an **iatrogenic** illness or injury since the fault would have been with the surgeons. (*DMSMH*, p. 172)

**ICDS, International Congress of Dianeticists and Scientologists.** (HCOB 29 Sept 66)

**IDEAL STATE,** what do we mean by an **ideal state.** A **state** somebody wanted to be in over which he had full power of choice. That would be an **ideal state.** (SH Spec 273, 6306C12)

**IDENTIFICATION, 1.** the inability to evaluate differences in time, location, form, composition, or importance. ( *SOS*, p. 153) **2. identification** is a monotone assignment of importance. (*SOS*, p. 153) **3.** the lowest level of reasoning is complete inability to differentiate, which is to say, **identification.** (*SOS*, p.153) **4.** Duplicating in one space continually, is in itself **identification.** (2ACC-25B, 5312CM17)

**IDENTITY RUNDOWN,** we have never before had a Dn process specifically directed to getting a pc into valence. The **Identity Rundown** now handles that. It specifically takes up and handles valences the pc may be in by using the New Era Dn tech. (HCOB 22 Jun 78R)

**ILL,** being medically diagnosed as suffering from a known, well defined physical **illness** susceptible to medical care and relief. (HCO PL 6 Oct 58)

**ILLUSION, 1.** a surface manifestation which disappears when experience is consulted. (SH Spec 70, 6607C21) **2.** a product of the actual. (SH Spec 70, 6607C21) **3.** any idea, space, energy, object or time concept which one creates himself. (*Scn 8-8008* Gloss)

**IMAGINARY CAUSE, imagining** they do or **cause** things bad or good. (HCOB 1 Nov 68 II)

**IMAGINARY VISIO,** the scenery **imagination** constructs. (*SOS,* p. 72) See DUB-IN.

**IMAGINATION, 1.** the recombination of things one has sensed, thought or intellectually computed into existence, which do not necessarily have existence. This is the mind's method of envisioning desirable goals or forecasting futures. (*DMSMH,* p. 14) **2.** the ability to create or forecast a future or to create, change or destroy a present or past. (*Scn 8-8008,* p. 7) **3.** if you take the word **imagination** apart, you will discover that it means merely the postulating of images or the assembly of perceptions into creations as you desire them. (*SA,* p. 158)

**IMMORTALITY,** infinite survival, the absolute goal of survival. The individual seeks this on the first dynamic as an organism and as a theta entity and in the perpetuation of his name by his group. On the second dynamic he seeks it through children and so on through the eight dynamics. Life survives through the persistence of theta. A species survives through the persistence of the life in it. A culture survives through the persistence of the species using it. There is evidence that the theta of an individual may survive as a personal entity from life to life through many lives on earth. (*SOS* Gloss)

**IMPACT,** cause and effect simultaneously. (PAB 30)

**IMPLANT, 1.** a painful and forceful means of overwhelming a being with artificial purpose or false concepts in a malicious attempt to control and suppress him. (*Aud 71 ASHO*) **2.** an electronic means of overwhelming the thetan with a significance. (HCOB 8 May 63) **3.** an unwilling and unknowing receipt of a thought. An intentional installation of fixed ideas, contra-survival to the thetan. (SH Spec 83, 6612C06)

**IMPLANT GOAL,** an **implanted goal**—a **goal** the thetan himself has not decided upon—but which has been induced in him by overwhelming force or persuasion. (HCOB 13 Apr 64, *Scn VI Part One Glossary of Terms*)

**IMPLANT GPM,** an **implanted goal problem mass.** An electronic means of overwhelming the thetan with a signficance using the mechanics of the actual pattern of living to entrap the thetan and force obedience to behavior patterns. (HCOB 13 Apr 64, *Scn VI Part One Glossary of Terms*)

**IMPLOSION,** something that could be likened to the collapse of a field of energy such as a sphere toward a common center point, making an inflow. It can happen with the same violence as an explosion; but does not necessarily do so. (*Scn 8-8008*, p. 49)

**IMPORTANCE,** is mass. In thinkingness when you say **importance** you mean mass. (SH Spec 39, 6108C15)

**IN,** things which should be there and are or should be done and are, are said to be **"in"**; i.e. "We got scheduling **in.**" (HCOB 19 Jun 71 III)

**INACCESSIBLE CASE,** that person who is bound and deter-mined to stay sick, who won't talk to you, will have nothing to do with being healed in any way, is an **inaccessible case.** (5011C22)

**INADVERTENT WITHHOLD, 1.** the pc thinks he is **withholding** because the auditor didn't hear or acknowledge. (HCOB 13 Sept 65) **2.** he didn't intend to **withhold** it, just nobody would acknowledge it. He never intended to **withhold** it at all. An **inadvertent withhold** will cause very near the same phenomenon as an actual withhold. (SH Spec 60, 6506C11)

**INCIDENT,** an experience, simple or complex, related by the same subject, location, perception or people that takes place in a short and finite time period such as minutes, hours or days; also, mental image pictures of such experiences. (HCOB 12 Dec 71 IX)

**INCREDIBLE CHAIN,** it's the things that have happened on his track which are, to him, **incredible.** And because they are so **incredible** he doesn't believe them, and neither does anybody else. But it's most because nobody else believed them. And he doesn't believe them himself so the **chain** itself remains hidden because it's **incredible; the incredible chain.** (ESTO 5, 7203C03 SO I)

**IND,** *"Ind"* for **indicated** to pc. (HCOB 26 Jun 71)

**INDICATOR,** a condition or circumstance arising in a session which indicates whether the session is running well or badly. (HCOB 28 Dec 63) **2.** the little flag sticking out that shows there is a possible situation underneath that needs attention. (HCO PL 15 May 70 II)

**INDICATORS,** those manifestations in a person or group that **indicate** whether it is doing well or poorly, signal an approaching change, or show that the auditing process has reached the desired end point. (HCOB 20 Feb 70)

**IN-DISPERSAL,** where the flows are all travelling toward a common center. One might call this an implosion. (*Scn 8-8008,* pp. 17-18)

**INDIVIDUAL, 1.** an **individual** is a collection of "memories" going back to his first appearance on earth. In other words, he is the composite of all his facsimiles plus his impulse to be. **Individual-ity** depends upon facsimiles. (*HFP*, p. 111) **2.** somebody who is operating in coordination with himself twenty-four hours a day. That's an **individual.** An organism which is unhappy, aberrated, is an organism which is working at cross purposes with itself twenty-four hours a day. (5110CM11B) **3.** when we say the **individual** we are talking about something as precise as an apple. We are not talking about a collection of behavior patterns which we all learned about in the study of rats. We are talking about something that is finite. We are talking about somebody. The somethingness that you are and the capabilities you can be and this is what we are talking about. We are not talking about the color of your hair or the length of your feet. We are talking about you. (*Abil Mi 5*)

**INDIVIDUATION,** a separation from knowingness. (5203CM10B)

**INDOC, indoctrination.** (HCOB 10 Apr 57)

**INERT INCIDENT, 1.** an **incident** which is an **inert incident** is not having any effect on the pc. It's not part of his aberrative picture. (SH Spec 300, 6308C28) **2.** an **incident**, unrestimulated. (SH Spec 300, 6308C28)

**IN ETHICS,** see ETHICS, Def. 5.

**INFINITY SYMBOL,** ∞. As seen in some Scientology books, stood upright —8. (HCOB 23 Aug 65)

Infinity Symbol

**INFINITY-VALUED LOGIC,** in Dn, there is a new way of thinking about things which underlies a great deal of its technology. Instead of two-valued logic or three-valued logic we have **infinity-valued logic.** Here is a gradient scale which permits no absolute at either end. In other words, there is not an absolute right and an absolute wrong, just as there is no absolute stillness and no absolute motion. Of course, it is one of the tenets of Dn that absolutes are not attainable but only approachable. (*SOS*, Bk. 2, pp. 249-250) See also LOGIC.

**INJURY RUNDOWN,** on an **injury,** after the Contact Assist, a Touch Assist and then an LIC on the **injured** member could be done. Dn actions would follow as necessary. This would include handling the **injury** fully as a narrative item and then fully handling all somatics connected with it, per New Era Dn Series tech. (HCOB 23 Jul 71R)

**INSANE, 1.** the truly **insane** cannot control or withhold their evil impulses and dramatize them at least covertly. The **insane** are not always visible. But they are visible enough. And they *are* malicious. (HCOB 10 May 72) **2.** having been pronounced **insane** by a psychiatrist or being incapable of any responsibility for social conduct. (HCO PL 6 Oct 58)

**INSANE CERTAINTY,** would be no **certainty** at all, or a **certainty** asserted by only one or two people and disagreed with by all others. (*Cert*, Vol. 10, No. 12)

**INSANE PC,** by **insane pc** is meant one who is subject to highly irrational and destructive behavior. (HCO PL 12 Jun 69)

**INSANITY, 1.** the overt or covert but always complex and continuous determination to harm or destroy. (HCOB 28 Nov 70) **2.** "**insanity**" is most often the suppressed agony of actual physical illness and injury. (HCOB 2 Apr 69) **3.** the obsessive adaptation of a solution to the exclusion of all other solutions in the absence of a problem. (SH Spec 27X, 6107C04) **4.** the inability to associate or differentiate properly. (*Scn 8-8008*, p. 44) **5. insanity** is an emotion which is brought about by the compulsion to reach and the inhibition not to reach or the compulsion not to reach and the inhibition to reach. (2ACC-18A, 5312CM08) **6.** the best definition of which I know would be: the person widely believes that the symbols are the things. (PDC 20) **7. insanity** is an individual assisting things which inhibit survival and destroying things which assist survival. (5109CM24A) **8.** if an individual is incapable of adjusting himself to his environment so as to get along with or obey or command his fellows, or, more importantly, if he is incapable of adjusting his environment, then he can be considered to be "**insane.**" But it is a relative term. (*DMSMH*, p. 380) **9.** the point between where a person who is sane goes thereafter **insane** is very precise. It's the exact point at which he begins to stop something. At that moment he is **insane.** At first he is **insane** on that one subject; then he can get another *idée fixe* and become **insane** on another subject, thus getting cumulative **insanity.** But there is no doubt of his **insanity** on that one subject, something that he is trying to stop. (6711C18SO) **10. insanity** itself is simply must reach—can't reach, must withdraw—can't withdraw. (SH Spec 98, 6201C10)

**IN-SCANNING,** taking energy manifestations that were in the incident as they flowed in toward the preclear. That's **in-scanning.** That's environment to the preclear in the incident. (5203CM04B)

**IN SESSION,** the definition of **in session** is interested in own case and willing to talk to the auditor. When this definition describes the session in progress, then of course the pc will be able to as-is and will cognite. (HCOB 26 Apr 73 I)

**INSTANT F/N, 1.** an **instant F/N** is an **F/N** which occurs **instantly** at the end of the major thought voiced by the auditor or at the end of the major thought voiced by the pc (when he originates items or tells what the command means). (HCOB 20 Sept 78) **2.** an **instant F/N** is a read. (HCOB 20 Sept 78) **3.** an **instant F/N** on an item means charge has just keyed out on that item, and that it can key back in again. (HCOB 20 Sept 78) **4.** in Dn an **instant**

**F/N** takes precedence over all other reads. This is because, the pc, having just keyed out the charge on that item, will find it most real. It will be the most runnable item. An **instantly F/Ning** item is taken up first. (HCOB 20 Sept 78)

**INSTANT READ, 1.** the correct definition of **instant read** is that reaction of the needle which occurs at the precise end of any major thought voiced by the auditor. All definitions which state it is fractions of seconds after the question is asked, are cancelled. Thus an **instant read** which occurs when the auditor assesses an item or calls a question is valid and would be taken up and latent reads, which occur fractions of seconds after the major thought, are ignored. Additionally, when looking for **reads** while clearing commands or when the preclear is originating items, the auditor must note only those **reads** which occur at the exact moment the pc ends his statement of the item or command. (HCOB 5 Aug 78)

**INSTANT ROCK SLAM,** that **"rock slam"** which begins at the end of the major thought of any item. *Symbol* IRS. (HCOB 8 Nov 62)

**INSTANT RUDIMENT READ,** on **rudiments,** repetitive or fast, the **instant read** can occur anywhere within the last word of the question or when the thought major has been anticipated by the preclear, and must be taken up by the auditor. This is not a prior read. Preclears poorly in session, being handled by auditors with indifferent TR-1, anticipate the **instant read** reactively as they are under their own control. Such a **read** occurs in the body of the last meaningful word in the question. It never occurs latent. (*EMD*, p. 37)

**INST CONF, Instructors' Conference.** (HCOB 29 Sept 66)

**INSTITUTIONALIZED,** having been committed to a public or private **institution** for the insane. (HCO PL 6 Oct 58)

**IN TECH,** when **tech** is **in,** we mean that Scn is being applied and is being correctly applied. (HCOB 13 Sept 65)

**INTEG, Integrity.** (BPL 5 Nov 72RA)

**INTEGRITY, (1.)** the condition of having no part or element taken away or wanting; undivided or unbroken state; wholeness. **(2.)** the condition of not being marred or violated; unimpaired or uncorrupted condition; soundness. **(3.)** soundness or moral principle; the character of uncorrupted virtue, especially in relation to truth and fair dealing; uprightness, honesty, sincerity. (BTB 4 Dec 72)

**INTEGRITY PROCESSING,** in an effort to get around what was thought to be a public relations scene, the name "security checking" was changed to **"Integrity Processing."** This was also a PR error because the actual truth of the matter is it originated as "confessional" and should have simply been changed back to "handling of confessions." This administrative demand of name alteration threw the original issues on "sec checking" into disuse. Additionally **"Integrity Processing"** did not include all the tech of sec checking. There should be no further confusion in this matter. "Sec checking," **"Integrity Processing"** and "confessionals" are all the exact same procedure and any materials on these subjects is interchangeable under these titles. (HCOB 24 Jan 77) *Abbr.* IP.

**INTELLIGENCE, 1.** is the ability to recognize differences, similarities and identities. (HCO PL 26 Apr 70R) **2.** the ability to perceive, pose and resolve problems. (*Scn 0-8*, p. 64) **3.** the ability of an individual, group or race to resolve problems relating to survival. (*Scn 0-8*, p. 61)

**INTELLIGENCE GAIN,** loss of restimulation by stupidity by reason of attempts to confront or experience the problems of life (**intelligence** appears when stupidity is keyed out or erased). **Intelligence** is a confronting ability. (HCOB 28 Feb 59)

**INTENSIVE,** an **intensive** is defined as any one single period of 12 1/2 hours or 25 hours of auditing delivered all within one single week or weekends on a set schedule. (HCO PL 20 Oct 71)

**INTENSIVE PROCEDURE,** the Standard Operating Procedure, 1954, given in *The Creation of Human Ability*, by L. Ron Hubbard. (*PXL*, p. 277)

**INTENTION, 1.** an **intention** is something that one wishes to do. He **intends** to do it; it's an impulse toward something; it's an idea that one is going to accomplish something. It's **intentional**, which means he *meant* to do it, he *means* to do it. (SH Spec 83, 6612C06) **2. intention** is the command factor as much as anything else. If you **intend** something to happen it happens if you **intend** it to happen. Verbalization is not the **intention**. The **intention** is the carrier wave which takes the verbalization along with it. (*Abil 270*) **3.** degree of relative beingness which an individual desires to assume as plotted on the tone scale. (5203CM04A)

**INTENTIONAL WITHHOLD,** one which is a **withhold** because he would be punished if he admitted it. (SH Spec 63, 6110C05)

**INTEREST, 1. interest** is more consideration than attention, and is therefore attention with intention. **Interest,** therefore, could be defined as this; attention with an intention to give or attract attention. (*COHA*, p. 103) **2. interest** does not mean happiness and joy. **Interest** is only absorbed attention and a desire to talk about it. (HCOB 1 Jul 63)

**INTERESTED/INTERESTING, 1.** a thetan is **interested,** and an object is **interesting.** A thetan is not **interesting.** He is **interested.** And when a person becomes terribly **interesting** he has lots of problems. That is the chasm that is crossed by all of your celebrities, anybody who is foolish enough to become famous. He crosses over from being **interested** in life to being **interesting,** and people who are **interesting** are really no longer **interested** in life. (*PXL*, p. 191) **2.** "A" has the intention of **interesting** "b." "B" to be talked to, becomes **interesting.** Similarly "b," when he emanates a communication, is **interested** and "a" is **interesting.** Cause is **interested,** effect is **interesting.** (*Dn 55!*, p. 66)

**INTERIORIZATION, 1.** the state or condition of being **interiorized.** "To go in" = the act of the *verb* **interiorizing.** "Went in" (past tense of the verb "to go in") = the past tense of the act of **interiorizing.** What you will be auditing [in the Interiorization Rundown] is times the "pc went in" or others were caused "to go in"—and not "was in" or "was stuck in" or "sat in," but the actual times when the action of *going in* occurred. (HCOB 4 Jan 71) **2. interiorization** means going into it too fixedly, and becoming part of it too fixedly. It doesn't mean just going into your head. (SH Spec 84, 6612C13) **3.** if the havingness of the preclear is low, he is apt to close in tight to the body because this gives him more havingness and if the preclear fears that the body is going to go out of control he will also move in closer to the body. Thus we get **interiorization** as no more complicated than fear of loss of control and drops in havingness. (*SCP*, p. 18) *Abbr.* Int.

Interested—Interesting (Def. 1)

# INTERIORIZATION RUNDOWN

**INTERIORIZATION RUNDOWN, 1.** also known as **Int-Ext RD** for **Interiorization-Exteriorization Rundown.** (HCOB 24 Sept 71R) **2.** the **Interiorization Rundown** is a remedy designed to permit the pc to be further audited after he has gone exterior. The **Int Rundown** is not meant to be sold or passed off as a method of exteriorizing a pc. (HCOB 17 Dec 71RB) See EXTERIORIZATION RUNDOWN.

**INTERN(E),** an advanced graduate or a recent graduate in a professional field who is getting practical experience under the supervision of an experienced worker. (HCOB 19 Jul 71)

**INTERN(E)SHIP,** serving a period as an **intern,** or an activity offered by a Church of Scientology by which experience can be gained. The apprenticeship of an auditor is done as a Scientology Church **intern.** A course graduate becomes an auditor by auditing. That means lots of auditing. (HCOB 19 Jul 71)

**INTERROGATION, (SILENT),** how to read an E-meter on a **silent subject.** When the person placed on a meter will not talk but can be made to hold the cans, it is still possible to obtain full information from the person asking questions, one expects no reply, asks for no pictures. The auditor just watches the needle for dips when questions are asked. (HCOB 30 Mar 60)

**INT-EXT, interiorization-exteriorization.** (HCOB 30 May 70)

**INT-EXT RD, Interiorization-Exteriorization Rundown.** (HCOB 24 Sept 71)

**IN THE WHITE,** *Slang.* on an OCA, the center line of 00 is the critical point of the graph. A little bit into the lower gray-shaded area is not too bad. But when they go down **into the white,** like a minus 62 or a minus 76 or even a minus 26, they're said to be **"in the white."** (7203C30SO)

**INT RD, Interiorization Rundown** also known as **Int-Ext RD** for **Interiorization-Exteriorization Rundown.** (HCOB 24 Sept 71)

**INTRODUCTION OF AN ARBITRARY,** an **arbitrary** may be considered as a factor **introduced** into a problem's solution when that factor does not derive from a known natural law but only from an opinion or authoritarian command. A problem resolved by data derived from known natural laws resolves well and smoothly and has a useful solution. When a problem is resolved by **introducing arbitraries** (factors based on opinion or command but not natural law) then that solution, when used, will ordinarily require more **arbitraries** to make the solution applicable. The harder one tries to apply the solution corrupted by **arbitraries** to any situation, the more **arbitraries** have to be **introduced.** (*SOS* Gloss)

**INTROSPECTION RUNDOWN,** the essence of the **Introspection Rundown** is looking for and correcting all those things which caused the person to look inward, worriedly and wrestle with the mystery of some incorrectly designated error. The end phenomena is the person extroverted, no longer looking inward worriedly in a continuous self-audit without end. (HCOB 23 Jan 74RA)

**INTROVERSION, 1.** looking in too closely. (*POW*, p. 92) **2.** a manifestation of the analytical mind trying to solve problems on improper data, and observing the organism being engaged in activities which are not conducive to survival along the dynamics. (*DTOT*, p. 105)

Introversion

**INTROVERTED,** he would look in on himself. (SH Spec 84, 6612C13)

**INT RUNDOWN CORRECTION LIST,** used when **Int-Ext** reads on any repair list and the **Int RD** has already been done or corrected, when a bog occurs on the **Int RD** itself, or if pc upset after **Int RD** and/or TA gone high or low immediately after. Don't re-run **Int RD**—use the **correction list.** EP is all reading items handled to F/N, EP of **Int RD**, and **INT-Ext** no longer reading. (BTB 11 Aug 72RA)

# INVADER FORCES

**INVADER FORCES, 1.** an electronics people. The electronics people usually happen to be an evolutionary line which is on heavy gravity planets and so they develop electronics. The reason you say **invader force** at all is because at some time along the line fairly early in its youth it took off to conquer the whole mest universe. You could expect almost anything in terms of physical form particularly physical form which matched the peculiar purpose of this group. They've usually got some gimmick like Fac One. Control has been the main thing. The way to control territory is control people. (5206CM27A) **2.** there are five **invader forces** active and one aborning, but the one aborning is not active. It will probably be several million years before you begin to see this one, some of you hit the track 60 trillion years ago mest universe and some of you didn't get into the mest universe until about 3 trillion years ago that is **invader force one** and **invader force two.** This is E-meter data confirmed from preclear to preclear. Now we don't see anything of **invader force three** here on earth. I just haven't found any threes. **Invader force four** is really holding the fort someplace or other. Every little while, a few million years, some planet will get taken over by an **invader force.** (5206CM27A) See also FIFTH INVADER FORCE.

**IN VALENCE,** what we mean by **"in valence"** is simply **in the valence** he was in when the engram occurred. Now when we say out of valence we mean simply and entirely the pc was not in the body he was occupying during the incident. (SH Spec 51, 6109C07)

**INVALIDATION, 1.** refuting or degrading or discrediting or denying something someone else considers to be fact. (HCOB 2 Jun 71 I) **2.** any thought, emotion or effort, or counter-thought, counter-emotion or counter-effort which denies or smothers the thought, emotion or effort of the individual. (*HOM*, p. 56) **3. invalidation** by words is the symbolic level of being struck. (2ACC-19B, 5312CM09) **4.** basically, non-attention. Attention itself is quite important for attention is necessary before an effect can be created. (PAB 8) **5. invalidation** is force applied. You apply enough force to anybody and you've **invalidated** him. How **invalidated** can he get? Dead! (5207CM24B) *Abbr.* Inval.

**INVALIDATION OF AUDITORS,** could be defined as (a) letting an auditor lose, (b) correcting things he does right. (HCOB 1 Sept 71 I)

**INVENTION PROCESSING,** this is done by having the preclear **invent** various ideas or considerations by which he creates stable data to displace aberrated stable data, and to handle confusions. (Op. Bull. No. 1)

**INVERSION, 1.** a switch to an opposite obsessive consideration such as from compulsion to inhibition. There may be many **inversions** on any consideration, each leading further from self-determinism. (*COHA* Gloss) **2.** his resistance has been overcome so that when it tries to outflow, it inflows. That's an **inversion** and that's what's meant by **inversion.** A person tries to outflow, he inflows—in other words, he exactly reverses his consideration on the thing. (8ACC-8, 5410CM12) **3.** the flows have exactly turned around and that's what we know as an **inversion** and that's exactly why we call it an **inversion;** because it's a flow going backwards. (SH Spec 6, 6106C02)

**INVERTED DYNAMICS,** we can take a person and actually have him be someplace else when he is right there. See, he'll still keep this body but he'll actually be and operate someplace else and you'll run into this every once in a while in a preclear. We call this **inverted dynamics.** (2ACC-1B, 5311CM17)

**INVISIBLE CASE,** cannot see mock-ups. They have no field and do not see anything when they close their eyes, everything is **invisible,** they have no facsimiles, no mock-ups. (PAB 154)

**INVISIBLE FIELD,** a part of some lock, secondary or engram that is **"invisible."** It like a black field responds to R3R. (HCOB 23 Apr 69)

**IP,** see INTEGRITY PROCESSING.

**IQ, 1. intelligence quotient. IQ** ratings are a measure of an individual's capacity for learning something new; they are scales based upon how old in years a person has become compared to how "old," he is mentally. (*SOS*, p. xxi) **2.** the degree that a person can observe, understand actions. (SH Spec 100, 6201C16)

**IRRATIONALITY,** the inability to get right answers from data. (*DMSMH*, p. 16)

**IRS, instant rock slam.** (HCOB 8 Nov 62)

**IS-ES, THE,** *Slang.* the four conditions of existence. (*PXL*, p. 214) [These four conditions are listed separately under AS-ISNESS, ALTER-ISNESS, IS-NESS, NOT-ISNESS.]

---

**IS-NESS, 1. is-ness** is an apparency of existence brought about by the continuous alteration of an as-isness. This is called, when agreed upon, reality. (*PXL*, p. 154) **2.** something that is persisting on a continuum. That is our basic definition of **is-ness**. (*PXL*, p. 91) **3.** the anatomy of reality is contained in **is-ness**, which is composed of as-is-ness and alter-is-ness. **Is-ness** is an apparency, it is not an actuality. The actuality is as-is-ness altered so as to obtain a persistency. (*PXL*, p. 175)

**"ISSUE I"**, first **issue** of that date. ["issue" as seen on HCOBs and HCO PLs.] (HCOB 4 Sept 71 III)

**ITEM, 1.** any one of a list of things, people, ideas, significances, purposes, etc., given by a preclear to an auditor while listing; any separate thing or article; in particular, one placed on a list by a pc. (*Dn Today*, p. 1028) **2.** somatic or sensation etc. (HCOB 27 May 70) **3.** any terminal, opposition terminal, combination terminal, significance, or idea (but not a doingness, which is called "a level") appearing on a list derived from the pc. (HCOB 8 Nov 62) *Symbol* IT.

**ITSA, 1.** the action of the pc saying **"It's a** this or **it's a** that." (HCOB 6 Nov 64) **2.** letting the pc say what's there that was put there to hold back a confusion or problem. (HCOB 1 Oct 63) **3.** pc saying what *is*, what is there, who is there, where it is, what it looks like, ideas about, decisions about, solutions to, things in his environment. The pc talking continuously about problems or puzzlements or wondering about things in his environment, is *not* **itsaing**. (HCOB 16 Oct 63) **4.** a pc who is **itsaing** is simply looking at and identifying some thing. (SH Spec 320, 6310C31) **5.** TA comes from saying **"It is . . ."** **Itsa** isn't even a comm line. It's what travels on a comm line from pc to auditor, if that which travels is saying with certainty **"It is."** (HCOB 1 Oct 63)

**ITSA LINE,** the pc's **line** to the auditor. (HCOB 23 May 71 III)

**ITSA MAKER LINE,** the pc's **line** to his bank. (HCOB 23 May 71 III)

**IVORY TOWER RULE,** the case supervisor is most successful when he supervises in seclusion. This is called the **Ivory Tower rule.** (HCOB 8 Aug 71)

# J

**JAMMING THE TRACK,** *Slang.* sticking, holding the **time track.** (PAB 106)

**JEALOUSY,** is basically an inability to confront the unknown. (SH Spec 43, 6108C22)

**JIGGLE-JIGGLE,** needle manifestation. A vibration. You've got somebody with an alternating current ridge. (SH Spec 1, 6105C07)

**JOBURG,** a comprehensive security checklist developed in **Johannesburg,** South Africa. (*Abil 218*)

**JOINT POSITION,** the recall of bodily attitudes. (*SOS* Gloss)

**JUDICIARY DIANETICS,** covers the field of **adjudication** within the society and amongst the societies of man. Of necessity it embraces **jurisprudence** and its codes and establishes precision definitions and equations for the establishment of equity. It is the science of **judgment.** (*DMSMH*, p. 402)

**JUMP CHAINS,** the main liability (in Dn auditing) of pushing a pc past a win is that he may **"jump chains"** and begin another **chain** with no assessment. (HCOB 23 Jun 69)

219

# JUNIOR CASE

**JUNIOR CASE,** if father was named George and the patient is called George, beware of trouble. The engram bank takes George to mean George and that is identity thought de luxe. A **junior case** is seldom easy. (*DMSMH*, p. 305)

**JUSTICE, 1.** the action of the group against the individual when he has failed to get his own ethics in. (HCOB 15 Nov 72 II) **2.** could be called the adjudication of the relative rightness or wrongness of a decision or an action. (*AP&A*, p. 10)

**JUSTIFICATION,** explaining away the most flagrant wrongnesses. Most explanations of conduct, no matter how far fetched, seem perfectly right to the person making them since he or she is only asserting self-rightness and other-wrongness. (HCOB 22 Jul 63)

**JUSTIFIED THOUGHT,** the attempt of the analytical mind to explain the reactive, engramic, reactions of the organism in the ordinary course of living. **Justified thought** is the effort of the conscious mind to explain away aberration without admitting, as it cannot do normally, that it has failed the organism. (*DTOT*, p. 42)

**JUSTIFIER, 1.** the technical term we apply to the "mock-up" or overt act demanded by a person guilty of an unmotivated act. (*COHA*, p. 156) **2.** a mocked up motivator. (8ACC-16, 5410CM21)

**JUSTIFIER-HUNGRY,** an act must be considered harmful or evil to be an overt act. To need a **justifier** a person must have believed his act to have been harmful. In that a thetan cannot possibly, actually, be harmed, any harmful act he performs is an unmotivated act. As the thetan cannot experience a motivator-overt act sequence, we have the dwindling spiral. He is always **justifier hungry.** Thus he punishes and restimulates himself. Thus he is always complaining about what others do to him. Thus he is a problem to himself. (*COHA*, p. 156)

# K

**KEEPER OF TECH,** is the highest technically trained personnel in the field. He/she is usually located in a very specific area (Church), where they can be contacted and communicated with any time. The major duty of any **Keeper of Tech** is to ensure that the standard of Dn and Scn **technology,** processing and case supervision is applied and maintained as originated by LRH, as its 100 per cent rate, in the area they are **keeping tech** in. (FO 2354)

**KERFUFFLE,** *Slang.* an upset. (SH Spec 45, 6411C03)

**KEYED-OUT CLEAR, 1.** when you find what lock words have been tied into the GPMs in this or even an earlier lifetime and key them out (destimulate them) (untie them from the main mass) the GPMs sink back into proper alignment and cease being effective. This makes a **key-out Clear.** This condition is valuable because the GPMs are now confrontable one by one (not dozens by dozens) and Routine 6 can be run easily on the preclear. (HCOB 17 Oct 64 III) **2.** this is a simulated Clear, we call it a **"keyed-out Clear"** quite properly. But it *isn't* a Clear, it's a release. The person has been released from his reactive mind. He still has that reactive mind but he is not *in* it. He is just released from it. (HCOB 2 Apr 65) [The following is a quote from HCOB 24 September 1978, Issue III, *Dianetic Clear.* "I have now determined there is no such thing as Keyed-Out Clear. There is only Dianetic Clear and he is a Clear." Please read this HCOB for full data on this subject.]

**KEYED-OUT OT, 1.** released OT. (HCOB 30 Jun 65) **2.** the pc is still a *pre*-clear though a **keyed-out OT.** This really isn't a thetan exterior. The thetan exterior is quite unstable and can be attained below an ordinary first stage release. **Keyed-out OT** is not done by routine auditing, being an offshoot of it that happens sometimes. (HCOB 28 Jun 65)

**KEY-IN,** *v.* **1.** the action of recording a lock on a secondary or engram. (HCOB 23 Apr 69) —*n.* **1.** the first time an engram is restimulated is called a **key-in.** A **key-in** is merely a special kind of lock, the first lock on a particular engram. (*SOS*, Bk. 2, p. 29) **2.** a moment when the environment around the awake but fatigued or distressed individual is itself similar to the dormant engram. At that moment the engram becomes active. It is **keyed-in** and can thereafter be dramatized. (*SOS*, Bk. 2, p. 136)

**KEY-OUT,** *v.* **1.** an action of the engram or secondary dropping away without being erased. (HCOB 23 Apr 69) —*n.* **1.** the person without knowing what the earlier instance was has had the lock vanish. That's a **key-out.** (SH Spec 122, 6203C19) —*adj.*

Key Out (Def. 1)

**1.** released from the stimulus-response mechanisms of the reactive mind. (*PXL*, p. 18) **2.** release or separation from one's reactive mind or some portion of it. (*PXL*, p. 252)

**KINESTHESIA, 1.** by **kinesthesia** we perceive motion through space and time. (*SOS*, p. 59) **2.** weight and muscular motion. (*DMSMH*, p. 46)

**KINETIC,** something which has considerable motion. (*Scn 8-80*, p. 43)

**KINETIC MOTION,** something that's moving. Or a potentiality of **motion.** (PDC 18)

**KNOW BEST,** a technical and admin term. In tech it refers to an auditor who in misapplying a process on a pc considers he **knows** more than is actually contained in the technical bulletins on the subject and uses this **"know best"** as a basis for altering technical procedure. In admin it refers similarly to a person who considers he has a better way of accomplishing something than is contained in the policy letters covering that subject and messes things up. Management then finds itself left with the task of correcting that person's goofs by applying the correct standard policy to the area. In English, it is a derogatory term meaning the person is pretending to **know** while actually being stupid. (LRH Def. Notes)

**KNOWING CAUSE,** the person at **cause** is there because he **knows** he is there and because he is willingly there. The person at **cause** is not at **cause** because he does not dare be at effect. He must be able to be at effect. If he is afraid to be at effect, then he is unwilling cause and is at cause only because he is very afraid of being at effect. (*SCP*, p. 9)

**KNOWINGNESS, 1.** being certainness. (PAB 1) **2.** a capability for truth; it is not data. (PDC 47) **3. knowingness** would be self-determined **knowledge.** (5405C20)

**KNOWLEDGE, 1.** by **knowledge** we mean assured belief, that which is **known**, information, instruction; enlightenment, learning; practical skill. By **knowledge** we mean data, factors and whatever can be thought about or perceived. (*FOT*, p. 76) **2. knowledge** is more than data; it is also the ability to draw conclusions. (*DAB*, Vol. II, p. 69) **3.** a whole group or subdivision of a group of data or speculations or conclusions on data or methods of gaining data. (*Scn 0-8*, p. 67)

**KNOW-POINT,** a **know-point** is senior to a viewpoint. An individual would not have dependency on space or mass or anything else. He'd simply **know** where he was. (*PXL*, p. 257)

**KNOW-TO-MYSTERY SCALE,** the **scale** of affinity from **know-ingness** down through lookingness, emotingness, effortingness, thinkingness, symbolizingness, eatingness, sexingness and so through to **not-knowingness-mystery.** The **know-to-sex scale** was the earlier version of this **scale.** (*PXL*, p. 49)

**KOT, Keeper of Tech.** (FO 2354)

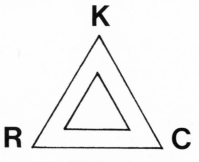

KRC Triangle

**KRC TRIANGLE,** the upper **triangle** in the Scn symbol. The points are **K** for **knowledge, R** for **responsibility,** and **C** for **control.** It is difficult to be **responsible** for something or **control** something unless you have **knowledge** of it. It is folly to try to **control** something or even **know** something without **responsibility.** It is hard to fully **know** something or be **responsible** for something over which you have no **control,** otherwise the result can be an overwhelm. Little by little one can make anything go right by: increasing **KNOWLEDGE** on all dynamics, increasing **RESPONSIBILITY** on all dynamics, increasing **CONTROL** on all dynamics. (HCO PL 18 Feb 72)

**KUCDEIOF, know, unknow, curious, desire, enforce, inhibit, none of it, false.** (SH Spec 296, 6308C20)

# L

**L,** all **lists** have been in HCOBs as **"L."** (HCOB 19 Aug 63) [In this dictionary, the Scn and Dn lists will be found under LIST.] See also CORRECTION LIST.

**LACC, London Advanced Clinical Course.** (HCOB 29 Sept 66)

**LAM, London Auditors' Meetings.** (HCOB 29 Sept 66)

**LAMBDA, 1.** Dianetic Axiom 11: A life organism is composed of matter and energy in space and time, animated by *theta. Symbol:* Living organism or organisms will hereafter be represented by the Greek letter **Lambda.** (*Dn Today,* p. 968) **2.** a chemical heat engine existing in space and time motivated by the life static and directed by thought. (*Dn Today,* p. 969)

**L & A, Logics and Axioms Lectures.** (HCOB 29 Sept 66)

**L & N, Listing and Nulling.** (HCOB 20 Apr 72 II)

**L&N LIST,** a list of items given by a pc in response to a listing question and written down by the auditor in the exact sequence that they are given to him by the preclear. An **L&N list** is always done on a separate sheet. (BTB 7 Nov 72 III)

# LANGUAGE

**LANGUAGE, 1.** the symbolization of effort. (*Scn 0-8*, p. 82) **2.** the communications of agreements and disagreements. (PDC 27) **3.** symbolized object or condition or state of being. (PDC 44)

**LANGUAGE LOCKS, locks** in which the main aberrative content is in terms of **language.** These may be considered symbolic restimulators of mest **locks,** which are more fundamental. (*SOS* Gloss)

**LARGE READS,** 1/3 of a dial or more at sensitivity 5. (HCOB 24 Jan 65)

**LARGE THETA BOP,** a quarter of a dial to a third of the dial. (*Cert*, Vol. 5, No. 9, 1958)

**LAST GPM,** closest to PT. (SH Spec 307, 6309C17)

**LATENT READ, 1.** a **read** which occurs later than completion of the major thought being expressed in words by the auditor. (HCOB 25 May 62) **2.** the correct definition of instant read is that reaction of the needle which occurs at the precise end of any major thought voiced by the auditor. All definitions which state it is fractions of seconds after the question is asked, are cancelled. Thus an instant read which occurs when the auditor assesses an item or calls a question is valid and would be taken up and **latent reads,** which occur fractions of seconds after the major thought, are ignored. (HCOB 5 Aug 78)

**LATER ON THE TRACK,** closer to PT. (HCOB 8 Apr 63)

**LAUDABLE WITHHOLD,** if it's **laudable** to have done it, then it's not **laudable** to **withhold** it. All right, if it's **laudable** to **withhold** it then it must be coupled with, "You shouldn't ought to have done it, it shouldn't be done." So one of the pair of the overt or the **withhold** is always **laudable** and always desirable. And the other one is undesirable. A **laudable withhold** is an undesirable action. (SH Spec 100, 6201C16)

**LAUGHTER, 1. laughter** plays a definite role in therapy. It is quite amusing to see a preclear, who has been haunted by an engram which contained great emotional charge, suddenly relieve it, for the situation, no matter how gruesome it was, when relieved, is in all its aspects a subject of great mirth. **Laughter** is definitely the relief of painful emotion. (*DMSMH*, p. 121) **2.** this **laughter** is the reversing of charge residual in the locks which depended for their fear content or antagonistic content upon the basic engrams. (*DTOT*, p. 99)

**LAW OF AFFINITY,** the **law of affinity** might be interpreted as the **law of cohesion;** "affinity" might be defined as "love" in both its meanings. Deprivation of or absence of affection could be considered as a violation of the **law of affinity.** Man must be in **affinity** with man to survive. (*DMSMH*, p. 106)

**LAWS,** the codified agreements of the people crystallizing their customs and representing their believed in necessities of conduct. (PAB 96)

**LCHP, London Congress** of **Human Problems.** (HCOB 29 Sept 66)

**LCNRH, London Congress** on **Nuclear Radiation** and **Health.** (HCOB 29 Sept 66)

**LD, long duration.** (HCOB 9 Aug 69)

**LEARNING DRILL, THE,** a **drill** used to improve the *ability* to study and increase the **learning** rate. (BTB 10 Dec 70R)

**LEAVE OF ABSENCE,** an authorized period of **absence** from a course granted in writing by a course supervisor and entered in the student's study folder. (HCOB 19 Jun 71 III)

**LECT, lecture.** (HCOB 29 Sept 66)

**LEFT-HAND BUTTON,** a suppressor-type **button.** The nearly-found-out is a **left-hand button** and does not necessarily read on the meter. Suppress, careful of, nearly found out, fail to reveal. They do not cause things to read, they prevent things from reading. All the other buttons cause things to read unnecessarily. Anxious about tends to be a **left-hand button.** Protest follows on a **left-hand button** so it tends to be the point where the **left** and right side tie together. (SH Spec 229, 6301C10)

**LEG OF A PROCESS,** in a **process** with more than one command, each command is called a **"leg."** (HCOB 21 Jul 63)

**L-11,** New Life Rundown. (CG&AC 75) See also L9S.

**L-11 EXPANDED,** New Life Expansion Rundown. (CG&AC 75)

**LETTING THE PC HAVE HIS WIN,** a session that tries to go beyond a big dial wide drifting floating F/N only distracts the pc from his **win. Big win.** Any **big win** (F/N dial wide, cog, VGIs) gives you this kind of persistent F/N. You at least have to let it go until tomorrow and **let the pc have his win.** That is what is meant by **letting the pc** *have* **his win.** When you get one of these dial wide F/Ns, cog, VGIs, Wow! you may as well pack it up for the day. (HCOB 8 Oct 70)

**LEVEL, 1.** grade and **level** are the same thing but when one has a grade one is a pc and when one has a **level** one is studying its data. (HCOB 2 Apr 65) **2.** a segment of technical information or performance for any application of Scn. (*Aud 72 UK*) **3. level** means "that body of Scn data for that point of progress of the individual." (*Aud 72 UK*) **4.** any doingness or not doingness on the pre-hav scale. Any word in the scale itself. (HCOB 7 Nov 62 III) *Abbr.* Lev.

**LEVEL 0,** see HRS.

**LEVEL I,** see HTS.

**LEVEL II,** see HCA.

**LEVEL III,** see HPA.

**LEVEL IV,** see HAA.

**LEVEL V,** see HVA.

**LEVEL (5), STATE OF CASE,** dub-in—some areas of track so heavily charged, pc is below consciousness in them. (HCOB 8 Jun 63) [For a complete list of the 8 levels of case of SOP 8-C, see STATE OF CASE SCALE.]

**LEVEL VI,** see HSS. [The SHSBC teaches to Level VI and results in a Class VI auditor. However Grade VI is a solo-audit grade and is not only done by a Class VI auditor but also by pcs who have attained Grade VA and have completed a special course which teaches them to solo audit.]

**LEVEL VII, Level VII** contains the materials necessary to totally erase the reactive mind. (SH Spec 71, 6607C26) [The Class VII *Course* is the course which teaches auditors to audit the power processes. Level VII or Clearing Course, as it is more often called, is done by pcs who have successfully solo audited to Grade VI Release, after which they may solo audit to Clear.]

**LEVEL OF AWARENESS,** by **level of awareness** is meant that of which a being is **aware.** There are about fifty-two **levels of awareness** from unexistence up to the state of Clear. A being who is at a **level** on this scale is aware only of that **level** and the others below it. (HCO PL 5 May 65)

**LF, long fall.** (HCOB 29 Apr 69)

**LFBD, long fall blowdown.** (HCOB 29 Apr 69)

**LGC, London Group Course.** (HCOB 29 Sept 66)

**LIE, 1.** a second postulate, statement or condition designed to mask a primary postulate which is permitted to remain. (*PXL,* p. 180) **2.** a statement that a particle having moved did not move, or a statement that a particle not having moved, did move. (*PXL,* p. 180) **3.** an alteration of time, place, event and form. (*PXL,* p. 187) **4.** invention with a bad connotation. (PAB 49)

**LIE FACTORY,** *Slang.* technically, a phrase contained in an engram demanding prevarication—it was originally called a fabricator. (*DMSMH,* p. 191)

**LIE REACTION,** questions originally used in Scientology only to study the needle pattern of the person being checked so that changes in it could then be judged in their true light. Some pcs for instance, get a slight fall every time *any* question is asked. Some get a fall only when there is heavy charge. Both can be security checked by studying the common pattern of the needle demonstrated in asking the **lie reaction** questions. (HCO PL 25 Mar 61)

**LIFE, 1.** (understanding), when we say **"life"** we mean understanding, and when we say "understanding" we mean affinity, reality and communication. To understand all would be to **live** at the highest level of potential action and ability. Because **life** is understanding it attempts to understand. When it faces the incomprehensible it feels balked and baffled. (*Dn 55!,* p. 36) **2.** a fundamental axiom of Dn is that **life** is formed by theta compounding with mest to make a living organism. **Life** is theta plus mest. (*SOS*, Bk. 2, p. 3) **3.** a static, which yet has the power of controlling, animating, mobilizing, organizing and destroying matter, energy and space, and possibly even time. (*HFP*, p. 24) **4.** a thought or mind or beingness that conceives there are forms, masses, spaces, and difficulties. (HPCA-64, 5608C--) **5.** that which is posing and solving problems. (UPC 11) **6. life** is a game consisting of freedom, barriers and purposes. (*Scn 0-8*, p. 119)

**LIFE AND LIVINGNESS ENVIRONMENT,** the workaday world of the pc. (HCOB 1 Oct 63)

**LIFE CONTINUUM, 1.** one individual attempting to carry on the **life** of another deceased individual or departed individual by means of generating in his own body the infirmities and mannerisms of the deceased or departed individual. (9ACC-24, 5501C14) **2.** it is the restimulation of an individual's desire to go on living when he's dying. (5112CM28B) **3.** it is simply this: somebody fails, departs or dies and the individual then takes on the burden of this person's habits, goals, fears, and idio-syncrasies. (5112CM28B)

**LIFE REPAIR PROGRAM,** handles **life** areas. (HCOB 15 Jun 70) [Note the referenced HCOB outlines the steps for this type of program.]

**LIFE RUDS,** as the person with out ruds makes no real gain it is wise to put **ruds** in **"in life."** This is done with, **"In life** have you had an ARC break?" **"In life** have you had a problem?" **"In life** have you had a withhold?" (HCOB 16 Aug 69)

**LIFE STATIC, 1.** a **life static** has no mass, no motion, no wave-length, no location in space or time. It has the ability to postulate and to perceive. (*PXL*, p. 146) **2.** the thought, soul, vital part of you which animates this mest, the body. (*HFP*, p. 75)

**LIFE UPSET INTENSIVE,** this is a five hour or so **intensive.** It is the ARC break routine mostly. (LRH ED 57 INT)

**LIGHT OBJECTIVE PROCESSES, light objective** (look outward, take attention off body) **processes.** (*Abil Mi 244*)

**LIGHT PROCESSING, 1. light processing** deals with postulates and effects and can be done either on an individual or co-auditing basis. (*DAB*, Vol. II, p. 173) **2.** includes analytical recall of conscious moments. It is intended to raise tone and increase perception and memory. (*SA*, p. 61)

**LIMITED PROCESS,** any process which makes the preclear create is a **limited process.** Such processes as "Tell a lie" are creative processes. (HCOB 11 Feb 60)

**LIMITED TECHNIQUE,** a **technique** which can be used only for a short time beneficially, and after a certain period of time will begin to cause deterioration. (2ACC 20B, 5312CM10)

**LINE CHARGE,** a prolonged spell of uncontrolled laughter or crying which may be continued for several hours. Once started a **line charge** can usually be reinforced by the occasional interjection of almost any word or phrase by the auditor. The **line charge** usually signals the sudden release of a large amount of charge and brings about a marked change in the case. (*COHA*, p. 281)

**LINE LISTING,** when a goal is found, you then have a number of **lines.** Called **lines.** And item by item you ask the question of these **lines.** You ask the question of the **lines** of the pc and he gives you the answer. And that is written down. And that is called **line listing.** And when you have finished all the **lines** completely there is a free needle on all of the **lines.** (SH Spec 195, 6309C27)

**LINE PLOT,** this consists of a heavy blue 13-inch (foolscap or legal) sheet of paper, kept in the pc's folder and kept up to date every time a reliable item (or even last item "in")is found. On this **line plot** one column, the left-hand one, is reserved for oppterms. The right-hand column is reserved for terms and **lines** indicate whenever terms or oppterms are derived from each other. A reliable item is designated as such on this **line plot** with the symbol R.I. Nonreliable items are not designated. The date each **line plot** item was found is added after the item so it can be found again in the auditor's reports without a scramble. (HCOB 8 Nov 62)

**LINES, BASIC FOUR,** (1) Who or what would want . . . ? (2) Who or what would not want . . . ? (3) Who or what would oppose . . . ? (4) Who or what would not oppose . . . ? (HCOB 7 Nov 62)

**LIST,** see CORRECTION LIST and L & N LIST.

**LISTEN STYLE AUDITING,** at Level 0 the style is **Listen Style auditing.** Here the auditor is expected to **listen** to the pc. The only skill necessary is **listening** to another. **Listen Style** should not be complicated by expecting more of the auditor than just this: **Listen** to the pc without evaluating, invalidating or interrupting. (HCOB 6 Nov 64)

**LISTING, 1.** the auditor's action in writing down items said by the pc in response to a question by the auditor. (HCOB 5 Dec 62) **2.** this is something **listed** by the pc. The pc says it. It is from a question. The auditor asks the question, the pc then gives him items which the auditor then writes down from the pc. (Class VIII No. 11) **3.** a special procedure used in some processes where the auditor writes down items said by the preclear in response to a question by the auditor in the exact sequence that they are given to him by the preclear. (*Scn AD*) **4.** in **listing,** today the correct L&N item must BD and F/N. (HCOB 20 Apr 72 II)

**LISTING AND NULLING, 1.** this is something **listed** by the pc, the pc says it. It is from a question. The auditor asks the question, the pc then gives him items which the auditor then writes down from the pc. (Class VIII No. 11) **2.** you ask a question of the pc, the pc gives you item, item, item, item. The auditor writes them down and then he **nulls** the **list.** And there must only be one item which has any read in it of any kind whatsoever on that **list.** (Class VIII No. 11) Also see LISTING, see NULLING.

**LISTING METER,** a real cheap **meter** that was beautifully designed, but basically one that would do a power of good as far as **listing** is concerned, so that you wouldn't miss reads. (SH Spec 256, 6304C02)

**LIST ONE, 1.** a **list** of Scn items. This includes Scn, Scn organizations, an auditor, clearing, auditing, Scientologists, a session, an E-meter, a practitioner, the auditor's name, Ron, other Scn persons, parts of Scn, past auditors, etc. This **list** is composed by the auditor, not the pc. (HCOB 23 Nov 62) **2.** this is the **list one** of Routine 2-12. The Scn **list** is called **List One.** (HCOB 24 Nov 62)

**LIST ONE R/Ser,** see ROCK SLAMMER

**LISTS,** all **lists** have been in HCOBs as "**L.**" (HCOB 19 Aug 63) [Below are some of the **lists** which begin with **L.** Other Scn and Dn **lists** and their usages will appear alphabetically as they occur (e.g. **WCCL** will be found under W.)] (a) **LCR=Confessional Repair List.** (FBDL 245) (b) **L1=List One.** (HCOB 23 Aug 65) (c) **L1C=List 1C,** used by auditors in session when an upset occurs, or as ordered by the C/S. Handles ARC broken, sad, hopeless or nattery pcs. (HCOB 19 Mar 71) [Earlier numbered L1, L1-A and L1-B.] (d) **L1R=Integrity Processing Repair List.** The rule of Integrity processing is that it should always end on an F/N. When it does not F/N however (which includes F/Ning at the pc examiner) or pc is upset, gets sick, or not doing well after Integrity processing, this **list** must be used to repair the pc. (HCOB 8 Jan 72R) (e) **L1X Hi-Lo TA List=**this assessment has been developed to detect all the reasons for high and low TA. It is used when a C/S Series 53 has been done and the high or low TA persists. (HCOB 1 Jan 72RA) (f) **L3B=**[the **Dn repair list** prior to the **L3RD,** which revised it.] (g) **L3EXD RB=**this is the prepared **list** for Expanded Dn. (HCOB 24 Oct 76R) (h) **L3RF=** Dn and Int RD Repair **List.** This **list** includes the most frequent Dn errors. (HCOB 11 Apr 71RC) (i) **L4BRA=**this prepared **list** **L4BRA** corrects L & N **lists.** It can be run on old **lists,** current **lists,** general **listing.** (HCOB 11 Apr 77) See CORRECTION LIST.

**LIVE QUESTION, 1.** unflat **question.** (HCOB 13 Dec 72R) **2. question** unflat, needle reaction on a **question.** (HCOB 19 Oct 61)

**LIVINGNESS,** is going along a certain course impelled by a purpose and with some place to arrive. It consists mostly of removing the barriers in the channel, holding the edges firm, ignoring the distractions and reinforcing and re-impelling one's progress along the channel. That's **life.** (SH Spec 57, 6504C06)

**LIVINGNESS REPAIR,** this is often the first action taken on a person by a professional auditor and can bring a great deal of brightness back into his **life.** (LRH ED 301 INT)

**L9S,** a process called **L9-Short** (originally called **L10s** but renamed for proper issue) *The New Life Rundown.* The New Life Rundown has exact steps. Well done it gives a new life in truth. (HCOB 17 Jun 71) [Now called L-11 per CG&AC 75.]

**LOC, locational.** (BTB 20 Aug 71R II)

**LOCATIONAL, 1.** a process called **locational.** Command: "Have you got an auditing room?" **Locational** is only one of many spotting processes. (*SCP*, pp. 27-28) **2.** "**Locate** the _____." The auditor has the preclear **locate** the floor, the ceiling, the walls, the furniture in the room and other objects and bodies. (HCOTB 6 Feb 57) **3.** "Look at that object". (HCOB 2 Nov 57RA)

**LOCATIONAL PROCESSING,** the object of **locational processing** is to establish an adequacy of communication terminals in the environment of the preclear. It can be run in busy thoroughfares, graveyards, confused traffic or anywhere there is or is not motion of objects and people. Commands: "Notice that (person)." (Op Bull No. 1) *Abbr.* Loc.

**LOCATIONAL SPOTTING,** one directs the pc's attention with "You notice that (object)" all about the room and at first only occasionally includes the pc's body and the auditor's body in the spotting. Then the auditor, using the same process, concentrates less and less upon the room and more and more upon the auditor and the pc. It will be found that the pc will eventually find the auditor with his attention so directed. (*SCP*, p. 20)

**LOCK, 1.** an analytical moment in which the perceptics of the engram are approximated, thus restimulating the engram or bringing it into action, the present time perceptics being erroneously interpreted by the reactive mind to mean that the same condition which produced physical pain once before is now again at hand. **Locks** contain mainly perceptics; no physical pain and very little misemotion. (*SOS*, p. 112) **2.** a situation of mental anguish. It depends for its force on the engram to which it is appended. The **lock** is more or less known to the analyzer. It's a moment of severe restimulation of an engram. (*EOS*, p. 84) **3.** those parts of the time track which contain moments the pc associates with key-ins. (HCOB 15 May 63) **4.** conscious level experiences which sort of stick and the individual doesn't quite know why. (SH Spec 72, 6607C28) **5.** mental image pictures of non-painful but disturbing experiences the person has experienced. They depend for their force on secondaries and engrams. (HCOB 12 Jul 65)

Lock

**LOCK END WORDS, words** that are not in the GPMs but which, occurring later, are close in meaning to significances that are part of the GPMs and so **lock** into a GPM and restimulate it. They keep large parts of the reactive mind in restimulation. (LRH Def. Notes)

**LOCK SCANNING,** one contacts an early **lock** on the track and goes rapidly or slowly through all such similar incidents straight to present time. One does this many times and the whole chain of **locks** become ineffective in influencing one. (*HFP*, pp. 99-100)

# LOCK WORDS

**LOCK WORDS, words** not in the GPMs but close in meaning. (HCOB 17 Oct 64 III)

**LOE, London Open Evening Lectures.** (HCOB 29 Sept 66)

**LOGIC, 1.** a gradient scale of association of facts of greater or lesser similarity made to resolve some problem of the past, present or future, but mainly to resolve and predict the future. **Logic** is the combination of factors into an answer. (*Scn 8-8008*, p. 46) **2.** the gradient scale and comparisons of data which work out a smooth network of terminals and communication lines which deliver data in a prediction of future form or state of beingness. (Spr Lect 6, 5303CM25) **3.** primitive **logic** was one-valued. Everything was assumed to be the product of a divine will, and there was no obligation to decide the rightness or wrongness of anything. Most **logic** added up merely to the propitiation of the gods. Aristotle formulated **two-valued logic.** A thing was either right or wrong. This type of **logic** is used by the reactive mind. In the present day, engineers are using a sort of **three-valued logic** which contains the values of right, wrong, and maybe. From three-valued logic we jump to an **infinity-valued logic**—a spectrum which moves from infinite wrongness to infinite rightness. (*NOTL*, p. 17) **4.** rationalism, for all **logic** is based upon the somewhat idiotic circumstance that a being that is immortal is trying to survive. (*Scn 8-8008*, p. 47) **5.** the subject of reasoning. (HCO PL 11 May 70)

**LOL, life or livingness.** (SH Spec 225, 6212C13)

**LONG FALL,** an E-meter read of two to three inches. (HCOB 29 Apr 69) *Abbr.* LF.

**LONG FALL BLOWDOWN,** a **long fall** followed by a **blowdown** or TA motion downward. (HCOB 29 Apr 69) *Abbr.* LFBD.

**LON LECT, London Lecture.** (HCOB 29 Sept 66)

**LOOP,** a redoubling of the time track, back on itself. In this case incidents are not in their correct place on the time track. (*DTOT*, p. 142)

**LOSE,** intending to do something and not doing it, and intending not to do something and doing it. (SH Spec 278, 6306C25)

Loss

**LOSS,** something has withdrawn from a thetan without his consent. This would be the definition of **loss.** (*COHA*, p. 210)

**LOSS OF HAVINGNESS,** see DEPLETION OF HAVINGNESS.

**LOSS OF VIEWPOINT,** where he has had an ally who is dead, he has once had a **viewpoint** which was alive and now can no longer use that **viewpoint.** This is the basic **loss** and the basic occlusion. It is the **loss of a viewpoint.** (PAB 2)

Love

**LOVE, 1. love,** as a word, has too many meanings, and so we use an old, old word, affinity, as meaning the **love** or brotherhood from one dynamic to another. (*HFP*, p. 41) **2.** the human manifestation of admiration. (PAB 8) **3.** an intensity of happiness addressed in a certain direction. (*SA*, p. 93)

**LOWER HARMONIC,** it is a **lower** similarity which is nutty which is actually based on something like it higher on the scale which isn't. It means a co-action or similar. (SH Spec 83, 6612C06)

**LOWER ON THE SCALE,** means **lower** toned or means in worse shape. (5707C17)

**LOW TA, 1.** below 2.0 on the tone arm. (HCOB 11 May 69 II) **2.** the **low TA** is a symptom of an overwhelmed being. When a pc's **TA** goes **low** he is being overwhelmed by too heavy a process, too steep a gradient in applying processes or by rough TRs or invalidative auditing or auditing errors. A **low TA** means that the thetan has gone past a desire to stop things and is likely to behave in life as though unable to resist real or imaginary forces. (HCOB 16 Jun 70)

**LOW-TONE CASE,** can be at clear read, unreactive on a sticky sort of needle. He cannot however *do* things in life. He or she cannot answer questions intelligently about help or control. (*EME*, p. 9)

**LPC, London Professional Course.** (HCOB 29 Sept 66)

**LPLS, London Public Lecture Series.** (HCOB 29 Sept 66)

**LRH, L. Ron Hubbard,** Founder and Source of Dianetics and Scientology and Commodore of the Sea Organization. (HCO PL 13 Jul 73)

**LT, lifetime.** (BTB 20 Aug 71R II)

**LTD,** designation on HCO Policy Letters and HCO Bulletins indicates dissemination and restriction as follows: Goes to HCO Area Secs, HCO Cont, HCO WW only but never to central organizations or field or public. (HCO PL 22 May 59)

**LTD CONT,** designation on HCO Policy Letters and HCO Bulletins indicates dissemination and restriction as follows: Goes to HCO **Cont** only plus HCO WW. (HCO PL 22 May 59)

**LTD WW,** designation on HCO Policy Letters and HCO Bulletins indicates dissemination and restriction as follows: Goes to HCO **WW** personnel only. (HCO PL 22 May 59)

**L-10,** there are now three **L-10s: L-10S** for "short," **L-10M** for "medium," for those not yet OT, and **L-10-OT** for those on OT grades III or above. (LRH OODs Command Item, 17 May 71)

**L-10M,** the Flag OT Executive Rundown, delivers OT capability to executives being trained on Flag. The technical name of it is "**L-10M.**" (HCOB 8 Jun 71 II) [Now called L-12 per CG&AC 75.]

**L-10-OT,** an upper level rundown whose basic tech comes from research into increasing **OT** powers. (CG&AC 75)

**L-12,** the Flag OT Executive Rundown. (CG&AC 75) See also L-10M.

**LUCK, 1.** by **luck** we mean "destiny not personally guided." **Luck** is only necessary amid a strong current of confusing factors. (*POW*, p. 21) **2.** the hope that some uncontrolled chance will get one through. Counting on **luck** is an abandonment of control. That's apathy. (*POW*, p. 25)

**LUMBOSIS, 1.** a very famous Scn disease. (1MACC-27, 5911C26) **2.** a weird disease that is only known in Scn. (SH Spec 66, 6509C09)

**LX LISTS,** there are now three "LX" lists: **LX3**=attitudes, **LX2**=emotions, **LX1**=conditions. Originally they were called "X" because they were **experimental.** These serve to isolate reasons a being is charged up to such an extent that he is out of valence. When a person is out of valence he does not easily as-is his bank. (HCOB 2 Aug 69, *LX Lists*)

**LYING, 1. lying** is an alteration of time, place, event or form. **Lying** becomes alter-isness, becomes stupidity. (*COHA*, p. 20) **2.** the lowest form of creativity. (*FOT*, p. 25)

# M

**M,** stands for **males** on the E-meter. (SH Spec 195A, 6209C27)

**MA,** designation on HCO Policy Letters and HCO Bulletins indicates dissemination and restriction as follows: **Magazine Article.** To go into any and all official **magazines.** (HCO PL 22 May 59)

**MAA, master at arms.** This is a naval term used in the Sea Org and is equivalent (but senior) to the ethics officer in a Scientology Church. (BTB 12 Apr 72R)

**MACC, Melbourne Advanced Clinical Course.** (HCOB 29 Sept 66)

**MACHINE, 1.** an actual **machine** in the mind, (like ordinary **machinery**) constructed out of mental mass and energy, that has been made by the individual to do work for him, usually having been set up so as to come into operation automatically under certain predetermined circumstances. (*Scn AD*) **2.** a very special kind of circuit, and they have wheels and cogwheels and belts and barrels and steam boilers and electronic electrodes and dials and switches and meters, almost anything you can think of as a **machine,** you will find in some thetan's bank as a **machine,** doing something that any **machine** does. (5 LACC-10, 5811C07) **3.** the individual got disinterested in what he was doing but he felt he had to go on doing it so he set it up automatically. (5410C10D)

**MAGNETIC FIELD,** strong electrical currents produce in the vicinity of their flow what are called **magnetic fields.** If you wrap an electrical wire around a bar of iron and run current through the wire, you have a **magnet.** When you put a new piece of iron near this **magnet** the **field** of the **magnet** snaps the piece of iron up against the **magnet.** (*HOM,* p. 53)

**MAJOR ACTION,** any—but any—**action** designed to change a case or general considerations or handle continual illness or improve ability. This means a *process* or even a series of processes like three flows. It doesn't mean a grade. It is any process the case hasn't had. (HCOB 24 May 70R)

**MAJOR THOUGHT,** by **major thought** is meant the complete **thought** being expressed in words by the auditor. (HCOB 25 May 62)

**MAN, 1. man** is actually a body run by an awareness of awareness unit which has infinite survival power—even though it can get into a great deal of trouble. (*Abil Mi 5*) **2.** a structure of cells which are seeking to survive, and only to survive. (*DMSMH,* p. 50) **3.** a composite being of four distinct and divisible actualities: these parts are termed the thetan, the memory banks, the genetic entity and the body. (*Scn 8-8008,* p. 7) **4. man** is basically a machine only as far as his body goes. **Man** is otherwise a spiritual entity which has no finite survival. It has, this entity, an infinite survival. (*Abil Mi 5*) See HOMO SAPIENS.

**MANAGEMENT POWER RUNDOWN,** the **Management Power Rundown** was developed at Flag to increase the trained skill of any church student and greatly enhance the most valuable final product of a Church Academy—a student able to use and apply brilliantly, the skills taught. This rundown solves the basic why of learning slowness, misunderstoods, third dynamic and **management** aberration, chronic illness and what is commonly referred to as "psychosis." (HCOB 11 Dec 70) *Abbr.* MPR.

**MANIC, 1.** a highly complimentary prosurvival engram. (*DMSMH,* p. 233) **2.** an engram which is highly complimentary and any compliment which it contains in it will be obeyed to its most literal fullest extent. (5009CM28) **3.** the extremes of too quiet and never quiet have a number of psychiatric names such as "catatonia" (withdrawn totally) and **"manic"** (too hectic). (HCOB 24 Nov 65)

**MANIC DEPRESSIVE,** symptomatic of a person being next to an undetected suppressive. (SH Spec 67, 6509C21)

**MARCAB CONFEDERACY,** various planets united into a very vast civilization which has come forward up through the last 200,000 years, is formed out of the fragments of earlier civilizations. In the last 10,000 years they have gone on with a sort of a decadent kicked-in-the-head civilization that contains automobiles, business suits, fedora hats, telephones, spaceships. A civilization which looks almost exact duplicate but is worse off than the current U.S. civilization. (SH Spec 291, 6308C06)

**MARRIAGE INTENSIVE,** this is where husbands and wives handle **marital** difficulties enabling them to lead happily **married** lives. (LRH ED 301 INT)

**MASS, 1.** problems have endurance. So you could say, on a thought level, that thought **mass** is basically problems. If thought **mass** is enduring, then it is basically composed of problems. If ridges are enduring, then they must be problems. Why would a problem endure? The problem is the two confusions and the two stable data counter-opposed, and one doesn't look at either of them or as-is either of them, so you get an endurance of energy **masses** in the mind. Mental **mass** is **mass**. It has weight; very tiny, but it has weight, and it actually has size and shape and so forth. (SH Spec 26X, 6107C03) **2.** (in the GPM) when we say **mass** we mean **mass**. It's electronic standing waves actually, and they usually appear black to the pc and these become visible. (SH Spec 96, 6112C21) **3.** a **mass** is no more and no less than a confusion of mismanaged communication. (*Dn 55!*, p. 65) **4.** there are two types of **mass**. There is the first type which is simply mocked up **mass** in mocked up space. This we know by agreement to be the physical universe. There is a second type of **mass**, which is the space-**mass** experience **mass**, which we call a facsimile or an engram. (PAB 52)

**MASTER PROCESS,** one which ran out all other **processes** and **processing.** (HCOB 14 May 62)

**MASTER PROGRAM,** the **master program** for every case is given on the Classification and Gradation Chart issued from time to time. (HCOB 12 Jun 70)

**MATCHED TERMINALS,** the way one does **matched terminals** is to have the preclear facing the preclear or his father facing his father; in other words, two of each of anything, one facing the other. These two things will discharge one into the other. Thus running off the difficulty. (*Scn 8-8008*, p. 127) See also DOUBLE TERMINALING.

**MATCHING TERMINALS,** putting up a person facing a person, the same person facing the same person. (5304M07) See also DOUBLE TERMINALING.

**MATERIALS OF SCIENTOLOGY,** the **materials of Scn** are not its tools. Its tools are processes—its **materials** are books, tapes, *Professional Auditor's Bulletins*, journals, letters and experience. (PAB 36)

**MATERIAL UNIVERSE,** the **universe** of matter, energy, space and time. (*Scn Jour 16-G*)

**MATTER, 1.** a group of particles of energy located in a relatively stable relationship to each other. (9ACC-24, 5501C14) **2.** a piece of **matter** is actually thought, effort and emotion all in one at the same time. (PDC 61) **3.** a particle with no space to go anyplace. (PDC 16) **4.** it is evidently a very solid thought which is chaotic enough in its arrangement of attention units that you can't do too much about it. (5206CM23B)

Matter (Def. 1)

**MAYBE, 1.** simply a counter-balance insistence on must and must not. It is and it is not. And these things equally insistent add up into the indecisions of **maybe.** (SH Spec 28, 6107C12) **2.** a **maybe** is a double flow or a controversion to such a degree that an individual is hung up on it. (Spr Lect 17, 5304CM08) **3.** a confusion of beingness, a confusion of doingness, and a confusion of havingness, and it's too badly balanced to resolve itself. (PDC 44) **4.** neither no nor yes. (PDC 15)

**MCSC, Mini Course Supervisor's Course.** (HCO PL 5 Nov 72R)

**MEAN GRAPH,** not an average **graph.** It's just a **graph** that a person isn't in too bad shape, just sort of loused up, but they kind of know it. (SH Spec 22, 6106C28)

**MECHANICAL ABERRATION,** there is a type of **aberration** source which is simply the amount of charge there is on the case. This might be called **mechanical aberration.** It does not stem from specific commands but stems from mental inefficiency by reason of cumulative entheta. Entheta by itself can charge up a case to the point where the case will behave in certain definite ways regardless of the command content of the engrams. (*SOS*, Bk. 2, pp. 102-103)

**MECHANICAL DEFINITION,** called **"mechanical"** as it is **defined** in terms of distance and position. **Mechanical** in this sense means interpreting or explaining the phenomena of the universe by referring to causally determined physical forces; **mechanistic.** A being can put out objects to view (or anchor points) and also put out points which will view them, even while the being himself is elsewhere. Thus one can achieve space. **"Mechanical"** also applies to "acting or performing like a machine—automatic." Thus a **"mechanical definition"** would be one which **defined** in terms of space or location such as "the car over by the old oak tree" or "the man who lives in the big house." Here "the old oak tree" and "the big house" are fixed objects and the unfixed objects ("car," "man") are a sort of viewpoint. One has identified things by location. (LRH Def. Notes)

**MECHANICS, 1.** when we say **mechanics** we mean space, energy, objects and time. And when something has those things in it we're talking about something **mechanical.** (*PXL*, p. 166) **2.** by **mechanics** we mean any and all of the objects, motions, or spaces which exist. **Mechanics** are always quantitative. There is always just so much distance or so much mass or so many hours. We have a word for **mechanics** compounded from matter, energy, space, and time which is MEST. By MEST we mean any or all arrangements of energy of whatever kind, whether in fluid or object form, in space or spaces. (*Dn 55!*, p. 8)

**MEDIUM CLEAN NEEDLE,** offers many prior and latent reads, but reads instantly when a question is asked. (HCOB 14 Jun 62)

**MEDIUM DIRTY NEEDLE,** agitated throughout check but with periods of no agitation when a read can be obtained easily. Reacts to checker's voice (rudiments checker). (HCOB 14 Jun 62)

**MEGALOMANIAC,** a person who has delusions of grandeur, wealth, power, etc. (HCOB 11 May 65)

Megalomania

**MEL 4, Melbourne 4.** Process from 1st Advanced Clinical Course in **Melbourne.** (BTB 20 Aug 71R II)

**MEMORY, 1.** a recording of the physical universe. Any **memory** contains a time index (when it happened) and a pattern of motion. As a lake reflects the trees and moving clouds, so does a **memory** reflect the physical universe. Sight, sound, pain, emotion, effort, conclusions, and many other things are recorded in this static for any given instant of observation. Such a **memory** we call a facsimile. (*Scn 8-80*, p. 13) **2. memory** in Dn is considered to be any concept of perceptions stored in the standard memory banks which is potentially recallable by the "I." (*DMSMH*, p. 61) **3. memory** usually means recalling data of recent times. (*HFP*, p. 26) **4.** memory would have the connotation of you simply know it had happened. (SH Spec 84, 6612C13)

**MEMORY BANKS, STANDARD,** the analytical mind has its **standard memory banks.** Just where these are located structurally is no concern of ours at this time. To operate, the analytical mind has to have percepts (data), memory (data), and imagination (data), whether or not the data contained in the **standard memory banks** is evaluated correctly or not, it is all there. (*DMSMH*, p. 45)

**MENTAL IMAGE PICTURES, 1.** copies of the physical universe as it goes by. (6101C22) **2.** in Scn we call a **mental image picture** a facsimile when it is a "photograph" of the physical universe sometime in the past. We call a **mental image picture** a mock-up when it is created by the thetan or for the thetan and does not consist of a photograph of the physical universe. We call a **mental image picture** an hallucination or more properly an automaticity (something uncontrolled) when it is created by another and seen by self. (*FOT*, pp. 56-57)

Mental Image Picture (Def. 1)

**MERCHANTS OF CHAOS,** there are in our civilization some very disturbing elements. These disturbing elements are the **Merchants of Chaos.** They deal in confusion and upset. Their daily bread is made by creating **chaos.** If **chaos** were to lessen, so would their incomes. It is to their interest to make the environment seem as threatening as possible, for only then can they profit. Their incomes, force, and power rise in direct ratio to the amount of threat they can inject into the surroundings of the people. (*NSOL*, pp. 17-18) **2.** Merchant of Fear or **Chaos Merchant** and which we can now technically call the suppressive person. (HCO PL 5 Apr 65)

**MERCHANTS OF FEAR, 1.** probably the truly aberrative personalities in our society do not number more than five or ten per cent. They have very special traits. Where you find in the preclear's bank a person with one or more of these character-istics, you will have the person who most thoroughly tried the preclear's sanity. Such people would be better understood if I called them the **"Merchants of Fear."** (PAB 13) **2.** We can now technically call the suppressive person. (HCO PL 5 Apr 65, *Handling the Suppressive Person*)

**MESMERISM, mesmerism** is no relation to hypnotism at all. **Mes-merism** is animal magnetism. It's a physiological rapport. Not a concentration on mental but on mental-physiological. To have rapport with something you can *be* it. When doing physical healing, if you stroke sympathetically (both sides) alternately inducing a rhythmic motion which is monotonous, you can **mes-merize** a person. In **mesmerism** there is an imposition on feeling. If you **mesmerize** a person and pinch your back, he will get red in the same place and feel the pain of the pinch. This is physiological rapport. No words are said during **mesmerism.** (BTB 7 Apr 72R)

**MEST, 1.** a coined word, meaning **matter, energy, space** and **time,** the physical universe. All physical phenomena may be considered as **energy** operating in **space** and **time.** The move-ment of **matter** or **energy** in **time** is the measure of **space.** All things are **mest** except theta. (*Abil 114-A*) **2.** the symbol for the physical universe in use hereafter is **mest,** from the first letters of the words **matter, energy, space** and **time,** or the Greek letter *phi* ($\phi$). (*HFP*, p. 166) **3.** simply a composite of **energies** and particles and **spaces** which are agreed upon and which are looked at. (*PXL*, p. 193) **4.** a solid object, and the **space** and **energy** and so forth which comprise such solid objects. (PDC 12)

**5.** any or all arrangements of **energy**, of whatever kind, whether in fluid or object form, in **space** or **spaces**. (*Dn 55!*, p. 9)

**MEST BODY, 1.** the physical **body**. The organism in all the **mest** aspects. (*SOS* Gloss) **2.** the **mest body** should not be thought of as a harbor or vessel for the theta being. A better example would be a sliver inserted unwantedly in the thumb where the thumb would be the theta being, the **mest body** the sliver. **Mest bodies** are good identification tags, they generate exciting emotions, they are fun to operate at times, but they are no end of existence. (*HOM*, p. 16)

**MEST CLEAR, 1.** by **mest clear** is meant a Book One clear. Here we defined **clear** in terms of facsimiles. This is a rather simple mechanical definition. It said in effect that so far as human beings were concerned our preclear finally arrived at a point where he had full color-visio-sonic, had no psychoses or neuroses and could recall what had happened to him in this lifetime. (*SCP*, p. 3) **2.** someone who knows he has reached the bottom rung of the ladder on his way up. He also knows the rest of humanity uncleared is below this state but that they don't know that they are. A **mest clear** still thinks of himself more or less as a body and is more or less subject to one. All engrams are effectually keyed out without being examined. For practical purposes they are erased. He has excellent recalls. They may or may not be eidetic. (*Abil 87*) **3.** if a fellow can exist without synthetic beingnesses, which are solutions to problems he can't confront, you've got a **mest clear**. He is still in a body. He's got body beingness yet, but he's gotten rid of these synthetic valences. (SH Spec 36, 6108C09)

**MEST LOCKS, locks** which come about through the inhibition or enforcement of the individual's experience or control of **matter** or **energy** or **space** or **time**. It is postulated that the reduction of the **mest locks** in which the individual was made to go up or not permitted to come down will make any bouncer phrases in the case inactive, and so on with all types of action phrases. (*SOS* Gloss)

**MEST PERCEPTICS,** common garden-variety sense data—**perceptions**, new and recorded, of **matter, energy, space,** and **time,** and combinations of these. (*SOS* Gloss)

**MEST PERCEPTION,** recordings the thetan takes from the organs of **perception** of the human body as a short cut to

**perception** (lazy **perception**). The body records actual wave emanations from the **mest** universe, the thetan uses these recordings. (*Scn 8-8008* Gloss)

**MEST REALITY,** the **reality** which can be sensed, measured, and experienced in the physical universe. (*SOS*, p. 97)

**MEST STRAIGHTWIRE,** self-analysis. (5209CM04A)

**MEST TECHNIQUE,** straightwire, repetitive straightwire (slow, auditor-managed lock scanning), and lock scanning on **mest** locks. Language locks are found by straightwire only as a clue to the underlying **mest** locks. **Mest technique** and validation technique may be combined and should be. (*SOS* Gloss)

**MEST UNIVERSE, 1.** that agreed-upon reality of **matter, energy, space** and **time** which we use as anchor points and through which we communicate. (*Scn 8-8008*, p. 27) **2.** a mutual system of barriers on which we have agreed so we can have a game. (5311CM17A) **3.** is a two-terminal universe. (*Scn 8-8008*, p. 31)

**METALOSIS,** *Osis*, Greek, action: process, condition abnormal or diseased condition caused by. *Metal,* any of a large group of substances (as bronze, steel) that typically show a characteristic luster, are good conductors of electricity and heat, are opaque, can be fused or are usually malleable or ductile. A psychosomatic condition caused by the interaction of body electric flows and the magnetic and other fields of metal. The effect takes a long time to occur. Engrams are formed. (LRH Def. Notes)

**METALOSIS RUNDOWN,** the procedure used in Expanded Dianetics to cure **metalosis.** (LRH Def. Notes)

**METAPHYSICS, 1.** it means **after physics** because the original classes in it were given in the period which immediately followed the **physics** period. That is where that gets its name, because it was the unexplained, inexplicable and upsetting things that no one knew the answer of. (Unidentified LRH tape) **2.** the study of the ultimate reality of all things. (*B&C*, p. 16)

**METER,** see E-METER.

250

**METER CHECK, 1.** the action of **checking** the reaction of a student to subject matter, words or other things, isolating blocks to study, interpersonal relations or life. It is done with an **E-meter.** (HCOB 19 Jun 71 III) **2.** the procedure whereby an ethics officer or trained auditor establishes the state of a person in regard to ethical or technical matters by using the technology of the **E-meter.** (*ISE*, p. 40)

**METER DEPENDENCE, meter dependence** is created by invalidation by or poor acknowledgment of the auditor. If the auditor seems not to accept the pc's data, then the pc may insist that the auditor "see it read on the meter." This can grow up into a formidable **meter dependence** on the part of the pc. (HCOB 13 Apr 64, *Scn VI Part One Tone Arm Action*)

**M 1 to 9 (WC),** see WORD CLEARING.

**METHOD 1 ASSESSMENT,** see ASSESSING, METHODS OF.

**METHOD 2 ASSESSMENT,** see ASSESSING, METHODS OF.

**METHOD 3 ASSESSMENT,** see ASSESSING, METHODS OF.

**METHOD 4 ASSESSMENT,** see ASSESSING, METHODS OF.

**METHOD 5 ASSESSMENT,** see ASSESSING, METHODS OF.

**METHOD 6 ASSESSMENT,** see ASSESSING, METHODS OF.

**METHODS OF WORD CLEARING,** see WORD CLEARING for definitions of Methods 1-9 word clearing.

**MID-CONFESSIONAL SHORT ASSESSMENT,** see MID-INTEGRITY PROCESSING SHORT ASSESSMENT.

**MGMT, management.** (BPL 5 Nov 72RA)

**MID-INTEGRITY PROCESSING SHORT ASSESSMENT,** for use during an integrity processing session if a question won't F/N but before starting that question, the TA range was 2-3, or there was an F/N. (BTB 7 Dec 72R)

**MIDDLE RUDIMENTS, 1. middle rudiments** are **rudiments** used one after another; inquiries about various **rudiments** during a session. Of course you are then to keep the session progressing and keep the **rudiments** in. (SH Spec 45, 6108C24) **2.** the **middle**

**rudiment** consists of a package question which handles suppressions, invalidations, missed withholds and "careful of." This is your standard, basic **middle rudiment**. (SH Spec 155, 6205C31) **3. middle rudiments** may also contain (this is less often, but may also contain) the half-truths, untruths, impress and damage **end rudiment**; the question or command **end rudiment**; and the influence of the E-meter **rudiment**. (SH Spec 155, 6205C31) **4. mid ruds** are called **mid ruds** because **middle** of session was the earliest use, plus **rudiments** of a session. (HCOB 14 Aug 64)

**MID RUDS, middle rudiments.** (HCOB 23 Aug 65)

**MIMICRY, 1.** a non-verbal technique wherein the auditor **mimics** the preclear and persuades the preclear to **mimic** the auditor. Various processes are used, such as passing a ball back and forth between them, nodding, shaking hands, sitting down, standing up, walking across the room and back and sitting down, all of which are effective. (*Dn 55!*, p. 110) **2.** he does something, you do something [the same thing], and therefore he becomes aware that he's doing it because he sees you doing it. (SH Spec 59, 6504C27)

**MIND, 1.** pictures which have been made of experiences and plotted against time and preserved in energy and mass in the vicinity of the being and which when restimulated are re-created without his analytical awareness. (SH Spec 72, 6607C28) **2.** a literal record of experience plotted against time from the earliest moment of aberration until now plus additional ideas the fellow got about it, plus other things he may have mocked up or created on top of it in mental mass, plus some machines, plus some valences. (SH Spec 70, 6607C21) **3.** a network of communications and pictures, energies and masses, which are brought into being by the activities of the thetan versus the physical universe or other thetans. The **mind** is a communication and control system between the thetan and his environment. (*FOT*, p. 56) **4.** the purpose of the **mind** is to pose and resolve problems relating to survival and to direct the effort of the organism according to these solutions. (*Scn 0-8*, p. 76) **5.** a natively self-determined computer which poses, observes and resolves problems to accomplish survival. It does its thinking with facsimiles of experience or facsimiles of synthetic experience. It is natively cause. It seeks to be minimally an effect. (*HFP*, p. 33) **6.** the **human mind** is an observer, postulator, creator and storage place of knowledge. (*HFP*, p. 163) **7.** the **mind** is a self-protecting mechanism and will not permit itself to be seriously overloaded so long as it can retain partial awareness of itself. (*DMSMH*, p. 165) **8.** the **mind** is composed of energy which exists in space and which condenses down into masses. (SH Spec 133, 6204C17)

**MINOR THOUGHT,** by **minor thoughts** is meant subsidiary **thoughts** expressed by words within the major thought. They are caused by the reactivity of individual words within the full words. Example: "Have you ever injured dirty pigs?" To the pc the words "you," "injured," and "dirty" are all reactive. Therefore, the **minor thoughts** expressed by these words also read on the meter. (HCOB 25 May 62)

**MINUS-FREEDOM,** freedom is not the plus of a condition where slavery is the minus unless we are dealing entirely with the political organism. Where we are dealing with the individual better terminology is necessary and more understanding of the anatomy of **minus-freedom** is required. **Minus-freedom** is entrapment. Freedom is the absence of barriers. Less freedom is the presence of barriers. Entirely **minus-freedom** would be the omnipresence of barriers. (*Dn 55!*, p. 55)

**MINUS RANDOMITY, 1.** from the viewpoint of the individual, that thing which has too little motion in it for his tolerance is **minus randomity.** (*Abil 36*) **2.** a good statement of **minus randomity** would be: things are too slow. Things are certainly slow around here, life is dull, there is nothing happening. (*Abil 36*)

**MINUS SCALE,** the **minus** awareness levels of the Classification Gradation and Awareness Chart. (HCOB 20 Sept 66)

**MINUS SCALE RELEASE,** there are several Grades of Release below Zero, in the **Minus Scale** of the original complete Gradation Chart. Many of the **Minus Scale** can be attained by simple assessment. (And ceasing to assess the moment the **release** occurs is vital—don't keep on assessing as the same session auditing action.) There are three specific Grades of **Release** below Zero and above the lower **Minus Scale.** These are, from lowest: Straightwire Release, Dianetic Secondary Release, Dianetic Engram Release. (HCOB 20 Sept 66)

**MINUS TONE SCALE,** the subtones below the Emotional Tone Scale which are so low as to constitute by the individual a no-affinity, no-emotion, no-problem, no-consequence state of mind on things which are actually tremendously important. (*Scn AD*)

**MIS-ACKNOWLEDGMENT,** there are many ways to **mis-acknowledge** a pc. But any **mis-acknowledgment** is only and always a failure to end the cycle of a command. If the pc is not sure he has answered and that the auditor has accepted the answer, the *pc will get no benefit from the auditing.* (PAB 145)

**MISASSESSMENT,** multiple item or narrative item or both or taking an item that doesn't read or in which pc has no interest. (HCOB 9 Aug 69)

**MISASSIST,** an incident wherein the preclear has tried to help on some dynamic and failed. (*HOM,* p. 75)

**MISCELLANEOUS REPORT,** a **report** such as an MO report, a D of P interview, an ethics report, a success story, etc. which is put in the pc's folder and gives a C/S more information about the case. (BTB 3 Nov 72R)

**MISDIRECTOR, 1.** a phrase which, when the auditor sends the preclear in one direction, makes the preclear go in another **direction.** (*SOS,* p. 106) **2.** a command which sends the preclear in the **wrong direction,** makes him go earlier when he should be going later, go later when he should go earlier, etc. "You can't go back at this point," "You're turned around," etc. (*DMSMH,* p. 213)

**MISEMOTION, 1.** anything that is unpleasant **emotion** such as antagonism, anger, fear, grief, apathy or a death feeling. (HCOB 23 Apr 69) **2. emotion** and **misemotion** include all levels of the complete tone scale except "pain"; **emotion** and **misemotion** are closely allied to **"motion,"** being only a finer particle action. (HCOB 19 Jan 67)

**MISEMOTIONAL, 1.** such a word would indicate that a person did not display the **emotion** called for by the actual circumstances of the situation. (*SOS*, p. 49) **2.** being **misemotional** is synonymous with being irrational. (*SOS*, p. 49)

**MIS-MEMORY,** forgettingness. (*Abil SW*, p. 11)

**MISPROGRAMMED,** the current **program** has neglected or misplaced an urgently needed action. (BTB 23 Oct 71 V)

**MISSED OVERT,** a done, that people didn't find out about. (SH Spec 181, 6208C07)

**MISSED WITHHOLD, 1.** an undisclosed contra-survival act which has been restimulated by another but not disclosed. (HCOB 3 May 62) **2.** a **missed withhold** is a should have known. The pc feels you should have found out about something and you didn't. (SH Spec 136, 6204C24) **3.** the **missed withhold** is something people nearly found out. It's another person's action. It's nothing the pc did or is doing. It is another person's action and the pc's wonder about it. (SH Spec 206, 6211C01) *Abbr.* M/W/H.

**MISSED WITHHOLD OF NOTHING, 1.** there is **nothing there,** yet the auditor tries to get it and the pc ARC breaks. This gives the pc a **missed withhold of nothing.** (HCO PL 16 Apr 65) **2.** "cleaning" a rudiment that has already registered null gives the pc a **missed withhold of nothingness.** His **nothingness** was not accepted. The pc has no answer. A **missed no-answer** then occurs. To ask again something already null is to leave the pc baffled—he has a **missed withhold** which is a **nothingness.** (HCOB 4 Jul 62)

**MISSED WITHHOLD PROGRAM,** where the auditor searched for and found when and where **withholds** had been available but had been **MISSED.** (HCOB 8 Feb 62)

**MISSION,** a group granted the privilege of delivering elementary Scn and Dn services. Does not have Church status or rights. (BTB 12 Apr 72R)

**MO, medical officer.** (*Abil 272*)

**MOCKERY BAND,** there is a little **band** down very close to death on the tone scale which is a **mockery band** and in that **band** anything that's in that **band** is a **mockery** of anything higher. (5405CM12)

**MOCK-UP,** *v.* **1.** to get an imaginary picture of. (*COHA,* p. 100) —*n.* **1.** "**mock-up**" is derived from the World War II phrase which indicated a symbolized weapon or area of attack. Here, it means in essence, something which a person makes up himself. (*Scn Jour, Iss 14-G*) **2.** a **mock-up** is more than a mental picture; it is a self-created object which exists as itself or symbolizes some object in the mest universe. It is a thing which one can be. (*Scn Jour, Iss 14-G*) **3.** a full perceptic energy picture in three dimensions created by the thetan and having location in space and time. Now, that's the ideal definition. A **mock-up** is something the thetan puts up and says is there. That's what a **mock-up** is. (9ACC-24, 5501C14) **4.** we call a mental image picture a **mock-up** when it is created by the thetan or for the thetan and does not consist of a photograph of the physical universe. (*FOT,* pp. 56-57) **5.** any knowingly created mental picture that is not part of a time track. (HCOB 15 May 63)

**MODEL SESSION, 1.** the same exact pattern and script (patter) with which an auditing session is begun and ended; the overall form of all Scn auditing sessions which is the same anywhere in the world. (*Scn AD*) **2.** its wording is very fixed. All refinements of **model session** are in the direction of causing less ARC breaks and getting more auditing done. (SH Spec 289, 6307C24) **3.** the patter wording of a **model session** is what is said and fixed. By always using the same words to open, continue and close a session, to begin and end processes, a duplication of sessions is achieved which as they continue, runs them out. The patter wording of a **model session** should be learned by heart and not changed. (HCOB 26 Aug 60)

**MODIFIER,** a **modifier** is that consideration which opposes the attainment of a goal and tends to suspend it in time. Example: goal, "to be a willow wand;" **modifier,** "so as never to be reached." (HCOB 7 Nov 61)

**MOISTURE PERCEPTION, moisture perception** permits us to sense the dampness or dryness of the atmosphere and so judge further our environment. (*SOS,* p. 59)

**M1 CS 1, 1. method 1** word clearing **CS 1.** [as in case supervisor direction.] (HCOB 14 Sept 71 II Revised 24 Sept 71) [Note this

HCOB has been cancelled by HCOB 14 June 73 *Word Clearing C/S No. 1R Cancelled.*] **2.** standard **C/S** for word clearing in session **Method 1.** (HCOB 30 Jun 71 II)

**M 1 WC, Method One word clearing.** (HCO PL 8 Jan 72 I) See WORD CLEARING.

**MONEY PROCESSING INTENSIVE,** this handles the inability to have **money** resulting in the ability to increase income. (LRH ED 301 INT)

**MONITOR,** could be called the center of awareness of the person. It, inexactly speaking, *is* the person. It has been approximated by various names for thousands of years, each one reducing down to "I." The **monitor** is in control of the analytical mind. (*DMSMH*, p. 43)

**MOOD DRILLS,** developed to handle stuck or fixated auditor **moods** or where some auditor's **mood** entered into the session would rough up or upset a pc or slow his progress. **Mood drills** consist of TRs 1 to 4 done out of session on each tone level of the *full* tone scale, hitting each **mood** up and down the scale. The coach calls the **mood,** the auditor does TRs 1 to 4 in that **mood.** It doesn't really require much coaching. "You just start low on the scale and TR that mood then the next, then the next. Like, all TRs done "hopeless," etc. Lots of laughs doing it really. Doing TRs as a dead auditor is pretty tricky." Once begun **mood drills** should be continued until the whole scale is flat so the auditor doesn't get stuck on the tone scale but can do any **mood** easily and without strain. (BTB 13 Mar 75)

**MORAL CODE, 1.** that series of agreements to which a person has subscribed to guarantee the survival of a group. (SH Spec 62, 6110C04) **2.** a series of solutions to problems which have not been confronted or analyzed. (SH Spec 27X, 6107C04)

**MORALS,** *n. pl.* **1.** the principles of right and wrong conduct. (HCO PL 3 May 72) **2. morals** should be defined as a code of good conduct laid down out of the experience of the race to serve as a uniform yardstick for the conduct of individuals and groups. Such a codification has its place; **morals** are actually laws. **Morals** are, to some degree, arbitraries, in that they continue beyond their time. All **morals** originate out of the discovery by the group that some act contains more pain than pleasure. (*SOS*, p. 129) **3.** are things which were introduced into the society to resolve harmful practices which could not be explained or treated in a rational manner. (5008C30) **4.** those things which are considered to be at any given time survival characteristics. A survival action is a **moral** action and those things are considered immoral which are considered contra-survival. (SH Spec 62, 6110C04) **5.** an arbitrary code of conduct not necessarily related to reason. (*Scn 8-8008*, p. 100)

**MORES,** are those things which make a society possible. They are the heavily agreed-upon, policed codes of conduct of a society. (PAB 40)

**MOTION, 1.** uncomfortable perceptions stemming from the reactive mind are called sensation. These are basically "pressure," **"motion,"** "dizziness," "sexual sensation," and "emotion and misemotion." **"Motion"** is just that, a feeling of being in **motion** when one is not. **"Motion"** includes the "winds of space," a feeling of being blown upon especially from in front of the face. (HCOB 19 Jan 67) **2.** dimension points, by shifting, can give the viewpoint the illusion of **motion.** The viewpoint, by shifting, can give the dimension points the illusion of **motion. Motion** is the manifestation of change of viewpoint of dimension points. (*Scn 8-8008*, p. 16) **3.** is a consecutive appear and disappear in infinitely small gradients. (2ACC-19A, 5312CM09) **4.** a change of position in space. (*HFP*, p. 110)

**MOTIVATOR, 1.** an aggressive or destructive act received by the person or one of the dynamics. It is called a **motivator** because it tends to prompt that one pays it back—it **"motivates"** a new overt. (HCOB 20 May 68) **2.** something which the person feels has been done to him, which he is not willing to have happen. (HCO Info Ltr 2 Sept 64) **3.** an act received by the person or individual causing injury, reduction or degradation of his being-ness, person, associations or dynamics. (HCOB 1 Nov 68 II) **4.** an overt act against oneself by another. In other words, a **motivator** is a harmful action performed by somebody else against oneself. (8ACC-14, 5410CM20)

**MOTIVATOR HUNGER, 1.** a **motivator** is called a "**motivator**" because it tends to prompt an overt. It gives a person a **motive** or reason or justification for an overt. When a person commits an overt or overt of omission with no **motivator** he tends to believe or pretends that he has received a **motivator** which does not in fact exist. This is a false **motivator.** Beings suffering from this are said to have "**motivator hunger**" and are often aggrieved over nothing. (HCOB 1 Nov 68) **2.** *Homo sapiens* goes around trying to get force applied hard enough so that he gets sympathy for it and we call that **motivator hunger.** (2ACC-30B, 5312CM21)

**MOTIVATORISH CASE,** a preclear who only gets off **motivators** in a session. The **motivator case** is well aware that each **motivator** answer is not truly real, but reactively he is incapable of looking at the cause side of the picture and considers any effort on the part of anyone to attempt to get him to do so as an effort on the part of that person to punish him or to make him guilty. Such a person has many overts of blaming others and uses any **motivator** as a justification of his overts against others. (BTB 12 Jul 62)

**MOTIVATOR-OVERT ACT,** whereby something is done to the preclear and then the preclear does the same thing to somebody else. (PAB 18)

**MOTOR CONTROL TIME TRACK,** this **time track** is not connected to the analytical mind and speech, but is apparently a parallel **time track** with greater reliability than the sensory track. The precision of data contained in the **motor control time track** is enormous. The **motor strip time track** can be asked questions down to the smallest moment of time, and the area of an engram can be so located and its character determined. (*DTOT*, pp. 88-89)

**MOTOR STRIP,** the pc's sensory perceptions. (*Exp Jour, Winter-Spring, 1950*)

**MOTOR STRIP TIME TRACK,** see MOTOR CONTROL TIME TRACK.

**MPR,** see MANAGEMENT POWER RUNDOWN.

**MS, model session.** (HCO PL 8 Dec 62)

**MSH, Mary Sue Hubbard.** (HCOB 23 Aug 65)

**M/U or MIS-U,** abbreviation for **misunderstood.** (BTB 12 Apr 72R)

**MULTIPLE DECLARE, declaring** Grades 0 to IV all at one time mostly without any mention of the end phenomena of the grade. (HCOB 30 Jun 70R)

**MULTIPLE ILLNESS,** the preclear is physically uncomfortable or **ill** from several engrams of different types all restimulated. (HCOB 23 Apr 69)

**MULTIPLE SOMATICS,** several **somatics** as one item. (HCOB 19 May 69, *Health Form, Use of*)

**MULTIVALENCE,** *valens* means "powerful" in Latin. It is a good term because it is the second half of **ambivalent** (power in two directions) and exists in any good dictionary. It is a good term because it describes (although the dictionary did not mean it to) the intent of the organism when dramatizing an engram. **Multivalence** would mean "many powerfuls." It would embrace the phenomena of split personality, the strange differences of personality in people in one and then another situation. **Valence** in Dn means the personality of one of the dramatic personnel in an engram. (*DMSMH*, p. 80)

**MURDER ROUTINE,** a *slang* title for the "worse than" technique. One gets the pc to give off his overts by inferring he has done very bad things, including **murder.** Auditor, "Did you **murder** your wife?" Pc, "Oh no! I only cheated on her!" Described in full in BTB 30 Aug 72 I, issued 28 Mar 74 Ex Dn Series 8. Actually developed in 1961 in South Africa. (LRH Def. Notes)

**MUTTER TR,** a drill to perfect the muzzled auditing comm cycle. (1) The coach has student give command. (2) Coach **mutters** an unintelligible answer at different times. (3) Student acknowledges. (4) Coach flunks if student does *anything* else but acknowledge. This is the *entirety* of this drill. It is not to be confused with any other training drill. (HCOB 1 Oct 65R)

**MUTUALLY RESTIMULATIVE,** two people may discover that they are **mutually restimulative**—which is to say each is a pseudo-person in the other's engrams or one is restimulated (voice tone, incidents) by the other. (*DMSMH*, p. 389)

**MUTUAL OUT RUDS,** this means two or more people who **mutually** have **ruds out** on the wider group or other dynamics and do not get them in. (HCOB 17 Feb 74)

**MUZZLED AUDITING, 1.** stating only the model session patter and commands and TRs. It *always* gets the best results. (HCOB 20 Jul 72 II) **2.** this could also be called rote style auditing. **Muzzled auditing** has been with us many years. It is the stark total of TRs 0 to 4 and not anything else added. Repetitive command auditing, using TRs 0 to 4, at Level I is done completely **muzzled.** (HCOB 6 Nov 64) **3.** in **muzzled auditing,** the auditor says only two things. He gives the command and acknowledges the answer to that command. If the pc says anything that is not an answer to that command, the auditor nods his head and awaits an answer before giving acknowledgment. (HCOB 25 Mar 59)

**MUZZLED COACHING,** the **coach** says fine when he thinks it is fine and otherwise keeps his mouth shut. This is **muzzled coaching.** (HCOB 29 Sept 59)

**MW/H** (also **M/W/H**), **missed withhold.** (HCOB 23 Aug 65)

**MYSTERY, 1.** the anatomy of **mystery** is unprediction, confusion and then total blackout. **Mystery** is the level of always pretending there's always something to know earlier than the **mystery.** (*PXL*, p. 170) **2.** oblivion of knowing. (*COHA*, p. 151) **3.** the glue that sticks thetans to things. (SH Spec 206, 6211C01)

**MYSTERY SANDWICH, 1.** the principle of **mystery** is, of course, this: the only way anybody gets stuck to anything is by a **mystery sandwich.** A person cannot be connected to his body, but he can have a **mystery** between him and his body which will connect him. You have to understand this thing about the **mystery sandwich.** It's two pieces of bread, one of which represents the body, and one of which represents the thetan, and the two pieces of bread are pulled together by a **mystery.** They are kept together by a volition to know the **mystery.** (PAB 66) **2.** a thetan stuck to anything is of course just a **mystery sandwich.** Thetan, **mystery,** object—**mystery sandwich.** (SH Spec 48, 6108C31)

**MYSTICAL MYSTIC,** *Slang.* a type of case. The person will be totally reasonable about anything that happens in his vicinity but not do anything about it, and see nothing but good in anything including murdering babies. (SH Spec 42, 6410C13)

**MYSTIQUE,** qualifications or skills that set a person or thing apart and beyond the understanding of an outsider. (HCO PL 29 Oct 71 III)

# N

**NARCOSYNTHESIS, 1.** a complicated name for a very ancient process quite well known in Greece and India. It is drug hypnotism. A shot of sodium pentothal is given intravenously to the patient and he is asked to count backwards. It is actually a depressant on the awareness of an individual so that those attention units which remain behind the curtain of his reactive mind can be reached directly. (*DMSMH*, p. 123) **2.** the practice of inducing sleep with drugs and then talking to the patient to draw out buried thoughts. (*EOS*, p. 24)

**NARRATIVE,** is a story, an account, a tale. (HCOB 18 Jun 78R)

**NARRATIVE CHAIN, 1.** a **chain** of similar experiences rather than a similar somatic. (HCOB 23 May 69) **2.** these are by repeating story. By incident description. (HCOB 27 Jan 70)

**NARRATIVE ITEM, 1.** is one which will land the pc in a single incident for which there is no chain. Flagrant example: "The time the horse Baldy dumped me in the Potomac." Obviously, there was only one such incident. (HCOB 27 Jan 70) **2.** a **narrative item** describes only one possible incident. (HCOB 27 Mar 71R)

**NATIVE STATE, 1.** the potentiality of knowing everything. (SH Spec 35, 6108C08) **2.** the list of no games conditions is a summary of the **native state** of a thetan. (HCOB 3 Sept 56) **3.** the thetan is not in contact with space, energy, mass. He doesn't have any dimension. (PAB 64) **4.** the **native state** thetan is total knowingness. (Op Bull 1)

**NATTER,** sometimes pcs who have big overts become highly critical of the auditor and get in a lot of snide comments about the auditor. Such **natter** always indicates a real overt. (HCOB 7 Sept 64 II)

**NATURAL AUDITOR,** the **natural auditor** ties right into it and does a workmanlike job. He or she gets lots of bulletin and tape passes in ratio to flunks, absorbs data well and gets it into practice, does a passable job on a pc even at the start of training, and improves casewise rapidly under the skilled training and auditing. (HCOB 8 Mar 62)

**NATURAL TRs,** spoken TRs are natural. TRs are for use in life and in the auditing room. There is no uncomfortable robot execution or straining of voice. (BTB 18 Aug 71R)

**NCG, no case gain** despite good and sufficient auditing. (HCO PL 12 May 72)

**NECESSITY LEVEL, 1.** that amount of urgency or commotion necessary in the environment to extrovert the individual and put him into motion in present time. (5501C14) **2.** a sudden heightened willingness which untaps a tremendous amount of ability. (PAB 129) **3.** the emergency factor. A sudden increase of randomity to a sufficiency that the individual makes a momentary adjustment to it. In other words, it momentarily increases his tolerance for unexpected motion. (*Abil 36*)

**NEEDLE PATTERN, 1.** it is a chronic and constant **needle behavior** on a particular pc when the auditor is saying and doing nothing. It's not a needle response. It's a **needle appearance** when the auditor is saying or doing nothing. (SH Spec 224, 6212C13) **2.** a **pattern** is a series of missed withholds culminating in a constantly active **needle.** A **pattern** can be a big dirty needle or a little dirty needle. In other words a wide dial dirty needle or a small dial dirty needle. (SH Spec 145, 6205C15)

**NEEDLE REACTIONS**, rise, fall, speeded rise, speeded fall, double tick (dirty needle), theta bop or any other action. (HCOB 25 Apr 63)

**NEEDLE REACTIONS ABOVE GRADE IV,** a response like a brief dirty needle on a pre-OT means "No" always. A real dirty needle is constant and continuous. The same small jerky needle action on a person Grade V or above means "No" or that the question is negative. (HCOB 18 Apr 68)

**NEEDLE READS,** see READ.

**NEGATIVE BLOWDOWN,** when a TA has gone below 2.0 and a relief of the condition occurs, the TA will **blow UP** to normal range. Hence, **negative blowdown,** as it is the reverse of a normal **blowdown.** Mentioned in BTB 7 Feb 71 II reissued 7 Aug 74, *Cancellation.* (LRH Def. Notes)

**NEGATIVE GAIN,** you can erase engrams, that's taking away. You get actually **negative gain.** By the removal of the harmful thing you can get a positive advance. That's called **negative gain.** (ESTO 6, 7203C03 SO II)

**NEGATIVE POSTULATE,** the **postulate** not to be. It cancels past postulates and it also cancels, in greater or lesser degree, the entire individual. (*AP&A*, p. 34)

**NERVOUSNESS, 1.** that condition which results from having one's space as occupied, made untenable. (PDC 48) **2.** distracted attention. (Spr Lect 14, 5304CM07)

**NEUROSIS, 1.** an emotional state containing conflicts and emotional data inhibiting the abilities or welfare of the individual. (*DTOT*, p. 58) **2.** the difference between **neurosis** and psychosis is that in psychosis, the guy is just generally the effect of everything, and in **neurosis** he's more or less singly the effect of things. He's a deranged being on some subject. (SH Spec 70, 6607C21) **3.** antisocial action or anti-survival action which is compulsively undertaken by the individual. (SH Spec 299, 6308C27) **4.** he's got some idea of what's happening, where he is on some things and some faint idea what's happening in his environment on some things. But generally unknowingness overbalances the knowingness and so you get a **neurosis**. (SH Spec 41, 6108C17) **5.** a habit which, worsening, flies entirely out of control. One is stopped so often in life that he becomes an enemy of stopping and dislikes stopping so intensely that he himself will not stop things. **Neurosis** and psychosis of all classes are entirely inabilities to start, to change or to stop. (*FOT*, p. 68)

**NEUROTIC, 1.** considered to be below 2.5. The **neurotic** has thorough concern about the future to the degree that he has many more fears about the future than he has goals in the future. He spends much of his time pondering the past. He acts and then wonders if he has acted correctly and is sure he has not. Thoughts to him are as solid as mest. He is overwhelmed by sudden counter-efforts. He is operating on a subcontrol center which has been itself very blunted. He is ill much of the time to a greater or lesser degree. He has colds. He brings "bad luck" and disaster. He is *Homo sapiens* at his "rational worst." (*AP&A*, p. 38) **2.** a **neurotic** is a person who has some obsession or compulsion which overmasters his self-determinism to such a degree that it is a social liability. (Spr Lect 9, 5303CM27) **3.** identified by the preclear having mock-ups which will not persist or which won't go away. (*COHA*, p. 232) **4.** a person who is mainly harmful to himself by reason of his aberrations, but not to the point of suicide. (*SOS*, pp. 25-26) **5.** the computation of present time only. (*Scn 0-8*, p. 89)

**NEW ERA DIANETICS,** a refinement of all previous **Dn** techniques from 1950 up to present time as well as the development of new technique giving much faster results and far higher gain per hour of auditing and speedy resolution of **Dn** cases. **NED** consists of at least 12 separate Rundowns. It occasionally makes a **Dn** Clear although this must not be promised. The only "trouble" with **NED** compared to earlier **Dn** is that it produces results very fast. One can achieve more result per hour of auditing time by about 100 to 1 over old **Dn** and when you realize that old **Dn** was the first and remains the only fast and effective processing known to Man you get some idea of where **NED** is at. (LRH ED 301 INT) *Abbr.* NED

**NEW ERA DIANETICS AUDITOR FOR OTs,** must be Class IV, OT III Hubbard Advanced Courses Specialists (HACS). (WIS, p. 36)

**NEW ERA DIANETICS CASE COMPLETION,** has successfully completed **NED** Rundowns on locks, secondaries and engrams. Ability gained: a truly well and happy human being. (WIS, p. 56)

**NEW ERA DIANETICS DRUG RUNDOWN COMPLETION,** has successfully completed **NED Drug Rundown** with the ability gained: freedom from the harmful effects of drugs, medicine and alcohol and free from need to take them. (WIS, p. 56)

**NEW ERA DIANETICS FOR OTs RUNDOWN, 1.** was developed especially for **Dn** and Scn Clears who have completed the Grade of **OT** III. L. Ron Hubbard's most major breakthrough since 1968 when he released **OT** III, it can only be delivered at Advanced Organizations and at Flag Land Base by Class IV, **OT** III Advanced Courses Specialists. The end phenomena of **"NED for OTs" Rundown** is: Cause over Life. (WIS, p. 13) **2.** the discovery and development of techniques by which the Second Wall of Fire can be overcome. This consists of 29 fantastic new confidential **Rundowns,** delivered by a specially trained **OT** auditor. Some of the miracles of life have been exposed to full view for the first time ever in **NED FOR OTs.** (LRH ED 301 INT)

**NEW ERA DIANETICS OBJECTIVES COMPLETION,** has successfully completed **New Era Dn Objective** Processes. Ability gained: in present time and havingness of present time environment. (WIS, p. 56)

**NEW PRECLEAR,** never before audited. (HCOB 5 Apr 69)

**NEW VITALITY RUNDOWN,** this was also called the "Special **Rundown**" when it was being developed in '75 and I trained a group of auditors on it at Flag. It has never been exported from Flag. It handled cases that had not progressed well due to suppression or other factors. (LRH ED 301 INT) *Abbr.* NVRD

**NINTH DYNAMIC, 1.** "the buck." (5203CM05A) **2.** aesthetics. (PDC 2)

**NIP,** you take two energy beams and you slap them together just back of a guy's ears. (PDC 27)

**NIPPING, 1.** you close down over the head of some mest body and you go "bat" and you really shoot the horsepower to him, the voltage, for just a split instant. (5206CM28A) **2.** an overt act of the thetan is **nipping** by which he harasses other thetans, **nipping** mest beings which usually kills them dead much to the thetan's surprise. (*HOM*, p. 50)

# NO AUDITING

**NO AUDITING,** while seeming to deliver auditing, actually getting nothing done. Going through endless, useless motions, perhaps in top form, perhaps perfectly, none of which are calculated to advance the pc's case one inch. (HCOB 30 Dec 62)

**NO CASE GAIN, 1.** persons with heavy overts on Scn make **no case progress.** (HCOB 23 Nov 62) **2.** no TA actions in auditing or "little TA" (less than ten divs per session). (HCO PL 5 Apr 65) **3.** no **case-change** despite good tries with the routine processes. (HCO PL 5 Apr 65 II)

**NO-GAIN-CASE, 1.** the suppressive person is a specialist in making others ARC break with generalized entheta that is mostly lies. He or she is also a **no-gain-case.** So avid are such for the smashing of others by covert or overt means that their case is bogged and won't move under routine processing. (HCO PL 5 Apr 65, *Handling the Suppressive Person*) **2.** such a person has withholds, he or she can't communicate freely to as-is the block on the track that keeps them in some yesterday. Hence, a **"no-case-gain."** (HCO PL 5 Apr 65, *Handling the Suppressive Person*) **3.** this **case** performs continual calculating covert hostile acts damaging to others. This **case** puts the enturbulence and upset into the environment, breaks the chairs, messes up the rugs and spoils the traffic flow with "goofs" done intentionally. (HCO PL 5 Apr 65, *Handling the Suppressive Person*) **4.** the "withholdy case that ARC breaks easily," "the blowy student" "unstable gain student." (HCO PL 5 Apr 65 II)

**NO-GAME,** preponderance of win or a preponderance of lose. (PAB 73)

**NO-GAME CONDITIONS, 1. no-game conditions** are: knowing all, not-knowing everything, serenity, namelessness, no-effect on opponent, effect on self or team, have everything, can't have nothing, solutions, pan-determinism, friendship with all, understanding, total communication, no communication, win, lose, no universe, no playing field, arrival, death. (*FOT,* p. 94) **2.** a totality of barriers and a totality of freedom alike are **no-game conditions.** (PAB 84) **3.** reached by a preponderance of win (**no-game**) or a preponderance of lose (**no-game**). (Op Bull No. 17)

**NO HAVINGNESS, 1.** is defined as something that a person can't reach or doesn't permit itself to be reached. (SH Spec 103, 6201C23) **2. no havingness** is prevented reach; in other words, the concept of no reach. (SH Spec 97, 6201C09)

**NO-INTERFERENCE AREA,** (zone) from R6 Solo to OT III one does not do anything except keep the pc winning for R6 Solo to OT III. This is the critical band of the gradation chart. From R6 to OT III you have a closed band for other major actions. (HCOB 23 Dec 71) **2.** where drugs have not been handled or only partially have been handled, the **no interference zone** rule is waived. (HCOB 31 May 74)

**NOMENCLATURE,** the set of terms used to describe things in a particular subject. (*Aud 73 ASHO*)

**NO MENTION,** a **no mention** of well done or very well done or anything simply means: (1) F/N did not get to examiner, (2) no major auditing errors exist in the session. (HCOB 21 Aug 70)

**NON-COMMUNICATION,** a **non-communication** consists of barriers. (*COHA*, p. 18)

**NON-CYCLICAL PROCESS,** a repetitive process which does not cause the preclear to cycle on the time track. (HCOB 29 Sept 65)

**NON-EXTANT ENGRAM,** an **"engram"** sometimes didn't exist. A pc can be trying to run being run over by a car when he never was. (HCOB 20 May 68)

**NON-READING ITEM,** one that did **not read** when originated or cleared and also did **not read** when called. (HCOB 28 Feb 71)

**NON-VOCAL LOCK SCANNING,** the preclear recognizes the phrases as he goes by them incident to incident, from early to late, but does not tell the auditor what phrases he is contacting. (*SOS*, Bk. 2, p. 126)

**"NO OVERTS" CASE,** a **case** that "has **never** committed any **overts.**" Such a person might for example **never** seem to have anything on F-2. (BTB 22 Oct 70R)

**NO RANDOMITY,** below minus randomity is **no randomity** of any kind. One could be at this point for two reasons: because he is shuddering away from confusion or he could be at that point because he has a tremendous tolerance for confusion and for motionlessness. (*Abil 36*, p. 9)

**NO RESPONSIBILITY, 1.** unwillingness to make a decision or unwillingness to make a condition of being is the highest essence of **no responsibility.** (PDC 7) **2.** the inability to handle force. (PDC 28)

**NORMAL,** type of case. The so-called **normal** is used here to be at around 2.5 to 3.0 on the tone scale. He is partially extroverted, partially introverted. He spends considerable time with his calculations. He evaluates slowly even when he has the data, and then postulates without realizing too much about his postulation. He has much in the past which he does not care to recall. He has much in his present which gives him concern. His future goals are rather well nullified by future fears. He is *Homo sapiens.* He is in terrible condition, taken from the viewpoint of *Homo novis.* He is in excellent condition from the viewpoint of past "ologies." (*AP&A*, p. 37)

**NORTH TO APATHY,** *Slang.* pcs, I discover, go from minus tone scale *up* to being able to have problems or tone or solids. Any case has some point that goes from no-effect or unreal or don't care, *up* **to apathy.** Cases go **north to apathy.** (HCOB 20 Aug 56)

**NO SYMPATHY, 1.** it's a blackout, it's an occlusion. "I'm **not** going to feel **sympathy** for it" is actually the phrase that goes with the concept. (5208CM07B) **2.** he's bound and determined **not** to be **sympathetic,** and that's the emotion of **no sympathy.** (5208CM07B) **3.** is an emotion and an action. One puts a black curtain before himself to prevent his feeling affinity with that which he is hurting. (*Scn 8-80*, p. 49)

**NO TA,** less than ten divisions per session (2 1/2 hours). (HCO PL 5 Apr 65, *Handling the Suppressive Person*) See also, TONE ARM ACTION.

**NOT BEINGNESS,** is an acceptance of control by the environment and abdication even of control of self. (*AP&A*, p. 51)

**NOT DOING THE AUDITING COMMAND,** is defined as simply not executing it, or doing something else, or executing the auditing command indifferently and then doing something else. (SH Spec 60, 6109C28)

**NOTHINGNESS, 1.** an absence of everything: no time, no space, no energy, no thought. (5501C14) **2.** an absence of quantities and locations. (5501C14)

**NO-TIME MOMENTS,** the only things which float on the time track are the moments of silence when no communication occurred. These are **no-time moments** and so have no time in which they can live, and so they float forward on the time track. (*Dn 55!*, p. 95)

**NOT IN PRESENT TIME,** a person who is talking on another subject than that to which cause was giving his attention. He has experienced such a scarcity of communication elsewhere, that he is still involved with communication elsewhere. This is what we mean by **"not in present time."** (*Dn 55!*, p. 76)

**NOT-IS-NESS, 1.** trying to put out of existence by postulate or force something which one knows, priorly, exists. One is trying to talk against his own agreements and postulates with his new postulates, or is trying to spray down something with the force of other is-nesses in order to cause a cessation of the is-ness he objects to. (*PXL*, p. 64) **2.** not-is-ness is the effort to handle is-ness by reducing its condition through the use of force. It is an apparency and cannot entirely vanquish an is-ness. (*PXL*, p. 154) **3.** there are two different conditions of **not-is-ness**: one is just vanishment. The other one is an is-ness which somebody is trying to postulate out of existence by simply saying, "It isn't." A **not-is-ness**, in our terminology, would be this second specialized case of an individual trying to vanish something without taking responsibility for having created it. (*PXL*, p. 100) **4.** not-is-ness is manifested as and is in itself the mechanism we know as unreality. (*PXL*, p. 55)

**NOT-IS STRAIGHTWIRE,** this is the direct cure of **not-is-ness**; and where you have a case that is running a bad **not-is** a process can evidently be invalidated or **not-ised** when the individual is out of session, or overnight. This is what **Not-is Straightwire** cures. (PAB 155)

**NOT KNOW, 1.** trying not to remember. (*FOT*, p. 84) **2.** an actual ability to **"not know"** is an ability to erase by self-command the past without suppressing it with energy or going into any other method. (PAB 87) **3.** in its most extreme manifestation is unconsciousness. **Not-know** in a lesser manifestation is death. The most extreme manifestation is when a person cannot go unconscious and we call that insanity. (SH Spec 15X, 6106C15)

**NOT KNOWINGNESS, 1.** being in present time and not in the past or the future. (PAB 88) **2.** mystery. (*COHA*, p. 16)

**NO TONE ARM ACTION,** there is **no** meter registry of change on the meter control lever (**tone arm**). (HCO PL 5 May 65) See also NO TA.

**NOT THERE,** dispersed, hiding himself, being vague, **not there** most of the time. (*FOT*, p. 29)

**NULLABLE,** the condition a list must be in order to have an item found on it. (HCOB 5 Dec 62)

**NULLABLE LIST,** is one where items just go out very easily and the needle doesn't dirty up to amount to anything. (SH Spec 220, 6211C29)

**NULLIFICATION,** the method of handling others wherein the individual seeks to minimize individuals, to be more than they and so to be able to control them. This category would rather see a man sick than well, because sick men are less dangerous than well men according to the "thinking" that takes place in this band. (*SOS,* p. 155)

**NULLING,** the auditor's action in saying items from a list to a pc and noting the reaction of the pc by use of an E-meter. (HCOB 5 Dec 62)

**NULL NEEDLE, 1.** means it doesn't get a change of pattern or a react on the question. (SH Spec 1, 6105C07) **2.** the **needle** continuing to behave in an action uninfluenced by the auditing question. (*BIEM,* p. 40)

**NULL SUBJECTS,** uncharged subjects. (HCOB 8 Oct 71 III)

**NUTRITION,** support of the organism by organic and inorganic means (food, water, air, sunlight) during all of the present life, from conception or thereabouts to death. The **nutrition** of a genetic line, of course, would pass from parents to children in the forms of organic inheritance and gestation environment. (*SOS* Gloss)

# O

**O=,** denotes an item which simply has the requirement of you reading, understanding and attesting in the space opposite the item on the checksheet. Your initials in the space provided indicate that you have read, understood and can apply the data concerned. (HCO PL 13 Apr 71)

**OBJECT, 1.** an **object** could be considered to be any unit manifestation of energy including matter. It has been found that the duration of an **object** roughly approximates its solidity. (*Scn 8-8008*, p. 14) **2. objects** consist of grouped particles. (PRO 13, 5408C20) **3.** a condensed piece of energy. (PDC 46)

Object

**OBJECTIVE,** dictionary definition "of or having to do with a material **object** as distinguished from a mental concept, idea or belief." Means here and now **objects** in PT as opposed to "subjective." (HCOB 2 Nov 57RA)

**OBJECTIVE ARC,** I have recently added a new process to be done before the full battery of **Objective** Processes. It is called **Objective ARC. Objective ARC** is the first **Objective Process** to be done on a pc. The end phenomena of this process would be a person in present time, cognition, and very good indicators, accompanied by an F/N. (HCOB 19 Jun 78)

**OBJECTIVE DUB-IN,** the manifestation of putting, unknowingly, perceptions which do not in actual fact exist, in the environment. (HCOB 11 May 65)

**OBJECTIVE ENVIRONMENT,** is the environment everyone agrees is there. (*HFP* Gloss)

**OBJECTIVE HAVINGNESS PROCESSES,** objective duplication increase. (HCOB 29 Sept 60)

**OBJECTIVE PROCESSES, 1. objective processes** deal with body motions and observing and touching **objects** in the auditing room. (HCOB 30 Sept 71 V) **2.** look around or physical contact processes are obviously **"objective."** Pcs who have been on drugs obviously have to be run on **objective** not subjective **processes.** Anyone can be brought more into present time with **objective processes.** (HCOB 2 Nov 57RA)

**OBNOSIS, 1.** the **observation of the obvious;** the ability to look at the **obvious.** (SH Spec 48, 6411C04) **2.** this is a coined (invented) word meaning **observing the obvious.** There is no English or any other language precise equivalent for it. (HCO PL 26 Jun 72)

**OBSERVER,** condition where the preclear cannot be anything— cannot occupy a source point or receipt point. (*COHA*, p. 169)

**OBSESSION,** he's just returning motion on something where he's had too much motion thrown at him on this subject. That's an **obsession,** and that's all an **obsession** is. It's just bouncing back the motion which has been bounced at him. (5206CM24C)

**OBSESSIVE COMMUNICATION,** an outflow which is not pertinent to the surrounding terminals and situation. In other words, compulsive or **obsessive communication** is an outflow which is not in reality with the existing reality. (*Dn 55!,* p. 93)

**OCA GRAPH, 1.** personality **graph, Oxford Capacity Analysis.** (HCOB 7 Sept 71) **2.** a specially prepared **graph** which plots ten traits of a pc's personality from a personality test taken by the pc. (BTB 5 Nov 72 IV)

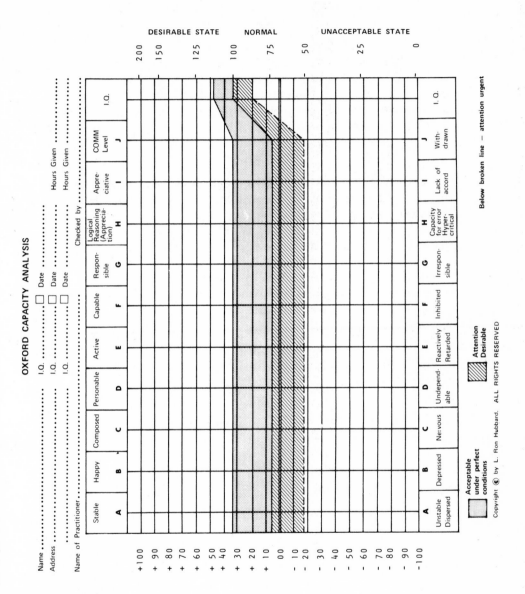

OXFORD CAPACITY ANALYSIS

DESIRABLE STATE    NORMAL    UNACCEPTABLE STATE

Name ...........
Address ...........
Name of Practitioner ...........

I.Q. ...... Date ......
I.Q. ...... Date ...... Hours Given ......
I.Q. ...... Date ...... Hours Given ......
Checked by ......

| Stable | Happy | Composed | Personable | Active | Capable | Respon-sible | Logical Reasoning (Apprecia-tion) | Appre-ciative | COMM Level | I.Q. |
|--------|-------|----------|------------|--------|---------|--------------|-----------------------------------|----------------|------------|------|
| A | B | C | D | E | F | G | H | I | J | |

| Unstable Dispersed | Depressed | Nervous | Undepend-able | Reactively Retarded | Inhibited | Irrespon-sible | Capacity for error Hyper-critical | Lack of accord | With-drawn | I.Q. |
|--------------------|-----------|---------|---------------|---------------------|-----------|----------------|-----------------------------------|----------------|------------|------|
| A | B | C | D | E | F | G | H | I | J | |

Below broken line — attention urgent

Acceptable under perfect conditions

Attention Desirable

OCA Graph

275

**OCCLUDED,** memory not available for recall. Someone who is **occluded** has a poor memory and poor recalls of the past. (*NSOL*, p. 144)

**OCCLUDED CASE, 1.** is fixed, most likely, in the effort of a heavy facsimile. The **occluded case** is using a service facsimile so heavily that it is in constant restimulation, and that service facsimile is occluded by heavy effort. The **occluded case** complains of illness, ordinarily. (*AP&A*, p. 41) **2.** your **occluded case** is simply a balled-up track. (5206CM24F) **3.** simply a heavily ridged case. (5203CM04B)

**OCCLUSION, 1.** something hidden, an **occlusion** of memory is something forgotten, i.e. not available to conscious recall. An **occluded** case is one whose memory is usually largely **occluded** and whose field of awareness is black or very dark. (*COHA* Gloss) **2. occlusion** is simply using remote viewpoints and then having the remote viewpoints go blank. (5410CM10B) **3.** loss of viewpoint of effects. When one has lost a viewpoint with which to perceive effects and upon which he depended for all perception of effect he is very **occluded.** (PAB 4)

**OCCLUSION TYPE OF CIRCUIT,** the **circuit** which drops curtains across certain pieces of information or may mask "I" from contact with the standard bank or the reactive bank. This **circuit** might be worded, "For your own good I have to protect you from yourself." (*SOS*, Bk. 2, p. 206)

**OCTSER, October series.** (HCOB 29 Sept 66)

**OFF, officer.** (BPL 5 Nov 72RA)

**OFF TECH, off technical.** (HCOB 23 Aug 65)

**OFF THE TRACK,** whenever you find a patient, returned, outside himself and seeing himself, that patient is **off the track.** (*DMSMH*, p. 320)

**OJ, overt justification** (a process name). (BTB 20 Aug 71R II)

**OKAY TO AUDIT,** an **okay to audit** means two things. There are two **okays to audit.** One is **okay to audit** as an intern. This means one has done the checksheet to the satisfaction of the intern supervisor. One can now audit for intern qualifications. The other is **okay to audit** as an HGC auditor. This means one has done the intern checksheet, has audited flublessly to many program completions and is passed by the HGC C/S. (HCO PL 24 Aug 71)

**OLD AGE,** is nothing more than a confirmed low tone on the physiological side. (5203CM05B)

**OLD CUFFS, 1.** [refers to a habit of writing on his **cuffs** of Ole Doc Methuselah's, a hero of an LRH science fiction book.] "Ole Doc sat in the sunlight and puffed his pipe and occasionally made intricate calculations on his gold **cuff**—his filing case was full of torn **cuffs** containing solutions which would have rocked even his brothers of the Universal Medical Society." (L. Ron Hubbard, *Ole Doc Methuselah*, p. 75) **2.** they're just suppositions and so forth, theories. (5410CM10C)

**OLD TIMER,** see FOUNDING SCIENTOLOGIST.

**OLFACTORY, 1.** with **olfactory** perception we perceive the minute particles of matter which register as smell. (*SOS*, p. 59) **2.** the sense of smell is evidently activated by small particles escaping from the object, which is thus sensed traveling through space and meeting the nerves. (*SA*, p. 87)

**-OLOGY,** means study. (5407C19)

**O-METER,** in 1955 a planned new and better E-meter than had ever been built before, under the trademarked name of **physio-galvanometer,** or **O-meter.** (PAB 52)

**ONE-FIVE (1.5 on the tone scale), 1.** numerical equivalent on the *Chart of Human Evaluation* for the person who is in overt hostility. Anger is his standard state. He is capable of taking destructive action and is characteristically trying to stop things. (*PXL* Gloss) **2.** total obstacle. The definition of **1.5** would be just that, total obstacle. (2ACC-30A, 5312CM21) **3.** a case of chronic anger or one which enturbulates easily into anger. (*SOS*, p. 51)

**ONENESS,** people have had the idea that there was a main body of theta and everybody became **"one"** when you got to the top of the tone scale. Fortunately that isn't true. But you go down tone scale and everybody becomes **one.** And the **oneness** is mest. There's no individuality whatsoever in mest. (PDC 6)

**ONE-SHOT CLEAR, 1.** there was a great deal of discussion in the '50s concerning the fact that there ought to be some chemical which one would load up into a syringe and the word **one-shot clear** became current. But it is actually a sarcastic word. I can absolutely assure you completely and 100 per cent that there is no magic single button. (Cl. VIII No. 9) **2.** the command "Be three feet back of your head." This is the **one-shot clear.** (5410CM10B) **3.** by **one-shot clear** we meant one phrase or one action given once or repeated, which would bring into being the **Clear** as described in *Dianetics: The Modern Science of Mental Health*, Chapter II. (*Dn 55!*, p. 134)

**ONE-VALUED LOGIC,** see LOGIC.

**ONE WITH THE UNIVERSE,** one of the control mechanisms which has been used on thetans is that when they rise in potential they are led to believe themselves **one with the universe.** This is distinctly untrue. Thetans are individuals. They do not as they rise up the scale, merge with other individualities. (*Scn 8-8008*, p. 25)

**ONLY ONE, 1.** if an individual can discover that he is **only** playing on the first dynamic and that he belongs to no other team it is certain that this individual will lose for he has before him seven remaining dynamics. And the first dynamic is seldom capable of besting by itself all the remaining dynamics. In Scn we call this condition the **"only one."** Here is self-determinism in the guise of selfish-determinism and here is an individual who will most certainly be overwhelmed. To enjoy life one must be some part of life. (PAB 84) **2.** just above zero on the tone scale. An individual must have no effect on self and total effect on everything and everybody else. Now that is the category of **only one.** This person can never communicate on a team basis. (5707C25) **3.** you can look at any person who is being dishonest or who is upsetting his environment or who is getting people into trouble all the time. You could look at that person and the actuality is he has no reality on his fellow man. He doesn't know they live. That's a very low-toned thing we call **"only one."** And when they get into that then they are able to do most anything. All criminals are in this bracket. (ASMC 2, 5506C03) **4.** the preclear has gotten into a state, ordinarily, where he is the **only**

**one** who can grant beingness, but he has so long restrained other people from granting life to things that he himself will no longer grant any life to things. (*COHA*, p. 56)

**OPENING PROCEDURE BY DUPLICATION**, gets the preclear to examine, communicate with and own two dissimilar objects. These objects are placed several feet apart and at a level so that the preclear can pick them up without bending over, but so he has to walk between them. (*COHA*, p. 48)

**OPENING PROCEDURE OF 8-C, 1.** the basic theory of **Opening Procedure of 8-C** is to make and break communication with the physical universe. Once an individual discovers that he can make and break communication with walls and objects, it will be discovered that he can let go of various pieces of his engram bank. (PAB 47) **2.** consists of having the preclear move his body around the room under the auditor's direction until (a) he finds he is in actual communication with many spots on the surface of things in the room, (b) until he can select spots in the room and know that he is selecting them and can communicate with them, and (c) select spots and move to them, decide when to touch them and when to let go. (*COHA*, p. 44)

**OPERATING**, able to act and handle things. (*Aud 10 UK*)

**OPERATING THETAN, 1.** a **thetan** exterior who can have but doesn't have to have a body in order to control or **operate** thought, life, matter, energy, space and time. (SH Spec 82, 6611C29) **2.** willing and knowing cause over life, thought, matter, energy, space and time. And that would of course be mind and that would of course be universe. (SH Spec 80, 6609C08) **3.** an individual who could **operate** totally independently of his body whether he had one or didn't have one. He's now himself, he's not dependent on the universe around him. (SH Spec 66, 6509C09) **4.** a Clear who has been refamiliarized with his capabilities. (HCOB 12 Jul 65) **5.** a being at cause over matter, energy, space, time, form and life. **Operating** comes from "able to **operate** without dependency on things" and **thetan** is the Greek letter **theta** (θ), which the Greeks used to represent "thought" or perhaps "spirit" to which an "**n**" is added to make a new noun in the modern style used to create words in engineering. (*BCR*, p. 10) **6.** by **operating thetan** we mean theta clear plus ability to operate functionally against or with mest and other life forms. (*SCP*, p. 3) **7.** this state of being is attained by drills and familiarity after the state of Clear has been obtained. A real **OT** has no reactive bank, is cause over matter, energy, space, time and thought and is completely free. (HCOB 12 Jul 65)

Operating Thetan Symbol

**OPERATION CLEAR,** it is **CLEAR** you, then **CLEAR** your environment, then **CLEAR** the country. (*Cert*, Vol. 5, No. 2, 1958)

**OPERATIVE SHOCK, a shock** to the person sufficient to blow up a few facsimiles. (5207CM24B)

**OPPOSE LIST, a list** in Routine 2-12 where if the reliable item found turned on pain, you list "Who or what would . . . (reliable item) **oppose?**" If it turned on sensation, list "Who or what would **oppose** . . . (the reliable item)?" (HCOB 23 Nov 62)

**OPPOSITE POSTULATE,** an individual who has made a postulate on a subject experiences "failure" when he has to make an **opposite postulate** later. The **opposite postulate** has the effect of a negative postulate. The **opposite postulate** is distinguished from a negative postulate because it depends upon effort which a negative postulate does not necessarily have to do. (*AP&A*, p. 34)

**OPPOSITE VECTOR CASE,** has private goals quite the reverse of getting better. (HCOB 24 Mar 60)

**OPPOSITION TERMINAL, 1.** a designation of a type of GPM item (R6 material). (HCOB 23 Aug 65) **2.** one of a pair of reliable items of equal mass and force, the significance of which the thetan has in **opposition** to his own intentions. (HCOB 13 Apr 64,

*Scn VI Part One Glossary of Terms*) **3.** an item or identity the pc has actually **opposed** (fought, been an enemy of) sometime in the past (or present) is called an **opposition terminal.** As the person identified himself as not it, he could experience from it only sensation. An **opposition terminal** when its mental residues (black masses) are recontacted in processing, produces only sensation, never pain. *Symbol:* oppterm. (HCOB 8 Nov 62)

**OP PRO BY DUP, Opening Procedure by Duplication.** (SH Spec 67, 6509C21)

**OPPTERM, opposition terminal.** (HCOB 8 Nov 62)

**OPTIMUM PRECLEAR,** would be one who had average response to noises and sights, who had accurate sonic and visio and who could imagine and know that he was imagining, in color-visio and tone-sonic. This person, understand clearly, may have aberrations which make him climb every chimney in town, drink every drop in every bar every night (or try it anyway), beat his wife, drown his children and suppose himself to be a jub-jub bird. In the psychosomatic line he may have arthritis, gall-bladder trouble, dermatitis, migraine headaches and flat feet. Or he may have that much more horrible aberration—pride in being average and "adjusted." He is still a relatively easy case to clear. (*DMSMH*, p. 191)

**OPTIMUM RANDOMITY, 1.** from the viewpoint of the individual, something which has in it the right amount of motion or unexpectedness for his tolerance. (*Scn AD*) **2.** the amount of unexpectedness and rapidness of motion he would be comfortable about. (*Abil 36*, p. 6) **3. optimum randomity** is a 50/50 ratio between cause and effect or a 50 percent offensive and 50 per cent defensive potential. (PAB 30)

**OPTIMUM SOLUTION,** the **solution** which brings the greatest benefit to the greatest number of dynamics. The infinitely perfect **solution** would be one which brought infinite survival on all dynamics. (*NOTL*, p. 96)

**O-RATING,** read and listen to the data and understanding of. (HCO PL 26 Jun 72 V) See also ZERO RATE.

**ORG, organization.** (HCOB 23 Aug 65)

ORGANIC, internal sensations and, by new definition, emotion. (*Abil 71*)

ORGANICALLY INSANE, missing or seared portions of the brain bringing about insanity, mainly genetic or iatrogenic and relatively rare except in institutions. (*DMSMH*, p. 172)

ORGANIC PERCEPTIONS, through **organic perceptions** we **perceive** the states of our own bodies, internally. (*SOS*, p. 59)

ORGANIC SENSATION, that **sense** which tells the central nervous system the state of the various **organs** of the body. (*SA*, p. 104)

ORGANISM, 1. a portion of mest which has been **organized** and is being controlled by theta. **Organisms** are alive. They are the physical manifestation of life. Theta is said, then, to be the "energy" of life. (It is not to be confused with physical energy, which is the "e" of "mest.") (*Abil 114A*) 2. an **organism** is composed of theta and mest and their altered form, entheta and enmest. (*SOS*, Bk. 2, p. 246)

ORIENTATION, determination of location in space and time and determination of energy quantity present. This applies to past, present, future. (*Scn 8-8008* Gloss)

ORIENTATION POINT, 1. that **point** in relation to which others have location. It is also that **point** from which the space containing the locations is being created. (*COHA*, p. 54) 2. a **point** of reference from which the position of other objects is judged. People are often found still using **orientation points** from childhood which may be thousands of miles from their present time location. The goal of Scientology is that the thetan be his own principal **orientation point**, and that he have the ability to use or discard any other point of reference. (*COHA* Gloss)

ORIGIN, a point of no-dimension, a point has neither length, breadth, nor depth. But it is something from which you could view length, breadth and depth. (PDC 11)

ORIGINAL ASSESSMENT SHEET, 1. this **sheet** is thoroughly filled out with the pc on the meter. It gives you the pc's history, what drugs and alcohol he has taken in this lifetime, illnesses, operations, present physical conditions, mental treatment, medicines and perception difficulties. (HCOB 22 Jun 78R) 2. the purpose of this form is to provide essential data regarding the preclear to the C/S, the D of P and the auditor, and to better acquaint the auditor with the preclear at the onset of auditing. (HCOB 24 Jun 78)

**ORIGINAL FORMULA,** the **original formula** which led us into Scientology was: having noted the conditions, I found it was necessary to communicate with them in order to perceive, orient myself in them, and with the resulting understandings find out what my purpose really was. And so that was a **formula**, and it was the **original formula** by which we moved in. (SH Spec 57, 6504C06)

**ORIGINAL ITEM,** the **original item** is a condition, illness, accident, drug, alcohol or medicine, etc. that has been given by the pc to the auditor. This will come from the **Original** Assessment Sheet, from another New Era Dn Rundown or may simply be offered by the pc. (HCOB 18 Jun 78R)

**ORIGINATION,** in TR-4 all **originations** concern the coach, his ideas, reactions or difficulties, none concern the auditor. By **originate** is meant a statement or remark referring to the state of the coach or fancied case. (HCOB 16 Aug 71 II)

**ORIGIN "I",** a viewpoint from which one can perceive anchor points. (PDC 13)

**ORIGIN OF THE PRECLEAR,** the **preclear** volunteers something all on his own. The **preclear** is as well as he can **originate** a communication. That means he can stand at cause on the communication formula. (PAB 151)

**O/R LISTING,** one clears **"overrun"** as "gone on too long" or "happened too often." Then one **lists** smoothly, calmly to the BD F/N item which simply appears. There is no nulling. (HCOB 19 May 71)

**-OSIS,** the condition of. (*Abil 180*)

**O.T., operating thetan,** highest state there is. (SH Spec 66, 6509C09)

**O.T. ACTIVITIES,** would be those programs conducted by OTs to assist Scientology. (SH Spec 84, 6612C13)

**OTHER-DETERMINED REALITY,** somebody has given him a facsimile and has really impressed him with it and so this looks more real to him than reality. (PRO 15, 5408CM20)

**OTHER-DETERMINISM, 1.** simply something else giving you orders or directions. (8ACC-6, 5410CM08) **2.** something has so thoroughly overwhelmed the pc that he is it. (HCOB 7 May 59)

**OTHER SIDE OF WITHHOLDS,** type of case, the person who is afraid to find out. (HCOB 15 Mar 62)

**OTHER TECH,** is defined as any **tech** which is not standard tech. (FO 800)

**OT METERS** (future **meters**), an entirely different **meter** for an entirely different purpose. It is for use above Clear up to **OT.** (*EME*, p. 26)

**OT-3A,** procedure tested and released in 1960 for use on staff clearing course, in the HGC, and co-audit to produce theta clears. (HCOB 24 Jan 60) [The full rundown is contained in the HCOB 25 Jan 1960, *OT-3 Procedure, HGC Allowed Processes.*]

**OT TR-0,** a drill to train students to be there comfortably and confront another person. The idea is to get the student able to be there comfortably in a position three feet in front of another person, to be there and not do anything else but be there. Student and coach sit facing each other with eyes closed. (HCOB 16 Aug 71 II)

**OUT,** things which should be there and aren't or should be done and aren't are said to be **"out,"** i.e. "Enrollment books are **out.**" (HCOB 19 Jun 71 III)

**OUT-CREATED,** created against too thoroughly. (PAB 85)

**OUT-ETHICS, 1.** an action or situation in which an individual is involved contrary to the ideals and best interests of his group. An act or situation or relationship contrary to the ethics standards, codes or ideals of the group or other members of the group. An act of omission or commission by an individual that could or has reduced the general effectiveness of a group or its other members. An individual act of omission or commssion which impedes the general well-being of a group or impedes it in achieving its goals. (HCO PL 3 May 72) **2.** a person who acts against his own moral codes and the mores of the group violates his integrity and is said to be **out-ethics.** (BTB 4 Dec 72)

**OUTFLOW, 1.** a person talking to somebody else, communicating to that person. (*Dn 55!*, p. 62) **2.** a thetan who is being interested is simply **outflowing.** Interested=**outflowing.** Interesting=inflowing. (*PXL*, p. 193)

**OUT LIST,** a wrong **list** item or a wrong **list.** (HCOB 20 Apr 72 II)

**OUT OF,** in heavily restimulated circumstances the person goes "out of." In such a condition people want to stop things, cease to act, halt life, and failing this they try to run away. As soon as the actual by-passed charge is found and recognized as the charge by the person, up goes affinity and reality and communication and life can be lived. (HCOB 19 Aug 63)

**OUT OF ARC PROCESS,** this is the command which asks for **out of affinity** moments, **out of reality** moments and **out of communication** moments. (HCOB 12 Jul 64)

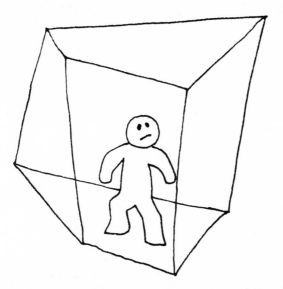

Out of Plumb

**OUT OF PLUMB,** a room has eight points at the baseboard and ceiling, and those will sometimes go completely askew. The eight points no longer make a box. They make a twisted space. The room looks like that to the person. (SH Spec 195A, 6209C27)

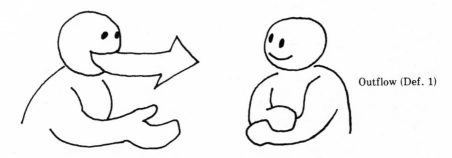

Outflow (Def. 1)

---

**OUT OF SESSION, 1.** when the preclear controls the session he is **out of session.** Therefore, it is necessary for the preclear not to stop or alter the course of action of an auditor. The moment that a preclear can satisfactorily, to himself, stop the auditor, that preclear is **out of session** and the probability of doing him much good while he is **out of session** is very remote. (HCOB 4 Oct 56) **2.** there are various degrees of being **out of session.** The most severe of these is the person who refuses auditing. The next degree is sitting in the chair but refusing to answer questions. The next degree is sitting in the chair and being uncooperative or even choppy. (HCOB 17 Nov 60) **3.** the definition of "in session" is (a) interested in own case, (b) willing to talk to the auditor. When either of these are violated the pc is **"out of session"** and is receiving no benefit from processing. (HCOB 17 Nov 60)

**OUT OF VALENCE, 1.** simply and entirely the pc was not in the body he was occupying during the incident. (SH Spec 51, 6109C07) **2.** in the pictures you get of old incidents, you may be seeing yourself "outside of yourself," not seeing the scene as you saw it then. This is being **out of valence.** (*HFP*, p. 92) **3.** it means the case is too heavily charged. It is very, very, very heavily charged. So the person cannot even come to the center of his bank, he can't be in the middle of his bank and look at it. He has been living for eons watching himself so that the pictures he takes are outside. (7203C30SO) **4.** if you look into suppressive person tech you will find an SP *has* to be **out of valence** to be SP. He does not know that he is because he is himself in a non-self **valence.** He is "somebody else" and is denying that he himself exists, which is to say denying himself as a self. (HCOB 17 Jul 71)

**OUT-POINT LIST,** these are the elements of illogic and insanity. (HCOB 28 Aug 70RA)

**OUT RUDIMENT,** a **rudiment** is **out** if it reads and in if it does not read. (*EMD*, p. 37)

**OUT RUDS,** are easy to spot. The person with an ARC break, won't talk or is misemotional or antagonistic. A problem produces fixated attention. Natter and 1.1 remarks means a withhold. (HCOB 15 Oct 74)

**OUT-SCANNING,** you get the energy emanating from the pre-clear to the environment in the incident. That's **out-scanning.** (HCL 4, 5203CM04B)

**OUT TECH,** means that Scientology is not being applied or is not being correctly applied. (HCOB 13 Sept 65)

**OUT THE BOTTOM,** *Slang.* the individual drops down the tone scale so far he can go no further down. It symbolized being worse off than merely being on the **bottom** of the ladder. Gone downward from the **bottom.** (LRH Def. Notes)

**OVER ACKNOWLEDGEMENT, 1. acknowledging** before the pc has said all. (HCOB 13 Apr 64, *Scn VI Part One Tone Arm Action*) **2.** giving an unnecessary number of Goods, Thank yous, etc., which will have the same effect as under acknowledging. (BTB 29 Jun 62)

**OVERAUDITING, auditing** beyond a grade of release attained. (*Aud 10 UK*)

**OVERBURDEN,** the incident is too charged in one place to be confronted. (HCOB 15 Jul 70)

**OVERLISTED LIST,** the pc is just kind of in apathy about it all and upset and sort of audited into the ground, and it's all sort of tight and the mass is tight and the needle is tight. The auditor had a complete **list** and didn't know when to stop. (SH Spec 255, 6304C04)

**OVER-PERCEPTION,** this is not necessarily imagination, but it can go to the length of seeing and hearing things which are not there at all, which happens to be a common insanity. (*DMSMH,* p. 189)

**OVER-RESTIMULATION, 1.** pc goes into more charge than he or she can itsa easily. The TA slows down. (HCOB 13 Apr 64, *Scn VI Part One Tone Arm Action*) **2.** something that is **over-restim-ulated** is not easily discharged because in some fashion or another the discharge has been prevented. It comes from getting a hold of too much and not discharging it. (SH Spec 300, 6308C28) **3.** there is a condition of **over-restimulation.** Its definition is, it will not discharge by ordinary means. (SH Spec 300, 6308C28)

**OVERRUN, 1.** an **overrun** means doing something too long that has engrams connected with it which means an engram chain with too many engrams on it being restimulated by life or auditing. Hence **overrun.** If this **overrun** persisted unhandled eventually the pc would be overwhelmed and one in theory, would have a low TA. (HCOB 16 Jun 70) **2.** gone on too long or happened too often. (HCOB 3 Jun 71) **3.** means the pc came out of the bank and the pc went back into it again. (Class VIII, No. 2) **4.** continuing a process past the optimum point. (*Abil 218*) **5.** running past a free, floating needle on any type of process. (HCOB 2 Aug 65)

**OVERRUNNING,** means accumulating protests and upsets about it until it is just a mass of stops. Anyone can do anything forever unless he begins to stop it. (HCOB 2 Jun 71 I)

**OVERSHOOTING,** going beyond a completion or completing a completion. (HCOB 16 Aug 70)

**OVERSHOT,** entered the case too high. (PAB 61)

**OVERT ACT, 1.** an **overt act** is not just injuring someone or something; an **overt act** is an **act** of omission or commission which does the least good for the least number of dynamics or the most harm to the greatest number of dynamics. (HCO PL 1 Nov 70 III) **2.** an intentionally committed harmful **act** committed in an effort to resolve a problem. (SH Spec 44, 6410C27) **3.** that thing which you do which you aren't willing to have happen to you. (1SH ACC 10, 6009C14)

**OVERT HOSTILITY,** here is the occasional grouch, the complaining individual who yet makes no mistake about what he finds wrong. The "blunt, honest" type who tactlessly tears up the tenderer feelings of companions is found in this band. (*SOS*, p. 20)

**OVERT-MOTIVATOR SEQUENCE, 1.** if a fellow does an **overt**, he will then believe he's got to have a **motivator** or that he has had a **motivator**. (AHMC 2, 6012C31) **2.** the **sequence** wherein someone who has committed an **overt** has to claim the existence of **motivators**. The **motivators** are then likely to be used to justify committing further **overt** acts. (*PXL* Gloss)

**OVERT OF OMISSION,** a failure to act resulting in the injury, reduction or degradation of another or others in their beingness, persons, possessions or dynamics. (HCOB 1 Nov 68 II)

**OVERWHELMING, 1.** as a person begins to be unwilling to **overwhelm,** he, of course, begins to be unwilling to win and so loses pan-determinism and sinks into self-determinism. Games are, for our auditing purposes, "contests in **overwhelmings.**" The primary **overwhelming** is to take space. (PAB 80) **2. overwhelming** does not consist of space, energy et al. It is the idea that an **overwhelming** has occurred. The winner is convinced that he has **overwhelmed** the opposing player. The loser is convinced that he has been **overwhelmed.** (PAB 80) **3.** to push in too tight. (SH Spec 57, 6109C21)

**OVERWHUMPED,** *Slang.* over-restimulated. (SH Spec 302A, 6309C03)

**O/W, overt/withhold.** (HCOB 23 Aug 65)

**O-W BY TRANSFER,** most pcs are on **O-W by transfer** which is to say when they kick George in the head they get a headache themselves. This makes them think they are George. (HCOB 22 Dec 60)

**OWN,** to **own** is not to label or cart away. To **own** is to be able to see or touch or occupy. (*FOT*, p. 33)

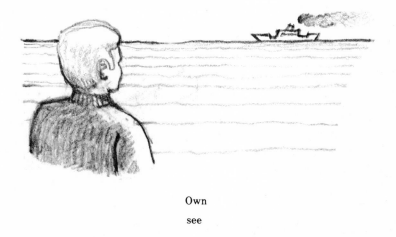

Own

see

touch

occupy

see definition on previous page

**OWNERSHIP, 1. ownership** is a problem of havingness. If you **own** something you can have it, if you don't **own** it you can't have it. (2ACC-29B, 5312CM20) **2. ownership** could be said to be that area being covered and protected by the preclear. (PAB 8)

**OWN VALENCE,** his **own** concept of himself. (PAB 95)

# P

**PAB, Professional Auditors Bulletin** (a series of technical booklet issues.) (BTB 20 Aug 71R II)

**PACK,** a **pack** is a collection of written materials which match a checksheet. It is variously constituted—such as loose-leaf or a cardboard folder or bulletins in a cover stapled together. A **pack** does not necessarily include a booklet or hardcover book that may be called for as part of a checksheet. (HCOB 19 Jun 71 III)

Pack

**PACKAGE,** always consists of two RIs that are terminals and two RIs that are oppterms. (HCOB 27 Jan 63)

# PACKAGE RUDIMENT QUESTION

**PACKAGE RUDIMENT QUESTION,** four **rudiments** in one **question** and therefore four major thoughts in one sentence. It's just a fast way of doing four **rudiments** in one sentence. (HCOB 25 May 62)

**PACKED UP METER,** a **meter** is "**packed up**" when the TA goes high or too low and the needle freezes and won't read. (HCOB 23 Sept 66)

Pain

**PAIN, 1.** is composed of heat, cold, electrical, and the combined effect of sharp hurting. If one stuck a fork in his arm, he would experience **pain.** When one uses **PAIN** in connection with clearing one means awareness of heat, cold, electrical or hurting stemming from the reactive mind. According to experiments done at Harvard, if one were to make a grid with heated tubes going vertical and chilled tubes going horizontal and were to place a small current of electricity through the lot, the device, touched to a body, would produce the feeling of **PAIN.** It need not be composed of anything very hot or cold or of any high voltage to produce a very intense feeling of **pain.** Therefore what we call **PAIN** is itself, heat, cold and electrical. If a pc experiences one or more of these from his reactive mind, we say he is experiencing **PAIN.** *Symbol:* PN. (HCOB 8 Nov 62) **2.** the sharp impulse or dull impulse of heat, cold and electrical. (SH Spec 202A, 6210C23) **3.** the sensation of **pain** is actually a sensation of loss. It is a loss of beingness, loss of position and awareness. (*COHA,* p. 210) **4.** too much motion too fast. (5203CM05B) **5. pain,** technically, is caused by an effort counter to the effort of the individual as a whole. (*Scn Jour 5-G*) **6. pain**

is the randomity produced by sudden or strong counter-efforts. (*AP&A*, p. 100) **7.** the sudden impact of theta and mest together could be considered a turbulence which creates dissonance in theta. This is registered and recorded as **pain**. (*SOS*, p. 40) **8.** theta and mest coming together too hard get into a turmoil which we call **pain**. (*SOS*, p. 5) **9. pain** is a warning of non-survival or potential death. (*SA*, p. 27)

**PAIN ASSOCIATION,** the person is made to **associate** his "wrong ideas" with **pain** so that he "will not have these ideas," or will be "prevented from doing these things." A crude current example is to electric shock a person every time he smokes a cigarette. After several "treatments" he is supposed to **associate** the **pain** with the idea and so "give up smoking." (HCOB 16 Jul 70)

**PAINFUL EMOTION ENGRAM, 1.** similar to other engrams. It is caused by the shock of sudden loss such as the death of a loved one. (*DMSMH*, p. 62) **2.** the death, departure or denial by an ally is a certain **painful emotion engram**. (*DMSMH*, p. 353)

**PAINFUL INCIDENT,** any **incident** which was **painful**; a death, an operation, a big failure, big enough to render you unconscious such as an accident. (*HFP*, p. 99)

**PAN-DETERMINISM, 1.** would mean a willingness to start, change and stop on any and all dynamics. That is its primary definition. A further definition, also a precision definition, is: the willingness to start, change and stop two or more forces, whether or not opposed, and this could be interpreted as two or more individuals, two or more groups, two or more planets, two or more like-species, two or more universes, two or more spirits whether or not opposed. This means that one would not necessarily fight, he would not necessarily choose sides. (*Dn 55!*, p. 100) **2.** defined as **determining** the activities of two or more sides in a game simultaneously. (PAB 84) **3.** the ability to regulate the considerations of two or more identities, whether or not opposed. (*COHA*, p. 110) **4.** full responsibility for both sides of a game. (*Scn 0-8*, p. 119)

**PAN-KNOWINGNESS,** in his native state, a thetan knows everything without looking, or anything, but he doesn't know any particulars of data. These are all invented. So what you would really call this would be a potentiality, or **pan-knowingness**. (PAB 64)

**PAPER TRICK,** there are cases around that have been "audited" for years who have never really done a process. This can be whipped by a Comm Process done with **paper** and pencil. [The comm process discussed in the reference HCOB is "From where could you communicate to a victim?"] You locate the terminal with an E-Meter and then you lay the instrument aside, give the pc a sheet of **paper** and a pencil, and every time he answers your auditing question, you have him or her draw the answer on the **paper.** As the Comm Process exceeds language, it can be easily checked. Even if the pc seems to be having some success but could succeed faster you can boost it along with the **"paper trick"** as this is called. (HCOB 27 Aug 59)

**PARANOID, 1.** a person with delusions, as of grandeur or, especially, persecution. (HCOB 11 May 65) **2.** is one on whom everything is impinged. There isn't really any such thing as a **paranoid.** There's such a thing as collapsed space. (PDC 26)

**PARA-SCIENTOLOGY, 1.** includes all of the uncertainties and unknown territories of life which have not been completely explored and explained. (PAB 85) **2.** that large bin which includes all greater or lesser uncertainties. Here are the questionable things, the things of which the common normal observer cannot be sure with a little study. Here are theories, here are groups of data, even groups commonly accepted as "known." (*COHA*, p. 188) **3.** those things which are uncertainties, such as metaphysics, spirits, other worlds, space opera, whole track, GE line, are all being put into the bin called **para-Scientology.** (PAB 2)

**PARTICLE,** energy is subdivisible into a large motion, such as a flow, a dispersal, or a ridge, and a small motion which is itself commonly called a **particle** in nuclear physics. Agitation within agitation is the basic formation of **particles** of energy, such as electrons, protons and others. (*Scn 8-80*, p. 43)

**PARTS OF MAN, 1.** the individual **man** is divisible (separable) into three **parts** (divisions). The first of these is the spirit, called in Scn the *Thetan*. The second of these **parts** is the *Mind*. The third of these **parts** is the *Body*. (*FOT*, p. 54) **2.** thetan, thetan machinery, body and the reactive-somatic mind. (8ACC 14, 5410C20)

**PAST,** on the time track, everything which is earlier than present time. (*SOS* Gloss)

**PASTORAL COUNSELING,** Dianetics is practiced in the Church of Scientology as **pastoral counseling,** addressing the spirit in relation to his own body and intended to increase well-being and *peace of mind.* (BPL 24 Sept 73RA XIII)

**PAST POSTULATES,** decisions or conclusions the preclear has made in the **past** and to which he is still subjected in the present. **Past postulates** are uniformly invalid since they cannot resolve present environment. (*HFP* Gloss)

**PATHOLOGY, THREE STAGES OF,** *predisposition,* by which is meant the factors which prepared the body for sickness, *precipitation,* by which is meant the factors which cause the sickness to manifest itself, and *perpetuation,* by which is meant the factors which cause the sickness to continue. (*DMSMH,* pp. 91-92)

**PATIENT,** preclear. (PAB 87)

**PATTY-CAKED,** *Slang.* the auditor left off simply because the preclear was having difficulty doing the process. (*COHA,* p. 113)

**PC, preclear.** (HCOB 23 Aug 65)

**PC EXAMINER,** that person in a Scn Church assigned to the duties of noting **pcs'** statements, TA position and indicators after session or when **pc** wishes to volunteer information. (HCO PL 4 Dec 71 V)

**PCRD, Primary Correction Rundown: a corrective** action. Purpose: to get the person through the PRD. (HCOB 20 Jul 72 I)

**PC TYPE A,** has few personal problems. Even when they occur he isn't upset by them. Handles life easily. Is energetic generally and able to work efficiently at things. Takes setbacks optimistically. Feels good most of the time. (HCOB 29 Jun 64)

**PC TYPE B,** is deluged with personal problems. Can't see any way out. Gets upset easily or is just in plain apathy and is never upset because things aren't real anyway (like a boulder wouldn't get upset). Has a hard time in life. Is generally tired and can't work very long at anything. Takes setbacks emotionally or just collapses. Feels ill most of the time. A **type B** can't be cause. (HCOB 29 Jun 64)

**PDH, 1.** stands for **pain drug hypnosis.** It is known to some psychiatrists as a means of compelling obedience. They sometimes use it on psychotics. (LRH ED 2 US and 2WW Only) **2. pain drug hypnosis**—a **drug** is administered to a person, the person is put into a trance and is told things. (5203CM05D)

**PE, Personal Efficiency Foundation.** (HCOB 23 Aug 65)

**PECULIAR CASES,** all **peculiar cases** were **cases** that weren't run by standard tech. (Class VIII, No. 1)

**PE FOUNDATION,** a programmed drill calculated to introduce people to Scn and to bring their cases up to a high level of reality both on Scn and on life. (HCOB 29 Sept 59)

**PERCEPTS,** see PERCEPTICS, def. 2.

**PERCEPTICS, 1.** sense messages. (*SOS*, p. 9) **2.** specialized data from the standard memory or reactive banks which represent and reproduce the sense messages of a moment in the past. The sense messages of present time, also; (formerly the word **"percepts"** was used to mean the sense messages of present time, but usage has dropped this distinction). (*SOS* Gloss)

**PERCEPTION, 1. perception** is the process of recording data from the physical universe and storing it as a theta facsimile. (*HFP*, p. 181) **2.** channels through which one can contact the physical universe. (*SA*, p. 64) **3.** any means of communicating below the level of knowingness. There are more than fifty **perceptions** used by the physical body, the best-known of which are sight, hearing, touch, taste and smell. (*COHA* Gloss)

**PERCEPTION POINT,** there would be a viewpoint, which is a **perception point,** which would consist of look, and smell, and talk and hear, and all sorts of things could be thrown in under this category, viewpoint. Ordinarily we simply mean at that level of the scale, looking, but you can throw all the rest of the **perceptions** in at that level of the scale. (*PXL*, p. 257)

**PERFECT COMMUNICATION,** a **perfect communication** is one which is duplicated **perfectly** at the effect point whatever emanated from the cause point. (UPC 1, 5406CM05)

**PERFECT DUPLICATE, 1.** a **perfect duplicate** is an additional creation of the object, its energy, and space, in its own space, in its own time, using its own energy. This violates the condition that two objects must not occupy the same space, and causes a vanishment of the object. (*Scn 0-8*, p. 31) **2.** it means a copy in its own space with its own particles in its own time. It'll disappear if you do that. (5410CM10B)

**PERFECT DUPLICATION,** cause and effect in the same point in space. (*PXL*, p. 114)

**PERMANENT CERTIFICATE,** in the case of an auditor, an internship or formal auditing experience is required. When actual honest evidence is presented to C&A that he has demonstrated that he can produce flubless results his **certificate** is validated with a gold seal and is a **permanent certificate**. With other courses the person must demonstrate that he can apply the materials studied by producing an actual, honest statistic in the materials studied. He presents this evidence to C&A and receives a validation gold seal on his **certificate**. (HCO PL 31 Aug 74 II)

**PERMANENT RESTIMULATION,** the mechanism of **permanent restimulation** consists of opposing forces of comparable magnitude which cause a balance which does not respond to current time and remains "timeless." (HCOB 13 Apr 64, *Scn VI Part One Tone Arm Action*)

**PERPETUATION,** by which is meant the factors which cause the sickness to continue. (*DMSMH*, p. 92)

**PERSISTENCE,** the ability to exert continuance of effort toward survival goals. (*Scn 0-8*, p. 73)

**PERSISTENT F/N,** unkillable **F/N**. It's **persistent** at least for that day. (HCOB 8 Oct 70)

**PERSONAL IDENTITY,** the composite of all your experience plus an initial decision to be and occasional decisions not to be. You do not die as an identity or a personality or an individual. You and the mest body "separate" and the mest body gets a funeral. (*HFP*, p. 76)

**PERSONAL INTEGRITY,** is knowing what you know. What you know is what you know, and to have the courage to know and say what you have observed. And that is **integrity** and there is no other **integrity.** (*B&C*, p. 21)

**PERSONALITY, 1.** the individual, the **personality,** is the awareness of awareness unit, and the awareness of awareness unit is the **person.** (*Dn 55!*, p. 17) **2.** a complex of inherited (mest, organic, theta) and environmental (aberration, education, present time environment, nutrition, etc.) factors. (*SOS* Gloss)

**PERSONALITY ACCESSIBLE,** means a **person** who will talk to you about his condition without being antagonistic. (*NOTL,* p. 34)

**PERSONALITY GRAPH,** a picture of a valence. On any human being, he himself is not really enough there to have a **personality.** (SH Spec 70, 6607C21) See also OCA GRAPH.

**PERSONAL MOTION,** this is awareness of change of position in space. This perception is assisted by sight, the feel of wind, changes in body weight, and by the observation of external environment. (*SA*, p. 106)

**PERSONAL PRESENCE ALTITUDE,** the individual who leads or makes an impression upon others merely by his **presence,** by his example and the fact of his existence, has **personal presence altitude.** Ghandi had this to a very high degree. (*SOS* Gloss)

**PERSONAL ROLLER COASTER,** (From HCOB 5 Dec 68). Same as **roller coaster.** (LRH Def. Notes)

**PERSONNEL PROGRAMMER,** a **Personnel Programmer** works with individual staff members and draws up workable **personnel programmes** and sees that they are fully executed. The purpose of a **Personnel Programmer** is to help LRH to expertly **programme** each staff member to a point of real success on their own post, to operate well as a member of the group and attain higher and higher levels of skill, knowledge and ability, through full use of the technology of Dn and Scn. (HCO PL 22 Jan 72 II)

**PGM, Program** (FO 2192)

**PHANTOM SLAM,** always comes on and goes off and comes on and goes off and a **phantom slam** has this characteristic; that it never obeys the auditor. The **phantom slam** may turn on and louse you up on the list as to which item is **rockslamming.** You don't ever get a **phantom slam** on an uncharged list. The list has to be "hotter than a pistol" to turn the **slam** on. Completely aside from the **phantom slam** this type of case will never do what you tell them. You say, "Has anything been suppressed?" and they don't think about suppressing something, they think about something else. (SH Spec 225, 6212C13)

**PHC, First Phoenix Congress.** (HCOB 29 Sept 66)

**PHD, Philadelphia Doctorate Course.** (HCOB 29 Sept 66)

**PHI (φ),** mest. (*NOTL,* p. 142)

**PHILOSOPHY, 1.** the pursuit of knowledge. The knowledge of the causes and laws of all things. (*SPB,* p. 1) **2.** a love or pursuit of wisdom or a search for the underlying causes and principles of reality. (Ron's Jour 68)

**PHRASE,** can be an enforced command thing which an individual then takes as a superior command or even can take as his own postulate. (PDC 7)

**PHS, Philadelphia Doctorate Course Supplementary Lectures.** (HCOB 29 Sept 66)

**PHYSICALLY ILL PC,** he is in suppressed pain and each time he gets a *change,* he puts on full stops as it started to hurt. He won't get the same gain again and tomorrow the same process or type of process won't work. He stops the pain if it starts to hurt, puts a new stop on his case. Slow gain, poor result is a **physically ill pc.** (HCOB 12 Mar 69)

**PHYSICAL PAIN,** the alarm reaction to theta that the organism has been too heavily impinged upon mest. **Physical pain** is an abrupt and sharp warning of non-survival. (*SOS,* Bk. 2, p. 22) **2.** theta and mest are many times brought together in disorderly collision. This creates the phenomenon known as **physical pain.** (*SOS,* Bk. 2, p. 4)

**PHYSICAL UNIVERSE, 1.** the **universe** of matter, energy, space and time. It would be the **universe** of the planets, their rocks, rivers, and oceans, the **universe** of stars and galaxies, the **universe** of burning suns and time. In this **universe** we would not include theta as an integral portion, although theta obviously impinges upon it as life. (*SOS,* p. 4) **2.** the **physical universe** is reducible to motion of energy operating in space through time. (*Scn 0-8,* p. 71)

**PHYSICAL WELL-BEING,** absence of factors which predispose him to illness. (*SOS,* p. 15)

**PHYSIO-ANIMAL BRAIN,** the **physio-animal** section of the **brain,** contains the motor controls, the sub-brains, and the physical nervous system in general, including the physical aspect of the analytical section of the brain. The control of all voluntary and involuntary muscles is contained in this section. It commands all body fluids, blood flow, respiration, glandular secretion, cellular construction, and the activity of various parts of the body. (*DTOT,* p. 23)

**PHYSIOGALVANOMETER,** see O-METER.

**PHYSIO-ANIMAL MIND,** the **physio-animal mind** has specific methods of "thinking." These are entirely reactive; **animal** experimentation—rats, dogs, etc.—is experimentation on and with precisely this **mind** and little more. It is a fully conscious **mind.** There is no period in the life of the organism from conception to death when this mind is not awake, observing, and recording perceptics. This is the **mind** of a dog, cat or rat and is also the basic **mind** of a man so far as its operating characteristics are concerned. (*DTOT,* p. 24)

**PIANOLA CASE, 1.** a **case** that was wide open, had sonic recall, visio recall, no pain shut-offs or anything and you just said "Go back to the earliest moment of pain or unconsciousness" and the fellow went and you say, "Go to the beginning of the engram" and he goes, and you run it out and it erases. Well, they'd begun to call this the **pianola case,** because it plays itself. (5009CM23B) **2.** in a **pianola case,** the file clerk works with you. The somatic strip does what you tell it to do. (*NOTL,* p. 68) **3.** a **case** that has easy running in all perceptics. (*NOTL,* p. 25)

**PICTURE,** facsimile. (PAB 136) See FACSIMILE.

**PICTURE AND MASSES REMEDY, 1.** it is usual to do a **PICTURE AND MASSES REMEDY** to find and handle restimulated engram chains which are causing the TA to be high. (HCOB 16 Aug 70R) **2.** the anaten pc—dopes off in session—high TA. The handling of the pcs or pre-OTs that fall under the above category, even though they were well rested before session consists of: the case supervisor sends the pc or pre-OT to a Dn auditor who would list: "What **pictures** or **masses** have you touched on in life or in auditing that have been left unflat?" The Dn auditor would get the best reading item from the list, gets the somatic or pain, or sensation or unwanted emotion or attitude that goes with that **picture** or **mass**, makes sure that it reads well, and he would follow down to basic and erasure that item that read with the **picture** or the **mass** by standard R3R. The list is reassessed and is exhausted as above. (BTB 3 Oct 69R) [Note: The referenced BTB gives two additional remedies for handling the anaten pc—dopes off in session—high TA.]

**PINCH TEST,** for demos you can do a **"pinch test"** where you explain to the pc that to show him how the meter registers mental mass—you will give him a **pinch** as part of the demo. Then get him to think of the **pinch** (while he is holding the cans) showing him the meter reaction and explaining how it registers mental mass. (BTB 8 Jan 71R)

**PINK SHEET, pink sheets** are issued by a course supervisor as a corrective measure. A student is given a **pink sheet** when something earlier was missed that should have been learned. The principle of the **pink sheet** is that a student is responsible for all the material he has studied earlier. If he is unable to apply or use any of this material then the **pink sheet** is issued to remedy the situation. It gives the student a study assignment calling for restudy and checkout of the specific materials pertaining. It is a quick and precise remedy. (HCOB 19 Jun 71 III)

**PL, policy letter.** (BPL 5 Nov 72RA)

**PLATEN,** a card with holes in it that is put on another paper and has in it the line plot mostly written out. (HCOB 8 Dec 64)

**PLAY, 1.** somebody invented the difference between work and **play. Play** was seen to be something interesting and work was seen to be something arduous and necessary. **Play** is almost purposeless. Work has a purpose. **Play** should be called work without a purpose. Activity without a purpose. (*POW*, p. 32) **2.** unreal or delusory motion about which you are not supposed to be serious; you are not supposed to as-is it. (SH Spec 19, 6106C23)

**PLEASURE, 1.** the Dn definition of **pleasure** is that the organism tending toward survival obtains **pleasure** by survival actions and the seeking of survival goals. (*SOS,* Bk. 2, p. 84) **2.** the perception of well being or an advance toward the ultimate goal. (*DTOT*, p. 20) **3.** creative and constructive effort. (*DASF*)

# PLEASURE MOMENTS

**PLEASURE MOMENTS,** mental image pictures containing **pleasure** sensations. They respond to R3R. One seldom addresses them unless the preclear is fixated on some type of **"pleasure"** to a point where it has become highly aberrated. (HCOB 23 Apr 69)

Pleasure Moment

**PLOTTING,** the action of obtaining goals or items from the pc and positioning them in their correct sequence on their respective **plots.** (HCOB 13 Apr 64, *Scn VI Part One Glossary of Terms*)

**PLS, Public Lecture Series** (American). (HCOB 29 Sept 66)

**PLUS-POINT LIST,** they are the elements of logic and sanity. (HCOB 28 Aug 70RA)

**PLUS RANDOMITY,** from the viewpoint of the individual, something which has in it too much motion or unexpectedness for his tolerance is **plus randomity.** (*Abil 36*)

**P.M., pleasure moment.** (*Hubbard Chart of Human Evaluation*)

**PN,** symbol for **pain** or electrical. (HCOB 19 Jan 67)

**POINT OF VIEW, point** from which he was looking, rather than his opinions. (*Dn 55!,* p. 69)

**POINTS,** the arbitrary assignment of a credit value to a part of study materials. "One page equals one **point.**" "That drill is worth 25 **points.**" (HCOB 19 Jun 71 III)

**POINTS SYSTEM,** the **system** of assigning and counting up **points** for studies and drills that give the progress of a student and measure his speed of study. They are kept track of by the student and course administrator and added up each week as the student's statistic. The statistic of the course is the combined study **points** of the class. (HCOB 19 Jun 71 III)

**POLE THETA TRAP,** the being is shot into the implant area put on a post wobbled around and then ran through this implant of goals, on a little monowheel **pole trap** which had the effigy of a body on it, the being didn't have a body and was put on a **pole trap.** The **pole trap** has a body on it. (SH Spec 266, 6305C21)

**POLITICAL DIANETICS,** embraces the field of group activity and organization to establish the optimum conditions and processes of leadership and inter-group relations. (*DMSMH*, p. 152)

**POOR CASE CONDITION OR INCOMPLETE,** a staff member who is in a state of chronic repair or who is not in good physical condition or good **case condition** as they are defined. (HCO PL 21 Oct 73R)

**POOR MEMORY,** a **poor memory** means a curtained **memory**, the **memory** being complete. Every perception observed in a lifetime is to be found in the banks. (*EOS*, p. 54)

**POSITIONAL ALTITUDE,** deriving from an arbitrarily assigned **position.** Military officers and bureaucrats often depend heavily upon **positional altitude.** (*SOS* Gloss)

**POSITIVE POSTULATE,** it's not only that there is no negative given attention to, but it does not assume that any negative is possible. (ESTO 6, 7203C03 SO II)

**POSITIVE PROCESSING,** this consists of addressing the theta on the case and bringing it to view. (*SOS*, Bk. 2, p. 281)

**POST INJURY,** after **injury.** (HCOB 12 Mar 69)

**POSTOPERATIVE,** after **operation.** (HCOB 12 Mar 69)

**POSTPARTUM PSYCHOSIS,** mental upset due to delivery of a baby. (HCOB 15 Jan 70)

**POST PURPOSE CLEARING,** an essential part of hatting; to get the person's **post purpose cleared** by an auditor. This requires an auditor, an E-meter, and is done in session. Staff member must bring hat folder to the **PPC** session so if there is any confusion on **purposes** in it they can be **cleared** up from the hat folder. (HCOB 4 Aug 71R) *Abbr.* PPC.

**POSTULATE,** *n.* **1.** a self-created truth would be simply the consideration generated by self. Well, we just borrow the word which is in seldom use in the English language, we call that **postulate.** And we mean by **postulate,** self-created truth. He **posts** something. He puts something up and that's what a **postulate** is. (HPC A6-4, 5608C--) **2.** a **postulate** is, of course, that thing which is a directed desire or order, or inhibition, or enforcement, on the part of the individual in the form of an idea. (2ACC 23A, 5312CM14) **3.** that self-determined thought which starts, stops or changes past, present or future efforts. (*AP&A*, p. 33) **4.** is actually a prediction. (5112CM30B) —*v.* **1.** in Scn the word **postulate** means to cause a thinkingness or consideration. It is a specially applied word and is defined as causative thinkingness. (*FOT,* p. 71) **2.** to conclude, decide or resolve a problem or to set a pattern for the future or to nullify a pattern of the past. (*HFP,* p. 155) **3.** to generate or "thunk" a concept. A **postulate** infers conditions and actions rather than just plain thinks. It has a dynamic connotation. (SH Spec 84, 6612C13)

**POSTULATE OFF, 1. postulate off** = erasure. (HCOB 24 Sept 71R) **2.** the EP of a Dn chain is always always always the **postulate** coming **off.** The **postulate** is what holds the chain in place. Release the **postulate,** the chain blows. That's it. (HCOB 16 Sept 78) **3.** only when the **postulate** has come off to F/N and VGIs can one consider that the full EP of a Dn incident or chain has been reached. (HCOB 26 Jun 78RA II)

**POSTULATE PROCESSING, 1.** that **processing** which addresses the **postulates,** evaluations and conclusions of the preclear at the level of self-determined thought, yet **postulate processing** has some value when addressed to stimulus-response ideas. **Postulate processing** is the primary and highest method of **processing** a thetan. With creative processing, it constitutes *Scn 8-8008.* (*Scn 8-8008,* p. 37) **2.** the **process** or any **process** which permits an individual to change his **postulates.** (PDC 37)

**POSTULATED REALITY,** a second type of **reality** is **postulated reality,** which is brought into being by creative or destructive imagination. (*SOS,* p. 97)

**POTENTIAL TROUBLE SOURCE, 1.** a person or preclear who "roller-coasters," i.e., gets better, then worse. This occurs only when his connection to a suppressive person or group is unhandled and he must, in order to make his gains from Scn permanent, receive processing intended to handle such. (*ISE,* p. 48) **2.** somebody who is connected with an SP who is invalidating him, his beingness, his processing, his life. (SH Spec 63,

6506C08) **3.** means the case is going to go up and fall down. He's a **trouble source** because he's going to get upset. He's a **trouble source** because he's going to make **trouble.** And he's **trouble** for the auditor and he's **trouble** for us and he's **trouble** for himself. (SH Spec 68, 6510C14) **4.** it means someone connected to a person or group opposed to Scn. It is a technical thing. It results in illness and roller-coaster and is the cause of illness and roller-coaster. (HCOB 17 Apr 72) *Abbr.* PTS.

**POTENTIAL VALUE, 1.** the **potential value** of the individual is derived from his ability to think and his power in the following fashion, where **PV** equals **potential value,** A equals ability to think and D equals power. $PV=AD^x$. (*DASF*) **2.** equal to intelligence multiplied by the dynamics of the individual to a certain power. This might be restated as meaning that the **potential value** of any man was equal to some numerical factor, denoting his structural intelligence and capability, multiplied by his free theta to a power. This was written in the handbook in an effort to encourage some psychologist to discover what the power of the dynamic might be and conclude some means of establishing **potential value** by psychometry. (*SOS*, p. 126) **3.** the **potential value** of an individual or a group may be expressed by the equation $PV=ID^x$ where I is intelligence and D is dynamic. The worth of an individual is computed in terms of the alignment, on any dynamic, of his **potential value** with optimum survival along that dynamic. (*DMSMH*, p. 40)

**POWER, 1.** the amount of work which can be accomplished in a unit of time, or the amount of force which can be applied in a unit of time. **Power** has the connotation of being potential. **Power** does not necessarily mean application of it. (SH Spec 83, 6612C06) **2.** the ability to maintain a position in space. (PAB 131)

**POWER AUDITOR,** a graduate of the Saint Hill Special Briefing Course who has also served the Saint Hill Internship. Only they are qualified to do the **power** processes of Grade V. They are Class VII **auditors.** (*ISE*, p. 45)

**POWER PROCESSES,** the **processes** audited only by Class VII auditors which make Grade V Power Releases. (*Scn AD*)

**PPC, Post Purpose Clearing.** (HCOB 4 Aug 71R)

**PR, process.** (BTB 20 Aug 71R II)

**PR (PUBLIC RELATIONS), 1.** *Slang.* to cover up, putting up a lot of false reports to serve as a smoke screen for idleness or bad actions. (HCO PL 4 Apr 72) **2. public relations** cheery false-hoods. (HCOB 22 Sept 71) **3.** a technique of communicating ideas. (HCO PL 13 Aug 70 I)

**PRACTICAL,** the drills which permit the student to associate and coordinate theory with the actual items and objects to which the theory applies. **Practical** is application of what one knows to what one is being taught to understand, handle or control. (HCOB 19 Jun 71 III)

**PRACTICAL INSTRUCTOR,** assists the **practical** supervisor, handles all **practical** administration and acts as auditing supervisor. (HCO PL 18 Dec 64)

**PRACTICAL SUPERVISOR,** handles all **practical** instruction, acts as auditing **supervisor.** (HCO PL 18 Dec 64)

**PR AUDITING REPORT,** meaning **promoting** instead of auditing. A false **auditing report.** (HCOB 16 Aug 70)

**PRD, Primary Rundown.** (HCOB 20 Jul 72 I)

**PREASSESSMENT, 1.** is a new procedure in New Era Dn. It is done with a prepared **Preassessment** List and determines what categories of somatics are connected to the original item, and which of these is the most highly charged. (HCOB 18 Jun 78R) **2.** this is a new procedure on the handling and running of Dn. It ensures that every somatic is gotten off in connection with whatever you are handling. (HCOB 22 Jun 78R) **3.** the **Preassessment** is done to get running items. (HCOB 18 Jun 78R)

**PREASSESSMENT ITEM,** this is in turn the largest reading **item** on the **Preassessment** List and then subsequently lesser reading **items** from the same list are taken up. (HCOB 18 Jun 78R)

**PREASSESSMENT LIST,** this is found in New Era Dn Series 4-1. A prepared **list** of categories of somatics which is assessed in connection with the original item. (The **list** includes pains, sensations, feelings, emotions, attitudes, misemotions, unconsciousnesses, sorenesses, compulsions, fears, aches, tirednesses, pressures, discomforts, dislikes, numbnesses.) (HCOB 18 Jun 78R)

**PRECIPITATION,** the factors which cause the sickness to manifest itself. (*DMSMH*, p. 92)

**PRECLEAR, 1.** a person who, through Scn processing, is finding out more about himself and life. (*PXL*, p. 20) **2.** a spiritual being who is now on the road to becoming Clear, hence *pre*clear. (HCOB 5 Apr 69) **3.** one who is discovering things about himself and who is becoming clearer. (HCO PL 21 Aug 63)

**PRECLEAR ASSESSMENT SHEET,** the purpose of this form is to establish auditor control over the preclear, to better acquaint the auditor with his preclear, and to provide essential information required. (BTB 24 Apr 69R)

**PRECURSOR,** earlier engram. (*DTOT*, p. 98)

**PREDICTION, 1.** when we speak of **prediction** we mean that he should be in communication with his environment as it will exist, as well as it exists. (*Dn 55!*, p. 62) **2.** the process of knowing the future. Living only for today is the process of not knowing the future. (*FOT*, p. 85)

**PREDISPOSITION, 1.** before the fact, the guy is disposed to get sick. (7204C07SO III) **2.** the factors which prepared the body for sickness. (*DMSMH*, p. 92)

**PREFRONTAL LOBOTOMY,** uses a scalpel or ice pick to perform an operation on the **prefrontal lobes** of the brain. (*DMSMH*, p. 151)

**PRE-HAVE,** before one attained **havingness** he ran a "**before-havingness**" process hence "**pre (before) have.**" When the full scale was achieved he could **have.** (LRH Def. Notes)

**PREHAVINGNESS BUTTONS,** the things that prevent people from **having.** (SH Spec 18, 6106C22)

**PREHAVINGNESS SCALE, 1.** an assessment **scale** which takes in most possible formulas and regimens: **Havingness** is the make-break point of a case. Before **havingness** can be tested for, all heavy areas on the lower part of the **scale** must be flat. The most elementary use of the **scale** is to assess the points on the **scale** upwards until a fall is observed and then to run this fall out. (HCOB 28 Jan 61) **2.** any **scale** giving degrees of doingness or not doingness. (HCOB 7 Nov 62 III)

Preclear

# PREMATURE ACKNOWLEDGEMENT

**PREMATURE ACKNOWLEDGEMENT,** occurs when you "coax" a person to talk after he has begun with a nod or a low "yes" you ack, make him forget, then make him believe you haven't got it and then make him tell you at great length. He feels bad and doesn't cognite and may ARC break. Any habit of agreeable noises and nods can be mistaken for **acknowledgement,** ends cycle on the speaker, causes him to forget, feel dull, believe the listener is stupid, get cross, get exhausted explaining and ARC break. The missed withhold is inadvertent. One didn't get a chance to say what one was going to say because one was stopped by **premature acknowledgement.** Result, missed W/H in the speaker, with all its consequences. (HCOB 7 Apr 65)

**PRENATAL ESP,** another manifestation of charge and circuits. A circuit may exist which says, "I know what you're thinking about," and when returned to its vicinity the preclear seems to get the thoughts of mother and father by **ESP.** Actually these "thoughts" are composites of phrases which occur in the reactive and standard banks of the preclear. There may well be **extra-sensory perception,** but **"prenatal ESP"** is false. (*SOS,* Bk. 2, p. 209)

**PRENATALS,** a Dn term used to denote engrams received before birth. (BTB 12 Apr 72R)

**PRENATAL VISIO,** there actually is a **prenatal visio,** but it is black. The blackness of the **prenatal,** when the individual is stuck in a **prenatal** engram, will actually blot out his **visio.** There is no mechanism save that of the imagination which is known to produce the pictures that come about with **"prenatal visio."** (*SOS,* p. 209)

**PRE-OT,** a thetan beyond the state of Clear who, through the advanced courses, is advancing to the full state of **operating thetan.** (*PRD* Gloss)

**PREPARED ASSESSMENT FORM,** this New Era Dn process list dredges up the unwanted conditions that wait in the future so they can be handled before they hit the pc. (LRH ED 301 INT)

**PREPARED LIST, 1. prepared** by the auditor, **prepared** by me, **prepared** by somebody else. It is not given by the pc—it is made up, **listed** by somebody else, not the preclear. (Class VIII, No.

11) **2. lists** designed to find by-passed charge and repair a faulty auditing action or life situation. (HCOB 28 May 70) **3.** is one which is issued in an HCOB and is used to correct cases. There are many of these. Notable amongst them is C/S 53 and its corrections. (HCOB 15 Oct 73)

**PREPCHECK, 1.** sec checking=security checking, so it couldn't be used as a purely auditing action for the pc. So I had to have a new word. **Prep** for **preparatory** to auditing. It's a forerunner of ruds. (LRH Def. Notes) **2. preparatory check.** A process. (HCOB 23 Aug 65) **3.** on a **prepcheck** run each reading item (SF, F, LF, BD) from the assessed list of items on the **prepcheck** buttons. Each button is run to F/N, Cog. Take up each reading button in turn until you get full EP for the subject. (BTB 10 Apr 72R)

**PREPCHECK BUTTONS,** the following order and number of **prepcheck buttons** should be used wherever an **"18-button prepcheck"** is recommended. Do not use the older order of buttons. For all uses the 18 **prepcheck buttons** now are: suppressed, careful of, didn't reveal, not-ised, suggested, mistake been made, protested, anxious about, decided, withdrawn from, reached, ignored, stated, helped, altered, revealed, asserted, agreed (with). (HCOB 14 Aug 64)

**PREPCHECKING, 1.** a way of cleaning up a case in order to run Routine 3D Criss Cross. I developed **prepchecking** in order to get around an auditor's difficulty in "varying the question" in pulling withholds. Auditors had a hard time doing this, hence **prepchecking. Prepchecking** became more important than a "rote procedure for sec checking." The target of a **prepcheck** question is a chain of withholds. The purpose of **prepchecking** is to set up a pc's rudiments so they will stay in during further clearing of the bank. (HCOB 1 Mar 62) **2.** the reason this is called **prepchecking** and the reason it isn't called withhold system and it isn't called anything else but **prepchecking** is it's **preparatory to clearing.** (SH Spec 114, 6202C21) **3.** is the system of getting each rudiment in with a crunch, so it's more or less permanently in during the auditing in 3DXX and that's **prepchecking.** (SH Spec 110, 6202C13)

**PREPCLEARING, 1. preparatory to clearing. Prepclearing** for short. Abandon all further reference to security checking or sec checking. The task of the auditor in **prepclearing** is to prepare a pc's rudiments so that they can't go out during 3D Criss Cross. We have just risen well above security checking in ease of auditing and in case gains. (HCOB 12 Feb 62) **2.** prepchecking is synonymous at the present moment. (SH Spec 114, 6202C21)

**PRE-RELEASE,** any patient who is entered into therapy to accomplish a **release** from his chief difficulties, psychosomatic or aberrational. (*DMSMH* Gloss)

**PRESENT TIME, 1.** the **time** which is now and which becomes the past almost as rapidly as it is observed. It is a term loosely applied to the environment existing in now, as in "The preclear came up to **present time**," meaning the preclear became aware of the existing matter, energy, space, and time of now. The point on anyone's time track where his physical body (if alive) may be found. "Now." (HCOB 11 May 65) **2.** when we say that somebody should be in **present time** we mean he should be in communication with his environment. We mean, further, that he should be in communication with his environment as it exists, not as it existed. (*Abil Mi 246*) **3.** a response to the continuous rhythm of the physical universe, resulting in a hereness in nowness. (HCOB 15 May 63) **4.** the ground, sky, walls, objects, and people of the immediate environment. In other words, the anatomy of **present time** is the anatomy of the room or area in which you are at the moment when you view it. (PAB 35) **5.** a continuing series of instants in which, moment to moment, theta goes on changing mest. (*SOS*, p. 36) **6.** an ever extending moment; and a person who is free on his time track is generally in **present time**, moving forward through the consecutive moments of **time**. (*SOS*, p. 102) **7.** an arbitrary **time**, agreed upon, and is the same across a whole universe. It is the point of coincidence of three universes. (PAB 29) **8.** people go out of **present time** because they can't have the mest of **present time**. That's it. **Present time** is the only referral point that exists. In its absence all becomes "bank." (HCOB 29 Sept 60) *Abbr.* PT.

**PRESENT TIME ENVIRONMENT,** the whole area covering the pc's life and livingness over a definite period. It may be the last day, the last week, the last year, depending on the pc. (HCOB 16 Oct 63)

**PRESENT TIME PROBLEM, 1.** technically, a special **problem** that exists in the physical universe now, on which the pc has his attention fixed. (HCOB 31 Mar 60) **2.** is one that exists in **present time,** in a real universe. It is any set of circumstances that so engages the attention of the preclear that he feels he should be doing something about it instead of being audited. (HCOB 3 Jul 59) **3.** a **present time problem** is one which has its elements in the material universe in **present time,** which is going on now, and which would demand the preclear's attention to such an extent that he would feel he had better be doing something about it rather than be audited. (HCOB 16 Dec 57) **4.** any worry that keeps a pc out of session, which worry must exist in **present time** in the real universe. (PAB 142) *Abbr.* PTP.

**PRE-SESSION PROCESS, 1.** a **process** that is used to get into session (a) a stranger who isn't receiving well; (b) a person antagonistic to Scn; (c) a person who ARC breaks easily in session; (d) a person who makes few gains in auditing; (e) a person who relapses after being helped; (f) a person who makes no gains in auditing; (g) a person who, having been audited, refused further auditing; (h) any person being audited as a check-off before session, aloud to pc or silently by auditor. (HCOB 21 Apr 60) **2.** designed as classes of **processes** to handle these four points: (1) help factor; (2) control factor; (3) pc communication factor; (4) interest factor. These four are vital to auditing itself and without them auditing doesn't happen. (HCOB 21 Apr 60)

**PRESSOR BEAM, 1.** the **pressor** is a **beam** which can be put out by a thetan which acts as a stick and with which one can thrust oneself away or thrust things away. The **pressor beam** can be lengthened, and in lengthening, pushes away. **Pressor beams** are used to direct action. (*Scn 8-8008*, pp. 48-49) **2.** a **pressor beam** which is exerting **pressure** expands when it is energized. (PDC 8)

**PRESSOR RIDGE,** that **ridge** formed by two or more **pressor** beams operating against each other in conflict. (*Scn 8-8008,* p. 49)

**PRESSOR-TRACTOR RIDGE,** a combination of **pressor-tractor** flows in sufficient collision as to form a solidification of energy. (*Scn 8-8008*, p. 49)

**PRESSURE,** if one took a fork and **pressed** it against the arm, that would be **pressure.** A bank solidity is a form of **pressure.** (HCOB 19 Jan 67)

**PRESSURE SOMATIC,** is, in Dn, considered to be a symptom in a lock, secondary or engram, simply part of the content. (HCOB 23 Apr 69)

**PRETENDED DEATH CASE,** the **pretended death case** has come to a point where he considers the environment so fraught with menace that nothing in the environment has any intent save to kill him and that **death** is immediate. He has insufficient energy or reason remaining even to appeal for help and, indeed, he considers that there is no person or object to which he can so appeal, and so he attempts to demonstrate to anything in the environment that it has won and that he is already **dead.** (*SOS*, p. 172)

**PRETENDED KNOWINGNESS,** is actually denial of **knowingness.** (SH Spec 35, 6108C08)

**PRETENSE,** a false reason or excuse. A mere show without reality. (HCO PL 3 May 72)

**PREVENT,** is to a large degree an anatomy of a problem. (SH Spec 29, 6107C14)

**PREVENTIVE DIANETICS,** a large subject, infiltrating the fields of industry and agriculture and other specialized activities of man, its basic principle is the scientific fact that engrams can be held to minimal content or **prevented** entirely with large gains in favor of mental health and physical well-being as well as social adjustment. (*DMSMH*, pp. 152-153)

**PREVENTIVE SCIENTOLOGY,** in this branch of processing, an individual is freed from assuming states lower than those he has already suffered from. In other words, the progress of tendencies, neuroses, habits and deteriorating activities can be halted by **Scn** or their occurrence can be **prevented.** This is done by processing the individual on standard **Scn** processes without particular attention to the aberration involved. (*FOT*, pp. 87-88)

**PRICE OF FREEDOM,** constant alertness, constant willingness to fight back. There is no other **price.** (AHMC-1, 6012C31)

**PRIDE, pride** is aesthetic sensitivity. (5208CM07D)

**PRIMAL CAUSE,** communication origin. (*Dn 55!*, p. 85)

**PRIMARY CORRECTION RUNDOWN, 1.** it consists of auditing and study correction actions. The **Primary Correction Rundown** takes care of people who have trouble on the **Primary Rundown.** (HCOB 4 Apr 72R) **2.** the **rundown** consists of ethics orientation on the first dynamic, potential trouble source handling for connections with hostile elements, drug handling, case handling, the why of not using study tech or study, the Study Correction List and handling, Method 7, a review of grammar, and then back to a **Primary RD.** (HCOB 30 Mar 72R) *Abbr.* PCRD.

**PRIMARY ENGRAM,** one that contains physical pain and unconsciousness. (*NOTL*, p. 46)

**PRIMARY LOCK,** the key-in of an engram takes place at some future date from the time the engram was actually received. The key-in moment contains analytical reduction from weariness or slight illness. A situation similar to the engram, which contained "unconsciousness," came about and keyed-in the engram. This is a **primary lock.** (*DMSMH*, p. 304)

**PRIMARY MID-RUDS,** suppress and invalidate. Those are the **primary mid-ruds.** (SH Spec 229, 6301C10)

**PRIMARY RUNDOWN, 1.** the **Primary Rundown** consists of word clearing and study tech. It makes a student super-literate. (HCOB 4 Apr 72R) **2.** consists of Method 1 word clearing and Method 8 on study tapes and *Student Hat.* (HCOB 30 Mar 72R) *Abbr.* PRD.

**PRIMARY SCALE,** a list of NOUNS or CONDITIONS which are key items in mental reaction. When these are assessed one assessed the VERB needed to complete a command from the SECONDARY SCALE. (HCOB 23 May 61) See HCOB 23 May 61, *Prehav Scale Revised* for the actual **scale.** (LRH Def. Notes)

**PRIMARY UNIVERSE,** the physical **universe.** (*Abil 34*)

**PRIMARY UNMOTIVATED ACT,** as any energy or space condition survives only because it has been and is being altered, the **primary unmotivated act** would be changing the condition of energy, space and objects. (*COHA*, p. 159)

**PRIME CAUSE, prime** postulate: "to be." (*DAB*, Vol. II, 1951-52, p. 229)

**PRIME POSTULATE, 1.** a **postulate** may spring from past effort or **prime** thought. A **prime postulate** is the decision to change from a state of not beingness to a state of beingness. (*AP&A*, p. 34) **2.** we call the **prime postulate** the basic purpose of the individual in *Dianetics: Modern Science of Mental Health*, or his goal. (SH Spec 168, 6207C10)

**PRIME THOUGHT,** the decision moving the original potential being from the state of not beingness to the state of beingness. **Prime thought** can occur at any moment during any lifetime, moving the individual from the state of not beingness to the state of beingness. A common name for this phenomenon is necessity level. (*AP&A*, p. 22)

**PRINCIPLE OF A-R-C,** the **A-R-C** triangle is **affinity, reality,** and **communication.** The basic **principle** here is that as one raises or lowers any of the three, the others are raised or lowered, and that the key entrance point to these is **communication.** (*PXL*, p. 38)

**PRIOR ASSESSMENT, 1.** the person looked on drugs or alcohol as a cure for unwanted feelings. One has to assess what was wrong before or prior to the cure. All it requires is a special **assessment** called a **prior assessment.** (HCOB 19 May 69, *Drug and Alcohol Cases Prior Assessing*) **2.** AESPs listed separately and run R3R, prior to first drug or alcohol taken. (HCOB 31 Aug 74)

**PRIOR CAUSE,** it is one of the "facts" of objects that space and energy must have been **caused** before the object could exist in the mest universe. Thus any object has **prior cause.** (*Scn 8-8008*, p. 68)

**PRIOR CONFUSION, 1.** all sticks on the time track stick because of a **prior confusion.** The most stuck point on the track is a problem. The **confusion** occurred minutes, days, weeks before this problem. (HCOB 9 Nov 61) **2.** all somatics, circuits, problems and difficulties including ARC breaks are all preceded by a **prior confusion.** Therefore it is possible to eradicate somatics by sec checking the area of **confusion** which occurred just before the pc noticed the somatic for the first time. (HCOB 2 Nov 61)

**PRIOR READS, 1. reads** which occur **prior** to the completion of the major thought. (*EMD*, p. 38) **2.** any non-instantaneousness before the end of the sentence. (SH Spec 148, 6205C24)

**PRO, Professional Course.** (HCOB 29 Sept 66)

**PROB, problem.** (BTB 20 Aug 71R II)

**PROB INT, problems intensive.** (BTB 20 Aug 71R II)

**PROBLEM, 1.** a **problem** is postulate-counter-postulate, terminal-counter-terminal, force-counter-force. It's one thing versus another thing. You've got two forces or two ideas which are interlocked of comparable magnitude and the thing stops right there. All right, now with these two things one stuck against the other you get a sort of a timelessness, it floats in time. (SH Spec 82, 6111C21) **2.** a **problem** is a postulate-counter-postulate resulting in indecision. That is the first manifestation of **problems,** and the first consequence of a **problem** is indecision. (SH Spec 27, 6107C11) **3.** a multiple confusion. (SH Spec 26X, 6107C03) **4.** an intention counter-intention that worries the preclear. (HCOB 23 Feb 61) **5.** a **problem** is the conflict arising from two opposing intentions. A present time **problem** is one that exists in present time, in a real universe. (HCOB 3 Jul 59) **6.** something which is persisting, the as-is-ness of which cannot be attained easily. (PRO 16, 5408CM20)

**PROBLEMS INTENSIVES, 1.** can key out present time problems of long duration, chronic somatics, circuits and hidden standards. To give a **problems intensive** the auditor first fills in the *Preclear Assessment Form* on the preclear. The auditor then asks the preclear for all self-determined changes the preclear has made this life. (HCOB 9 Nov 61) **2.** each change or turning point, was preceded by a period of confusion. Find the persons present in the confusion. Assess the persons for most reaction, take the one with most reaction and run a processing check on that person to get the withholds the pc had from that person. (HCOB 17 Oct 61) [This rundown was later revised as follows.] **3.** get the self-determined changes, handle each reading change in order of largest read. Locate the prior confusion to the change by asking the pc for it. You want the *time*. Predate the *time* of the prior confusion by one month. Prepcheck "Since (date) has anything been (prepcheck button)?" References are HCOB 30 July 1962, *A Smooth HGC 25 Hour Intensive* and HCOB 27 Sept 62, *Problems Intensive Use* (BTB 9 Oct 71RA III) [The above is a very brief summary only. The full series of steps can be found in the referenced HCOBs and BTB.]

**PROBLEMS LONG DURATION,** is spotted by no real change in characteristics or OCA or general case. (LRH Def. Notes)

**PROBLEMS RELEASE,** expanded Grade I release. (CG&AC 75) See GRADE I RELEASE.

**PROCEDURE CCH, CCH** is a very sloppy title, for **Procedure CCH** is really **C** for **control,** D for duplication, **C** for **communication, Ct** for **control** of thought=**havingness;** and that is the real name of it. First, we get the person under **control,** get him into the capability of duplicating and then we move him up into **communication** more or less on a person level. Now we take the mind. The mind consists of mental image pictures and if duplication is addressed to the mind we get **communication.** The third zone is the **control** of the thetan, which brings us to the **control** of thinkingness, **Ct.** (PAB 122)

**PROCEDURE 30,** the special auditing **procedure** of which Opening Procedure by Duplication (R2-17 *Creation of Human Ability*) is the first step. (*PXL* Gloss)

**PROCESS,** a set of questions asked by an auditor to help a person find out things about himself or life. More fully, a **process** is a patterned action, done by the auditor and preclear under the auditor's direction, which is invariable and unchanging, composed of certain steps or actions calculated to release or free a thetan. There are many **processes** and these are aligned with the levels taught to students and with grades as applied to preclears, all of which lead the student or the preclear gradiently to higher understanding and awareness. Any single **process** is run only so long as it produces change and no longer. (*Scn AD*)

**PROCESS BITING**, *Slang.* If the TA is moving, the **process** is **biting** and if it is not moving the **process** is not **biting**. No motion on the tone arm dial=no action in the bank. (SH Spec 1, 6105C07)

**PROCESS BY TONE ARM**, theoretically when I say **process by the tone arm** I mean keeping the needle somewhere in the vicinity of set and that gives you your **tone arm** motion. (SH Spec 3, 6105C19)

**PROCESS COMPLETION**, defined as the end phenomena of the **process**. (HCOB 26 May 71)

**PROCESS CYCLE**, selecting a **process** to be run on the preclear, running the tone arm action into it (if necessary) and running the tone arm action out of it. (HCOB 7 Apr 64)

**PROCESSED**, drilled in Scn with Scn exercises. (PAB 82)

**PROCESSES OF SCIENTOLOGY**, methods of "unhypnotizing" men to their own freer choice and better life. (*COHA*, p. 251)

**PROCESS FLAT**, see FLAT PROCESS.

**PROCESSING, 1.** called "auditing" by which the auditor (practitioner) "listens and commands." The auditor and the preclear (patient) are together out of doors or in a quiet place where they will not be disturbed or where they are not being subjected to interrupting influences. The purpose of the auditor is to give the preclear certain and exact commands which the preclear can follow and perform. The purpose of the auditor is to increase the ability of the preclear. The *Auditor's Code* is the governing set of rules for the general activity of auditing. (PAB 87) **2.** the principle of making an individual look at his own existence, and improve his ability to confront what he is and where he is. (*Aud 23 UK*) **3.** a series of methods arranged on an increasingly deep scale of bringing the preclear to confront the no-confront sources of his aberrations and leading him to a simple, powerful, effective being! (HCO PL 18 Sept 67) **4.** the verbal exercising of a patient (preclear) in exact Scn **processes.** (PAB 87) **5. processing** is not getting data out of the preclear; it is not assembling his life for him as a complete, consecutive play—it is increasing his self-determinism and his right to reason. (*DAB*, Vol. II, p. 70 1951-52) **6.** a procedure by which an individual recovers his self-determinism. No procedure which does not bring about increased self-determinism is **processing.** (*Abil 114A*)

**PROCESSING CHECKS,** you will see **processing checks** in literature going out, so don't let it throw you. I'm talking about security **checks.** (SH Spec 91, 6112C12)

**PROCESS LAG, 1.** the length of time it takes the whole circuit to clean or clear or get free and of course that length of time is how long it takes you to run out that question and we call that a **process lag.** If you are running Opening Procedure 8-C and you have to run it on a preclear fourteen hours before he seems to be in good shape on the thing, you have done then a **process lag** and you've cleaned up a **process lag.** How long did it take for this **process** to be effective on the preclear, fourteen hours. (5411CM05) **2.** this is the length of time it requires for the preclear to obtain a result from a **process.** (PAB 43) **3.** the length of time it takes to reduce all communication lag from a type of question or action in auditing. (PAB 43) **4.** another kind of communication **lag** is simply a **processing lag.** It's the length of time that it takes the **process** to be effective on the preclear. (5410CM06)

**PRODUCTION,** an org must **produce** to survive. By **production** is meant training auditors who can audit, auditing pcs to a good result and making money, or in a total socialism obtaining adequate support in ratio to **production.** (HCOB 21 Nov 71 I)

**PRODUCT PROGRAM,** is an experimental **program.** It remains experimental and has not been released. (BTB 1 Nov 72)

**PROFESSION INTENSIVE,** enables a person to overcome difficulties that he may encounter in his **profession** or in any given subject. (LRH ED 301 INT)

**PROFESSIONAL AUDITING,** sessions given by a trained **auditor** who is governed by ethical codes and technical skill, who directs the pc's attention to areas which when examined by the preclear will cause a release of sufficient charge to cause tone arm action, thus reaching the eventual state of Clear. (HCO PL 21 Aug 63)

**PROFESSIONAL SCIENTOLOGIST,** one who expertly uses **Scn** on any area or level of the society. (HCOB 10 Jun 60)

**PROFESSIONAL STUDENTS,** are defined as (1) those **students** who are holding a valid, in force and in hand Class IV or above certificate; (2) those **students** who are holding a valid, in force and in hand old HCA/HPA certificate or (3) those **students** who are fully paid up through HAA and actually on the course. At a Church of Scientology SH organization, a **student** to receive the **professional** discount would have to be either (a) on the SHSBC or (b) holding a valid, in force and in hand SHSBC Class VI certificate. A valid in force cert has a fully paid up membership. (HCO PL 6 Aug 72R)

**PROFILE,** an APA or OCA **profile** was a picture of a valence or of valences—artificial overlays. (PAB 138)

**PROGRAM, 1.** is defined as the sequence of actions session by session to be undertaken on a case by the C/S in his directions to the auditor or auditors auditing the case. (HCOB 12 Jun 70) **2.** any series of actions designed by a C/S to bring about definite results in a pc. A program usually includes several sessions. (HCOB 23 Aug 71) **3.** the consecutive layout of what has to be done in the next many sessions. (HCOB 14 Jun 70)

**PROGRAM COMPLETION,** a **program** is **complete** when the end phenomena of the **program** is attained. (HCOB 26 May 71)

**PROGRAM CYCLE,** selecting an action to be performed, performing that action and completing it. (HCOB 7 Apr 64)

**PROGRAMMING, 1.** the overall planning for a person of the courses, auditing and study he should follow for the next extended time period. (HCOB 19 Jun 71 III) **2.** is simply how we are going to take the charge off the case. (SH Spec 271, 6305C30)

**PROGRAM SHEET,** a **sheet** which outlines the sequence of actions, session by session, to be run on the pc to bring about a definite result. (BTB 30 Nov 72R)

# PROGRESS PROGRAM

**PROGRESS PROGRAM, 1.** when you are doing something to bring a case back up to where the case ought to be on his grade chart. (7204C07 SO I) **2.** a Scn auditing **program** to clean up upsets in life. (HCOB 6 Sept 71) **3.** a **program** to eradicate case mishandling by current life or auditing errors. (*Aud 58 UK*) **4.** what is called a "Repair Program" on the first issue of C/S Series HCOB is renamed a **progress program.** (HCOB 25 Jun 70 II)

**PROLONGATION,** continuously gone on with. (7204C07 SO III)

**PROMPTERS, THE,** in Listen Style Auditing if the auditor believes the pc has stopped because of embarrassment or some similar reason, the auditor has **the prompters,** the only things he is allowed to use. **Prompter** (a) "Have you found something you think would make me think less of you?" **Prompter** (b) "Is there something you thought of that you think I wouldn't understand?" **Prompter** (c) "Have you said something you felt I didn't understand? If so, tell me again." **Prompter** (d) "Have you found something *you* haven't understood? If so, tell me about it." (HCOB 10 Dec 64)

Propitiation

**PROPITIATION, 1.** the strange manifestation of the individual attempting to buy off the imagined danger by **propitiation.** Cases which are far down on the tone scale will, when they reach 1.0, quite commonly offer the auditor presents and attempt to do things for him. (*SOS*, p. 57) **2. propitiation** is an apathy effort to hold away a dangerous "source" of pain. To nullify the possible anger of a person perhaps long since dead but living now again in a partner, is the hope of **propitiation.** (*DMSMH*, p. 309) **3.** this conciliation is an effort to feed or sacrifice to an all destructive force. (*DMSMH*, p. 307)

**PRO-SURVIVAL ENGRAM, 1.** an **engram** which seems to be in favor of **survival.** (*DMSMH*, p. 62) **2. pro-survival engrams** containing the ally computation can be described as those which contain personnel who defended the patient's existence in moments when the patient conceived that his existence was under attack. (*DMSMH*, p. 244) **3.** any **engram** which, by content only, not by any real aids to the individual containing it, pretended to assist **survival.** (*DMSMH*, p. 264)

**PROTEST READ,** an item, possibly already run, is seen to **read.** The pc frowns. He is **protesting** and the meter is registering **protest,** not the item. A **protest** almost never blows down the TA. (HCOB 29 Apr 69)

**PROVISIONAL,** meaning "not permanent." (HCO PL 9 May 65)

**PROVISIONAL CERTIFICATE,** the student graduate is given a **provisional certificate.** This looks like any other **certificate** but is not gold-sealed and has **provisional** plainly on it. **Provisional certificates** expire after one year if not validated. (HCO PL 31 Aug 74 II) See also PERMANENT CERTIFICATE.

**PR PR, power processes.** (Class VIII No. 17)

**PSEA, pain, sensation, emotion, attitude.** (7203C30S0)

**PSEUDO-ALLY, 1.** a person about whom the preclear has a similar computation as an **ally** not based directly on an engram recording but on a similarity to an **ally.** (*SOS*, Bk. 2, p. 112) **2.** a person whom the reactive mind has confused with the real **ally.** (*DMSMH*, p. 251)

**PSEUDO-CENTERS,** the personalities of people whom you've tried to help and have failed. These are "valences." (*HFP*, p. 96)

**PSYCHE, 1.** a thetan, the spirit, the being himself. (SH Spec 31, 6407C29) **2.** soul. (5506C03) **3.** a Greek word meaning spirit. (PAB 82)

**PSYCHIATRY,** the primary difference between Scn and **psychiatry** is that **psychiatry** is authoritarian and tells the person what's wrong with him, often introducing a new lie. Scn finds out what's wrong with the person from the person. (SH Spec 294, 6308C14)

**PSYCHO,** *Slang.* the bank has total effect upon him and he has no effect of any kind on the bank. A **psycho** is actually an engram bank in full dramatization. (SH Spec 4, 6105C26)

**PSYCHO-,** *combining form:* refers to mind. (*DMSMH*, p. 92)

**PSYCHO-ANALYSIS,** is a system of mental therapy developed by Sigmund Freud in Austria in 1894 and which depends upon the following practices for its effects: the patient is made to discourse (free associate) on and recall his childhood for years while the practitioner effects a transfer of the patient's personality to his own and searches for hidden sexual incidents believed by Freud to be the only cause of aberration; the practitioner reads sexual significance into all discourse and evaluates it for the patient along sexual lines; the entirety of the cases of **psycho-analysis** have never been tabulated and little or no testing has been done to establish the validity of the system. (PAB 92)

**PSYCHOLOGY, 1.** defined this way: **psyche-ology;** spirit, study of. (AHMC 1, 6012C31) **2.** that body of practice devoted to the creation of an effect on living forms. It is not a science since it is not an organized body of knowledge. In actual use it is a dramatization of Axiom 10, wholly reactive. In this wise the word can be used by Scientologists, and this definition can be used legally to prove Scn isn't **psychology.** (HCOB 22 Jul 59) **3.** the study of the spirit (or mind) that came into the peculiar position of being a study of the spirit which denied the spirit. (PAB 82) **4.** a study of the brain and nervous system and its reaction patterns. (ASMC 3, 5506C03) **5.** an anglicized word, not today true to its original meaning. **Psychology** is composited from *psyche* and *ology*, and *psyche* is mind or soul, but leading **psychological** texts begin very, very carefully by saying that today the word does not refer to the mind or to the soul. To quote one, it "has to be studied by its own history," since it no longer refers to the soul, or even to the mind. So we don't know what **psychology** refers to today. (*PXL*, p. 2) **6.** the study of the human brain and stimulus-response mechanism and its code word was "man to be happy, must adjust to his environment." In other words—man, to be happy must be a total effect. (2ACC 1B, 5311CM17)

**PSYCHOPOLITICS**, the technical name for brainwashing. (Op Bull No. 9)

**PSYCHOSIS, 1.** the root word **"psyche"** refers only to a being or soul and the **"osis"** could loosely be defined as "the condition of." (*Cert*, Vol. 13, No. 2) **2. psychosis** could be technically called an inability to be; so it naturally is an inability to communicate because beingness is a problem in anchor points and that's a problem in communication. (Spr Lect 9, 5303CM27) **3.** an inability to cope with the routine problems of the first and second dynamics. (Spr Lect 9, 5303CM27) **4. psychosis** is a complete inability to assign time and space. (*Scn 8-80*, p. 44) **5.** any major form of mental affliction or disease. (*SOS*, p. 25) **6.** a conflict of commands which seriously reduce the individual's ability to solve his problems in his environment to a point where he cannot adjust some vital phase of his environmental needs. (*DTOT*, p. 58) **7.** the difference between neurosis and **psychosis** is that in **psychosis**, the guy is just generally effect of everything, and in neurosis he's more or less singly the effect of things. He's a deranged being on some subject. (SH Spec 70, 6607C21) **8.** is simply an evil purpose. It means a definite obsessive desire to destroy. (ESTO No. 3, 7203C02 SO I)

**PSYCHOSOMATIC, 1. psycho** of course refers to mind and **somatic** refers to body; the term **psychosomatic** means the mind making the body ill or illnesses which have been created physically within the body by derangement of the mind. (*DMSMH*, p. 92) **2.** a chronic pain which amounts to a physical illness with which the pc has been afflicted for a very long time. They turn on and they don't turn off. (SH Spec 92, 6112C13)

**PSYCHOSOMATICALLY ILL CASE,** one in which the entheta side of the engram is suppressed and the **somatic** side of the engram is in restimulation. (*SOS*, p. 82)

# PSYCHOSOMATIC ILLNESS

**PSYCHOSOMATIC ILLNESS, 1.** it is the pain contained in a past experience or the physical malfunction of a past experience. The facsimile of that experience gets into present time and stays with the person until a shock drops it out of sight again or until it is processed out. A shock or necessity however permits it to come back. (*NSOL*, pp. 139-140) **2.** this we call physical **illness** caused by the mind. In brief, such **illness** is caused by perceptions received in the reactive mind during moments of pain and unconsciousness. (PAB 85) **3.** physiological insanity. It is being expressed by the body rather than by the mind. (8ACC 6, 5410CM08) **4. illnesses** which have a mental origin but which are nevertheless organic. (*DMSMH*, p. 91)

**PSYCHOTHERAPY, 1.** is an effort to remove neurosis and psychosis from man by immediate address to the individual and the group. (LPLS 1, 5510C08) **2.** a series of processes by which the past is addressed to remedy the present or by which physical matter, such as the human brain, is rearranged (as in a prefrontal lobotomy) in order to inhibit odious conduct in present time. (*Scn Jour 14-G*)

**PSYCHOTIC, 1.** does not know what is going on in his environment and does not know what is going on inside himself. It is all unknown and therefore unobservational—unobserved. He doesn't know what's happening inside himself and he doesn't know what's happening with himself and he doesn't know what's happening where he is and he doesn't know what's happening in front of him or behind him at any given time of the day or night. This is the one common denominator of all **psychosis.** (SH Spec 41, 6108C17) **2.** that person who cannot receive orders of any kind, who sits unmoving or goes berserk at the thought of doing anything told him by another determinism. (HCOB 25 Aug 60 II) **3.** the complete subject of one or more unknown causes to which he is the unwilling effect and any effort on his part to be cause is interfered with by the things to which he is the effect. (PAB 144) **4.** when a person has lost his ability to impose time and space upon his facsimiles and his memories he's **psychotic,** he's gone. (5209CM04B) **5.** an avoidance of both the future and present time and a shift into the past. (PAB 17) **6.** the case which cannot observe but thinks obsessively is known to us as the **psychotic.** (PAB 8) **7.** that person according to Dn definition whose theta has become entheta completely, and who is either entirely locked up in an engram or chain of engrams and does nothing but dramatize them or who is under the command of a control circuit and does some computation, if limited and unreasonable. (*SOS*, Bk. 2, p. 190) **8.** an individual who cannot handle himself or his environment well enough to survive and who must be cared for to protect others from him or to protect him from himself. (*SOS*, p. 25) **9.** a person who is physically or mentally harmful to those about him out of proportion to the amount of use he is to them. (*SOS*, p. 26) **10.** computation only of past situations. (*Scn 0-8*, p. 89)

**PSYCHOTIC BREAK, 1.** when a person drops below the 2.0 level he has so much entheta compared to his theta that a sudden shock may simply enturbulate the remaining theta and send him into a **psychotic break.** When all the theta is enturbulated, its reaction is to kick apart theta and mest, in other words, cause death and remove the organism from the path of other organisms. (*SOS*, p. 28) **2.** some person disorients a human being one time too many and it's just that, disorientation. The person tells him he's here when he's there and fouls him up one way or the other and pulls the space out, or tells him he can't stay there anymore, or tells him that he can't have that space, or tells him that he can't have that matter which also contains space. He loses something in other words. But what he loses most importantly is space. So he loses this space, and one day he feels with several facsimiles a clank, and he doesn't feel good at all. (PDC 25) **3.** a neurotic person has not given up the strain of keeping some of his attention in present time, and will not do so until forced by chronic, constant restimulation to do so. When this happens the neurotic suddenly becomes **psychotic.** A **psychotic break** has occurred. (*DAB*, Vol. I, No. 6, 1950)

**P.T., present time.** (SH Spec 72, 6607C28)

**PT ENVIRONMENT LIST, 1.** an Expanded Dianetics Rundown. The auditor finds out what is charged in the pc's **present time environment,** then gets PSEAs connected with that and runs standard R3R on the items. (7203C30S0) **2.** life and livingness environment, the workaday world of the pc is a source of restimulation. (HCOB 1 Oct 63)

**PTP, present time problem.** (*BCR*, p. 21)

**PTP,** basically the inability to confront the dual-terminal nature of the universe. It is an inability to span attention and denotes that the pc who is having lots of **PTPs** has his attention *very* fixed on something. (HCOB 31 Mar 60)

**PTP OF LONG DURATION, 1.** by **long duration** we mean this lifetime absolute maximum limit. As soon as we exceed this lifetime we have case. (SH Spec 42, 6108C18) **2.** the attention is fixed on something in present time all right but it's also been fixed on this thing for a long time and is usually subjective. (SH Spec 42, 6108C18)

**PTP OF SHORT DURATION,** fixed attention on the immediate environment. (SH Spec 42, 6108C18)

**PTS, 1.** means **potential trouble source** which itself means a person connected to a suppressive person. All sick persons are **PTS.** All pcs who roller-coaster (regularly lose gains) are **PTS.** Suppressive persons are themselves **PTS** to themselves. (HCOB 20 Apr 72) **2.** is the manifestation of a postulate-counter-postulate. (SH Spec 68, 6510C14) **3.** the mechanism of **PTS** is environmental menace that keeps something continually keyed in. This can be a constant recurring somatic or continual, recurring pressure or a mass. The menace in the environment is *not* imaginary in such extreme cases. The action can be taken to key it out. But if the environmental menace is actual and persists it will just key in again. This gives recurring pressure unrelieved by usual processing. (HCOB 5 Dec 68)

**PTS RD CORRECTION LIST,** this **correction list** is assessed and handled after a **PTS Rundown** has been done on the pc. It also serves as a check list of expected actions with the **Rundown.** It is always assessed M5. EP is pc no longer upset, each reading item taken to EP. (BTB 11 Aug 72RA)

**PTS TYPE A,** a person intimately connected with persons (such as marital or familial ties) of known antagonism to mental or spiritual treatment or Scn. (HCO PL 5 Apr 72 I)

**PTS TYPE ONE,** the SP on the case is right in present time, actively suppressing the person. **Type one** is normally handled by an ethics officer in the course of a hearing. (HCOB 24 Nov 65)

**PTS TYPE TWO, type two** is harder to handle than type one, for the apparent suppressive person in present time is only a restimulator for the actual suppressive. The pc who isn't sure, won't disconnect, or still roller-coasters, or who doesn't brighten up, can't name any SP at all is a **type two.** (HCOB 24 Nov 65)

**PTS TYPE THREE,** the **type three PTS** is mostly in institutions or would be. On this case the type two's *apparent* SP is spread all over the world and is often more than all the people there are—for the person sometimes has ghosts about him or demons and they are just more apparent SPs but imaginary as beings as well. (HCOB 24 Nov 65)

**PURE RESEARCH,** study without thought of possible application. (HCOB 30 Aug 65)

**PURPOSE,** the survival route chosen by an individual, a species, or a unit of matter or energy in the accomplishment of its goal. (NOTE: the **purpose** is specific and may be closely defined being a subdivision of one of the sub-dynamics. It has been tentatively established by investigation that an individual human being has established his **purpose** for life at the age of two years and that the actual **purpose** is not derived in any degree from engrams but is only warped by them.) (*DTOT* Gloss)

**PV=AD$^x$,** see POTENTIAL VALUE.

**PV, potential value.** (*DMSMH*, p. 40)

**PV=ID$^x$,** see POTENTIAL VALUE.

# Q

**Q, 1. Q,** came from *quod* in **Q.**E.D. or "therefore" in geometry. "It follows." (LRH Def. Notes) **2.** a mathematical designation. It can be defined this way: it is the level from which we are now viewing which is a common denominator to all experience which we can now view. The highest level from which we're operating. (PDC 6)

**Q AND A, 1.** means **"Question and Answer."** When the term **Q and A** is used it means one did not get an answer to his **question.** It also means not getting compliance with an order but accepting something else. Example: Auditor, "Do birds fly?" Pc, "I don't like birds." Auditor, "What don't you like about birds?" Flunk. It's a **Q and A.** The right reply would be an **answer** to the **question** asked and the right action would be to get the original **question answered.** (HCOB 5 Dec 73) **2.** the origin of the term comes from "changing when the pc changes." The basic **answer** to a **question** is, obviously, a **question** if one follows the duplication of the comm formula completely. A later definition was **"Questioning** the pc's **Answer."** Another effort to overcome it and explain **Q & A** was the Anti-**Q and A** drill. But none of these reached home. The new definition is this: **Q and A** is a failure to complete a cycle of action on a preclear. An auditor who starts a process, just gets it going, gets a new idea because of pc cognition, takes up the cognition and abandons the original process is **Q and A-ing**. (HCOB 7 Apr 64)

**Q AND A'D,** did what the preclear did. Any time the preclear changed the auditor changed. (PAB 151)

**QEO,** the **Qualifications Establishment Officer (QEO).** Establishes and maintains the Qual Division. (HCO PL 7 Mar 72)

**Qs, THE,** there is a series, numbering about five above the level of logic and above the level of axiom. I have been calling these things **the Qs,** just the letter "**Q,**" the mathematical symbol. We call them **the Qs** to differentiate them from other things. Actually **Q** can be defined this way: it is the level from which we are now viewing, which is the common denominator to all experience which we can now view. This is the level from which we're viewing all experience and which acts as a common denominator to all this experience and **the Q** is the highest level from which we are operating. (PDC 6)

**QUACK,** is anyone who pretends to be something which he is not, or one who is not able to do what he claims to do, especially if he takes money for this pretense. (HCO Info Ltr 22 Sept 63)

**QUAD, quadruple.** (HCOB 4 Apr 71-1R)

**QUAD DIANETICS, Quadruple Dianetics** is **four** flow items, **Dianetic** items into **four** flows. F-1 is flow one, something happening to self. F-2 is flow two, doing something to another. F-3 is flow three, others doing things to others. F-0 is flow zero, self doing something to self. Standard R3R commands are used on **Quad Dianetics.** (HCOB 4 Apr 71-1R)

**QUAD FLOWS, F-1** is **flow one,** something happening to self. **F-2** is **flow two,** doing something to another. **F-3** is **flow three,** others doing things to others. **F-0** is **flow zero,** self doing something to self. (HCOB 4 Apr 71-1R)

**QUAL,** the **Qualifications** Division (Division 5 of a church) where the student is examined and where he may receive cramming or special assistance and where he is awarded completions and certificates and where his **qualifications** as attained on courses or in auditing are made a permanent record. (HCOB 19 Jun 71 III)

**QUAL CONF, Qualifications Division Conference** tape. (HCOB 29 Sept 66)

**QUAL DIV, Qualifications Division.** (HCOB 23 Aug 65)

**QUAL I&I, Qual Interview and Invoice.** (7109C05SO)

**QUAL SEC, Qualifications Secretary.** (HCOB 23 Aug 65)

**QUESTION CLEAN,** gives no instant read. (HCOB 24 Jun 62)

**QUICKIE,** in the dictionary you will find **"Quickie** also **quicky:** something done or made in a hurry. Also: a hurriedly planned and executed program (as of studies)." Anything that does not fully satisfy all requirements is **quickie.** So **"quickie"** really means "omitting actions for whatever reason that would satisfy all demands or requirements and doing something less than could be achieved." In short a **quickie** is not doing all the steps and actions that could be done to make a perfect whole. (HCOB 19 Apr 72)

**QUICKIE LOWER GRADES,** (also called "Triple Grades") means one F/N for each of three flows or three F/Ns per **grade.** There

**QUICKIE GRADES, 1.** a derogatory term denoting **grades** "run" without running all the processes of the **grades** each to full end phenomena thus reducing the effectiveness of Scn by failure to apply it properly. (BTB 12 Apr 72R) **2.** pc didn't actually reach full abilities in earlier Scn auditing. (HCOB 25 Jun 70 II)

**QUICKIE LOWER GRADES,** (also called "Triple Grades") means one F/N for each of three flows or three F/Ns per **grade.** There are not just three F/Ns per **grade.** There are dozens of F/Ns. (HCOB 30 Oct 71)

**QUICKIE PROGRAMS,** those which omit essential steps like vital lists or 2wcs to get data. FESes for past errors are often omitted. (HCOB 19 Apr 72)

**QUICK STUDY,** a **quick study** by which is meant a student who learns rapidly or a person who grasps a subject **quickly,** has a high ability to confront that subject. (HCOB 2 Jun 71 I)

# R

**R, 1. routine**—prefix on process designations. (HCOB 23 Aug 65) See ROUTINE for process designations like **R3R, R3N, R6EW,** etc. **2.** example, R2-25, **"Routine"** followed by the research code number of the process. When processes are being researched and developed they are given numbers and some become known by these numbers rather than names. (BTB 20 Aug 71R). **3. reality.** (SH Spec 304, 6309C10) **4.** when an issue is cancelled, the number is followed by **R** on the next issue meaning **revised.** (HCO PL 2 May 72)

**RABBIT,** *n.* person who runs from everything including his bank. (HCOB 26 Apr 71 II) —*v.* to run away from the bank. (HCOB 10 Apr 72)

**RABBITING,** frightened and running away. (HCOB 23 Dec 71)

**RADIATION,** is either a particle or wave-length, nobody can say for sure. Let's define it as a capability of influencing matter, and that that capability can be exerted across space. (*AAR,* p. 68)

**RANDOMITY, 1.** the amount of predicted and unpredicted motion a person has, in ratio. He likes 50/50. (PAB 30) **2.** the degree of **randomity** is measured by the **randomness** of effort vectors within the organism, amongst organisms, amongst races or species of organisms or between organisms and the physical universe. (*Scn 0-8,* p. 79) **3.** a component factor and necessary part of motion, if motion is to continue. The three degrees of **randomity** consist of **minus randomity, optimum randomity,** and **plus randomity.** (*Scn 0-8*, p. 79) **4.** the misalignment through the internal or external efforts by other forms of life or the material universe of the efforts of an organism, and is imposed on the physical organism by counter-efforts in the environment. (*Scn 0-8*, p. 78)

**RANDOM RUDIMENT,** a **rudiment** put into the session at any time the pc seems to need it. Example: pc seems ARC broken so one asks if he is and handles. Or pc is antagonistic so one asks for a W/H. Or pc seems restless, one asks if there is a PTP. (It is far safer to do an L1C prepared list or a C/S 53RJ as then one can be sure which **rudiment** went out. (LRH Def. Notes)

**RAPID TR-2,** see CR0000-2.

**RAPPORT, rapport** is mutual feelingness. To have **rapport** with something you can *be* it. (BTB 7 Apr 72R)

**RATIONAL CONFLICT,** while man is concerned with any of the eight dynamics, any one of them may become antipathetic to his own survival. This is **rational conflict** and is normally and commonly incidental to survival. It is non-aberrative in that it is **rational** within the educational limitation. (*DTOT*, p. 32)

**RATIONALITY, 1.** is ability to recognize and meet the magnitude of effort (counter-effort) being applied to the individual. (*DAB*, Vol. II, p. 100, 1951-52) **2.** the computational accuracy of the individual modified by aberration, education and viewpoint. (*DASF*)

**RATIONALIZATION,** is wholly an attempt to shunt responsibility. (*AP&A*, p. 58)

**RATIONAL THOUGHT,** optimum type of **thought.** This is used by a Clear. (*DTOT*, p. 43)

**RAVE SUCCESS STORY,** one given voluntarily without coercion or threat by the pc which expresses actual improvement and benefit due to auditing received in complimentary terms which may include to Scientology, the Founder, the C/S and/or the Auditor. (HCO PL 21 Oct 73R)

**RAW MEAT PRECLEAR, 1.** one who has never had Scn processing. (HCOB 16 Jan 68) **2.** the guy thinks he's a brain. He doesn't know he's a thetan, he isn't up there and he thinks he's deteriorated into a bit of matter, he thinks he's a body and so forth. Hence this jocular term **"raw meat."** (SH Spec 43, 6410C20)

**RD, rundown.** (HCOB 24 Sept 71)

**REACH AND WITHDRAW, 1. reach and withdraw** are the two fundamentals in the action of theta. (*COHA*, p. 241) **2.** to grasp and let go. (PAB 9) ["Reach" and "Withdraw" process commands can be found in HCOB 1 Apr 70, *Ethics Program No. 1 Case Actions.*]

**REACTION TIME,** it's how fast thought can recognize a situation and act upon it. (UPC 3)

**REACTIVATED,** an engram is **reactivated** when an individual with an engram receives something in his environment similar to the perceptions in the engram. The engram puts everything it contains into greater or lesser operation. (*DMSMH*, p. 73) See RESTIMULATION.

**REACTIVE, 1.** irrational, **reacting** instead of acting. (*Scn AD*) **2.** that means instantaneous response. (SH Spec 292, 6308C07)

**REACTIVE ACTION,** this is the essence of **reactive action.** A thetan unwilling to or actually unable to duplicate a something-ness tries to make nothing of everything as he counts upon the environment to fix his attention and himself does not fix it by choice; when he is in a very bad state a thetan then sees only those things which have mass and are in **action** and neglects those things which do not have mass and are not in **action.** (*Abil 23*)

**REACTIVE BANK, 1.** a stimulus-response machine of some magnitude. (*PXL*, p. 217) **2.** unconscious mind. (*Cert*, Vol. 14, No. 7) See REACTIVE MIND.

**REACTIVE CONDUCT,** when the **reactive** mind is able to exert its influence upon a person far better than the thetan himself can, we say this person is suffering from **reactive conduct**. He has a **reactive** mind. In other words, his association has become too blatantly in error for him any longer to conceive differences and we get identification: A=A=A=A. (5702C28)

**REACTIVE MIND, 1.** a portion of a person's **mind** which works on a totally stimulus-response basis, which is not under his volitional control, and which exerts force and the power of command over his awareness, purposes, thoughts, body and actions. Stored in the **reactive mind** are engrams, and here we find the single source of aberrations and psychosomatic ills. (*Scn 0-8*, p. 11) **2.** comprises an unknowing, unwanted series of aberrated computations which bring about an effect upon the individual and those around him. It is an obsessive strata of unknown, unseen, uninspected data which are forcing solutions, unknown and unsuspected, on the individual—which tells you why it remained hidden from man for so many thousands of years. (*Scn 0-8*, p. 11) **3.** is basically that area of occlusion which the pc is unable to contact and which contains within itself a total identification of all things with all things, and until released into the realm of knowingness continues to **react** upon the person compelling him into actions, dramatizations and computations which are not optimum to his or anyone else's survival. (SH Spec 35, 6108C08) **4.** the **reactive mind** is a stimulus-response mechanism, ruggedly built, and operable in trying circumstances. The **reactive mind** never stops operating. Pictures of the environment, of a very low order, are taken by this mind even in some states of unconsciousness. The **reactive mind** acts below the level of consciousness. It is the literal stimulus-response **mind.** Given a certain stimulus it gives a certain response. (*FOT*, p. 58) **5.** once called the "unconscious" **mind.** It is a tough, rugged **mind** which is alert during any moment of life, regardless of the presence of pain, and which records everything with idiotic faithfulness. It stores up the entheta and enmest of an accident with all the perceptics (sense messages) present during the "unconsciousness" resulting from the accident. (*SOS*, p. 9) **6.** once known as the "unconscious **mind,**" but this terminology is highly misleading, because the **reactive mind** is the **mind** which is always conscious. (*SOS*, Bk. 2, p. 182) **7.** also known as the R6 bank. (HCOB 12 Jul 65)

**REACTIVE PLEASURE,** in the organism below 2.0 (on the tone scale) tending toward death, a **reactive pleasure** is taken in the performance of acts which lead to succumbing on any of the dynamics. In other words, above 2.0 **pleasure** is survival, and below 2.0 **pleasure** is obtained only by succumbing or by bringing death to other entities, or by causing self or other entities to be suppressed on the tone scale. (*SOS*, Bk. 2, p. 84)

**REACTIVE THOUGHT, 1. thought** established by counter-efforts as in *Homo sapiens* and governed entirely in a stimulus-response basis. (*Scn 8-8008*, p. 36) **2. reactive thought** is wholly in terms of everything in an engram equals everything in an engram equals all the restimulators in the environment and all things associated with those restimulators. (*DMSMH*, p. 79)

**READ, 1.** a "tick" or a "stop" is not a **read. Reads** are small falls or falls or long falls or long fall blowdown (of TA). (HCOB 27 May 70) **2.** the action of the needle on the E-meter dial falling (moving to the right). A **"reading** question" is one which causes the meter needle to fall to the right to a greater or lesser extent when the question is asked of the preclear or student with the person holding the electrodes. In word clearing a **reading** word is one which causes the meter needle to fall to the right when said, thought or read by the student or called by the word clearer with the student holding the electrodes. (BTB 12 Apr 72R)

**READING ITEM,** the **read** is taken when the pc first says it or when the question is cleared. This is the valid time of **read.** This **reading** defines what is a **reading item** or question. Calling it back to see if it **read** is not a valid test as the surface charge may be gone but the **item** or question will still run or list. (HCOB 28 Feb 71)

**READING QUESTION,** see READING ITEM.

**READING WORD,** see READ.

**REALITY, 1.** is, here on earth, agreement as to what is. This does not prevent barriers or time from being formidably **real.** It does not mean either that space, energy or time are illusions. It is as one knows it is. (*COHA*, p. 249) **2.** that sequence which begins with postulates and ends with mass, which we originally defined as an agreed-upon thing. **Reality** is the agreed-upon apparency of existence. (*CMSCS*, p. 11) **3.** the **reality** of something is the ability to place it in time and space. That's **reality. Reality** is an agreement. (5203CM05A) **4.** is not what the individual thinks **reality** is. **Reality** is what the majority agrees it is. (SH Spec 105, 6201C25) **5.** the degree of agreement reached by two ends of a communication line. In essence, it is the degree of duplication achieved between Cause and Effect. That which is **real** is **real** simply because it is agreed upon, and for no other reason. (*Dn 55!*, p. 35) **6. reality** is a postulated **reality. Reality** does not have to persist to be a **reality**. The condition of **reality** is simply is-ness. That is the total condition of **reality**. (*PXL*, p. 62) **7.** the agreement upon perceptions and data in the physical universe. (*Scn 0-8*, p. 83) **8.** agreement in the mental plane and solids in the physical plane. (*POW*, p. 92) **9.** the solid objects, the **real** things of life. (HCOB 21 Jun 71 I) **10.** that which is made and which is commonly experienced by agreement; that which is made, or one or many make, and can be commonly experienced. That, we will define as **reality**. (PDC 5) **11.** is composed of the degree of duplication possible, and this is also describable under the heading of agreement. **Reality** is a quality which depends upon duplication and in the action of duplication expertly or poorly done we find agreement and disagreement. (PAB 44) **12. R**=Mass or agreement. (HCOB 27 Sept 68 II)

**REALITY BREAK,** actually disagreements on **reality**, usually resulting only from a different viewpoint and not from actual differences in **reality** itself. (*Scn 0-8*, p. 103)

**REALITY SCALE,** see SCALE OF REALITY.

**REAL UNIVERSE,** one which contains space, energy and time. (*Cert*, Vol. 10, No. 12)

**REASON, 1. reason** could be said to be the orderly handling of mest by theta. This postulates that the entirety of **reason** depends upon a harmony of conquest of mest. Theta could be said to be complete **reason**; mest could be said to be complete force. (DAB, Vol. II, p. 132) **2.** effort plus intention is **reason. Reason** has to include the thought plus the effort. Thought plus effort is **reason.** (5203CMO6A.) **3.** the ability to extrapolate new data from the existing data. **Reason** is hand in glove with self-determinism. The rehabilitation of a person's self-determinism is the rehabilitation of his ability to **reason**. (DAB, Vol. II, p. 70.)

Reality

**REBALANCING,** letting the case settle to bring it back to a workable state. (*DMSMH*, p. 294)

**RECALL, 1.** present time remembering something that happened in the past. It is not re-experiencing it, re-living it or re-running it. **Recall** does not mean going back to when it happened. It simply means that you are in present time, thinking of, remembering, putting your attention on something that happened in the past—all done from present time. (HCOB 14 Oct 68 II) **2.** the process of regaining perceptions. (*Scn 0-8*, p. 85) **3.** implies that you bring it up to present and look at it. (SH Spec 84, 6612C13)

**RECALL PROCESSES, processes** which deal with the pc remembering things that happened in his past. (HCOB 30 Sept 71 V)

**RECALL RELEASE,** expanded ARC Straightwire release. (*CG&AC* 75) See ARC STRAIGHTWIRE RELEASE.

**RECEIPT POINT,** effect is the **receipt point** of the communication. (*Dn 55!*, p. 70)

Receipt Point

**RECESSION, 1.** you may find you get into a little light engram and you find it won't lift and you go over it and then it faded away. This is **recession.** You can do this and three days later have a stalled case on your hands. This engram you have beaten down comes back in full force in three days. (*NOTL*, p. 108) **2.** during a **recession** the somatic of the engram first reduces slightly and then continues constant. In the reduction, the somatic, little by little each recounting, reduces. In a **recession,** the somatic remains steady. If a **recession** takes place, it means simply that an engram similar to the one which is being re-experienced is earlier on the case, or that a tremendous quantity of entheta in secondaries and locks exists above the engram that is being **recessed. Recessions** occur only where the auditor has not taken off enough entheta from the case in the form of locks and secondaries to permit engrams to be run. It is a premature address to engrams or it is caused by auditing in violation of the file clerk's data. (*SOS*, Bk. 2, p. 173)

**RECOUNTING,** the principle of **recounting** is very simple. The preclear is merely told to go back to the beginning of the incident and to tell it all over again. He does this many times. As he does it the engram should lift in tone on each **recounting.** (*DTOT*, p. 103)

**RECURRING WITHHOLDS,** the pc that gives the same **withhold** over and over to the same or different auditors, has an unknown incident underlying it. All is not revealed on that chain. (HCOB 21 Mar 62)

**RED-HERRING,** *Slang.* to go chasing after facsimiles. (*SLP,* Iss. 7R)

**RED SHEET,** Repair Programs (now called Progress Programs) are on **red sheets.** (HCOB 25 Jun 70)

**RED TAG,** a large **red** card placed on the outside front cover of a pc folder which indicates that a repair session must be done within 24 hours or if a full FES is required, within 72 hours. (BTB 20 Jan 73RB)

**REDUCE, 1.** to take all the charge or pain out of an incident. This means to have the preclear recount the incident from beginning to end (while returned to it in reverie) over and over again, picking up all the somatics and perceptions present just as though the incident were happening at that moment. To **reduce** means, technically, to render free of aberrative material as far as possible to make the case progress. (*DMSMH*, p. 287) **2.** to render an engram free from somatic or emotion by recountings. (*NOTL* Gloss)

**REDUCED FACSIMILE,** is a **facsimile** which no longer has the capability of absorbing your attention units into a mock-up of it. (5206CM24B)

**REDUCTION,** a **reduction** is done exactly as an erasure, but the engram will not completely erase, remaining, after a few recountings, in a more or less static condition of low aberrative power and with no physical pains remaining in it. (*SOS*, Bk. 2, p. 172)

**RE-EXPERIENCE,** you **re-experience** a facsimile by seeing it, hearing it, feeling everything in it including, especially, your own thoughts and conclusions. Just as though you were there again. (*HFP*, p. 86)

**REFLEXIVE EFFECT POINT,** a causative action, calculated to result in an **effect** on the **cause point.** (*NSOL*, p. 23)

**REGIMEN, 1.** a certain settled schedule of things. (7204C07 SO III) **2.** the workhorse combination of processes, that boosts the case to clear after it has been started. (HCOB 1 Dec 60)

**REGISTER,** a falling needle. (*EME*, p. 14) See FALL.

**REGRESSION,** was a technique by which part of the individual's self remained in the present and part went back to the past. These abilities of the mind were supposed native only in hypnotism and were used only in hypnotic technique. (*DMSMH*, p. 12)

**REGRET, 1.** is what inverts the time track, one wishes it hadn't happened and so he tries to collapse the track on the point. Actually overt acts collapse the track but the emotion of **regret** is experienced at that level. (5904C08) **2.** the action of trying to make time run backwards. (5206CM24E) **3.** simply an effort to take something out of the timestream, "I'm sorry it happened. I wish it hadn't happened." (5112CM29A) **4.** entirely the study of reversed postulates. One intended to do something good and one did something bad or one intended to do something bad and accidentally did something good. Either incident would be **regretted.** (PAB 91)

**REHAB, rehabilitate.** (HCOB 4 Jan 71)

**REHABBING DRUGS,** using the data from the *Pc Assessment Form*, **rehab** in turn each **drug** by counting the number of times released for each type of **drug** to F/N. (BTB 25 Oct 71R II) See also CHEMICAL RELEASE.

**REHABILITATION,** when the person was originally released he had become aware of something that caused the reactive mind to *de*-stimulate at that point or become weak. And so he released. You have to find that point of sudden awareness again. To regain a former release (or thetan exterior or keyed-out OT; released OT). (HCOB 30 Jun 65) *Abbr.* Rehab.

**REJECTION LEVEL,** the condition in which a person or object must be, in order that the preclear be able to **reject** it freely. (*COHA* Gloss)

**RELEASE,** *n.* **1.** one who knows he or she has had worthwhile gains from Scn processing and who knows he or she will not now get worse. (HCOB 9 Aug 63) **2.** a person whose case "won't get any worse." He begins to gain by living rather than lose. (HCOB 17 Mar 59 II) **3.** a person who has been able to back out of his bank. The bank is still there but the person isn't sunk into it with all its somatics and depressions. (HCOB 2 Apr 65) **4.** a **release** purely and simply is a person who has obtained results in processing and has a reality on the fact that he has attained those results. That severely is the definition of **release.** (SH Spec 159, 6206C19) **5.** a **release** is an individual from whom have been **released** the current or chronic mental and physical difficulties and painful emotion. (*DMSMH*, p. 170) **6.** a series of gradual key-outs. At any given one of those key-outs the individual detaches from the remainder of his reactive bank. (SH Spec 65, 6507C27) —*v.* the act of taking the perceptions or effort or effectiveness out of a heavy facsimile or taking away the preclear's hold on the facsimile. (*HFP* Gloss)

**RELEASED OT, 1.** if a being is a first, second or third stage **release** and has also become exterior to his body in the process, we simply add **"OT"** to the state of **release.** It is secondary in importance to the fact of being a **release.** As soon as the being seeks to exert his **"OT"** powers he tends to restimulate his R6 bank and so goes back into his body. (HCOB 12 Jul 65) **2.** temporarily up and feeling high and great but he can fall on his head. (SH Spec 82, 6611C29)

**RELEASE OF AFFECT, 1.** by first getting the patient to find and say what shock occurred when the sickness began, getting when, and getting it recounted, the "illness" will lessen, the emotional state will alter—called a **release of affect.** (HCOB 2 Apr 69) **2.** a misemotional discharge. (SH Spec 65, 6507C27)

**RELIABLE ITEM, 1.** *Symbol:* **R.I.** any **item** that rock slams well on being found and at session end and which was the last **item** still in after assessing the list. Can be a terminal, opposition terminal, a combination terminal or a significance, provided only that it was the **item** found on a list and rock slammed. (HCOB 8 Nov 62) **2.** an **item** which the pc got after the list was nulled, and it's **reliable** and can be used to obtain further **items.** That is a **reliable item.** (SH Spec 202A, 6210C23) **3.** can be an oppterm or a terminal and that meant one that slams when found. (SH Spec 203A, 6210C23) **4.** a black mass with a significance in it which is dominated by a goal and which is part of a GPM. (HCOB 13 Apr 64, *Scn VI Part I Glossary of Terms*)

**RELIEF RELEASE,** expanded Grade II release. (CG&AC 75) See GRADE II RELEASE.

**RELIEF RUNDOWN,** where the Original Assessment Sheet has shown losses by death or other severe changes in a person's life such as losses of position or pets or objects it will be found that the person's life changed for the worse at that point. The auditor spots these points of change either on the Original Assessment Sheet or by asking the preclear. These points are then run narrative R3RA Quad. When all such great changes in a person's life have been found and erased the person should experience a considerable sense of **relief** about life. (HCOB 3 Jul 78R)

**RELIGION, 1.** the ritual of worship or regard about spiritual matters. (4 LACC-18, 5510C13) **2.** a study of wisdom. (HCO PL 6 Mar 69) **3.** the word **religion** itself can embrace sacred lore, wisdom, knowingness of gods and souls and spirits, and could be called, with very broad use of the word, a philosophy. We could say there is **religious** philosophy and there is **religious** practice. (*PXL*, p. 13)

**RELIGIOUS PHILOSOPHY,** implies study of spiritual manifestations; research on the nature of the spirit and study on the relationship of the spirit to the body; exercises devoted to the rehabilitation of abilities in a spirit. (HCOB 18 Apr 67)

**RELIGIOUS PRACTICE,** implies ritual, faith-in, doctrine based on a catechism and a creed. (HCOB 18 Apr 67)

**RELIVING,** where a man is so thoroughly in the past for the moment that while he. was recalling an infant experience, if startled he would react just as he would have when a baby. (*DMSMH*, p. 197)

**REM, remedy.** (BTB 20 Aug 71R II)

**REMEDY, 1.** by **remedy** one means the correction of any aberrated condition. (PAB 50) **2.** something you do to get the pc into condition for routine auditing. (HCOB 27 Sept 64) **3.** an auditing process which is designed to handle a non-routine situation. (HCOB 11 Dec 64)

**REMEDY A, 1.** locates the misunderstoods a person has in Scn. (HCOB 9 Nov 67) **2.** has to do with definitions in Scn or the present subject. You must not miss that, it's present subject, immediate subject. It's the immediate subject the guy's trying to study. It's not just applicable to Scn. This guy is trying to study engineering and he hasn't understood a term in engineering. Well, you could handle that with **Remedy A.** (SH Spec 47, 6411C17)

**REMEDY B, 1.** seeks out and handles a former subject, conceived to be similar to the immediate subject, in order to clear up misunderstandings in the immediate subject or condition. (HCOB 12 Nov 64) **2. Remedy B** is former subject. He's got the present immediate subject mixed up with some former subject. So now you've got to find the former subject and find the word in it which hasn't been defined. (SH Spec 47, 6411C17)

**REMEDY OF HAVINGNESS, 1. remedy of havingness** does not mean stuffing the preclear with energy. It means remedying his ability to have or not have energy. (*Dn 55!*, p. 117) **2.** by **"remedy"** one means the correction of any aberrated condition. By **"havingness"** one means mass or objects. It means the **remedy** of a preclear's native ability to acquire things at will and reject them at will. (PAB 50) **3.** means **remedy** of the condition of **having** to **have**. (9ACC-1, 5412CM06)

**REMEDY OF LAUGHTER** (R2-26), in the **Remedy of Laughter** the preclear can be made simply to stand up and start **laughing**. The goal of the process is to regain the ability to **laugh** without reason. This process is done until the preclear can actually enjoy a **laugh** without any reason whatsoever, without believing that **laughing** without reason is insane, without feeling self-conscious about **laughing,** and without needing any boost from the auditor. (*COHA*, pp. 68-70)

**REMEMBERING, 1.** one could recall the fact that one had seen a dog chase a cat. That would be **remembering**. (*HFP*, p. 26) **2.** the process of knowing the past. (PAB 86)

**REMIMEO,** Churches which receive this must **mimeograph** it again and distribute it to staff. (HCOB 4 Sept 71 III)

**REMOTE VIEWPOINT, 1.** a **viewpoint** without the consideration by the thetan that he is located at that point. The thetan may have any number of **remote viewpoints.** (*COHA* Gloss) **2.** a technical term meaning a thetan who is afraid to look from where he is. He puts out **viewpoints** over there and looks from that. (5410CM10B)

**REPAIR, 1.** patching up past auditing or recent life errors. This is done by prepared lists or completing the chain or correcting lists or even two-way comm or prepchecks on auditors, sessions, etc. (HCOB 23 Aug 71) **2. repair** is undertaken to eradicate errors made in auditing or the environment which impede the use of major processes. (HCOB 12 Jun 70)

# REPAIR CORRECTION LIST

**REPAIR CORRECTION LIST,** use this list to clean up bypassed charge on improperly done or unnecessary prepared lists or **repair** actions. This list is done when a pc protests a prepared **list** or **repair** action, when BIs are present on the subject of **repair** or prepared **lists** or when improper past **repair** or use of correction **lists** reads on a correction **list.** (HCOB 16 Oct 78)

**REPAIR OF HAVINGNESS,** we used to call **repair of havingness** "giving him some **havingness.**" (PAB 72)

**REPAIR PROGRAM, 1.** takes the case from where it has falsely gotten to on the class chart and gets off the overwhelm with light processes. (HCOB 14 Jun 70) **2. program** to eradicate case mishandling by current life or auditing errors (called a set-up program). (HCOB 12 Jun 70) **3.** progress **program.** (HCOB 30 Jun 70R)

**REPEATER TECHNIQUE, 1.** the **repetition** of a word or phrase in order to produce movement on the time track into an entheta area containing that word or phrase. Repeating or "rolling" a phrase in an engram in order to de-intensify the phrase or reduce the engram is not **repeater technique.** (*SOS*, Bk. 2, p. 68) **2.** after he has placed the patient in reverie, if he discovers the patient, for instance, insists he "can't go anyplace," the auditor makes him **repeat** the phrase. **Repetition** of such a phrase, over and over, sucks the patient back down the track and into contact with an engram which contains it. It may happen that this engram will not release—having too many before it—but it will not release only in case it has that same phrase in an earlier engram. So the **repeater technique** is continued with the auditor making the patient go earlier and earlier for it. If all goes on schedule the patient will very often let out a chuckle or a laugh of relief. The phrase has been sprung. (*DMSMH*, p. 215) **3.** the file clerk is asked for data on certain subjects, particularly those affecting the return and travel on the time track, and which aid the ability of the preclear to contact engrams. (*DMSMH*, p. 225)

**REPETITIVE AUDITING CYCLE,** is a specialized activity. There's the **auditing cycle** of one cycle. Then there's the **auditing cycle** of the next cycle etc. You must complete all comm cycles of an **auditing cycle.** (SH Spec 290, 6307C25)

**REPETITIVE COMMAND AUDITING,** using TRs 0 to 4, at Level I is done completely muzzled. This could be called muzzled

**repetitive auditing** style but will be called "muzzled style" for the sake of brevity. At Level I we don't expect the auditor to do anything but state the command (or ask the question) with no variation, acknowledge the pc's answer and handle the pc origins by understanding and acknowledging what the pc said. (HCOB 6 Nov 64)

**REPETITIVE PREPCHECKING, prepchecking** by **repetitive** command. This type of **prepchecking** is more easily done and more thorough than **prepchecking** by the withhold system and its earlier forefather security checking. (HCOB 3 Jul 62)

**REPETITIVE PROCESS, 1.** is simply a **process** that is run over and over with the same question of the pc. The pc answers the thing and the auditor gives him an acknowledgment. Gives him TR-4 on his origins and it is run until it is flat. (SH Spec 169, 6207C10) **2. process** which permits the individual to examine his mind and environment and out of it select the un-importances and importances. (SH Spec 67, 6509C21)

**REPETITIVE RUDIMENTS,** (1) run the **rudiment** as a **repetitive** process until pc has no answer; (2) consult meter for a hidden answer; (3) if meter reads use it to steer ("that" "that" each time the meter flicks) the pc to the answer; (4) lay aside the meter and do (1) and (2) and (3). The process is flat when there is no instant read to the question. (HCOB 2 Jul 62)

**REPETITIVE STRAIGHTWIRE, straightwire** to one incident done over and over until the incident is de-sensitized. (*AP&A*, p. 22)

**REPLAY,** a bad habit some preclears have of playing over what they remember they said the last time instead of progressing through the engram freshly on each recounting and contacting what is contained in the engram itself. (*DMSMH*, p. 279)

**REPRESENT LIST, 1.** in Routine 2-12 a **list** from the line question "Who or what does . . . **represent** to you?" (HCOB 23 Nov 62) **2.** search and discovery as a process is done exactly by the general rules of listing. One lists for persons or groups who are or have suppressed the pc. The list is complete when only one item reads on nulling and this is the item. If the item turns out to be a group, one does a second **list** of "Who or what would **represent** (item)?" gets the **list** long enough to leave on nulling only one item reading, and that is the SP. (HCOB 24 Nov 65)

**REPRESSIONS, 1.** things pc must prevent himself from doing. (BTB 24 Apr 69R) **2.** a command that the organism must not do something. (*DTOT*, p. 58)

**REPUTATIONAL WITHHOLD,** he must **withhold** it because it will damage his beingness, in other words his **reputation.** (SH Spec 63, 6110C05)

**RESERVATION,** is entering into an outgoing flow an impetus to make it flow less hard and hit less hard. (HCL-5, 5203CM05A)

**RESISTIVE CASE, 1.** symptoms of a **resistive case** are thick review folder, roller-coasters, complains, blows courses or churches, long sessions, hard to get F/Ns, doesn't want auditing, makes trouble for auditors, and/or does not respond to auditing. (HCOB 8 Sept 71) **2.** TA in normal range but not responding well to auditing. (BTB 11 Aug 72RA)

**RESISTIVE CASE RUNDOWN,** the **resistive case rundown** is an VIII development to handle those who cannot make the grades. It was put into the *Green Form* as GF 40 so as to preserve it. (HCOB 30 Jun 70R)

**RESISTIVE V,** severely occluded case. (PAB 15) See also BLACK V.

**RESISTOR,** is a device placed along an electrical line to limit the flow of current to a known value. It is used here to find the actual values of TA positions 2 and 3, which may be different from those given in the manufacturer's markings. (*EMD*, p. 16A)

**RESPON,** responsibility. (BTB 20 Aug 71R II)

**RESPONSIBILITY, 1.** the ability and willingness to assume the status of full source and cause for all efforts and counter-efforts on all dynamics. (*AP&A*, p. 57) **2.** when one speaks of **responsibility** he means "the determination of the cause which produced the effect." (*AP&A*, p. 62) **3.** full **responsibility** is not fault; it is recognition of being cause. (*AP&A*, p. 58) **4.** willingness to make or unmake barriers. (PAB 30) **5.** the feeling that one can operate something. (PAB 31) **6.** the area or sphere of influence the individual can rationally affect around other people, life, mest and the general environment. (*SOS*, p. 142) **7.** admission of control of space, energy and objects. (PDC 4) **8.** it is willingness to own or act or use or be. (PDC 56) **9.** the concept of being able to care for, to reach or to be. (HCO PL 17 Jan 62) **10.** "admit causing," "able to withhold." (HCOB 21 Jan 60, *Responsibility*)

**RESPONSIBILITY (A PROCESS), 1.** has three commands. "You look around here and find something you could be **responsible** for." "You look around here and find something you don't have to be **responsible** for." "You look around here and find something you would permit somebody else to be **responsible** for." (*SCP*, p. 22) **2.** "What part of that incident could you be **responsible** for?" (SMC-5, 6001C02)

**RESPONSIBILITY RD,** see R/S HANDLING.

**RESPONSIBLE FOR CONDITION CASES,** is meant the person who insists a book or some auditor is "wholly **responsible** for the terrible condition I am in." (HCO PL 27 Oct 64)

**RESTIMULATION, 1.** the reactivation of a past counter-effort by appearance in the organism's environment of a similarity toward the content of the past randomity area. (*Scn 0-8*, p. 85) **2.** means the reactivation of an existing incident. (SH Spec 84, 6612C13) **3.** where the environment reactivates a facsimile, which then acts back against the body or awareness of awareness unit of the person. This is a very simple system of stimulus-response. (*Dn 55!*, p. 15) **4.** where the perceptics of the engram are approximated by those of the present time environment. (*SOS*, Bk. 2, p. 118)

**RESTIMULATION LOCK,** merely brings to the person perceptions which approximate those of an engram. If the individual is tired or weary, these perceptions, sights, sounds, smells, or whatever they may be, will **restimulate** the engram which has similar perceptics; and the incident becomes a **lock** on the engram and charges it to some small degree. (*SOS*, p. 113)

**RESTIMULATOR, 1. restimulators** are those approximations in the environment of an individual of the content of an engram. (*DTOT*, p. 42) **2.** an approximation of the reactive mind's content or some part thereof continually perceived in the environment of the organism. (*DTOT*, p. 27) **3.** the individual with an engram receives something in his environment similar to the perceptions in the engram. (*DMSMH*, p. 73) **4.** words, voice tones, music, whatever they are—things which are filed in the reactive mind bank as parts of engrams. (*DMSMH*, p. 74)

**RESTIMULATOR LAG,** when a keyed-in engram was **restimulated** it often required two or three days for action to take place. (Example: say a migraine headache has as its **restimulator** a rhythmic burping sound; that sound is heard by the individual who has the engram; three days later he suddenly has a migraine.) (*DMSMH*, p. 380)

**REST POINT,** an individual in a high-games condition is in motion. The game gets too high, and he drops out. So he goes into a no-games condition. You can call this a **rest point** on the track. (PAB 98)

**RESULTS,** defined: case achieves a reality on change of case, somatic, behavior or appearance, for the better. (HCOB 28 Feb 59)

**RETRACTOR,** it is possible for a wave to act as a **retractor.** That is to say, it is possible for certain waves to pull back instead of push out. Thetans can put out such a **retractor** wave. (*HOM*, p. 54)

**RETRACTOR BEAM,** a **retractor beam** or a **retractor** loop is a **beam** which goes out here from the source, hits the target then drags the target in. It's to grab hold of something and hold it and pull it in. That's one of its uses and the other use is to nail you into a body. (5207CM24A)

**RETRAIN,** is the entire course as any green student would take it from beginning to end. (ESTO 4, 7203C02 SO II)

**RETRAINING,** occurs where the student has continually flubbed sessions or tech actions or flunked exams. It is assumed he does not have a grasp of the data. In **retraining** the student may be ordered to redo the full requirements of the checksheets. (HCO PL 22 Jul 70 III)

**RETREAD, 1.** means picking up the materials that the auditor is weak on. It's a review course. But it does mean going through the pack and the materials of the particular level being **retreaded.** It's mostly a check of misunderstood words, Method 4 style word clearing, on the different sections of the materials of the course, emphasis being placed on what the auditor is weak on. (HCO PL 22 Feb 72) **2. retreading** is different than retraining. **Retread** is brushing up one's study and knowledge and application of tech on the course one is redoing. It is a commendable action on one's own determinism. (HCO PL 22 Jul 70 III)

**RETURN,** regression in its simplest form, hereafter called **return** is employed in Dn auditing. **Return** is the method of retaining the body and the awareness of the subject in present time while he is told to go back to a certain incident. (*DTOT*, p. 87)

**RETURNING, 1.** the word used to go back and re-experience an incident. (HCOB 14 Oct 68 II) **2.** the technique in which the preclear is sent as early as possible on his track before therapy itself is engaged upon. (*DMSMH*, p. 225) **3.** the person can "send" a portion of his mind to a past period on either a mental or combined mental and physical basis and can re-experience incidents which have taken place in his past in the same fashion and with the same sensations as before. (*DMSMH*, p. 11)

**RETURN PROGRAM, 1.** Advance Program. (HCOB 30 Jun 70R) **2.** consists simply of writing down in sequence every needful step and process missed on the class chart by the case which are now to be done. (HCOB 14 Jun 70) **3.** the **return** to the false point on the *Classification and Gradation Chart* reached by getting honestly done all the points missed on the road. (HCOB 14 Jun 70)

**REV!,** "This preclear is in trouble, please do a **review hard.**" (HCOB 23 Aug 65)

**REVELATION,** means disclosure—a veil has been lifted—something previously hidden is now **revealed.** (*B&C*, p. 22)

**REVERIE, 1.** in **reverie** the preclear is placed in a light state of "concentration" which is not to be confused with hypnosis. The mind of the preclear will be found to be to some degree detachable from his surroundings and directed interiorly. (*DTOT*, p. 135) **2.** Dn **reverie** leaves a preclear fully aware of everything which is taking place and with full recall of everything which has happened. (*DMSMH*, p. 165)

**REVERSAL OF POSTULATE,** one intends to do something by making a **postulate** that it will take place, yet something else takes place. This is a **reversal of postulate.** (PAB 91)

**REVERSE CURVE, THE,** is the emotional **curve** rising from below 2.0 to above 2.0. It happens in a short space of time. It is important because it locates allies. (*AP&A*, p. 24)

**REV FL?,** "Could you please find out if this process is **flat** for me?" (HCOB 23 Aug 65)

**REVIEW, 1.** the Department of **Review** is in the Qualifications Division. The entire purpose of the Department of **Review** is repair and correction of auditing and training difficulties. **Review** is an extension of my own case cracker hat and my own fast instruction hat. (HCO PL 24 Apr 65) **2.** that area where standard tech is corrected back to standard tech. (Class VIII No. 2)

**REVIEW CODE,** the **code** has four symbols, REV!, REV FL?, DECLARE?, ETH? REV! means "This pc is in trouble! Please do a review hard." REV FL? means "Could you please find out if this process if flat for me?" DECLARE? means "Pc has reached a grade or release. Please look at pc and if okay, pass on to Certs and Awards." ETH? means "This pc may be an ethics case, roller-coasters or no case gain." (HCO PL 4 Jul 65)

**REVIV, revivification.** (HCOB 23 Aug 65)

**REVIVIFICATION, 1. revivification** is the bringing back to life of an engram in which a preclear is stuck. The engram or some portion thereof is being acted out in present time by the preclear. It is called a **revivification** because the engram is suddenly more real to the preclear than present time has ever been. He re-lives that moment briefly. He does not merely recall or remember it. This is not the same thing as the "returning" to an incident or engram that is employed in Dianetic auditing. *Return* is the method of retaining the body and the awareness of the subject in present time while he is told to go back to a certain incident. **Revivification** is the re-living of an incident or a portion of it as if it were happening *now*. (HCOB 6 Dec 78) **2.** the hypnotic subject could be sent back to a moment "entirely" so that he gave every appearance of being the age to which he was returned with only the apparent faculties and recollections he had at that moment: this was called **"revivification"** (**re-living**). (*DMSMH*, p. 12) *Abbr.* reviv.

**REVIVIFY, relive.** (HCOB 11 May 65) *Abbr.* reviv.

**R-FACTOR, 1. R** or **reality; reality factor.** (HCOB 21 Dec 61) **2.** telling the pc what you are going to do at each new step. (HCOB 23 Jun 62)

**RHYTHM,** actually a part of the time sense, but is also the ability to tell the spaces between sound waves which are pulsing regularly, as in the beating of a drum. (*SA*, p. 85)

**RHYTHMIC, KINESTHETIC,** weight and motion. (*Abil 149*)

**RI, reliable item.** (HCOB 4 Aug 63)

**RIDGE, 1.** it's a standing apparent motionlessness of some kind or other, an apparent solidity, an apparent no-outflow—no-inflow, that's a **ridge.** Flows have direction. **Ridges** have location. (5904C08) **2.** a **ridge** is caused by two energy flows coinciding and causing an enturbulence of energy, which, on examination, is found to take on a characteristic which in energy flows is very like matter, having its particles in chaotic mixture. (*Scn 8-80*, p. 43) **3.** a **ridge** is formed from two flows and these two flows hitting will pile things up. (PDC 18) **4.** a **ridge** is essentially suspended energy in space. it comes about by flows, dispersals or **ridges** impinging against one another with a sufficient solidity to cause an enduring state of energy. (*Scn 8-8008*, p. 18) **5.** a solid body of energy caused by various flows and dispersals which has a duration longer than the duration of flow. Any piece of matter could be considered to be a **ridge** in its last stage. **Ridges,** however, exist in suspension around a person and are the foundation upon which facsimiles are built. (*Scn 8-8008*, p. 49) **6.** facsimiles, or pictures, of motion. (*Scn 8-80*, p. 45) **7.** areas of dense waves. (*Scn 8-8008*, p. 78) **8.** electronic densities. (*Scn Jour 6-G*)

**RIDICULE, 1.** it's somebody grabbing hold of one of your anchor points, claiming it and holding it away from you. (5311CM17A) **2.** pushing the anchor points in and then pulling them out and holding them out. (Spr Lect 17, 5304M08)

**RIGHT,** this would be forwarding a purpose not destructive to the majority of the dynamics. (*Abil Ma 229*)

**RIGHT-HAND BUTTONS,** mistake, suggest, decide, protest, these all make things read. They don't keep things from reading, **right-hand side.** (SH Spec 229, 6301C10)

**RIGHTNESS,** is conceived to be survival. Any action which assists survival along the maximal number of dynamics is considered to be a **right** action. Theoretically, how **right** can one be? Immortal! (*Scn 8-8008*, p. 58)

**RIGHT THOUGHT,** a **thought** which would promote the optimum survival of the optimum number of dynamics. (5410CM20)

**RIGIDITY,** fixation in space. (2ACC-26A, 5312CM17)

**RISE,** is exactly opposite to a "fall"—the needle moves to your left instead of to the right. (*BIEM*, p. 42)

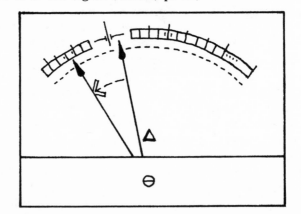

Rise

**RISING NEEDLE, 1.** means "no confront." The preclear has struck an area or something he isn't confronting. One never calls his attention to this. But one knows what it is. It is a steady constant movement of the needle, rather slow, from right to left. (*EME*, p. 16) **2.** a **rising needle** tells you that the pc can't confront, therefore has exceedingly low reality, responsibility, and knowingness on whatever significance it's **rising** on. (HCOB 12 Jun 61)

**RISING SCALE PROCESSING, 1.** in this **process**, an individual was asked to get one of the lower postulates on the *Chart of Attitudes* and then carry it "upward" until he could get the higher idea. In this particular case one would ask the preclear to get the idea of losing and would then ask him to change that as nearly as he could to the idea of winning. (PAB 91) **2.** is another way of doing postulate processing. One takes any point or column of the *Chart of Attitudes* which the preclear can reach, and asks the preclear then to shift his postulate upwards toward a higher level. **Rising-Scale processing** is simply a method of shifting postulates upward toward optimum from where the preclear believes he is on the chart. It is essentially a process directed toward increasing belief in self by using all the "buttons" on the *Chart of Attitudes. (Scn 8-8008,* p. 84)

**ROBOT, 1.** the individual with an evil purpose has to withhold himself because he may do destructive things. When he fails to withhold himself he commits overt acts on his fellows or other dynamics and occasionally loses control and does so. This of course makes him quite inactive. To overcome this he refuses any responsibility for his own actions. Any motion he makes must be on the responsibility of others. He operates then only when given orders. Thus he *must* have orders to operate. Therefore one could term such a person a **robot** and the malady could be called **robotism.** (HCOB 10 May 72) **2.** a **robot** is a machine that somebody else runs. (5611C15)

**ROCK, THE, 1.** was something which we audited for and assessed out, meaning a shape of something which we could then run a process on. We at that time were running on the theory that it was the first object the fellow had made on the track. (SH Spec 83, 6612C06) **2.** that which a person has used to reach people or things with and is determined in value by its creativeness or destructiveness. It is simply a reach and withdraw mechanism which makes a ridge and this causes the stick of the needle. The **rock** is an object not a significance. (HCOB 29 Jul 58)

**ROCKET READ, 1.** an **RR** is characterized by a spurted, accelerated beginning, which gives it its name. It looks like something taking off, like being shot; shot away from its start. It's a spurting beginning, and then its other characteristic is a curled end. (SH Spec 266, 6305C21) **2.** it takes off. It always goes to the right. It takes off with a very fast spurt and does a rapid decay. Like a bullet fired into water. It's very fast. It looks like its got all of its motive power from its first instance of impulse with no additional motive power being imparted to it by anything. It's kicked off and it has no further kick so it rapidly dies out. (SH Spec 224, 6212C13) **3.** is the read of the goal or the rock itself. (HCOB 6 Dec 62) **4.** called a **rocket read** because it takes off like a **rocket** and slows down. (SH Spec 202A, 6210C23)

**ROCK SLAM, 1.** the following is the only valid definition of an **R/S**: The crazy, irregular *left-right* slashing motion of the needle on the E-Meter dial. **R/Ses** repeat left and right slashes unevenly and savagely, faster than the eye easily follows. The needle is frantic. The width of an **R/S** depends largely on sensitivity setting. It goes from one-fourth inch to whole dial. But it **slams** *back and forth*. A **rock slam (R/S)** means a hidden evil intention on the subject or question under auditing or discussion. Valid **R/Ses** are not always instant reads. An **R/S** can read prior or latently. One slash doesn't *begin* to be an **R/S**. Nor two or three for that matter. The correct definition of an **R/S** includes that it slashes savagely *left and right*. A dirty needle is not to be confused with an **R/S**. They are distinctly different reads. You never mistake an **R/S** if you have ever seen one. A dirty needle is far less frantic. The difference between a **rock slam** and a dirty needle is in the *character of the read*, not the size. Persistent use of "fish and fumble" can sometimes turn a dirty needle into a **rock slam**. However until it does it is simply a dirty needle. Auditors, C/Ses, supervisors must must must know the difference between these two types of reads cold. (HCOB 3 Sept 78) **2.** The term was taken from a process in the 50s which sought to locate "A **rock**" on the pc's early timetrack; the "**slam**" is a description of the needle violence, meaning it "**slams**" back and forth. For a time all left right motions of the needle were considered and called "**Rock-slams**" until it was found that a *smooth* left right flow was a symptom of release or key out and this became the "Floating

Needle." There is yet another left right motion of the needle called the "Theta Bop." This occurs when the person has or is trying to exteriorize. "Theta" is the symbol for the person as a spirit or goodness; "bop" is an electronic term for a slight hitch in the sweep of a needle. A "Theta Bop" hitches evenly at each end of the sweep left and right and is very even in the middle of the sweep. Neither the "Floating Needle" nor the "Theta Bop" can be confused with a "**Rockslam.**" The difference of the **Rockslam** is uneven, frantic slashing left and right; even the distances traveled left and right are likely to be different in each swing from the last. A **rockslam** means a hidden evil intention on the subject or question under discussion or auditing. (HCOB 10 Aug 76R)

**ROCK SLAM CHANNEL, 1.** the pathway through the pairs of items that compose a cycle of the GPM and lead to the **rock** and goal. (HCOB 6 Dec 62) **2.** that hypothetical course between a series of pairs consisting of terminals and opposition terminals. (HCOB 8 Nov 62)

**ROCK SLAMMER, 1.** there are, for our purposes, two kinds of **R/Sers.** (a) those who **R/S** on subjects not connected with Scn and (b) those who **R/S** on subjects connected to Scn. The latter is a "List One **R/Ser**" and it is of great importance to us that they be located and moved off lines when they are part of staffs as their intent is solely to destroy us whatever else they say: their intent is solely to destroy us whatever else they say: their long run actions will prove it. The definition of a List One **R/Ser** is anyone who has **R/Sed** on List One. Staff concerned must be able to identify an **R/Ser** which is different from someone with an **R/S**. (HCOB 1 Nov 74R)

**ROCKSLAMMING LIST,** things **R/Sing** when they were written down. One **rockslam** on it at least. (SH Spec 225, 6212C13)

**ROLL BOOK,** the master record of a course giving the student's name, local and permanent address and the date of enrollment and departure or completion. (HCOB 19 Jun 71 III)

**ROLLER-COASTER, 1.** a case that betters and worsens. A **roller-coaster** is always connected to a suppressive person and will not get steady gains until the suppressive is found on the case or the *basic* suppressive person earlier. Because the case doesn't get well he or she is a potential trouble source to us, to others and to himself. (HCOB 8 Nov 65) **2.** a slump after a gain. Pcs who do not hold their gains are PTS. (HCOB 9 Dec 71RA) **3.** gets better, gets worse, gets better, gets worse. (SH Spec 63, 6506C08)

**ROLLER-COASTERING,** the PTS is known by **roller-coastering** (Coney Island fast up and down quarter-mile of aerial railway). They slump. (HCOB 3 Apr 66)

**ROLLING A PHRASE,** repeating or **rolling a phrase** in an engram in order to de-intensify the **phrase** or reduce the engram. This is not repeater technique. (*SOS*, Bk. 2, p. 68)

**ROLLYCOASTER CASE,** *Slang.* a potential trouble source, and just on the other side of him there is a suppressive person invalidating his gains. He's never going to get any better, not until he is labeled a potential trouble source and told to handle. (SH Spec 61, 6505C18)

**ROTE STYLE AUDITING,** muzzled **auditing** or repetitive command **auditing.** (HCOB 6 Nov 64)

**ROUGH CASE, 1.** no case gain. (HCO Exec Ltr, 3 May 65) **2.** unreality **case.** (HCOB 6 Dec 58)

**ROUGH PC,** the characteristic of the **rough pc** is not a **pc's** tendency to ARC break and scream but something much more subtle. The **pc** who makes no gain is the **pc** who will not as-is, who will not confront, who can be audited forever without cogniting on anything. The person whose "thought has no effect on his or her bank" he's been remarked on by me for years. This person is so afraid to find out that he or she will not permit anything to appear and therefore nothing will as-is, therefore, no cognition. (HCOB 15 Mar 62)

**ROUTE 1, ROUTE 2,** intensive procedure: outline in the use of this procedure, only two types of case are considered, and the procedure is adapted to these two types. The sole criteria of the case is whether or not it can be exteriorized. This is promptly established by the use of ARC straightwire. When there is no noticeable communication lag, then **Route 1** is employed in this procedure. When there is any noticeable communication lag, **Route 2** is employed. (*COHA*, p. 23) [Route 1 and Route 2 are fully covered in *Creation of Human Ability*.]

**ROUTINE,** a standard process, designed for the best steady gain of the pc at that level. (HCOB 11 Dec 64) *Abbr.* R

**ROUTINE 1, 1.** is CCHs and Joburg security checks. (SH Spec 7, 6106C05) **2.** applying control so as to get him into communication so that he can have. (SH Spec 18, 6106C22)

**ROUTINE 1A, 1.** is simply familiarization with problems and getting off the fellow's withholds with security checks. (SH Spec 27, 6107C11) **2.** any combination of processes which combines problems and security checks, and that is all. (SH Spec 27, 6107C11)

**ROUTINE 1C, R-1C,** consists of (1) finding something that moves the TA; (2) running the TA out of that subject to F/N, cog, VGIs. The usual method of finding what to run in general **R-1C** is by assessment of dynamics. Assessment by dynamics gives a series of questions covering each of the dynamics. This is assessed by tone arm as given in E-meter Drill 23. Take up the reading question by use of further questions on that same subject. (BTB 4 Dec 71R I)

**ROUTINE 1CM, R-1CM,** that's fishing with TA on the meter. It's picking up the things that blew down the meter while the guy was itsaing. It was actually a specialized application of R-1C. (SH Spec 14, 6404C10)

**ROUTINE 2, 1.** is a general run of the Pre-hav scale, Joburg security check, and the havingness and confront processes all run in model session. (SH Spec 7, 6106C05) **2.** getting out of the road the fixed reactive buttons which prevent him from having things. (SH Spec 18, 6106C22)

**ROUTINE 2C, 1. R-2C Slow Assessment by Dynamics.** This form is a breakdown of the eight dynamics into areas where important itsa may be developed. The stress of this assessment is on

TA motion. (BTB 17 Oct 63R) **2.** a process which is discussion by lists. (SH Spec 14, 6404C10)

**ROUTINE 2-G,** a goal finding activity. (HCOB 13 Apr 63)

**ROUTINE 2-G1, R2-G1** is a special goals precheck administered before a goal is found. This is a refined version of the problems intensive, slanted directly at goals. (HCOB 13 Apr 63)

**ROUTINE 2-GPH, R2-GPH** is a special goals precheck done by pre-hav levels with a new assessment for each button. This is a refined use of the original **Routine 2.** (HCOB 13 Apr 63)

**ROUTINE 2-GX,** is a **goal** finding **routine** consisting of the nearly exact pattern of a problems intensive but asking a different question, which adds up to listing times in the pc's life when his purpose was baulked and assessing and running as in a problems intensive. (HCOB 4 Mar 63, *Urgent*)

**ROUTINE 2-GX1,** is a **goals** intensive by precheck. (SH Spec 251, 6303C21)

**ROUTINE 2-H,** it is a very valuable unlimited process that undercuts repetitive processes and produces tone arm action on cases that have none on repetitive processes. **R2-H** combines the most difficult steps of engram running, dating, assessing, locating and indicating by-passed charge. It disposes of ARC breaks. (HCOB 25 Jun 63)

**ROUTINE 2-10,** (**R2-12** short form for beginners). The short form of **R2-12** can be used by untrained auditors with some effect until they are trained in mid ruds and other niceties. (HCOB 5 Dec 62)

**ROUTINE 2-12, 1.** method of discharging the influence of a rock slamming item is actually taken from 3GA Criss Cross (3GAXX), and is a specialized **routine** from Routine 3. We will, however, since it does not touch goals, designate it as **Routine 2.** (HCOB 23 Nov 62) **2.** is simply an effort to locate one of the GPM items as it seems to be in present time to the pc. It's an effort to locate that item in present time and find its opposition. (SH Spec 218, 6211C27) **3.** the action of **Routine 2-12** is not the key-out of the pc's bank as in prechecking but the actual eradication of those items which have been keyed in by present time which then and thereafter keep the pc in the grip of a present time problem. (SH Spec 218, 6211C27) **4.** is to put the case in condition so that it can show progress toward clearing and does actually progress the case toward clearing and is a clearing procedure. (SH Spec 218, 6211C27)

**ROUTINE 2-12A,** simply dropped out some unnecessary points in **2-12,** threw away tiger drilling and so forth. (SH Spec 236, 6302C12)

**ROUTINE 2-16,** Opening Procedure of 8-C. (*COHA*, p. 44)

**ROUTINE 2-17,** Opening Procedure by Duplication. (*COHA*, p. 47)

**ROUTINE 3, 1.** consists solely of finding a goal, then finding a terminal that matches the goal and running the terminal, and then finding another terminal for that goal, and another terminal for that goal, till that goal disappeared. And then finding that the goal had probably disappeared, and finding another goal, and finding a terminal for that goal, and so on. And finding and auditing that and then finding another terminal and auditing that, and finally it disappeared. And eventually you got into the situation where you'd find a goal and it would blow up and you'd find a terminal and it would blow up, and then you just couldn't find anything, and you got a free needle. What you've done in essence was to pick off a number of pieces of the goals problem mass so the pc was floating free of the goals problem mass. (SH Spec 139, 6204C26) **2.** getting out of the road all these unrealized goals each one of which has been a defeat for him at some time or another, all of which goals had as their end product havingness. (SH Spec 18, 6106C22) **3.** SOP goals assessment with a Joburg security check. (SH Spec 7, 6106C05)

**ROUTINE 3A, 1.** in **R-3A** you took the goal and the modifier and you found the terminal with goal and modifier. (SH Spec 139, 6204C26) **2.** a way to undercut the speed of a goals terminal run. This consists of a discovery of a new piece of the puzzle—the modifier. By use of the modifier the basic terminal of a goals chain may be isolated without running off the upper terminal. (HCOB 7 Nov 61)

**ROUTINE 3D, 1.** in **Routine 3D** you found the goal and the modifier and the terminal and then the opposition terminal. (SH Spec 139, 6204C26) **2.** in **3D** you're actually taking apart, from a distance, the component parts of the goals problem mass. (SH Spec 82, 6111C21) *Abbr.* R-3D.

## ROUTINE 3D CRISS CROSS

**ROUTINE 3D CRISS CROSS, 1.** a process which addresses the goals problem mass. (SH Spec 137, 6204C24) **2.** why do we say **criss cross**? That's just because you go from one channel to the other channel, and then you go back to the other channel. What do we mean by Channel? We mean what the pc has been and what the pc has opposed. (SH Spec 202A, 6210C23) **3.** earlier version of 3GAXX. (LRH Def. Notes) *Abbr.* 3DXX.

**ROUTINE 3D CRISS CROSS ITEMS,** the **items,** the identities and the beingnesses which the person has actually been. Don't call them so much a beingness as an identity. They are a package of conduct, they are a package of training patterns and so forth, which are residual from that particular life. (SH Spec 116, 6202C27)

**ROUTINE-3G, Routine Three employing goals.** (SH Spec 141, 6205C01)

**ROUTINE 3 GA CRISS CROSS,** see THREE GA XX.

**ROUTINE 3H, R-3H,** ARC break process (R-4H renamed **R-3H**). (HCOB 22 Sept 65)

**ROUTINE 3M, R3M** is a clearing technique. (HCOB 22 Feb 63)

**ROUTINE 3-MX,** is called **X** because it's still **experimental** and therefore its designation is really **Routine 3M.** (SH Spec 235, 6302C07)

**ROUTINE 3-N, R3N** is a stripped down directive **Routine Three** which uses line plots. (SH Spec 263, 6305C14)

**ROUTINE 3N2, R3N2** is an abbreviated form of **R3N.** (SH Spec 266, 6305C21)

**ROUTINE 3-R, 1. R3R** *Engram Running by Chains* is designated "**Routine 3-R**" to fit in with other modern processes. (HCOB 24 Jun 63) **2. Routine 3 Revised.** (BTB 20 Aug 71R II)

**ROUTINE 3RA,** engram running by chains is designated "**Routine 3RA.**" It is a new triumph of simplicity. It does not demand visio, sonic or other perception at once by the pc. It develops them. (HCOB 26 Jun 78RA II)

**ROUTINE 3-SC, 1. Routine Three, Service Facsimile Clear.** (HCOB 1 Sept 63) **2.** in **R3SC** you are only trying to end the compulsive character of the service facsimile so found and get it off automatic and get the pc to see it better. (HCOB 1 Sept 63)

**ROUTINE THREE SC-A,** full service facsimile handling updated with New Era Dn. We are into a new echelon of service facsimile running. New Era Dn has opened the door to a more complete and finite handling of a service fac, with precision and exactness, than we have had heretofore. We no longer just find a service fac, audit off the automaticities, key it out and forget it. We audit it out fully and terminatedly, using New Era Dn to take it down to its basics and erase those. (HCOB 6 Sept 78 III)

**ROUTINE 4-H, R4H, Routine Four.** Process used to relieve ARC breaks. (HCOB 23 Aug 65)

**ROUTINE 4-SC, R4SC, Routine Four.** Process used to locate and run service facsimiles. (HCOB 23 Aug 65)

**ROUTINE 6 END WORDS (R6EW),** when the pc has taken the locks off the reactive mind itself, using **R6EW,** he attains Fourth Stage Release. (HCOB 30 Aug 65) [Grade VI Release]

**RR, rocket read**—type of meter **read.** (HCOB 23 Aug 65)

**R/S, rock slam,** type of meter **read.** (HCOB 23 Aug 65)

**R/Ser,** see ROCK SLAMMER.

**R/S HANDLING,** also called the **Responsibility RD,** is done as OCA right-hand side **handling.** A list of all **R/Sing** statements is made, then each taken up. The idea is an **R/S** will occur in connection with a terminal which will read when checked and that's what you want to run. (HCOB 28 Mar 74, *Expanded Dianetics Series No. 21*)

**RSM, "Royal Scotman".** (FO 1483) [The Flagship's name before it became the "Apollo"]

**R/S PC, RSes**=psychosis=succumb, is trying to die (evil purpose) and the auditor is trying to make him live. This gives you an intention-counter-intention=problem, so all such **pcs** are *problems* to audit. (BTB 30 Aug 72 II)

**R/S STATEMENTS, statements** which the pc said that **R/Sed** when he said it. (BTB 8 Nov 72R II)

**R6, 1. Routine Six.** (HCOB 23 Aug 65) **2.** abbreviation for **Routine 6.** It means the exact processes and aspects of case handled at **Level VI** of Scn. (BTB 12 Apr 72R)

**R6 BANK,** *the* reactive mind. (HCOB 12 Jul 65)

**R6EW, Routine 6 End Words.** (HCOB 23 Aug 65)

**R6-EW P, Routine 6 End Word Plot.** (HCOB 4 Jan 65)

**R6-EW S, Routine 6 End Word Sixes.** (HCOB 4 Jan 65)

**R6GPMI, Routine Six Running GPMs by Items.** (HCOB 23 Aug 65)

**R6O, Routine Six Original Bank.** (HCOB 23 Aug 65)

**R6R, Routine 6 Review** of all bank run. (HCOB 23 Aug 65)

**RUDIMENTS, 1.** setting the case up for the session action. This includes ARC breaks, PTPs, W/Hs, GF or O/R listing or any prepared list. (HCOB 23 Aug 71) **2.** the **rudiments** apply to present time and this universe now. They are a nowness series of processes. (SH Spec 31, 6205C13) **3.** a **rudiment** is that which is used to get the pc in shape to be audited that session. (SH Spec 147, 6205C17) **4.** the reason you use and clean **rudiments** is to get the pc in session so you can have the pc (1) in communication with the auditor and (2) interested in own case. The purpose of **rudiments** is to set up a case to run, not to run a case. (HCOB 19 May 61)

**RUDS, rudiments.** (HCOB 23 Aug 65)

**RUN,** undergo processing. (*SOS*, p. 75)

**RUNDOWN,** a series of steps which are auditing actions and processes designed to handle a specific aspect of a case and which have a known end phenomena. Example: **Introspection Rundown.** (LRH Def. Notes)

**RUNNING ITEM, 1.** the auditor chooses the largest reading **item** the pc has given and checks interest for the next chain. This is the **running item.** (HCOB 18 Jun 78R) **2.** the auditor takes the best reading **item** on the **running item** list (possibly an LF or an LFBD or an F/N) and checks with the pc, "Are you interested in this **item**?" and if so it becomes the **running item** which you will run by R3RA Quad. (HCOB 18 Jun 78R)

**RUNNING ITEM LIST,** the auditor now takes the preassessment **item** and makes a **list** on a separate sheet of paper and asks the pc, "What (preassessment item found) are/is connected with (original item found?" The auditor writes down exactly what the pc says in a column and notes the meter reads at the exact moment the pc ends the statement of the **running item.** The result is a list called the **"Running Item List."** (HCOB 18 Jun 78R)

**RUN OUT,** erase. (*FOT*, p. 95)

# S

**SAAC, South African Anatomy Congress.** (HCOB 29 Sept 66)

**SA ACC, South African Advanced Clinical Course.** (HCOB 29 Sept 66)

**SAD EFFECT, 1.** when an ARC break is permitted to continue over too long a period of time and remains in restimulation a person goes into a **sad effect,** which is to say they become **sad** and mournful, usually without knowing what is causing it. This condition is handled by finding the earliest ARC break on the chain. Finding whether it was a break in affinity, reality, communication or understanding, and indicating it to the person, always of course, in session. (LRH Def. Notes) **2.** this is a state of great **sadness,** apathy, misery and desire for suicide and death. (HCOB 14 Mar 63)

**SADNESS,** is a small volume of grief. (*SA*, p. 93)

**SAFE TECHNIQUE,** is that **technique** which always deals in things of which the preclear is certain. (*COHA*, p. 220)

**SAG, 1.** an engram not basic is subject to **sag** which is to say that it may be brought to the two point zero (2.0) tone, but after a certain length of time has elapsed—from one to two days—it will be found to have **sagged** and to be, for instance, in a one point one (1.1) tone. It can be successfully lifted until it is apparently in a three point zero (3.0) tone, at which point much of its content will disappear. (*DTOT*, p. 114) **2.** any engram may be exhausted to a point where it will recede. It is temporarily and momentarily lost to the individual and apparently does not trouble him. That engram which has been exhausted in a chain without the basic having been reached will **sag** or reappear within twenty-four to sixty hours. (*DTOT*, p. 139)

**SAINT HILL (SH)**, the name of LRH's home in East Grinstead, Sussex, England, and location of the world-wide headquarters of Scn, and the UK Advanced Organization and **SH** (AOSH UK). LRH taught the original **Saint Hill** Special Briefing Course at **Saint Hill** from 1961 to 1965. The term **SH** now applies to any organization authorized to deliver those upper level Scn services hence we also have the "American **Saint Hill** Organization" (**ASHO**) and the "Advanced Organization and **Saint Hill** in Denmark" (AOSH DK) and **"Saint Hill** Europe" (**SH** EU). (BTB 12 Apr 72R)

Saint Hill

**SAINT HILL SPECIAL BRIEFING COURSE**, the **Saint Hill Special Briefing Course** has certain distinct purposes. The **course** was begun to do two things: (1) to study and resolve training and education; (2) to assist people who wanted to perfect their Scn. There has been no change in these purposes. The first is succeeding very well. The second is achieving world-wide recognition through people who have graduated the **SHSBC**. (HCO PL 9 Jul 62) *Abbr.* SHSBC.

**SALVAGE,** to save from ruin. (HCO PL 23 Oct 65)

**S AND D, search** and **discovery.** (HCOB 13 Jan 68)

**S AND D TYPE S,** is "Who or what are you trying to **stop?**" (HCOB 13 Jan 68)

**S AND D TYPE U,** there are several types of **S** and **D** (**Search** and **Discovery**). The **type** is determined by the first letter of the key word in the listing question. **S and D Type U** is "Who or what has attempted to **unmock** you?" (HCOB 13 Jan 68)

**S AND D TYPE W,** is "Who or what are you trying to **withdraw** from?" (HCOB 13 Jan 68)

**SANDERSON R/D,** the "Wants Handled R/D" as outlined in *Expanded Dianetic Series 9*, HCOB 10 Jun 72 was originally called the "**Sanderson R/D**" on Flag. (BTB 30 Aug 72)

**SANITY, 1.** the ability to recognize differences, similarities and identities. (HCO PL 26 Apr 70 R) **2.** a tolerance of confusion and an agreed-upon stable datum on which to align the data in a confusion are at once necessary for a **sane** reaction on the eight dynamics. This defines **sanity.** (*Scn 0-8*, p. 36) **3.** the computation of futures. (*Scn 0-8*, p. 89) **4.** a balance of creation and destruction is **sanity.** The individual is **sane** wherever he will create and destroy. (*Scn 8-8008*, p. 99) **5.** the legal definition of **sanity** is the "ability to tell right from wrong." (PAB 63) **6.** the ability to tell differences. The better one can tell differences, no matter how minute, and know the width of those differences, the more rational he is. The less one can tell differences and the closer one comes to thinking in identities (A=A) the less **sane** he is. (*DMSMH*, p. 338) **7. sanity** is the measure of how ably an individual assists things which assist survival, and inhibits things which inhibit survival. (5109CM24A) **8.** the degree of rationality of an individual. (*DASF*) **9.** rationality. A man is **sane** in the ratio that he can compute accurately, limited only by information and viewpoint. (*EOS*, p. 42) **10.** an absolute perfection in reasoning, which would resolve problems to the optimum good of all those concerned. (5203CM03A) **11. sanity** is certainty, providing only that that certainty does not fall beyond the conviction of another when he views it. (*COHA*, p. 187)

**SC, Success Congress.** (HCOB 29 Sept 66)

**SCALE OF REALITY, 1.** the **reality scale** refers to the individual's hold on **reality** and his agreement with others on what **reality** is. (*NOTL*, p. 103) **2.** at the bottom there is nothing, above that there is a communication line, the line becomes more solid, then above that terminals begin to materialize lightly and the line becomes less solid, then above that you have the terminals and you don't have any lines, and above that the terminals are there mostly by agreement, above that there is agreement, and above agreement there is consideration, individual consideration, and above that there is postulate. That is the **Scale of Reality.** (PAB 154)

**SCANNING, 1.** the action of rapidly glancing through an incident from beginning (earliest moment of the incident) to the end of the incident. (HCOB 12 Dec 71 IX) **2.** one contacts an incident and recognizes it as a concept of an incident. The preclear then goes forward from this incident to the next one of a similar type that he can recognize. (*SOS*, Bk. 2, p. 126)

**SCHEDULING,** the hours of a course or the designation of certain times for auditing. (HCOB 19 Jun 71 III)

**SCHIZO,** nickname for **schizophrenic.** It is an odd misnomer in that it means split personality and the trouble with a **schizo** is that he needs splitting, not that he's split. He's in another's valence and what is required is to remove or split the preclear out of that other's valence. (PAB 106)

**SCHIZOPHRENIC, 1.** the original definition of **schizophrenic** or "scissors personality" was in observation of shift of identity. A case which is very heavily charged goes into valences so completely that the person sharply and distinctly changes personality and appearance when shifted from one valence to another. (*SOS*, Bk. 2, p. 200) **2.** the **schizophrenic** is an individual who has several portions of the analyzer segmented off by different circuits, which are actually valences, and who goes from one to another of these portions of the analyzer, only occasionally, if ever, becoming himself. (*SOS*, Bk. 2, p. 49) **3.** an idea that one is two persons, which is remediable by a discovery of the life continuums being dramatized by the individual. (PDC 14) **4.** the multi-valent aberee. (*DMSMH*, p. 125)

**SCIENCE, 1.** a **science** is an organized body of knowledge which, proceeding from certain definite axioms, is able to predict knowledge, where, when you look, knowledge will be found. It doesn't have variables in it. (5009CM 23) **2.** a **science** is not merely a collection of facts, neatly arranged. An essential of a **science** is that observations give rise to theories which, in turn, predict new observations. When the new observations are made, they, in turn, give rise to better theories, which predict further observations. (*Scn 8-80*, p. 8)

**SCIENTIFIC TRUTH,** something which was workably and invariably right for the body of knowledge in which it lay. (*DASF*)

**SCIENTOLOGIST, 1.** one who betters the conditions of himself and the conditions of others by using **Scn** technology. (*Aud 73 UK*) **2.** one who controls persons, environments and situations. A **Scientologist** operates within the boundaries of the *Auditor's Code* and the *Code of a Scientologist*. (PAB 137) **3.** one who understands life. His technical skill is devoted to the resolution of the problems of life. (*COHA*, p. 12) **4.** a specialist in spiritual and human affairs. (*Abil Ma 1*)

**SCIENTOLOGY, 1.** it is formed from the Latin word *scio*, which means *know* or *distinguish*, being related to the word *scindo*, which means *cleave*. (Thus, the idea of differentiation is strongly implied.) It is formed from the Greek word *logos*, which means THE WORD, or OUTWARD FORM BY WHICH THE INWARD THOUGHT IS EXPRESSED AND MADE KNOWN: also THE

# SCIENTOLOGY CLEAR

INWARD THOUGHT or REASON ITSELF. Thus, **SCIEN-TOLOGY** means KNOWING ABOUT KNOWING, or SCIENCE OF KNOWLEDGE. (*Scn 8-80*, p. 8) **2. Scientology** addresses the thetan. **Scientology** is used to increase spiritual freedom, intelligence, ability, and to produce immortality. (HCOB 22 Apr 69) **3.** an organized body of scientific research knowledge concerning life, life sources and the mind and includes practices that improve the intelligence, state and conduct of persons. (HCOB 9 Jul 59) **4.** a religious philosophy in its highest meaning as it brings man to total freedom and truth. (HCOB 18 Apr 67) **5.** the science of knowing how to know answers. It is a wisdom in the tradition of ten thousand years of search in Asia and Western civilization. It is the science of human affairs which treats the livingness and beingness of man, and demonstrates to him a pathway to greater freedom. (*COHA*, p. 9) **6.** an organization of the pertinences which are mutually held true by all men in all times, and the development of technologies which demonstrate the existence of new phenomena not hitherto known, which are useful in creating states of beingness considered more desireable by man. (*COHA*, p. 9) **7.** the science of knowing how to know. It is the science of knowing sciences. It seeks to embrace the sciences and humanities as a clarification of knowledge itself. Into all these things—biology, physics, psychology and life itself—the skills of **Scientology** can bring order and simplification. (*Scn 8-8008*, p. 11) **8.** the study of the human spirit in its relationship to the physical universe and its living forms. (*Abil 146*) **9.** a science of life. It is the one thing senior to life because it handles all the factors of life. It contains the data necessary to live as a free being. A reality in **Scientology** is a reality on life. (*Aud 27 UK*) **10.** a body of knowledge which, when properly used, gives freedom and truth to the individual. (*COHA*, p. 251) **11.** knowledge and its application in the conquest of the material universe. (HCL 1, 5203CM 03A) **12.** an applied philosophy designed and developed to make the able more able. In this sphere it is tremendously successful. (HCO PL 27 Oct 64) **13.** an applied religious philosophy dealing with the study of knowledge, which through the application of its technology, can bring about desirable changes in the conditions of life. (HCO PL 15 Apr 71R)

**SCIENTOLOGY CLEAR**, see CLEAR.

**SCIENTOLOGY CROSS,** a **cross** about three inches high and is of simple but effective design without lettering or other ornament. The model of the **cross** came from a very ancient Spanish mission in Arizona, a sand casting which was dug up by Ron. The **cross** is a regular Roman **cross** with four additional short points between the four long points, a true eight dynamic **Scn cross;** the sunburst **cross.** (*Abil 14*)

Scientology Cross

**SCIENTOLOGY 8-8008, 1.** was a formula. It said: the attainment of **infinity**, that is the first **eight** is achieved by the reduction of the physical universe from **infinity**, that is the second **eight**, to **zero**, which is the first **zero** and the building of one's own universe from **zero** to an **infinity** of one's own universe and by that one achieves the attainment of **infinity**. (9ACC 14, 5412CM24) **2.** the roadmap of a process. And it says, the attainment of **infinity** by the reduction of the apparency of the mest universe is **infinity** to **zero** and the increase of one's own apparent **zero** to an **infinity** of his own universe. (PDC 31) **3.** the original definition of **Scientology 8-8008** was the attainment of **infinity** by the reduction of the apparent **infinity** and power of the mest universe to a **zero** for himself, and the increase of the apparent **zero** of one's own universe to an **infinity** for oneself. **Infinity** (∞) stood upright makes the number **eight.** (*Scn 8-8008,* p. 31)

371

# SCIENTOLOGY FIVE

**SCIENTOLOGY FIVE, Scn** applied at a high echelon to social, political and scientific problems. This requires the earlier levels and a high state of training on theoretical and wide application levels and the personal state of OT. (HCO PL 2 Aug 63)

**SCIENTOLOGY FOUR,** processes to OT, Saint Hill Special Briefing Course, 1963 type technology and targets. (HCO PL 2 Aug 63)

**SCIENTOLOGY GRADATION CHART,** see CLASSIFICATION, GRADATION AND AWARENESS CHART.

**SCIENTOLOGY LIBRARY AND RESEARCH LTD.,** took charge of the millions of words on tapes, the tons of original **Scn** materials and the manufacture of all the new course books and level manuals of **Scn.** (HCO Info Ltr 5 Feb 64) *Abbr.* S.L.R.

**SCIENTOLOGY, LIST ONE,** see LIST ONE.

**SCIENTOLOGY ONE, Scn** is now partitioned into five levels. **Scn One:** usable data about living and life, applicable without training, presented in continental magazines and booklets. This is for anyone. It contains assists as its auditing level. **Scn One** is itself divided into theory (data about life, the mind, beingness and the universe), practical (drills one can do to raise one's ability to handle others and situations), and auditing (assists, ways to get relaxed, ways to cheer up, ways to handle situations etc. in the everyday business of living, ways to process people without knowing much about processing, ways to get people to pass exams, do their work, get along). (HCO PL 2 Aug 63)

**SCIENTOLOGY PRECLEAR,** a well and happy human being who is being processed toward total ability and spiritual freedom. (HCOB 6 Apr 69)

**SCIENTOLOGY PROCESSES,** could be described as methods of "unhypnotizing" men to their own freer choice and better life. (*COHA,* p. 251)

**SCIENTOLOGY RELEASE,** a series of major levels of gain wherein Scn processing frees the person from the principal life difficulties or personal "blocks" stemming from the mind. Called

**release** grades, each of these levels must be completed for one to be ready to undertake Scn clearing. (*DTOT*, p. 151)

**SCIENTOLOGY SYMBOL, 1.** the S and double triangle. The S stands for **scio** (knowing in the fullest sense). The lower triangle is the ARC triangle, its points being affinity, reality, communication which combined give understanding. The upper triangle is the KRC triangle. The points are K for knowledge, R for responsibility and C for control. (6001C03)

Scientology Symbol

**SCIENTOLOGY THREE,** clearing and OT preparatory levels including advanced auditing above HPA/HCA level. The work on this was more or less suspended when it became obvious that OT had to be attained. Includes key-out clearing and other sub OT states. However, much technology exists on it. This is the level of the better human being. (HCO PL 2 Aug 63)

**SCIENTOLOGY TWO,** academy HPA/HCA accomplishment level. **Scn** for use in spiritual healing. This is a healing strata, using the wealth of past processes which produced results on various illnesses. The auditing level is reach and withdraw and repetitive processes. The target is human illness. (HCO PL 2 Aug 63)

**SCIENTOLOGY ZERO, 1. Scientology Zero** is the problems and confusions and wrongnesses, zones of chaos of existence and the identification of those zones of chaos. At **Scientology Zero** you merely want the people to become aware of the fact of what the problem is. (SH Spec 310, 6309C25) **2.** descriptions of the environment and what is wrong with it. **Scientology Zero** simply takes care of the environment in which the person lives. The whole subject is instantly summatable in it's own heading which is "the dangerous environment." (SH Spec 328, 6312C10)

**SCIENTOMETRIC TESTING,** IQ and personality tests reworked and modernized and co-ordinated with an electro-psycho-galvanometer. The results are more accurate than psychological tests. This is **Scientometry.** This is not psychology. These tests are more modern, being electronically co-ordinated. (HCO PL 24 Nov 60)

**SCL, Study Correction List.** (BTB 1 Nov 72)

**SCN, Scientology.** (HCOB 23 Aug 65)

**SCOUTING,** this is a two-way comm activity. Guide the pc carefully around his life until he gets on a sticky point. Then sort it out, attempting to get parts of it to clear up. Do not let pc linger on matters which do not stick. *Responsibility* sorts the matter out. His realization (cognition) of various zones are what does him good. (HCOB 28 Jul 58)

**SCP, Standard Clearing Procedure.** (HCOB 29 May 58)

**SCRAMBLER, scrambles** incidents and phrases. (I'm confused, I'll take mine **scrambled,** stir it up, it's all mixed up and I'm in the middle.) (*SOS* Gloss)

**SCRATCHY NEEDLE,** for some reason or other the term **scratchy needle** didn't survive but **dirty needle** did. (SH Spec 202A, 6210C23)

**SCREAMER, 1.** a case which has maximum charge but not a great deal of circuitry. The supercharge on the case is so great on the reactive bank that the case bleeds quickly. This is your **screamer.** Emotion releases suddenly. (*NOTL*, p. 70) **2.** people who ordinarily "run" (undergo processing) in Dn quite noisily. (*SOS*, p. 75)

**SCREEN, 1.** the cycle of the preclear who has been taught to hate things is that he begins to resist them and eventually piles up energy against them to such a degree that he makes an actual deposit which is an occlusion and which has on his side of it complete blackness and on the reverse side of it the piled-up facsimiles of that thing which he is resisting. This **screen,** then, has a hunger for the thing which it was resisting; and if this **screen** is fed whatever it was set up to resist, it will dissolve. (PAB 8) **2.** the **screen** is actually a ridge that is formed for a special purpose of protection. (*Scn 8-80*, p. 43)

**S-C-S, Start-Change-Stop.** (HCOB 23 Aug 65)

**SEA ORGANIZATION, 1.** in 1968 the **Sea Org** became a good-will activity and an efficient administrative arm of Scientology. The **Sea Org** runs the advanced organizations and is the custodian of the Clear and OT processing materials. (Ron's Journal 1968) **2.** is that **organization** which functions at a high level of confront and standard. Its purpose is to get ethics in on the planet and eventually the universe. This **organization** operates with a fleet of ships dedicated to this purpose around the world. Being mobile and separate from the pull of land is an absolute necessity to accomplish its plans, missions and purpose: to get ethics in. (FO 508)

Sea Organization Symbol

**SEARCH AND DISCOVERY,** as a process is done exactly by the general rules of listing. One lists for persons or groups who are or have suppressed the pc. The list is complete when only one item reads on nulling and this is the item. (HCOB 24 Nov 65) *Abbr.* S AND D. (HCOB 13 Jan 68)

**SEC CHECK, security check.** (HCOB 23 Aug 65)

**SECONDARY, 1.** a mental image picture of a moment of severe and shocking loss or threat of loss which contains misemotion such as anger, fear, grief, apathy or "deathfulness." It is a mental image recording of a time of severe mental stress. It may contain unconsciousness. Called a **secondary** because it itself depends upon an earlier engram with similar data but real pain, etc. (HCOB 23 Apr 69) **2.** depends for its charge on an engram which contains pain and unconsciousness. It's **secondary**. It does not contain pain and unconsciousness. It contains emotion, any emotion or misemotion. But of course pleasure doesn't make a **secondary** and it also doesn't make an incident. (SH Spec 70, 6607C21) **3.** every moment of great emotional shock, where loss occasions near unconsciousness, is fully recorded in the reactive mind. These shocks of loss are known as **secondaries**. (*SOS*, p. xiii) **4.** a mental image picture containing misemotion (encysted grief, anger, apathy, etc.) and a real or imagined loss. These contain no physical pain—they are moments of shock and stress and depend for their force on earlier engrams which have been restimulated by the circumstances of the **secondary**. (*PXL*, p. 250) **5.** a moment of misemotion where loss is threatened or accomplished. **Secondaries** contain only misemotion and communication and reality enforcements and breaks. (*SOS*, p. 112) **6.** a very severe moment of loss. It's either anger against losing, fear of losing, or fear because one has lost, or the recognition that

Secondary

one has lost. (PDC 4) **7.** a mental image picture of a moment of severe and shocking loss or threat of loss which contains unpleasant emotion such as anger, fear, grief, apathy or "deathfulness." It is a mental image recording of a time of severe mental stress. A **secondary** is called a **secondary** because it itself depends upon an earlier engram with similar data but real pain. (*DPB*, p. 6)

**SECONDARY ENGRAM, 1.** defined as a period of anguish brought about by a major loss or a threat of loss to the individual. The **secondary engram** depends for its strength and force upon physical pain **engrams** which underlie it. (*SOS*, Bk. 2, p. 136) **2.** the **secondary engram** is called **secondary** because it depends upon an earlier physical pain **engram** to exist being itself occasioned by a conscious moment of loss. It is called an **engram** in order to focus the attention of the auditor on the fact that it must be run as an **engram** and that all perceptics possible must be exhausted from it. (*SOS*, Bk. 2, p. 149) **3. secondary** (A-R-C) **engrams,** have more charge than locks. These charges on the A-R-C are so-called because they charge up the case. **Engrams** won't have charge without later incidents. If you could get all the grief off a case and do nothing else, you would have a release. You are trying to blow these charges so the engrams will not very badly affect a person. (*NOTL*, p. 35) **4.** there are three types of **secondary engrams** impinged on physical pain **engrams:** (1) painful emotion—grief—broken affinity, (2) encysted communication, (3) invalidated reality. (*NOTL*, p. 29)

**SECONDARY SCALE,** the pre-havingness **scale** contains a primary scale and a **secondary scale.** The **secondary scale** contains nearly all simple verbs in the English language, properly placed for level and repeated on other levels. (HCOB 23 May 61)

**SECONDARY STYLE,** every level has a different primary style of auditing. But sometimes in actual sessions or particularly in assists this style is altered slightly for special purposes. The style altered for assists or for a particular process in a regular session is called a **secondary style.** It is done a precise but different way to accomplish assists or to assist a pc in a regular session. This variation is called the **secondary style** of that level. (HCOB 21 Feb 66)

**SECONDARY UNIVERSE,** it isn't really his universe. It's pictures of the physical universe which he retains in lieu of. We're talking of the reactive mind, the facsimiles, engrams, energy pictures, as a **secondary universe** which is formed by reason of not being able to have the physical universe. And that's how the reactive mind gets born and where it comes from. These **secondary universes** could just as well be called reactive universes. (*Abil 34*, 1956)

**SECOND-DYNAMIC,** see DYNAMICS.

**SECOND FACSIMILES,** are "photographs" of the memories of another. They are still pictures usually. Their characteristic is that they show up with only two or three pictures of some long situation. (*HOM*, p. 36)

**SECOND GPM,** the next-to-the-latest **GPM** on the track. (SH Spec 251, 6303C22)

**SECOND ORIGINAL ASSESSMENT,** at the point in the New Era Dn Program, when the pc has fully completed his Drug Rundown and handled the items on the **Original Assessment** Sheet, the **Original Assessment** Sheet is REDONE. The **Second Original Assessment** Sheet gives a comparison. The somatics and pains not mentioned in the **second assessment** can be considered to be gone. A **second** form done gives the auditor and the C/S an indication of the actual improvement. Additionally, the pc's memory will have improved if you've done a good job of auditing. So we reassess the **Original Assessment** Sheet and handle any additional items which come up. (HCOB 4 Jul 78R)

**SECOND PHENOMENON,** the **second phenomenon** is the overt cycle which follows a misunderstood word. When a word is not grasped, the student then goes into a non-comprehension (blankness) of things immediately after. This is followed by the student's solution for the blank condition which is to individuate from it—separate self from it. Now being something else than the blank area, the student commits overts against the more general area. These overts, of course, are followed by restraining himself from committing overts. This pulls flows toward the person and makes the person crave motivators. This is followed by various mental and physical conditions and by various complaints, fault-finding and look-what-you-did-to-me. This justifies a departure, a blow. But the system of education, frowning on blows as it does, causes the student to really withdraw self from the study subject (whatever he was studying) and set up in its place a circuit which can receive and give back sentences and phrases. We now have "the quick student who somehow never applies what he learns." The specific **phenomena** then is that a student can study some words and give them back and yet be no participant to the action. The student gets A+ on exams but can't apply the data. (HCO PL 24 Sept 64)

**SECOND POSTULATE,** know. (PAB 66)

**SECOND STAGE RELEASE,** see STAGES OF RELEASE.

**SECOND WIND,** is really getting enough environment and enough mass in order to run out the exhaustion of the last race. There is no such thing as **"second wind."** There is such a thing as a return to extroversion on the physical world in which one lives. (*POW*, pp. 97-98)

**SECRET, 1.** withheld thought. (PAB 131) **2.** it is the answer which was never given and that is all a **secret** is. (*Dn 55!*, p. 76)

**SECURITY, 1. security** itself is an understanding. Men who know are **secure**. Insecurity exists in the absence of knowledge. All **security** derives from knowledge. (*POW*, p. 16) **2.** self-confidence alone is **security**. Your ability is your **security**. There is no **security** but you. (*HFP*, p. 53) **3.** is not a static thing. **Security** would lie only in a man's confidence in reaching his goals and indeed, in his having goals to reach. (*SOS*, Bk. 2, p. 86)

**SECURITY CHECKING, 1.** remedying the compulsion or obsession to commit actions which have to be withheld, i.e. we are remedying unreasonable action. (SH Spec 100, 6201C16) **2.** withholds don't add up to withholds. They add up to overts, they add up to secrecies, they add up to individuation, they add up to games conditions, they add up to a lot more things than O/W. Although we carelessly call them withholds, we're asking a person to straighten out their interpersonal relationships with another terminal. Our normal **security check** is addressed to the individual versus the society or his family. It's what people would consider reprehensible that makes a withhold. In a Catholic society, not having kept Mass would be a reprehensible action. In a non-Catholic society, nobody would think twice about it. So, most of our **security checks** are aimed at transgressions against the mores of the group. That is the basic center line of the **security check**. It's a moral code that you're processing in one way or the other. You're straightening out somebody on the "Now I'm supposed to's." They've transgressed against a series of "Now I'm supposed to's." Having so transgressed, they are now individuated. If their individuation is too obsessive, they snap in and become the terminal. All of these cycles exist around the idea of the transgression against the "Now I'm supposed to."

That's what a **security check** clears up and that is all it clears up. It's a great deal more than a withhold. (SH Spec 58, 6109C26) *Abbr.* Sec Checking or Sec √ ing.

**SECURITY FORM 7A, security check** devised specifically to check applicants for employment. (HCOB 28 Sept 61)

**SECURITY FORM 7B, security check** devised specifically to check personnel already employed. (HCOB 28 Sept 61)

**SEE,** is just the **sight** band of perception. The photon wave-length of perception which is a manufactured energy. (PDC 5)

**SELF,** thetan, plus machines plus body plus reactive bank (in Dn). (8ACC-13, 5410C19)

**SELF ANALYSIS IN SCIENTOLOGY,** is a group technique aimed at the rehabilitation of one's own universe so as to bring it up to a level of comparability with one's own observation of the mest universe, and can be delivered to groups of children or adults by a person trained only through the text of *Self Analysis in Scientology.* (*COHA,* p. 245)

**SELF ANALYSIS LISTS, 1.** the **lists** of questions by which the individual can explore his past and improve his reactions toward life. Dianetically speaking, this self-processing section could be called "straight wire." It is not "auto processing." The reader is actually being processed by the author. (*SA,* p. 62) **2.** the auditor is assisted by these **lists** in that they open a case for the running of engrams and secondaries and raise the preclear on a tone scale. These **lists** are used repetitively; that is to say the individual goes over them again and again. There is no finite period to the work. The reason the recall of these questions is important is that they reveal and discharge locks which have formed above the basic engrams (moments of physical pain and unconsciousness) and secondaries (moments of acute loss as death of a loved one). The discharging of these locks renders engrams and secondaries relatively ineffective. (*SA,* p. 62)

**SELF AUDITING, 1.** the manifestation of going around running concepts or processes on one's **self.** One is doing this because he has been made afraid, through his failure on others, of his ability to control his own engrams, facsimiles, thoughts and concepts, and he seeks to control them through **auditing.** (*Dn 55!,* p. 121) **2.** solo auditing occurs in session with a meter. **Self-auditing** is out-of-session wondering and chewing on bank. (HCOB 10 Apr

72) **3.** the manifestation of being overwhelmed by masses etc., and pulling only think out of the bank. Pulling out think then pulls in more force which gives more **self-audit**. (HCOB 19 Jun 70 II) **4. self-auditing** is done ordinarily out of valence and results in the preclear expending counter-efforts against himself. Thus he succeeds only in hurting himself. (*AP&A*, p. 31)

**SELF-COACHING,** the student tending to introvert and look too much at how he is doing and what he is doing rather than just doing it. (HCOB 24 May 68)

**SELF-CONFIDENCE, 1.** nothing more than belief in one's ability to decide and in one's decisions. (*HFP*, p. 142) **2.** is self-determinism. It is one's belief in one's ability to determine his own causes. (*DAB*, Vol. II, 1951-52, p. 166)

**SELF-DETERMINED,** one can only be **self-determined** when one can observe the actual situation before one; otherwise a being is delusion-determined or other-determined. (HCOB 6 Nov 64)

**SELF-DETERMINISM, 1.** the ability to locate in space and time, energy and matter; also the ability to create space and time in which to create and locate energy and matter. (*Scn 0-8*, p. 25) **2. self-determinism** in the field of motion consists of, by own power of choice, permitting the object or body to be still or not to be still; permitting a thing to be changed or not to be changed; permitting a thing to be started or not to be started. (*CMSCS*, p. 18) **3. self-determinism** is that state of being wherein the individual can or cannot be controlled by his environment according to his own choice. In that state the individual has self-confidence in his control of the material universe and the organisms within it along every dynamic. He is confident about any and all abilities or talents he may possess. He is confident in his interpersonal relationships. He reasons but does not need to react. (*AP&A*, p. 53) **4.** entirely and solely the imposition of time and space upon energy flows. Imposing time and space upon objects, people, self, events, and individuals, is causation. (*Scn 8-80*, p. 44) **5.** the theta control of the organism. (*Scn 0-8*, p. 83) **6.** full responsibility for **self**, no responsibility for other side of game. (*Scn 0-8*, p. 119) **7.** means the ability to direct himself. (2 ACC 30A, 5312CM21) **8.** the individual can only **determine** something from his own viewpoint. (SH Spec 83, 6612C06) **9.** a condition of **determining** the actions of **self**. It is a first (**self**) dynamic action and leaves the remaining seven undetermined or, in actuality, in opposition to the **self.** Thus if one wants to take on the rest of life in a free-for-all fight, one could be entirely insistent upon total **self-determinism.** One is **Self-determined,** then, in any situation in which he is fighting. He is pan-determined in any situation which he is controlling. (*FOT*, p. 50) **10. self-determinism** meant, in essence, control by the awareness of awareness unit of that which it conceived to be its identity. (*Dn55!*, p. 98)

**SELF-INVALIDATING ENGRAM,** the **engram** which contains the phrases, "never happened," "can't believe it," "wouldn't possibly imagine it," and so on. (*DTOT*, p. 129)

**SELF-INVALIDATION,** a person who makes huge overts out of every little action, which is in essence **self-invalidation,** has behind that someplace a huge overt—big enough to set the police of several galaxies after them. (BTB 11 Dec 72R)

**SELFNESS,** not selfishness but just being himself. (*Aud Spec Iss. 1973 ASHO*)

**SELF-PERPETUATING ENGRAM,** implies that "It will always be this way," and "It happens all the time." (*DTOT*, p. 130)

**SELF-PROCESSING,** the action of a person trying to run **processes** on **himself** or continually thinking about his own case or trying to work out what is wrong with himself. It is an improper action which will only lead to a worsening of the person's case. (BTB 12 Apr 72) See also SELF-AUDITING.

**SEMI-ACKNOWLEDGEMENT, half acknowledgements.** When you **acknowledge** what the pc said without ending the cycle of the auditing command and then say the next auditing commands. (SH Spec 25, 6107C05)

**SEN, sensation.** (HCOB 23 Aug 65)

**SENSATION, 1.** uncomfortable perceptions stemming from the reactive mind (except pain) are called **sensation.** These are basically "pressure," "motion," "dizziness," "sexual sensation," and "emotion" and "misemotion." There are others, definite in themselves but definable in these five general categories. If one took a fork and pressed it against the arm, that would be "pressure." "Motion" is just that, a feeling of being in motion when one is not. "Motion" includes the "winds of space." A feeling of being blown upon, especially from in front of the face. "Dizziness" is a feeling of disorientation and includes a spinniness, as well as an out-of-balance feeling. "Sexual sensation" means any feeling, pleasant or unpleasant, commonly experienced during sexual restimulation or action. "Emotion" and "misemotion" include all levels of the complete tone scale except "pain"; emotion and misemotion are closely allied to "motion," being only a finer particle action. A bank solidity is a form of "pressure," and when the **sensation** of increasing solidity of masses in the mind occurs, we say "The bank is beefing up." All these are classified as **sensation**. *Symbol:* Sen. (HCOB 8 Nov 62) **2.** all **sensation** is energy. (2 ACC 26A, 5312CM17)

**SENSING DEVICES, sensory** organs. (*EOS*, p. 45)

**SENSITIVITY BOOSTER,** the meter can be made more **sensitive** by turning the **sensitivity booster** to 32 which will double the **sensitivity** or to 64 which quadruples the **sensitivity** (64 or 128 in later models). (*BIEM*, p. 25)

**SENSITIVITY KNOB, 1.** on the E-meter the **sensitivity knob** magnifies the movement of the needle. (*BIEM*, p. 25) **2.** the **sensitivity knob** increases the swing of the needle. (*EME*, p. 13)

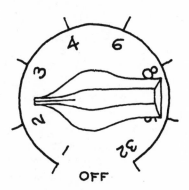

Sensitivity Knob

**SENSORY CHANNELS,** the nerves. (*HFP*, p. 32)

**SENTIENT,** responsive to or conscious of **sense** impressions. (*EOS*, p. 43)

# SEPARATENESS

**SEPARATENESS,** the object of **separateness** in locational processing is to establish and run out identifications. Commands: Select an object from which you are **separate.** Select an object which is **separate** from you. (Op Bull No. 1, 20 Oct 55)

**SERENE VALENCES,** when people are in **serene valences** it means they are wholly overwhelmed as a thetan. (HCOB 5 Jun 61)

**SER FAC, service facsimile.** (HCOB 23 Aug 65)

**SERIES,** see GOAL SERIES.

**SERIOUS,** when interest is important because of penalty. (PDC 59)

**SERIOUSLY PHYSICALLY ILL CASES, cases** where the **illness** makes too much PTP in PT. (HCOB 25 Nov 71 II)

**SERVICE FACSIMILE, 1.** these are called **"service facsimiles."** **"Service"** because they **serve** him. **"Facsimiles"** because they are in mental image picture form. They explain his disabilities as well. The **facsimile** part is actually a self-installed disability that "explains" how he is not responsible for not being able to cope. So he is not wrong for not coping. Part of the "package" is to be right by making wrong. The **service facsimile** is therefore a picture containing an explanation of self condition and also a fixed method of making others wrong. (HCOB 15 Feb 74) **2.** this is actually part of a chain of incidents which the individual uses to invite sympathy or cooperation on the part of the environment. One uses engrams to handle himself and others and the environ after one has himself conceived that he has failed to handle himself, others and the general environ. (*AP&A*, p. 7) **3.** it is simply a time when you tried to do something and were hurt or failed and got sympathy for it. Then afterwards when you were hurt or failed and wanted an explanation, you used it. And if you didn't succeed in getting sympathy for it, you used it so hard it became a psychosomatic illness. (*HFP*, p. 89) **4.** every time you fail, you pick up this **facsimile** and become sick or sadly noble. It's your explanation to yourself and the world as to how and why you failed. It once got you sympathy. (*HFP*, p. 89) **5.** that facsimile which the preclear uses to apologize for his failures. In other words, it is used to make others wrong and procure their cooperation in the survival of the preclear. If the preclear well cannot achieve survival, he attempts an illness or disability as a survival computation. The workability and necessity of the **service facsimile** is only superficially useful. The **service facsimile** is an action method of withdrawing from a state of beingness to a state of not beingness and is intended to persuade others to coax the individual back into a state of beingness. (*AP&A*, p. 43) **6.** that computation generated by the preclear (not the bank) to make self right and others wrong, to dominate or escape domination and enhance own survival and injure that of others. (HCOB 1 Sept 63)

**SESSION,** see AUDITING SESSION.

**SESSION ARC BREAK,** occurs when the **session** inadvertently brought into view someplace on the back track, something which was not acknowledged. A heavy charge on the back track moved in just to the fringes of consciousness of the pc and he reacted, and his **affinity,** and **reality,** and **communication** went by the boards. (SH Spec 60, 6505C11)

**SESSION MISSED WITHHOLD,** a **missed withhold** picked up in a **session** is anything the pc thinks, anything the pc is **withholding.** It doesn't matter. That's a **session missed withhold.** Pc didn't tell the auditor he was uncomfortable, etc. (SH Spec 142, 6205C03)

**SETTLE OUT, 1.** which is to say, permits the temporarily enturbulated theta to disenturbulate and the "frozen" entheta to convert, in some minute quantity, to free theta. (*SOS*, Bk. 2, p. 8) **2.** destimulate. (HCOB 16 Aug 70)

**SET UP,** getting an F/N showing and VGIs before starting any major action. Such may require a repair action and rudiments as well. (HCOB 23 Aug 71)

**SETUP PROGRAM,** a repair **program** to eradicate case mishandling by current life or auditing errors. (HCOB 12 Jun 70)

# SEVEN RESISTIVE CASES

**SEVEN RESISTIVE CASES,** these are the only **cases** which hang up: (1) unaudited **cases** (lies about grades, etc.); (2) drug **cases** (who seek in processing the delusions or madness which exhilarated them on drugs); (3) former therapy **cases** (in this or past lives); (4) out of valence **cases;** (5) **cases** who continue to commit overts on Scn; (6) **cases** "audited" with their ruds out or grades out; (7) seriously physically ill **cases** (where the illness makes too much PTP in PT). (HCOB 23 Sept 68)

**SEVEN SPECIAL CASES, Seven Resistive Cases.** (HCOB 8 Sept 71)

**SEVENTH DYNAMIC,** see DYNAMICS.

**SEVENTY-FIVE RATING, 75 rating.** Passing grade **75** per cent on simple written examination of which true and false questions can comprise **75** per cent or more of the questions asked. (HCO PL 15 Mar 63)

**SEVERITY,** an increase in that discipline believed necessary by the people to guarantee their security. (PAB 96)

**SEX, 1.** the body's single effort to make something out of nothing is resident in **sex,** and in this culture at our time **sex** is a degraded and nasty thing which must be hidden at best and babies are something not to have but to be prevented. Thus even **sex** has been made to parallel the something-into-nothing impulse. (PAB 14) **2. sex** has been overweighted in importance in old psychotherapy, an importance more or less disgraced at this time. **Sex** is only one of numerous creative impulses. An anxiety about **sex,** however, occurs when an individual begins to believe that there will not be a body for him to have during the next lifetime. (*FOT,* p. 67) **3. sex** finds no space tolerable for present beingness but looks to other and future beingnesses as the only chance for universes. (PAB 33) **4.** a harmonic of aesthetics and pain. (*Scn Jour 18-G*) **5.** an interchange of condensed admiration particles which forwards new bodies into being. (*COHA,* p. 205) **6.** the super-condensed many times via'd activity of creating other life forms. The only thing which makes it more complex is the fact that it is considered to be more complex. (5410CM20)

**SEXUAL SENSATION,** any feeling, pleasant or unpleasant, commonly experienced during **sexual** restimulation or action. (HCOB 19 Jan 67)

**SF, small fall,** (a quarter to half an inch). (HCOB 29 Apr 69)

**SH, Saint Hill.** (HCOB 23 Aug 65)

**SH ACC, Saint Hill Advanced Clinical Course.** (HCOB 29 Sept 66)

**SHAME, 1.** effect one creates is unworthy, shouldn't have done it. (HCOB 6 Feb 60) **2.** being other bodies, that's **shame.** There is an emotion of **shame** connected with being other bodies; one is **ashamed** to be oneself, he is somebody else. (5904C08)

**SH DEMO, Saint Hill Demonstration.** (HCOB 29 Sept 66)

**SHIFT OF VALENCE,** that merely means taking on the identity of another mass. (5410CM12)

**SHOCK, 1.** a person can be broken down on the emotional scale so steeply, sharply and suddenly that they can be killed. That's what's known as **shock.** (5203CM05A) **2.** an expression of an unwillingness to duplicate. (5410CM21)

**SHORT 8,** a short form of Standard Operating Procedure 8 of *Scn 8-8008.* (*COHA,* p. 243)

**SHORT LIST,** by **short,** we don't mean 539 pages, or three items either. A **short list** is enough items to get the pc sure he or she has covered the lot. (HCOB 1 Jul 65)

**SHORT SESSIONING, 1.** starting, continuing for a few minutes, a **session,** and ending the **session.** It has good gain qualities for a pc who has poor concentration. (HCOB 24 Mar 60) **2.** means that two or more **sessions** can be run in one auditing period. (HCOB 21 Dec 61)

**SHORT SPOTTING, 1.** one version of TR-10, "You notice that (nearby object)." It is **spotting** right up close. (*SCP,* p. 10) **2.** a process called **short spotting,** wherein the auditor has the preclear **spot** things that are very close to him. (*SCP,* p. 22)

**SHORT TERM PTP,** is in terms of months or weeks. (SH Spec 5, 6106C01)

**SHPA, Special Hubbard Professional Auditors Course** (London). (HCOB 29 Sept 66)

**SHSBC, 1. Saint Hill Special Briefing Course.** (HCO PL 11 Feb 63) **2.** the purpose of the **Saint Hill Special Briefing Course** was first foremost and only to make clearing auditors. (HCO PL 12 Nov 62)

**SHUT-OFFS,** there is a whole species of commands which **shut off** pain and emotion simultaneously. "I can't feel anything" is the standard, but the command varies widely and is worded in a great many ways. (*DMSMH*, p. 347)

**SICK BEING,** one who has been bent upon violence and was suppressed, or one who was bent upon constructiveness and was suppressed. (HCO Info Ltr 2 Apr 64)

**SICKNESS, 1.** the result of engram chains in restimulation. (HCOB 16 Aug 69) **2.** is a covert effort to die. (SH Spec 40, 6108C16) **3.** invalidation of a terminal. (SH Spec 46, 6108C29)

**SIGHT,** light waves, coming from the sun, moon, stars or artificial sources, reflect from objects and the light waves enter the eyes and are recorded for present time action or as memory for future reference. Light sources are also recorded. This is the sense perception called **sight.** (*SA*, p. 79)

**SIGNIFICANCE, 1.** a word which is used in the special sense to denote any thought, decision, concept, idea or meaning in the mind in distinction to its masses. (The mind is basically composed of masses and **significances.**) (*Scn AD*) **2.** engrams, secondaries, locks all add up to mental masses, forces, energies, time, which express themselves in countless different ways such as pain, misemotion, feelings, old perceptions and a billion billion thought combinations buried in the masses as **significances.** A thetan can postulate or say or reason anything. Thus there is an infinity of **significances.** A thetan is natively capable of logical thought. This becomes muddied by out-points held in by mental forces such as pictures of heavy experiences. As the masses and forces accumulated and copied from living build up, the logic potential becomes reduced and illogical results occur. The *pc* is continually searching for the *significance* of a mass or force— what is it, why is it. All forces in the bank contain **significances.** The amount of **significance** recovered or realized by the pc only shows up as cognitions. (HCOB 16 Jun 70)

**SIGNIFICANCE PROCESSING, significance processing** had the preclear take some picture or object and assign innumerable **significances** to it. This is an excellent **process** for those who are always looking for deeper **significances** in everything. (*COHA*, p. 79)

**SIMULATED CLEAR,** we called it a "keyed-out **clear**" quite properly. The person has been *released* from his reactive mind. He still has that reactive mind but he's not *in* it. (HCOB 2 Apr 65)

**SINCE MID RUDS,** see BIG MIDDLE RUDIMENTS, MIDDLE RUDIMENTS.

**SINGLE,** by **"single"** is meant "to self" flow 1. (HCOB 5 Oct 69)

**SIX BASIC PROCESSES, THE,** (1) Two-Way Communication; (2) Elementary Straightwire; (3) Opening Procedure of 8C; (4) Opening Procedure by Duplication; (5) Remedying Havingness; (6) Spotting Spots in Space. (PAB 42)

**SIX LEVELS OF PROCESSING, 1. level one**—rudiments, **level two**—locational and not-know processes, **level three**—decisional processing, **level four**—opening procedure by duplication, **level five**—remedy of communication scarcity, **level six**—remedy of havingness and spotting spots in space. (*Scn 8-8008*, p. 137) **2.** a method of auditing and a new auditing atmosphere which articulates the attitude best calculated to maintain continuing stable data in a case. The auditing atmosphere is A-R-C with gain marked by continuing rises in ARC. (*Scn 8-8008*, pp. 137-141)

**SIXTH DYNAMIC,** see DYNAMICS.

**SKIPPED GRADIENT,** a **skipped gradient** means taking on a higher degree or amount before a lesser degree of it has been handled, one has to go back and handle the missed degree or thing or else one will have just loses on a subject thereafter. (HCOB 2 Jun 71 I)

**SKUNK, "skunk"** has a slang definition of "to lose out," to be **"skunked."** (LRH Def. Notes)

**SKUNKED,** a list with RSes on it in listing that failed to produce a reliable item. (HCOB 5 Dec 62)

**SLAM,** see ROCK SLAM.

**SLANT (/), 1.** if the item is alive constantly or sporadically but doesn't go null for three consecutive reads you put a **slant.** (SH Spec 137, 6204C24) **2.** the auditor, to null the list marks each item that stays in with a (/). (HCOB 5 Dec 62)

**SLAVERY,** being positioned in another's time and space. (*Scn 8-8008* Gloss)

**SLOW ASSESSMENT,** by **slow assessment** is meant letting the pc itsa while **assessing.** This consists of *rapid auditor action,* very crisp to get something that moves the TA and then immediate shift into letting the pc itsa during which, "Be quiet!" The **slowness** is overall action. It takes hours and hours to do an old preclear **assessment** form this way but the TA *flies.* (HCOB 1 Oct 63)

**SLOW BOAT AUDITING, auditing** done without an ability to estimate the ARC of the pc or know where the basic processes fit on the tone scale. (*Abil Ma 5*)

**SLOW GAIN CASE,** committing overts the auditor doesn't see. Therefore a little discipline in the environment speeds the **slow gain case.** (HCOB 29 Sept 65)

**SLP, Six Levels** of **Processing.** (*Scn 8-8008,* p. 137)

**S.L.R., Scientology Library** and **Research Ltd.** (HCO PL 30 Sept 64)

**S.M., straight memory.** (*Hubbard Chart of Human Evaluation*)

**SMALL TIGER,** it is however simply called **Tiger Drill.** Big Tiger is always called Big Tiger. Only the following buttons are used in **Small Tiger:** suppressed, invalidated, suggested, failed to reveal and mistake. (HCOB 29 Nov 62)

**SMC, State** of **Man Congress.** (HCOB 29 Sept 66)

**SMELL,** is evidently activated by small particles escaping from the object, which is thus sensed traveling through space and meeting the nerves. Taste is usually considered to be a part of the sense of **smell.** (*SA,* p. 87)

**SNAPPING TERMINALS,** the reason an engram comes into being and expresses itself on a preclear's body is a lack of communication. The communication has become solid. It expresses itself as an engram, as a facsimile, as a lock, as a secondary. This expression comes about through absence of two-way communication. The moment that one runs two-way communication in upon the process, the spot has a tendency to go back to its original location. This is the phenomenon known as **snapping** or closing **terminals.** (PAB 51)

**S.O., Sea Organization.** (FO 508)

**SOCIAL COUNSELOR COURSE,** the **course** covers the basic materials of Dn and Scn and teaches the student how to audit. (SO ED 135, INT, 18 Jan 72)

**SOCIAL MACHINERY,** action without awareness. He's doing it all the time but he never noticed it. What the individual is aware of and what the individual is doing are not the same thing, ever. (*Aud 31*)

**SOCIAL PERSONALITY,** the **social personality** naturally operates on the basis of the greatest good. He is not haunted by imagined enemies but he does recognize real enemies when they exist. The **social personality** wants to survive and wants others to survive. Basically the **social personality** wants others to be happy and do well. (*ISE*, p. 19)

**SOFT TRs,** there has been such a thing as "**soft TRs**". In being "**soft**" and "nice" about **TRs,** you are not doing anyone a favor. If anything, it would be the greatest disservice you could give a being. In Scn we get results and we get them by following our technology relentlessly to the letter. (BTB 18 Aug 71R)

**SOLDERED-IN,** the engram acts as if it were a **soldered-in** connection to the life function regulator and the organic coordinator and the basic level of the analytical mind itself. By **soldered-in** is meant "permanent connection." This keying in is the hook-up of the engram as part of the operating machinery of the body. (*DMSMH*, p. 78)

**SOLID,** when the meter needle is not floating the TA is registering mass, mental mass. When you see a TA going up, up, up you know the picture isn't erasing but is getting more **solid.** The **solidness** is visible right on the TA dial. (HCOB 25 May 69)

**SOLIDITY, 1.** could be said to be stupidity. (*COHA*, p. 139) **2.** barriers. (HCOB 10 Mar 70)

**SOLNS, solutions.** (BTB 20 Aug 71R II)

**SOLO AUDITING, 1.** the action of **"solo auditing"** is not self-auditing. **Solo auditing** is done in a regular session in model session form. (HCOB 8 Dec 64) **2.** in **solo auditing** the auditor is also the pc. This means that once the auditor has duplicated and understood the item or question the pc has also. (BTB 12 Dec 71 IV)

**SOLUTION, 1.** what will cause the problem to dissipate and disappear. (*PXL*, p. 182) **2.** something which **solves** the problem. Thus the as-isness of the problem *is* the **solution** for it would vanish the problem. (*COHA*, p. 109)

**SOM,** symbol for **somatic.** (HCOB 19 Jan 67)

**SOMA,** body. (HCOB 23 Apr 69)

**SOMATIC, 1.** by **somatic** is meant a pain or ache sensation and also misemotion or even unconsciousness. There are a thousand different descriptive words that could add up to a feeling. Pains, aches, dizziness, sadness—these are all feelings. Awareness, pleasant or unpleasant, of a body. ( HCOB 26 Apr 69) **2.** body sensation, illness or pain or discomfort. **"Soma"** means body. Hence **psychosomatic** or pains stemming from the mind. (HCOB 23 Apr 69) **3.** this is a general word for uncomfortable physical perceptions coming from the reactive mind. Its genus is early Dn and it is a general, common package word used by Scientologists to denote "pain" or "sensation" with no difference made between them. To the Scientologist anything is a **somatic** if it emanates from the various parts of the reactive mind and produces an awareness of reactivity. *Symbol:* SOM. (HCOB 8 Nov 62) **4.** the word **somatic** means, actually, bodily or physical. Because the word pain is restimulative, and because the word pain has in the past led to a confusion between physical pain and mental pain, the word **somatic** is used in Dn to denote physical pain or discomfort, of any kind. It can mean actual pain, such as that caused by a cut or a blow; or it can mean discomfort, as from heat or cold; it can mean itching—in short, anything physically uncomfortable. It does not include mental discomfort such as grief. Hard breathing would not be a **somatic**; it would be a symptom of misemotion suppression. **Somatic** means a non-survival physical state of being. (*SOS*, p. 79)

**SOMATIC CHAIN, 1. chains,** held together by **somatics.** The body condition or **somatic** is what keeps the **chain** in association. **Somatic chains** go quickly to basic and are the important **chains.** (HCOB 23 May 69)

**SOMATIC LOCATION,** the technique available to the auditor by which the moment of reception of the **somatic** is **located,** in an effort to discover whether it is received in this engram or to find an engram containing it. (*DMSMH*, p. 226)

**SOMATIC MIND, 1.** the mind that works in a purely stimulus response way, contains only actingness, no thinkingness, and can be used to set up certain physical machines. (HCO Info Ltr 2 Sept 64) **2.** that mind which, directed by the analytical or reactive mind, places solutions into effect on the physical level. (*Scn 0-8*, p. 65) **3.** this is an even heavier type of mind than the reactive mind since it contains no thinkingness and contains only actingness. The impulses placed against the body by the thetan through various mental machinery, arrive at the voluntary, involuntary, and glandular levels. These have set methods of analysis for any given situation and so respond directly to commands given. (*FOT*, p. 61) **4.** the **somatic mind** would be that **mind** which takes care of the automatic mechanisms of the body, the regulation of the minutiae which keep the organism running. (*SOS*, Bk. 2, p. 233)

**SOMATIC SHUT-OFF,** the **somatic** may be **shut-off** in the incident or elsewhere, either earlier by command or late by painful emotion. The patient who wriggles a great deal or who does not wriggle at all is suffering from a pain or emotion **shut-off** or late painful emotional engrams or both. There is a whole species of commands which **shut-off** pain and emotion simultaniously: this is because the word "feel" is homonymic. "I can't feel anything" is the standard, but the command varies widely and is worded in a great many ways. (*DMSMH*, pp. 346-347)

**SOMATIC STRIP,** the **somatic strip** is so called because it seems to be a physical indicator mechanism which has to do with time.

The auditor orders the **somatic strip.** There is this difference between the file clerk and the **somatic strip:** he works with the file clerk but commands the **somatic strip.** On command, the **somatic strip** will go to any point of the preclear's life, unless the entheta on the case is so heavy that the **somatic strip** is frozen in one place. The **somatic strip** goes to the point of return, but it is not the same as completely returning since the preclear's "I" can stay in present time and the **somatic strip** can be sent back to earlier periods of his life. This is a very useful mechanism. The **somatic strip** can be sent back to the beginning of an engram and will go there. The **somatic strip** will advance through an engram in terms of minutes counted off by the auditor, so that the auditor can say that the **somatic strip** will go to the beginning of the engram, then to the point five minutes after the engram began, and so forth. (*SOS*, Bk. 2, p. 163)

**SONIC, 1.** ability to hear the **sound** in pictures. (HCOB 20 May 69) **2.** by the word **sonic** in Dn is usually meant **sonic** recall, rather than hearing **sounds** outside the body. **Sonic** means hearing the **sounds** which have been remembered. Those **sounds** which the individual has heard in the past are all recorded, either in the analytical standard memory bank or in the reactive bank. (*SOS*, p. 65) **3.** recalling a **sound** by hearing it again is called **"sonic"** in Dn and is a desirable circumstance which can be returned to the individual. (*SA*, p. 85)

**SONIC CIRCUITS,** are very easily recognized, for they speak audibly inside the head of the preclear or give him faint **sonic** impressions. (*SOS*, Bk. 2, p. 205)

**SONIC SHUT-OFF, 1.** it's a person trying to stop the energy wave of **sound.** (5110CM01B) **2. sonic shut-off** may be quite selective: the individual may be able to hear **sounds** but not voices. Selective **shut-offs** are caused both by charge on the case and by selective **sonic shut-off** commands, such as "You cannot hear your wife," or "You pay no attention to me." (*SOS*, p. 66)

**SOP, Standard Operating Procedure.** (*Scn 8-8008*, p. 85)

**SOP-8, Standard Operating Procedure 8.** This **operating procedure** retains the most workable methods of preceding **procedures** and, in itself, emphasizes positive gain and the present and future rather than negative gain of eradication of the past. The goal of this **procedure** is not the rehabilitation of the body but of the thetan. Rehabilitation of a body incidentally ensues. The goal of this **procedure** is Operating Thetan. (*Scn 8-8008*, p. 115)

**SOP 8A,** a process; employed the moment it is discovered the pc's very uncertain of his own mock-ups or if he is occluded. (PAB 2)

**SOP-8-C,** might be called **SOP-8** modified for clinical, laboratory, and individual human applications. The goal of the system of operation is to return to the individual his knowledge, skill and knowingness, and to enhance his perception, his reaction time and serenity. (*COHA*, p. 246)

**SOP 8-D,** this **procedure** is for use by a trained Scientologist. Its primary goal is the delivery of heavy cases; however it can be extensively applied to all cases. (*COHA*, p. 174)

**SOP GOALS,** this is **Standard Operating Procedure Goals.** There is a great deal to know about **SOP Goals.** It is the right way to use the pre-hav scales. With skilled use this can produce releases and Clears. (HCOB 23 Mar 61)

**SOUND, 1. sound** consists of the perception of waves emanating from moving objects. An object moves rapidly or slowly, and sets into vibration the air in its vicinity which pulses. When these pulses strike the eardrum they set into motion the individual's **sound** recording mechanism and the **sound** is registered. **Sound** is absent in a vacuum and is actually merely a force wave. (*SA*, p. 84) **2. sound** is a by-product of communication. It is the carrier wave of communication and is not itself communication. (*Dn 55!*, p. 131) **3. sound** has several parts. The first is pitch. This is the number of vibrations per unit of time of any object from which **sound** is coming. The second is quality or tone which is simply the difference between a jagged or ragged **sound** wave and a smooth **sound** wave as in a musical note. The third is volume, which merely means the force of the **sound** wave, its loudness or quietness. (*SA*, p. 85)

**SOURCE, 1.** the point of origin, or it would be the originator, or where something was begun or dreamed up or mocked up. (Class VIII, No. 18) **2.** that from which something comes or develops; place of origin: cause. (HCOB 11 May 65)

# SOURCE LIST

**SOURCE LIST, 1.** the goal oppose as covered in steps 1-7 (of R3M). This is called a **"source list."** (HCOB 22 Feb 63)
**2.** there are only two of these **"source lists."** (a) the "most likely list" at the start of each GPM, done before RIs are found. "Who or what would be most likely to achieve this goal?" And (b) the "goal as an RI oppose list" at the bottom of the GPM, done *after* all the RIs of the GPM are found. "What goal would (the goal just done) oppose?" (HCOB 8 Apr 63)

**SOURCE-POINT,** if you consider a river flowing to the sea, the place where it began would be the **source-point** or cause and the place where it went into the sea would be the effect-point and the sea would be the effect of the river. (PAB 86)

Source Point

**SOUTH,** very, very rough cases. The common denominator is: nothing they think has any effect on anything. They're all on automatic and what they've got left under analytical control is so scrappily tiny that it's a wonder they move at all. (6102C14) See ALL THE WAY SOUTH.

**SOUTH OF THE AUKS,** "South" is used as "below" or more basic or "more lost." **South of the AUKS** would be even further **south** than the South Pole, Antartica being inhabited by a flightless bird, the **AUK.** (LRH Def. Notes)

**SP, suppressive person.** (HCOB 5 Feb 66)

**SPACATION, 1.** the subject of **space.** We call the process **spacation,** and **spacation** would be the subject of **space.** (PDC 1)
**2.** a process having to do with the rehabilitation of the creation

of **space**. (PDC 1) **3.** constructing own **space** with eight anchor points and holding it stable without effort. (*Scn 8-8008*, pp. 116-117) **4.** the subject of the creation, handling of, or concept of **space**. (PDC 11)

**SPACE, 1. space** is a viewpoint of dimension. It doesn't exist without a viewpoint. (5311CM17A) **2. space** is not nothingness. **Space** is the viewpoint of dimension, and that is what **space** is. It is how far we look and if you didn't look you wouldn't have any **space**. (5608C00) **3. space** is caused by looking out from a point. The only actuality of **space** is the agreed-upon consideration that one perceives through something and this we call **space**. (*FOT*, p. 71) **4. space** is made by the attitude of a viewpoint which demarks an area with anchor points. (*Scn 8-8008*, p. 17) **5.** can be defined of course in reverse by its own terms in terms of time. **Space** is something that to go from the left side of the table over to the right side of the tabletop would require **space**. They define against each other (time and **space**). (5203C03B)

Space

**SPACE OPERA,** a novel, motion picture, radio or television play, or comic strip usually of a stock type featuring interplanetary travel, beings of outer space often in conflict with the people of earth and other similar science fiction themes. (*Websters Third International Dictionary*)

**SPECTRUM,** gradations of something which are really the same thing but which have wider and wider scope or range. (*DMSMH*, p. 196)

**SPECTRUM PRINCIPLE,** a yardstick whereby gradations from zero to infinity and infinity to infinity were used and absolutes were considered utterly unobtainable for scientific purposes. (*DMSMH*, p. 336)

**SPEECH, 1.** a specialized portion of sound and sight. **Speech** is learned by the mimicry of the sounds of action. (*NOTL*, p. 39) **2.** a symbolized package of perception. (Spr Lect 3, 5303M24)

**SPERM DREAM,** patients sometimes have a feeling that they are **sperms** or ovums at the beginning of the track; in Dn this is called the **sperm dream.** (*DMSMH*, p. 294)

**SPHERES OF INTEREST,** the **spheres of interest** are the eight dynamics. A series of concentric **spheres** each one larger than the last with the first dynamic at center and the eighth dynamic at the extreme of any universe gives a spatial picture of **interest.** (*COHA*, p. 99)

**SPINNER, THE,** a chair device was used to **spin** the thetan until he had no orientation. This is the probable source of the slang term, **spinning,** meaning going insane. (*HOM*, pp. 72-73)

**SPINNING,** slang term meaning going insane. (*HOM*, p. 73)

**SPIRALS, 1.** the thetan lives his life in segments: the largest segment is composed of **spirals,** as he goes through the mest universe, he is involved in a series of **spirals** each one less in terms of years, ordinarily, than the last. The length of this **spiral** might serve to indicate how much longer the thetan can continue. By a **spiral** would be meant a more or less continuous cycle of action. (*HOM*, p. 50) **2.** a term of lives, or a term of existences, or a single existence which bear an intimate relation, one to the other. (PDC 16)

**SPIRIT,** a thetan, after the Greek symbol of thought (Θ) and spirit—theta. (*Abil 146*)

**SPORADIC SLAM,** this **slam** is occasionally turned on. (SH Spec 194, 6209C25)

**SPOT,** a simple location, not a **spot** that has a mass, temperature, or characteristics. A location is simply a location, it does not have mass, it does not have color, it does not have any temperature. (*Dn 55!*, p. 119)

**SPOTTING SPOTS, 1.** the goal of the process is to bring the preclear to a point where he can **spot** locations in space which do not have color, mass or shape, but which are simply locations, and spot that same location repeatedly without variation. (PAB 51) **2.** this is a precision action—you want him to **spot** a **spot** in space and then be able to **spot** it again. That **spot** is only a location. It doesn't have mass, and you want him to be able to put his finger on it and take his finger off of it, and put the finger of his other hand on it, and take it off, and move his body into it and move his body out of it and so forth. This is a location and the more certain he becomes of these locations the better he is, and the next thing you know—why, he's able to tolerate space. (*PXL*, p. 262)

**SPRINGY,** needle reaction—reads which bounce back to set position. (HCOB 8 Jul 64 II)

**SPR LECT, London Spring Lectures.** (HCOB 29 Sept 66)

**SQUIRREL, 1.** a **squirrel** is doing something entirely different. He doesn't understand any of the principles so he makes up a bunch of them to fulfill his ignorance and voices them off on a pc and gets no place. (SH Spec 77, 6111C08) **2.** those who engage in actions altering Scn, and offbeat practices. (*ISE*, p. 40) —*v.* change and invent processes. (HCOB 22 Jul 69)

**SQUIRRELLING, 1.** it means altering Scn and offbeat practices. It is a bad thing. (HCO PL 14 Feb 65) **2. squirrelling** is not really different processes—it is careless, incomplete, messed up auditing procedure. (HCOB 15 Jan 70 II)

**SRI, Student Rescue Intensive.** (BTB 9 Aug 70R)

**SSSA, six steps for self auditing.** (PAB 7)

**STABILITY,** what we will call a **stability** for want of a better word at this time would be one who can, without the assistance of mest eyes, perceive with complete certainty the three universes from many viewpoints, a Clear. (PAB 2)

**STABLE DATUM, 1.** until one selects one **datum,** one factor, one particular in a confusion of particles, the confusion continues. The one thing selected and used becomes the **stable datum** for the remainder. (*POW,* p. 23) **2.** any body of knowledge is built from one datum. That is its **stable datum.** Invalidate it and the entire body of knowledge falls apart. A **stable datum** does not have to be the correct one. It is simply the one that keeps things from being in a confusion and on which others are aligned. (*POW,* p. 24) **3.** a **datum** which keeps things from being in a confusion and around which other data align. (*NSOL,* p. 66) See also DOCTRINE OF THE STABLE DATUM.

**STAFF STAFF AUDITOR, 1.** purpose: to keep **staff** morale high, by keeping missed withholds cleaned up. To see to it that **staff** gets best auditing possible. To release and clear **staff.** (HCO PL 17 May 62) **2. audits staff** members, handles auditing emergency assists on **staff.** (HCO PL 18 Dec 64)

**STAGE FOUR NEEDLE, 1.** means somebody who isn't registering by reason of being stuck in machinery. A **stage four needle** rises and sticks and then falls. (5811C07) **2.** this is the sole survivor of an old system (20th ACC) that used **four stages** of meter reaction as a test of state of case. A **stage four needle** is still important to identify when met as it means this preclear is from no place as a case. A **stage four** is below a merely stuck needle. A **stage four needle** goes up about an inch or two (always the same distance) and sticks and then falls, goes up, sticks, falls, about once a second or so. It is very regular, always the same distance, always the same pattern, over and over on and on, and nothing you say or the preclear says changes it (except body reactions). It's a disheartening phenomenon. Until you break it, there's no case change. (*EME,* p. 19)

**STAGES OF RELEASE, First Stage Release. 1.** this occurs in auditing up to Grade IV. It is not very stable. The person is *very* well off and definitely a release, but he or she can now postulate and in postulating sometimes gets into the R6 bank. The **first stage release** is eased out of the bank but subject to call back. (HCOB 28 Jun 65) **2.** to obtain **first stage release**, one must have had lower grade auditing of some sort. This removes the locks (the distressful moments of life) off the reactive mind. As these pinned one to it, one can now get out of it. (HCOB 5 Aug 65)

**Second Stage Release.** Power Process Release. This is very stable and should be called a **Second Stage Release** or a Power Release to be technically exact. You can run only power processes on a **First Stage Release.** These knock out all factors of the track that force a person back into the R6 bank and leave the person able to go into or get out of the R6 bank easily. This **second stage release** is definitely *Homo novis.* The person ceases to respond like a *Homo sapiens* and has fantastic capability to learn and act. (HCOB 28 Jun 65)

**Third Stage Release. 1.** certain advanced power processes make a **Third Stage Release.** These mainly recover knowledge and smooth out one's understanding of the awareness of the environment achieved by **Second Stage Release** on power processing. (HCOB 12 Jul 65) **2.** (called for a few days a **second stage** before terminology was firm) is an improved **Second Stage Release** in that selective areas of learning are handled to return special skills to the person. The case state does not necessarily improve but certain zones of knowledge have been polished up. (HCOB 28 Jun 65)

**Fourth Stage Release.** to obtain **Fourth Stage Release** one has to take the lock end words off the R6 bank. He has to be an R6 auditor himself to do this properly. With these gone, the R6 bank is left on its naked basics and one can be very free of it for quite a while. (HCOB 5 Aug 65)

**Fifth Stage Release. 1.** to obtain a **Fifth Stage Release,** one has to have run out the whole remaining reactive mind. That's done by a process known as R6-GPMI or GPM's by Items (HCOB 5 Aug 65) **2. Fifth Stage Release** would be Clear. (SH Spec 65, 6507C27)

**STALE-DATED C/S,** a **C/S** that is a week or two old. This is called a **stale-dated C/S** meaning it is too old to be valid. (HCOB 23 Aug 71)

**STALE-DATED PROGRAM,** a **repair (progress) program** that is a month or two old. This is called a **stale-dated program** meaning it is too old to be valid. (HCOB 23 Aug 71)

**STANDARD, 1.** a definite level or degree of quality that is proper and adequate for a specific purpose. (Class VIII, No. 4) **2.** "**Standard**" in **standard** tech auditing is a precise activity, done with good TRs, exact grade processes and exact actions. (HCOB 10 Sept 68)

**STANDARD AUDITING CYCLE,** a **standard auditing cycle** includes only those items which appear on the paid completions HCOB 30 Aug 71RA Issue II, Revised 21 Oct 73, *Paid Completions—Second Revision.* (HCO PL 21 Oct 73R)

**STANDARD DIANETICS,** modern Dn auditing is called **Standard Dianetics** and **new Dianetics.** It is a precision activity. (LRH ED 9, 11 May 69)

**STANDARD MEMORY BANKS, 1.** the analytical mind has its **standard memory banks.** To operate, the analytical mind has to have percepts (data), memory (data), and imagination (data). Whether or not the data contained in the **standard memory banks** is evaluated correctly or not, it is all there. The various senses receive information and this information files straight into the **standard memory bank.** (*DMSMH*, p. 45) **2.** those in which experience is stored for use in the estimation of the effort necessary for survival and are concerned with analytical thought. (*Scn 8-8008*, p. 8) **3.** recordings of everything perceived throughout the lifetime up to present time by the individual except physical pain, which is not recorded in the analytical mind but is recorded in the reactive mind. (*SOS*, Bk. 2, p. 230)

**STANDARD PATTERN OF A TRACK,** the **standard pattern of a track** should be counter-effort, overt act, thought pattern. (5206CM24F)

**STANDARD TECH, 1.** a **standardization** of processes so that they apply to 100 per cent of the cases to which they are addressed.

(Class VIII, No. 19) **2.** the accumulation of those exact processes which make a way between humanoid and OT, the exact method of organizing them, the exact method of delivering them, and the exact repair of any errors made on that route. (Class VIII, No. 2) **3.** that terribly narrow path which we now call **standard tech** is composed of those things which if they are out inhibit and prohibit all case gain. (Class VIII, No. 1) **4. standard tech** is not a process or a series of processes. It is following the rules of processing. (HCOB 26 Feb 70) **5.** that **tech** which has absolutely no arbitraries. (HCOB 23 Aug 68)

**STANDING WAVE,** a **wave** form comes up and either because it meets another **wave** form or for some other reason it just becomes a rigid form. If you could imagine an ocean **wave** not any longer rolling but just sitting there all peaked. Well, electricity strangely enough will do this, and a thetan is very good at this. (7204C07 SO III)

**STARRATE CHECKOUT,** a very exact **checkout** which verifies the full and minute knowledge of the student, of a portion of study materials and tests his full understanding of the data and ability to apply it. (HCOB 21 Sept 70)

**STAR-RATED,** 100 per cent letter perfect in knowing and understanding, demonstrating and being able to repeat back the material with no comm lag. (HCO PL 8 Mar 66)

**START-CHANGE-STOP,** the anatomy of control. This is a cycle of action. There is continue (persist) on the middle of the curve and other cycles within cycles of action, but the most important factors are **start, change,** and **stop.** These three parts of control are run flat individually. Then pick up the other part of the cycle and run that flat in this order: we run **change** flat, and then run **start** very flat and then we run **stop** flat. (PAB 97)

**STATE OF CASE SCALE, 1.** this is the **state of case scale.** All levels given are major levels. Minor levels exist between them. Level (1), no track—no charge. Level (1) is of course an O.T. (HCOB 8 Jun 63) Level (2), full visible time track—some charge. Level (2) is the clearest clear anybody ever heard of. (HCOB 8 Jun 63) Level (3), sporadic visibility of track—some heavily charged areas. Level (3) can run engrams. (HCOB 8 Jun 63)

# STATES OF RELEASE

Level (4), invisible track (black or invisible field), very heavily charged areas exist. Level (4) can run early track engrams if the running is skilled. Level (4) includes the Black V case. (HCOB 8 Jun 63) Level (5), dub-in—some areas of track so heavily charged pc is below consciousness in them. Level (5) has to be run on general ARC processes. (HCOB 8 Jun 63) He has an uncertainty about everything. He has to figure about everything; he has to know before he goes, and he has to hide but he knows he can't hide, and he depends on logic to serve for all of his predictions because he can't look. (PAB 2) This guy can't confront it to the degree that if he tries to confront it he makes a picture of it. He's got a picture of a picture. (SH Spec 275, 6306C18) Level (6), dub-in of dub-in. Many areas of track so heavily charged, the dub-in is submerged. Level (6) has to be run carefully on special ARC processes with lots of havingness. (HCOB 8 Jun 63) A (6) is neurotic. He's unable to easily recall the things in the next to the last list of *Self Analysis;* something really real, a time he was really in communication, and so forth. (5304M07) There's nothing that distinguishes the (6) from the dub-in case except the degree of franticness which the case goes into, and the amount of delusion which can turn on. What characterizes this case is the terrible automaticity of the bank. (SH Spec 274, 6306C13) Level (7), only aware of own evaluations —track too heavily charged to be viewed at all. Level (7) responds to the CCHs. (HCOB 8 Jun 63) Level (8), unaware—pc dull, often in a coma. Level (8) responds only to reach and withdraw CCHs. (HCOB 8 Jun 63) In actuality on some portion of every time track in every case you will find each of the levels except (1) momentarily expressed. The above scale is devoted to *chronic* case level and is useful in programming a case. Now, what makes these levels of case? It is entirely charge. The more heavily charged the case, the lower it falls on the above scale. It is charge that prevents the pc from confronting the time track and submerges the time track from view. (HCOB 8 Jun 63)

**STATES OF RELEASE,** there are five **states of release** (Grades 0-IV) up to Power Release (Grade V). Above this is a Whole Track Release (Grade VI) and above that is a state we call Clear. Clear is followed by the state of OT (Operating Thetan), attained in sections. (*Aud 107 ASHO*)

**STATIC, 1.** a **static** is something without mass, without wave-length, without time, and actually without position. That's a **static** and that is the definition of zero. (5410CM06) **2.** a **static** by definition, is something that is in a complete equilibrium. It isn't moving and that's why we've used the word **static.** Not in an engineering sense but in its absolute dictionary sense. (5608C--) **3.** an actuality of no mass, no wave-length, no position in space or relation in time, but with the quality of creating or destroy-ing mass or energy, locating itself or creating space, and of re-relating time. (*Dn 55!*, p. 29) **4.** something which has no motion. The word is from the Latin, *sto* meaning *stand.* No part of mest can be **static,** but theta is **static.** Theta has no motion. Even when the mest it controls is moving in space and time, theta is not moving, since theta is not in space or time. (*Abil 114A*) **5.** has no motion, it has no width, length, breadth, depth; it is not held in suspension by an equilibrium of forces; it does not have mass; it does not contain wave-lengths; it has no situation in time or space. (*Scn 8-8008*, p. 13) **6.** the simplest thing there is is a **static,** but a **static** is not nothingness. These are not synonyms. We speak of it carelessly as a nothingness. That's because we say nothingness in relationship to the space and objects of the material universe. Life has a quality. It has an ability. When we say nothingness we simply mean it has no quantity. There is no quantitative factor. (5411CM05) **7.** a **static,** in physics, is called something which is "an equilibrium of forces." (*Dn 55!*, p. 27)

**STEERING THE PC, 1.** this is the only use of latent or random reads. You see a read the *same* as the instant read occurring again when you are not speaking but after you have found a whole thought reacting you say, "There" or "That" and the pc, seeing what he or she is looking at as you say it recovers the knowledge from the reactive bank and gives the data and the whole thought clears or has to be further worked and cleared. (HCOB 25 May 62) **2.** each time the needle twitches the auditor says, "That" or "There" to help the pc see what is twitching. This prompting is the only use of latent reads in Scn. (HCOB 3 May 62)

**STENOGRAPHIC AUDITING,** the auditor is writing down every word the pc says (like a **stenographer**). (BTB 10 Jul 69)

**STEP V,** Black V. (*PXL,* p. 167) See also STATE OF CASE SCALE.

**STEP SIX, 1.** I had known about help for some years and in 1957, autumn, used it with **Step 6** in clearing people. The first clears made easily by others were done with meter assessments and five way help brackets on terminals. It was found that **Step 6,** being a creative process, was bad on some cases. The clearing formula was help and **Step 6.** (HCOB 12 May 60) **2.** establish pc's control over mest subjective. (HCOB 13 Mar 75) [The full rundown is contained in *Scientology Clear Procedure, Issue One.*]

**STEP SIX PHENOMENON (OF SCIENTOLOGY CLEAR PRO-CEDURE),** when what you are asking the pc to do is at great variance with the basic goal of the pc, you get an increase of mass in the bank by reason of mocking things up. (SH Spec 160, 6206C12)

**STEP 6 SOP-8C,** that **step** which includes the solution of problems posed by symbolism. The solution which resolves symbolism is the definition of **Step 6.** (2ACC-11B, 5311CM27)

**STHIL, Saint Hill.** (HCOB 23 Aug 65)

**STICK,** needle definitely *stops* (if it was moving) or simply remains fixed with no movement in either direction. (HCOB 30 Apr 60)

**STICKERS,** they are **stuck** phrases in modifiers. "Stay right here and wait no matter how long it takes." That would not be unusual to find in a modifier. It parks the person on the track very effectively. (SH Spec 81, 6111C16)

**STICKY NEEDLE (sticky or rigid needle),** one which does not change, but if it does, changes very slightly and with a jerk. (*Scn Jour 1-G 1952*)

**STICTUIVITY (STICK-TO-IVITY),** *Slang.* the ability to **stick to** a purpose, to keep on going. The ability to persist. (LRH Def. Notes)

**STILL TA, 1.** occurs when the auditor did not have to move the **TA** in order to read the needle. (SH Spec 234, 6302C07) **2.** only one-eighth of a division of motion on the **tone arm dial**—e.g., an eighth of the distance from 4 to 5. (HCOB 11 Apr 61)

**STIMULUS-RESPONSE,** mechanism whereby the individual is restimulated or upset or **stimulated** by the environment. (*HFP*, p. 32)

**STO,** a **Staff Training Officer** (**STO**) is the head of the **staff training** section of the Qualifications Division. (HCO PL 21 Sept 69)

**STOP, 1.** motionlessness. (*SCP*, p. 17) **2.** a **stop** is made out of vias. (*COHA*, p. 108)

**STOPPED READ,** would be one that froze the needle. (HCOB 3 Jun 71)

**STOP SUPREME,** a variation of S-C-S processes. **Stop Supreme** is a heavy emphasis on **stop** and it will be found that after the three processes of start, change and **stop** are flat, one can move rather easily into **Stop Supreme.** The idea behind **Stop Supreme** is that **stop** or motionlessness, is probably the most thetan ability a thetan has. Thus the rehabilitation of this particular ability is worthwhile and does produce considerable results. (*SCP*, p. 17)

**STP, Standard Procedure Lectures.** (HCOB 29 Sept 66)

**ST PTS, student points.** (FBDL 279)

**STRAIGHT LINE MEMORY,** in **straight line memory** you don't put the preclear in reverie or let him close his eyes. It can cure a person by remembering pleasant things in the past. You don't want him to remember only the concept, but to remember the exact moment. (*NOTL*, p. 113)

**STRAIGHT MEMORY, 1.** the process of recovering data, springing locks by **straight memory** and setting up the case in such a way that it'll go into reverie. It's getting your earliest locks, getting him to remember this and that and the bad things he thinks about himself. (5011CM30) **2.** straight wire. (*SOS*, Bk. 2, p. 64)

**STRAIGHTWIRE, 1.** when we say **straightwire,** we're simply talking about stringing a line from cause to effect through the past. (5410CM07) **2.** straight memory is also called **straightwire** because the auditor is directing the memory of the preclear and in doing so is stringing **wire,** much on the order of a telephone line, between "I" and the standard memory bank. (*SOS*, Bk. 2, p. 64) **3.** a technique of direct memory. (5009CM23B) **4.** in 1950 in the early HDA lectures we described this as the act of stringing a line between present time and some incident in the past, and stringing that line directly and without any detours. (*Abil SW*, p. 11) **5. straightwire** is—the recovery of the actual, time, place and object. (5410CM07)

**STRAY RI,** a **stray RI** is an **RI** from a GPM of another goal than the one being worked. (HCOB 18 Mar 63)

**STRESS ANALYSIS,** using the E-meter to isolate the exact point of a man's difficulty with a subject or equipment and clearing this up, or finding the exact point where equipment is not well adapted to man. Its use in study can pin-point the exact thing that has halted the flow of comprehension. Thus it can be cleared up. (HCOB 13 Jun 70 II)

**STRIPPING,** the action of **stripping** is done by taking every aspect of every factor in the problem and running it back to the postulate the preclear made to be concerned about that aspect of the factor. (*AP&A*, p. 46)

**STUCK FLOW, 1.** a **flow** which runs too long in one direction can "stick." It will not **flow** longer in that one direction. It now has to have a reverse **flow** run. (HCOB 5 Oct 69) **2.** one-way communication. The **flow** can be **stuck** incoming or it can be **stuck** outgoing. (*Dn 55!*, p. 79)

**STUCK IN A WIN,** a person is **stuck in "wins"** only when he intended to lose and won. A runner never expected to **win.** He was simply part of the field most of his career and then spectacularly and almost by accident, he won. It is certain that he will be **stuck in** that **win.** Therefore the only **wins** that a person gets **stuck in** are those which were not intentional. (PAB 91)

**STUCK IN PRESENT TIME, 1.** the condition of a person being incapable of moving on the time track into the past. In actuality the preclear is in some incident which forces him to be in the apparent **present.** (HCOB 11 May 65) **2.** a person cannot be **stuck in present time.** The engram might give him the illusion of being **stuck in present time,** but actually he is **stuck in** an engram. (*NOTL*, p. 127) **3.** when a case is **stuck in present time**

it is highly charged with occluded emotion and it is obeying a restimulated engram to the effect that it must go all the way to now and stay there. (*DMSMH*, p. 285)

**STUCK IN THE PAST,** one holds onto things **in the past** on the postulate that they must not happen in the future. This **sticks** the person in the **past.** (PAB 17)

**STUCK NEEDLE, 1.** in a totally **stuck needle** the preclear would not even register being pinched. It looks stiff. (*EME*, p. 14) **2.** you ask the pc a question and the **needle** just stays **stuck** with no movement whatsoever. (*BIEM*, p. 40) **3.** it simply means that the fellow has flowed out or flowed in too long in one direction. (5207CM24B)

**STUCK ON THE TRACK, 1.** a phenomenon where a person can believe himself to be at some distant point in the past. (*Dn 55!*, p. 15) **2.** that means he's got too much energy in one lump about something that he has nothing further to do with. (PDC 54) **3.** the anatomy of being **stuck on the track** is "this part of the **track** must not duplicate, and I must stay here to make sure that it doesn't." (2ACC-24A, 5312CM15)

**STUCK PICTURE,** is when a pc can't audit the chain he should be on because the **picture** keeps coming in. (HCOB 13 May 69)

Student

**STUDENT,** a **student** is one who **studies.** He is an attentive and systematic observer. A **student** is one who reads in detail in order to learn and then apply. As a **student studies** he knows that his purpose is to understand the materials he is **studying** by reading, observing, and demonstrating so as to apply them to a specific result. He connects what he is **studying** to what he will be doing. (BTB 26 Oct 70 II)

**STUDENT ADMIN, 1.** the **Administrator's** function of service to **students** is important, he must see the data on the course being held is available and in sufficient quantity and quality. (HCO PL 11 May 69) **2.** gives flawless service to **students** and classrooms so that there is never a stop on **student** or classroom functions. (HCO PL 14 Oct 70)

**STUDENT AUDITOR,** a **student** enrolled on a course **auditing** as stipulated on his checksheet for course requirements. (HCO PL 4 Dec 71 V)

Student Auditor

**STUDENT BOOSTER RUNDOWN,** this is a specialty on Flag which also trains the executives of orgs and has to have a fast study remedy. It is also given to business executives so that they can absorb effortlessly and with greater speed the vast quantities of data that pass across an executive's desk. (LRH ED 301 INT)

**STUDENT CONSULTATION,** the personal handling of **student** problems or progress by a qualified **consultant.** (HCOB 19 Jun 71 III)

**STUDENT FOLDER,** the **folder** contains *all* of the routing forms and attached invoices, all pink sheets issued to the **student,** all essays the **student** has done on the checksheet, all written drills, and the finished checksheet itself. (HCO PL 18 Jul 71 II)

**STUDENT HAT,** a course; the product of this course is a **student** who has a good working knowledge of study tech, completion of this checksheet does not entitle the **student** to superliterate status which is granted only on full completion of Primary Rundown or Primary Correction Rundown. (HCO PL 12 Apr 72RA-1 II)

**STUDENT RESCUE INTENSIVE, 1.** this is a speed up for **study**. It is terribly effective providing always that the person's case is in normal condition. (LRH ED 57 INT, 14 Dec 69) **2.** a rundown which came about when a supervisor found that engrams and secondaries gather around the subject of **study** and developed some material on it which I tested and redeveloped. (HCOB 23 Nov 69R III)

**STUDENTS' RABBLE ROUSE LINE,** this is the **line** on which **students** can scream when there is an outness on their course which is not being immediately corrected. (HCO PL 20 Nov 70 II)

**STUDY,** to apply the mind in order to acquire knowledge or skill. (BTB 4 Mar 65R)

**STUDY CORRECTION LIST,** used to handle outnesses in a person's earlier **studies** which prevent him from progressing well on current **study** or make him antipathetic towards **study**. Done as part of the Primary Correction Rundown. It is not used as a substitute for correct application of **study** tech on the person's current course. Assessed M5. EP is all reading items fully handled and an F/Ning list on final assessment. The full EP of pc willing and able to **study** well would require each step of Primary Correction RD completed in sequence if pc had been having **study** trouble. (BTB 11 Aug 72RA)

**STUDY GREEN FORM,** a rundown which isolates and handles anything that could be wrong with any student or pupil. (LRH ED 301 INT)

**STUDY STRESS ANALYSIS,** see STRESS ANALYSIS.

**STUPIDITY, 1.** the mechanical definition of **stupidity** is the unknownness of time, place, form and event. (5408CM20) **2.** the definition of **stupidity** is simply this—having lost the time, the place, and the object. (AX-3, 5410CM07) **3. stupidity** is the unknowness of consideration. (*PXL*, p. 182)

**S2,** "From where could you communicate to a victim?" (BTB 9 Oct 71RA II)

**STYLE,** a method or custom of performing actions. (HCOB 6 Nov 64)

411

**SUB-APATHY,** a state of disinterest, no affinity, no reality, no communication. There will be social machinery, valences, circuits, etc., but the pc himself will not be there. (BTB 6 Feb 60)

**SUB-ITSA,** significances or masses so charged that the pc is unable to locate, identify or describe them. They are below the depth he is able to itsa to. (HCOB 13 Apr 64, *Scn VI Part One Glossary of Terms*)

**SUBJECTIVE** (a standard dictionary definition), "proceeding from or taking place in an individual's mind." (HCOB 2 Nov 57RA)

**SUBJECTIVE CONFRONT PROCESSES, subjective** duplication increase. (HCOB 29 Sept 60)

**SUBJECTIVE DUB-IN,** the manifestation of putting, unknowingly, perceptions which do not in actual fact exist, into incidents on the time track. (HCOB 11 May 65)

**SUBJECTIVE ENVIRONMENT,** is the **environment** the individual himself believes is there. (*HFP*, p. 153)

**SUBJECTIVE HAVINGNESS,** one way to run this is to ask the preclear what he can mock up. Then have him mock up what he can, and shove it into his body. That is the most elementary way of running this. (PAB 154)

**SUBJECTIVE PROCESSES, 1. processes** which intimately address the internal world of the preclear. (*COHA*, p. 166) **2.** an out of sight, in-his-own-mind process. (*Dn 55!*, p. 121) **3.** consultation with the preclear's own universe, with his mock-ups, and with his own thoughts and considerations. (*COHA*, p. 167) **4.** think **processes.** (HCOB 29 Oct 57) **5.** recall, think, remember or return on the time track **processes** are **subjective.** (HCOB 2 Nov 57RA)

**SUBMIND,** the reactive mind. (*SOS*, p. xii)

**SUBVOLITIONAL,** actions, decisions, choices and goals occurring below the level at which the pc has any conscious control. Inevitable activities. (HCOB 13 Apr 64, *Scn VI Part One Glossary of Terms*)

**SUB ZERO RELEASE,** the Awareness Levels from the Gradation Chart are assessed from the bottom **-34** up. When the PC's awareness level is called the needle will float. This will be most real to the PC and he will probably comment on it. The Examiner stops at that instant, indicates the floating needle. The examiner notifies the Auditor that a **Sub Zero Release** has been obtained. (HCOB 2 Jan 67) See also MINUS SCALE RELEASE.

**SUCCESS STORY, 1.** means an originated written statement by the pc. (HCO PL 29 Aug 71) **2.** the statement of benefit or gains or wins made by a student or a preclear or pre-OT to the **success** officer or someone holding that post in an org. (HCOB 19 Jun 71 III) See also RAVE SUCCESS STORY.

**SUCCUMB, 1.** survive has its dichotomy, **succumb.** When one is below 2.0 on the tone scale, all survival looks evil to him. Live=evil in the **succumbing** case. (*COHA*, p. 147) **2.** the point marked by what one might call the death of the consciousness of the individual. (*SA*, p. 22) **3.** The failure to survive is to **succumb.** (*SOS*, Bk. 2, p. 31) **4. succumbing** is the ultimate penalty of non-survival activity. This is pain. Failures bring pain and death. (*SOS* Gloss)

**SUICIDE, suicides** are assisted normally by engrams which specifically demand **suicide.** But **suicide** is a natural manifestation, apparently, a fast means of separating theta and mest and gaining death quickly. **Suicide** is always psychotic. (*SOS*, p. 28)

**SUMMARY REPORT FORM,** a **report** written by the auditor after the session on a fill-in type standard **form** and is simply an exact record of what happened and what was observed during the session. (BTB 3 Nov 72R)

**SUPER, 1. superiority** in size, quality, number or degree. (*Aud 77 ASHO*) **2. supervisor.** (HCO PL 16 Mar 71R)

**SUPER POWER, a super** fantastic, but confidential series of rundowns that can be done on anyone whether Dn Clear or not that puts the person into fantastic shape unleashing the **Super Power** of a Thetan. This is the means that puts Scientologists into a new realm of ability enabling them to create the New World. It puts world Clearing within reach in the future. This is a parallel rundown to **Power** in Saint Hills which is taken by the Dn Clear. It consists of 12 separate high-**power** rundowns which are brand new and enter realms of the tech never before approached. **Power** is still very much in use on the Grade Chart but is for those who didn't go Clear on Dn. (LRH ED 301 INT)

**SUPER-LITERATE, 1.** the ability to comfortably and quickly take data from a page and be able at once to apply it. (HCOB 7 Sept 74) **2.** being a **super-literate** is like hearing and seeing and reading for the first time. Reading a text or instruction or book is comfortable. One has it in conceptual form. One can apply the material learned. It is a new state. (HCOB 21 Jun 72 IV) **3. super**—superiority in size, quality, number or degree. **Literacy**—the ability to read and write. What is really needed is the ability to comfortably and quickly take data from a page and be able at once to apply it. Anyone who could do that would be **Super-Literate. Super-Literacy** is the end product of a Primary Rundown or a Primary Correction Rundown. (HCOB 7 Sept 74)

**SUPERSTITION,** an effort, for lack of education, to find pertinent data in too wide a zone or to fix the attention upon irrelevant data. (*SOS*, Bk. 2, p. 9)

**SUPERVISOR,** a course must have a **supervisor.** He may or may not be a graduate and experienced practitioner of the course he is **supervising** but he must be a trained course **supervisor.** He is not expected to teach. He is expected to get the students there, rolls called, checkouts properly done, misunderstoods handled by finding what the student doesn't dig and getting the student to dig it. The **supervisor** who tells students answers is a waste of time and a course destroyer as he enters out data into the scene even if trained and actually especially if trained in the subject. The **supervisor** is NOT an "instructor" that's why he's called a **"supervisor."** (HCO PL 16 Mar 71R)

**SUPERVISOR CHECKOUT,** a **checkout** done by the **supervisor** of a course or his assistant. (HCOB 19 Jun 71 III)

**SUPERVISOR'S DUTY,** communication of the data of Scn to the student so as to achieve acceptance, duplication and application of the technology in a standard and effective manner. (HCOB 16 Oct 68)

**SUPPRESS,** to squash; to sit on, to make smaller, to refuse to let reach, to make uncertain about his reaching, to render or lessen in any way possible by any means possible, to the harm of the individual and for the fancied protection of a **suppressor.** (SH Spec 84, 6612C13)

**SUPPRESSED LIST,** no further items on the assessment **list** read but the pc still has some symptoms. The **list** isn't null. It is **suppressed** or invalidated. (HCOB 29 Jan 70)

**SUPPRESSED PERSON RUNDOWN,** a magical **rundown** just now being released to Class IV and other orgs. It utilizes a principle found in an early ACC but never fully developed and released till '78 that one could bring the **Suppressive** in a person's life to communicate to him and seek peace, without ever contacting him. When expertly done on a person who has been the target of **suppression** by antagonistic people it brings him back to freedom and handles his environment as well. When one realizes that most illness is precipitated by **suppression** one can understand the need and use of such a miraculous **rundown**. (LRH ED 301 INT)

**SUPPRESSION, suppression** is "a harmful intention or action against which one cannot fight back." Thus when one can do *anything* about it, it is less **suppressive.** (HCO PL 26 Dec 66)

**SUPPRESSIVE ACTS, 1. acts** calculated to impede or destroy Scn or a Scientologist. (HCO PL 23 Dec 65) **2. actions** or omissions undertaken to knowingly **suppress,** reduce or impede Scn or Scientologists. (HCO PL 23 Dec 65)

**SUPPRESSIVE GROUPS,** are defined as those which seek to destroy Scn or which specialize in injuring or killing persons or damaging their cases or which advocate **suppression** of mankind. (HCO PL 29 Jun 68)

**SUPPRESSIVE PERSON, 1.** he's solving a present time problem which hasn't in actual fact existed for the last many trillenia in most cases, and yet he is taking the actions in present time which solve that problem. The guy's totally stuck in present time, that is the whole anatomy of psychosis. (SH Spec 61, 6505C18) **2.** a person who rewards only down statistics and never rewards an up statistic. He goofs up or vilifies any effort to help anybody and particularly knifes with violence anything calculated to make human beings more powerful or intelligent. A **suppressive** automatically and immediately will curve any betterment activity into something evil or bad. (SH Spec 73, 6608C02) **3.** a person who doesn't get case gain because of continuing overts. (SH Spec 67, 6509C21) **4.** the person is in a mad, howling situation of some yesteryear and is "handling it" by committing overt acts today. I say condition of yesteryear but this case thinks it's today. (HCO PL 5 Apr 65) **5.** an **SP** is a no-confront case because, not being in his own valence he has no viewpoint from which to erase anything. That is all an **SP** is. (HCO PL 20 Oct 67) **6.** those who are destructively antisocial. (HCO PL 30 Aug 70) **7.** a person with certain behavior characteristics and who **suppresses** other people in his vicinity and those other people when he **suppresses** them become PTS or potential trouble sources. (SH Spec 78, 6608C25) **8.** is one that actively seeks to **suppress** or damage Scn or a Scientologist by **suppressive** acts. (*ISE,* p. 48) **9.** a person who has had a counter-postulate to the pc you are handling. (SH Spec 68, 6510C14) *Abbr.* SP

**SUPPRESSOR,** the impulse to forbid revelation in another. This of course, being an overt, reacts on one's own case as an impulse to keep oneself from finding out anything from the bank, and of course **suppresses** as well the release of one's own withholds. So it is more fundamental than a withhold. A **"suppressor"** is often considered "social conduct" insofar as one prevents things from being revealed which might embarrass or frighten others. (HCOB 15 Mar 62)

**SUPREME TEST,** the **supreme test** of a thetan is his ability to make things go right. (HCOB 19 Aug 67)

**SURGES** (NEEDLE REACTIONS), sudden long sweeps to the right. (LRH Def. Notes)

**SURPRISE,** rapidity of change of state, unpredicted. (HCOB 17 Mar 60)

**SURVIVAL, 1.** is a condition susceptible to non-survival. If one is **"surviving,"** one is at the same moment admitting that one can cease to **survive,** otherwise one would never strive to **survive.** (*Scn 8-8008*, p. 47) **2. survival** might be defined as an impulse to persist through time, in space, as matter and energy. (*Scn 8-8008*, p. 5) **3. survival** is understood to be the basic single thrust of life through time and space, energy and matter. **Survival** is subdivided into eight dynamics. (*SOS*, p. x)

**SURVIVAL GOAL,** an optimum solution to existing problems. (*DAB*, Vol. II, p. 37, 1951-52)

**SURVIVAL SUPPRESSOR,** is the combined and variable threats to the **survival** of the race or organism. (*DMSMH*, p. 25)

**SURVIVE,** the dynamic principle of existence is **survive.** At the opposite end of the spectrum of existence is *succumb.* (*SOS* Gloss)

**SW, Straightwire.** (BTB 20 Aug 71R II)

**SWEAT PROGRAM, 1.** some of these new drugs, like the intelligence drug, LSD (developed to poison and paralyze whole cities) or Angel Dust (developed by crooked gamblers to handle race horses and fix races) have a nasty habit of remaining in the body and popping up unexpectantly to send people on "trips." **The Sweat Program** has been refined to handle this. (LRH ED 301 INT) **2.** will be necessary if the person has taken LSD or Angel Dust. It may also be indicated when a person has been subjected to exposure to toxic substances which have lodged in the tissue and fat of the body. In future times psychiatrists or others of ill repute may develop other compounds such as LSD which lodge in the systems; a **sweat program** may be indicated in these. (HCOB 22 Jun 78R)

**SWEETNESS AND LIGHT,** a person who cannot conceive of ever having done anything bad to anybody or anything. (HCOB 3 Sept 59)

Sweetness and Light

**SYMBIOTE, 1.** the Dn meaning of **symbiote** is extended beyond the dictionary definition to mean "any or all life or energy forms which are mutually dependent for survival." The atom depends on the universe, the universe on the atom. (*DMSMH*, p. 32) **2.** all entities and energies which aid survival. (*EOS*, p. 101)

**SYMBOL, 1.** an object which has mass, meaning and mobility. (*COHA*, p. 54) **2.** something which could represent an idea. It is a piece of energy which is agreed to represent a certain idea. (2ACC-20A, 5312CM10) **3.** an idea which is cloaked in energy of any kind is actually a **symbol.** That is the definition of a **symbol.** It's any idea which is fixed in any space with energy. (2ACC-22A, 5312CM13) **4.** pieces of thought, which represent states of being in the material universe. (5203CM06A) **5.** a **symbol** is an idea fixed in energy and mobile in space. (*COHA*, p. 259)

Symbol for Theta

**SYMBOL FOR THETA,** eighth letter of the Greek alphabet. Ancient Greeks used this to represent spirit or thought. *Symbol:* Θ. (HCOB 23 Aug 65)

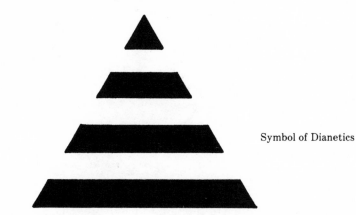

Symbol of Dianetics

**SYMBOL OF DIANETICS,** the Greek letter Delta is the basic form. Green for growth, yellow for life. The four stripes represent the four dynamics of Dianetics: Survival as I Self, II Sex and Family, III Group and IV Mankind. This **symbol** was designed in 1950 and has been used since. (*Dn Today*)

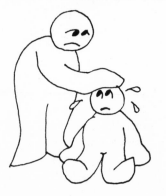

Sympathy

**SYMPATHY, 1.** a terrible thing but is considered to be a very valuable thing. The survival value of **sympathy** is this: when an individual is hurt or immobilized, he cannot fend for himself. He must count on another or others to care for him. His bid for such care is the enlistment of the **sympathy** of others. This is practical. If men weren't **sympathetic,** none of us would be alive. The non-survival value of **sympathy** is this: an individual fails in some activity. He then considers himself incapable of surviving by himself. Even though he isn't sick actually he makes a bid for **sympathy.** A psychosomatic illness is at once an explanation of failure and a bid for **sympathy.** (*HFP*, p. 122) **2. sympathy** is commonly accepted to mean the posing of an emotional state similar to the emotional state of an individual in grief or apathy. It is on the tone scale between 0.9 and 0.4. **Sympathy** follows or is based upon overt action by the preclear. **Sympathy** can be mechanically considered as the posing of any emotion so as to be similar to the emotion of another. (*AP&A*, p. 23) **3. sympathy** is a co-flow, it's sort of a co-beingness. One individual goes onto the wave-length of another individual. (PDC 23) **4.** "I am him" which is what **sympathy** is; it's a low level interchange of energy. (5209CM04B) **5.** equal motion, equal plane, similar space. (Spr Lect 1, 5303CM23)

**SYMPATHY COMPUTATION,** if a patient had a tough engramic background, then broke his leg and got **sympathy** he thereafter tends to go around with a simulated broken leg—arthritis, etc. etc. This is the **sympathy computation.** It makes a patient "want to be sick." Sickness has a high survival value says the reactive mind. So it tailors up a body to be sick. (*EOS*, p. 93)

**SYMPATHY ENGRAM, 1.** an **engram** of a very specific nature, being the effort of the parent or guardian to be kind to a child who is severely hurt. (*DTOT*, p. 95) **2.** a **sympathy engram** would go something like this: A small boy, much victimized by his parents, is extremely ill. His grandmother attends him and while he is delirious soothes him and tells him she will take care of him, that she will stay right there until he is well. This puts a high "survival" value on being sick. He does not feel safe around his parents; he wants his grandmother present (she is a winning valence because she orders the parents around), and he now has an engram. (*DMSMH*, p. 107) **3.** the **sympathy engram** is one which comes forward and stays chronic as a psychosomatic illness. (*DMSMH*, p. 107)

**SYMPATHY EXCITER,** a **sympathy exciter** is any entity on any dynamic for which the individual has felt **sympathy** of the variety between 0.9 and 0.4. **Sympathy exciters** are most commonly parents, allies and pets. (*AP&A*, pp. 44-45)

**SYMPTOMS, 1.** pains, emotional feelings, tiredness, aches, pressures, sensations, unwanted states of the body, etc. (HCOB 19 May 69) **2.** is from either the body directly (such as a broken bone, a gallstone, or immediate physical cause) or is part of the content of a mental image picture—lock, secondary or engram. (HCOB 23 Apr 69)

**SYNTHETIC,** dub-ins. (PAB 99)

**SYNTHETIC VALENCE, 1.** an artificial person. (*SOS*, Bk. 2, p. 201) **2.** those **valences** which have never actually confronted the preclear in the flesh. The Devil of course is the championship **synthetic valence** of all time. (PAB 95) **3. valence** described to pc and assumed. (HCOB 14 Jul 56) **4.** a **synthetic valence** is a description by one personality of a non-present personality. (5703C10)

# T

**TA, 1. tone arm action.** A technical term for a quantitative measure of case gain in the Scn processing of a preclear for a given unit of time. (*ISE*, p. 38) **2. tone arm** refers to the tone arm or its motion. (HCOB 13 Apr 64, *Scn VI Part One Glossary of Terms*) **3.** the total number of divisions down, a **tone arm** has moved accurately in a unit of time. (HCOB 24 Jul 64) **4.** a measure of the amount of encysted force which is leaving the case. ( SH Spec 291, 6308C06)

**TACIT CONSENT, 1.** in the case of two preclears working on each other, each one assuming in his turn the auditor's role, a condition can arise where each prevents the other from contacting certain engrams. This is **tacit consent.** A husband and wife may have a mutual period of quarrels or unhappiness. Engaged upon clearing each other, working alternately as auditor, they avoid, unknowingly, but by reactive computation, the mutual period, thus leaving in place painfully emotional engrams. (*DMSMH*, p. 319) **2.** mutual avoidance of certain subjects. (SH Spec 63, 6110C05)

**TACTILE, 1.** by **tactile** we perceive the shape and texture of surfaces and compounds. (*SOS*, p. 59) **2.** touch. (*DMSMH*, p. 14)

# TALKING THE TA DOWN

**TALKING THE TA DOWN,** it is done by the simple time-honored action of asking the right question, getting it answered, and letting the **tone arm blow down.** To ask the right question on this technique, you must first know what you are trying to accomplish. Why do you want to bring the **TA down?** The answer is simply, that the TA being high (3.5 or above), indicates that there is some mass the preclear's attention is on. You want that mass out of way so that you can direct the preclear's attention where *you* want it. So what you simply do is get the preclear to tell you what is in restimulation so that it will key out without driving the preclear further into his bank—and thus restimulating more mass. (BTB 14 Mar 71 II)

**TAO, 1.** it meant the way to solving the mystery which underlies all mysteries. It wasn't simply "The Way." (7ACC-25, 5407C19) **2.** means knowingness. Now that is the literal translation of the word if you want to translate it that way; in other words, it's an ancester to the word Scn just as such. (5407C19)

**TAPE COURSE,** a **course** relayed by **tape** recorded lectures or translations. (BTB 12 Apr 72R)

**TAPE LECTURE NUMBER,** 6408C11 SH Spec 35, *Study—Evaluation of Information* (example of **tape lecture number** and title). The first two **numbers** (64) give the year, 1964. The second two (08) give the month, August, the eighth month. (C) stands for copy. The third two **numbers** (11) give the day, the 11th. SH Spec gives the course, the Saint Hill Special Briefing Course, and then the title. From all this you know the lecture was given on 11 August, 1964, that the (35) is one of the consecutive numbers assigned for record purposes. (HCOB 23 Aug 65)

**TAPE PLAYERS,** are the machines used on a **tape** course for **playing** back on already recorded magnetic **tape.** Tape recorders are the machines used to record the tapes in the first place. (BTB 22 Nov 71 II)

**TAPE RECORDERS,** the machines used to **record** the **tape** in the first place. (BTB 22 Nov 71 II)

**TA SINK,** drops below 2.0 (HCOB 9 Jun 71 I)

**TCC, Theta Clear Congress.** (HCOB 29 Sept 66)

**TD, Tiger Drill.** (HCOB 8 Nov 62)

**TEACHER OR SUPERVISOR INTENSIVE,** for any person involved in **teaching** or **supervising** or education and enables him to become a vastly better **teacher** or **supervisor.** (LRH ED 301 INT)

**TEARACULI APATHIA MAGNUS,** Latinated nonsense for sad effect. (HCOB 14 Mar 63)

**TECH, 1.** by **tech** is meant **technology,** referring of course to the application of the precise scientific drills and processes of Scn. (HCOB 13 Sept 65) **2.** abbreviation for "**technology**" or "**technical,**" depending on context. The **technology** referred to is normally that contained in HCOBs. It also means the "Technical Division" in a Scientology Church (Division 4, the division of the org that delivers training and processing). (BTB 12 Apr 72R) **3.** technical. (HCOB 23 Aug 65)

**TECH DIV, Technical Division.** (HCOB 23 Aug 65)

**TECH IS IN,** Scn **is** being applied and **is** being correctly applied. (HCOB 13 Sept 65)

**TECHNICAL EXPERTISE,** is composed of all the little and large bits of technique known to the skilled painter, musician, actor, any artist. He adds these things together in his basic presentation. He knows what he is doing. And how to do it. And then to this he adds his message. (HCOB 29 Jul 73)

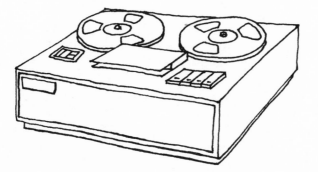

Tape Recorder

# TECHNICAL HIERARCHY

**TECHNICAL HIERARCHY,** a sort of *ex officio* **technical** committee on the subject of **technical** matters composed generally of the Senior C/S, C/Ses, Qual Sec, Cramming Officer and Intern Supervisor that monitors the quality of HGC auditing. (HCOB 1 Sept 71 I)

**TECHNICAL TERM,** it's something that has a specialized meaning in one subject which doesn't have any broader meaning, but may *appear* in another subject meaning something *else.* (HCO PL 22 Sept 72)

**TECHNIQUE,** a process or some action that is done by auditor and pc under the auditor's direction. A **technique** is a patterned action, invariable and unchanging, composed of certain steps or actions calculated to bring about tone arm action and thus better or free a thetan. (HCOB 26 Nov 63)

**TECHNIQUE 8-80,** a specialized form of Scn. It is, specifically the electronics of human thought and beingness. The **"8-8"** stands for **"Infinity-Infinity"** upright, the **0** represents the static, **theta.** (*Scn 8-80*, p. 9)

**TECHNIQUE 80, 1.** is a method; an application which can be applied to (1) mest bodies; (2) one lifetime; (3) some segment of the whole track; or (4) which can be applied to the whole track. When I say segment of the whole track I mean that you can take and specialize with **Technique 80** on addressing the genetic line of the mest body only. You can take someone and process only space opera (the two or ten million years somebody spent in space). The process is **Technique 80.** We use motivators, overts and deds. (5206CM27A) **2.** we call **Technique 80** the "to be or not to be" **technique** which balances out the motivator, the overt act and the ded. It's the anatomy of maybe. It becomes an entire subject of how to take apart maybe. How to get an indecision, how to get an involved grouped series of incidents apart. Any method which does this falls under the category of **Technique 80.** (5206CM23A)

**TECHNIQUE 88, 1.** a **technique** is in there for everything. And that's why we say **Technique 88.** There's an infinity of **techniques** inside of **Technique 88. Technique 88** includes all of the technology of doing anything that man or any other being has ever done. (5206CM25B) **2.** is processing the theta body and actually anything that pertains to processing the theta body can

424

be lumped into **Technique 88.** (5206CM27A) **3.** the knowledge and know-how necessary to clear a theta body. (5206CM27A)

**TECHNOLOGY, 1.** the methods of application of an art or science as opposed to mere knowledge of the science or art itself. (HCOB 13 Sept 65) **2.** a body of truths. (Class VIII No. 4)

**TECH SEC, 1. technical secretary.** (HCOB 23 Aug 65) **2.** abbreviation for **technical secretary.** The title of the person who is head of the Technical Division in the Church of Scientology. (BTB 12 Apr 72)

**TECH (TECHNICAL) SERVICES,** the activity which enrolls, routes, schedules, distributes the mail of and assists the housing of students. (HCOB 21 Sept 70)

**TECH TRAINING CORPS,** the purpose of the **TTC** is to produce well trained auditors, C/Ses and supervisors for the Church in excess of its delivery demands so as to bring about a 1:1 Tech Admin Ratio and a superlative level of tech delivery that does credit to LRH and Scn. All persons currently on full-time training are automatically part of the **TTC.** Every Church of Scientology (Class IV), Saint Hill Organization, Advanced Organization and Flag has its own **TTC.** (BPL 13 Apr 75) *Abbr.* TTC.

**T80, Technique 80 lectures.** (HCOB 29 Sept 66)

**T88, Technique 88 lectures.** (HCOB 29 Sept 66)

**TEMPERATURE ASSIST, assist** for a pc running a **temperature.** The **temperature** process is most effective on a low order persistent fever that goes on and on for days or even weeks. (HCOB 23 Jul 71)

**TEMPORARILY ENTURBULATED THETA, entheta** can exist as **temporary enturbulence** in the individual's life force or reason when he is confronted by unreasonable or non-survival circumstances in his environment. This could be called **temporarily enturbulated theta.** (*SOS*, Bk. 2, p. 118)

**TEN, 1.** a preclear carried through to a chronic somatic release. The **tenth** act 'consists of running out, by effort, emotion and thought, the service facsimile. (*AP&A*, pp. 18-20) **2.** a case advanced to the point of released service facsimile. (*HFP* Gloss)

**TENSION,** a collapsed communication line. (Spr Lect 18, 5304 CM08)

**TENSOR BEAM,** tractor beam. (*Abil 34*)

**TENTH DYNAMIC,** would probably be ethics. (PDC 2)

**TEO,** the **Technical** Division **Establishment Officer (TEO) establishes** and maintains the **tech** division. (HCO PL 7 Mar 72)

**TERM, terminal**—designation of a type of GPM item (R6 materials). (HCOB 23 Aug 65)

**TERMINAL, 1.** it would be any fixed mass utilized in a communication system. That, I think, is the best of the various definitions that have come out for this. Any mass used in a fixed position in any communications system. Thus you see a man would be a **terminal,** but a post could also be a **terminal.** (5703PM01) **2.** something that has mass and meaning which originates, receives, relays and changes particles on a flow line. (HCO PL 25 Jul 72) **3.** anything used in a communication system; something that has mass in it. Something with mass, meaning and mobility. Anything that can receive, relay or send a communication. (HCOB 25 Jan 65) **4.** any point of no form or any form or dimension from which energy can flow or by which energy can be received. (*Scn 8-8008*, p. 32) **5.** a **terminal** is what you need in order to get a perception. (Spr Lect 3, 5303M24) **6.** one of a pair of reliable items of equal mass and force, the significance of which the thetan has aligned with his own intentions. (HCOB 13 Apr 64, *Scn VI Part One Glossary of Terms*) **7.** an item or identity the pc has actually been sometime in the past (or present) is called a **terminal.** It is "the pc's own valence" at that time. In the goals problem mass (the black masses of the reactive mind) those identities which, when contacted, produce pain, tell us at once that they are **terminals.** The person could feel pain only as himself (thetan plus body) and therefore identities he has been produce pain when its mental residues (black masses) are recontacted in processing. *Symbol:* term. (HCOB 8 Nov 62)

**TERMINAL ASSESSMENT,** locating the **terminals** in the case which, when run, will produce an increase in the responsibility and reality level of the preclear. (HCOB 3 Jul 59)

**TERRIBLE TRIO,** well, amongst all havingness, what is the super-gold process? There is one. It is **terribly** certain, it does not fail in our experience and its gains are permanent. It is a process known as the **Terrible Trio.** The commands of the **Terrible Trio** are "Look around the room and tell me what you could have." "Look around the room and tell me what you would let remain." And, "Look around the room and tell me what you could dispense with." When I originally gave the triple havingness process to staff auditors somebody sensing its effectiveness, dubbed it "the **Terrible Trio.**" (PAB 80)

**TERROR, 1.** the result of something having appeared engramically and then later on threatening to appear again. (SH Spec 122, 6203C19) **2. terror** is a magnitude of fear. (*NOTL*, p. 21) **3.** fear with lots of volume. (*SOS*, p. 13)

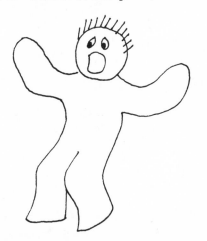

Terror

**TERROR STOMACH,** simply a confusion in a high degree of restimulation in the vicinity of the vagus nerve. This is one of the larger nerves and it goes into agitation under restimulation. (PAB 107)

**TESTED RELEASE,** stable **release,** which would be the fellow who had no adverse needle reactions on the buttons of help, control and communication.(SH Spec 4, 6105C26)

**THAT'S IT!,** when the coach says **"That's it"** he means "we are through. We are going to take a breather." (PAB 152)

**THEETIE-WEETIE, 1.** *Slang.* it's from England, means "sweetness and light" (but they can't face mest or any outness). Cannot go deeper into the bank than a thought. (LRH Def Notes) **2.** a person with a terribly high OCA who is absolutely for the birds. The *Chart of Human Evaluation* will tell you the truth. (7203C30)

**THEETIE-WEETIE CASE, 1.** he operates in a totally psychotic way while being totally serene. The valence is all the way up at tone 40 and the pc is all the way down at minus eight. (SH Spec 2, 6105C12) **2.** a "sweetness and light" case at the extreme top of the graph who will go to graph bottom before the **case** starts up again as though the profile were a cylinder which when it goes off the top, then appears on the bottom when people are in "serene" valences (meaning they are wholly overwhelmed as a thetan). (HCOB 5 Jun 61) **3.** is high on the OCA/APA yet makes no progress. This is because such **cases** believe you ought to know what they are thinking about, so every moment around them you are missing withholds. (BTB 12 Jul 62)

**THEFT,** the **theft** of objects is really an effort to steal a self. Objects represent selves to others. **Thieves** and what they steal cannot be understood by the logic of their material needs. They steal tokens of selves and hope to assume thereby another self. (HCOB 2 May 58)

**THEORY,** the data part of a course where the data as in books, tapes and manuals is given. (HCOB 19 Jun 71 III)

**THEORY INSTRUCTOR,** assists the **theory** supervisor. Acts as auditing supervisor. Handles all **theory** administration. (HCO PL 18 Dec 64)

**THEORY OF EPICENTERS,** see EPICENTER THEORY.

**THEORY SUPERVISOR,** handles all **theory** instruction of the course and acts as auditing supervisor. (HCO PL 18 Dec 64)

**THERMAL, 1.** by **thermal** we perceive temperature, hotness and coldness, and so can evaluate further our current environment by comparing it to our past environments. (*SOS*, p. 59) **2.** a vibration of material, air, and so on—if one material is vibrating fast, we say it's hot, and if another one is vibrating more slowly, we say it's cold. (5203CM09A) **3.** temperature. (*DMSMH*, p. 14) **4.** the recall of temperature. (*SOS* Gloss)

**THETA, 1. theta** is thought, life force, *élan vital*, the spirit, the soul, or any other of the numerous definitions it has had for some thousands of years. (*SOS*, p. 4) **2.** the life force, life energy, divine energy, *élan vital*, or by any other name, the energy peculiar to life which acts upon material in the physical universe and animates it, mobilizes it and changes it. It is susceptible to alteration in character or vibration, at which time it becomes enturbulated theta or entheta. (*SOS*, Bk. 2, p. 21) **3. theta** is thought, an energy of its own universe analogous to energy in the physical universe but only occasionally paralleling electromagnetic-gravitic laws. The three primary components of **theta** are affinity, reality, and communication. (*SOS*, Bk. 2, p. 3) **4.** reason, serenity, stability, happiness, cheerful emotion, persistence, and the other factors which man ordinarily considers desirable. (*SOS*, Bk. 2, p. 12) **5.** an energy existing separate and distinct from the physical universe. (*SOS*, p. 4) **6.** Greek for thought or life or the spirit. (*Aud 10 UK*) **7.** not a nothingness. It just happens to be an exterior thing to this universe—so you couldn't talk about it in this universe's terms. (PDC 6)

**THETA BEING, 1.** the "I," it is who the preclear is. (*HOM*, p. 15) **2.** the **theta being** is close to a perpetual motion picture machine in that it can create energy and impulses. It thinks without facsimiles, it can act without experience, it can know simply by being. (*HOM*, p. 43)

**THETA BODY,** a thetan very often carries with him a **theta body** which he mocked up on the past track and which is a number of facsimiles of old bodies he has misowned and is carrying along with him as control mechanisms which he uses to control the body he is using. (PAB 130)

**THETA BOP, 1.** is a small or wide steady dance of the needle. Over a spread of one-eighth of an inch, say (depending on sensitivity setting—it can be half an inch), the needle goes up and down perhaps five or ten times a second. It goes up, sticks, falls, sticks, goes up, sticks, falls, sticks, etc., always the same distance, like a slow tuning fork. It is a constant distance and a constant speed. A **theta bop** means "death," "leaving," "don't want to be here." It is caused by a yoyo of the preclear as a thetan vibrating out and into the body or a position in the body. It's as if the needle is jumping between two peaks across a narrow valley. (*EME*, p. 16) **2.** a small or wide steady dance of the needle. Depending on the sensitivity setting it can be anything from one-eighth to half an inch wide. It is very rapid, perhaps five or ten times a second. (*BIEM*, p. 43) **3.** a diagnostic read, a sort of yoyo—in and out. It does not matter a continental how wide the **theta bop** is. It can be a whole dial wide. Most **theta bops** do it repetitively. One dip and one recovery at the exact same speed over the same area would be a one-motion **theta bop**. A **theta bop** has the equal halt at both ends. (SH Spec 1, 6105C07)

**THETA CLEAR, 1.** it is a person who operates exterior to a body without need of a body. (SH Spec 59, 6109C27) **2.** that state wherein the preclear can remain with certainty outside his body when the body is hurt. (PAB 33) **3.** a **theta clear,** then can be defined as a person who is at cause over his own reactive bank and can create and uncreate it at will. Less accurately he is a person who is willing to experience. **Theta clear** *is* stable. (*Abil 92M*) **4. theta clear** would mean clear of the mest body or cleared of the necessity to have a mest body. (5206CM26A) **5.** there are two types of **theta clear,** the theta being which is cleared of its necessity or compulsion to have a body and a theta being which is cleared all the way on the track. (5206CM26B) **6.** the basic definition of **theta clear** is: no further necessity for beingnesses. (SH Spec 36, 6108C09) **7.** this is a relative not an absolute term. It means that the person, this thought unit, is clear of his body, his engrams, his facsimiles, but can handle and safely control a body. (*COHA*, p. 248) **8.** in its highest sense, means no further dependency on bodies. (*SCP*, p. 3) **9.** an individual who, as a being, is certain of his identity apart from that of the body, and who habitually operates the body from outside, or exteriorized. (*PXL*, p. 16)

**THETA CLEARING, 1.** to create a **theta clear** it is only necessary to bring the being up to a point where it can leave and return upon a mest body. (*HOM*, p. 59) **2.** the emancipation or exteriorization of a soul. (*PXL*, p. 26)

**THETA E, earth theta line.** (HCL-15, 5203CM10A)

**THETA FORCE, theta force** is reason. (*SOS*, p. 158)

**THETA I, theta individual** which is the individual you are and are aware of being. (HCL-15, 5203CM10A)

**THETA LINE, 1.** a timeless, spaceless, influence capable of making recordings, capable of animating and motivating, controlling, forming, destroying, conserving matter, energy, space and time. (HCL-19, 5203CM10A) **2.** that **line** where the individual uses the genetic line to make one or many bodies that pass through time and the theta body inhabits the other body from just before conception until slightly after death. This **theta line** is subject to several different bodies. (HCL-20, 5203CM10B) **3.** life monitoring energy and making bodies. (HCL-15, 5203CM10A)

**THETA-MEST THEORY, 1.** a **theory** generated by myself in the fall of 1950 as an effort to explain (just a theory) the phenomena of an analyzer working in one direction and a reactive mind working in quite another, the reactive mind being interesting, and the analyzer being interested. (5410CM06) **2.** the idea is that life is a no-substance thing, up against a physical universe which is a substance thing. Here is nothingness up against a some-thingness interacting where the nothingness or the no-substance thing is actually giving orders to and handling the all substance thing, the physical universe. (UPC 3 5406CM——) **3.** the idea that there was a universe and that there was thought—theta without wave-length, without mass, without time, without position in space: this was life. And that was impinged upon something else called the physical universe, which was a mechanical entity which did things in a peculiar way, and these two things together, **theta-mest** interacting, gave us life forms. (*PXL*, p. 140)

**THETAN, 1.** the living unit we call, in Scn, a **thetan**, that being taken from the Greek letter **theta**, the mathematic symbol used

in Scn to indicate the source of life and life itself. (*Abil Ma 1*)
**2.** the awareness of awareness unit which has all potentialities
but no mass, no wave-length and no location. (HCOB 3 Jul 59)
**3.** the being who is the individual and who handles and lives in
the body. (HCOB 23 Apr 69) **4.** (spirit) is described in Scn as
having no mass, no wave-length, no energy and no time or
location in space except by consideration or postulate. The spirit
is not a thing. It is the creator of things. (*FOT*, p. 55) **5.** the
personality and beingness which actually is the individual and is
aware of being aware and is ordinarily and normally the
"person" and who the individual thinks he is. The **thetan** is
immortal and is possessed of capabilities well in excess of those
hitherto predicted for man. (*Scn 8-8008*, p. 9) **6.** the name given
to the life source. It is the individual, the being, the personality,
the knowingness of the human being. (*Scn 8-80*, p. 46) **7.** energy-
space production unit. (*COHA*, p. 247) **8.** in the final analysis
what is this thing called **thetan**? It is simply you before you
mocked yourself up and that is the handiest definition I know of.
(5608C——) **9.** the person himself—not his body or his name, the
physical universe, his mind, or anything else; that which is
aware of being aware; the identity which is the individual. The
**thetan** is most familiar to one and all as *you*. (*Aud 25 UK*) **10.** a
static that can consider, and can produce space and energy and
objects. (*PXL*, p. 121)

**THETAN EXTERIOR, 1.** a being who knows he is a spirit with a
body and not just a body. (*Aud 18*) **2.** he's out but if the body
were to be injured he would be back in. (PDC 52) **3.** a being not
influenced by a body. (SH Spec 82, 6611C29) **4.** a **thetan** who is
clear of the body and knows it but is not yet stable outside. (*Scn
8-8008* Gloss)

**THETAN PLUS BODY** (on the tone scale), a bunch of social
responses stimulus-response mechanisms that are built into the
being by the society. (PDC 1)

**THETAN TONE SCALE,** the sub-zero to 40.0 **scale** is the range
of the **thetan.** A **thetan** is lower than body death since it
survives body death. It is in a state of knowingness below 0.375
only when it is identifying itself as a body and is to its own
thinking, the body. (*Scn 8-80*, p. 52)

**THETA PERCEPTICS,** communication with the theta universe. Such **perceptics** may include hunches, predictions, ESP at greater and lesser distances, communication with the "dead," **perception** of the Supreme Being, etc. (*SOS* Gloss)

**THETA PERCEPTION,** that which one perceives by radiating towards an object and from the reflection perceiving various characteristics of the object such as size, odor, tactile, sound, color, etc. Certainty of perception is increased by drilling in certainties as above. **Theta perception** is dependent upon willingness to handle and to create space, energy and objects in view of the fact that the mest universe can be established easily to be an illusion. One must have an ability to perceive illusions before one can clearly perceive the mest universe. The **thetan** who cannot perceive the mest universe easily will also be found to be incapable of handling and orientating other kinds of illusions with certainty. **Theta perception** is also a direct index to responsibility, for responsibility is the willingness to handle force. (*Scn 8-8008* Gloss)

**THETA POSTULATE,** a **postulate** made without regard to evaluations, conclusions, or time. (PDC 7)

**THETA TIME,** only now, but some of it gets left back in mest time in an engram. (*NOTL,* p. 15)

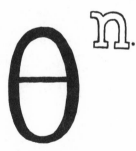

Theta to the Nth Degree

**THETA TO THE NTH DEGREE,** meaning unlimited or vast. $\Theta^n$. (HCOB 23 Aug 65)

**THETA TRAPS,** how can you **trap** a **thetan?** By curiosity, by giving him awards and prizes (of an implant), by retractor screens, by mock-ups, by ornate buildings which he will enter unsuspectingly to be electroniced down: by many such means the thetan is reduced from knowing to a colonist, a slave, a MEST body. All **theta traps** have one thing in common: they use electronic force to knock the thetan into forgetting, into unknowingness, into effect. Their purpose is to rid the area of those nuisances, the thetans who cannot be policed, and gain personnel—always the former, not always the latter. (*HOM*, pp. 71-72)

**THETA UNIVERSE, 1.** thought matter (ideas), thought energy, thought space, and thought time, combined in an independent universe analogous to the material universe. One of the purposes of **theta** is postulated as the conquest, change, and ordering of mest. (*SOS* Gloss) **2.** is a postulated reality for which there exists much evidence. (*SOS*, p. 99)

**THINKING, 1.** that process in which a person engages by which he hopes he will someday come to know. (2ACC 1B, 5311CM17) **2.** the combination of past observations to derive a future observation. (PAB 8) **3.** a substitution for an ability to predict. (2ACC 21A, 5312CM11) **4.** condensed effort. (2ACC 21A, 5312CM11) **5.** comparing a particular datum with the physical universe as it is known and observed. (Lecture: *Education and the Auditor*, 1951, p. 9)

**THINKINGNESS, 1.** down the scale at the level below effort. It comes in as figure-figure-figure-figure-figure. "I'll just figure this out and I'll get a computation and a calculation and I'll add it up to . . . Now let me see . . ." We don't know how all of this mechanic got into a postulate, but they've let it get in there. So that's the level, **thinkingness.** (*PXL*, p. 169) **2.** the potential of considering. (*COHA* Gloss)

**THIRD DYNAMIC,** see DYNAMICS.

**THIRD PARTY LAW,** the **law** would seem to be: a **third party** must be present and unknown in every quarrel for a conflict to exist. (HCOB 26 Dec 68)

**THIRD POSTULATE, 1.** forget. (PAB 66) **2.** forgettingness. (SH Spec 35, 6108C08)

**THIRD RAIL,** is a special form of factual havingness. Commands and position: are the same as in factual havingness. However the commands are run in a special ratio of: 8 commands of "vanish," 2 commands of "continue" and 1 command of "have." Purpose: to remedy extreme conditions of not-isness, to remedy obsessive waste, to permit use of the process without bogging preclear in any one of the commands. (HCOB 3 Jul 59)

**THIRD STAGE RELEASE,** see STAGES OF RELEASE.

**THOUGHT, 1.** the perception of the present and the comparison of it to the perceptions and conclusions of the past in order to direct action in the immediate or distant future. (*Scn 0-8*, p. 78) **2.** direct observation is infinitely superior to **thought** which seeks to know before looking. **Thought** could be said to be the manifestation of evolving a low-level certainty of observation from a number of past observations. The combination of past observations to derive a future observation could be said to be the process of thinking itself. (PAB 8) **3.** a static of unlimited capabilities, which has itself no wave-length, no space, and no time. It is impinged upon a physical universe which has space, time, energy and matter. The mission of **thought** is survival in the physical universe and in order to do this it is effecting a conquest of the physical universe. (5203CM03B) **4. thought** is the phenomenon of combining, imagining or postulating theta facsimiles for the estimation of future physical efforts. (*AP&A*, p. 22) **5. thought** is not motion in space and time. **Thought** is a static containing an image of motion. (*HFP*, p. 25) **6.** the subject matter of Scn. It is considered as a kind of "energy" which is *not* part of the physical universe. It controls energy, but has no wave-length. It uses matter but it has no mass. It is found in space, but it has no position. It records time but it is not subject to time. In Scn the Greek word (and letter), *theta*, is used as a symbol for thought. (*Abil 114A*) **7.** the causal agent in an organism. It is **thought** which causes everything both structural and functional that happens in an organism. An organism without **thought** is already dead. (*Abil 114A*)

**THREE D,** written **3D**. See ROUTINE 3D.

**THREE D CRISS CROSS,** written **3DXX**. See ROUTINE 3D CRISS CROSS.

**THREE FLOWS,** see TRIPLE FLOWS.

# THREE GA XX (3GAXX)

**THREE GA XX (3GAXX), 1.** it's a research numbering for a process called **Three GA Criss Cross**. It lists and handles some types of implants. (LRH Def. Notes) **2. 3GA Criss Cross** is an activity engaged upon by the auditor to unburden the case and locate goals. (SH Spec 218, 6211C27) *Abbr.* 3GAXX.

**3 MAY [72] PL, Hubbard Communications Office Policy Letter 3 May 1972** *Important—Executive Series 12—Ethics and Executives,* executive or officers steps for getting in Ethics on a staff member. (HCO PL 3 May 72)

**3MC, Third Melbourne Congress.** (HCOB 29 Sept 66)

**THREE M's,** a symbol has **three M's,** mass, meaning and mobility. (*COHA,* p. 91)

**THREE (3) S & Ds,** (1) is a specific rundown for doing **S & Ds** covered fully in HCOB 30 Jun 71R. (2) **3 S & Ds** as a rundown is used in the PTS Rundown without change. (HCOB 9 Dec 71RA)

**THREE UNIVERSES, 1.** the **universes,** then, are **three** in number: the **universe** created by one viewpoint, the **universe** created by every other viewpoint, the **universe** created by the mutual actions of viewpoints which is agreed to be upheld—the physical universe. (*COHA,* p. 185) **2.** the first of these is one's own **universe.** The second **universe** would be the material **universe,** which is the **universe** of matter, energy, space and time, which is the common meeting ground of all of us. The third **universe** is actually a class of **universes,** which could be called "the other fellow's **universe,**" for he and all the class of "other fellows" have **universes** of their own. (*COHA,* p. 188)

**THREE-VALUED LOGIC,** see LOGIC.

**THROUGH A CHECKSHEET,** means **through** the entire **checksheet**—theory, practical, all drills—and done in sequence. (BPL 27 Jul 69)

**THROW A CURVE,** see CURVE.

**THUMB SYSTEM,** an auditor trick that permits better attention on pcs' answers and less command mistakes on alternate command processes, when you give the plus command put your **thumb** on your index finger. Hold it there until it is answered. When the minus command is given, put your **thumb** on the second fingertip until it is answered. This sets up a physical universe tally and keeps one from mucking up the command sequence without having to "hold it in mind." This permits better observation of the pc. (HCOB 1 Sept 60)

**THUNK,** *Slang.* thinkingness. (SH Spec 143, 6205C03)

**TICK,** small jerk of needle, (meter read). (HCOB 29 Apr 69)

**TIGER,** someone who has been repeatedly associated with goofed projects and operations and who actually has caused such to occur. He is a person who is continually out-ethics. He has failed to get ethics in on himself and he is in a group of people as a **tiger** would be dangerous. (FO 872) [This is the derogatory form of this term and when it is used by LRH is not always meant in the above sense.]

**TIGER DRILL, 1.** a **drill** where the coach can give different reads and different goals for the student auditor to work on, the only condition being that the goals selected be those which would be most unlikely on anyone's goals list. The goal used in this **drill** is: To be a **tiger.** (HCOB 1 Aug 62 II) **2.** the use of the word **tiger** was so that a null, unmeaningful word would be on the **drill** or not restimulate anyone. Later, because of the **drill, tiger**=SP. (LRH Def. Notes) **3.** that series of buttons which are capable of preventing a right goal or level from reading or making a wrong level read, combined in an appropriate exercise. (HCOB 7 Nov 62 III) **4.** this **drill** is used in Routine 2-12 to sort out the last three or four items left in on each nulling. In 3GAXX it is used on the last three or four items left in and on any goals list. (HCOB 29 Nov 62)

**TIME, 1. time** is basically a postulate that space and particles will persist. (The rate of their persistence is what we measure with clocks and the motion of heavenly bodies.) (PAB 86) **2. time** is actually a consideration but there is the experience of **time.** There is a distance, there is a velocity of particle travel—and the movement of that particle in relationship to its starting point and in relationship to its ending point, itself is the consideration of **time.** (5410CM13) **3.** exists in those things a thetan creates. It is a shift of particles, always making new space, always at an agreed-upon rate. (*COHA*, p. 249) **4.** simply a consideration, the considerations of **time** itself are mechanically tracked by the alteration of the position of the particles in space. (PAB 46) **5.** a further investigation and inspection of **time** has demonstrated it to be the action of energy in space, and it has been found that the duration of an object roughly approximates its solidity. **Time** could be considered to be a manifestation in space which is varied by objects. An object could be considered to be any unit manifestation of energy including matter. (*Scn 8-8008*, p. 14) **6.** an abstract manifestation which has no existence beyond the idea of **time** occasioned by objects, where an object may be either energy or matter. (*Scn 8-8008*, p. 26) **7. time** is the co-action of particles. You can't have action of particle at all unless you have space, and when you have a change in space then you have a different **time**. (*PXL*, p. 135) **8. time** is a consideration which brings about persistence. And the mechanic of bringing about that persistence is, by alteration. And so we have alter-is-ness taking place immediately after an as-is-ness is created, and so we get persistence. In other words, we have to change the location of a particle in space. (*PXL*, p. 114)

Time (Def. 4)

**TIMELESSNESS,** merely means something that endures across long spans of time. (PDC 13)

**TIME LIMITER,** the auditor prefaces a question with a **time limiter** such as, "In this lifetime . . ." "In auditing . . ." or whatever applies. (HCOB 3 Jul 62)

**TIME SHIFT, 1.** the auditor can take a preclear straight through an incident by announcing "It is one minute later, it is two minutes later. Three minutes have gone by," and so forth. The auditor does not have to wait for those minutes to elapse; he just announces them. The **time shift** is generally used when the auditor is trying to get the preclear ahead of an incident to make sure that he really has a beginning. (*DMSMH*, p. 224) **2.** the technique by which a preclear can be moved short or long distances on the track by specific announcement of the amount of **time** forward the preclear is to go or **time** backwards, or return or progression through intervals of **time**. (It is also useful to find out if the preclear is moving or which direction he is moving on the time track in order to discover the action some engram may be having upon him.) (*DMSMH*, p. 226)

**TIME TAB,** thoughts are filed by your concept of when they happened. As long as you know the **time tab** of any thought, it is yours completely. When you do not know the **time tab** of a thought, you no longer control it. (*HFP*, p. 111)

Time Track (Def. 1)

**TIME TRACK, 1.** the consecutive record of mental image pictures which accumulates through the preclear's life or lives. It is very exactly dated. (HCOB 23 Apr 69) **2.** the **time** span of the individual from beingness to present time on which lies the sequence of events of his total existence. (HCOB 9 Mar 60) **3.** the endless record, complete with fifty-two perceptions of the pc's entire past. The **time track** is a very accurate record of the pc's past, very accurately timed, very obedient to the auditor. If motion picture film were 3D, had fifty-two perceptions and could fully react upon the observer, the **time track** could be called a motion picture film. It is at least 350,000,000,000,000 years long, probably much longer, with a scene about every 1/25 of a second. (HCOB 15 May 63) **4.** consists of all the consecutive moments of "now" from the earliest moment of life of the organism to present time. Actually, the **track** is a multiple bundle of perceptics; and it might be said that there is a **time track** for each perceptic, all tracks running simultaneously. The **track** might also be considered as a system of filing recordings made of the environment and the organism, filed according to time received. All the perceptions of the environment and the organism during the entire lifetime, up to now, or present time, are recorded, faintly or deeply, upon the **time track**. (*SOS*, p. 102)

**TIP, Technical Individual Program.** This form of issue is originated so that personal **programs** may be issued for students and pcs and published. It is **individually** written for the student or pc. It is on green paper. (TIP 1 FAO, 20 Jun 71)

**TOCKY,** needle reaction—small RS. (HCOB 8 Jul 64 II)

**TOKEN, 1.** the term **token** is defined to embrace the objects and habits which an individual or society keeps by not knowing they are extensions of an ally. (*DMSMH*, p. 354) **2.** the **token** is a very special kind of restimulator. The **token** is any object, practice or mannerism which one or more allies used. By identity thought the ally is survival, anything the ally used or did is, therefore, survival. (*DMSMH*, p. 355)

**TONE, 1. tones** have to do with physics, they have to do with vibration, they have to do with corresponding vibrations in the physical sciences. It merely means a condition. (5904C08) **2.** sound quality; the difference between a jagged or ragged sound wave and a smooth sound wave as in a musical note. (*SA*, p. 85) **3.** the emotional condition of an engram or the general condition of an individual. (*DTOT* Gloss)

**TONE 0 SOCIETY,** a **society** governed by the mystery and superstition of some mystic body. (*DMSMH*, p. 405)

**TONE 1 SOCIETY,** a **society** managed and dictated to by the whims of one man or a few men. (*DMSMH*, p. 405)

**TONE 2 SOCIETY,** a **society** hindered by arbitrary restrictions and oppressive laws. (*DMSMH*, p. 405)

**TONE 4 SOCIETY,** a free **society,** working in complete cooperation toward common goals; any Golden Age is a **tone 4.** (*DMSMH*, p. 405)

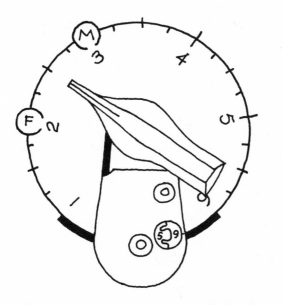

Tone Arm

**TONE ARM, 1.** meter control lever. (HCO PL 5 May 65) **2.** the measure of accumulation of charge. (Class VIII No. 6) **3.** registers density of mass (ridges, pictures, machines, circuits) in the mind of the preclear. This is actual mass, not imaginary, and can be weighed, measured by resistance etc. Therefore the **tone arm** registers state of case at any given time in processing. The **tone arm** also registers advance of case during processing by moving. (*EME*, p. 9) **4.** the **tone arm** reads at 5000 ohms female and 12,500 ohms male for the body. It reads the body. When a person is Clear the E-meter ceases to read. That tells you why a dead thetan reads at 2 or 3. (SH Spec 1, 6105C07) **5.** the instrument which measures the adequacy of restimulation. That shows you that an adequate amount of charge is being restimulated in the session, and that it is being adequately dispelled on the itsa line. This shows you that the cycle of what's-it-itsa is in progress and the amount of restimulation is adequate to get auditing done. (SH Spec 295, 6308C15) *Abbr.* TA.

**TONE ARM ACTION,** is measured by divisions down per 2 1/2 hour session or per hour of auditing. **TA action** is not counted by up and down, only down is used. Usually the decimal system is used. (HCOB 25 Sept 63)

**TONE ARM BLOWDOWN,** a sudden downwards motion of the **tone arm.** (*EMD*, p. 27)

**TONE ARM COUNTER,** records the distance of downward movements traversed by the tone arm. It is recorded in numbers of divisions—from 4 to 3 would be one division. (*BIEM*, p. 33)

**TONE ARM MOTION,** the amount of divisions, down, measured for a 2 1/2 hour session. (*EMD*, p. 25) See also TONE ARM ACTION.

**TONE FOUR, 1.** denotes a person who has achieved rationality and cheerfulness. (*DTOT*, p. 60) **2.** the emotional state of enthusiasm. (*DTOT*, p. 10) **3. tone 4** indicates eager pursuit of activity, with complete freedom of choice for other activities as desired. (*NOTL*, p. 99)

**TONE 40, 1.** defined as "giving a command and just knowing that it will be executed despite any contrary appearances." **Tone 40** is positive postulating. (PAB 133) **2.** a positive postulate with no counter-thought expected, anticipated or anything else; that is, total control. (PAB 152) **3.** an execution of intention. (HCOB 23 Aug 65) **4.** means unlimited space at will. (5707C25)

**TONE 40 AUDITING, 1.** positive, knowing, predictable control toward the preclear's willingness to be at cause concerning his body and his attention. (HCOB 3 Jul 59) **2.** control by direct **tone 40** command. (HCOB 2 Apr 58)

**TONE 40 BOOK AND BOTTLE,** is not Opening Procedure by Duplication. You have to be ready to assume total control of the preclear to run **tone 40 Book and Bottle.** The commands are the same, except that you never acknowledge anything but the execution of the auditing commands. (PAB 153)

**TONE 40 COMMAND,** intention without reservation. (HCOB 1 Dec 65)

**TONE 40 8-C,** a total accurate estimation of effort with no halts or jagged motions—that is, smooth. (PAB 152)

**TONE SCALE, 1.** we have a gradient **scale** from space to matter which starts at the arbitrary number of 40.0 for our purposes and goes down to 0.0 for the purposes of *Homo sapiens* and to —8.0 for the purposes of estimating a thetan. This gradient **scale** is called the **tone scale.** (*Scn 8-8008*, p. 20) **2.** the main gradient **scale** of Scn. One of the most important observations which led to the formulation of this **scale** was the change in emotional manifestation exhibited by a person who was being processed. The progress from painful emotions to pleasant emotions was so reliable and evident on indication of success, that it became the main measuring stick of the progress of a case. (*Abil 114A*) **3.** essentially an assignation of numerical value by which individuals can be numerically classified. It is not arbitrary but will be found to approximate some actual governing law in nature. (*DTOT*, p. 59) **4.** under affinity we have the various emotional **tones** ranged from the highest to the lowest and these are, in part, serenity (the highest level), enthusiasm (as we proceeded downward towards the baser affinities), conservatism, boredom, antagonism, anger, covert hostility, fear, grief, apathy. This in Scn is called the **tone scale.** (*FOT*, p. 40) **5.** a **scale** which plots the descending spiral of life from full vitality and consciousness through half-vitality and half-consciousness down to death. (*SA*, p. 37) **6.** the range of emotion. The **tone scale** goes in harmonics of movement, and that is all. (5203CM04B) **7.** a study of varying degrees of ARC. (*COHA*, p. 162)

**TOPECTOMY,** operation which removes pieces of brain somewhat as an apple corer cores apples. (*DMSMH*, p. 193)

**TOP OPPTERM,** the final achievement of the goal. (SH Spec 329, 6312C12)

**TOP TRIANGLE,** it is the KRC **triangle.** The points are K for knowledge, R for responsibility and C for control. (HCO PL 18 Feb 72)

Top Triangle

**TOTAL FREEDOM,** would be existence without barriers. (SH Spec 20, 6106C26)

**TOTAL KNOWINGNESS,** the static has the capability of **total knowingness. Total knowingness** would consist of total ARC. (*COHA,* p. 16)

**TOTAL POWER,** occurs when an individual can selectively confront or not confront anything. (SH Spec 84, 6612C13)

**TOUCH,** the sense of **touch** is that communication channel which informs the central control system of the body whenever some portion of the body is in contact with the material universe, other organisms, or the organism itself. It has four subdivisions: pressure, friction, heat or cold and oiliness. An aberrated sense of **touch** is partially responsible for a dislike of food as well as impotency and antipathy for the sexual act. (*SA,* p. 90)

**TOUCH ASSIST, 1.** an **assist** which brings the patient's attention to injured or affected body areas. (HCOB 2 Apr 69) **2.** this is run on both sides of the body. It is run until the pain is gone, cog, F/N. It is run around the injury and especially below the injury;

i.e. further from the head than the injury. Use a simple command like "Feel my finger. Thank you." (BTB 9 Oct 67R)

**TOUGH CASE,** the **tough case** (who is also the difficult student) is the sole reason one has an urge to alter a process. The poor TA type case or the "no change" response to routine processes. (HCO PL 5 Apr 65 II)

**TR, training regimen** or **routine.** Often referred to as a **training drill. TRs** are a precise **training** action putting a student through laid out practical steps gradient by gradient, to teach a student to apply with certainty what he has learned. (HCOB 19 Jun 71 III)

**TR-0,** a drill to train students to confront a preclear with auditing only or with nothing. The whole idea is to get the student able to be there comfortably in a position three feet in front of a preclear, to be there and not do anything else but be there. (HCOB 16 Aug 71 II)

**TR-1,** a drill to train the student to deliver a command newly and in a new unit of time to a preclear without flinching or trying to overwhelm or using a via. A phrase is picked out of the book *Alice in Wonderland* and read to the coach. It is repeated until the coach is satisfied it arrived where he is. **TR-1** is called "Dear Alice." (HCOB 16 Aug 71 II)

**TR-2,** a drill to teach students that an acknowledgement is a method of controlling preclear communication and that an acknowledgement is a full stop. (HCOB 16 Aug 71 II)

**TR2½,** a drill to teach the student that a **half** acknowledgement is a method of encouraging a pc to communicate. (HCOB 16 Aug 71R II)

**TR-3,** a drill to teach a student to duplicate without variation an auditing question, each time newly, in its own unit of time, not as a blur with other questions, and to acknowledge it. It is to teach that one never asks a second question until he has received an answer to the one asked. (HCOB 16 Aug 71 II)

**TR-4,** a drill to teach the student not to be tongue-tied or startled or thrown off session by originations of the preclear and to maintain ARC with the preclear throughout an origination. (HCOB 16 Aug 71 II)

**TR-5, 1.** a drill called "Hand Mimicry," a drill to educate students that verbal commands are not entirely necessary. To make students physically telegraph an intention and to show the students the necessity of having preclear obey commands. (HCOB 11 Jun 57) **2.** first in auditing we have to get the pc to sit there and be willing to be audited. We have for this many processes. Best is **TR-5**. "You make that body sit in that chair." "Thank you." (HCOB 8 Apr 58, *Auditing the PC on Clear Procedure*)

**TR-5N, 1.** is ARC break handling. (HCOB 7 Dec 58) **2.** the commands are "What has anyone done wrong to you?" and "What have you done wrong to people?" and other ARC break questions. (HCOB 17 Dec 58 II) [Later revised to] **3.** to handle charge on the auditor, **TR-5N** should be run, if charge does not blow on a little two way comm. **TR-5N** is: "What have I done to you?" "What have you done to me?" (HCOB 25 Jan 61)

**TR-6,** called 8-C (body control) the first part of this drill is to accustom students to moving another body than their own without verbal communication. The second part is to accustom students to moving another body, by and while giving commands, only, and to accustom students to proper commands of 8-C. (HCOB 7 May 68)

**TR-7,** a drill to train a student never to be stopped by a person when he gives a command. To train him to run fine control in any circumstances; to teach him to handle rebellious people and to bring about his willingness to handle other people. (HCOB 7 May 68)

**TR-8,** a drill to make students clearly achieve tone 40 commands. To clarify intentions as different from words. To start students on the road to handling objects and people with postulates and to obtain obedience not wholly based on spoken commands. (HCOB 7 May 68)

**TR-9,** a drill to make students able to maintain tone 40 under any stress or duress. (HCOB 7 May 68)

**TR-10,** for the case who cannot handle a PT problem with a process there is always locational (**TR Ten**). Many a person with a PT problem can only participate in a session to the extent of **TR Ten,** "You notice that object (wall, floor, chair, etc.)" (*SCP*, p. 8)

**TR-101,** the purpose of **TR-101** is to get the student able to give all R3R commands accurately in correct order without hesitation or having to think what the next command should be. (BTB 9 Oct 71R VII)

**TR-102,** a drill called "Auditing a Doll." Its purpose is to familiarize the student with the materials of auditing and coordinate and apply the commands and processes of Standard Dianetics in an auditing session. (BTB 9 Oct 71R VII)

**TR-103,** this drill is to give the student auditor total certainty on the R3R procedure, handling the meter and the admin at the same time. (BTB 20 May 70)

**TR-104,** this drill is to train the student auditor to deliver a standard session, with standard procedure, using standard commands, without session additives, and to train the student auditor to apply TRs 0-4 in the R3R procedure, here having a "real" pc, E-meter and admin handled with skill. (BTB 20 May 70)

**TRACK,** the time **track**—the endless record, complete with fifty-two perceptions of the pc's entire past. (HCOB 13 Apr 64, *Scn VI Part One Glossary of Terms*)

**TRACTOR BEAM, 1.** an energy flow which the thetan shortens. If one placed a flashlight beam upon a wall and then, by manipulating the **beam,** brought the wall closer to him by it, he would have the action of a **tractor beam. Tractor beams** are used to extract perceptions from a body by a thetan. (*Scn 8-8008*, p. 49) **2.** a method of contracting. The **tractor beam** contracts when energized. (PDC 8) **3.** a pulling wave. (*Scn 8-80*, p. 38) **4. in-tractors** are **tractors** put on the preclear by the environment. **Out-tractors** are **tractors** which the preclear puts on the environment. (5203CM04B)

**TRACTOR RIDGE,** that **ridge** formed by two **tractor** beams in conflict operating against each other. (*Scn 8-8008*, p. 49)

**TRAINED SCIENTOLOGIST,** someone with a special knowledge in the handling of life. (*Aud 75 UK*)

**TRAINING,** a formal activity imparting the philosophy or technology of Dn and Scn to an individual or group and culminates in the award of a grade or certificate. (*Aud 2 UK*)

**TRAINING AND SERVICES BUREAU,** that **bureau** on Flag, responsible for training, processing and other technical matters. (BTB 12 Apr 72R)

**TRAINING PATTERN, 1.** that stimulus-response mechanism resolved by the analytical mind to care for routine activity or emergency activity. It is held in the somatic mind and can be changed at will by the analytical mind. (*DMSMH*, p. 39)

**TRAINING 13 HC, 1.** this is a general understanding, answering the student or trainee's origin exercise, for use in stress analysis; a version of **"Training 13"** revised for **HC** from HCOB 11 Jun 57 Rev 12 May 72, *Training and CCH Processes.* (BTB 25 Jun 70R II)

**TRANSFERENCE, 1.** the patient flipped into another valence. (SH Spec 65, 6507C27) **2.** the **transference** of the patient into the valence of the practitioner. (*Cert*, Vol. 9, No. 7)

**TRANSGRESSION,** an action against a person or being or thing with which one has a moral code or an understanding or a co-action. (SH Spec 62, 6110C04)

**TRANS-ORBITAL LEUCOTOMY,** an operation which, while the patient is being electrically shocked, thrusts an ordinary dime store ice pick into each eye and reaches up to rip the analyzer apart. (*DMSMH*, p. 194)

**TRANSPOSITION,** that act of taking a person who is here and under influence, like hypnosis or something of this sort, and persuading him to be somewhere else, and then monitoring him somewhere else by addressing the body which is kept in a state of trance or drugs here. (PDC 24)

**TRAP, 1.** one is **trapped** by those things to which he will not grant havingness. A game condition demands that one denies havingness. Therefore games **trap. Traps** are part of games. That is all they are. (PAB 94) **2.** all a **trap** is, is being inside something, interiorized. (5410CM10C) **3.** theta and mest interconnected too strongly are the components of a **trap**. Theta is mixed up with mest, mest is mixed up with theta. (*SCP*, p. 21)

**TRAVELING RR,** in listing the **RR travels** down the list. It comes from the goal charge. Therefore it can **travel.** (HCOB 18 Mar 63)

**TREBLE ASSESS,** (Expanded Dianetics term from tape 7203C30, *Expanded Dianetics*) The act of making up a list of things the pc wants handled from the pc or worksheets or health form, **assessing** it for the best reading item (**assessment 1**) then by laws of listing and nulling finding who or what would have that to a single BD F/N item (**assessment 2**) then by laws of listing and nulling finding what intention the result of **assessment 2** would have (**assessment 3**) and running the result with Dianetics. (LRH Def. Notes)

**TRIO,** CCH 8 "Look around the room and tell me what you could have", "Look around the room and tell me something you would permit to remain", "Look around the room and tell me what you could dispense with". Originally called the **"Terrible Trio".** (HCOB 11 Jun 57)

**TRIPLE FLOWS, 1.** a being has a minimum of **three flows.** By "flow" is meant a directional thought, energy or action. The **three flows** are: inward to oneself, outward to another or others, and crossways, others to others. Examples: **Flow 1,** to self, drinking. **Flow 2,** self to another or others, pc giving them drinks. **Flow 3,** others to others, people giving other people drinks. (HCOB 5 Oct 69)

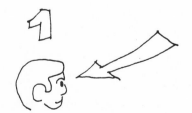

Triple Flows

inflow

# TRIPLE GRADES

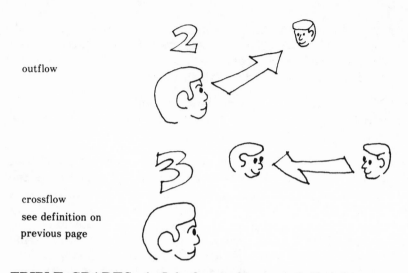

outflow

crossflow
see definition on
previous page

**TRIPLE GRADES, 1.** I had not discovered that lower grades were gone out of use and I let be published *Triple Grades* which seemed to condense all lower grades. The major process or major grade process is definitely not enough, to make a pc make a lower grade. (HCOB 30 Jun 70R) **2.** quickie lower grades also called **"Triple Grades"** means one F/N for each of three flows or three F/Ns per grade. There are not just three F/Ns per grade. There are dozens of F/Ns. (HCOB 30 Oct 71)

**TRIPLES,** items run **triple** flow. (HCOB 12 Oct 69)

**TRIPPER,** meaning somebody who has taken drugs. (HCOB 23 Sept 68)

**TRs WENT OUT,** is another way of saying he ceased to be with the pc. (Class VIII, No. 14)

**TRUNCATED GPM, 1.** one that is cut off at the top. (SH Spec 235, 6304C04) **2.** incomplete. (HCOB 28 Sept 63)

**TRUTH, 1. truth** is the exact consideration. **Truth** is the exact time, place, form and event. (*PXL*, p. 183) **2.** that which works. And that which works most broadly to that which it is applied. (PDC 19) **3.** by definition—is what is. (Class VIII, No. 4)

**T/S, Tech Services.** (HCOB 5 Mar 71)

**TTC, Tech Training Corps.** (BPL 13 Apr 75)

**TVD, television demonstration.** (HCOB 23 Aug 65)

**TWC (2WC), two-way comm.** (HCOB 17 Mar 74)

**12,500 OHMS,** the exact value for tone arm position 3 on the E-meter. **Ohms** is the term for the unit used in measuring electrical resistance on a line. (*EMD*, p. 16A)

**TWENTY-TEN,** that's **twenty** minutes of withholds pulled, and **ten** minutes of havingness. (SH Spec 97, 6201C09)

**TWIN,** the study partner with whom one is paired. Two students studying the same subject who are paired to checkout or help each other are said to be "**twinned.**" (HCOB 19 Jun 71 III)

**TWIN CHECKOUT,** when **two** students are paired they **check** each other **out.** (HCOB 21 Sept 70)

**TWO-VALUED LOGIC,** see LOGIC.

**TWO-WAY COMM, 1.** the precise technology of a process used to clarify data with another for the other. It is not chatter. It is governed by the rules of auditing. It is used by supervisors to clear up blocks to a person's progress in study, on post, in life or in auditing. It is governed by the communication cycle as discovered in Scn. (HCOB 19 Jun 71 III) **2.** is an inquiry of the pc as to what is going on and an invitation to him to look at it, and that is all. (SH Spec 43, 6108C22) **3.** a **two-way** cycle of **communication** would work as follows: Joe, having originated a **communication,** and having completed it, may then wait for Bill to originate a **communication** to Joe, thus completing the remainder of the **two-way** cycle of **communication.** Thus we get the normal cycle of a **communication** between two terminals. (*Dn 55!*, p. 84) **4.** the cycle is Cause, Distance, Effect, with Effect then becoming Cause and **communicating** across a distance to the original Source, which is now Effect and this we call a **two-way communication.** (*Dn 55!*, p. 64) *Abbr.* 2WC or TWC.

**TYPE THREE,** see PTS TYPE THREE.

# U

**UC, Unification Congress.** (HCOB 29 Sept 66)

**UGLINESS, 1.** a disharmony of wave motion, no matter how high the wave length, is ugliness. But **ugliness** is also a wave, a disharmony with the wave-length of beauty but very close to it. (*Scn 8-80*, p. 26) **2. ugliness** is a disharmony in wave discord with theta. (*Scn 8-80*, p. 26)

**UNBURDENING, 1.** as a basic is not at once available on any chain, one usually **unburdens** it by running later engrams, secondaries and locks. The act of **unburdening** would be digging off the top to get at the bottom as in moving sand. (HCOB 23 Apr 69) **2.** the technique of thoroughly bringing to view everything contained in an engram by scanning its locks. Alternate running of the engram and scanning its locks should bring about a maximal release of entheta. (*SOS*, Bk. 2, pp. 280-281)

**UNCHANGING GRAPH,** if a **graph** is **unchanging** there was a PTP. Present time problem is what keeps a **graph** from **changing.** (SH Spec 56, 6503C30)

**UNCONSCIOUS, 1.** any person who is unaware, to a great degree is **unconscious.** (HCOB 3 Jul 59) **2.** means a greater or lesser reduction of awareness on the part of "I." An attenuation of working power of the analytical mind. (*DMSMH*, p. 46)

**UNCONSCIOUS, THE,** reactively hidden pictures plus circuits plus machinery make up the totality of what Freud called **the unconscious.** (5810C29)

**UNCONSCIOUS MIND, 1.** the **"unconscious mind"** is the **mind** which is always conscious. So there is no **unconscious mind,** and there is no **unconsciousness.** (*EOS*, p. 39) **2.** the only **mind** which is always conscious. This submind is called the reactive **mind.** (*SOS*, p. xii) See REACTIVE MIND.

**UNCONSCIOUSNESS, 1.** an excess of randomity imposed by a counter-effort of sufficient force to cloud the awareness and direct function of the organism through the mind's control center. (*Scn 0-8*, p. 81) **2.** when the analytical mind is attenuated in greater or lesser degree. (*Scn 0-8*, p. 66) **3.** actually a manifestation of one's self-determinism being upset by a counter-effort. (5203CM08) **4.** a condition wherein the organism is discoordinated only in its analytical process and motor control direction. (*DTOT*, p. 25) **5.** is the intensification of unknowingness. (SH Spec 15X, 6106C15) **6.** a halfway end of cycle. (2ACC 8B, 5311CM24) **7. unconsciousness,** light or deep, is merely a slide in toward death. (HCL 11, 5203CM08)

**UNCONTROLLED LISTING,** the pc is permitted to **list** on and on with no stops or checks. (HCOB 24 Apr 63)

**UNDERCUTS,** runs on a lower case than. (*SCP*, p. 22)

**UNDERLISTED LIST,** more than one item RRs or RSes or everything on the **list** is alive. (SH Spec 255, 6304C04)

**UNDER-RESTIMULATION,** is just an auditor not putting the pc's attention on anything. (HCOB 1 Oct 63)

**UNDERSHOOTING,** to leave a cycle incomplete and go off to something else. (HCOB 26 Aug 70)

**UNDERSTANDING, 1. understanding** is composed of affinity, reality and communication. (SH Spec 79, 6609C01) **2.** knowingness could simply be a potential **understanding.** It could be an ability being carried forward, an action taking place; **understanding** is an action. **Understanding** is knowingness of life to a certain direction and object and thing or action. The **understanding** is knowingness in action. We break down this and we get affinity, reality and communication. (5411CM05) **3. understanding** is a sort of a total solvent, it's the universal solvent, it washes away everything. (SH Spec 79, 6609C01)

**UNETHICAL CONDUCT,** is actually the **conduct** of destruction and fear; lies are told because one is afraid of the consequences should one tell the truth; thus, the liar is inevitably a coward, the coward is inevitably a liar. (*SOS,* pp. 128-129)

**UNHAPPINESS, unhappiness** is only this: the inability to confront that which is. (*NSOL,* p. 25)

**UNHAPPY PERSON,** one whose acceptance levels are continually being violated. (UPC 13, 5406C——)

**UNINTENTIONAL WITHHOLD,** he doesn't **intend** to **withhold** it but he finds himself in a position of doing so because nobody will listen. (SH Spec 63, 6110C05)

**UNION STATION DESTROY,** a process; "You invent a way of **destroying** that (indicated) person." This is run outside on people chosen at random. It is done to take over **destructive** automaticities. (HCOB 17 Mar 75, *HGC Clear Procedure Outline of February 6, AD8*)

**UNIT FACSMILE,** would be any consecutive related experience in motion and so forth. It would contain as many recordings or as many separate pictures as sight needs in order to produce motion, 75 to 125 pictures a second. This experience may have lasted for a week. (5112CM29B)

**UNITS,** in 1965 the Saint Hill Special Briefing Course was organized as follows. It was divided into four **units.** Unit A covering Level 0. **Unit** B covering Levels I and II. **Unit** C covering Levels III and IV. **Unit** D covering Level VI. (HCO PL 27 Feb 65)

**UNIVERSE, 1.** a **universe** is defined as a "whole system of created things." There could be and are, many **universes,** and there could be many kinds of **universes.** (*Scn 8-8008*, p. 27) **2.** is an effort to locate oneself. (SH Spec 51, 6109C07)

**UNIVERSE OF THOUGHT,** theta. (*NOTL*, p. 13)

**UNIVERSE O/W,** this consists of doing an E-meter assessment of the person on the four points (1) the thetan, (2) the mind, (3) the body and (4) the physical universe, taking the most different needle reaction from the rest and running what was found with *Overt-Withhold Straightwire,* Ex: "Recall something you have done to the physical universe," alternated with "Recall something you have withheld from the physical universe." (HCOB 5 Oct 59)

**UNMOCK, 1.** take down or destroy. (HCO PL 13 Jul 74 II) **2.** make nothing of. (HCOB 19 Jan 68)

**UNMOTIVATED ACT,** an overt act delivered in the absence of a **motivator.** (*COHA*, p. 156)

**UNREALITY, 1.** the consequence and apparency of the practice of not-isness. (*Scn 0-8*, p. 32) **2.** a substitute of an unknown for a known. (SH Spec 15X, 6106C15) **3. unreality** is not-is-ness, our effort trying to make something disappear, with energy. (PRO 15, 5408C20) **4. unreality** is force and invalidation. (SH Spec 294, 6308C14)

**UNREDUCED FACSIMILE,** it is a **facsimile** which still has the capability of absorbing your attention unit output. (5206CM24B)

**UNUSUAL SOLUTIONS, 1.** a phrase describing actions taken by an auditor or a case or auditing supervisor when he or she has not spotted the gross auditing error. The **"unusual solution"** seldom resolves any case because the data on which it is based (the observation or report) is incomplete or inaccurate. (HCOB 16 Nov 64) **2.** an **"unusual solution"** is one evolved to remedy an abuse of existing technology. (*ISE*, p. 46)

**UNWILLING CAUSE,** if he is afraid to be at effect, then he is **unwilling cause** and is at **cause** only because he is very afraid of being at effect. Having to be at **cause** because he doesn't dare be at effect. (*SCP*, p. 9)

**UPC, Universe Process Congress.** (HCOB 29 Sept 66)

**UPPER INDOCTRINATION,** training processes 6 to 9. The 18th ACC in Washington, July 8 to August 16, 1951, was taught in three units composed as follows: communication course, **upper indoctrination** course, CCH course. (HCOB 8 Jun 57)

**UPPER LEVEL,** is very simply defined as anything from Power on up. (ED 110R FLAG)

**UP SCALE,** there is a downward spiral on the tone **scale** and an upward spiral. These spirals are marked by decreasing or increasing awareness. To go **up scale** one must increase his power to observe with certainty. (*COHA,* p. 200)

**URGES,** drives, impulses. (*IFR,* p. 8)

# V

**VACUUM, 1.** a **vacuum** is a supercold object which, if brought into contact with bank, drinks bank. Objects at 25°F or less have high electrical capacitance, low resistance. (PAB 106) **2.** a **vacuum** is a supercold object that attracts electronically into it, the whole track. (PAB 97)

**VALENCE, 1.** a **valence** is an identity complete with bank mass or mental image picture mass of somebody other than the identity selected by oneself. In other words, what we usually mean by **valence** is somebody else's identity assumed by a person unknowingly. (17ACC-10, 5703C10) **2.** the **valence** mechanism produces whole people for the preclear to be and will include habits and mannerisms which are not mentioned in engrams but are a result of the preclear's compulsion to copy certain people. (*SOS*, Bk. 2, p. 202) **3.** a **valence** is a false or true identity. The preclear has his own **valence.** Then there are available to him the **valences** of all persons who appear in his engrams. (*SOS*, p. 106) **4.** just an identity that is so dominant that it balls-up a whole section of the whole track. It takes a large section of the whole track and bundles it all up in a black ball and it's full of pictures. (SH Spec 105, 6201C25) **5.** a **valence** is a substitute for self taken on after the fact of lost confidence in self. (SH Spec 68, 6110C18) **6.** the combined package of a personality which one assumes as does an actor on a stage except in life one doesn't usually assume them knowingly. (5707C17) **7.** a **valence** is a commanded mimicry of another person or thing or imagined entity. These commands would be in engrams. The **valence** is not contained in a circuit. The **valence** and the circuit are two different things. The **valence** is a whole person, a whole thing, or a large number of persons or things. The circuit robs "I" of attention units. The **valence** transplants "I." It takes "I" and puts him somewhere else. (*NOTL*, p. 82) **8.** the personality of one of the dramatic personnel in an engram. (*DMSMH*, p. 81) **9.** the form and identity of the preclear or another, the beingness. (HCOB 23 Apr 69) **10.** a **valence** is a synthetic beingness, at best, or it is a beingness which the pc is not, but is pretending to be or thinks he is. That beingness could have been created for him by a duplication of an existing beingness, or a synthetic beingness built up by the descriptions of somebody else. (SH Spec 41, 6108C17) **11.** a facsimile personality made capable of force by the counter-effort of the moment or receipt into the plus or minus randomity of unconsciousness. **Valences** are assistive, compulsive or inhibitive to the organism. A control center is not a **valence.** (*Scn 0-8*, p. 86) **12.** there are many **valences** in everyone. By a **valence** is meant an actual or a shadow personality, one's own **valence** is his actual personality. (*SA*, p. 159) **13.** *valens* means "powerful" in Latin. It is a good term because it is the second half of ambivalent (power in two directions). It is a good term because it describes the intent of the organism when dramatizing an engram. **Multivalence** would mean "many powerfuls." It would embrace the phenomena of split personality, the strange differences of personality in people in one and then another situation. **Valence** in Dn means the personality of one of the dramatic personnel in an engram. (*DMSMH*, p. 80)

**VALENCE BOUNCER,** which prohibits an individual from going into some particular **valence.** (*SOS*, p. 182)

**VALENCE CASE,** the schizophrenic of psychiatry, the person who shifts from one identity to another, in Dn, we call a **valence case.** (*SOS*, p. 75)

**VALENCE CLOSURE,** you snap terminals and obsessively become the thing you have overts against. (SH Spec 53, 6109C13)

**VALENCE DENYER,** which may even **deny** that the person's own **valence** exists. (*SOS*, p. 182)

**VALENCE GROUPER,** which makes all **valences** into one **valence.** (*SOS*, p. 182)

**VALENCE SHIFT,** pc will cognite on having been out of **valence** and will return to his own **valence.** It's a cognition on *beingness*, not doingness or havingness. (BTB 26 Nov 71 III)

**VALENCE SHIFTER, 1.** a **valence shifter** is anything that indicates the person should be somebody else, with such a phrase a person is liable to **shift** instantly into another **valence.** (*NOTL*, p. 110) **2.** a phrase which causes the individual to **shift** into another identity. The phrase "you ought to be in his shoes" and the phrase "you're just like your mother" are **valence shifters,** which change the preclear from his own identity into the whole identity of another person. (*SOS*, p. 106) **3.** the phrase known as the **"valence shifter"** may force the person to be in any or every **valence** (grouper), or may force him to be barred out of a **valence** (bouncer) so that he cannot imitate some human being such as father, who may have had very good qualities well worth imitating. Typical **valence shifters** are such phrases as "you're just like your father," "I'll have to pretend I'm somebody else." (*SOS*, Bk. 2, p. 201) [This term has since been used to also denote the name of an auditing action.] **4.** a list process to handle "out of **valence.**" (HCOB 10 Sept 68)

**VALENCE WALL,** can actually exist in the individual to a point where he can be either one of two persons, himself and another person. In the very highly-charged case, in the case of the obvious psychotic, these **valence walls** are so well defined that the auditor can almost watch the person click from one **valence** to another. (*SOS*, p. 75)

**VALIDATION EFFORT PROCESSING,** this consists of discovering moments when the preclear is successfully approaching goals, when he is successfully exerting an **effort,** when his self-determined **effort** is winning. (5110CM01)

**VALIDATION STRAIGHTWIRE,** the theory of which was to **validate** all the good moments of the preclear's past by having him recall them. (*Abil SW*, p. 7)

**VAMPIRE IDEA,** the personality which absorbs the life and lives on the life of others. (PAB 8)

**VBIs, very bad indicators.** (BTB 6 Nov 72RA IV)

**VEDA, 1.** we find Scn's earliest certainly known ancestor in the **Veda.** The **Veda** is a study of the whereins and whereases and who made it and why. It is a religion. It should not be confused as anything else *but* a religion. And the word **veda** simply means: lookingness or knowingness. (*PXL*, p. 10) **2. veda** itself means simply knowingness or sacred lore and don't think that is otherwise than a synonym. Knowingness has always been considered sacred lore. (*PXL*, p. 12)

**VERBATIM, 1.** in the same words as the text. (HCO PL 4 Mar 71) **2.** word for word. (HCO PL 17 Mar 74 II)

**VERY WELL DONE, 1.** if the auditor did the C/S, did a correct session, got an F/N at exam and did the admin and next C/S is correct, then the C/S marks **"very well done."** (HCOB 5 Mar 71) **2.** an auditor gets a **"very well done"** when the session by worksheet inspection, exam report inspection is: (1) F/N, VGIs at examiner, (2) the auditing is totally flubless and by the book, (3) the whole C/S ordered was done without departure and to the expected result. (HCOB 21 Aug 70)

**VGIs, 1.** abbreviation for **very good indicators.** It means **good indicators** to a **very** marked degree. Extremely **good indicators.** (BTB 12 Apr 72R) **2.** pc happy. (HCOB 20 Feb 70)

**VIA, via** means a relay point in a communication line. To talk **via** a body, to get energy **via** eating alike are communication by-routes. Enough **vias** make a stop. A stop is made out of **vias.** (*COHA*, p. 108)

Via

**VICTIM, 1.** a destroyed, or threatened with destruction receipt point. (1MACC-7, 5911C12) **2.** a **victim** is an unwilling and unknowing effect of life, matter, energy, space and time. (HCOB 3 Sept 59)

**VIEWPOINT, 1.** a **point** of awareness from which one can perceive. (PAB 2) **2.** that thing which an individual puts out remotely, to look through. A system of remote lookingness— we'll call it just remote **viewpoint.** That's a specialized kind of **viewpoint.** And the place from which the individual is himself looking, we'll call flatly a **viewpoint.** (2ACC 17A, 5312CM07) **3.** evaluation is the reactive mind's conception of **viewpoint.** The reactive mind does not perceive, it evaluates. To the analytical mind it may sometimes appear that the reactive mind has a **viewpoint.** The reactive mind does not have a **viewpoint,** it has an evaluation of **viewpoint.** Thus the **viewpoint** of the analytical mind is an actual point from which one perceives. Perception is done by sight, sound, smell, tactile, etc. The reactive mind's 'viewpoint' is an opinion based on another opinion and upon a very small amount of observation, and that observation would be formed out of uncertainties. Thus the confusion of the word **viewpoint** itself. It can be a point from which one can be aware, which is its analytical definition, and it can be somebody's ideas on a certain subject which is the reactive definition. (*COHA*, pp. 208-209)

**VIEWPOINT PROCESSING, 1.** this **process** seeks to resolve the problems set up by the evaluation of one being for another. It resolves in particular dependence upon people, objects, bodies and special systems of communication. **Viewpoint processing** resolves dependencies. (PAB 8) **2.** what we are trying to do here, then, is not to run out all the engrams in the bank but to release and free the **viewpoints** which are being resisted. (PAB 8)

**VIEWPOINT STRAIGHTWIRE, 1.** the formula of this process is: all the definitions and axioms, arrangements and scales of Scn should be used in such a way as to bring about a greater tolerance of such **viewpoints** on the part of the preclear. That means that any scale there is, any arrangement of fundamentals in thinkingness, beingness, could be so given in a **straightwire** process that it would bring about a higher state of tolerance on the part of the preclear. (*PXL*, p. 248) **2.** this process is to increase the preclear's ability to tolerate **views.** (*COHA*, p. 66)

**VIRUS,** matter and energy animated and motivated in space and time by theta. (*Scn 0-8*, p. 75)

**VISIO, 1.** recalling a scene by seeing it again is called in Dn **visio,** by which is meant **visual** recall. (*SOS*, p. 72) **2.** with **visio** we perceive light waves, which, as sight, are compared with experience and evaluated. (*SOS*, p. 59) **3.** the ability to **see** in facsimile form something one has seen earlier so that one sees it again in the same color, dimension scale, brightness and detail as it was originally viewed. (*PXL*, p. 230)

**VISIO IMAGERY,** when a person can recall things he has seen simply by seeing them again, in color, in his mind. (*Exp Jour, Winter-Spring, 1950*)

**VISIO SEMANTIC,** the recordings of words read. These are special parts of the sound and sight files. (*DMSMH*, p. 46)

**VITAL INFORMATION RUNDOWN,** simply stated I found that WHERE **VITAL INFORMATION** WAS NOT BEING RELAYED OR WAS HIDDEN OR FALSIFIED, THE PEOPLE RESPONSIBLE WERE DRAMATIZING WITHHOLDS. The answer that fits all cases is a failure to relay **information**, brief, instruct, train or supervise stemming from a general past and current OVERT OF WITHHOLDING **VITAL INFORMATION**. It is not simple withholding **information**. It is (or once was) the intentional overt of withholding **VITAL information**. It would be a very long chain and would influence general conduct. This **RD** is very powerful. (HCOB 6 Oct 74R)

**VITAMIN E,** the apparent acting of this **vitamin** is to oxygenate the blood and inhibit the body from pulling in mental masses due to oxygen-energy starvation. (HCOB 27 Dec 65)

**VITAMINS, vitamins** are not drugs. They are nutrition. (*Aud 71 ASHO*)

**V UNIT, 1.** in 1962 a Saint Hill Special Briefing Course **unit** for co-auditing heavily supervised R2-10 or R2-12 directed toward results. There were no checksheets beyond course regulations. (HCO PL 8 Dec 62) **2.** the purpose of **V** unit is to: (1) get the student into some kind of shape to finish the SHSBC, (2) give the student a win as an auditor, (3) establish an auditing reality on Scn. (HCO PL 13 Feb 63)

# W

**WALKING OUT PROCESSES,** type of **process** where the student takes his preclear **out** into some populated area. (PAB 70)

**WANTS HANDLED, 1.** the thing (somatic, intention, terminal, condition, doingness) the pc really **wants handled.** (HCOB 28 Mar 74) **2.** a **"wants** to get rid of" not a **"wants** to achieve." (HCOB 28 Mar 74)

**WANTS HANDLED RUNDOWN,** an Ex Dn **rundown.** The important points of the **RD** are to run it as a **"wants** to get rid of," not a **"wants** to achieve" and to complete each thing the pc **wants handled** before going on. **Handling** of each thing the pc **wants handled** is dictated by what the "thing" (somatic, intention, terminal, condition, doingness) is. (HCOB 28 Mar 74)

**WAR, 1.** a means of bringing about a more amenable frame of mind on the part of the enemy. (SH Spec 63, 6506C08) **2.** is the antithesis of organization. **War** is chaos. (SH Spec 131, 6204C03)

**WASTE-HAVE,** a person can't **have** something. You can have him **waste** it enough and he'll find out after a while, he'll say "Well, I can **have** it." (5702C26)

**WATERLOO STATION,** a process where, in a populated area (park, railroad **station,** etc.) you have the pc tell the auditor something he wouldn't mind not-knowing about persons, or the persons not-knowing about him which auditor spots for him. (PAB 69)

**WAVE,** a path of flow or a pattern of flow. (PDC 18)

**WAVE-LENGTH,** the relative distance from node to node in any flow of energy. In the mest universe **wave-length** is commonly measured by centimeters or meters. (*Scn 8-8008*, p. 18)

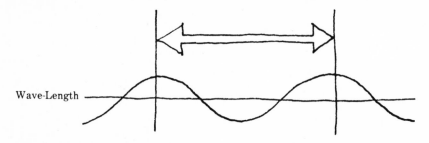

Wave-Length

**WC (-ER) (-D) (-NG), word clear** (-er) (-ed) (-ing). (BPL 5 Nov 72RA)

**WCCL, Word Clearing Correction List.** (BTB 11 Aug 72RA)

**WDAHs, well done auditing hours.** (FBDL 279)

**WELL DONE, 1.** "well done" given by the C/S for a session means the pc had F/N VGIs at the examiner immediately after the session. (HCOB 21 Aug 70) **2.** is only given to those where the session ran off like a clock exactly on standard tech. (Class VIII, No. 2)

**WELL DONE AUDITING HOURS, 1.** "well done auditing hours" is defined as number of **auditing hours** in the chair which are **well done** by C/S grading, with F/N, VGIs at end of session and examiner, to which can be added admin time up to and no higher than 10 per cent of the actual **well done hours audited.** (FO 3076) **2. well done hours** are defined as those **hours** given a **well done** by the C/S—the session having concluded on F/N VGIs and the pc having F/N VGIs at the examiner immediately after the session, and no gross technical outnesses in the session. (HCO PL 23 Nov 71 II)

**WELL DONE BY EXAMS,** if the **exam** form F/Ned, but the admin is not okay and the session actions were not okay the C/S writes **"well done by exam."** (HCOB 5 Mar 71)

**WFMH, World Federation** of **Mental Health.** (*Aud 71 ASHO*)

**WF-1, 1. why finding drill-one.** (BTB 2 Sept 72R) **2. WF-2, why finding drill-two.** (BTB 2 Sept 72 II)

**WH (W/H), withhold.** (HCOB 23 Aug 65)

**WHAT QUESTION,** the formulation of the **what question** is done as follows: the pc gives an overt in response to the zero question which does not clean the needle of the instant read on the zero. The auditor uses that overt to formulate his **what question.** Let us say the zero was "Have you ever stolen anything?" The pc says "I have stolen a car." Testing the zero on the meter, the auditor says "I will check that on the meter: Have you ever stolen anything?" (He mentions nothing about cars, Heaven forbid!) If he still gets a read, the auditor says "I will formulate a broader question," and says, to the meter, **"What** about stealing cars? **What** about stealing vehicles? **What** about stealing other people's property?" the auditor gets the same zero question read on **"What** about stealing other people's property?" So he writes this down on his report. Now as he has his **question,** the auditor sits up, looks at the pc and says, meaning it to be answered (but without accusation) **"What** about stealing other people's property?" (HCOB 24 Jun 62 *Prepchecking*)

**WHAT'S IT,** *v.* a coined word, coming from the phrase, **"What is it?"** It basically means to ask a question. However, it has come to mean "to dwell on problems, confusions or uncertainties rather than to resolve them." —*n.* **1.** an unanswered question; a puzzlement about something. (*Scn AD*) **2.** the rise of the TA is a "What's it?" The pc's groping (**what's it**). The pc says **"What's it?"** The auditor must begin to ask occasionally "Well, **what's it** seem to you?" And the pc will find his own "It's a . . ." and the TA will fall. (HCOB 4 Aug 63)

**WHAT'S-IT LINE, 1.** is from the auditor to the pc. And the auditor is saying **what's it.** (SH Spec 291, 6308C06) **2.** it's called

**what's it** because those exact words raise the tone arm and the itsa line is called itsa because those exact words lower the TA. (SH Spec 294, 6308C14)

**WHAT TO AUDIT,** a book now called *A History of Man* and is a fragmentary account of the GE line. (PDC 9)

**WHITE FLOW,** a **white flow** is a moving **flow** and a black area is a stopped flow. And a black area is stopped because there's a **white flow** around there somewhere ready to run. (5207CM24B)

**WHITE FORM,** PC Assessment **Form** (HCOB 23 Aug 71)

**WHOLE TRACK,** the **whole track** is the moment to moment record of a person's existence in this universe in picture and impression form. (HCOB 9 Feb 66)

**"WHY", 1.** that basic outness found which will lead to a recovery of statistics. (HCO PL 13 Oct 70) **2.** the real reason found by the investigation. (HCO PL 29 Feb 72 II)

**WIDE OPEN CASE, 1.** a **case** that has pictures and everything and is impatient to get on with it but does not markedly alter the bank with thinking alone. (*SCP*, p. 9) **2.** is possessed of full perception except somatic, which is probably light even to the point of anesthesia. **Wide open** does not refer to a high tone individual but to one below 2.5 who should be easy to work but is often inaccessible and who finds it difficult to regain a somatic but simple to regain perception. (*AP&A*, p. 40) **3.** your **wide open case** is somebody who has had all of his past shut off from him and is living in a demon circuit. That's all that's left of him is a demon circuit. (5206CM24F) **4.** a tremendously heavily charged track brings the individual into a psychotic level. The inability of the mind to occlude and encyst charge gives us the strange picture of an individual who can move on the track and who can run through engrams and who has sonic and visio but who is psychotic. (*SOS*, p. 109)

**WIDE ROCK SLAM,** a quarter of a dial **rock slam** to a full dial **rock slam.** (HCOB 12 Sept 62)

**WILDCAT,** meaning springing up anywhere. (HCO PL 5 Oct 69)

**WILLPOWER,** in this mest universe it consists of the relative ability to impose time and space on energy or matter. That's **willpower** and that's self-determinism, and that is controlling people and people controlling you. (5209CM04B)

**WIN,** intending to do something and doing it or intending not to do something and not doing it. (SH Spec 278, 6306C25)

**WINNING VALENCE, 1.** is a synthetic **valence.** It is not actually the personality of the person who won. It is the individual's mock-up of that person which is diminished, or augmented by other people's opinions and by one's own postulates. (PAB 83) **2.** in the case of the woman beaten by her husband, the engram contains just two **valences.** Who **won?** The husband. Therefore it is the husband who will be dramatized. She didn't win, she got hurt. When restimulators are present, the thing to do is to be the **winner,** the husband, to talk like him, to say what he did. Hence, when the woman is restimulated into this engram by some action she dramatizes the **winning valence.** (*DMSMH*, p. 81) **3.** the **valence** of greatest determinism. (*COHA*, p. 99)

**WINS,** if a pc is getting **wins** then the pc gets more able, earns more or finds more wherewithal, and accomplishes more in a given period of time, leaving more time to use for auditing and the minor upsets or discomforts which accompany even the smoothest auditing are disregarded. (*BCR*, p. 17)

**WITH A SESSION,** is defined as "interested in own case and willing to talk to the auditor." (HCOB 19 Aug 63)

**WITHDRAWAL SYMPTOMS,** the most wretched part of coming off hard drugs is the reaction called **withdrawal symptoms.** People go into convulsions. These are so severe that the addict becomes very afraid of them and so remains on drugs. The reaction can produce death. The theory is that withdrawal symptoms are muscular spasms. (HCOB 5 Nov 74)

**WITHHELD COGNITION,** see CUT COGNITION.

**WITHHOLD, 1.** a **withhold** is an unspoken, unannounced transgression against a moral code by which the person was bound.

# WITHHOLD OF OMISSION

(SH Spec 62, 6110C04) **2.** the unwillingness of the pc to talk to the auditor or tell him something. (SH Spec 108, 6202C01) **3.** a **withhold** is something that a person believes that if it is revealed it will endanger their self-preservation. (SH Spec 113, 6202C20) **4.** when the person should be reaching and is withdrawing that's a **withhold.** (SH Spec 98, 6201C10) **5.** a **withhold** is a **withhold** if it is a violation of the mores the pc has subscribed to and knows about. (SH Spec 75, 6111C02) **6.** a **withhold** is something the pc did that he isn't talking about. (SH Spec 206, 6211C01) **7.** a **withhold** is what the pc is **withholding** and it does not have to include what the pc considers is a **withhold.** (SH Spec 98, 6201C10) **8.** it is restraining self from communicating. (SH Spec 98, 6201C10) **9.** is always the manifestation which comes after an overt. Any **withhold** comes after an overt. (SH Spec 181, 6208C07)

**WITHHOLD OF OMISSION,** he should be reaching and he is not and that's just a **withhold of omission.** (SH Spec 98, 6201C10)

**WITHHOLDS LONG DURATION,** are spotted by a nattery, critical or hostile sort of life. The case would be anywhere from 2.2 on down to 1.0 on the tone scale. (LRH Def. Notes)

**WITHHOLD SYSTEM,** I have finally reduced clearing **withholds** to a rote formula which contains all the basic elements necessary to obtain a high case gain without missing any **withholds.** The **system** has five parts: (0) the difficulty being handled, (1) what the **withhold** is, (2) when the **withhold** occurred, (3) all of the **withhold,** (4) who should have known about it. (HCOB 12 Feb 62)

**WITHHOLDY CASE,** routinely ARC breaking and having to be patched up, commonly blows, has to have lots of hand-holding. (HCO PL 5 Apr 65 II)

**WITHHOLDY PC,** a **pc** who seems to have a lot of ARC breaks, the **pc** is a **withholdy pc** not an ARC breaky pc. Any auditor miss causes a pc blowup. If you call such a case that ARC breaks a lot a **"withholdy pc** that ARC breaks a lot" then you can solve the case, for all you have to do is work on **withholds.** (HCOB 4 Apr 65)

**WITH SCIENTOLOGY,** "interested in subject and getting it used." (HCOB 19 Aug 63)

**WOG, 1. worthy Oriental gentleman.** This means a common ordinary run-of-the-mill garden-variety humanoid. (SH Spec 82, 6611C29) **2. a wog** is somebody who isn't even trying. (SH Spec 73, 6608C02)

**WOOF AND WARP,** (rug terms; weaving). [Consult your regular dictionary for full description.] (SH Spec 46, 6411C10)

**WORD, 1.** a symbolic sound code of the physical universe in action or in static and refers to nothing more than a condition or lack of condition of being of the physical universe. **Words** are all physical universe because they are designed to go on a physical universe system. (5203CM07A) **2.** a **word** is a whole package of thought. (PRO 14, 5408C20) **3. words** are only symbols which represent actions. (*SA*, p. 63) **4. words** are sounds in syllabic form delivered with a definite timbre, pitch, and volume or sight recognition in each case. **Words** are a highly specialized form of audio-perceptics. The quality of the sound in uttering the **word** is nearly as important as the **word** itself. The written **word** belongs in part to visio-perceptics. (*DTOT*, p. 38)

**WORD CLEARER,** one who is qualified in and uses the technology of **word clearing.** (BTB 12 Apr 72R)

**WORD CLEARING (W/C),** a technique for locating and handling (**clearing**) misunderstood **words.** There are nine methods of **word clearing.** (BTB 12 Apr 72R)

**WORD CLEARING CORRECTION LIST (WCCL),** used to handle any upsets or high or low TA occurring during or shortly after **word clearing.** Assessed M5. EP is all reading items handled to F/N and pc again running well. (BTB 11 Aug 72RA)

**WORD CLEARING METHOD ONE, 1.** by meter in session. A full assessment of many, many subjects is done. The auditor then takes each reading subject and **clears** the chain back to earlier **words** and or **words** in earlier subjects until he gets an F/N. (HCOB 24 Jun 71) **2.** assess, take the reading items from the best read on down and with E/S pull each one to F/N. Get each word you find to F/N. There can be many F/Ns per subject. End off with a win on the subject. (HCOB 30 Jun 71RB II) **3.** the action taken to clean up all misunderstoods in every subject one has studied. It is done by a **word clearing** auditor. The result of a properly done **Method One word clearing** is the recovery of one's education. (*Aud 87 ASHO*) *Abbr.* M1.

**WORD CLEARING METHOD 2, 1.** by meter in classroom. The earlier passage is read by the student while on a meter and the misunderstood **word** is found. Then it is fully defined by dictionary. The **word** is then used several times in sentences of the student's own verbal composing. The misunderstood area is then reread until understood. (HCOB 24 Jun 71) **2. (M2)** means **word clearing Method 2.** A **method** of locating and handling misunderstood **words,** using a meter, in which the student reads aloud from written materials and each reading **word cleared.** (BTB 12 Apr 72R) **3. Method 2** is done with the pc reading the materials aloud and each reading **word** is taken to F/N before re-reading the relevant section and proceeding. (BTB 10 Oct 71R) *Abbr.* M2.

**WORD CLEARING METHOD 3, 1.** verbal in classroom. The student says he does not understand something. The supervisor has him look earlier in the text for a misunderstood **word,** gets the student to look it up, use it verbally several times in sentences of his own composition, then read the text that contained it. Then come forward in the text to the area of the subject he did not understand. (HCOB 24 Jun 71) **2.** a **method** of **word clearing** used in the classroom where the misunderstood **word** is located and handled without the use of a meter. In the study materials **M3** means only **word clearing Method 3.** (BTB 12 Apr 72R) *Abbr.* M3.

**WORD CLEARING METHOD 4, 1. Method 4** fishes for the misunderstood **word,** finds it, clears it to F/N, looks for another in the area until there are no more with an F/N VGIs. Then moves to another area, handles that, eventually all misunderstoods that resulted in the cramming order or non-F/N student are handled. (HCOB 22 Feb 72RA) **2.** a **method** of **word clearing** in which a meter is used to rapidly locate any misunderstoods in a subject or section of materials. It is used in the classroom by the course supervisor. (BTB 12 Apr 72R) *Abbr.* M4.

**WORD CLEARING METHOD 5,** a system wherein the **word clearer** feeds **words** to the person and has him define each. It is called material **clearing.** Those the person cannot define must be looked up. This **method** is the **method** used to **clear words** or auditing commands or auditing lists. (HCOB 21 Jun 72 I) *Abbr.* M5.

**WORD CLEARING METHOD 6,** is called key **word clearing.** It is used on posts and specific subjects. The **word clearer** makes a list of key (or most important) **words** relating to the person's duties or post or the new subject. The **word clearer** without showing the person the definitions, asks him to define each **word.** The **word clearer** checks the definition on his list for general correctness. Any slow or hesitancy or misdefinition is met with having the person look the **word** up. (HCOB 21 Jun 72 II) *Abbr.* M6.

**WORD CLEARING METHOD 7,** whenever one is working with children or foreign-language persons or semi-literates **Method 7** Reading Aloud is used. The procedure is have him read aloud. Note each omission or **word** change or hesitation or frown as he reads and take it up at once. Correct it by looking it up for him or explaining it to him. (HCOB 21 Jun 72 III) *Abbr.* M7.

**WORD CLEARING METHOD 8,** is an action used in the *Primary Rundown* where one is studying study tech or where one is seeking a full grasp of a subject. Its end product is super-literacy. Usually an alphabetical list of every **word** or term in the text of a paper, a chapter or a recorded tape is available or provided. The person looks up each **word** on the alphabetical list and uses each in sentences until he has the meaning concep-tually. (HCOB 21 Jun 72 IV) *Abbr.* M8.

**WORD CLEARING METHOD 9,** the procedure is: (1) student or staff member reads the text out loud. He is not on the meter. (2) the **word clearer** has a copy of the text and reads along with the student silently. (3) if the student leaves out a **word** or stumbles or exhibits any physical or verbal manifestation while reading the text, the **word clearer** immediately asks for the misunderstood **word** or term and gets the meanings **cleared** with a dictionary and put into sentences until the **word** is understood and VGIs are present. (BTB 30 Jan 73RA II) *Abbr.* M9.

**WORD LIST,** is simply a **list** of **words** taken from a body of data. A **word list** can be made for a tape lecture, a mimeo issue, a chapter of a book, etc. The **word list** contains all the **words listed** in alphabetical order. (BTB 6 Jan 74 III)

**WORK, 1. work,** in essence, is simply the handling of effort, the use of effort. (2ACC-30B, 5312CM21) **2.** play should be called "**work** without a purpose." It could also be called "activity without purpose." That would make **work** be defined as "activity with purpose." (*POW*, p. 32)

**WORKABILITY,** the capability of starting, changing and stopping. And the degree of capability of starting, changing and stopping would demonstrate for this universe, **workability.** (PDC 19)

**WORKSHEETS,** a **worksheet** is supposed to be the complete running record of the session from beginning to end. (HCOB 7 May 69 VI) *Abbr.* W/S.

**WORRIED,** means he is unable to unbalance the balance between yes and no. (PDC 15)

**WORRY, 1.** that's "Was it yes?" "Was it no?" "Was it yes?" "Was it no?" (5112CM30B) **2.** contradictory engram commands which cannot be computed. (*DMSMH,* p. 210)

**WORSENED GRAPH,** if the pc's **graph worsens,** the only thing that can **worsen** a pc in auditing, so that his **graph worsens,** markedly in processing is an ARC break. (SH Spec 56, 6503C30)

**WRAPPED AROUND A TELEGRAPH POLE,** *Slang.* the pc who has been so poorly audited that "auditing" has created a charged up condition on the case or the individual is so restimulated in his environment that the same condition occurs. In both cases the charge which has been restimulated causes the person to get **wrapped** up in his case resulting in severe upset and dispersal. Taken from U.S. West where a tangled up man in a confused condition was likened to a person, horse or cow who had run into **a telegraph pole** and gotten **wrapped around** it. It infers the situation or person needs to be untangled and straightened out. (LRH Def. Notes)

**WRONG,** that which was minimal survival for the minimal number, for the maximal number of dynamics, whichever way you want to look at it, was **wrong.** (PDC 15)

**WRONGNESS,** always miscalculation of effort. (*Scn 0-8*, p. 74)

**WRONG SOURCE,** in the R2-12 steps opposing a wrong item. (HCOB 3 Jan 63)

**WRONG WAY,** in Routine 2, listing the **wrong way** (using the **wrong** question) you get an endless list that never completes and won't null. You have only two list questions to use in opposing a reliable item. These are "Who or what would oppose a . . . ?" and "Who or what would a . . . oppose?" For *every* reliable item there is only one of the above that is right. The other is **wrong.** If it happens that you start listing the **wrong way** this is because you failed to find out correctly if the RI you were about to list an opposition list to was a terminal (pain) or an opposition terminal (sensation). The pc said he had sensation but actually felt pain. (HCOB 3 Jan 63)

**WRONG WAY OPPOSE,** in Routine 2 listing having the wording reversed such as "Who or what would **oppose** a catfish?" As different from "Who or what would a catfish **oppose?**" A **wrong way oppose** list is of course "wrong source" as one is using "catfish" as a terminal instead of "catfish" as an oppterm or vice versa. (HCOB 3 Jan 63)

**WRONG WHY,** the incorrectly identified outness which when applied does not lead to recovery. (HCO PL 13 Oct 70 II)

**W/S, worksheet.** (BTB 6 Nov 72R VII)

**W.S.U., withdrawal, stop, unmock.** (Class VIII, No. 19)

**W UNIT,** in 1962 a Saint Hill Special Briefing Course **unit** specializing in the theory of the usual beginning course fundamentals but only GF Model Session, including mid ruds, big mid ruds, and meter, TRs, havingness, and CCHs. Practical included TRs, meter, GF Model Session only, CCHs and assist. (HCO PL 8 Dec 62)

**WW, world wide.** (HCO PL 4 Mar 65)

**W/W WOULD, who** or **what would.** (HCOB 23 Nov 62)

# X

**X, 1.** it doesn't mean this didn't RS, it doesn't mean this didn't RR, it means this does not produce any reaction of any kind on the meter. (SH Spec 255, 6304C04) **2.** didn't read. (HCOB 29 Apr 69) **3.** experimental. (SH Spec 235, 6302C07)

**X1,** code number of a process. (BTB 20 Aug 71R II)

**X2,** code number of a process. (BTB 20 Aug 71R II)

**X UNIT,** in 1962 a Saint Hill Special Briefing Course **unit** with theory covering everything relative to R2-12, data on mid ruds, tiger drilling and big tiger. Practical was all R2-12 practical, any drills omitted in W unit, tiger drilling and big tiger. (HCO PL 8 Dec 62)

# Y

**YELLOW SHEET,** a **sheet** detailing each correction list or set of commands which have been word cleared. It also lists the pc's current havingness process and the type of cans the pc uses. (BTB 3 Nov 72R)

**YELLOW TAB,** a C/S must put a **yellow tab** marked PTS on a PTS pc folder that stays on until the person is no longer PTS. (HCOB 17 Apr 72)

**Y UNIT,** in 1962 a Saint Hill Special Briefing Course **unit** with theory covering everything relative to finding goals and clearing; 3GAXX, Routine 3-21 and HCOBs on wrong goals. Practical—all clearing practical, free needle etc. (HCO PL 8 Dec 62)

# Z

**ZERO,** the proper and correct definition of **zero** would be: "something which had no mass, which had no wave-length, which had no location in space, which had no position or relationship in time. Something without mass, meaning or mobility. (*Dn 55!,* p. 28)

**ZERO,** zero on the tone scale is equivalent to death. An individual with a **zero** tone would be dead. (*DTOT,* p. 59)

**ZERO** "written (0)", denotes an item which simply has the requirement of you reading, understanding and attesting in the space opposite the item, on the checksheet. Your initials in the space provided indicate that you have read, understood and can apply the data concerned. (HCO PL 13 Apr 71)

**ZERO A & ZERO B QUESTIONS,** prechecking. When you obtain a generality early on after the **zero question,** you make it a **zero A.** One asks the **zero A,** "Have you ever disconcerted your mother?" The needle reacts. The auditor fishes around for a specific other incident. Finally gets, "I used to lie to her." So the auditor writes a **zero B,** "Have you ever lied to your mother?" And then nags away at the pc until a specific time is recovered. When the **zero B** is clean, ask the **zero A.** (HCOB 21 Mar 62)

**ZERO QUESTION,** in prepchecking (prepclearing) one uses the whole subject to be cleared as the **zero question.** (HCOB 1 Mar 62) See SEC CHECK FORMS, these are **zero questions.** (HCOB 24 Jun 62)

**ZERO RATE,** material which is only checked out on the basis of general understanding. (HCOB 21 Sept 70)

**ZERO RATING (0-RATING), 1.** passed by proof of having read or listened to the material (such as notes or a general verbal statement of the subject which assures the theory examiner that the material has been covered). (HCO PL 15 Mar 63) **2.** read and listen to the data and understanding of. (HCO PL 26 Jan 72 V)

**ZOMBIE,** an electric shock or neuro-surgical case. (*DMSMH*, p. 286)

**Z UNIT,** in 1962 a Saint Hill Special Briefing Course **unit** with theory covering additional clearing data, form of the course and Scn plans. Practical was a review of drills and TRs. (HCO PL 8 Dec 62)

# The Tone Scale

| TONE SCALE EXPANDED | | KNOW TO MYSTERY SCALE |
|---|---|---|
| SERENITY OF BEINGNESS | 40.0 | KNOW |
| POSTULATES | 30.0 | NOT KNOW |
| GAMES | 22.0 | KNOW ABOUT |
| ACTION | 20.0 | LOOK |
| EXHILARATION | 8.0 | PLUS EMOTION |
| AESTHETIC | 6.0 | |
| ENTHUSIASM | 4.0 | |
| CHEERFULNESS | 3.5 | |
| STRONG INTEREST | 3.3 | |
| CONSERVATISM | 3.0 | |
| MILD INTEREST | 2.9 | |
| CONTENTED | 2.8 | |
| DISINTERESTED | 2.6 | |
| BOREDOM | 2.5 | |
| MONOTONY | 2.4 | |
| ANTAGONISM | 2.0 | MINUS EMOTION |
| HOSTILITY | 1.9 | |
| PAIN | 1.8 | |
| ANGER | 1.5 | |
| HATE | 1.4 | |
| RESENTMENT | 1.3 | |
| NO SYMPATHY | 1.2 | |
| UNEXPRESSED RESENTMENT | 1.15 | |
| COVERT HOSTILITY | 1.1 | |
| ANXIETY | 1.02 | |
| FEAR | 1.0 | |

| | | |
|---|---|---|
| DESPAIR | .98 | |
| TERROR | .96 | |
| NUMB | .94 | |
| SYMPATHY | .9 | |
| PROPITIATION — (*HIGHER TONED-* *SELECTIVELY GIVES*) | .8 | |
| GRIEF | .5 | |
| MAKING AMENDS — (*PROPITIATION* *—CAN'T W/H ANYTHING*) | .375 | |
| UNDESERVING | .3 | |
| SELF-ABASEMENT | .2 | |
| VICTIM | .1 | |
| HOPELESS | .07 | |
| APATHY | .05 | |
| USELESS | .03 | |
| DYING | .01 | |
| BODY DEATH | 0.0 | |
| FAILURE | 0.01 | |
| PITY | -0.1 | |
| *SHAME (BEING OTHER BODIES)* | -0.2 | |
| ACCOUNTABLE | -0.7 | |
| BLAME — (*PUNISHING OTHER* *BODIES*) | -1.0 | |
| *REGRET—(RESPONSIBILITY AS* *BLAME*) | -1.3 | |
| CONTROLLING BODIES | -1.5 | EFFORT |
| PROTECTING BODIES | -2.2 | |
| OWNING BODIES | -3.0 | THINK |
| APPROVAL FROM BODIES | -3.5 | |
| NEEDING BODIES | -4.0 | SYMBOLS |
| WORSHIPPING BODIES | -5.0 | EAT |
| SACRIFICE | -6.0 | SEX |
| HIDING | -8.0 | MYSTERY |
| BEING OBJECTS | -10.0 | WAIT |
| BEING NOTHING | -20.0 | UNCONSCIOUS |
| CAN'T HIDE | -30.0 | |
| TOTAL FAILURE | -40.0 | UNKNOWABLE |

L. Ron Hubbard
Founder

# The Reference Summary

Following is a summary of all the references mentioned at the end of each definition in this Dictionary. They are written out here in full. You will find these very useful as a means of locating additional information about a given word or subject in Dianetics and Scientology.

The Reference Summary provides another extremely useful service to the student. Data about almost any area of Dianetics or Scientology can be gotten by merely looking up the word or subject concerned in the Dictionary and consulting those references mentioned. This serves the purpose of a large technical cross index which can be of valuable service to all auditors, supervisors, cramming officers, case supervisors, and students alike.

The Reference Summary is laid out as follows. Appearing first is a full list of the Abbreviations that are used in the references at the end of each definition and in the Reference Summary itself.

Next is an explanation about the new and exciting *LRH Definition Notes* which are fully explained under the heading LRH Definition Notes later on.

Appearing next are full lists or explanations about the books, booklets, DABs, Journals and articles, magazines, PABs, etc. that were consulted for definitions.

You are firmly advised to consult the list of abbreviations in looking up any references in the Dictionary or Reference Summary in order to fully understand the Abbreviations used.

**The Editors**

# Abbreviations

The following comprise the abbreviations that are used in the reference summary and also appear at the end of each word defined in the dictionary.

**AAR,** *All About Radiation*

**Abil,** *Ability Magazine*

**Abil Ma,** *Ability Major Magazine*

**Abil Mi,** *Ability Minor Magazine*

**Abil SW,** *Ability Straightwire*

**ACC,** Advanced Clinical Course

**ACSA,** South African Anatomy Congress

**AHD,** *American Heritage Dictionary*

**AHMC,** Anatomy of the Human Mind Congress

**A&L,** *Axioms and Logics*

**AP&A,** *Advanced Procedures and Axioms*

**ASHO,** American Saint Hill Organization

**ASMC,** Anatomy of the Spirit of Man Congress

**AUD,** *The Auditor Magazine*

**AUD ASHO,** *Auditor Magazine American Saint Hill Organization*

**AUDC,** Auditors Conference

**AUD DK,** *Auditor Magazine Denmark*

**Audit,** auditing

**AUD Spec Iss,** *Auditor Magazine Special Issue*

**AUD UK,** *Auditor Magazine United Kingdom*

**B&C,** *Background and Ceremonies of the Founding Church*

**BCR,** *The Book of Case Remedies*

**BIEM,** *The Book Introducing The E-meter*

**BPL,** Board Policy Letter

**BTB,** Board Technical Bulletin

**C,** Copy (tape)

**C&A,** Certificates and Awards

**CDN,** *Child Dianetics*

**Cert,** *Certainty Magazine*

**CFC,** *Ceremonies of the Founding Church*

**CG&AC,** The Classification Gradation and Awareness Chart

**Cl.,** Class

**Class VIII No._____,** Class VIII tape number_____

**CM,** Copy Master (tape)

**CMSCS,** *Control and the Mechanics of Start Change Stop*

**COHA,** *The Creation of Human Ability*

**Confid,** Confidential

**DAB Vol. II,** *Dianetic Auditors Bulletin, Volume II*

**DASF,** *Dianometry Astounding Science Fiction*

**Dec Conf,** December Conference Lectures

**Def,** Definition

**DMSMH,** *Dianetics: The Modern Science of Mental Health*

**Dn 55!,** *Dianetics 55!*

**Dn Today,** *Dianetics Today*

**DPB,** *The Basic Dianetic Picture Book*

**DTOT,** *Dianetics: The Original Thesis*

**ED Flag,** Executive Directive Flag

**EMD,** *The Book of E-meter Drills*

**EME,** *E-meter Essentials*

**EOS,** *Dianetics: The Evolution of A Science*

**ESTO 3,** Establishment Officer Tape Three

**Exp Jour,** *The Explorer's Journal*

**FAO,** Flag Administration Organization

**FBDL,** Flag Bureaux Data Letter

**FC,** Freedom Congress

**FO,** Flag Order

**FOT,** *The Fundamentals of Thought*

**FSO,** Flag Ship Order

**GAH,** *Scientology: Group Auditors Handbook*

**GL,** Glossary

**Gloss,** Glossary

**HCL,** Hubbard College Lectures

**HCOB,** Hubbard Communications Office Bulletin

**HCO Info Ltr,** Hubbard Communications Office Information Letter

**HCO PL,** Hubbard Communications Office Policy Letter

**HCOTB,** Hubbard Communications Office Technical Bulletin

**HCOTRB,** Hubbard Communications Office Training Bulletin

**HEV,** Human Evaluation Course

**HFP,** *Handbook for Preclears*

**HOA,** *Hymn of Asia*

**HOM,** *History of Man*

**HPC,** Hubbard Professional Course Lectures

**HPC A6,** Hubbard Professional Course August 1956

**HYLBTL?,** *Have You Lived Before This Life?*

**HTLTAE,** *How To Live Though An Executive*

**IFR,** *Information For Releases*

**ISE,** *Introduction to Scientology Ethics*

**Iss,** Issue or Issued

**LACC,** London Advanced Clinical Course

**LPLS,** London Public Lecture Series

**LRH Def. Notes,** L. Ron Hubbard Definition Notes

**LRH ED INT,** L. Ron Hubbard Executive Directive International

**Mimeo,** Mimeograph or Mimeograph Issues

**MIT,** *Mission Into Time*

**No.,** number

**NOTL,** *Notes on The Lectures*

**NSOL,** *Scientology A New Slant On Life*

**Oct Ser,** October Series

**OODs,** Orders of the Day of the Flagship Apollo

**Op Bull,** Operational Bulletin

**OS,** Organizational Series

**PAB,** Professional Auditors Bulletin

**PDC,** Philadelphia Doctorate Course

**PIP,** Printed Intensive Procedure Lectures

**PLS,** Public Lecture Series

**POW,** *The Problems of Work*

**PRD Gloss,** *Special Primary Rundown Glossary*

**PRO,** Professional Course

**PXL,** *The Phoenix Lectures*

**Reiss,** Reissued

**Rev,** Revised

**Ron's Jour 68,** Ron's Journal 1968 (tape)

**SA,** *Self Analysis*

**SC,** Success Congress

**Scn AD,** *Scientology Abridged Dictionary*

**Scn 0-8,** *Scientology 0-8*

**Scn 8-80,** *Scientology 8-80*

**Scn 8-8008,** *Scientology 8-8008*

**Scn Jour,** *Journal of Scientology*

**SCP,** *Scientology Clear Procedure*

**SH ACC,** Saint Hill Advanced Clinical Course

**SHPA,** Special Hubbard Professional Auditors Course (London)

**SH Spec,** Saint Hill Special

**SH TVD,** Saint Hill Television Demonstration

**SLP,** Six Levels of Processing

**SMC,** State of Man Congress

**SO,** Sea Organization

**SOED INT,** Sea Organization Executive Directive International

**SOS,** *Science of Survival*

**SPB,** *The Basic Scientology Picture Book*

**Spec Lect,** Special Lecture

**Spr Lect,** London Spring Lectures

**STCR,** *Scientology Twentieth Century Religion*

**STP,** Standard Procedure Lectures

**Sup,** Supplement or Supplementary Lecture

**T 80,** Technique 80 Lectures

**T 88,** Technique 88 Lectures

**TIP,** Technical Individual Program

**TVD,** Television Demonstration

**UPC,** Universe Process Congress

**U.S.,** United States

**Vol.,** Volume

**WW,** World Wide

**XDN No. 1,** Expanded Dianetics Tape Number One

**I, II, III,** Issue 1, 2 or 3, etc.

# LRH Definition Notes

Many of the LRH Definition Notes have been especially defined by Ron for thi dictionary to clear up terms frequently misunderstood by students and auditors alike.

Some are notes written by Ron to auditors in response to queries about definition during the training of Class VI and VIII auditors aboard Flag in 1968 and 1969.

# Books

*Advanced Procedure and Axioms* by L. Ron Hubbard. The American Saint Hil Organization, Los Angeles, California, First Hard Cover Edition, 1971.

*All About Radiation* by L. Ron Hubbard. The Publications Organization World Wide East Grinstead, Sussex, England, 1967.

*A History of Man* by L. Ron Hubbard. The Hubbard Communications Office Limited World Wide, East Grinstead, Sussex, England, Fifth Edition, 1965.

*Background and Ceremonies* by L. Ron Hubbard. The Church of Scientology o California, Los Angeles, California, 1972.

*Dianetics, The Evolution of A Science* by L. Ron Hubbard. Hubbard College o Scientology, East Grinstead, Sussex, England, 1967.

*Dianetics 55!* by L. Ron Hubbard. The Department of Publications World Wide, Sixth Edition, 1968.

*Dianetics: The Modern Science of Mental Health* by L. Ron Hubbard. The Publications Organization World Wide, East Grinstead, Sussex, England Fifteenth Printing, May 1968.

*Dianetics: The Original Thesis* by L. Ron Hubbard. Scientology Publications Organiza tion, Copenhagen, Denmark, 1970.

*Dianetics Today* by L. Ron Hubbard. The Church of Scientology of California Publications Organization United States, Los Angeles, California, First Printing 1975.

*Handbook for Preclears* by L. Ron Hubbard. The Publications Organization World Wide, Edinburgh, Scotland, Fifth Edition 1968.

*Have You Lived Before This Life?* by L. Ron Hubbard. The American Saint Hil Organization, Los Angeles, California, Reprinted April 1971.

*How To Live Though An Executive* by L. Ron Hubbard. The Hubbard College of Scientology, East Grinstead, Sussex, England, Third Edition 1965, Reprinted 1967.

*Hymn of Asia* by L. Ron Hubbard. The Church of Scientology of California Publications Organization United States, Los Angeles, California, First Printing 1974.

*Introduction to Scientology Ethics* by L. Ron Hubbard. The American Saint Hill Organization, Los Angeles, California, Third Edition 1970.

*Mission Into Time* by L. Ron Hubbard. The American Saint Hill Organization, Los Angeles, California, First Printing 1973.

*Notes on The Lectures* by L. Ron Hubbard. The American Saint Hill Organization, Los Angeles, California, Sixth Edition, 1968.

*Ole Doc Methuselah* by L. Ron Hubbard. Daw Books Inc., New York, New York, 1970.

*Science of Survival* by L. Ron Hubbard. The Hubbard Communications Office, East Grinstead, Sussex, England, Ninth Printing January 1964.

*Scientology A New Slant On Life* by L. Ron Hubbard. The Hubbard College of Scientology, East Grinstead, Sussex, England, Reprinted May 1966.

*Scientology: Group Auditors Handbook,* taken from the works of L. Ron Hubbard, The Hubbard Association of Scientologists International, Phoenix, Arizona, USA, 1954.

*Scientology Twentieth Century Religion,* The Church of Scientology World Wide, 1972.

*Scientology 0-8* by L. Ron Hubbard. Scientology Publications Organization, Copenhagen, Denmark, First Edition 1970.

*Scientology 8-80* by L. Ron Hubbard. The American Saint Hill Organization, Los Angeles, California, Reprinted 1971.

*Scientology 8-8008* by L. Ron Hubbard. The Publications Organization World Wide, Edinburgh, Scotland, Seventh Edition 1967.

*Self Analysis* by L. Ron Hubbard. The Publications Organization World Wide, Edinburgh, Scotland, First Hard Cover Edition 1968.

*The Creation of Human Ability* by L. Ron Hubbard. The Publications Organization World Wide, East Grinstead, Sussex, England, Reprinted 1968.

*The Fundamentals of Thought* by L. Ron Hubbard. The American Saint Hill Organization, Los Angeles, California, 12th Printing 1973.

*The Phoenix Lectures* by L. Ron Hubbard. The Publications Organization World Wide, Edinburgh, Scotland, First Edition 1968.

*The Problems of Work* by L. Ron Hubbard. The Publications Department A/S, Copenhagen, Denmark, 11th Printing September 1972.

# Booklets

*Axioms and Logics* by L. Ron Hubbard. The Publications Organization World Wide, East Grinstead, Sussex, England, 1967.

*Control and The Mechanics of S.C.S.* by L. Ron Hubbard. The Hubbard College of Scientology, East Grinstead, Sussex, England, 1967.

*Education and The Auditor* by L. Ron Hubbard. The Hubbard Dianetic Foundation Inc., Wichita, Kansas, 1951.

*E-meter Essentials* by L. Ron Hubbard. The Hubbard College of Scientology, East Grinstead, Sussex, England, Third Printing, 1967.

*Information For Releases,* taken from the works of L. Ron Hubbard. The Hubbard College of Scientology, 1967.

*Scientology Abridged Dictionary,* taken from the works of L. Ron Hubbard. The American Saint Hill Organization, Los Angeles, California, Tenth Printing, April 1973.

*Scientology: Clear Procedure Issue One* by L. Ron Hubbard. The Department of Publications World Wide, East Grinstead, Sussex, England, 1968.

*Special Primary Rundown Glossary,* Flag Publications, 1972.

*The Basic Dianetics Picture Book I,* taken from the works of L. Ron Hubbard. The American Saint Hill Organization, Los Angeles, California, Second Printing, January 1973.

*The Basic Scientology Picture Book, Vol. I,* taken from the works of L. Ron Hubbard. The American Saint Hill Organization, Los Angeles, California, Second Printing May 1972.

*The Book Introducing The E-meter* by L. Ron Hubbard. The Publications Organization World Wide, Edinburgh, Scotland, 1968.

*The Book of Case Remedies* by L. Ron Hubbard. The Department of Publications World Wide, East Grinstead, Sussex, England, 1968.

*The Book of E-meter Drills* by L. Ron Hubbard. The Publications Organization World Wide, East Grinstead, Sussex, England, 1968.

494

# Dianetic Auditor Bulletins

The Dianetic Auditors Bulletins were published as an information source on Dianetic development and research by the former Dianetic Research Foundation, Wichita, Kansas, USA.

*A Brief History of Psychotherapy* by L. Ron Hubbard. *The Dianetic Auditors Bulletins,* Vol. II, pages 147-149, July 1951-June 1952.

*An Essay on Authoritarianism* by L. Ron Hubbard. *The Dianetic Auditors Bulletins,* Vol. II, pages 132-146, July 1951-June 1952.

*Basic Reason—Basic Principles* by L. Ron Hubbard. *The Dianetic Auditors Bulletins,* Vol. II, pages 67-83, July 1951-June 1952.

*Cause and Effect* by L. Ron Hubbard. *The Dianetic Auditors Bulletins,* Vol. II, pages 228-239, July 1951-June 1952.

*Education and The Auditor* by L. Ron Hubbard. *The Dianetic Auditors Bulletins,* Vol. II, pages 3-53, July 1951-June 1952.

*Postulate Processing* by L. Ron Hubbard. *The Dianetic Auditors Bulletins,* Vol. II, pages 164-173, July 1951-June 1952.

*Self-Determined Effort Processing* by L. Ron Hubbard. *The Dianetic Auditors Bulletins,* Vol. II, pages 99-105, July 1951-June 1952.

# Articles and Scientology Journals

*Dianometry, Your Ability and State of Mind* by L. Ron Hubbard. *Astounding Science Fiction,* Vol. XLVI No. 5, pages 76-100, January 1951.

*Terra Incognita: The Mind* by L. Ron Hubbard. *The Explorers Journal,* Vol. XXVIII No. 1, Winter-Spring 1950.

*Journal of Scientology,* articles by L. Ron Hubbard. The Hubbard Association of Scientologists, Phoenix, Arizona, Issues 1G-43G, September 1952 to December 1954.

# Magazines

*Ability Magazine* is the official publication of Dianetics and Scientology in the Eastern United States. Published by the Hubbard Scientology Organization in Washington, D.C. *Ability Straightwire* was part of the *Ability* magazine series numbered *Ability Major 5, 1955.*

*The Auditor.* This is the monthly journal of Scientology. These are noted in the reference as to whether they are United Kingdom, Publications Organization Denmark or American Saint Hill Organization Issues.

*Certainty Magazine* is the official periodical of Dianetics and Scientology in the British Isles.

*Reality Magazine* is the official publication of the Church of Scientology of Los Angeles.

# Professional Auditor Bulletins

*Professional Auditor's Bulletins* by L. Ron Hubbard. The Publications Department Advanced Organization Saint Hill, Copenhagen, Denmark, 1973, Nos. 1-160, May 1953 to May 1959.

# Hubbard Communications Office Bulletins
## (also Board Technical Bulletins)

| | |
|---|---|
| 14 Jul 56 | A Rule Has Showed Up . . . |
| 20 Aug 56 | HGC Procedure of August 20 |
| 3 Sept 56 | Briefing Bulletin Staff and Seminar Leaders Games Congress, Shoreham Hotel 31 Aug-3 Sept 56 |
| HCOTB 12 Sept 56 | Executives in Washington and London . . . |
| 4 Oct 56 | High School Indoctrination |
| 26 Oct 56 | HPA-HCA Training Processes |
| HCOTB 6 Feb 57 | The following procedure . . . |
| 10 Apr 57 | To: Director of Training The HPA/HCA Full Course Must Teach Entirely . . . |
| 3 May 57 | Training—What It Is Today How We Tell People About It |
| 8 Jun 57 | The Teaching of the 18th ACC |

506

| 9 Oct 71RA<br>Issue II<br>Revised<br>21 Jul 73<br>Revised & Reissued<br>29 Jul 74 as BTB | Auditors Drills Series No. 2<br>Level 0 Process Drills |

9 Oct 71RA
Issue III
Revised & Reissued
10 Jun 74 as BTB
Revised
21 Feb 75

Auditor Drills Series No. 3RA
Level 1 Process Drills

BTB 9 Oct 71R
Issue VII
Revised
28 Mar 74

Auditor Drills Series No. 7
Drills for Auditor
Dianetic Drills

10 Oct 71R
Revised & Reissued
31 Jul 74 as BTB

Word Clearing Series 28R
Tech Points on a Word Clearing Festival

22 Oct 71
Reissued
19 Sept 74

Exteriorization

23 Oct 71R
Issue V
Revised & Reissued
28 Jul 74 as BTB

Personnel Programming Series 6R
Personnel Programmer Ethics
Intervention Rights

24 Oct 71

False TA

25 Oct 71R
Issue II
Revised
26 Aug 72
Revised
30 Jun 74
Reissued
29 Aug 74 as BTB

The Special Drug Rundown

29 Oct 71R
Revised
14 May 74

Int RD Correction List Revised

30 Oct 71

Triple Grades vs. Expanded

| | |
|---|---|
| 20 Nov 71<br>Revised<br>24 Mar 72 | HAS Specialist and Establishment Officer<br>Auditing Program (Revised) |
| 21 Nov 71<br>Issue I | Important — Tape Course Series No. 2<br>Dianetics and Scientology in Other Languages |
| 22 Nov 71 Issue II<br>Reissued<br>11 Aug 74 as BTB | Tape Course Series No. 5<br>Tape Players — Description and Care |
| 24 Nov 71<br>Issue II<br>Reissued<br>3 Jul 74 as BTB | Tape Course Series No. 7<br>Course Materials |
| 25 Nov 71<br>Issue II<br>Reissued<br>21 Sept 74 | Resistive Cases Former Therapy |
| 26 Nov 71<br>Issue III<br>Reissued<br>9 Sept 74 as BTB | Out of Valence — 220H |
| 1 Dec 71R<br>Issue IV<br>Revised & Reissued<br>24 Jul 74 as BTB | Effort Processing |
| 1 Dec 71RB<br>Issue II<br>Revised<br>6 Jan 75 | Triple Ruds Long Duration |
| 4 Dec 71R<br>Issue I<br>Revised & Reissued<br>5 Aug 74 as BTB | R-1C |
| 9 Dec 71RA<br>Revised<br>21 Oct 74 | PTS Rundown |
| 12 Dec 71R<br>Revised & Reissued<br>1 Aug 74 as BTB | C/S Series No. 69R<br>Mandatory C/Sing Checklist |

| | |
|---|---|
| 30 Mar 72<br>Revised<br>30 May 72 | The Primary Correction Rundown Revised |
| 2 Apr 72RB<br>Issue II<br>Revised<br>17 Mar 74 | Expanded Dianetics Series No. 3RB<br>L3EXD RB—Expanded Dianetics Repair List |
| 4 Apr 72<br>Revised<br>30 May 72 | Primary Rundown Revised |
| 7 Apr 72R<br>Revised & Reissued<br>23 Jun 74 as BTB | Touch Assists Correct Ones |
| 10 Apr 72 | C/S Series No. 75<br>Solo C/S Series No. 13<br>Pre-OTs Don't C/S |
| BTB<br>10 Apr 72R<br>Revised<br>17 Nov 74 | Prepchecks |
| 12 Apr 72R<br>Revised & Reissued<br>6 Sept 74 as BTB | Further Definitions of Scn Terms Contained in the<br>Student Hat and Not Elsewhere Defined |
| 15 Apr 72<br>Revised Issue of<br>31 Mar 72 | Expanded Dianetics Series No. 1R |
| 17 Apr 72 | C/S Series No. 76<br>C/Sing a PTS Rundown |
| 19 Apr 72 | Quickie Defined |
| 20 Apr 72 | Expanded Dianetics Series No. 4<br>Suppressed PCs and PTS Tech |
| 20 Apr 72<br>Issue II | C/S Series No. 78<br>Product, Purpose and Why and WC Error Correction |
| 26 Apr 72 | Study Series No. 8<br>The Glib Student |

| | |
|---|---|
| 2 May 72R<br>Revised & Reissued<br>10 Jun 74 as BTB | Clearing Commands |
| 10 May 72 | Robotism |
| 3 Jun 72R<br>Revised<br>15 Oct 74 | PTS Rundown, Final Step |
| 10 Jun 72<br>Issue I<br>Reissued<br>21 Sept 74 | By-passed Charge |
| 15 Jun 72 | C/S Series No. 80<br>"Dog PCs" |
| 19 Jun 72 | Word Clearing Series No. 37<br>Dinky Dictionaries |
| 21 Jun 72<br>Issue I | Word Clearing Series No. 38<br>Method 5 |
| 21 Jun 72<br>Issue II | Word Clearing Series 39<br>Method 6 |
| 21 Jun 72<br>Issue III | Word Clearing Series No. 40<br>Method 7 |
| 21 Jun 72<br>Issue IV | Word Clearing Series No. 41<br>Method 8 |
| 20 Jul 72<br>Issue I | Primary Correction Rundown Handling |
| 20 Jul 72<br>Issue II | Distractive and Additive Questions and Orders |
| 11 Aug 72RA<br>Revised<br>18 Sept 74 as BTB | C/S Series No. 83RA<br>Correction Lists |
| 30 Aug 72<br>Issue I<br>Issued<br>28 Mar 74 as BTB | Expanded Dianetics Series No. 8 |

| | |
|---|---|
| 30 Aug 72<br>Issue II<br>Issued<br>28 Mar 74 as BTB | Expanded Dianetics Series 9 |
| 2 Sept 72R<br>Revised & Reissued<br>27 Jun 74 as BTB | Why Finding Drill — One |
| 2 Sept 72<br>Issue II<br>Reissued<br>23 Aug 74 as BTB | Why Finding Drill — Two |
| 2 Sept 72R<br>Issue III<br>Revised & Reissued<br>27 Nov 74 as BTB | Cramming Series 10<br>Good Cramming is the Key to<br>Flubless Auditors and Auditing |
| 5 Sept 72RA<br>Revised & Reissued<br>20 Aug 74 as BTB<br>Revised<br>25 Nov 74 | Cramming Series No. 11RA<br>High Crime Checkouts |
| 18 Sept 72<br>Issued<br>28 Mar 74 as BTB | Expanded Dianetics Series 10 |
| 14 Oct 72R<br>Revises<br>31 Aug 72R | Confidential<br>Modern Sec Checking (Confessional) Procedure-R |
| 22 Oct 72<br>Reissued<br>28 Mar 74 as BTB | Expanded Dianetics Series 14 |
| 24 Oct 72<br>Issued<br>28 Mar 74 as BTB | Expanded Dianetics Series 15<br>Expanded Dianetics Case I |
| 1 Nov 72<br>Issued<br>28 Mar 74 as BTB | Expanded Dianetics Series 19<br>Expanded Dianetics Case M |

| | |
|---|---|
| 3 Nov 72R<br>Reissued<br>18 Sept 74 as BTB<br>Revised<br>7 Feb 73 | Auditor Admin Series 3R<br>The PC Folder and its Contents |
| 5 Nov 72R<br>Issue III<br>Revised & Reissued<br>9 Sept 74 as BTB | Auditor Admin Series 7R<br>The Folder Summary |
| 5 Nov 72<br>Issue IV<br>Reissued<br>2 Jul 74 as BTB | Auditor Admin Series 8<br>OCA Graphs |
| 6 Nov 72R<br>Issue II<br>Revised & Reissued<br>15 Jul 74 as BTB | Auditor Admin Series 9R<br>The Program Sheet |
| 6 Nov 72RA<br>Issue IV<br>Revised & Reissued<br>30 Aug 74 as BTB<br>Revised<br>20 Nov 74 | Auditor Admin Series 11RA<br>The Exam Report |
| 6 Nov 72R<br>Issue VI<br>Revised & Reissued<br>27 Aug 74 as BTB | Auditor Admin Series 13R<br>The Auditor Report Form |
| 6 Nov 72R<br>Issue VII<br>Revised & Reissued<br>25 Jul 74 | Auditor Admin Series 14R<br>The Worksheets |
| 7 Nov 72R<br>Issue I<br>Revised & Reissued<br>12 Aug 74 as BTB | Auditor Admin Series 16R<br>Correction Lists |
| 7 Nov 72R<br>Issue III<br>Revised & Reissued<br>28 Jul 74 as BTB | Auditor Admin Series 18R<br>L & N Lists |

| | |
|---|---|
| 7 Nov 72R<br>Issue IV<br>Revised & Reissued<br>27 Jul 74 as BTB | Auditor Admin Series 19R<br>Dianetic Assessment Lists |
| 8 Nov 72R<br>Issue I<br>Revised & Reissued<br>6 Aug 74 as BTB | Auditor Admin Series 21R<br>The Dianetic Flow Table |
| 8 Nov 72R<br>Issue II<br>Revised & Reissued<br>9 Sept 74 as BTB<br>Issue II | Auditor Admin Series 22R<br>Folder Error Summaries |
| 15 Nov 72<br>Issue II | Students Who Succeed |
| 4 Dec 72<br>Reissued<br>3 Jul 74 as BTB | Integrity Processing Series 1<br>Historical |
| 6 Dec 72R<br>Revised & Reissued<br>23 Aug 74 as BTB | Integrity Processing Series 3R<br>Hi-Lo TA Assessment for Integrity<br>Processing and Confessionals |
| 7 Dec 72R<br>Revised & Reissued<br>9 Jul 74 as BTB<br>Revised 1 Dec 74 | Integrity Processing Series 4R<br>Mid-Integrity Processing Short Assessment |
| 11 Dec 72R<br>Revised<br>12 Feb 73<br>Reissued<br>11 Jul 74 as BTB | Integrity Processing Series 8R<br>The Tech and Ethics of Integrity Processing |
| 13 Dec 72R<br>Revised & Reissued<br>1 Nov 74 | Integrity Processing Series 10R<br>Integrity Processing Questions<br>Must be F/Ned |
| 18 Dec 72<br>Reissued<br>9 Jul 74 as BTB | Integrity Processing Series 15<br>Aspects of Integrity Processing |
| 4 Jan 73<br>Reissued<br>6 Apr 74 | Study Series No. 9<br>Confront |

| | |
|---|---|
| 6 Jan 74 | Assist Summary Addition |
| BTB<br>6 Jan 74<br>Issue II | Hobson-Jobsoning in Tape Translations |
| BTB<br>6 Jan 74<br>Issue III | Word Lists, How to Do |
| 23 Jan 74RA<br>Revised<br>1 Nov 74 | The Technical Breakthrough of 1973!<br>The Introspection Rundown |
| 15 Feb 74<br>Amended &<br>Reissued<br>28 Mar 74 | Expanded Dianetics Series No. 20<br>Service Facsimile Theory and Expanded Dianetics |
| 17 Feb 74 | C/S Series 91<br>Mutual Out Ruds |
| 17 Mar 74 | TWC Checksheets<br>TWC, Using Wrong Questions |
| 28 Mar 74 | Expanded Dianetics Series No. 21<br>Expanded Dianetics Developments Since the Original Lectures |
| BTB<br>11 Apr 74 | ARC Break Handling |
| BTB<br>20 Jul 74 | Auditor Expertise Drills Series No. 1<br>Basic Auditing Drills |
| 31 Aug 74 | Urgent — C/S Series No. 93<br>New Grade Chart |
| 7 Sept 74 | Word Clearing Series No. 53<br>Superliteracy and the Cleared Word |
| 15 Oct 74 | Cramming Series 25<br>Cramming Over Out Ruds |
| 1 Nov 74R | Rock Slams and Rock Slammers |
| 5 Nov 74 | Drugs, More About |
| 8 Dec 74 | TR0 — Notes on Blinking |
| 13 Mar 75 | TRs Training Breakthrough |
| BTB<br>13 Mar 75 | Alternate Clear Sheet |

527

# Hubbard Communications Office Policy Letters

528

| | |
|---|---|
| 29 Aug 71<br>Corrected &<br>Reissued<br>14 Oct 71 | Urgent — Org Conditions<br>Stat Change — Important |
| 20 Oct 71 | Selling Intensives |
| 21 Oct 71<br>Revised & Reissued<br>22 Apr 72 | HQS Course Checksheet |
| 29 Oct 71<br>Issue III | Executive Series No. 2 Leadership |
| 23 Nov 71R<br>Issue II<br>Revised<br>18 Dec 71 | Tech Div Gross Divisional Statistics Clarification |
| 4 Dec 71<br>Issue V | Rules for Student Auditors |
| 8 Jan 72<br>Issue I | Inspection and Report Forms One |
| 26 Jan 72<br>Issue V | Scientology Level I Standard Academy Checksheet |
| 2 Feb 72<br>Issue II<br>Cancelled<br>26 Aug 72 | Mini Technical Division — 4 Stage<br>Two Org Board Cancelled |
| 16 Feb 72 | The Purpose of the Department<br>of Personal Enhancement |
| 18 Feb 72 | Executive Series No. 8 — The Top Triangle |
| 22 Feb 72 | Interneship Errors Found |
| 29 Feb 72<br>Issue II | Data Series No. 24<br>Handling, Policy, Plans, Programs, Projects and<br>Orders Defined |
| 7 Mar 72<br>Revised<br>13 Apr 72 | Establishment Officer Series No. 1R |
| 16 Mar 72<br>Issue V | High Crime — What Is A Course |
| 4 Apr 72 | Establishment Officer Series 14 — Ethics |
| 5 Apr 72<br>Issue I | PTS Type A Handling |

532

| | | |
|---|---|---|
| 14 Jan 74R<br>Issue I<br>Revised 27 Sept 74 as a BPL | | New Issues |
| BPL 9 Mar 74 | | Understanding Corporate Integrity<br>(HCO PL 23 Apr 73 Issue III Revised and Reissued<br>as a Board Policy Letter) |
| 17 Mar 74 | | Press Conferences, Preparation For |
| 13 Jul 74<br>Issue II | | Org Series 34<br>Working Installations |
| 31 Aug 74<br>Issue II | | Urgent - Important<br>Fast Flow Training Reinstated |
| BPL 13 Apr 75 | | Technical Training Corps |

# LRH Tape Recorded Lectures

**1950**

| | | |
|---|---|---|
| 5008C30 | LECT | Preventive Dianetics |
| 5009C23 | LECT | General Dianetics — Part 1 |
| 5009C23 | LECT | General Dianetics — Part 2 |
| 5009CM23A | LECT | Introduction to Dianetics |
| 5009CM23B | LECT | What Dianetics Can Do |
| 5009CM28 | LECT | Stalled Cases |
| 5011C22 | STP | Auditor's Code and Accessibility |
| 5011CM25 | LECT | ARC and Four Dynamics |
| 5011CM30 | LECT | Standard Procedure (Step 3) |

**1951**

| | | |
|---|---|---|
| 5108CM13A | HEV-2 | Human Evaluation — Lect 2 |
| 5108CM13B | HEV-3 | Human Evaluation — Lect 3 |
| 5109CM17A | LECT | Some Notes on Black Dianetics |
| 5109CM17B | LECT | The Cellular Postulate |
| 5109CM24A | OCTSER | Effort Processing Definition of Effort |
| 5109CM24B | OCTSER | Effort Processing |
| 5110CM01 | OCTSER | Self-Determinism — Effort Processing |

| | | |
|---|---|---|
| 5110CM08A | OCTSER | Effort Processing by LRH |
| 5110CM08B | OCTSER | Axioms & Effort Processing |
| 5110CM11A | OCTSER | Dianetic Axioms 33 to 51 |
| 5110CM11B | OCTSER | Theory of Epicenters — Self-Determinism |
| 5112CM28A | DEC CONF | Chart of Attitudes |
| 5112CM28B | DEC CONF | Life Continuum Theory |
| 5112CM29A | DEC CONF | The Goal of Processing (The Ideal State of Man) Part 1 Lecture 3 |
| 5112CM29B | DEC CONF | The Goal of Processing (The Ideal State of Man) Part 2 Lecture 3 |
| 5112CM30A | DEC CONF | Effort Processing — Notes on Children's Illnesses |
| 5112CM30B | DEC CONF | Processing Yes-No-Maybe Remarks |

**1952**

| | | |
|---|---|---|
| 5202C25 | HPC-1 | Review of Progress of Dianetics and Dianetics Business |
| 5203CM03A | HCL-1 | Introduction to Scientology — Milestone 1 |
| 5203CM03B | HCL-2 | Introduction to Scientology — Outline of Therapy |
| 5203CM03C | HCL-2A | Demonstration by Ron of E-meter, Running Entities |
| 5203CM04A | HCL-3 | Axioms (Intention) |
| 5203CM04B | HCL-4 | Thought, Emotion, Effort |
| 5203CM05A | HCL-5 | Thought and Preclears |
| 5203CM05B | HCL-6 | Emotion |
| 5203CM05D | HCL-6 Spec | Demonstration of Auditing |
| 5203CM06A | HCL-7 | Effort and Counter-Effort |
| 5203CM06B | HCL-8 | Attack on the Preclear |
| 5203CM07A | HCL-9 | How to Handle Facsimiles |
| 5203CM07B | HCL-10 | Indoctrination of the Preclear |
| 5203CM08 | HCL-11 | Resolution of Effort and Counter-Effort, Overt Acts |

| | | |
|---|---|---|
| 5203CM08A | HCL-12 | Indoctrination in use of E-meter (Parts 1 and 2) |
| 5203CM09A | HCL-13 | Thought, Emotion, and Effort, Counter-Effort |
| 5203CM09B | HCL-14 | Demonstration—Effort, Counter-Effort Straightwire |
| 5203CM10A | HCL-15 | Training Auditors; The Anatomy of Facsimile One |
| 5203CM10C | HCL-17 | Demo of New Method of Running Effort and Counter-Effort |
| 5203CM10 | HCL-18 | Entities (Demo cont'd) |
| 5203CM10A | HCL-19 | History of Man—Series 1—2 |
| 5203CM10B | HCL-20 | History of Man Series 3A |
| 5203CM——   | HCL-23 | Theta Body |
| 5203CM——   | HCL-25 | An Analyses of Memory Part 1 |
| 5203CM——A  | HCL-27 | How to Search for Incidents on the Track |
| 5203CM——B  | HCL-27A | How to Search for Incidents on the Track |
| 5205C20 | T-80-2A | Decision: Maybes, Time, Postulates, Cause and Effect in Relation to Dynamics |
| 5206CM23A | T88-1 | Thetan/Body, Anatomy of Maybe, The Time Scale, Decision to be "Course Outline," Disentangling Body from Thetan, Wide Open and Occluded Cases, What are Entities |
| 5206CM23B | T88-2 | Matter, Solid Thought, Home Universe Theory and Origin of Mest, Erasing. Law on Time Scale, Incidents, Space and Time, Restimulation, Forgetting, Emotional Curve, Identity, Auditing |
| 5206CM23C | T88-3 | Mechanics of Aberration, Tone Scale and Maybe, Axioms, Effort, Nowness and Thenness, Axioms of Knowingness, Pervasion, Q & A |
| 5206CM24A | T88-4 | Motions and Maybes, Attention Unit Flows, Glares, Hypnosis, Control, Shock |

536

| | | |
|---|---|---|
| 5212C17 | PDC-55 | Demonstration on Step One (cont'd) |
| 5212C17 | PDC-56 | Discussion of Demo: Above Agreement with Flows |
| 5212C17 | PDC-57 | Continued Demonstration Step 4 |
| 5212C18 | PDC-58 | About the Press' Tone Level: Psychometry |
| 5212C18 | PDC-59 | Chart of Havingness |
| 5212C18 | PDC-60 | How to Talk about Scientology |
| 5212C18 | PDC-61 | How to Talk to Friends about Scientology |
| 5212C18 | PDC-62 | Your Own Case: to You the Student |

**1953**

| | | |
|---|---|---|
| 5303CM23 | SPR LECT 1 | Review of Dianetics, Scientology and Para-Dianetics/Scientology |
| 5303CM23 | SPR LECT 2 | What's Wrong with the PC? |
| 5303CM24 | SPR LECT 3 | Steps 1-7 SOP Issue 5 |
| 5303CM24 | SPR LECT 4 | SOP Issues (cont'd) |
| 5303CM25 | SPR LECT 5 | The Elements with Stress on How to Run Matched Terminals |
| 5303CM25 | SPR LECT 6 | The Elements with Stress on How to Run Matched Terminals |
| 5303CM26 | SPR LECT 7 | How and When to Audit |
| 5303CM26 | SPR LECT 8 | Present Time |
| 5303CM27 | SPR LECT 9 | SOP Utility |
| 5303CM27 | SPR LECT 10 | SOP Utility (cont'd) |
| 5304CM07 | SPR LECT 13 | Data on Case Level 5 |
| 5304CM07 | SPR LECT 14 | More on Case Level 5 |
| 5304CM07 | SPR LECT 15 | Exteriorization — Demo and Explanation |
| 5304CM07 | SPR LECT 16 | Demonstration (cont'd) |
| 5304CM08 | SPR LECT 17 | Case Level 6 and 7 |
| 5304CM08 | SPR LECT 18 | Case Level 6 and 7 (cont'd) Psychotic |
| 5311CM17A | 2ACC-1A | Opening Lecture — Emotional Tone Scale |

| | | |
|---|---|---|
| 5312CM16 | 2ACC-24B | Technique to Assign Cause |
| 5312CM16 | 2ACC-25A | Comm Lines, Overt Act Motivator Sequence |
| 5312CM17 | 2ACC-25B | SOP 8-C Formulas |
| 5312CM17 | 2ACC-26A | The Only One |
| 5312CM18 | 2ACC-26B | Space Opera |
| 5312CM19 | 2ACC-28A | Mass |
| 5312CM20 | 2ACC-28B | Communication |
| 5312CM20 | 2ACC-29A | SOP 8-C: on Auditing |
| 5312CM20 | 2ACC-29B | Reach/Withdraw |
| 5312CM21 | 2ACC-30A | Ability to Accept Direction |
| 5312CM21 | 2ACC-30B | Knowingness and Certainty |
| 5312CM22 | 2ACC-31A | Havingness — Remedy of |
| 5312CM22 | 2ACC-31B | Postulates |

**1954**

| | | |
|---|---|---|
| 5405CM12 | 6ACC-5 | Basic Definitions |
| 5405C13 | 6ACC-6 | Definition: Cycle of Action and Time |
| 5405C20 | 6ACC-17 | Definitions, ARC |
| 5406CM05 | UPC-1 | Opening Lecture — History of Dianetics and Scientology |
| 5406CM-- | UPC-2 | Procedure 30 — Duplication |
| 5406CM-- | UPC-3 | Theta-Mest Theory — Tone Scale Freedom, Space, etc. |
| 5406CM-- | UPC-4 | Opening Procedure by Duplication (PRO-19) |
| 5406CM-- | UPC-5 | Lecture and Processing |
| 5406CM-- | UPC-6 | Group Processing(Look at that Object) |
| 5406CM-- | UPC-7 | Workbook 31-G |
| 5406CM-- | UPC-8 | Processing (Granting Beingness) Session I |
| 5406CM-- | UPC-9 | Processing (Granting Beingness) Session II |
| 5406CM-- | UPC-10 | Group Processing (What Do — Didn't Have) |

| | | |
|---|---|---|
| 5406CM-- | UPC-11 | Theta Mest Theory Being a Problem Aspect |
| 5406CM-- | UPC-12 | Group Processing (Solution to Something) |
| 5406CM-- | UPC-13 | Process of Exteriorization |
| 5406CM-- | UPC-14 | Group Processing (Straight Exteriorization Processing) |
| 5407C19 | 7ACC-25 | Scientology and Civilization; PRO-1 and PRO-3; also titled—Scientology: Its General Background, Part 1 and Part 3 |
| 5408CM20 | AX-1 | Axioms, Part I (PRO-13) |
| 5408CM20 | AX-2 | Axioms, Part II (PRO-14) |
| 5408CM20 | AX-3 | Axioms, Part III (PRO-15) |
| 5408CM20 | AX-4 | Axioms, Part IV (PRO-16) |
| 5410CM04 | 8ACC-1A | Introductory Lecture Part I |
| 5410CM04 | 8ACC-1B | Introductory Lecture Part II |
| 5410CM05 | 8ACC-3 | Elements of Processing |
| 5410CM06 | 8ACC-4 | Two-Way Comm |
| 5410CM07 | 8ACC-5A | Elementary Straightwire |
| 5410CM08 | 8ACC-6 | Opening procedure of 8-C |
| 5410CM08 & 10B | PIP | Route I, Steps 4, 5, 6, 7 |
| 5410CM10C | PIP | Route I, Steps 8, 9, 10, 11 |
| 5410CM10D | PIP | Route I, Steps 12, 13, 14, 15 |
| 5410CM11 | 8ACC-7 | Opening Procedure by Duplication |
| 5410CM12 | 8ACC-8 | Remedy of Havingness |
| 5410CM13 | 8ACC-9 | Spotting Spots |
| 5410CM19 | 8ACC-13 | Axioms of Dianetics |
| 5410CM20 | 8ACC-14 | Parts of Man |
| 5410CM21 | 8ACC-16 | Route 2-61; Route 2-62 |
| 5410CM22 | 8ACC-17 | Two-Way Communication |
| 5410CM25 | 8ACC-18 | Communication and Straightwire |
| 5410CM26 | 8ACC-19 | Survive |
| 5410CM27 | 8ACC-20 | Hypnotism |

| | | |
|---|---|---|
| 5410CM28 | 8ACC-21 | Process: What Would You Do If |
| 5411CM01 | 8ACC-23 | Two-Way Communication |
| 5411CM02 | 8ACC-24 | Homo Sapiens |
| 5411CM05 | 8ACC-27 | Factors Present in Good and Bad Auditing |
| 5411C29 | HCAP-8 | Two-Way Communication |
| 5412CM06 | 9ACC-1 | Introduction to 9th ACC — Havingness |
| 5412CM09 | 9ACC-4 | Communication Formula |
| 5412CM10 | 9ACC-5 | Practice of Dianetics and Scientology |
| 5412CM13 | 9ACC-6 | Conduct of the Auditor |
| 5412CM14 | 9ACC-7 | Mechanics of Communication |
| 5412CM16 | 9ACC-9 | Pan-Determinism and One-Way Flows |
| 5412CM20 | 9ACC-10 | Games (Fighting) |
| 5412CM21 | 9ACC-11 | Games (Anatomy of) |
| 5412CM22 | 9ACC-12 | One-Way Flows (in Processing) |
| 5412CM22 | 9ACC-12A | Q & A Period |
| 5412CM23 | 9ACC-13 | Havingness and Communication Formulas |
| 5413CM23 | 9ACC-13A | After Lecture Comments |
| 5412CM24 | 9ACC-14 | Pan-Determinism |
| 5412CM27 | 9ACC-15 | Training New People |

**1955**

| | | |
|---|---|---|
| 5501C14 | 9ACC-24 | Perfect Duplicate, Life Continuum |
| 5501C19 | PLS | Communication and ARC Triangle |
| 5501C21 | 9ACC-29 | Axioms: Laws of Consideration |
| 5504C16 | HPC LECT-5 | Service Facsimiles |
| 5506C03 | ASMC-2 | Practicalities of a Practical Religion |
| 5506C03 | ASMC-3 | History of Research and Investigation |
| 5506C06 | ASMC-15 | What Scientology is Doing |
| 5510C03 | 4LACC-1 | Fundamentals of Scientology and Rudiments |
| 5510C06 | 4LACC-7 | Communication and "I Don't Know" (Confusion) |

| | | |
|---|---|---|
| 5510C08 | LPLS-1 | Goals of Dianetics and Scientology |
| 5510C10 | 4LACC-12 | Communication and the Subject of Communication |
| 5510C13 | 4LACC-18 | Affinity, Reality and Communication |
| 5510C18 | 4LACC-23 | Beginning and Continuing a Session |
| 5511C05 | 4LACC-50 | End of Course Lecture |

## 1956

| | | |
|---|---|---|
| 5608C— — | HPC A6-4 | Axioms 1 — 5 |
| 5610C22 | 15ACC-6 | Scale of Reality |
| 5610C24 | 15ACC-8 | Cut Comm Lines (In and Out) |
| 5610C26 | 15ACC-10 | Learning Rates |
| 5610C30 | 15ACC-12 | Education |
| 5611C01 | OS-6 | How to Handle Audiences |
| 5611C15 | OS-10 | Definition of Organization: Part 2 |

## 1957

| | | |
|---|---|---|
| 5701C14 | 16ACC-9 | Control |
| 5701C17 | 16ACC-12 | Communication, Randomities of |
| 5702C26 | 17ACC-2 | ARC Triangle and Associated Scales |
| 5702C27 | 17ACC-3 | Communication and Isness |
| 5702C28 | 17ACC-4 | The Parts of Man |
| 5703C01 | 17ACC-5 | Problems: Their Handling and Running |
| 5703C10 | 17ACC-10 | Valences |
| 5707C05 | FC-7 | Purpose and Need of Training Drills |
| 5707C15 | 18ACC-1 | What is Scientology? |
| 5707C16 | 18ACC-2 | CCH Related to ARC |
| 5707C17 | 18ACC-3 | Theory and Definition of Auditing |
| 5707C25 | 18ACC-9 | Scales (Effect Scale) |
| 5707C26 | 18ACC-10 | The Mind: Its Structure in Relation to Thetan and Mest |

**1961**

| 6101C02 | 22ACC-1 | Present Time Problems — Why Cases Don't Move |
| 6101C22 | ACSA-5 | Cycle of Action, Time Track, Terminals, Stable Datum, Reactive Thought |
| 6102C14 | 35A ACC-14 | Fundamentals of Auditing |

## Saint Hill Special Briefing Course Tape Lectures

| 6105C07 | SH Spec 1 | E-Meter Talk and Demo |
| 6105C12 | SH Spec 2 | Assessment |
| 6105C19 | SH Spec 3 | E-meter |
| 6105C26 | SH Spec 4 | On Auditing |
| 6106C01 | SH Spec 5 | Flattening Process and E-meter |
| 6106C02 | SH Spec 6 | Flows, Pre-hav Scale, Primary Scale |
| 6106C05 | SH Spec 7 | Routine One, Two and Three |
| 6106C06 | SH Spec 8 | Routine One, Two and Three |
| 6106C07 | SH Spec 9 | Points in Assessing |
| 6106C08 | SH Spec 10 | Q & A Period and Ending an Intensive |
| 6106C09 | SH Spec 11 | Reading E-meter Reactions |
| 6106C12 | SH Spec 12 | E-meter Actions, Errors in Auditing |
| 6106C13 | SH Spec 13 | Seminar — Q & A Period |
| 6106C14 | SH Spec 14 | Seminar — Withholds |
| 6106C15 | SH Spec 15X | Not Know |
| 6106C16 | SH Spec 16X | Confront and Havingness — Routine 1, 2, & 3 |
| 6106C19 | SH Spec 15 | Q & A Period — Auditing Slowdowns |
| 6106C20 | SH Spec 16 | Sec Check Questions — Mutual Rudiments |
| 6106C21 | SH Spec 17 | Seminar at Saint Hill |
| 6106C22 | SH Spec 18 | Running CCHs |
| 6106C23 | SH Spec 19 | Q & A Period — CCHs — Auditing |
| 6106C26 | SH Spec 20 | Dealing with Attacks on Scientology |

| | | |
|---|---|---|
| 6302C19 | SH Spec 240 | Rundown on Processes |
| 6302C20 | SH Spec 241 | Finding RRs |
| 6302C21 | SH Spec 242 | R-2 and R-3 Current Auditing Rundown |
| 6302C26 | SH Spec 243 | R-3M Current Rundown by Steps |
| 6303C05 | SH Spec 245 | R-2 and R-3 Urgent Data |
| 6303C07 | SH Spec 247 | When Faced with the Unusual, Do the Usual |
| 6303C19 | SH Spec 250 | R3M How to Find Goals |
| 6303C20 | SH TVD 18 | Rudiments and Havingness Session and Short Lecture (aud: LRH; pc: R. Sharpe) |
| 6303C21 | SH Spec 251 | R2-G Series |
| 6303C27 | SH Spec 254 | TVD 19, Sec Checking (aud: R. Sharpe; pc: Leslie Van Der Statten) Talk by LRH |
| 6304C04 | SH Spec 255 | Anatomy of the GPM |
| 6304C02 | SH Spec 256 | Line Plot, Items |
| 6304C18 | SH Spec 258 | Directive Listing |
| 6304C23 | SH Spec 259 | Goals Problems Mass |
| 6304C25 | SH Spec 260 | Finding Goals |
| 6304C30 | SH Spec 261 | Directive Listing |
| 6305C14 | SH Spec 263 | Implant GPMs |
| 6405C15 | SH Spec 264 | TVD 20, Blocking Out and Dating Items and Incidents Prior to Implants |
| 6305C16 | SH Spec 265 | The Time Track |
| 6305C21 | SH Spec 266 | The Helatrobus Implants |
| 6305C22 | SH Spec 267 | TVD 21, Engram Running—Helatrobus Implant, Goal "To be serious" (aud: LRH; pc: M.S. Hubbard) |
| 6305C23 | SH Spec 268 | State of OT |
| 6305C28 | SH Spec 269 | Handling ARC breaks |
| 6305C29 | SH Spec 270 | Programming Cases Part 1 |
| 6305C30 | SH Spec 271 | Programming Cases Part 2 |
| 6306C11 | SH Spec 273 | Engram Chain Running |

| | | |
|---|---|---|
| 7203C04 SO I | ESTO 7 | Hold the Form of the Org |
| 7203C04 SO II | ESTO 8 | Hold the Form of the Org |
| 7203C05 SO I | ESTO 9 | Revision of Prod/Org System |
| 7203C05 SO II | ESTO 10 | Revision of Prod/Org System |
| 7203C06 SO I | ESTO 11 | F/Ning Staff Members |
| 7203C06 SO II | ESTO 12 | F/Ning Staff Members |
| 7203C30 | SO | Expanded Dianetics |
| 7204C07 | SO I | Expanded Dianetics and Word Clearing |
| 7204C07 | SO II | Auditor Administration |
| 7204C07 | SO III | Illness — Breakthrough |

# Miscellaneous References

### Executive Directives

| | | |
|---|---|---|
| ED 110R FLAG | Upper Level Data | 21 Feb 72 |

### Flag Bureaux Data Letters

| | | |
|---|---|---|
| FBDL 245 | The Modern Confessional | 23 Nov 72 |
| FBDL 245-1 | Integrity Processing and the Hubbard Integrity Processing Specialist Course | 7 Jan 73 |
| FBDL 279 | Weekly Stat Briefing Sheet W/E 29 Mar 73 | 30 Mar 73 |
| FBDL 328 | The Hubbard Senior Course Supervisor Course (HSCSC) | 14 Aug 73 |

### Flag Orders

| | | |
|---|---|---|
| FO 1483 | Personnel | 17 Oct 68 |
| FO 2192 | Programming Unit Basic Hat | 14 Nov 69 |
| FO 2354 | The Keeper of Tech Duties and Responsibilities | 28 Jan 70 |
| FO 3076 | Non Sea Org Tech Pay and Bonuses | 20 Nov 71 |
| FO 3179 (CBO 190) | Aide and A/Aide Responsibility | 25 Apr 72 |

### Flag Orders of the Day

| | | |
|---|---|---|
| Flag OODs | LRH Command Item | 17 May 71 |

**Flag Ship Orders**

| | | |
|---|---|---|
| FSO 65 | Student Orientation Checksheet | 21 Jun 70 |
| FSO 529 | Esto Apprentice Training | 18 Mar 72 Corr & Reiss 22 Mar 72 |

**HCO Information Letters**

| | | |
|---|---|---|
| HCO Info Ltr | Who are the Quacks? | 22 Sept 63 |
| HCO Info Ltr | Ron's Journal No. 8 | 5 Feb 64 |
| HCO Info Ltr | Two Types of People | 2 Apr 64 |
| HCO Info Ltr | Anatomy of the Human Mind Course | 2 Sept 64 |

**LRH Executive Directives**

| | | |
|---|---|---|
| LRH ED 2 INT | Attestation Reinstated | 20 Jan 69 |
| LRH ED 2 US and 2 WW only | PDH | 9 Mar 69 |
| LRH ED 9 | Urgent Dianetics | 11 May 69 |
| LRH ED 18 INT | Dianetic Case Gain | 17 Jul 69 |
| LRH ED 57 INT | What to Sell | 14 Dec 69 |
| LRH ED 143 INT | The World Begins with TR 0 | 21 May 71 |
| LRH ED 257 | Delivery Repair Lists | 1 Dec 74 |

**Operational Bulletins**

| | | |
|---|---|---|
| Op. Bull 1 | The following Auditing Commands . . . | 20 Oct 55 |
| Op. Bull 5 | Limited Company Proceeding . . . | Undated |
| Op. Bull 9 | The Turn of the Tide | 19 Dec 55 |
| Op. Bull 13 | Operational Bulletins Growing Up | 17 Jan 56 |
| Op. Bull 17 | Fur Flying in Washington | 14 Feb 56 |

**Six Levels of Processing**

| | | |
|---|---|---|
| SLP Issue 7 Rev | Special Western Congress Release | Undated |

**Sea Organization Executive Directives**

| | | |
|---|---|---|
| SO ED 96 INT | Central Authority New Command and Communication Lines | 17 Dec 70 |
| SO ED 135 INT | The Social Counselor Course | 18 Jan 72 |

**Technical Individual Programs**

| | | |
|---|---|---|
| TIP 1 | Technical Individual Programs | 20 Jun 71 |

# About the Author

**L. RON HUBBARD** was born on the 13th of March, 1911, in Tilden, Nebraska, USA, to Commander Harry Ross Hubbard of the US Navy and Dora May Hubbard (nee Waterbury de Wolfe).

He grew up in Montana with old frontiersmen and cowboys, and had an Indian medicine man as one of his best friends. Here in Montana, L. Ron Hubbard had his first encounter with another culture, the Blackfoot (Pikuni) Indians. He became a blood brother of the Pikuni and was later to write about them in his first published novel, *Buckskin Brigades*.

By the time he was twelve years old, he had read a good number of the world's greatest classics and began to take interest in the fields of religion and philosophy. During this time, while living in Washington, D.C., he became a close friend of President Calvin Coolidge's son, Calvin Jr., whose early death accelerated L. Ron Hubbard's interest in the mind and spirit of Man.

From 1925 to 1929, his father's career took the family to the Far East where L. Ron Hubbard journeyed throughout Asia, exploring out-of-the-way places, and saw many new peoples and customs.

In 1929 with the death of his grandfather, the Hubbard family returned to the United States and there L. Ron Hubbard continued his formal education. He attended Swavely Prep School in Manassas, Virginia, and went to high school at Woodward School for Boys in Washington, D.C.

In 1930, he graduated from Woodward with honors, and enrolled at George Washington University Engineering School in the fall. He became the associate editor of the university newspaper and was a member of many of the university's clubs and societies, including the Twentieth Marine Corps Reserve and the George Washington College Company.

While at George Washington University, he learned to fly and discovered a particular aptitude as a glider pilot. Here, also, he was enrolled in one of the first nuclear physics courses ever taught in an American university.

As a student, barely twenty years old, he supported himself by writing, and within a very few years he had established himself as an essayist in the literary world.

Even though he was very busy during these college years, L. Ron Hubbard still found time for his exploring. In 1931, at the age of twenty, he led the Caribbean Motion Picture Expedition as a director, and underwater films made on that journey provided the Hydrographic Office and the University of Michigan with invaluable data for the furtherance of their research. And again in 1932, at twenty-one years of age, L. Ron Hubbard led another expedition conducting the West Indies Mineralogical Survey and made the first complete mineralogical survey of Puerto Rico.

Although very active now in several areas, L. Ron Hubbard continued his writing. Under about twenty different pen names millions of words poured from his pen and into print, including both fact and fiction, travel articles, stories of exploration and adventure, essays and anecdotes, science fiction, and western stories appearing in over ninety magazines and journals.

In 1935, L. Ron Hubbard went to Hollywood and worked under motion picture contracts as a scriptwriter. He is still very active in Hollywood's movie production.

While in Hollywood he continued his study of "What makes men tick," and in his own statement, L. Ron Hubbard dates the discovery of the primary law of life, summarily expressed by the command "Survive!" at 1938.

In 1940, as a duly elected member of the Explorers Club of New York, L. Ron Hubbard conducted the Alaskan Radio Experimental Expedition. He was awarded the Explorers Club flag for conducting this expedition. Also, in 1940, he earned his "License to Master of Steam and Motor Vessels," and within four and a half months obtained a second certificate attesting to his marine skill: "License to Master of Sail Vessels" ("Any Ocean").

In 1941, like many other young men of his generation, L. Ron Hubbard was commissioned in the US Navy. He served in all five theaters of the war. In 1944 he was severely wounded and was taken crippled and blinded to Oak Knoll Naval Hospital. It was here that L. Ron Hubbard did much of his early research on the human mind. At this time, he already had a great deal of data on what was known about the mind. Earlier, between the years of 1923 and 1928, he had received an extensive education in the field of the human mind from Commander Thompson of the Medical Corps of the US Navy, a friend of his father and a personal student of Sigmund Freud. Injured, L. Ron Hubbard faced an almost non-existent future, yet he worked his way back to fitness, strength and full perception in less than two years, using only what he knew and could determine about Man and his relationship to the universe.

Some of his early research was spent determining whether the mind regulated the body or the body regulated the mind. If the mind was capable of putting restraint upon the physical body, then obviously the fact that was commonly held to be true, that the body regulated the mind, was false. He went about proving this.

And so, L. Ron Hubbard continued studying, researching, and synthesizing this knowledge with what he had learned of Eastern philosophy, his understanding of nuclear physics, and his experiences among men, to form some of the basic tenets of Dianetics and Scientology.

After leaving Oak Knoll, the study, work, writing and research continued at a rapid pace. And then in 1948, he wrote *Dianetics: The Original Thesis,* his first formal report of the mysteries of the mind and life, which was a thirty-thousand word revelation.

The interest in Dianetics spread like wildfire. Letters asking for clarifications and advice and more data poured in, and just answering them was becoming a full-time occupation.

So the work continued, work on an extensive popular text on the subject of Dianetics that would answer all questions. In May of 1950, *Dianetics: The Modern Science of Mental Health* exploded onto the booklists, leapt to the top of the *New York Times* Best-Seller List and stayed there. It is still a best seller today.

L. Ron Hubbard then founded in 1950 the Hubbard Dianetic Foundation in Elizabeth, New Jersey to facilitate auditing and training the public in Dianetics.

During the next twenty-five years many, many churches and missions were established all over the planet to professionally deliver L. Ron Hubbard's technology standardly to the peoples of the world.

The founder of Dianetics and Scientology, L. Ron Hubbard, lives with his wife, Mary Sue, and their children: Quentin, twenty-one; Suzette, twenty; and Arthur, sixteen. Their eldest daughter, Diana, twenty-two, is happily married.

Today, L. Ron Hubbard continues his life's work unabated, writing, researching and exploring new avenues and hitherto unexplored realms of life and the human spirit.

\*  \*  \*

# Contact your nearest Church or Mission

## UNITED STATES

### ADVANCED ORGANIZATION

Church of Scientology of California
Advanced Organization
of Los Angeles
1306 N. Berendo Street
Los Angeles, California 90027

### SAINT HILL ORGANIZATION

Church of Scientology
American Saint Hill Organization
1413 N. Berendo Street
Los Angeles, California 90027

### PUBLICATIONS ORGANIZATION

Church of Scientology
Publications Organization
4833 Fountain Avenue,
East Annex
Los Angeles, California 90029

### CELEBRITY CENTRES

Church of Scientology
Celebrity Centre
1551 No. LaBrea Avenue
Hollywood, California 90028

Church of Scientology
Celebrity Centre New York
65 East 82nd Street
New York, New York 10028

Organizacion de Dianetica
Celebrity Centre Mexico
120 Alta Vista
San Angel Inn
Mexico 20 DF, Mexico

Church of Scientology
Celebrity Center
344 Carlton Avenue
Toronto, Ontario, Canada

### LOCAL CHURCHES

#### WASHINGTON, D.C.

Founding Church of Scientology
2125 S Street, N.W.
Washington, D.C. 20008

#### AUSTIN

Church of Scientology
2804 Rio Grande
Austin, Texas 78705

#### HAWAII

Church of Scientology
143 Nenue Street
Honolulu, Hawaii 96821

#### SAN DIEGO

Church of Scientology
926 "C" Street
San Diego, California 92101

#### SAN FRANCISCO

Church of Scientology
414 Mason Street
San Francisco, California 94102

LAS VEGAS

Church of Scientology
2108 Industrial Road
Las Vegas, Nevada 89102

LOS ANGELES

Church of Scientology of California
4810 Sunset Blvd.
Los Angeles, California 90027

PORTLAND

Church of Scientology
333 S.W. Park
Portland, Oregon 97205

SEATTLE

Church of Scientology
1531 4th Avenue
Seattle, Washington 98101

ST. LOUIS

Church of Scientology
3730 Lindell Boulevard
St. Louis, Missouri 63108

TWIN CITIES

Church of Scientology
730 Hennepin Avenue
Minneapolis, Minnesota 55403

BOSTON

Church of Scientology
448 Beacon Street
Boston, Massachusetts 02115

BUFFALO

Church of Scientology
1116 Elmwood Avenue
Buffalo, New York 14222

DETROIT

Church of Scientology
3905 Rochester Road
Royal Oak, Michigan 48067

MIAMI

Church of Scientology of Florida
120 Giralda
Coral Gables, Florida 33134

NEW YORK

Church of Scientology
28-30 West 74th Street
New York, New York 10023

SACRAMENTO

Church of Scientology
819 19th Street
Sacramento, California 95814

PHILADELPHIA

Church of Scientology
8 West Lancaster Avenue
Ardmore, Pennsylvania 19003

CHICAGO

Church of Scientology
1555 Maple Street
Evanston, Illinois 60201

# CANADA

TORONTO

Church of Scientology
385 Yonge Street
Toronto, Ontario M5B 1S1

VANCOUVER

Church of Scientology
4857 Main Street
Vancouver 10
British Columbia

OTTAWA

Church of Scientology
292 Somerset Street, West
Ottawa

## MONTREAL

Church of Scientology
15 Notre Dame Quest
Montreal, Quebec H2Y 1B5

## SCOTLAND

HAPI
Fleet House
20, South Bridge
Edinburgh, Scotland

# UNITED KINGDOM

## ADVANCED ORGANIZATION/ SAINT HILL

Hubbard College of Scientology
Advanced Organization Saint Hill
Saint Hill Manor East Grinstead
Sussex RH19 4JY, England

## LOCAL CHURCHES

Saint Hill Foundation
Saint Hill Manor East Grinstead
Sussex RH19 4JY, England

## PLYMOUTH

Hubbard Scientology Organization
39, Portland Square
Sherwell, Plymouth
Devon, England PL4 6DJ

## MANCHESTER

Hubbard Scientology Organization
48 Faulkner Street
Manchester M1 4FH, England

## LONDON

Hubbard Scientology Organization
68 Tottenham Court Road
London W. 1, England

# AUSTRALIA/ NEW ZEALAND

## ADELAIDE

Church of the New Faith
57 Puleteney Street
Adelaide 5000
South Australia

## MELBOURNE

Church of the New Faith
724 Inkerman Road
North Caulfield 3161
Melbourne, Victoria, Australia

## PERTH

Church of the New Faith
Pastoral House
#156 St. George's Terrace
Perth 5000
Western Australia

## SYDNEY

Church of the New Faith
1 Lee Street
Sydney 2000
New South Wales, Australia

## AUCKLAND

Church of Scientology
New Imperial Buildings
44 Queen Street
Auckland, New Zealand

# EUROPE

## ADVANCED ORGANIZATION

Church of Scientology
Advanced Organization Denmark
Jernbanegade 6
1608 Copenhagen V
Denmark

## SAINT HILL ORGANIZATION

Church of Scientology
Saint Hill Denmark
Jernbanegade 6
1608 Copenhagen V
Denmark

## PUBLICATIONS ORGANIZATION

Church of Scientology
Publications Organization
c/o SH Denmark
Jernbanegade 6
1608 Copenhagen V
Denmark

## LOCAL CHURCHES

### COPENHAGEN

Church of Scientology
Hovedvagtsgade 6
1103 Copenhagen K
Denmark

Church of Scientology of Copenhagen
Frederiksborgvej 5
2400 Copenhagen NV
Denmark

### PARIS

Church of Scientology
12 rue de la Montagne Ste
Genevieve, 75005 Paris
France

### VIENNA

Scientology-Osterreich
A-1070 Wien
Mariahilferstrasse 88A/Stg. 3/1/9
Vienna, Austria

### BRUSSELS

Church of Scientology
45A Rue de l'Ecuyer
1000 Brussels
Belgium

### AMSTERDAM

Church of Scientology
Singel 289-293
Amsterdam C. Netherlands

### MUNICH

Church of Scientology
8000 Munich 2
Lindwurmstrasse 29
West Germany

### GÖTEBORG

Church of Scientology
Kungsgatan 23
411 19, Goteborg, Sweden

### STOCKHOLM

Church of Scientology
Kammakaregatan 46
S-111 60 Stockholm
Sweden

### MALMÖ

Church of Scientology
Skomakaregatan 12
S-211 34 Malmö
Sweden

# AFRICA

## JOHANNESBURG

Church of Scientology
99 Polly Street
Johannesburg, South Africa, 2001

## CAPE TOWN

Church of Scientology
3rd Floor Garmor House
127 Plein Street
Cape Town, South Africa, 8001

## DURBAN

Church of Scientology
57 College Lane
Durban, South Africa, 4001

## PORT ELIZABETH

Church of Scientology
2 St. Christopher's
27 West Bourne Road
Port Elizabeth, South Africa 6001

## PRETORIA

Church of Scientology
224 Central House
Cnr Central & Pretorious Streets
Pretoria, South Africa, 0002

## BULAWAYO

Church of Scientology
210-211 Kirrie Bldgs
Cnr Abercorn & 9th Avenue
Bulawayo, Rhodesia

# MISSION LIST

## IN U.S.A.

Scientology Mission of Albuquerque
613 San Mateo Blvd NE.
Albuquerque, New Mexico 87108

Scientology Mission of Amarillo
2046 S. Hayden
Amarillo, Texas 79109

Scientology Mission of Berlin
1240a Farmington Avenue
Berlin, Connecticut 06037

Scientology Mission of Boston
69 Broad Street
Boston, Massachusetts 02110

Scientology Mission of Boulder
Box 995
Boulder, Colorado 80302

Scientology Mission of Cambridge
8 Essex Street
Cambridge, Massachusetts 02139

Scientology Mission of Central Ohio
3894 N. High Street
Columbus, Ohio 43214

Scientology Mission of Charlotte
1000 Dilworth Rd.
Charlotte, North Carolina 28203

Scientology Mission of Chicago
108 East Oak Street
Villa Park, Illinois 60181

Scientology Mission of Delaware Valley
Suite 924, 1 Cherry Hill Mall
Cherry Hill, New Jersey 08034

Scientology Mission of Denver
375 S. Navajo
Denver, Colorado 80223

Scientology Mission of El Paso
7308A Alameda
El Paso, Texas 79915

Scientology Mission of Fifth Avenue
30 Fifth Avenue
New York, New York 10011

Scientology Mission of Ft. Lauderdale
423 N. Andrews Ave.
Ft. Lauderdale, Florida 33301

Scientology Mission of Houston
4034 Westheimer
Houston, Texas 77027

Scientology Mission of Huron Valley
203 East Ann
Ann Arbor, Michigan 48108

Scientology Mission of Kansas City
4528 Main St.
Kansas City, Missouri 64111

Scientology Mission of Lakeview
1928 W. Montrose
Chicago, Illinois 60613

Scientology Mission of New Hope
4144 Shady Oak Road
Minnetonka, Minnesota 55343

Scientology Mission of New Jersey
5 Main St.
Flemington, New Jersey 08822

Scientology Mission of New York
500 West End Ave., Suite 2B
New York, New York 10024

Scientology Mission of North Manhattan
Apt. 2A, 251 West 98th Street
New York, New York 10025

Scientology Mission of Omaha
103 S. 35 Ave.
Omaha, Nebraska 68131

Scientology Mission of Peoria
920 W. Main Street
Peoria, Illinois 61606

Scientology Mission of Puerto Rico
1395 Americo Salas
Santurce
Puerto Rico 00909

Scientology Mission of Richardson
114 N. McKinney
Richardson, Texas 75080

Scientology Mission of San Antonio
Colonies North Mall,
3723 Colony Dr.
San Antonio, Texas 78230

Scientology Mission of Southwest
P. O. Box 8386
Dallas, Texas 75205

Scientology Mission of Urbana
Grenada House, 1004 S. 4th
Champaign, Illinois

Scientology Mission of Waterbury
42 Bank Street
Waterbury, Connecticut 06702

Scientology Mission of Westchester
11 Parrott Street
Cold Spring, New York 10516

Scientology Mission of Adams Avenue
6911 El Cajon Blvd.
San Diego, California 92115

Scientology Mission of Berkeley
1918 Bonita Avenue
Berkeley, California 94704

Scientology Mission of Castro Valley
20730 Lake Chabot Road
Castro Valley, California 94546

Scientology Mission of Orlando
Box 14045
Orlando, Florida 32807

Scientology Mission of Sacramento
1725 23rd Street
Sacramento, California 95816

Scientology Mission of East Bay
411-15th Street
Oakland, California 94612

Scientology Mission of Flagstaff
4469 Mountain Meadow Drive
Flagstaff, Arizona 86001

Scientology Mission of Hawaii
1282 Kapiolani Blvd.
Honolulu, Hawaii 96814

Scientology Mission of Lake Tahoe
P. O. Box 1540
South Lake Tahoe, California 95705

Scientology Mission of Long Beach
1261 Long Beach Blvd.
Long Beach, California 90813

Scientology Mission of Los Gatos
10 Jackson Street, No. 111
Los Gatos, California 95030

Scientology Mission of Meadows
1326 Las Vegas Blvd. S.
Las Vegas, Nevada 89101

Scientology Mission of Orange County
1451 Irvine Blvd.
Tustin, California 92680

Scientology Mission of Palo Alto
600 Middlefield Road
Palo Alto, California 94301

Scientology Mission of Pasadena
634 E. Colorado Blvd.
Pasadena, California 91101

Scientology Mission of Phoenix
1722 E. Indian School Rd.
Phoenix, Arizona 85016

Scientology Mission of Phoenix
331 N. 1st Avenue
Phoenix, Arizona 85003

Scientology Mission of Riverside
3485 University Street
Riverside, California 92501

Scientology Mission of Sacramento
5136 Arden Way
Carmichael, California 95608

Scientology Mission of Salt Lake City
253 East 2nd S.
Salt Lake City, Utah 84111

Scientology Mission of Santa Barbara
746 State Street
Santa Barbara, California 93101

Scientology Mission of Santa Clara
4340 Stevens Creek, No. 180
San Jose, California 95129

574

Scientology Mission of SCS
3802 Riverside Dr.
Burbank, California 91505

Scientolgy Mission of South Bay
607 S. Pacific Coast Highway
Redondo Beach, California 90277

Scientology Mission of Tucson
2100 E. Speedway
Tucson, Arizona 85719

Scientology Mission of Valley
13561A Ventura Blvd.
Sherman Oaks, California 91403

Scientology Mission of Washoe Valley
319 E. 6th
Reno, Nevada 89501

Scientology Mission of Westwood/Wilshire
10930 Santa Monica Blvd.
Los Angeles, California 90025

Scientology Mission of Albany
141 Brunswick Road
Troy, New York 12180

Scientology Mission of Arlington
818 N. Taylor Street
Arlington, Virginia 22203

Scientology Mission of Chadds Ford
Baltimore Pike
Chadds Ford, Pennsylvania 19317

Scientology Mission of Cleveland
PO Box 636, 4192 E. 187th Street
Cleveland, Ohio 44122

Scientology Mission of Elmira
111 N. Main Street
Elmira, New York 14902

Scientology Mission of Erie
528 West 18th
Erie, Pennsylvania 16502

Scientology Mission of New London
398 Broad Street
New London, Connecticut 06230

Scientology Mission of Putney
Wabena Stables
Putney, Vermont 05346

Scientology Mission of Anderson
PO Box 664
Anderson, Indiana 46016

Scientology Mission of Carbondale
417 S. Illinois Avenue
Carbondale, Illinois 62901

Scientology Mission of Cincinnati
2417 Vine Street
Cincinnati, Ohio 45219

Scientology Mission of Colorado Springs
1119 No. Cooper
Colorado Springs, Colorado 80905

Scientology Mission of St. Charles
138 North Main Street
St. Charles, Missouri 63301

Scientology Mission of Chula Vista
192 Landis Street
Chula Vista, California 92010

Scientology Mission of Fresno
1350 "O" St.
Fresno, California 93721

Scientology Mission of Goldengate
1807 Union Street, No. 2
San Francisco, California 94128

Scientology Mission of Newport Beach
341 Bayside Dr.
Newport Beach, California 92660

Scientology Mission of Portland
709 SW Salmon Street
Portland, Oregon 97205

Scientology Mission of Santa Rosa
806 Sonoma Avenue
Santa Rosa, California 95402

Scientology Mission of Sheridan
RT 2 Box 195
Sheridan, Oregon 97378

Scientology Mission of Stockton
47 W. Acacia St.
Stockton, California 95204

Scientology Mission of Walnut Creek
2363 Blvd. Circle No. 5
Walnut Creek, California 94595

Scientology Mission of Davis
1046 Olive Drive
Davis, California 95616

Scientology Mission of Burbank
124 N. Golden Mall
Burbank, California 91502

Mission of Scientology
1640 Welton
Denver, Colorado 80202

Mission of Scientology
9610 82nd Ave.
Edmonton, Alberta, Canada

Mission of Scientology
264 Weybosset
Providence, R.I. 02903

Mission of Scientology
250 Main St.
Worcester, Mass. 01608

Mission of Scientology
P. O. Box 4-830
Anchorage, Alaska 99509

Celebrity Center Las Vegas
2004 S. Western St.
Las Vegas, Nev. 89102

Mission of Scientology
3352 Jefferson Ave.
Cincinnati, Ohio 45220

Mission of Scientology of Central Oklahoma
P. O. Box 101
Edmond, Oklahoma 73034

Mission of Scientology of Maumee Valley
1941 Jermain Dr.
Toledo, Ohio 43606

Mission of Scientology of Columbus
45 Euclid Ave.
Columbus, Ohio 43201

Mission of Scientology Greenbrier
Coleman Drive
Lewesburg, W. Va. 24901

Mission of Scientology of Santa Fe
330 Montezuma
Santa Fe, New Mexico 87501

Mission of Scientology of Quebec City
781 Blvd. Charest Est #3
Quebec, P.Q., Canada

Mission of Scientology of Charlottetown
139 Kent St.
Charlottetown, P.E.I., Canada

## CANADA

Scientology Mission of Hamilton
28½ John Street N.
Hamilton, Ontario, Canada

Scientology Mission of Niagara
455 St. Paul St. St. Catherine's
Ontario, Canada

Scientology Mission of Vancouver
1524 West 6th Avenue
Vancouver 8, British Columbia
Canada

Scientology Mission of Winnipeg
410 Spence Street
Winnipeg, Manitoba, Canada

Scientology Mission of London
148 Dundas St.
London, Ontario, Canada

Scientology Mission of Windsor
437 Oulette Street
Windsor, Ontario, Canada

Scientology Mission of Regina
2023 St. John
Regina, Sasketchewan

Scientology Mission of Halifax
1585 Barrington Street, No. 208
Halifax, Nova Scotia, Canada

Scientology Mission of St. John
15 Charlotte Street
St. John, New Brunswick, Canada

Scientology Mission of Kitchener
241 King Street West, No. 14
Kitchener, Ontario, Canada

Scientology Mission of Edmonton
PO Box 1198
Edmonton, Alberta, Canada

Scientology Mission of Calgary
340  15th Avenue South West
Calgary, Alberta, Canada

## NEW ZEALAND

Scientology Mission of Christchurch
35 Rapaki Road
Christchurch 2, New Zealand

Scientology Mission of Ellerslie
1 Ranier Street
Ellerslie
Auckland, New Zealand

## SOUTH AFRICA

Dianetic Counselling Center Johannesburg
    (in S.A. [Pty.] Ltd.)
608 African City Bldg., Sixth Floor
100 Eloff Street
Johannesburg

Scientology Mission of Pietermaritzburg
    (in S.A. [Pty.] Ltd.)
411 Alexandra Road
Pietermaritzburg

Scientology Mission of Welkom
PO Box 33
Welkom 9460

Scientology Mission of Windhoek
PO Box 21039
Windhoek 9100 South West Africa

## AUSTRALIA

The New Faith Mission of Melville
15 Birdwood Road
Melville, Western Australia 6156

## EUROPE

Scientology Mission of Angers
43, rue Proust
49000 Angers, France

Scientology Mission of Berlin
1000 Berlin 12,
Giesebrechstrasse 10, Germany

Bogenhausen College fur Angewandte
    Philosophie
D-8 Munchen 80
Widenmayerstrasse 28/0
West Germany

Scientology Mission of Brabant
rue du Pacifique 4
Bruxelles, Belgium B-1180

Scientology Mission of Franken
D-71 Heilbronn
Rosenberg Str 44, W. Germany

Scientology Mission of Frankfurt
6000 Frankfurt Am Main
Kennedy Allee 33
West Germany

Scientology Mission of Hamburg
2000 Hamburg 36,
Gerhofstrasse 18, W. Germany

Institut fur Angewandte Philosophie
D-8 Munchen 70
Kidlerstrasse 10, Germany

Scientology Mission of Paris
147 Rue St. Charles
75 Paris 15, France

Strandvejens Scientology Center
Skellebaekvej 2
3070 Snekkersten
Denmark

Scientology Mission of Stuttgart
7000 Stuttgart 1
Neuebrucke 3
West Germany

Scientology Mission of Zurich
Mulibachstrasse 423/6
8185 Winkel-Ruti, Switzerland

Scientology Mission of Basel
Gerbergasslein 25
CH-4051 Basel, Switzerland

Scientology Mission of Bern
Hotelgasse 3,
3011, Bern Switzerland

Dianetic College Frankfurt
6000 Frankfurt-Fechenheim
Lachnerstrasse 6, West Germany

Scientology Mission of Helsingborg
Lidangsgatan 23
253 71 Helsingborg, Sweden

Scientology Mission of Lucerne
Talackerhalde 22,
6010 Kreins, Switzerland

Institut de Philosophie Appliquee
29 bis rue des Noailles
78000 Versailles, France

## UNITED KINGDOM

Scientology Mission of Birmingham
128A Alcester Road
Moseley,
Birmingham 13, England

Scientology Mission of Helensburgh
121 West King Street
Helensburgh, Dunbartonshire
Scotland

Scientology Mission of Southampton
33 Runnymede
West End, Southampton, Hampshire
England

Scientology Mission of Swansea
1 Highpool Close, Newton,
Mumbles, Swansea, Wales

Scientology Mission of Reading
"St. Michael's", Shinfield Rd.
Reading, Berkshire, England

Scientology Mission of Charnwood Forest
109 Meeting Street, Quorn
Loughborough, Leicestershire

Scientology Mission of Kirkwood
"Kirkwood House", Biggar
Lanarkshire, Scotland

Scientology Mission of Leeds
27 Manor Drive
Leeds LS6 1DE Yorkshire

## OTHER AREAS

Scientology Mission of Mexico
Avenida Nuevo Leon 159 1°,
Mexico 11 DF, Mexico

Scientology Mission of Mexico
AP 21875
Mexico 21 DF, Mexico

Scientology Mission of Mexico
Campos Eliseos 205
Mexico 5 DF, Mexico

Scientology Mission of Negev
P. O. Box 698
Beer Sheva, Israel

Scientology Mission of Rio de Janeiro
Praia de Botafogo 472, Apt 913
Rio de Janeiro, GB, Brazil